MCSE Guide to
Managing a Microsoft® Windows® Server 2003 Network, Enhanced

Jason W. Eckert
M. John Schitka
Brian McCann

THOMSON

COURSE TECHNOLOGY

Australia • Canada • Mexico • Singapore • Spain • United Kingdom

Herzing College, Atlanta Campus

THOMSON
————————★————————
COURSE TECHNOLOGY

MCSE Guide to Managing a Microsoft® Windows® Server 2003 Network, Enhanced
is published by Thomson Course Technology

Managing Editor:
William Pitkin III

Product Manager:
Nick Lombardi

Production Editors:
Elena Montillo
Kelly Robinson

Manufacturing Coordinator:
Susan Carroll

MQA Technical Leader:
Christian Kunciw

Senior Marketing Manager:
Karen Seitz

Associate Product Manager:
Sarah Santoro

Editorial Assistant:
Jenny Smith

Cover Design:
Steven Deschene

Text Designer:
GEX Publishing Services

Compositor:
GEX Publishing Services

Copy Editor:
Mary Kemper

Proofreadrer:
Chris Smith

Indexer:
Paul Kish

ISBN -13: 978-0-619-21753-2
ISBN -10: 0-619-21753-7

_{BRIEF} Contents

TABLE OF
Contents

Introduction

MCSE Guide to Managing a Microsoft Windows Server 2003 Network, Enhanced is your opportunity to explore the networking features of Microsoft's newest server operating system. This book is designed to introduce the reader to the major areas of network and network service configuration on Windows Server 2003. In addition, this book contains information that meets the objectives for the Microsoft Certified Systems Engineer certification exam #70-291, Implementing, Managing, and Maintaining a Microsoft Windows Server 2003 Network Infrastructure. If you are new to network administration, this book can give you the knowledge you need to manage Windows Server 2003 computers on a small, medium, or large network. If you are an experienced server administrator, the book provides a fast way to get up to speed in Windows Server 2003 networking.

Each chapter includes many features, including extensive screen reproductions and illustrations, designed to help you quickly learn and retain what you have learned. The objectives appearing at the beginning of every chapter give you an overview of what you will be able to accomplish, and can also be used for a fast review of the chapter contents. At the end of each chapter, there are chapter summaries for more in-depth point-by-point review. Throughout each chapter, you'll find many hands-on activities, so that you can immediately practice and apply what you are learning. This approach not only makes learning more interesting, but it helps prepare you for real-life administration activities. Besides the hands-on activities, each chapter gives you experience through realistic case studies that put you in the shoes of a Windows Server 2003 consultant who works in all kinds of situations fulfilling the needs of clients. Other learning tools include a list of key terms that you have encountered in the chapter and a set of review questions.

Intended Audience

MCSE Guide to Managing a Microsoft Windows Server 2003 Network, Enhanced is intended for anyone who wants to learn and practice using Windows Server 2003 in a network environment. The computer concepts that you need to know are typically explained as you encounter them. However, for best understanding (although not required) it is helpful to have some prior experience with a Windows operating system, such as Windows 2000 or Windows XP, and a very basic knowledge of the purpose of network servers.

- A new, full-color interior design brings the material to life, and full-color screen shots provide a more accurate look at the Microsoft Windows XP interface.

xiv   MCSE Guide to Managing a Microsoft® Windows® Server 2003 Network

New to this Edition

■ A new, full-color interior design brings the material to life, and full-color screen shots provide a more detailed look at the Microsoft Windows XP interface.

■ Appendix B provides detailed lab setup instructions to assist instructors in preparing their labs for class.

■ Appendix C features expanded and more comprehensive chapter summaries to assist students in reviewing the material covered in each chapter.

■ Two new Practice Exams are provided. One is located in the back of the textbook and is printed on perforated pages so that it can be handed in as a homework assignment or test. The second is posted on *www.course.com* in the password protected Instructor Resources section, along with the Solutions to both exams. The questions on these Practice Exams are modeled after the types of questions students will see on the actual MCSE 70-291 certification exam. In addition to helping students review what they have learned, the questions have the added benefit of preparing students for the certification exam.

■ Our CoursePrep ExamGuide content is now included in PDF format on the CoursePrep CD that accompanies this textbook. The content features key information, bulleted memorization points, and review questions for every exam objective in an easy-to-follow, two-page spread layout. This is an excellent resource for self-study before taking the 70-291 certification exam.

Chapter Descriptions

There are fourteen chapters in this book. The beginning chapters provide an introduction to configuring protocols, including the TCP/IP protocol, on the Windows Server 2003 operating system. The middle chapters address how to configure name resolution, as well as vital network services such as DNS, WINS, DHCP, and IPSec. The chapters at the end of the book focus on configuring remote access, RADIUS, routing, and security, as well as troubleshooting network connectivity.

Chapter 1, "Networking Overview" defines the role of a network server and discusses each of the Windows Server 2003 operating systems: Standard Edition, Web Edition, Enterprise Edition, and Datacenter Edition. The chapter also provides more detailed information about network types, the OSI model, the Windows networking model and common network services.

Chapter 2, "Configuring Network Protocols" explains how to configure protocols on Windows Server 2003. More specifically, this chapter details the structure of the TCP/IP protocol and the various methods that may be used configure TCP/IP parameters. This chapter also addresses the addition of other protocols such as IPX/SPX and Appletalk, and configuring protocol binding order.

Chapter 3, "TCP/IP Architecture" examines the structure of the TCP/IP protocol suite and how it relates to the OSI model. In addition, this chapter focuses on the structure of the protocols used at the Transport, Internet, and Network Interface layers.

Chapter 4, "Dynamic Host Configuration Protocol" explains how DHCP may be used to simplify network administration as well as how to configure it on Windows Server 2003. This chapter discusses the installation of the DHCP service, the creation of DHCP scopes and the configuration of DHCP server options, reservations, classes, and DHCP relay agents.

Chapter 5, "Managing and Monitoring DHCP" teaches you how to manage the DHCP database. This includes DHCP database backup, scope maintenance, as well as gathering DHCP statistics, reading event logs and audit logs to troubleshoot common problems related to the DHCP service.

Chapter 6, "Name Resolution" provides information about the different types of names used on Windows networks and how to configure them. In addition, you learn how to manage host name and NetBIOS name resolution on the network.

Chapter 7, "Domain Name System" shows you how to configure the DNS service on Windows Server 2003. More specifically, you learn how to install the DNS service, as well as how to plan, create, and manage DNS zones. Also, this chapter discusses the integration of DNS and Active Directory, as well as common DNS troubleshooting tools and procedures.

Chapter 8, "Windows Internet Naming Service" focuses on how to install and configure the WINS service on a Windows Server 2003 network to provide NetBIOS name resolution. WINS replication, proxy agents, and troubleshooting procedures are also addressed.

Chapter 9, "Securing Network Traffic Using IPSec" enables you to learn how to configure IPSec on Windows Server 2003 to provide security for the TCP/IP protocol. You learn the different modes and authentication types that IPSec uses, how to create IPSec policies, and how to apply IPSec policies to a computer. In addition, you learn how to troubleshoot computers that use IPSec.

Chapter 10, "Remote Access" discusses the use of remote access on a Windows Server 2003 network. More specifically, you learn how to configure the Routing and Remote Access service on Windows Server 2003 to allow dial-up and VPN connections. As well, you learn how to use RRAS policies to restrict remote access connections.

Chapter 11, "Internet Authentication Service" teaches you how the Internet Authentication Service may be used on Windows Server 2003 to create RADIUS servers and centralize the authentication and logging among several remote access servers. More specifically, you learn how to configure Windows Server 2003 as a RADIUS server, RADIUS client, and a RADIUS proxy.

Chapter 12, "Routing" examines how Windows Server 2003 can provide routing for different IP networks. The first half of this chapter introduces you to the structure of routing tables and the different methods that can be used to create routing table entries. Common routing protocols, packet filters, and demand-dial routing are introduced in the second half of this chapter.

Chapter 13, "Security Templates" teaches you how to create and apply security templates to computers on a Windows Server 2003 network to maximize network security. This chapter introduces you to default security templates and their application, as well as how to create and modify security templates to meet organizational needs.

Chapter 14, "Troubleshooting Windows Server 2003 Networks" enables you to develop problem-solving strategies for handling server difficulties. Specifically, you learn how to resolve connectivity problems, monitor key services, and use standard utilities to troubleshoot various networking-related problems.

Features and Approach

MCSE Guide to Managing a Microsoft Windows Server 2003 Network, Enhanced is one in a series of Course Technology Hands-on books that differ from other server and networking books by offering a unique hands-on approach and orientation to real-world situations and problem solving. To help you comprehend how Microsoft Windows Server 2003 and network management concepts and techniques are applied in real-world organizations, this book incorporates the following features:

- **Chapter Objectives** — Each chapter begins with a detailed list of the concepts to be mastered. This list gives you a quick reference to the chapter's contents and is a useful study aid.

- **Activities** — Hands-on activities are incorporated throughout the text, giving you practice in setting up, managing, and troubleshooting a network system. The activities give you a strong foundation for carrying out network administration tasks in the real world. Because of this book's progressive nature, completing the hands-on activities is essential before moving on to the end-of-chapter projects and subsequent chapters.

- **Chapter Summary** — Each chapter's text is followed by a summary of the concepts introduced in that chapter. These summaries provide a helpful way to recap and revisit the ideas covered in each chapter.

- **Key Terms** — All of the terms within the chapter that were introduced with boldfaced text are gathered together in the Key Terms list at the end of the chapter. This provides you with a method of checking your understanding of all the terms introduced.

- **Review Questions** — The end-of-chapter assessment begins with a set of review questions that reinforce the ideas introduced in each chapter. Answering these questions will ensure that you have mastered the important concepts.

- **Case Projects** — Each chapter closes with a section that proposes certain situations. You are asked to evaluate the situations and decide upon the course of action to be taken to remedy the problems described. This valuable tool will help you sharpen your decision-making and troubleshooting skills, which are important aspects of network administration.

- **Tear-Out Practice Exam** — A 50 question tear-out practice exam is included in the back of the text. The questions are modeled after the actual MCSE certification exam and are on perforated pages so students can hand them in as an assignment or an exam. The answers to the Practice Exam are included as part of the Instructor Resources.

- **On the CD ROM** — The CD-ROM includes CoursePrep® test preparation software, which provides sample MCSE exam questions mirroring the look and feel of the MCSE exams. The CD also contains a complete CoursePrep ExamGuide workbook in PDF format. It devotes an entire two-page spread to every exam objective, featuring bulleted memorization points and review questions for self-study before exam day.

Text and Graphic Conventions

Additional information and exercises have been added to this book to help you better understand what's being discussed in the chapter. Icons throughout the text alert you to these additional materials. The icons used in this book are described below.

Tips offer extra information on resources, how to attack problems, and time-saving shortcuts.

Notes present additional helpful material related to the subject being discussed.

The Caution icon identifies important information about potential mistakes or hazards.

Each Activity in this book is preceded by the Activity icon.

Case project icons mark the end-of-chapter case projects, which are scenario-based assignments that ask you to independently apply what you have learned in the chapter.

Instructor Resources

The following supplemental materials are available when this book is used in a classroom setting. All of the supplements available with this book are provided to the instructor on a single CD-ROM.

Electronic Instructor's Manual. The Instructor's Manual that accompanies this textbook includes additional instructional material to assist in class preparation, including suggestions for classroom activities, discussion topics, and additional activities.

Solutions. Solutions are provided for the end-of-chapter material, including Review Questions, and, where applicable, Hands-on Activities and Case Projects. Solutions to the Practice Exams are also included.

ExamView®. This textbook is accompanied by ExamView, a powerful testing software package that allows instructors to create and administer printed, computer (LAN-based), and Internet exams. ExamView includes hundreds of questions that correspond to the topics covered in this text, enabling students to generate detailed study guides that include page references for further review. The computer-based and Internet testing components allow students to take exams at their computers and also save the instructor time by grading each exam automatically.

Practice Exam. A second 50-question Practice Exam is included as part of the Instructor Resources. Like the Tear-out Practice Exam in the text, the questions are modeled after the actual MCSE certification exam. The answers to this exam are also included as part of the Instructor Resources.

PowerPoint presentations. This book comes with Microsoft PowerPoint slides for each chapter. These are included as a teaching aid for classroom presentation, to make available to students on the network for chapter review, or to be printed for classroom distribution. Instructors, please feel at liberty to add your own slides for additional topics you introduce to the class.

Figure files. All of the figures and tables in the book are reproduced on the Instructor's Resource CD, in bitmap format. Similar to the PowerPoint presentations, these are included as a teaching aid for classroom presentation, to make available to students for review, or to be printed for classroom distribution.

Minimum Lab Requirements

■ Hardware

All hardware in the computer should be listed on the Hardware Compatibility List available at *www.microsoft.com*.

Component	Requirement
CPU	Pentium 133 MHz (550 MHz or higher is recommended)
Memory	128 MB RAM (256 MB RAM recommended)
Disk Space	2 GB of free space (4 GB of free space recommended)
Drives	CD-ROM Floppy Disk
Networking	Two network interface cards per computer for network communications and labs Internet access via a router or NAT device All lab computers should be networked. Students will work in pairs for some lab exercises. Every computer should have two network adapters. A crossover cable is required for each pair of computers during later exercises.

■ Software

Microsoft Windows Server 2003 Enterprise Edition

The latest Windows Server 2003 Service Pack (if available)

■ Set Up Instructions

To successfully complete the Activities, set up the classroom computers as listed below:

(1) Ensure that all hardware used in the classroom is compatible with Windows Server 2003. To do this, it may be necessary to perform a test installation. Once the installation process is complete, use Device Manager to ensure that all devices are functioning correctly.

Windows Server 2003 will be installed onto drive C: of the instructor and student servers in the first chapter. The following specific parameters will be configured on individual servers during and after the installation process:

Parameter	Setting
Disk Partitioning	Students create a 2-GB NTFS partition during the installation process.
Computer Names	Instructor (instructor computer), StudentX (student servers)
Administrator Password	Secret
Components	Default Settings

Parameter	Setting
Network Adapter	IP Address: 192.168.1.X for the first NIC in each computer. This address will be configured on each student server during a lab in Chapter 3 of the text. The instructor computer should be allocated a unique IP address on the same subnet as client computers. The suggested IP address for the Instructor machine is 192.168.1.250. Subnet Mask: 255.255.255.0 DNS: The IP address of the classroom DNS computer used for Internet access Default Gateway: The IP address for the classroom default gateway used for internet access
Workgroup Name	Workgroup

Note: In the table above, "X" should represent a unique number to be assigned to each student. For example, student "1" would be assigned a computer name of Student1 and an IP address (in Chapter 3) of 192.168.1.1.

(2)   Students will work in pairs for some lab exercises. Each student will be required to configure a second NIC and use a crossover cable for these exercises.

ACKNOWLEDGMENTS

This text is product of the talents of many individuals. First, we wish to thank the staff at Course Technology for an enjoyable experience writing a networking textbook on Windows Server 2003. More specifically, we wish to thank our Project Manager, Nick Lombardi, for his patience and insight, as well as our Developmental Editor, Dave George, for his cheerfulness and wit while working our text into its current state. As well, we wish to thank Moirag Haddad at Digital Content Factory for her advice and guidance, our campus director David Anderson for freeing us up to write this book, and our administrative assistant Julie Kennedy, who has been an eager beaver and ardent supporter on all of our projects to date.

We would also like to thank the following reviewers, whose insightful comments were of invaluable assistance in the creation of this text:

Patty Gillilan	Sinclair Community College
CJ Gray	Pittsburg Technical Institute
Robert Sherman	Sinclair Community College
Duncan Ton	Minneapolis Community and Technical College

Jason W. Eckert: I must take this time to thank my co-author, M. John Schitka, for the hard work, long hours, and dedication he spent on this book. As well, I thank the Starbucks Coffee company for keeping me on schedule. Finally, and most importantly, I thank my daughter Mackenzie for providing me with many of the examples used in the textbook as well as teaching me that having fun playing a Harry Potter game is more important than writing a textbook.

M. John Schitka: First I want to thank my mentor and co-author Jason W. Eckert for his insight, patience, and wisdom during the long hours and late nights that went into the creation of this book. More importantly, I must thank my wife Jill, and children Kyra, Luke, and Noah for their support, tolerance, and patience during the time it took to write the book. Hopefully the readers will find it enlightening and of benefit in their educational journey.

Readers are encouraged to e-mail comments, questions, and suggestions regarding *MCSE Guide to Managing a Microsoft Windows Server 2003 Network* to the authors:

Jason W. Eckert: jasonec@trios.com

M. John Schitka: johnsc@trios.com

DEDICATION

In memory of Wallace Weber

## CHAPTER 1

NETWORKING OVERVIEW

After reading this chapter, you will be able to:

- Define a network and describe its usage
- Describe some of the features of Windows Server 2003
- Understand the differences in the editions of Windows Server 2003
- Identify the different types of networks commonly found in industry
- Describe common network protocols and their usage
- Outline the Open Systems Interconnection (OSI) model and how it is used as a model for transmission of information across a network
- Recognize the components in the Windows Server 2003 networking architecture
- List common networking services available in Windows Server 2003

In order to manage and maintain a network based on Windows Server 2003 technology, you need to understand some basic networking concepts, gain an understanding of several aspects of the Windows Server 2003 operating system, and then acquire the skills necessary to configure and manage Windows Server 2003. This book focuses on configuring, managing, and troubleshooting networking features and services in a Windows 2003 Server environment. This chapter presents basic networking concepts and protocols, and introduces services available in the Windows Server 2003 product family. It also discusses how information is passed to and from computers on a network using the OSI model and the Windows Server 2003 networking architecture. An in-depth discussion of these topics will be the subject of later chapters.

DEFINING NETWORKS

Most functions that computers perform today involve the sharing and exchange of information between computers. Information is usually transmitted from computer to computer via **media** such as fiber-optic, telephone, coaxial, shielded twisted-pair (STP) or unshielded twisted-pair (UTP) cable, though it can also be transmitted via wireless media such as radio, microwaves, or infrared waves. This media typically attaches to the computer via a peripheral card known as an **adapter**, such as a network interface card (NIC) or modem device.

Two or more computers connected with media that can exchange information are called a **network**. Computers on a network that share information or other resources, such as printers, are called **servers**, whereas computers that access those resources are referred to as **clients**. A single computer may be referred to as both a server and a client if it shares resources to other computers on a network as well as accesses resources on other computers on the network.

Windows Server 2003 is an operating system designed to share many resources to other operating systems on a network; thus it is often called a **network operating system (NOS)**.

Windows Server 2003 is the latest NOS from Microsoft. It retains and enhances the functionality and services found on Microsoft's previous NOS releases, Windows 2000 and Windows NT4.

WINDOWS SERVER 2003 EDITIONS

There are multiple versions (or editions) of Windows Server 2003. Each version is designed to meet the needs of certain market segments that Microsoft has targeted. The four versions are: Web Edition, Standard Edition, Enterprise Edition, and Datacenter Edition. The following section will explore their features and differences.

Web Edition

Windows Server 2003, Web Edition, is a lower-cost version of Windows Server 2003 that is optimized to be a dedicated Web server. This version is meant to counter **Linux** in the market for utility servers. Windows Server 2003, Web Edition, provides the easy manageability and performance of Windows without the complexity of Linux.

Some unique features of Web Edition are:

- The server must be a member server or standalone server.
- Load balancing is supported.
- Clustering is not supported.
- Virtual private network (VPN) support is limited.

- Services for Macintosh are not supported.
- Internet Authentication Service is not supported.
- Remote Installation Services are not supported.
- Windows Media Services are not supported.
- Terminal Services are not supported.

Standard Edition

Windows Server 2003, Standard Edition, is the version most likely to be used as a departmental file and print server or application server. It has a wide variety of available services such as **Remote Installation Services (RIS)** and application deployment through Group Policy.

Some unique features of Standard Edition are:

- The server can be a domain controller, member server, or standalone server.
- Load balancing is supported.
- Clustering is not supported.
- Full VPN support is available.
- Services for Macintosh are supported.
- Windows Media Server is supported.
- Terminal Services are supported.

Enterprise Edition

Windows Server 2003, Enterprise Edition, is designed to enable large enterprises to deliver highly available applications and Web services. It is available in 32-bit and 64-bit editions. This version of Windows Server 2003 is the logical upgrade from Windows 2000 Advanced Server for enterprises that are implementing Web services using the **Common Language Runtime (CLR)**.

Some unique features of Enterprise Edition are:

- The server can be a member server, domain controller, or standalone server.
- Load balancing is supported.
- Clustering is supported.
- **Metadirectory Services** are supported.
- 64-bit processing is supported.
- Hot add memory is supported.
- **Non-Uniform Memory Access (NUMA)** is supported.

Datacenter Edition

Windows Server 2003, Datacenter Edition, is designed for mission-critical applications that require the highest levels of availability and scalability. It is available in 32-bit and 64-bit editions.

Unlike other versions of Windows Server 2003, Datacenter Edition cannot be bought as retail software. It can only be bought through qualified Microsoft partners. Most of the Microsoft partners are original equipment manufacturers (OEMs). Microsoft partners submit a server and drivers to Microsoft for testing. Only after Microsoft has approved the hardware and driver combination can it be sold to customers.

A team from Microsoft and the Microsoft partner provide support. Only this team is allowed to install and support Datacenter Edition. The customer can add users and make application adjustments, but cannot add, update, or remove drivers and hardware.

Some unique features of Datacenter Edition are:

- The server can be a member server, domain controller, or standalone server.
- Load balancing is supported.
- Clustering is supported.
- Metadirectory Services are not supported.
- 64-bit processing is supported.
- Hot add memory is supported.
- Non-Uniform Memory Access (NUMA) is supported.
- Datacenter program is required.
- Internet Connection Firewall (ICF) is not supported.

Since each edition of Windows Server 2003 has different features and purposes, the minimum hardware requirement for each also differs. Also, since Windows Server 2003 is available on the Intel 32-bit Pentium platform as well as the Intel 64-bit Itanium platform, minimum requirements are different for each platform as well. Table 1-1 compares the minimum hardware requirements for each edition of Windows Server 2003.

Table 1-1   Hardware requirements for Windows Server 2003

Hardware	Web	Standard	Enterprise	Datacenter
Minimum CPU speed	133 MHz	133 MHz	133 MHz	400 MHz
			733 MHz (Itanium)	733 MHz (Itanium)
Recommended CPU speed	550 MHz	550 MHz	733 MHz	733 MHz
Minimum RAM	128 MB	128 MB	128 MB	512 MB

Table 1-1   Hardware requirements for Windows Server 2003 (continued)

Hardware	Web	Standard	Enterprise	Datacenter
Recommended RAM	256 MB	256 MB	256 MB	1 GB
Disk space for setup	1.5 GB	1.5 GB	1.5 GB 2.0 GB (Itanium)	1.5 GB 2.0 GB (Itanium)
Maximum RAM	2 GB	4 GB	32 GB 64 GB (Itanium)	64 GB 512 GB (Itanium)
Maximum processors	2	4	8	64

ACTIVITY

Activity 1-1: Installing Windows 2003 Server

Time Required: Approximately 3 hours

Objective: Install a functional version of Windows Server 2003.

Description: As the administrator of network services for Great Arctic North University, you are the proud owner of a copy of Microsoft's latest network operating system, Windows Server 2003, Enterprise Edition. You want to install and test the operating system (OS) before committing to further purchases and rolling it out.

Before installing Windows Server 2003, ensure that all hardware in your computer is listed on the hardware compatibility list available at *www.microsoft.com*, and that the requirements outlined in Table 1-2 are met.

Table 1-2   Windows Server 2003 installation hardware requirements

Hardware Components	Microsoft Windows Server 2003 Enterprise Edition Requirements
CPU	Pentium 133MHz or higher (Pentium III 550 MHz is recommended)
Memory	128 MB RAM (256 MB RAM recommended)
Disk Space	2 GB of free space (4 GB of free space recommended)
Drives	CD-ROM Floppy disk
Networking (configured later)	All lab computers should have a functional network adapter connected to a network. Every second computer should have two network adapters.

Once you have confirmed the suitability of your computer, install Windows 2003 Server by performing the following steps:

1. Place the Windows Server 2003 CD in your CD-ROM drive and boot your computer.

2. Press **Enter** at the Setup Notification screen to acknowledge the message and continue with the installation.

3. At the Welcome to Setup screen, press **Enter** to continue to set up Windows Server 2003.

4. At the Windows Licensing screen, press **F8** to accept the Windows Server 2003 Licensing Agreement.

5. At the partitioning screen, ensure that no partitions exist on your hard disk drive (remove them if necessary). Next, create a 2-GB partition by pressing the **C** key, and enter the number **2000** in the box supplied. Press **Enter** when finished.

 If your hard disk is larger than 2 GB, you may specify a larger size for your partition; simply enter a number greater than 2000 during Step 5.

6. Ensure that the C: partition that is marked New (Raw) is selected, and press **Enter** to install Windows Server 2003 on that partition.

7. Select **Format the partition using the NTFS file system**, and press **Enter**.

8. Once the format and file copy is complete, the computer has been rebooted and the Windows environment has been loaded, press **Next** at the Regional and Language Options screen.

9. At the Personalize Your Software screen, enter *your name* in the Name box and *your school or organization* in the Organization box. Press **Next** when finished.

10. At the Your Product Key screen, enter the product key that came with your copy of Windows Server 2003. Press **Next** when finished.

11. At the Licensing Modes screen, ensure that **Per server** is selected, and enter **20** in the concurrent connections box. Press **Next** when finished.

12. At the Computer Name and Administrator Password screen, enter the computer name **studentx** where *x* is a unique student number that is assigned to you by your instructor. If you are performing this installation outside a classroom environment, use the name student1 for the first computer, student2 for the second computer, and so on. Enter the password **secret** in both the Administrator password and Confirm password dialog boxes, and press **Next** when finished. Press **Yes** when a message appears warning you about the simplicity of your password.

 Normally, for the sake of security, you should choose a complex password that is not based on dictionary words and consists of letters, numbers and special characters. For simplicity and convenience in the classroom, we shall leave the administrator password as secret.

13. At the Date and Time Settings screen, ensure that your date, time, and time zone are correct before pressing **Next**.

1

14. At the Networking Settings screen, ensure that **Typical settings** is selected, and press **Next**.

15. At the Workgroup or Computer Domain screen, verify that **No, this computer is not on a network, or is on a network without a domain** is selected and that the name of the workgroup is **WORKGROUP**. Press **Next**.

16. After the installation has been completed, your computer will automatically reboot. Remove the CD-ROM from your CD-ROM drive.

17. At the login dialog box, press **Ctrl+Alt+Del** simultaneously and ensure that **Administrator** is listed as the user name. Enter **secret** as the password, and press **Enter**.

18. When the Manage Your Server screen appears, select the **Don't display this page at logon** checkbox in the bottom-left corner of window, and close the window.

19. Navigate to **Start**, **All Programs**, **Activate Windows**. When the Activate Windows wizard appears, follow the directions to activate your copy of Windows Server 2003.

ACTIVITY

Activity 1-2: Determine the Currently Installed Version of Windows Server 2003

Time Required: 10 minutes

Objective: Find the edition of Windows Server 2003 that is installed on a running server.

Description: You are a new network administrator at Great Arctic North University. One of the departments has a computer running Windows Server 2003 that was installed on a trial basis by someone who has since left the university. No one knows what version it is. You need to get a proper inventory before the full roll out of Windows 2003 Server. In this activity, you will identify the edition of Windows Server 2003 that is running on a given machine.

1. If necessary, start your server and log on as **Administrator**.

2. Click the **Start** button, and click **Manage Your Server**.

3. In the Tools and Updates box, click **Computer and Domain Name Information**.

4. Click the **General Tab**.

5. Observe and record the version of Windows Server 2003 that is installed.

6. Close all windows.

Activity 1-3: Discover the Features of Windows Server 2003 Enterprise Edition

Time Required: 15 minutes

Objective: Identify the unique features of Windows Server 2003, Enterprise Edition.

Description: You are a member of the Information Technology (IT) development and deployment team at Great Arctic North University and are evaluating the need for Windows Server 2003, Enterprise Edition servers. In this activity, you will use the Microsoft Web site to find more information on Windows Server 2003, Enterprise Edition.

1. If necessary, start your server and log on as **Administrator**.

2. Click the **Start** button, point to **All Programs**, and click **Internet Explorer**. If this is the first time Internet Explorer has been started, then a warning window will appear. In the warning window, click **In the future, do not show this message**, and click **OK**.

3. Type **www.microsoft.com/windowsserver2003** in the Address box, and press **Enter**. If this is the first Web site you are visiting, then you will receive a warning about blocked content. In the warning window, click **Continue to prompt when Web site content is blocked** to deselect it, and click **Close**.

4. Click the **Product Information** link.

5. Click the **Product Overviews** link.

6. Click the **Windows Server 2003, Enterprise Edition Overview** link.

7. Review the information and close Internet Explorer when you are finished.

NETWORK TYPES AND PROTOCOLS

Networks that connect computers within close proximity are called **local area networks (LANs)**. LANs are the most common type of network used today; they are used to connect computers within a particular building or location such as doctor's office, school, or office building. They normally utilize twisted-pair cabling or a small wireless network, as well as switches, hubs and routers to connect the computers. Networks that connect computers that are separated by moderate distances (usually within the same city) are called **metropolitan area networks (MANs)**. A MAN is a network that connects computers in the same region such as a computer network used by different police offices in the same city. Networks that span larger distances than MANs are called **wide area networks (WANs)** and typically connect computers between cities, across countries, or even around the world. Technologies such as fiber-optic, satellite, asynchronous transfer mode (ATM), and frame relay are used to carry WAN traffic. WANs are often used to connect disparate LANs.

Many companies use LANs to allow employees to connect to databases and other shared resources, such as printers. Home users may also use LANs to connect several home computers, or a WAN to connect home computers to an Internet service provider (ISP) to gain access to resources (such as Web sites) on the worldwide public network called the Internet.

 The **Internet** (Internetwork) is merely many public networks that are interconnected; both home and company networks may be part of the Internet. Special computers called **routers** transfer information from one network to another.

Computers that are connected via network media still require a method for sending and receiving information to and from other computers on the network. This is achieved by using a network **protocol** that formats information into packages of information called **packets**, as well as a **media access method** that can send these packets onto the media itself.

There are many different network protocols that one may configure in Windows Server 2003 including, but not limited to:

- **TCP/IP (Transmission Control Protocol/Internet Protocol) Version 4** (commonly called **IPv4**).

- **TCP/IP (Transmission Control Protocol/Internet Protocol) Version 6** (commonly called **IPv6**).

- **IPX/SPX (Internetwork Packet eXchange/Sequenced Packet eXchange)**

- **AppleTalk**

The most common LAN protocol used today is TCP/IP Version 4 (IPv4); it is the standard protocol used to transmit information across the Internet and the one discussed in this textbook. IPv4 is normally referred to as TCP/IP without referencing a version number.

IPv6 is a newer version of TCP/IP and offers a number of enhancements. The most important enhancement is the expansion of the number of computers that are allowed to participate on a network such as the Internet. It is not commonly in use yet, but will be in the next 5 to 10 years.

Internetwork Packet eXchange/Sequenced Packet eXchange (IPX/SPX) is used primarily for backward compatibility with older networks running Novell Netware. Some older applications also require IPX/SPX. AppleTalk is used to communicate with Apple Macintosh computers.

 When transmitting information across a WAN, you may also use a WAN protocol in addition to a specific LAN protocol to format packets for safer transmission. The most common WAN protocol used today is **PPP (Point-to-Point Protocol)**; it will be discussed in a later chapter.

Once a protocol is used to format data into packets, those packets must be placed on the network media itself via a **media access method**. Although there are many media access methods available, the most common one used to send TCP/IP packets onto network media is called **Ethernet**; it ensures that any TCP/IP packets are retransmitted onto the network if a network error occurs. Another popular media access method is called **Token Ring**, which allows the computer that has a special token the ability to transmit information on a network. The media access method is usually contained within the hardware on the NIC or modem.

Activity 1-4: Viewing Available Protocols

Time Required: 15 minutes

Objective: Verify the protocols available for installation.

Description: As part of the network design team for Great Arctic North University, you need to verify the protocols that are available for Windows Server 2003 and report back to the team as part of the planning process for network services design. You must review the list of available protocols in the properties of a network connection and compile a report as to what is available.

1. Turn on your server and log on as **Administrator**, if necessary.

2. To open the properties of your local area network connection click **Start,** point to **Control Panel**, point to **Network Connections**, right-click **Local Area Connection**, and then click **Properties**.

3. Notice that the TCP/IP protocol is already installed.

4. Click the **Install** button.

5. Click **Protocol**, and click **Add**.

6. Notice that TCP/IP is not in the list because it is already installed.

7. Make a list of what other protocols are available

8. Click **Cancel** to close the Select Network Protocol window.

9. Click **Cancel** to close the Select Network Component Type window.

10. Click **Cancel** to close the Local Area Connection Properties window.

11. Click **Close** to close the Status window.

NETWORK ARCHITECTURE

Network architecture refers to the various hardware and software components that allow computers on a network to transfer information among themselves. In order to understand how Windows Server 2003 communicates with other computers on a network, you must first examine the different steps that computers use to send information across a network as well as the different software components that Microsoft provides to achieve these steps.

The OSI Model

The **Open System Interconnection (OSI) model** is a seven-layer model that is commonly used to explain the different components that computers use when sending or receiving data from one computer to another across a network. Figure 1-1 shows how these seven layers are used when a client computer requests information from another computer such as a Web server.

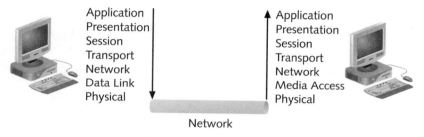

Figure 1-1   The OSI model

Say, for example, that the leftmost computer in Figure 1-1 is a server computer, and that it is sending information such as a Web page to the client computer on the right. The program that is sending the Web page will interact with software at the Application layer first. The Application layer redirects this information to the Presentation layer, which converts the information into a form that is easier to manipulate by the lower layers. Next, this information is sent to the Session layer that attaches a logical session identifier to it for uniqueness and synchronization. The Transport layer then accepts this information and divides it up into packets of information. These packets are then sent to the Network layer where they are addressed for the remote computer, and then to the Data Link layer that sends it to the Physical layer using a media access method such as Ethernet. The Physical layer comprises the network interface, which sends the data on to the network media to the client computer.

The client computer receives the data at its Physical layer and then sends it to the Media Access layer, which interprets the data, performs an error check, and sends it to the Network layer in packets. The Network layer determines whether the packets are addressed to the client computer; if they are, the packets are sent to the Transport layer where packets are checked to ensure that they are complete. These packets are then reassembled into their original data and sent to the Session layer for synchronization and then to the Presentation layer that formats the data for use by applications. The Application layer then delivers the data in its proper form to the application on the client computer that requested it.

The Windows Network Architecture

Windows Server 2003 provides four main software components that comprise the OSI model: client, **service**, protocol, and adapter. Client software makes requests for resources on servers on the network. Service software on those servers responds to requests from client software and provides access to resources, such as Web pages, for example. To communicate, the client and service software must use a common protocol, which defines the language that the client and service use. The adapter is the driver for the network card or modem. The operating system uses the network driver to communicate with the network card.

Windows Server 2003 also has two interfaces to make it easier for developers to create clients, services, protocols, and adapter software. The **Network Driver Interface Specification (NDIS)** resides between protocols and the adapter software. The **Transport Driver Interface (TDI)** resides between clients and protocols, as well as between services and protocols. Figure 1-2 shows how the OSI model relates to the main software components as well as NDIS and TDI.

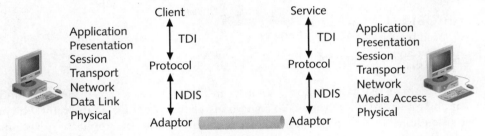

Figure 1-2   The Windows network architecture

NDIS

Network Driver Interface Specification (NDIS) is a specification created by Microsoft and 3Com to speed the development of device drivers and enhance networking capabilities. Before a standard interface was defined, the developers of network card drivers had to write code to interact with each protocol being used by each hardware device to which the network card was attached.

Now with a standard specification in place, the developers of network card drivers write code that communicates with NDIS, and protocol developers also write code that communicates with NDIS. Neither the developers of network card drivers nor protocol developers need to be aware of what the other is doing. NDIS acts as an intermediary for all communication between the protocol and the network card driver.

Bindings between protocols and adapters are controlled by NDIS. A single adapter can be bound to multiple protocols. A single protocol can also be bound to multiple adapters. This is very important in a computer that is acting as a router or a server that communicates with clients using multiple protocols.

Windows Server 2003 uses NDIS version 5.1. Network drivers written for NDIS 4.0 or later are also supported. In Windows 9x operating systems, NDIS 4.0 was included, starting with Windows 95 OSR2. Windows NT 4.0 was the first NT-based operating system to support NDIS 4.0. Network drivers written for these operating systems or later versions should function properly in Windows Server 2003.

Windows Server 2003 does not support the use of ISA network cards.

TDI

The **Transport Driver Interface (TDI)** layer provides clients and services with access to network resources. Applications talk to the TDI layer and the TDI layer passes on the requests to the protocols.

TDI emulates two network access mechanisms: **Network Basic Input Output System (NetBIOS)** and **Windows Sockets (WinSock)**. NetBIOS is an older network interface that is used by Windows 9x and Windows NT to access network resources. WinSock is used by Internet applications such as Internet Explorer and Outlook Express to access network resources. Starting with Windows 2000, WinSock can also be used by Windows to access Active Directory–based resources. Windows Sockets Direct (WinSock Direct) is a new enhancement to WinSock that is used to access resources on system area networks.

Developers write services and clients that communicate with NetBIOS or WinSock to access network resources. The applications communicate with the TDI layer, which emulates these interfaces. Developers creating protocols code them to communicate with the TDI layer. For a client and service to communicate, they must both be using the same network access mechanism and protocol.

Activity 1-5: Research Networking Architecture

Time Required: 15 minutes

Objective: Use the Windows Server 2003 Help and Support utility to glean additional information about NDIS and TDI.

Description: You are one of the Network administrative team at Great Arctic North University. One of the students has contacted you and wants to use you as a resource to further her learning. She is curious about the NDIS and TDI, and you are meeting with her in 45 minutes. You want to be sure you understand the difference between the TDI layer and NDIS. You decide to use the Help and Support utility built into Windows Server 2003 to discover more information.

1. Start your server and log in as **Administrator**, if necessary.

2. Click **Start**, and then click **Help and Support**.

3. Click the **Index** button.

4. Type **glossary** in the Type in the keyword to find box.

5. Double-click the **main glossary** item.

6. Click the **N** button in the browse pane.

7. Scroll the browse pane to **Network Driver Interface Specification (NDIS)**, and read the description and make notes.

8. Click the **T** button in the browse pane.

9. Scroll the browse pane to **Transport Driver Interface (TDI)**, and read the description and make notes.

10. Close the Help and Support window.

COMMON NETWORK SERVICES

Recall from the previous section that services running on servers are used to provide information to clients across the network. There are a wide variety of network services available in Windows Server 2003 that you may utilize and configure. Most of these services are updated versions of those available on Windows 2000 and Windows NT and will be discussed in depth in later chapters of this textbook. Here is a list of some features and services you will learn about in this book:

Dynamic Host Configuration Protocol (DHCP) is an automated mechanism used to assign IP addresses to client computers. Automating this process saves hours of work for a network administrator. In addition to assigning the IP address, DHCP can also provide IP configuration options such as subnet masks, the default gateway, and DNS servers.

Domain Name System (DNS) is a service that converts host names to IP addresses. Client computers require this to access resources through a host name. Active Directory uses DNS to store service location information.

Windows Internet Naming Service (WINS) converts NetBIOS names to IP addresses. Client computers require this to access resources through a NetBIOS name. Windows 9x and NT use WINS for service location.

Routing and Remote Access Service (RRAS) allows Windows Server 2003 to act as a router, VPN server, and dial-in server. Windows Server 2003 can route IPv4, IPv6, IPX/SPX, and AppleTalk packets. **Point-to-Point Tunneling Protocol (PPTP)** and **Layer Two Tunneling Protocol/IP Security (L2TP/IPSec)** connections are supported for VPN access. The L2TP/IPSec VPN has been improved to allow connections through Network Address Translation (NAT). A dial-in server allows remote users to connect to office networks using a modem and phone line.

Network Address Translation (NAT) allows an entire office of computers to share a single IP address when accessing the Internet. If Windows Server 2003 is used as a router to connect with an ISP, then only a single IP address is required. As packets are routed through the server running NAT, packet headers are modified to look as though the router created them. When response packets return, the router delivers them to the proper host on the internal network.

Internet Connection Sharing (ICS) is an automated way to set up DHCP, NAT, and a DNS proxy for small networks. DHCP automatically provides IP addresses and configuration options that define the ICS server as both the default gateway and the DNS server. The DNS proxy takes client DNS requests and forwards them to the DNS server it is configured to use. NAT allows all of the client computers to share a single IP address from an ISP.

Internet Authentication Service (IAS) allows a company to use Active Directory for centralized authentication of remote access clients on many different remote access servers. A company using IAS can have remote users dial in to an ISP and use the user ID and password of their Active Directory account for authentication. In addition, IAS can centralize the logging of internal dial-up servers.

IP Security (IPSec) is an enhancement to IPv4 that creates secure IP-based communications. In **Authentication Headers (AH) mode**, IPSec digitally signs packets to verify they were not modified in transit. In **Encapsulating Security Payload (ESP) mode**, IPSec digitally signs packets and encrypts the data to ensure that only the proper recipient can read the information.

Internet Connection Firewall (ICF) is a simple firewall that is suitable for small businesses using Windows Server 2003 as the router connecting to their ISP. ICF can be used in conjunction with ICS, RRAS, and NAT. It works with LAN, dial-up, **virtual private network (VPN),** and PPPOE connections. If there is already a firewall between the office network and the Internet, then ICF is not required.

Public key infrastructure (PKI) is an increasingly important part of network and Internet security. **Certificates** can be used to secure e-mail and Web sites or to provide authentication using smart cards. Windows Server 2003 can generate and manage certificates for internal use.

Network load balancing has been added as a standard feature to all versions of Windows Server 2003. In high-traffic environments, a single server may not be able to keep up with the level of service that is required. This is particularly likely for Web-based applications that may be available to thousands of users. Load balancing transparently spreads the traffic between two or more servers. From the client perspective, it appears as if there is still only one server.

Automated System Recovery allows a single step recovery of the operating system, system state, and hardware configuration.

The default configuration for **Internet Information Server (IIS)** 6.0 is locked down to be more secure. In addition, it offers enhanced scalability and improved load balancing.

Internet Protocol version 6 (IPv6) is the future of Internet connectivity and will replace the current **Internet Protocol version 4 (IPv4)** protocol over time. The implementation of IPv6 is designed to allow for backward compatibility with networks still running IPv4.

Point-to-Point Protocol over Ethernet (PPPoE) is used by many high-speed **Internet service providers (ISPs)** to control traffic on their networks. Windows Server 2003 can access these networks without installing third-party client software.

For network bridging, Windows NT/2000 Server could be used as a router but not as a **bridge**. In smaller networks, Windows Server 2003 can be used as a bridge to allow multiple network segments to communicate without introducing the complexity of routing.

Windows Server 2003 has built in support for wireless networks. This includes extensions to Group Policy that can push out wireless configuration information to clients and a **Microsoft Management Console (MMC)** snap-in to view wireless access statistics on clients or access points.

IP Security (IPSec) has been enhanced to allow transmission of encrypted packets through Network Address Translation (NAT). Management of IPSec can now be accomplished through the command-line utility NETSH.

Volume Shadow Copy is a new feature that is used by backup software to make a copy of files to be backed up. This system allows files to be backed up when they are open, allowing an administrator to back up files while they are in use without errors.

Windows Server 2003 includes the ability to provide streaming audio and video using **Windows Media Services**. This is used in combination with Windows Media Player on the client computers.

The Enterprise and Datacenter versions of Windows Server 2003 support 64-bit processing on Intel **Itanium** Processors.

Several services and features are installed and enabled by default at installation. This setup can be modified by choices made during installation, particularly if a custom (rather than a typical) installation is performed. In addition, services can be installed or removed after installation. The next two exercises will explore what services are currently installed and what services are available for you to install on your Windows Server 2003 computer.

Activity 1-6: Viewing the Status of Services Installed on a Windows Server 2003 Computer

Time Required: 15 minutes

Objective: Identify installed network services currently enabled on your server.

Description: You are a new network administrator at Great Arctic North University. One of the departments is having trouble connecting to one of its servers. Because some staff members in the department have permission to configure the server as needed, you think that the Internet Connection Firewall might have been inadvertently installed and configured. In this activity, you will verify that ICF is not running and see what other services are running or stopped on the server.

1. If necessary, start your server and log on as **Administrator**.

2. Click **Start**, point to **Administrative Tools**, and click **Services**.

3. Locate and double-click the **Internet Connection Firewall (ICF) / Internet Connection Sharing (ICS)** service. (The services should be listed in alphabetical order.)

4. Verify that the status of the service is stopped and the Startup type is Disabled. This means that the service is not currently running and will not start when the server is rebooted.

5. Read and explore the list. What services are listed? Do any have the Startup type listed as Disabled? List five. Are these services started or stopped? Why? Do any of the services have the Startup type listed as Automatic? List five. Are these services started or stopped? Why?

6. Click **Cancel** to close the properties window.

7. Close the Services window.

ACTIVITY

Activity 1-7: View Networking Services Available for Installation

Time Required: 10 minutes

Objective: View the network services that are available for installation on your Windows Server 2003 computer.

Description: You are a network administrator at Great Arctic North University. The university is designing a new network. For your planning process, you need to identify the network services that are available to install on the Windows Server 2003 computers. In this activity, you will use Add/Remove Programs to see which network services are available for installation.

1. If necessary, start your server and log on as **Administrator**.

2. Click **Start**, point to **Control Panel**, and click **Add or Remove Programs**.

3. Click **Add/Remove Windows Components**.

4. Scroll through the list to see which services are available. Make a list of three available services.

5. Click **Networking Services**, and click the **Details** button.

6. View the Networking Services, and then click **Cancel** to close the Networking Services window.

7. Click **Cancel** to close the Windows Components Wizard.

8. Close the Add or Remove Programs window.

Chapter Summary

- Windows Server 2003 is the latest version of the Windows network operating system released by Microsoft. There are many new features, including enhanced Active Directory, the .NET Framework, Web Services, IPv6, network bridging, PPPOE support, built-in wireless support, Internet Connection Firewall, and 64-bit support.

- There are four different editions of Windows Server 2003: Web Edition, Standard Edition, Enterprise Edition, and Datacenter Edition. Each is designed to work in a certain environment and support different hardware.

- Networks consist of two or more computers that share information. Small, medium-sized and large networks are often referred to as LANs, MANs, and WANs, respectively.

- Information must be formatted using a network protocol before being sent onto the network itself. Four network protocols are supported by Windows Server 2003: IPv4, IPv6, IPX/SPX, and AppleTalk.

- OSI is a general network architecture model that describes how information is sent to and received from a network. The Windows Server 2003 network architecture is composed of four main networking components that fit the OSI model: clients, services, protocols, and network adapters.

- The TDI layer resides between clients and protocols or between services and protocols. It emulates NetBIOS and WinSock.

- NDIS is responsible for binding protocols to network adapters. It also makes the development of protocols and network adapter drivers easier by providing a consistent interface.

- Many network services are available in Windows Server 2003, including: DHCP, DNS, WINS, RRAS, IAS, NAT, ICS, ICF, IPSec, and PKI.

Key Terms

adapter — The networking component that represents the network interface card and driver.

AppleTalk — A protocol that is used when communicating with Apple Macintosh computers.

Authentication Headers (AH) mode — An IPSec operating mode that digitally signs packets but does not encrypt them.

Automated System Recovery — A part of the Backup utility in Windows 2003 that allows for the backup and restoration of the operating system, system services and disks, though it should only be used as a final resort.

binding — The process of configuring a network protocol to use a network adapter.

bridge — A network component that controls the movement of packets between network segments based on MAC addresses.

certificate — A combination of a public key and a private key that can be used to encrypt or digitally sign information.

client — A computer that requests resources across a network. Client software refers to the software on the client computer that performs the request.

Common Language Runtime (CLR) — A common component that runs code developed for the .NET framework regardless of the language in which it is written.

Domain Name System (DNS) — A service used by clients running TCP/IP to resolve host names to IP addresses. Active Directory uses DNS to store service location information.

Dynamic Host Configuration Protocol (DHCP) — A service used by the Windows operating system to automatically assign IP addressing information to clients.

Encapsulating Security Payload (ESP) mode — The mode used to encapsulate and encrypt the data portion of a packet to provide a secure and confidential means of communication.

Ethernet — The most popular media access method used today on networks.

Internet — A worldwide public network.

Internet Authentication Service (IAS) — The Microsoft implementation of a RADIUS server. It allows distributed authentication for remote access clients.

Internet Connection Firewall (ICF) — A simple firewall suitable for home use or small offices when connecting to the Internet.

Internet Connection Sharing (ICS) — An automated way to configure DHCP, NAT, and DNS proxy to share a single IP address and configuration information from an ISP.

Internet Information Services (IIS) — A popular suite of Internet services that includes a Web server and FTP server.

Internet Protocol version 4 (IPv4) — This is the version of the Internet protocol (IP) that is used on the Internet. It is the IP part of TCP/IP.

Internet Protocol version 6 (IPv6) — An updated version of Internet protocol that uses 128-bit addresses and provides many new features.

Internet service provider (ISP) — A company that sells Internet access.

Internetwork Packet eXchange/Sequenced Packet eXchange (IPX/SPX) — The protocol required to communicate with servers running Novell NetWare 4 and earlier.

IP Security (IPSec) — A service used with IPv4 to prevent eavesdropping on communication and to prevent data from being modified in transit.

Itanium — A 64-bit processor family manufactured by Intel.

Layer Two Tunneling Protocol (L2TP) — A protocol that places packets inside an L2TP packet to move them across an IP-based network. This can be used to move IPX or AppleTalk packets through a network that is not configured to support them.

Linux — An open source operating system that is very similar to UNIX.

local area network (LAN) — A network where computers are located in close physical proximity of one another.

media — The material used to transfer information between computers.

media access method — The method used to send data that is formatted using a protocol to a network interface so that it may be transmitted to other computers.

Metadirectory Services — A service in Windows that synchronizes Active Directory content with other directories and databases.

metropolitan area network (MAN) — A network where computers are located in the same city or geographic region.

Microsoft Management Console (MMC) — The generic utility used to manage most features and components of Windows Server 2003. Snap-ins are required to give MMC the functionality to manage components.

network — Two or more computers that share information.

Network Address Translation (NAT) — A service that allows multiple computers to access the Internet by sharing a single public IP address.

network architecture — The physical layout and arrangement of the various components, hardware and software that make up a computer network.

Network Basic Input/Output System (NetBIOS) — An older interface used by programmers to access network resources.

Network Driver Interface Specification (NDIS) — An interface for developers that resides between protocols and adapters. It controls the bindings between protocols and adapters.

network load balancing — When two or more computers share a single IP address to provide a service to clients. The load-balanced computers share the responsibility of providing the service.

network operating system (NOS) — An operating system that is optimized to act as a server rather than a client.

Non-Uniform Memory Access (NUMA) — A memory architecture for servers with multiple processors. It adds a third level of cache memory on motherboards.

Open Systems Interconnection (OSI) model — An industry standard that is used as a reference point to compare different networking technologies and protocols.

packet — The smallest unit of information that has been formatted by a network protocol for transmission across a network.

Point-to-Point Protocol (PPP) — The most common WAN protocol used today.

Point-to-Point Protocol over Ethernet (PPPoE) — A protocol used by some high-speed ISPs to authenticate and control IP traffic on their network.

Point-to-Point Tunneling Protocol (PPTP) — A protocol that can be used to provide VPN connectivity between a Windows client and VPN server. PPTP is supported by Windows 95 and later.

protocol — The language that two computers use to communicate on a network. Two computers must use the same protocol to communicate.

public key infrastructure (PKI) — A system to create and manage public keys, private keys, and certificates.

Remote Installation Services (RIS) — A service in Windows that automates the installation of Windows 2000 Professional or Windows XP Professional on client workstations.

router — A network device that forwards packets from one network to another. TCP/IP, IPX/SPX, and AppleTalk can be routed.

1

Routing and Remote Access Service (RRAS) — A service in Windows that controls routing, dial-in access, and VPN access on a Windows Server 2003.

server — A computer that hosts resources for other computers on a network.

service — A networking component that provides information to network clients. Each service communicates with corresponding client software.

Token Ring — A common media access method that allows each computer equal access to the network.

Transmission Control Protocol/Internet Protocol (TCP/IP) — The standard protocol used to send information across the Internet.

Transport Device Interface (TDI) — A software layer that exists between client or service software and protocols. Clients and services use this layer to access network resources.

virtual private network (VPN) — Encrypted communication across a public network.

Volume Shadow Copy — Allows the Backup Utility to copy files even if they are open, and also allows users and applications to access the data during the backup procedure.

wide area network (WAN) — A network where computers are separated by large physical distances.

Windows Internet Naming Service (WINS) — A service used to resolve NetBIOS names to IP addresses as well as store NetBIOS service information.

Windows Media Services — A service that provides streaming audio and video to clients.

Windows Sockets (WinSock) — A programming interface used by developers to access TCP/IP based services.

REVIEW QUESTIONS

1. What does the acronym NIC stand for?
   a. network installation and configuration
   b. network IP configuration
   c. network interface card
   d. Nothing; a NIC is what connects a computer.

2. A WAN covers a greater geographic area than a LAN. True or false?

3. What is the standard protocol used for communication on the Internet?
   a. TCP/IP
   b. IPX
   c. DLC
   d. AppleTalk

4. Which of the following editions of Windows Server 2003 cannot be bought as retail software?

   a. Web Edition

   b. Standard Edition

   c. Enterprise Edition

   d. Datacenter Edition

5. Which of the following editions of Windows Server 2003 supports clustering? (Choose all that apply.)

   a. Web Edition

   b. Standard Edition

   c. Enterprise Edition

   d. Datacenter Edition

6. Which of the following new features of Windows Server 2003 allows servers to connect to high-speed Internet service providers without adding third-party software?

   a. wireless support

   b. PPPoE

   c. Internet Connection Firewall (ICF)

   d. Windows Media Services

7. The TDI layer allows multiple protocols to be bound to a network adapter. True or false?

8. How many processors does Windows Server 2003, Enterprise Edition support?

   a. 2

   b. 4

   c. 8

   d. 16

   e. 32

9. What is the maximum amount of RAM that can be used in Windows Server 2003, Standard Edition?

   a. 2 GB

   b. 4 GB

   c. 32 GB

   d. 128 GB

10. A network that consists of computers that are separated by large physical distances is called a LAN. True or false?

11. Which of the following network components requests services across the network?

    a. client

    b. service

    c. protocol

    d. NDIS

    e. TDI

12. Which of the following network components emulates NetBIOS?

    a. client

    b. service

    c. protocol

    d. NDIS

    e. TDI

13. What term describes the manner in which information is sent onto a network interface?

    a. protocol

    b. media access method

    c. TDI

    d. client

14. What model is commonly used to describe network architecture?

    a. TDI

    b. NAT

    c. OSI

    d. NDIS

15. Which of the following network services automatically assigns IP addresses and configuration information to client computers?

    a. NAT

    b. WINS

    c. DHCP

    d. PPTP

16. The OSI model consists of four layers. True or false?

17. Which of the following network services is used for remote authentication?

    a. IAS

    b. DNS

    c. ICF

    d. ICS

18. Which of the following services allows an office of computers to connect to the Internet using a single IP address? (Choose all that apply.)

    a. DNS

    b. DHCP

    c. NAT

    d. ICS

    e. ICF

19. WINS is used by a client to convert host names to IP addresses. True or false?

20. Which of the following is a feature of NDIS? (Choose all that apply.)

    a. It acts as an intermediary for communications between protocols and network card drivers.

    b. It allows multiple protocols to be bound to a single adapter.

    c. It provides clients and services with access to network resources.

    d. It is the language clients and services use to communicate.

CASE PROJECTS

Case Project 1-1: Choosing a Network Operating System

As the person in charge of implementing network services for Great Arctic North University, you are responsible for ordering Windows Server 2003 for the faculties. To decide what software needs to be ordered, you are meeting with the head of each faculty. Create a document describing the benefits and drawbacks to each edition of Windows Server 2003 and when it is appropriate to use each. You can distribute this document to each faculty head before the meetings.

Case Project 1-2: Choosing Network Services

You are a member of the IT team at Great Arctic North University. The university is designing a new network. As part of the planning process, you are meeting with the rest of the IT Department to brainstorm on what services may be required on the network. Make a list of the network services that you think may be required and describe why.

Case Project 1-3: Choosing Network Drivers

You are one of the network administrators at Great Arctic North University. A colleague is concerned that some network card drivers will not function after the existing Windows NT and Windows 2000 servers are upgraded to Windows Server 2003. What can you tell your colleague about network driver compatibility with previous versions of Windows and the role that NDIS plays in this?

Case Project 1-4: Researching Features of Network Services

You are a network administrator at Great Arctic North University. As part of the ongoing professional development program, you are to give one of a series a brief presentations to interested faculty. Your presentation is to be on the features of three network services available with Windows Server 2003. Choose three network services you generated during Activity 1-7 (redo the lab if necessary), and research them using the Help and Support utility built in to Windows Server 2003 to prepare your report.

2

CONFIGURING NETWORK PROTOCOLS

After reading this chapter, you will be able to:

- ♦ Understand TCP/IP addressing
- ♦ Define TCP/IP parameters
- ♦ Configure TCP/IP parameters
- ♦ Work with TCP/IP networks
- ♦ Understand the process of subnetting a TCP/IP network
- ♦ Supernet several smaller networks
- ♦ Configure other network protocols
- ♦ Use bindings to optimize network connectivity

As described in Chapter 1, Windows has four main components that are used to send information across a network: clients, services, protocols, and adapters. The client and service software are designed to talk to each other. In the case of Windows Server 2003, the server service software may talk to the workstation (or client) service of another computer using another operating system such as Windows XP. For the client and service to be able to communicate with each other, they must speak the same language. From a computer's perspective this means that they must be using the same protocol. The most common protocol used today is TCP/IP; however, other protocols include IPX/SPX (NWLink) and AppleTalk. In this chapter you will explore the different protocols that are available for Windows Server 2003 and their configuration.

OVERVIEW OF TCP/IP

Transmission Control Protocol/Internet Protocol (TCP/IP) is the most commonly used network **protocol** today. There are several reasons why TCP/IP is so prevalent:

- *It has wide vendor support*—Vendors understand that their products will be more popular if their products can be integrated with products from other vendors. Most vendors support TCP/IP, and therefore all new products are developed with TCP/IP support to make them interoperable.

- *It is an open protocol*—No single company or individual controls an open protocol; a standards process controls it. This means that companies choosing to use TCP/IP do not need to be concerned that the owner of the protocol will charge expensive royalties or make changes that will affect their products.

- *It provides access to the Internet*—Internet access is required in business today and TCP/IP is the only protocol that is used on the Internet. There are many **service** protocols such as **Hypertext Transfer Protocol (HTTP)**, **File Transfer Protocol (FTP)**, and **Simple Mail Transfer Protocol (SMTP)** that only work on TCP/IP networks; these services and the TCP/IP protocol are collectively called the **TCP/IP protocol suite**. Other services that are required for Internet access such as **Domain Name Service (DNS)** work only with the TCP/IP protocol.

Although Windows Server 2003 has the ability to use several protocols, it has been designed so that many of its main features require the use of TCP/IP. For example, TCP/IP enables **Active Directory** to integrate with DNS for service location. TCP/IP also enables Windows client computers, such as Windows XP Professional, to use DNS to locate **domain controllers** for logging on to the network. The version of TCP/IP that is commonly used in industry and discussed in this text is IPv4.

Occasionally, when the TCP/IP protocol was installed on older versions of Windows, it would become corrupt in some way. The solution to this problem was to uninstall TCP/IP and reinstall it. This is no longer possible in Windows Server 2003, as TCP/IP is automatically installed and cannot be removed. If the configuration of TCP/IP becomes corrupt, you must repair the connection.

ACTIVITY

Activity 2-1: Repairing a Network Connection

Time Required: 5 minutes

Objective: Repair a connection that has a corrupt TCP/IP configuration.

Description: One of the servers you have installed in your test lab has mysteriously stopped communicating with the other servers. You have recently been installing and removing a number of services and you suspect that, as part of the process, the TCP/IP protocol has somehow become corrupt. To fix this, you need to repair the network connection.

2

 The connection on your server is not really corrupted, but these are the steps you would follow if it were.

NOTE

1. If necessary, start your server and log on as **Administrator**.

2. Click **Start**, point to **Control Panel**, point to **Network Connections**, right-click **Local Area Connection**, and click **Repair**.

3. Click **OK** to close the Repair Connection dialog box.

DEFINING TCP/IP PARAMETERS

To participate on a TCP/IP network, your computer must have a valid Internet Protocol (IP) address and subnet mask. Optionally, you may configure a default gateway, DNS server information, or WINS server information.

IP Addresses

The **IP address** is a unique number assigned to the computer that identifies itself on the network, similar to a unique postal address that identifies your location in the world. If any two computers have the same IP address, it is impossible for information to be correctly delivered to them. Directed communication from one computer to another single computer using TCP/IP is referred to as a **unicast**.

The most common format for IP addresses is four numbers called **octets** that are separated by periods. Each octet represents an 8-bit binary number (0–255). An example of an IP address in this notation is 192.168.5.69.

You may convert between decimal and binary numbers; an 8-bit binary number represents the decimal binary powers of two in the following order:

128   64   32   16   8   4   2   1

Thus, the number 255 is 11111111 (128 + 64 + 32 + 16 + 8 + 4 + 2 + 1) in binary, and the number 69 is 01000101 (64 + 4 + 1) in binary. When the computer looks at an IP address, the numbers are converted to binary. It is only in binary that some of the more complex features of TCP/IP are more understandable.

All IP addresses are composed of two parts: the network ID and the host ID. The **network ID** represents the network on which the computer is located, whereas the **host ID** represents a single computer on that network. No two computers on the same network can have the same host ID; however, two computers on different networks can have the same host ID.

You can compare the network ID and the host ID to a postal mailing address. A postal mailing address is composed of two portions: the street name and the house number. The street name is similar to a network ID. No two streets can have the same name, just as no two networks can have the same network ID. The host ID is like the house number. Two houses can have the same house number as long as they are on different streets, just as two computers can have the same host ID as long as they are on different networks.

Only computers with the same network ID can communicate amongst each other without the use of a **router**. This allows administrators to logically separate computers on a network; computers in the Accounting Department could use one network ID, whereas computers in the Sales Department could use a different network number. If the two departments are connected by a router, then computers in the Accounting Department may communicate with computers in the Sales Department and vice versa.

If your TCP/IP network is not connected to the Internet, then the choice of IP address is entirely up to the network administrator. However, if your network is connected to the Internet, you may need to use preselected IP addresses for the computers on your network. IP addresses that can be used on the Internet are assigned by an **Internet service provider (ISP)**. When you sign up with an ISP, you are given at least one IP address. Generally, if you want more than one or two IP addresses, you have to pay a monthly fee for them. To minimize the use of IP addresses, most companies use **Network Address Translation (NAT)** or a **proxy server**.

The organization with overall authority for IP address assignments on the Internet is the Internet Corporation for Assigned Names and Numbers (ICANN). ICANN then works with regional authorities to manage addresses within a given region. Your ISP obtains IP addresses from these organizations. There are three regional authorities:

- American Registry for Internet Numbers (ARIN) is responsible for North America, Central America, South America, and sub-Saharan Africa.
- Asia Pacific Network Information Center (APNIC) is responsible for the Asia and Pacific region.
- Réseaux IP Européens (RIPE) is responsible for Europe and surrounding regions.

Subnet Masks

Each computer is configured with a **subnet mask** to define which part of its IP address is the network ID and which part is the host ID. Subnet masks are composed of four octets just like an IP address. The simplest subnet masks use only the two values of 0 and 255. Wherever there is a 255 in the subnet mask, that octet is part of the network ID. Wherever there is a 0 in the subnet mask, that octet is part of the host ID. Table 2-1 shows two examples of how the network ID and host ID of an IP address can be calculated using the subnet mask.

Table 2-1   Examples of using a subnet mask to find network and host IDs

IP address	192.168.100.33
Subnet mask	255.255.255.0
Network ID	192.168.100.0
Host ID	0.0.0.33
IP address	172.16.43.207
Subnet mask	255.255.0.0
Network ID	172.16.0.0
Host ID	0.0.43.207

No matter how many octets are included in the network ID, they are always contiguous and start on the left. If the first and third octets are part of the network ID, then the second must be as well. Table 2-2 shows examples of valid and invalid subnet masks.

Table 2-2   Examples of valid and invalid subnet masks

Valid Subnet Masks	Invalid Subnet Masks
255.0.0.0	0.255.255.255
255.255.0.0	255.0.255.0
255.255.255.0	255.255.0.255

Recall that a computer uses its subnet mask to determine what network it is on and whether other computers with which it is communicating are on the same network or a different network. If two computers on the same network are communicating, then they can deliver packets directly to each other. If two computers are on different networks, then they must use a router to communicate. An example of two computers that are on the same network is shown in Figure 2-1.

Computer A   Computer B

IP Address: 192.168.23.77   IP Address: 192.168.23.228
Subnet Mask: 255.255.255.0   Subnet Mask: 255.255.255.0

Figure 2-1   A simple network

In Figure 2-1, there are two computers. Computer A has an IP address of 192.168.23.77 and a subnet mask of 255.255.255.0. Computer B has an IP address of 192.168.23.228 and a subnet mask of 255.255.255.0.

While you can look at the IP addresses of Computer A and Computer B and intuitively guess that they are on the same network, a computer cannot. Instead, Computer A must use its subnet mask to find out whether it is on the same network as Computer B before communicating with Computer B.

Following are the steps that Computer A must follow before sending a message to Computer B:

1. Computer A compares its subnet mask and IP address to find its own network ID. Table 2-3 shows the calculation of the network ID for Computer A.

Table 2-3   Network ID calculation for Computer A

IP address of Computer A	192.168.23.77
Subnet mask of Computer A	255.255.255.0
Network ID of Computer A	192.168.23.0

2. Computer A compares its subnet mask and the IP address of Computer B to find out whether they are on the same network. Table 2-4 shows the calculation of the network ID for the IP address of Computer B using the subnet mask of Computer A.

Table 2-4   Network ID calculation for Computer B

IP address of Computer B	192.168.23.228
Subnet mask of Computer A	255.255.255.0
Network ID of Computer B	192.168.23.0

3. Both network IDs are the same, so Computer A delivers the packet directly to Computer B.

Default Gateway

In TCP/IP jargon, **default gateway** is another term for router. If a computer does not know how to deliver a packet, it gives the packet to the default gateway to deliver. This happens every time a computer needs to deliver a packet to a network other than its own.

A router is often a dedicated hardware device from a vendor such as Cisco, D-link, or Linksys. Other times, a router is actually a computer with multiple network cards. Operating systems such as Windows Server 2003, **Linux**, and **NetWare** have the ability to perform as routers.

The one consistent feature of routers, regardless of the manufacturer, is that they can distinguish between different networks and move (or route) packets between them. Routers can also figure out the best path to use to move a packet between different networks.

It is important to note that routers keep track of networks, not computers.

NOTE

2

A router has an IP address on every network to which it is attached. When a computer sends a packet to the default gateway for further delivery, the address of the router must be on the same network as the computer, because computers can only talk directly to devices on their own network. An example of a computer using a default gateway to communicate with another computer on a different network is shown in Figure 2-2.

In Figure 2-2, Computer A is sending a packet to Computer C. Computer A uses its subnet mask to determine whether the default gateway is required.

1. Computer A compares its subnet mask and IP address to find its own network ID. Table 2-5 shows the calculation of the network ID for Computer A.

Table 2-5   Network ID calculation for Computer A

IP address of Computer A	192.168.23.77
Subnet mask of Computer A	255.255.255.0
Network ID of Computer A	192.168.23.0

2. Computer A compares its subnet mask and the IP address of Computer C to see if it is on the same network. This step does not calculate the network ID for Computer C. It only tests whether it is the same as Computer A. Computer A is not configured with the subnet mask of Computer C. So, it is impossible for Computer A to find the network ID for Computer C. Table 2-6 shows the results of the test for the network ID for the IP address of Computer C using the subnet mask of Computer A.

Table 2-6   Network ID test for Computer C

IP address of Computer C	172.30.34.228
Subnet mask of Computer A	255.255.255.0
Network ID of Computer C	172.30.34.0

3. The two network IDs are different, so Computer A sends the packet to the router (default gateway) for delivery.

4. The router looks in its routing table to see if it knows where the network 172.30.34.0 is located.

5. Because the router is attached to network 172.30.34.0, it delivers the packet to Computer C. If the router were not attached to network 172.30.34.0, then it would forward it to another router until the network was reached.

Computer A

IP Address: 192.168.23.77
Subnet Mask: 255.255.255.0
Default Gateway: 192.168.23.1

IP Address: 192.168.23.1
Subnet Mask: 255.255.255.0

Router

IP Address: 172.30.34.222
Subnet Mask: 255.255.255.0

Computer C

IP Address: 172.30.34.228
Subnet Mask: 255.255.255.0

Figure 2-2   A routed network

DNS

Domain Name Service (DNS) is essential to a Windows Server 2003 network. It is used to resolve host names to IP addresses, find domain controllers, as well as resources on the Internet such as Web server and e-mail servers.

The most common use for DNS is resolving host names to IP addresses. When you access a Web site, you normally specify a **fully qualified domain name (FQDN)** such as www.microsoft.com in a Web browser program. FQDNs are otherwise known as Internet names and consist of two parts: a **host name**, and a **domain name**. The host name is the friendly name of the computer and the domain name is the name of the organization in which that computer is located. Domain names conform to a hierarchical naming scheme called the DNS (Domain Name Service) namespace or BIND (Berkeley Internet Name Domain) since it was originally developed at the University of California at Berkeley.

DNS consists of an imaginary root domain (.) with several top-level domain names that identify the type of organization that runs the network that a given computer is on. There are several thousands of second-level domains existing underneath each top-level domain name to identify the name of the organization, and the host names for computers are typically listed underneath the second-level domains, as shown in Figure 2-3.

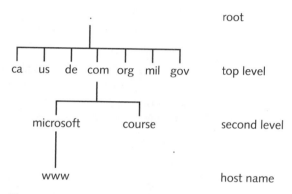

Figure 2-3   The DNS namespace

Since many programs (such as the Internet Explorer Web browser) use FQDNs to specify other computers, there must be some method to resolve FQDNs to IP addresses so that the TCP/IP protocol can locate the destination computer by IP address.

The local %windir%\system32\drivers\etc\hosts file on a Windows Server 2003 computer can be used to resolve FQDNs to IP addresses; however, since this file may grow too large to search efficiently, it should only contain extra or private computer names. FQDN name resolution is best achieved by contacting a DNS server that will contain records that associate FQDNs with IP addresses. There are several thousand DNS servers on the public Internet alone that may be used to resolve FQDNs to IP addresses.

WINS

In the past, Microsoft networks primarily used NetBIOS names to refer to other computers on a network. This works well for small network environments, however is cumbersome for larger networks and impossible for the Internet.

Over the past decade, however, several applications have been made for Windows that use NetBIOS names to locate other computers. Thus, NetBIOS is supported on the TCP/IP protocol by default and one may use the NetBIOS name of a computer when connecting to remote resources.

3

NetBIOS name resolution was performed in the past using broadcasts on the network; unfortunately, these broadcasts reduce the available bandwidth. Alternatively, Windows Server 2003 can use the local %windir%\system32\drivers\etc\lmhosts file to resolve NetBIOS names to IP addresses; however, this should only contain extra or private computer names. NetBIOS name resolution is best achieved by contacting a **WINS (Windows Internet Name Service) server**. If WINS is configured, Windows Server 2003 registers its IP address and services with the WINS server during startup. When Windows Server 2003 is shut down, it contacts the WINS server and tells it to release the registration of its IP address and services. Also, any NetBIOS names that are resolved successfully by contacting a WINS server are stored in a **NetBIOS name cache** on the local computer to speed up future resolution.

There is a sample lmhosts file (called lmhosts.sam) in the %windir%\system32\drivers\etc directory that you may rename to lmhosts.

Normally, preceding a line in a script file with # marks it as a comment, to be ignored by the system when executing the file. While this holds true for the LMHOST file, there are some exceptions to the rule. Preceding the following reserved words, the # symbol will not comment them out, but acts as a flag to the system to take a special action, as shown here:

    #PRE

    #DOM:<domain>

    #INCLUDE <filename>

    #BEGIN_ALTERNATE

    #END_ALTERNATE

The #PRE tag will cause the entry to be preloaded into the NetBIOS name cache. The #DOM tag will associate the entry with a specified domain affecting how the logon service functions. The #INCLUDE causes the system to locate and parse another system's LMHOSTS file, treating the contents as if they were part of the local file. The #BEGIN_ and #END_ALTERNATE reserved words cause several #INCLUDEs placed between them to be grouped together. Successful location and parsing of any one of these will cause the whole section to be seen as having succeeded. For more information on this and the structure of the LMHOSTS file in general, you can view the LMHOSTS sample file on your system.

CONFIGURING TCP/IP PARAMETERS

All IP configuration information can be manually entered on each workstation; this is called **static IP configuration**. Unfortunately, configuring IP information manually is not efficient and is sometimes problematic. With each manual entry, there is a risk of a typographical error. In addition, if the IP configuration changes, it is a very large task to visit each workstation to modify it.

Dynamic Host Configuration Protocol (DHCP) is an automated mechanism to assign IP addresses to clients; a computer configured to obtain its IP configuration using DHCP will contact a DHCP server on the local network and obtain unique IP information from it. Other TCP/IP configurations settings such as the local router or default gateway can also be handed out by a DHCP server; this is covered in more detail in Chapter 4.

Using DHCP to assign IP configuration to client computers on your network avoids the problem of IP information being entered incorrectly and simplifies administration. Take, for example, a 200-workstation network. If you were to manually change the IP addressing information on all of these workstations, it might take several days. With DHCP, the DHCP server can be updated with the new information and, on the next reboot, all workstations will receive the new information.

The network 169.254.0.0 is reserved for **Automatic Private IP Addressing (APIPA)**. Windows 2000/XP workstations automatically generate an address in this range if they are configured to obtain an address from a DHCP server and are unable to contact one. These addresses are not routable on the Internet. Windows Server 2003 also uses APIPA addresses if the server is configured to obtain a DHCP address and a DHCP server cannot be reached. However, most servers have static IP addresses to reduce network connectivity problems.

As an alternative to APIPA addresses, Windows Server 2003 can be configured to use an alternate IP configuration. If a DHCP server cannot be contacted, then the alternative static IP settings are used.

Activity 2-2: Configure TCP/IP Parameters

Time Required: 10 minutes

Objective: View the current IP address settings on a server.

Description: The test lab in your office contains a new computer that will be used by other technical staff at Great Arctic North University. This computer must have access to the network. You check the properties of the network card in device manager, and it appears to be functioning properly. Next, you must configure the TCP/IP protocol for this network card and document it for future reference.

1. If necessary, start your server and log on as **Administrator**.
2. Click **Start**, point to **Control Panel**, point to **Network Connections**, right-click **Local Area Connection**, and click **Properties**.
3. Click the **Internet Protocol (TCP/IP)** option, and click the **Properties** button.
4. Select the **Use the following IP address** option button and enter the following IP configuration information:
   - IP address: **192.168.1.x**, where x is your student number
   - Subnet mask: **255.255.255.0**

■ Default gateway: The default gateway used for Internet access in your classroom

■ Preferred DNS server: The DNS server used for Internet access in your classroom

Document your settings for later exercises.

5. Click the **Advanced** button.

6. Click the **WINS** tab.

7. Click the **Add** button and add the IP address of the WINS server in your classroom (if one is present).

8. Click the **OK** button to close the Advanced TCP/IP Settings screen.

9. Click the **OK** button to close the Internet Protocol (TCP/IP) Properties screen.

10. Click the **Close** button to close the Local Area Connection Properties screen.

Activity 2-3: Using IPCONFIG to View IP Configuration

Time Required: 5 minutes

Objective: View the current IP settings using the IPCONFIG utility.

Description: As part of documenting the configuration of a test server you need to get the IP configuration from it. You are not sure whether the server is using DHCP, or is configured with a static IP address. If the server is using DHCP, you cannot view the current IP configuration in the properties of the network connection. The IPCONFIG utility can be used to view IP configuration information whether the IP address is assigned through DHCP or statically.

1. If necessary, start your server and log on as **Administrator**.

2. Click **Start**, and then click **Run**.

3. Type **cmd.exe** in the Open text box. Click **OK**.

4. Type **ipconfig /all** and press **Enter** to view your IP configuration settings.

5. Close the command prompt window.

Activity 2-4: Test APIPA

Time Required: 15 minutes

Objective: Test the APIPA functionality in Windows Server 2003.

Description: Some of your fellow technical staff have seen workstations on your network with IP addresses in the 169.254.*x.x* range. You have explained that this is an automatic

2

function of Windows 2000/XP and Windows Server 2003 when they cannot contact a DHCP server. You are now going to demonstrate this for your colleagues.

1. Confirm that no DHCP servers are running on your network.

2. If necessary, start your server and log on as **Administrator**.

3. Click **Start**, point to **Control Panel**, point to **Network Connections**, right-click **Local Area Connection**, and click **Properties**.

4. Click the **Internet Protocol (TCP/IP)** option, and click the **Properties** button.

5. Click the **Obtain an IP address automatically** option, and click **OK**.

6. Close the Local Area Connection Properties window.

7. Click **Start**, click **Run**, type **cmd.exe**, and press **Enter**.

8. Type the **ipconfig** command to view your IP settings, and then press **Enter**.

9. If you do not see an address on the 169.254.*x.x* network, then wait for a few moments and repeat Step 8. Your Local Area Connection is configured with an APIPA address.

10. Close the command prompt, and reopen the Local Area Connection Properties window.

11. Click the **Internet Protocol (TCP/IP)** option, and click the **Properties** button.

12. Click the **Use the following IP address** option; type your IP address, subnet mask, and default gateway; and then click **OK**. You documented these settings in Activity 2-2.

13. Click **Close** to exit the Local Area Connection Properties window.

Activity 2-5: Alternative IP Configuration

Time Required: 10 minutes

Objective: Configure alternative IP address information to be used when a DHCP server is unavailable.

Description: Great Arctic North University has a portable computer-based testing system that moves from location to location. Normally, the server for the testing system gets an address from a DHCP server at the remote site. However, the Iqualuit branch of the Great Arctic North University campus does not use DHCP. You need to configure the server to use an IP address from the Iqualuit location when a DHCP-based address is not available.

1. Confirm that no DHCP servers are running on your network.

2. If necessary, start your server and log on as **Administrator**.

3. Open the Local Area Connection Properties window (see Activity 2-2 if necessary).

4. Click the **Internet Protocol (TCP/IP)** option, and click the **Properties** button.

5. Click the **Obtain an IP address automatically** option.

6. Click the **Alternate Configuration** tab.

7. Click **User configured**.

8. Enter the following IP configuration information:

   ■ IP address: **172.30.0.x**, where x is your student number.

   ■ Subnet mask: **255.255.0.0**

   ■ Default gateway: **172.30.0.254**

   ■ Preferred DNS server: **172.30.0.253**

9. Click **OK** to save the IP configuration changes, and click **Close** to exit the Local Area Connection Properties window.

10. Open a command prompt (see Activity 2-4, if necessary).

11. Type **ipconfig** and press **Enter**.

12. If you do not see the address on the 172.30.0.x network, then wait a few moments and repeat Step 11.

13. Close the command prompt window.

14. Open the Local Area Connections Properties window (see Activity 2-4, if necessary).

15. Click the **Internet Protocol (TCP/IP)** option, and click the **Properties** button.

16. Click the **Use the following IP address** option; type your IP address, subnet mask, and default gateway; and then click **OK**.

17. Click **Close** to exit the Local Area Connection Properties window.

WORKING WITH TCP/IP NETWORKS

Now that you have examined TCP/IP configuration parameters, you may start to manage TCP/IP networks. Before you work with TCP/IP networks, there are some key topics that you must know about how TCP/IP information applies to networks. This includes IP address classes, classless inter-domain routing, and reserved addresses.

IP Address Classes

IP addresses are divided into classes. The class of an IP address defines the default subnet mask of the device using that address.

All of the IP address classes can be identified by the first octet of the address, as shown in Table 2-7.

2

Table 2-7   IP address classes

Class	Address Range	Default Subnet Mask
A	1-127. x . x . x	255.0.0.0
B	128-191. x . x . x	255.255.0.0
C	192-223. x . x . x	255.255.255.0
D	224-239. x . x . x	N/A
E	240-255. x . x . x	N/A

Class A addresses that have not been subnetted use 8 bits for the network ID and 24 bits for the host ID. You can identify this from the subnet mask of 255.0.0.0. The value of the first octet will always be in a range from 1 to 127. This means there are only 127 potential Class A networks available for the entire Internet, and even this small number of Class A networks is reduced by reserved address ranges. Class A networks are only assigned to very large companies and Internet providers.

The number of hosts available on a Class A network is 16,777,214, as shown in Table 2-8; however, it is not reasonable to have this many hosts on a single unmanaged network. In the rare cases where a Class A network is in use, it is subnetted. **Subnetting** is the process in which a single large network is subdivided into smaller networks to control traffic flow. Subnetting will be covered later in this chapter.

Table 2-8   Hosts and networks for IP address classes

Class	Subnet Mask	Number of Networks	Number of Hosts
A	255.0.0.0	127	16,777,214
B	255.255.0.0	16,384	65,534
C	255.255.255.0	2,097,152	254

Class B addresses use 16 bits for the network ID and 16 bits for the host ID. The subnet mask of 255.255.0.0 defines this. The value of the first octet ranges from 128 to 191. There are 16,384 Class B networks with 65,534 hosts on each network.

The number of Class B networks is reduced slightly by reserved address ranges, but there are many more Class B networks than Class A networks. Class B networks are assigned to many larger organizations, such as governments, universities, and companies with several thousand users.

Class C addresses use 24 bits for the network ID and 8 bits for the host ID. This is defined by the subnet mask 255.255.255.0. The value of the first octet ranges from 192 to 223. There are 2,097,152 Class C networks, with 254 hosts on each network. Although there are very many Class C networks, they have a relatively small number of hosts, and thus are suited only to smaller organizations.

Class D addresses are not divided into networks, and they cannot be assigned to computers as IP addresses; instead, Class D addresses are used for multicasting. The value of the first octet ranges from 224 to 239.

Multicast addresses are used by groups of computers. A packet addressed to a multicast address is delivered to each computer in the multicast group. This is better than a **broadcast** message because routers can be configured to allow multicast traffic to move from one network to another. In addition, all computers on the network process broadcasts, while only computers that are part of that multicast group process multicasts.

Class E addresses are considered experimental and not used. The first octet of Class E addresses ranges from 240 to 255.

Classless Inter-domain Routing

At one time, IP address classes were used by routers on the Internet to move packets. The routers used the network address and default subnet mask. This is called **classful routing**.

With classful routing, each Internet backbone router would potentially need to keep 2,097,152 entries in its routing table for Class C networks alone. As the number of assigned Class C networks grew, this became unsustainable. Classful routing also wasted many IP addresses. If an organization needed 20 IP addresses, they required an entire Class C address. Out of the 254 hosts on a Class C network, 234 would be unused.

To make Internet routing and the assignment of IP addresses more efficient, **classless inter-domain routing (CIDR)** was introduced. CIDR does not use the default subnet masks for routing. Instead, the subnet mask must be defined for each network. A configurable subnet mask is more flexible and efficient because a single network can be subnetted and organizations can be assigned only a small part of a Class C network. For example, a company that needs 20 IP addresses can be assigned a block of addresses as small as 32. This would waste only 12 addresses instead of 234 from the previous example. CIDR also reduces the number of routing table entries that Internet backbone routers must hold. A single routing table entry can replace hundreds or thousands of entries for Class C networks.

CIDR notation is a common mechanism to indicate the number of bits in the network ID of an IP address. After the IP address, /xx is added, with xx being the number of bits in the network ID, as shown in Table 2-9.

Table 2-9   CIDR notation

CIDR Notation	Subnet Mask
192.168.1.0/24	255.255.255.0
172.16.0.0/16	255.255.0.0
10.0.0.0/8	255.0.0.0

Reserved Addresses

There are a number of IP addresses and IP networks that are reserved for special purposes and either cannot be assigned to hosts or cannot be used on the Internet.

2

Broadcasts are packets that are addressed to all computers on a network. There are two different types of broadcasts: local and directed. A local broadcast is delivered to all computers on a local network and is discarded by routers. The IP address 255.255.255.255 is a local broadcast; all bits in the address are set to 1.

A directed broadcast is a broadcast on a specific network. These packets can be routed to get to the network to which it is aimed. The IP address for a directed broadcast is set to the network ID to which it is directed, and then all host bits are set to 1. Routers can be configured to block directed broadcasts, but forward them by default. Table 2-10 shows some examples of IP networks and directed broadcasts for those networks.

Table 2-10   Directed broadcasts on specific networks

Network	Directed Broadcast
192.168.1.0/24	192.168.1.255
172.16.0.0/16	172.16.255.255
10.0.0.0/8	10.255.255.255

Any IP address with all host bits set to 0 refers to the network itself and cannot be assigned to a host. Table 2-11 shows some examples of IP addresses with all host bits set to 0.

Table 2-11   Host bits in IP addresses

IP Address	Network ID	Host ID
192.168.1.0/24	192.168.1.0	0.0.0.0
172.16.0.0/16	172.16.0.0	0.0.0.0
10.0.0.0/8	10.0.0.0	0.0.0.0

Any IP address with 127 as the first octet cannot be assigned to a host. These are referred to as **loopback** addresses. The most commonly used loopback address is 127.0.0.1. However, all of these addresses starting with 127 are actually the local host. These addresses are used to test the IP stack software because this function works even if the network card is not functioning.

Several networks are reserved for internal use and are discarded by Internet routers. However, they can be routed internally within a corporate network. In order to provide Internet access to computers using these addresses, a proxy server or Network Address Translation is required. It is very common to use these addresses in a corporate environment. Table 2-12 shows the network addresses that are reserved for internal networks.

Table 2-12   Addresses for internal networks

CIDR Notation	IP Address Range
192.168.0.0/16	192.168.0.0 - 192.168.255.255
172.16.0.0/12	172.16.0.0 - 172.31.255.255
10.0.0.0/8	10.0.0.0 - 10.255.255.255

SUBNETTING TCP/IP NETWORKS

A single network is appropriate for many small and midsized companies. However, larger companies with multiple physical locations or a very large single location usually need to use multiple networks. Subnetting refers to the process of separating a network into several smaller networks to improve performance. Subnetting is used because it can:

- Reduce collisions
- Limit broadcasts
- Control traffic

After a network has been subnetted, a router is required to move packets from one subnet to another.

Reducing Collisions

When two computers on an Ethernet network using CSMA/CD as a media access method attempt to transmit at the same time, a **collision** occurs. All of the computers involved in the collision wait a random period of time after the collision occurs before attempting to send data again.

On a very busy Ethernet network, the actual throughput may be only 30 to 40% of capacity because of lost efficiency due to collisions. A busy 10-Mbps network may only actually carry 3 to 4 Mbps and a busy 100-Mbps network may actually carry only 30 to 40 Mbps. Subnetting reduces the number of hosts on each network, and therefore reduces the amount of traffic on the network. With less traffic on each network, the number of collisions is reduced, and the actual throughput is improved. In a routed network, each network is a separate collision domain. Collisions that occur on one network do not affect another network. In a subnetted network, collisions that do occur affect a smaller number of hosts. This increases actual throughput.

Limiting Broadcasts

Broadcast messages are generated by a variety of network services. For example, NetBIOS name resolution, router communication, service advertisements, and other services send broadcast messages when the destination address of hosts is unknown.

A packet addressed to a broadcast address is read and processed by every computer on the network. This is not a problem when there are only a few broadcast packets on the network, but as more computers are added, broadcasts not only can become a drain on the processing resources of workstations and servers, but also can increase network traffic significantly. Subnetting a network creates multiple networks with fewer hosts on each network. The presence of fewer hosts on each network results in fewer broadcast messages, which reduces the processing load on each host.

Routers do not forward packets addressed to the IP address 255.255.255.255. This address is a broadcast on the local network and is processed by every computer on the local network. Depending on configuration, most routers forward directed broadcasts such as 192.168.4. 255. Packets addressed to this address are routed to the appropriate network, and then processed by all computers on that network.

Controlling Traffic

Introducing routers into a network allows a greater degree of control over network traffic. Most routers have the ability to implement rules about which packets they forward. This lets you control which hosts can talk to each other, as well as which protocols they can use to communicate. On a nonrouted network, the hosts can use any protocol they wish and communicate with any other host on the local network.

IP addresses are expressed in dotted decimal notation. Most utilities and other software use IP addresses in this format as well. Internally, however, a computer looks at an IP address as a single group of 32 **binary** digits. The subnet mask determines which **bits** are part of the network ID and which bits are part of the host ID. You don't normally use binary when configuring and working with computers. Values expressed in binary are very long compared to decimal and are difficult to work with. However, subnetting is based on binary. In order to understand subnetting, you must understand binary.

Binary is a base two numbering system, which means that there are only two potential values for each digit, 0 and 1.

Conversion between Binary and Decimal

Since most IP address configuration is done with dotted decimal notation, you need to convert any subnetting work you do from binary back to decimal. Fortunately, the largest number of bits you need to work with at any given time is eight. These are the octets in dotted decimal notation.

To convert a binary octet to a decimal value, you must multiply the digit in each column by the value of each column and then determine the sum of those products. Binary digits are always either 1 or 0, so you multiply the value of each column by 1 or 0. Table 2-13 shows the conversion of the binary number 10011011 to decimal.

Table 2-13   Binary to decimal conversion

Value in Decimal	128	64	32	16	8	4	2	1	
Binary Number	1	0	0	1	1	0	1	1	
Value of Column	128	0	0	16	8	0	2	1	155

While you can convert binary to decimal and decimal to binary using charts such as Table 2-13, most people use Windows Calculator to do the conversion.

ACTIVITY

Activity 2-6: Converting Binary Numbers to Decimal Using Windows Calculator

Time Required: 5 minutes

Objective: Convert numbers between binary and decimal numbering systems.

Description: You will be working on subnetting plans for Great Arctic North University later this week and want to be sure that you understand how to covert binary numbers to decimal and decimal numbers to binary.

1. If necessary, start your server, and log on as **Administrator**.

2. Click **Start**, point to **All Programs**, point to **Accessories**, and click **Calculator**.

3. Click the **View** menu, and click **Scientific**.

4. Convert the decimal number 177 to binary. To do this, type **177** in the calculator window, and click the **Bin** radio button. The answer should be 10110001. If there are less than eight digits, the leading zeros are not shown.

5. Convert the binary number 11001100 to decimal. To do this, type **11001100** in the calculator, and click the **Dec** radio button. The answer should be 204.

6. For more practice, convert the numbers in the following chart from decimal to binary.

Decimal	Binary
43	
19	
255	
240	
192	

7. For more practice, convert the numbers in the following chart from binary to decimal.

Binary	Decimal
00110011	
11001010	
11111100	
00000011	
01010101	

Working with Binary IP Addresses and Subnet Masks

The subnet masks that you have seen are in dotted decimal notation. However, when your computer calculates the host ID and network ID of an IP address, it is working in binary.

Where there is a 1 in the subnet mask, that bit is part of the network ID. Where there is a 0 in the subnet mask, that bit is part of the host ID. Table 2-14 shows an example of calculating the host ID and network ID of an IP address using binary.

Table 2-14   Calculating host ID and network ID

	Decimal	Binary
IP Address	192 . 168 . 5 . 20	11000000 . 10101000 . 00000101 . 00010100
Subnet Mask	255 . 255 . 255 . 0	11111111 . 11111111 . 11111111 . 00000000
Network ID	192 . 168 . 5 . 0	11000000 . 10101000 . 00000101 . 00000000
Host ID	0 . 0 . 0 . 20	00000000 . 00000000 . 00000000 . 00010100

The binary process used by your computer to find the network ID is called **ANDing**. This is a mathematical operation that compares two binary digits and gives a result of 1 or 0. If both binary digits being compared have a value of 1, then the result is 1. If one digit is 0 and the other is 1, or if both digits are zero, then the result is 0.

When an IP address is ANDed with a subnet mask, the result is the network ID. Each bit in the IP address is ANDed with the corresponding bit in the subnet mask. For example, in Table 2-14, the rightmost bit of the IP address is 0, and the far right bit of the subnet mask is 0. When 0 is ANDed with 0, the result is 0, and this is shown in the network ID. The far left bit of the IP address is 1, and the far left bit of the subnet mask is 1. When 1 is ANDed with 1, the result is 1, and this is shown in the network ID.

The host ID is the part of the IP address that is not the network ID.

NOTE

All of the 1s in a subnet mask must be contiguous. There must be no 0s interspersed with the 1s. Table 2-15 shows several examples of invalid subnet masks.

Table 2-15   Invalid subnet masks

Decimal	Binary
255.255.15.0	11111111 . 11111111 . 00001111 . 00000000
255.254.255.0	11111111 . 11111110 . 11111111 . 00000000
254.255.0.0	11111110 . 11111111 . 00000000 . 00000000
255.192.240.0	11111111 . 11000000 . 11110000 . 00000000

Activity 2-7: ANDing

Time Required: 20 minutes

Objective: Find the network ID of several IP addresses based on the given subnet mask.

Description: When you are troubleshooting IP address configuration problems, you may need to find the network ID on which an IP address is located. To practice, complete the chart below. First, convert the decimal numbers to binary, and then calculate the network ID by ANDing the IP address and the subnet mask.

	Decimal	Binary
IP Address	130.179.16.67	
Subnet Mask	255.255.255.0	
Network ID		
IP Address	192.168.32.183	
Subnet Mask	255.255.255.240	
Network ID		
IP Address	10.155.244.2	
Subnet Mask	255.224.0.0	
Network ID		

Creating Subnets

To subnet a network, you take some bits from the host ID and give them to the network ID. As the manager and designer of a network, you have the freedom to do this.

A Class B address is very large and generally needs to be subnetted to handle routing between different physical locations. To keep subnetting simple, bits are often taken from the host ID in a group of eight. This keeps the entire octet intact. Table 2-16 shows an example of subnetting a Class B address by taking 8 bits from the host ID and giving them to the network ID. Originally, the third octet was part of the host ID, but it is now part of the network ID. Using an entire octet for subnetting gives you 256 possible subnets. Traditionally the subnets with all 1s and all 0s are discarded, leaving 254 usable subnets. Subnets of all 1s and all 0s are utilized by routers to indicate network and broadcast IDs, which are discussed in Chapter 11.

Table 2-16 Simple subnetting

	Decimal	Binary
Original Network	172.16.0.0	10101100 . 00010000 . 00000000 . 00000000
Original Subnet Mask	255.255.0.0	11111111 . 11111111 . 00000000 . 00000000
New Subnet Mask	255.255.255.0	11111111 . 11111111 . 11111111 . 00000000
Subnet 1	172.16.0.0	10101100 . 00010000 . 00000000 . 00000000
Subnet 2	172.16.1.0	10101100 . 00010000 . 00000001 . 00000000
Subnet 3	172.16.2.0	10101100 . 00010000 . 00000010 . 00000000
Subnet 4	172.16.3.0	10101100 . 00010000 . 00000011 . 00000000
Subnet 5	172.16.4.0	10101100 . 00010000 . 00000100 . 00000000
Subnet 6	172.16.5.0	10101100 . 00010000 . 00000101 . 00000000
Subnet 7	172.16.6.0	10101100 . 00010000 . 00000110 . 00000000
Subnet 256	172.16.255.0	10101100 . 00010000 . 11111111 . 00000000

When simple subnetting is used, it is still very easy to find the network ID and host ID of an IP address, because each octet is still whole. However, sometimes you need to subdivide an octet to get the number of subnets or hosts that you desire.

Complex subnetting takes less than a full octet from the host ID. Table 2-17 shows an example of subnetting a Class B network by taking 3 bits from the host ID. Traditionally, subnet 1 and subnet 8 are not used because all the subnet bits are set to 0 and 1, respectively. However, today, with classless routing, both subnet 1 and subnet 8 can be used.

Table 2-17 Complex subnetting

	Decimal	Binary
Original Network	172.16.0.0	10101100 . 00010000 . 00000000 . 00000000
Original Subnet Mask	255.255.0.0	11111111 . 11111111 . 00000000 . 00000000
New Subnet Mask	255.255.224.0	11111111 . 11111111 . 11100000 . 00000000
Subnet 1	172.16.0.0	10101100 . 00010000 . 00000000 . 00000000
Subnet 2	172.16.32.0	10101100 . 00010000 . 00100000 . 00000000
Subnet 3	172.16.64.0	10101100 . 00010000 . 01000000 . 00000000
Subnet 4	172.16.96.0	10101100 . 00010000 . 01100000 . 00000000
Subnet 5	172.16.128.0	10101100 . 00010000 . 10000000 . 00000000
Subnet 6	172.16.160.0	10101100 . 00010000 . 10100000 . 00000000
Subnet 7	172.16.192.0	10101100 . 00010000 . 11000000 . 00000000
Subnet 8	172.16.224.0	10101100 . 00010000 . 11100000 . 00000000

The number of subnets can be calculated using the formula $2n - 2$. In this formula n is the number of bits taken from the host ID and used for subnetting. The minus 2 is only used for traditional subnetting where the subnets of all 1s and all 0s are removed.

Activity 2-8: Complex Subnetting

Time Required: 30 minutes

Objective: Subnet a single large network into 10 smaller networks.

Description: A large internal network address such as 172.20.0.0 is too large to be used without subnetting. To practice subnetting, divide the 172.20.0.0 network into 10 subnets using as few bits from the host as possible. List the 10 subnets in the following chart.

	Decimal	Binary
Original Network	172.20.0.0	10101100 . 00010100 . 00000000 . 00000000
Original Subnet Mask	255.255.0.0	11111111 . 11111111 . 00000000 . 00000000
New Subnet Mask		
Subnet 1		
Subnet 2		
Subnet 3		

	Decimal	Binary
Subnet 4		
Subnet 5		
Subnet 6		
Subnet 7		
Subnet 8		
Subnet 9		
Subnet 10		

The number of hosts available on a subnetted network follows the same pattern as the classful IP networks you have already seen. When the host bits are all set to 0, that address represents the subnet. When the bits are all set to 1, that address is a broadcast on that subnet. Table 2-18 shows the usable hosts for several subnetted networks.

Table 2-18   Usable hosts

	Decimal	Binary
Original Network	172.16.0.0	10101100 . 00010000 . 00000000 . 00000000
Original Subnet Mask	255.255.0.0	11111111 . 11111111 . 00000000 . 00000000
New Subnet Mask	255.255.224.0	11111111 . 11111111 . 11100000 . 00000000
Subnet 1	172.16.0.0	10101100 . 00010000 . 00000000 . 00000000
First Host on Subnet 1	172.16.0.1	10101100 . 00010000 . 00000000 . 00000001
Last Host on Subnet 1	172.16.31.254	10101100 . 00010000 . 00011111 . 11111110
Broadcast on Subnet 1	172.16.31.255	10101100 . 00010000 . 00011111 . 11111111
Subnet 2	172.16.32.0	10101100 . 00010000 . 00100000 . 00000000
First Host on Subnet 2	172.16.32.1	10101100 . 00010000 . 00100000 . 00000001
Last Host on Subnet 2	172.16.63.254	10101100 . 00010000 . 00111111 . 11111110
Broadcast on Subnet 2	172.16.63.255	10101100 . 00010000 . 00111111 . 11111111
Subnet 3	172.16.64.0	10101100 . 00010000 . 01000000 . 00000000
First Host on Subnet 3	172.16.64.1	10101100 . 00010000 . 01000000 . 00000001
Last Host on Subnet 3	172.16.95.254	10101100 . 00010000 . 01011111 . 11111110
Broadcast on Subnet 3	172.16.95.255	10101100 . 00010000 . 01011111 . 11111111

The formula $2n - 2$, which is used to calculate the number of subnets that can be created from a certain number of bits, is also used to calculate the number of usable hosts on a subnet. In both situations, the formula finds the total number of combinations that can be created from n bits. However, when used to calculate the number of usable hosts on a subnet, n is the number of bits in the host ID, and two combinations are removed for the broadcast on the subnet and the subnet itself. Table 2-19 shows the number of usable hosts available for certain numbers of bits.

Table 2-19   Usable hosts formula

Host Bits	Formula	Usable Hosts
6	26-2	64-2=62
8	28-2	256-2=254

Table 2-19   Usable hosts formula (continued)

Host Bits	Formula	Usable Hosts
10	210-2	1024-2=1022
12	212-2	4096-2=4094

Activity 2-9: Finding Valid Hosts

Time Required: 30 minutes

Objective: Calculate the number of valid hosts on a subnet.

Description: Once you have calculated the network ID for your subnets, you must find out the number of valid hosts on each subnet. These are the IP addresses you can assign to the hosts on your network. Using three subnets from Activity 2-8, find the first host, last host, and broadcast address for each subnet.

	Decimal	Binary
Subnet Mask	255.255.240.0	11111111.11111111.11110000.00000000
Subnet 1		
First Host on Subnet 1		
Last Host on Subnet 1		
Broadcast on Subnet 1		
Subnet 2		
First Host on Subnet 2		
Last Host on Subnet 2		
Broadcast on Subnet 2		
Subnet 3		
First Host on Subnet 3		
Last Host on Subnet 3		
Broadcast on Subnet 3		
First Host on Subnet 2		
Last Host on Subnet 2		
Broadcast on Subnet 2		
Subnet 3		
First Host on Subnet 3		
Last Host on Subnet 3		
Broadcast on Subnet 3		

SUPERNETTING TCP/IP NETWORKS

Supernetting is the opposite of subnetting. Subnetting is used to create several smaller networks from a large network, whereas supernetting is used to create one large network from several smaller ones. Subnetting takes bits from the host ID and moves them to the network ID. Supernetting takes bits from the network ID and gives them to the host ID. All of the networks being combined for supernetting must be contiguous. The IP addresses from the first network to the last must be one single range with no breaks. In the first network being supernetted, the bits being taken from the network ID must be zero. In the final network being supernetted, the bits being taken must be one.

Table 2-20 shows an example of supernetting two Class C networks into one larger network.

Table 2-20   Supernetting two Class C networks

	Decimal	Binary
Original Network 1	192.168.10.0	11000000 . 10101000 . 00001010 . 00000000
Original Network 2	192.168.11.0	11000000 . 10101000 . 00001011 . 00000000
Original Subnet Mask	255.255.255.0	11111111 . 11111111 . 11111111 . 00000000
Supernetted Network	192.168.10.0	11000000 . 10101000 . 00001010 . 00000000
New Subnet Mask	255.255.254.0	11111111 . 11111111 . 11111110 . 00000000
First Host	192.168.10.1	11000000 . 10101000 . 00001010 . 00000001
Last Host	192.168.11.254	11000000 . 10101000 . 00001011 . 11111110
Broadcast	192.168.11.255	11000000 . 10101000 . 00001011 . 11111111

Table 2-21 shows an example of supernetting four Class C networks into one larger network.

Table 2-21   Supernetting four Class C networks

	Decimal	Binary
Original Network 1	192.168.76.0	11000000 . 10101000 . 01001100 . 00000000
Original Network 2	192.168.77.0	11000000 . 10101000 . 01001101 . 00000000
Original Network 3	192.168.78.0	11000000 . 10101000 . 01001110 . 00000000
Original Network 4	192.168.79.0	11000000 . 10101000 . 01001111 . 00000000
Original Subnet Mask	255.255.255.0	11111111 . 11111111 . 11111111 . 00000000
Supernetted Network	192.168.76.0	11000000 . 10101000 . 01001100 . 00000000
New Subnet Mask	255.255.252.0	11111111 . 11111111 . 11111100 . 00000000
First Host	192.168.76.1	11000000 . 10101000 . 01001100 . 00000001
Last Host	192.168.79.254	11000000 . 10101000 . 01001111 . 11111110
Broadcast	192.168.79.255	11000000 . 10101000 . 01001111 . 11111111

Reasons for Supernetting

Supernetting is used when a range of IP addresses larger than a Class C network is required, but a full Class B network is not required. For example, a midsized company with 300 computers requires IP addresses from their ISP that are usable on the Internet. It would be wasteful to assign an entire Class B address to the company because thousands of IP addresses would go unused. Instead, the ISP can supernet two Class C addresses. This allows the company to have 510 Internet-usable IP addresses.

Supernetting may also be done to reduce routing complexity. For example, an older network running at 10 Mbps may have been configured with multiple Class C networks to reduce packet collisions. With current technology, the routers could be replaced with switches running at 100 Mbps. The switches still reduce packet collisions, and the complexity of the network is reduced. When the routers are removed, the computers on the network need to be reconfigured with supernetted addresses. If DHCP is being used, then this change is very easy to implement.

CONFIGURING OTHER PROTOCOLS

IPX/SPX

The most common protocol in use on **local area networks (LANs)** in the late 1980s and early 1990s was **Internetwork Packet eXchange/Sequenced Packet eXchange (IPX/SPX)**. It is much less common now because most companies have migrated their networks to TCP/IP. The main reason companies started to move away from IPX/SPX was the development of the Internet. To use the Internet, companies had to implement TCP/IP. Rather than maintain two protocols, most companies chose to use TCP/IP only.

The primary reason IPX/SPX was so popular is that NetWare, a common network operating system (NOS), required it at the time. Even today, most companies that use IPX/SPX require it for connectivity with a NetWare server. IPX/SPX is a routable protocol that is easy to configure. Because it is routable, it can be used on large networks. Easy configuration means there is very little maintenance of the client computers.

NWLink is the name Microsoft uses for the IPX/SPX-compatible protocol that it created. For Microsoft networks, the terms NWLink and IPX/SPX are often used interchangeably.

Activity 2-10: Installing NWLink

Time Required: 5 minutes

Objective: Install the NWLink protocol.

Description: One of the servers on which you are installing Windows Server 2003 requires the NWLink protocol to support an older application. In this activity, you will install NWLink on the server before it is rolled out to the Arts faculty.

1. If necessary, start your server and log on as **Administrator**.

2. Open the **Local Area Connection Properties** window.

3. Click the **Install** button.

4. Click the **Protocol** option, and click **Add**.

5. Click the **NWLink IPX/SPX/NetBIOS Compatible Transport Protocol** option, and click **OK**.

6. Click **Close** to close the Local Area Connection Properties windows.

Service Location

When using TCP/IP, Windows Server 2003 with Active Directory uses DNS for service location. Older Windows servers and clients use WINS for service location. The primary disadvantage to both of these systems is that they require the clients to be configured with the IP address of the DNS or WINS server. However, the client configuration can be automated through DHCP.

IPX/SPX uses **Service Advertising Protocol (SAP)** to locate services. Each device that is providing IPX-based services sends a broadcast packet every 60 seconds to advertise its availability. Routers do not forward broadcasts, but IPX routers maintain a list of services of which they are aware and broadcast it out to all of the networks to which they are attached. In this way, service availability is eventually advertised throughout the entire network.

The broadcast of SAP packets every 60 seconds makes IPX/SPX very unpopular with **wide area network (WAN)** support staff. WAN support staff always wants to minimize the amount of traffic crossing the WAN links, and the SAP packets need to cross WAN links for services to be available across them. The constant advertising is considered unnecessary because the services being advertised do not change most of the time.

Addressing

Like a TCP/IP address, an IPX/SPX packet is composed of a network ID and a computer ID. The network ID is an eight-character hexadecimal number. The computer ID is a 12-character hexadecimal number. IPX/SPX does not require a subnet mask because the length of the network ID and the computer ID are always consistent. When written out, an IPX address includes the network ID and the computer ID, separated by a colon, as follows: A1A1A1A1:1234567890AB

The computer ID portion of the address is taken from the **MAC address** of the network card. Each network card has a unique 12-character hexadecimal address built into the card. IPX uses this as a convenient unique identifier on the network. This configuration is automatic.

The network ID portion of the address can be manually configured, but is normally automatically detected during the boot up of the server or workstation. It is detected from packets that are seen on the network.

Internal Network Address

When Windows Server 2003 provides IPX/SPX-based services other than basic file and print, it must be configured with an **internal network address**. An internal network address is an eight-character hexadecimal number. This address must be different from any real IPX network address or the internal address of any other servers.

Applications running on Windows Server 2003 advertise their availability via SAP packets. In the SAP packets, services are advertised as available on the internal network address. The most common application that advertises via SAP is Microsoft SQL Server.

IPX routers must also be configured with an internal network address. This includes Windows Server 2003 when routing IPX.

IPX/SPX is not available for the 64-bit version of Windows Server 2003—only 32-bit versions.

Frame Type

One unique characteristic of IPX/SPX is that it has multiple **frame types**. **Frame** is the term for a packet when it is fully built just before it is put onto the network cabling. Different frame types use slightly different formatting for the packet.

Two computers with IPX/SPX installed, but configured with different frame types, cannot communicate, even though the difference between the packet formats is small. This is similar to a system where information is placed in different colored envelopes. Each computer is configured to read one or more colors of envelopes. If a computer receives an envelope color that it is not configured to read, it throws it away. Frame types are like the envelope colors in this example. Table 2-22 shows examples of different frame types and when they are used.

Table 2-22   Frame types

Frame Type	Common Use
Ethernet 802.3	NetWare 3.11 and earlier
Ethernet 802.2	NetWare 3.12 and above
Ethernet SNAP	Token Ring

A frame type can be manually configured, but is normally automatically detected during the initialization of network services. If multiple frame types are detected, Windows Server 2003 uses Ethernet 802.2. If Windows Server 2003 needs to be configured with multiple frame types, you must manually configure them in the protocol properties.

If you would like to view the IPX configuration that your system is using, including the frame type, you can use the ipxroute config command.

Activity 2-11: Configuring NWLink

Time Required: 10 minutes

Objective: Configure NWLink to use a specific frame type, IPX network address, and internal network number.

Description: You are configuring a server with Windows Server 2003. The NWLink protocol is installed on the server, but there have been autoconfiguration problems where the server sometimes automatically detects an incorrect frame type. To fix this, you need to configure the server with a specific frame type. In addition, this server will be hosting IPX services and requires an internal IPX number.

1. If necessary, start your server and log on as **Administrator**.

2. Open the **Local Area Connection Properties** window (see Activity 2-2, if necessary).

3. Click the **NWLink IPX/SPX/NetBIOS Compatible Transport Protocol** option, and click the **Properties** button.

4. Type **BADBAD01** in the Internal network number box.

5. Click **Manual frame type** detection.

6. Click **Add**.

7. Verify that the Ethernet 802.2 frame type is selected.

8. Type **A1A1A1A1** in the Network number box, and click **OK**.

9. Click **OK**, and then **Close** to close the window.

10. Open a command prompt.

11. Type **ipxroute config** and press **Enter** to view your IPX settings.

12. Close the command prompt.

Appletalk

The **AppleTalk** protocol is used for connectivity with Macintosh computers. When it is installed along with File Server for Macintosh or Print Server for Macintosh, Windows Server 2003 can emulate a Macintosh file or print server for Macintosh clients.

AppleTalk is a routable protocol and can be used on larger networks. However, there is no need for it if Macintosh clients are not supported.

Print Server for Macintosh is not available for the 64-bit versions of Windows Server 2003.

Activity 2-12: Installing AppleTalk

Time Required: 5 minutes

Objective: Install the AppleTalk protocol.

Description: To support Macintosh computers in the Fine Arts faculty, you must install AppleTalk on Windows Server 2003.

1. If necessary, start your server and log on as **Administrator**.

2. Open the **Local Area Connection Properties** window.

3. Click the **Install** button.

4. Click the **Protocol** option, and click **Add**.

5. Click the **AppleTalk Protocol** option, and click **OK**.

6. Click **Close** to exit the Local Area Connection Properties window.

Obsolete Protocols

There are several protocols that were available in earlier versions of Windows that are not available in Windows Server 2003.

Data Link Control (DLC) is a nonroutable protocol that was used for connectivity to mainframe computers. It was also used for connectivity to Hewlett-Packard printers on a network.

NetBIOS Enhanced User Interface (NetBEUI) was one of the most common protocols used for early Windows networks. It is a fast, nonroutable, autoconfiguring protocol. The major advantage of this protocol was that all older Windows operating systems supported it. The lack of configuration options also made it very easy to use. As TCP/IP became more popular, the use of NetBEUI was phased out because it was not suited to larger routed networks and could not be used to access the Internet.

CONFIGURING PROTOCOL BINDINGS

Binding is the process where a network protocol is configured to use a **network adapter**. When a protocol is added to a network connection, it is bound to the network adapter and the services that are part of that connection.

Windows Server 2003 allows you to optimize your network connectivity by adjusting the order in which protocols are used and defining the priority of network services. These settings are found in the Advanced Settings item of the Advanced menu in the Network Connections window.

For each adapter you can choose which **clients** and services are bound, and which network protocols are bound to each client or service. You can also choose the order of the bindings. The protocols used most often should be at the top of the list.

For example, you could remove the NWLink protocol from File and Printer Sharing for Microsoft Networks if you decided that it was not required. This would mean that clients could access shared folders and printers on this server only if they were using TCP/IP. However, this server would still be able to access other NWLink-based resources on Microsoft networks because NWLink would still be bound to the Client for Microsoft Networks.

Activity 2-13: Optimizing Binding Order

Time Required: 10 minutes

Objective: Modify the binding order of protocols to optimize network communication.

Description: The server you are configuring for the Arts faculty has TCP/IP and NWLink installed. In this activity, you will configure NWLink to be the protocol with the highest priority for File and Printer Sharing for Microsoft Networks. TCP/IP will have the second highest priority. The Microsoft Client for Microsoft Networks will be configured with TCP/IP as the highest priority and NWLink as the second highest priority.

1. If necessary, start your server and log on as **Administrator**.

2. To open the Network Connections window, click **Start**, point to **Control Panel**, right-click **Network Connections**, and click **Open**.

3. Click the **Advanced** menu, and click **Advanced Settings**.

4. If necessary, click **Local Area Connection**, then in Bindings for Local Area Connection under File and Printer Sharing for Microsoft Networks, click the **Internet Protocol (TCP/IP)** option, and click the **up (↑) arrow** button.

5. In Bindings for Local Area Connection under Client for Microsoft Networks, click the **Internet Protocol (TCP/IP)** option, and click the **up (↑) arrow** button twice.

6. Click **OK** to exit the Advanced Settings window.

7. Leave the Network Connections window open for the next activity.

Activity 2-14: Removing Unnecessary Protocols

Time Required: 5 minutes

Objective: Remove protocols that are no longer required.

Description: You would like to do a performance test on one of the servers in your test lab. To ensure peak performance, you need to remove all protocols except TCP/IP.

1. Open the **Local Area Connection Properties** window.

2. Select the **AppleTalk Protocol** option, and click the **Uninstall** button.

3. Click **Yes** to confirm the removal.

4. Click the NWLink **IPX/SPX/NetBIOS Compatible Transport Protocol** option, and click the **Uninstall** button.

5. Click **Yes** to confirm the removal.

6. You will be requested to restart your computer. Click **Yes** to the request.

CHAPTER SUMMARY

- Windows Server 2003 uses TCP/IP as its primary networking protocol. An IP address comprises both a network ID and a host ID. A subnet mask is used to define which part of the IP address is the network ID and which part is the host ID. A default gateway is required to deliver packets of information from one network to another.

- There are several ranges of IP addresses reserved for internal use and are not routable on the Internet. These address ranges are 10.*x.x.x*, 172.16.*x.x*–172.31.*x.x* and 192.168.*x.x*.

- DHCP is used to automatically allocate IP addresses and other IP configuration information to clients.

- If a DHCP server cannot be contacted, then clients use APIPA, which randomly generates an IP address in the range 169.254.*x.x*.

- Subnetting is used to divide a single large network into multiple smaller networks. It also reduces packet collisions on a network, limits broadcasts, and controls network traffic.

- Binary is a base-two numbering system. Only 0 and 1 are valid binary values. Computers work with IP addresses as 32-digit binary numbers.

- A 1 in a subnet mask corresponds with a bit that is part of the network ID. A 0 in a subnet mask corresponds with a bit that is part of the host ID.

- Subnetting takes bits from the host ID and uses them as part of the network ID.

- The formula $2n - 2$, where n is the number of host bits, can be used to calculate the number of useable hosts on a network.

- Supernetting combines multiple smaller networks into a single larger network. To supernet, the networks being combined must be contiguous.

- The IPX/SPX protocol can be used with the 32-bit version of Windows Server 2003. This protocol is primarily used in networks where Novell NetWare is present. The frame type is automatically detected when IPX/SPX is initialized during the boot process. If multiple frame types are present, then 802.2 is used.

- The AppleTalk protocol is available for Windows Server 2003. It is used for connectivity with Apple Macintosh computers.

- Bindings can be adjusted to optimize networking performance. The most-used protocols should be listed first in the bindings.

KEY TERMS

Active Directory — A directory service for Windows 2000/2003 Servers that stores information about network resources.

ANDing — The process in which a computer compares IP addresses against a given subnet mask to see if the IP addresses are on the same subnet or not.

AppleTalk — A protocol that is used when communicating with Apple Macintosh computers.

Automatic Private IP Addressing (APIPA) — A feature of newer Windows operating systems that automatically generates an IP address on the 169.254.*x.x* network when a DHCP server cannot be contacted.

binary — A base two numbering system, which has only two valid values for each digit: 0 and 1.

binding — Configuring a network protocol to use a network adapter.

bits — A single binary digit.

broadcast — A packet that is addressed to all computers on a network. A broadcast for the local network is addressed to 255.255.255.255.

classful routing — An older style of routing in which routing table entries would be based on Class A, B, and C networks with default subnet masks.

classless inter-domain routing (CIDR) — An addressing scheme that uses a defined number of bits for the subnet mask rather than relying on default lengths based on address classes. The number of bits in the network ID is defined as */XX* after the IP address. *XX* is the number of bits.

client — A networking component that is installed in computers requesting network services. Client software communicates with a corresponding service.

collision — When two computers attempt to send a packet on the network at the same time, the signals collide and become unreadable.

Data Link Control (DLC) — A nonroutable protocol originally developed for mainframe computers. Windows Server 2003 does not support it.

default gateway — A dedicated hardware device or computer on a network that is responsible for moving packets from one IP network to another. This is another term for IP router.

domain controller — A Windows 2000/2003 server that holds a copy of the Active Directory information for a domain.

domain name — The portion of DNS namespace that can be registered and controlled by an organization or individual.

Domain Name Service (DNS) — A service used by clients running TCP/IP to resolve host names to IP addresses. Active Directory uses DNS to store service location information.

Dynamic Host Configuration Protocol (DHCP) — A protocol used to automatically assign IP addressing information to clients.

File Transfer Protocol (FTP) — The protocol used by FTP clients and servers to move files. By default, it uses TCP port 21 for control information and TCP port 20 for data transfer.

frame — A packet of information that is being transmitted on the network.

frame types — The format of IPX/SPX packets. Multiple frame types are available and two computers must be using the same frame type to communicate.

fully qualified domain name (FQDN) — The combination of a host name and domain name that completely describes the name of a computer within the global DNS system.

host ID — The portion of an IP address that uniquely identifies a computer on an IP network.

host name — The name of a computer using the TCP/IP protocol.

Hypertext Transfer Protocol (HTTP) — The protocol used by Web browsers and Web servers. By default, it uses TCP port 80.

Internal network address — A unique eight-character hexadecimal identifier used by Windows computers that are providing IPX/SPX-based services. Services are advertised as available on this network.

Internet service provider (ISP) — A company that sells Internet access.

Internetwork Packet eXchange/Sequenced Packet eXchange (IPX/SPX) — The protocol required to communicate with servers running Novell NetWare 4 and earlier.

IP address — A unique address assigned to each computer with the TCP/IP protocol installed. It is 32 bits long and is composed of a network ID and a host ID.

Linux — An open source operating system that is very similar to UNIX.

local area networks (LANs) — A group of computers and other devices networked together over a relatively short distance.

loopback — Any IP address that begins with 127.$x.x.x$. These addresses represent the local host.

MAC address — A number that uniquely identifies a network node. This address is hard-coded onto the NIC.

multicast — A packet that is addressed to a specific group of computers rather than a single computer. Multicast addresses range from 224.0.0.0 to 239.255.255.255.

NetBIOS Enhanced User Interface (NetBEUI) — A nonroutable protocol commonly used in smaller Windows networks. Windows Server 2003 does not support it.

NetBIOS name cache — A cache or temporary store in memory used to hold information on recently resolved NetBIOS names

NetWare — A network operating system from Novell that traditionally uses the IPX/SPX protocol.

network adapter — In Windows networking, this represents the network interface card and the driver that goes with it.

network address translation (NAT) — A service that allows multiple computers to access the Internet by sharing a single IP address.

network ID — The portion of an IP address that designates the network on which a computer resides. This is defined by the subnet mask.

NWLink — An IPX/SPX-compatible protocol created by Microsoft for Windows operating systems.

octets — A group of 8 bits. An IP address is composed of four octets, with each expressed as a decimal number.

protocol — The language that two computers use to communicate on a network. Two computers must use the same protocol to communicate.

proxy server — A server that can be used to control and speed up access to the Internet. It also allows multiple computers to access the Internet through a single IP address.

router — A network device that moves packets from one network to another. TCP/IP, IPX/SPX, and AppleTalk can be routed.

service — A networking component that provides resources to network clients. Each service communicates with corresponding client software.

Service Advertising Protocol (SAP) — A protocol used by IPX/SPX to advertise the availability of services by sending out a broadcast message every 60 seconds.

Simple Mail Transfer Protocol (SMTP) — A protocol used by e-mail clients to send messages to e-mail servers. It uses TCP port 25.

static IP configuration — TCP/IP configuration settings and information manually entered onto a device such as a computer

subnet mask — A string of 32 bits that is used to define which portion of an IP address is the host ID and which part is the network ID.

subnetting — The process of dividing a single IP network into several smaller IP networks. Bits are taken from the host ID and made part of the network ID by adjusting the subnet mask.

supernetting — The process of combining several smaller networks into a single large network by taking bits from the network ID and making them part of the host ID.

TCP/IP protocol suite — A collection of related communication and information transfer protocols vital to communication on the Internet

Transmission Control Protocol/Internet Protocol (TCP/IP) — A suite of protocols that allows interconnected networks to communicate with one another. It is the most common protocol in Windows networking and must be used to access the Internet.

unicast — Communication from one computer to a single destination computer on a TCP/IP network.

wide area network (WAN) — Geographically dispersed networks with more than one physical location. The links between each location are relatively slow compared to local area networks.

WINS (Windows Internet Name Service) server — A Windows service used to resolve NetBIOS names to IP addresses as well as store NetBIOS service information.

REVIEW QUESTIONS

1. How many octets are there in an IP address?
   a. 2
   b. 4
   c. 8
   d. 16

2. How many bits are there in an octet?
   a. 2
   b. 4
   c. 8
   d. 16

3. Which of the following organizations is responsible for the management of IP addresses in North America?
   a. American Registry for Internet Numbers (ARIN)
   b. Asia Pacific Network Information Center (APNIC)
   c. Réseaux IP Européen (RIPE)
   d. Internet Corporation for Assigned Names and Numbers (ICANN)

4. Which of the following defines the part of an IP address that is the host ID and the part that is the network ID?
   a. default gateway
   b. DNS server
   c. WINS server
   d. subnet mask

5. What is the default subnet mask for a Class C IP address?
   a. 255.0.0.0
   b. 255.255.0.0
   c. 255.255.255.0
   d. 0.255.255.255

6. A computer will use a default gateway if the destination IP address is on a different network. True or false?

7. Which of the following is another name for default gateway?

    a. router

    b. switch

    c. hub

    d. host

8. IP address 227.43.76.109 is an example of which of the following classes of IP addresses?

    a. Class A

    b. Class B

    c. Class C

    d. Class D

    e. Class E

9. The IP address 169.254.226.4 can be routed on the Internet. True or false?

10. What was introduced to make Internet routing and the assignment of IP addresses more efficient?

    a. subnet masks

    b. switches

    c. DHCP

    d. CIDR

11. How many octets are part of the network ID when using the subnet mask 255.255.255.0?

    a. 1

    b. 2

    c. 3

    d. 4

12. What type of server does a Windows client use to resolve NetBIOS names to IP addresses?

    a. DNS

    b. DHCP

    c. WINS

    d. remote access

13. What type of server does a Windows client use to resolve host names to IP addresses?

    a. DNS

    b. DHCP

    c. WINS

    d. remote access

14. Which of the following protocols is used to communicate with Apple Macintosh computers?
    a. TCP/IP
    b. IPX/SPX
    c. AppleTalk
    d. NetBEUI

15. Which of the following protocols was commonly used in small, older Windows networks, but is not available in Windows Server 2003?
    a. TCP/IP
    b. IPX/SPX
    c. AppleTalk
    d. NetBEUI

16. Which of the following features of IPX/SPX is automatically detected during bootup?
    a. frame type
    b. internal network address
    c. subnet mask
    d. default gateway

17. Which of the following terms is often used interchangeably with IPX/SPX when talking about Microsoft networks?
    a. NWLink
    b. IPv6
    c. default gateway
    d. DNS

18. Which of the following is not a reason to subnet a network?
    a. to reduce collisions on the network
    b. to limit the number of collisions on the subnet
    c. to combine smaller networks into a larger network
    d. to control the amount of traffic on the network
    e. to reduce the number of IP addresses in use on the network

19. What is 10101011.11111110.11100111.00011111 in decimal notation?

20. Your computer has an IP address of 172.18.56.17 with a subnet mask of 255.255.
    248.0. Which of the following IP addresses are on your local subnet? (Choose all
    that apply.)

    a. 172.18.47.200

    b. 172.18.60.100

    c. 172.18.89.157

    d. 172.18.54.3

    e. 172.18.65.117

    f. 172.18.57.42

21. What is the maximum number of workstations the subnet mask 255.255.240.0 can
    support on the local subnet?

    a. 2,048

    b. 2,046

    c. 4,096

    d. 4,094

    e. 8,190

22. You have been assigned the network address 172.32.0.0 to use on your LAN. You
    need to divide the network into seven subnets. What subnet mask do you use?

    a. 255.240.0.0

    b. 255.224.0.0

    c. 255.255.248.0

    d. 255.255.240.0

23. A packet sent to all workstations on the network is called a _____ .

    a. directed packet

    b. unicast

    c. multicast

    d. broadcast

24. Combining smaller subnets into a single, larger subnet is called

    _____ .

    a. subnetting

    b. supernetting

    c. complex subnetting

    d. classful subnetting

25. You have been assigned the network ID 172.16.5.0 with a subnet mask of 255.255. 255.0. What is the maximum number of workstations you can have on the subnet?

    a. 255

    b. 254

    c. 253

    d. 126

26. You need to connect to a computer on your local subnet. Your computer's IP address is 172.28.17.5, and the other computer's IP address is 172.28.30.252. Which subnet mask(s) can you use? (Choose all that apply.)

    a. 255.0.0.0

    b. 255.255.0.0

    c. 255.255.252.0

    d. 255.255.240.0

    e. 255.255.248.0

27. You are using the network ID 10.0.0.0. You need to divide the network into smaller subnets that can support 6,000 workstations on each subnet. Which of the following subnets supports 6,000 workstations? (Choose all that apply.)

    a. 255.192.0.0

    b. 255.255.192.0

    c. 255.255.224.0

    d. 255.255.240.0

    e. 255.255.248.0

28. Your computer has been assigned the IP address 192.168.148.72 with a subnet mask of 255.255.252.0. Which of the following IP addresses is on your local subnet? (Choose all that apply.)

    a. 192.168.140.12

    b. 192.168.150.55

    c. 192.168.148.73

    d. 192.168.151.250

    e. 192.168.155.32

29. How many bits are required to supernet seven Class C addresses?

    a. 1

    b. 2

    c. 3

    d. 4

    e. 5

30. Which of the following can you adjust to optimize networking performance on Windows Server 2003?

   a. subnet mask

   b. bindings

   c. default gateway

   d. frame type

CASE PROJECTS

Because Great Arctic North University is in a remote part of the north, Internet access has not been available. Now, thanks to a new satellite system, you will be able to receive Internet access from ZAP Internet Services, despite your remote location.

Most of the university network consists of Windows-based computers. However, individual professors have independent funding for projects and can buy any equipment they want. As a result, some departments have Novell NetWare servers, the Engineering Department has Linux workstations, and the Fine Arts Department has Macintosh workstations.

Now that Great Arctic North University is connecting to the Internet, many existing systems need to be modified so that they are part of a single, well-organized network. Later cases will take you through several exercises required as part of the reorganization.

Case Project 2-1: Documenting the Existing Network

In order to make sound decisions, your boss, Jerry, needs information about the protocols in use on your network. Write a short report for Jerry documenting all of the protocols that are required on your network, why they are required, and any configuration options that might be required.

Case Project 2-2: Choosing IP Addresses

Jerry is unsure whether you should use Internal IP addresses for your network or get Internet-accessible addresses from ZAP Internet Services. Write a short list of pros and cons for each option that you can use when discussing this matter in the weekly technical staff meeting.

Case Project 2-3: Solving an Upgrade Problem

On Monday morning, you receive an e-mail asking for your help. Over the weekend, one of your colleagues upgraded a departmental Windows NT server to Windows Server 2003. Now, over half of the department can no longer log on to the server or access resources from it. What ideas do you have that may help your colleague?

Case Project 2-4: Choosing Subnets for Each Location

There are six different physical locations used by Great Arctic North University to deliver classes. Each of these locations has a minimum of 50 computers and a maximum of 1,000 computers. The IP addressing plan needs to be presented at the IT staff meeting this week. Write a short report indicating the range of addresses that should be used for each location and the reasons you chose those address ranges.

2

Case Project 2-5: Choosing Subnets for Lab Expansion

Because of increased enrollment, Great Arctic North University is expanding its student computer services by adding an additional six computer labs located on the main campus. Each lab will contain 100 new Windows XP–based computers. To reduce the amount of network traffic and increase control, you recommend that each new lab be configured as a separate subnet. The new computer labs can use the network ID 172.16.0.0. What subnet mask will you use to subnet the labs? What range of IP addresses can you assign to each lab? Use a table similar to the one shown here to record your answers.

Custom Subnet Mask:

	Beginning IP Address	Ending IP Address
Subnet 1		
Subnet 2		
Subnet 3		
Subnet 4		
Subnet 5		
Subnet 6		

Case Project 2-6: Supernetting to Reduce Routing

A router connecting two small test labs has failed and needs to be replaced. The first lab has 10 computers and is assigned the network ID 192.168.21.0 with a subnet mask of 255.255.255.0. The second lab has 25 computers with the network ID 192.168.23.0 and a subnet mask of 255.255.255.0. Instead of replacing the failed router, you recommend that the two subnets be combined into a single supernet. What subnet mask would you use? What IP addresses are valid for the new supernet?

3

TCP/IP ARCHITECTURE

After reading this chapter, you will be able to:

♦ Describe the overall architecture of TCP/IP

♦ Identify Application layer protocols in the TCP/IP protocol suite

♦ Compare and contrast the TCP and UDP Transport layer protocols

♦ Understand the role of various Internet layer protocols including IP, ICMP, and ARP

♦ Describe different Network Interface layer protocols

In Chapter 1, you were introduced to the OSI model and Windows Server 2003 network architecture. In Chapter 2, you learned how to configure protocols on Windows Server 2003, with specific emphasis on TCP/IP. This chapter discusses the various architectural components within the TCP/IP protocol suite and how they map to the OSI model.

TCP/IP ARCHITECTURE OVERVIEW

As we discussed in Chapter 1, the **Open Systems Interconnection (OSI) reference model** is an industry standard model that uses seven layers to describe how computers can communicate on a network. Since the OSI model is simply a standard model, protocols by individual makers may vary slightly from the OSI definition. This is the case with the TCP/IP protocol suite.

The TCP/IP protocol architecture is represented by a four-layer model that may be compared to the OSI model. The four architectural layers in the TCP/IP model are Application, Transport, Internet, and Network Interface. Each of these architectural layers will contain the TCP/IP protocols that compose the TCP/IP protocol suite.

Figure 3-1 shows the protocols that exist in each of the four layers in the TCP/IP model and how they relate to the OSI model.

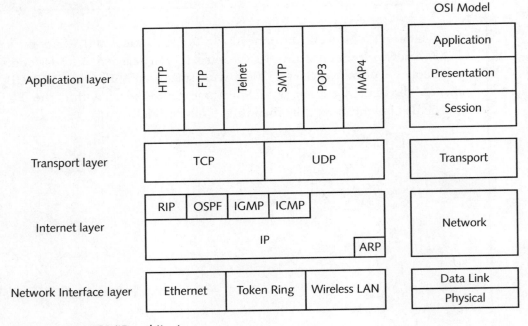

Figure 3-1   TCP/IP architecture

The **Application layer** provides access to network resources. It defines the rules, commands, and procedures that client software uses to talk to a service running on a server. It also contains a series of protocols that are useful on TCP/IP networks such as the Internet. As an example, the HTTP protocol is an Application layer protocol that defines how Web browsers and Web servers communicate.

The **Transport layer** is responsible for preparing data to be transported across the network. This layer breaks large messages into smaller **packets** of information and tracks whether they arrived at their final destination.

The **Internet layer** is responsible for logical addressing and routing. IP addresses are logical addresses. Any protocol that is network-aware exists in this layer.

The **Network Interface layer** consists of the network card driver and the circuitry on the network card itself.

APPLICATION LAYER PROTOCOLS

The Application layer accepts information from applications on the computer and sends this information on to the network. In addition, there are many Application layer protocols that are only available on TCP/IP networks, each of which is associated with a client application and service. For example, FTP clients use the FTP protocol and Telnet clients use the Telnet protocol. However, some client software is capable of using more than one protocol. For example, Web browsers are capable of using HTTP to communicate with Web servers, and FTP to communicate with FTP servers.

HTTP

Hypertext Transfer Protocol (HTTP) is the most common protocol used on the Internet today. This is the protocol used by Web browsers and Web servers. HTTP defines the commands that Web browsers can send and how Web servers are capable of responding. For example, when requesting a Web page, a Web browser sends a GET command. The server then responds by sending the requested Web page. Many commands are defined as part of the protocol.

Information can also be uploaded using the HTTP protocol. A survey form on a Web page is an example of information moving from a Web browser to a Web server. The capabilities of Web servers can also be extended by using a variety of mechanisms that allow Web servers to pass data from forms to applications or scripts for processing. Some of the common mechanisms for passing data from a Web server to an application are:

- **Common Gateway Interface (CGI)**
- **Internet Server Application Programmer Interface (ISAPI)**
- **Netscape Server Application Programmer Interface (NSAPI)**

The World Wide Web consortium (W3C) is the standards body responsible for defining the commands that are part of HTTP.

FTP

File Transfer Protocol (FTP) is a simple file-sharing protocol. It includes commands for uploading and downloading files, as well as requesting directory listings from remote servers. This protocol has been around the Internet for a long time and was originally implemented on UNIX during the 1980s. The first industry distributed document, or **Request for Comment (RFC)**, describing FTP was created in 1985.

 Although there are still FTP servers running on the Internet, they number fewer than in previous years. This is because HTTP is capable of uploading and downloading files, which is slowly making FTP obsolete.

FTP is implemented on standalone FTP clients as well as on Web browsers. It is safe to say that most FTP users today are using Web browsers.

Activity 3-1 : Using FTP to Download a File

Time Required: 10 minutes

Objective: Use FTP to download a utility.

Description: There is a utility that you wish to download from the Microsoft FTP server. Normally, you would use Internet Explorer to download this file, but Internet Explorer is not functioning properly on your workstation. As a result, you need to use the command-line FTP client to download the index of available files.

1. If necessary, start your server and log on as **Administrator**.

 For all activities, log on as the Administrator.

2. Click the **Start** button, and then click **Run**.
3. Type **ftp** and press **Enter**.
4. Type **open ftp.microsoft.com** and press **Enter**.
5. Type **anonymous** and press **Enter**.
6. Type your e-mail address, and press **Enter**.
7. Type **ls** and press **Enter**.
8. Type **cd softlib** and press **Enter**.
9. Type **dir** and press **Enter**.

3

10. Type **get index.txt** and press **Enter**. This command will retrieve the file index.txt from the remote server. All retrieved files are placed in the current directory on the local machine. In this instance, the current directory is C:\Documents and Settings\Administrator.

11. Type **bye** and press **Enter**.

Telnet

Telnet is a terminal emulation protocol that is primarily used to remotely connect to UNIX and Linux Systems. The Telnet protocol specifies how a Telnet server and Telnet client communicate.

The most common reason to connect to a server via Telnet is to remotely manage UNIX or Linux systems. All of the administration for these systems can be done through a character-based interface. This is important because Telnet does not support a **graphical user interface (GUI)**, only text.

Telnet is similar to the concept of a mainframe and dumb terminal. The Telnet server controls the entire user environment, processes the keyboard input, and sends display commands back to the client. A Telnet client is responsible only for displaying information on the screen and passing input to the server. There can be many Telnet clients connected to a single server at one time. Each client that is connected receives its own operating environment; however, these clients are not aware that other users are logged in to the system.

SMTP

Simple Mail Transfer Protocol (SMTP) is used to send and receive e-mail messages between e-mail servers. It is also used by e-mail client software, such as Outlook Express, to send messages to the server. SMTP is never used to retrieve e-mail from a server when you are reading it. Other protocols control the reading of e-mail messages.

Activity 3-2: Using Telnet to Verify SMTP

Time Required: 10 minutes

Objective: Use Telnet to verify the functionality of an SMTP server.

Description: A client is having a problem sending e-mail to a person at Microsoft. You want to verify that Microsoft's SMTP server is responding on the Internet. If you can telnet to the mail server on port 25, that will indicate that the server is operational and accepting connections.

1. If necessary, start your server and log on as **Administrator**.

2. Click the **Start** button, and then click **Run**.

3. Type **cmd** and click **OK**.

4. Type **telnet** and press **Enter**.

5. Type **set localecho** and press **Enter**. This displays the commands that you type in the Telnet window.

6. Type **open maila.microsoft.com 25** and press **Enter**.

7. Type **help** and press **Enter**. What commands does the mail server support?

8. Type **help** and press **Enter**. What is the FQDN of the mail server?

9. Type **quit** and press **Enter**.

10. If you are prompted to press a key to continue, then press **Enter** twice.

11. Type **quit** and press **Enter** to close the Telnet utility.

12. Close the command prompt.

POP3

Post Office Protocol version 3 (POP3) is the most common protocol used for reading e-mail messages. This protocol has commands to download messages and delete messages from the mail server. POP3 does not support sending messages. By default, most e-mail client software using POP3 copies all messages onto the local hard drive and erases them from the server. However, you can change the configuration so that messages can be left on the server. POP3 only supports a single inbox and does not support multiple folders for storage on the server.

IMAP4

Internet Message Access Protocol version 4 (IMAP4) is another common protocol used to read e-mail messages. The abilities of IMAP4 are beyond those of POP3. For example, IMAP can download message headers only, then allow you to choose which messages to download. In addition, IMAP4 allows for multiple folders on the server side to store messages.

TRANSPORT LAYER PROTOCOLS

Transport layer protocols are responsible for getting data ready to move across the network. The most common task performed by Transport layer protocols is breaking entire messages down into packets. For instance, if an entire file is being moved across the network, then a Transport layer protocol breaks it down into smaller pieces that can move more easily across the network.

One of the defining characteristics of Transport layer protocols is the use of **port** numbers. Each service running on a server listens at a port number. Each Transport layer protocol has its own set of ports. When a packet is addressed to a particular port, the Transport layer protocol knows to which service to deliver the packet. The combination of an IP address and port number is referred to as a socket.

A port number is like an apartment number for the delivery of mail. The network ID of the IP address ensures that the packet is delivered to the correct street (network); the host ID ensures that the packet is delivered to the correct building (host); the Transport layer protocol and port number ensure that the packet is delivered to the proper apartment (service).

The two Transport layer protocols in the TCP/IP protocol suite are **Transmission Control Protocol (TCP)** and **User Datagram Protocol (UDP)**. Table 3-1 shows well-known services and the ports they use.

Table 3-1   Common services and ports

Service	Port
FTP	TCP 21,20
Telnet	TCP 23
SMTP	TCP 25
HTTP	TCP 80
DNS	TCP 53, UDP 53
Trivial FTP (TFTP)	UDP 69
POP3	TCP 110
NNTP	TCP 119
IMAP	TCP 143
Secure HTTP	TCP 443

Activity 3-3: Using Port Numbers

Time Required: 5 minutes

Objective: Connect to resources using TCP and UDP port numbers.

Description: You have been explaining the concept of port numbers to a colleague. He is still unsure that he understands how they are used. You have explained that a Web browser automatically uses the default port for a protocol. In this activity, you demonstrate for your colleague what happens when an incorrect port number is used.

1. If necessary, start your server and log on as **Administrator**.

2. Open Internet Explorer.

3. Type **http://www.microsoft.com** in the address bar, and press **Enter**. The Web browser will automatically connect you to port 80 on this server.

4. Type **http://www.microsoft.com:21** in the address bar, and press **Enter**. The Web browser will not be able to connect because port 21 is not used for HTTP.

5. Type **http://www.microsoft.com:80** in the address bar, and press **Enter**. The Web browser will connect and give you the same Web page as in Step 3.

6. Type **ftp://ftp.microsoft.com** in the address bar, and press **Enter**. The Web browser will automatically connect you to port 21 when using FTP.

7. Type **ftp://ftp.microsoft.com:80** in the address bar, and press **Enter**. The Web browser will not be able to connect because port 80 is not used for FTP.

8. Click OK to clear the error message window.

9. Type **ftp://ftp.microsoft.com:21** in the address bar, and press **Enter**. The Web browser will connect and give you the same information as in Step 6.

10. Close Internet Explorer

TCP

Transmission Control Protocol (TCP) is the most commonly used Transport layer protocol. TCP is connection-oriented and reliable. **Connection-oriented** means that TCP creates and verifies a connection with a remote host before sending information. This verifies that the remote host exists and is willing to communicate before starting the conversation.

The establishment of a connection is a three-packet process between the source and destination host. It is often called a three-way handshake. Figure 3-2 shows the packets involved in the three-way handshake performed when a connection is established between Computer A and Computer B.

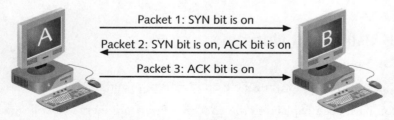

Figure 3-2   TCP three-way handshake

In Figure 3-2, you can see that the connection is initiated by Computer A. An option in the packet called the SYN bit is turned on. The **SYN bit** indicates that this packet is a request to negotiate a connection. This request includes parameters for the conversation such as the maximum packet size.

The response packet from Computer B to Computer A has the ACK and SYN bits turned on. The **ACK bit** is an option in a packet that indicates this packet is a response to the first packet. The SYN bit is on because this packet contains the parameters that Computer B would like to use when communicating with Computer A. If Computer B is able to use the parameters received in the first packet, then those are the parameters sent in this packet. If Computer B cannot use a parameter from the first packet, then it replaces that parameter with one that it can use in this packet.

The third packet is the final agreement from Computer A indicating that it has accepted the terms of the Computer B. This packet has the ACK bit turned on to indicate that it is a response to the second packet.

TCP is considered reliable because it tracks each packet and makes sure that it arrives at its destination. If a packet is lost or damaged as part of the communication process, then the packet is transmitted again. The overall process is called a **sliding window**.

If a thousand packets are waiting to be sent as part of the communication process, not all of the packets are sent at once because it would be too difficult to track them. Only a few packets are sent at a time. The number of packets is negotiated as part of the process of establishing the connection and is considered as being the size of the sliding window. For example, if the sliding window size is set to 10 packets, then only 10 packets are sent at a time. When the destination computer acknowledges receipt of the first 10 packets, then the window slides forward and another 10 packets are sent.

The sliding window cannot be moved past a packet that has not been received and acknowledged by the destination. If a packet goes missing, it must be retransmitted and acknowledged before the sliding window can move past that point. A common reason why there is a pause in the middle of large downloads from the Internet is that a packet has been lost and must be retransmitted before the conversation can continue.

Being reliable and connection-oriented are generally desirable qualities. Consequently, TCP is the Transport layer protocol used for most Internet services. HTTP, FTP, SMTP, POP3 and IMAP4 all use TCP.

Activity 3-4: Installing Network Monitor

Time Required: 5 minutes

Objective: Install Network Monitor to enable packet capturing.

Description: You would like to see exactly how some of the data packets on your network are addressed. To see packet details, you install the application Network Monitor, which is included with Windows Server 2003.

1. If necessary, start your server and log on as **Administrator**.

2. Click the **Start** button, point to **Control Panel**, and then click **Add or Remove Programs**.

3. Click **Add/Remove Windows Components**.

4. Scroll down in the Components section, then double-click **Management and Monitoring Tools**.

5. Click the check box beside Network Monitor Tools to select it, and click **OK**.

6. Place your Windows Server 2003 Enterprise Edition CD-ROM into your CD-ROM drive. Click the **Next** button.

7. Click the **Finish** button, and close the Add or Remove Programs window.

Activity 3-5: Viewing a TCP Connection in Network Monitor

Time Required: 30 minutes

Objective: Capture and view TCP connection packets in Network Monitor.

Description: You are going to be configuring the University firewall in the next few weeks and would like to be familiar with the detailed packet information that is used when creating a TCP connection. In this exercise, you capture and view the packets used when a TCP connection is created with HTTP.

1. If necessary, start your server and log on as **Administrator**.

2. Open Internet Explorer.

3. Click the **Start** button, point to **Administrative Tools**, and click **Network Monitor**.

4. Click **OK**.

5. Click the **+** (plus sign) beside Local Computer, click **Local Area Connection**, and click **OK**.

6. Press **F10** to start capturing packets.

7. In Internet Explorer, type **www.yahoo.com** in the address bar, and press **Enter**.

8. In Network Monitor, press **F11** to stop capturing packets.

9. Press **F12** to view the captured packets.

10. Filter the display to only show packets with a TCP source port or a TCP destination port of 80. This shows all packets addressed to the Web server or coming from the Web server.

    a. Click the **Display** menu and click **Filter**.

    b. Double-click the green **AND** to change it to **OR**.

    c. Double-click **Protocol==Any**.

    d. Click the **Property** tab.

    e. Double-click **TCP** in the Protocol: Property box; then, underneath TCP, click **Destination Port**, click the **Decimal** radio button, type **80** in the Value box, and click **OK**.

    f. In the Add box, click **Expression**.

    g. Under TCP, click **Source Port** and click **OK**.

    h. Click **ANY<--> ANY** and then click **Line** in the Delete box.

    i. Click **OK**.

11. View the first packet in a TCP handshake.

    a. Double-click the first packet in the Capture:l(Summary) window.

    b. Expand the **IP** section of the middle window to view the source and destination IP addresses. The source IP address is your computer. The destination IP address is the Web server.

    c. Expand the **TCP** section of the middle window to view the source and destination TCP ports. The source port varies, but the destination port is World Wide Web HTTP. Network Monitor substitutes the phrase World Wide Web HTTP for the number 80 to make the location easier to read and understand.

    d. Expand the **TCP: Flags** section of the middle window to view the acknowledgement (ACK) and synchronize (SYN) flags. In this packet, the ACK flag is set to 0 and the SYN flag is set to 1.

    e. Expand the **TCP: Options** and **TCP: Maximum Segment Size Option** to view the packet size that is being requested.

12. View the second packet in a TCP handshake.

    a. Click the second packet in the top window.

    b. In the **IP** section of the middle window, view the source and destination IP addresses. The source IP address is the Web server. The destination IP address is your server.

    c. In the **TCP** section of the middle window, view the source and destination TCP ports. The destination port is the same as the source port in the first packet. The source port is World Wide Web HTTP.

    d. In the **TCP: Flags** section of the middle window, view the acknowledgement (ACK) and synchronize (SYN) flags. In this packet, the ACK flag is set to 1 and the SYN flag is set to 1.

    e. In the **TCP: Options** and **TCP: Maximum Segment Size Option**, view the packet size that is being requested. This is the same as the size of the first packet or smaller.

13. View the third packet in a TCP handshake.

    a. Click the third packet in the top window.

    b. In the **IP** section of the middle window, view the source and destination IP addresses. The source IP address is your server. The destination IP address is the Web server.

    c. In the **TCP** section of the middle window, view the source and destination TCP ports. The source port is the same as the first packet and the destination port is World Wide Web HTTP.

    d. In the **TCP: Flags** section of the middle windows, view the acknowledgement (ACK) and synchronize (SYN) flags. In this packet, the ACK flag is set to 1 and the SYN flag is set to 0.

    e. TCP: Options does not exist in this packet.

14. Click the fourth packet in the top window to view an HTTP GET request. This packet is the request for the Web page.

15. Click the fifth packet in the top window to view the response to the GET request. This is the information returned from the Web server based on the GET request.

16. Close Network Monitor (click **No** as many times as is necessary if prompted to save changes) and Internet Explorer.

UDP

User Datagram Protocol (UDP) is not as commonly used as TCP and is used for different services. UDP is connectionless and unreliable. **Connectionless** means that UDP does not attempt to negotiate terms with a remote host before sending information. UDP simply sends the information. If any terms need to be negotiated, the Application layer protocol has to do it. There is no handshake for UDP. Unreliable means that UDP does not track or guarantee delivery of packets between the source and destination. UDP just sends a stream of packets without waiting for acknowledgement. There is no sliding window for UDP.

UDP is the appropriate Transport layer protocol to use when you are unconcerned about missing packets or would like to implement reliability in a special way. Streaming audio and video are in this category. If streaming audio were to pause and wait for missing packets to be sent again, then there could be long pauses in the sound. Most people prefer a small amount of static or silence be inserted for the missing packet and the rest of the audio track continue to play. UDP does this because it does not keep track of packets that are missing or need to be sent again. In the case of streaming audio, resent packets are handled by the Application layer protocol.

Connectionless communication also makes sense when the amount of data being exchanged is very small. Using three packets to set up a connection for a two-packet conversation is very inefficient. The resolution of a DNS name is a two-packet communication process and is done via UDP.

Activity 3-6: Capturing UDP Packets in Network Monitor

Time Required: 15 minutes

Objective: Capture and view UDP packets in Network Monitor.

Description: As preparation for configuring the University firewall in the next few weeks, you would like to be familiar with the detailed packet information that is used in UDP packets. In this activity, you view DNS packets.

1. If necessary, start your server and log on as **Administrator**.

2. Open Internet Explorer.

3. Open Network Monitor (see Activity 3-5, if necessary).

4. Click the **Start** button, and click **Run**.

5. Type **ipconfig /flushdns** and press **Enter**. This removes any cached DNS lookup information. This ensures that, later in the activity, a DNS lookup will be performed rather than DNS information being retrieved from the cache.

6. In Network Monitor, press **F10** to start capturing packets.

7. In Internet Explorer, type **www.yahoo.com** in the address bar, and press **Enter**.

8. In Network Monitor, press **F11** to stop capturing packets.

9. Press **F12** to view the captured packets.

10. Filter the display to only show packets with a TCP source port or a TCP destination port of 53. This shows all packets addressed to the DNS server or coming from the DNS server.

   a. Click the **Display** menu and click **Filter**.

   b. Double-click the green **AND** to change it to **OR**.

   c. Double-click **Protocol==Any**.

   d. Click the **Property** tab.

   e. Double-click **UDP** in the Protocol: Property box, and then, underneath UDP, click **Destination Port**, click the **Decimal** radio button, type **53** in the Value box, and click **OK**.

   f. In the Add box, click **Expression**.

   g. Under UDP, click **Source Port** and click **OK**.

   h. Click **ANY<--> ANY** and then click **Line** in the Delete box.

   i. Click **OK**.

11. View the first UDP DNS packet.

   a. Double-click the packet with the description **Std Qry for www.yahoo.com**.

   b. Expand the **IP** section of the middle window to view the source and destination IP addresses. The source IP address is your computer. The destination IP address is the DNS server.

   c. Expand the **UDP** section of the middle window to view the source and destination UDP ports. The source UDP port varies. The destination UDP port is Domain Name Server.

   d. Expand the **DNS** section of the middle window to view the DNS-specific information.

12. View the second UDP DNS packet.

   a. Click the packet with the description **Std Qry Resp. Auth NS is www.yahoo.com**.

   b. In the **IP** section of the middle window, view the source and destination IP addresses. The source IP address is the DNS server. The destination IP address is your server.

c. In the **UDP** section of the middle window, view the source and destination UDP ports. The source UDP is the Domain Name Server. The destination UDP port is the same as the source UDP port in the previous packet.

d. In the **DNS** section of the middle window, view the DNS-specific information.

13. Close Network Monitor (click **No** as many times as is necessary if prompted to save changes) and Internet Explorer.

TCP versus UDP

TCP is connection-oriented and reliable. This is similar to delivering a letter by registered mail. Inside the letter each page is numbered so that it can be read in the proper order. When the message is received the sender receives notice that it arrived properly at its destination.

UDP is connectionless and unreliable. If you were to take the same message as in the previous example and place it on several postcards, take all of the postcards and dump them in the mail box separately, then the likelihood is that the recipient would be able to put them in the proper order and understand the message. However, if one postcard was missing it would be very difficult for the recipient to understand the complete message.

INTERNET LAYER PROTOCOLS

Internet layer protocols are responsible for all tasks related to logical addressing. An IP address is a logical address. Any protocol that is aware of other networks, as in how to find them and how to reach them, exists at this layer. Each Internet layer protocol is very specialized. They include: IP, RIP, OSPF, ICMP, IGMP, and ARP.

IP

Internet Protocol (IP) is responsible for the logical addressing of each packet created by the Transport layer. As each packet is built, IP adds the source and destination IP address to the packet.

When a packet is received from the network, IP verifies that it is addressed to that computer. IP looks at the destination IP address of the packet to verify that it is the same as the IP address of the receiving computer, or a broadcast address of which that computer is a part. For example, if a computer has an IP address of 192.168.1.50/24, then IP would accept packets addressed to 192.168.1.50, 192.168.1.255, and 255.255.255.255.

RIP and OSPF

Routing Information Protocol (RIP) and **Open Shortest Path First (OSPF)** are both routing protocols. They are responsible for defining how paths are chosen through the internetwork from one computer to another. They also define how routers can share information about the networks of which they are aware.

ICMP

Internet Control Messaging Protocol (ICMP) is used to send IP error and control messages between routers and hosts. The most common use of ICMP is the ping utility.

The ping utility uses ICMP packets to test connectivity between hosts. When you use ping to communicate with a host, your computer sends an ICMP Echo Request packet. The host that you are pinging sends an ICMP Echo Response packet back. If there is a response, you can be sure that the host you have pinged is up and functional. However, if a host does not respond, that does not guarantee it is nonfunctional. Many firewalls are configured to block ICMP packets.

The **Internet Assigned Numbers Authority (IANA)** maintains a complete list of ICMP packet types at *www.iana.org/assignments/icmp-parameters*. Table 3-2 lists the most common ICMP packet types.

Table 3-2   Common ICMP packet types

Packet Type	Packet Name	Description
0	Echo Reply	Used in response to an Echo Request packet from a host
3	Destination Unreachable	Used by routers to indicate that the intended destination IP address cannot be reached
4	Source Quench	Used by routers to indicate that packets are being sent too fast and should be slowed down; this is seldom used
8	Echo	Used to generate an Echo Reply packet from a host
11	Time Exceeded	Used by routers to indicate that the time to live (TTL) of a packet has expired

The Time Exceeded ICMP packet type indicates that a packet could not reach its destination because delivery took too long. The **time to live (TTL)** of a packet is a combination of router hops and seconds. Each router that forwards a packet reduces the TTL of the packet by one. If it takes longer than 1 second to forward the packet, then the TTL is also reduced by one for each second that it is delayed.

The default TTL of Windows Server 2003 is 128. The default TTL used by other operating systems varies widely, but 64 is recommended by IANA.

Activity 3-7: Testing Host Functionality

Time Required: 5 minutes

Objective: Test the functionality of a host using the ping command.

Description: One of your users has called with a problem. She is unable to connect to *www.hotmail.com* with her Web browser. In this activity, you will use the ping utility to test Internet connectivity by connecting to *www.hotmail.com*.

1. If necessary, start your server and log on as **Administrator**.

2. Open a command prompt (see Activity 3-2, if necessary).

3. Type **ping www.hotmail.com** and press **Enter**. There is no response because Hotmail has configured its firewall to block ping packets by default. No response may also mean that the server is not functioning or that Internet connectivity is down.

4. Type **ping www.yahoo.com** and press **Enter**. This server responds. This confirms that the server is definitely functional and Internet connectivity is working.

5. Close the command prompt.

6. Open Internet Explorer.

7. Type **www.hotmail.com** in the address bar, and press **Enter**. The Hotmail Web site appears. This confirms that the Web site is functional.

8. Close Internet Explorer.

Activity 3-8: Viewing TTL

Time Required: 5 minutes

Objective: View the TTL of a ping packet.

Description: One of your users is complaining of slow Internet connectivity. To test the distance from Great Arctic North University to the site, you use the ping utility. The ping utility shows the TTL of the packet, giving an approximation of how fast the connection is. Since the TTL is reduced by one for each router that is crossed, a smaller TTL means that there are more routers between you and the remote host.

1. If necessary, start your server and log on as **Administrator**.

2. Open a command prompt (see Activity 3-2, if necessary).

3. Type **ping 192.168.1.10** and press **Enter**. The TTL in the response is the TTL when no routers are passed through.

4. Type **ping www.yahoo.com** and press **Enter**. You can figure out the number of routers between you and *www.yahoo.com* by calculating the TTL from pinging the default gateway minus the TTL from pinging *www.yahoo.com*. For example, if you received a TTL of 128 when pinging your default gateway and a TTL of 113 when pinging *www.yahoo.com*, then the number of routers between your computer and *www.yahoo.com* is $128 - 113 = 15$.

5. Type **ping –i 1 www.yahoo.com** and press **Enter**. This forces a TTL of 1. This results in an ICMP error message indicating that the TTL expired in transit.

6. Close the command prompt.

IGMP

Internet Group Management Protocol (IGMP) is used for the management of multicast groups. Hosts use IGMP to inform routers of their membership in multicast groups. Routers use IGMP to announce that their networks have members in particular multicast groups. The use of IGMP allows multicast packets to be distributed only to routers that have interested hosts connected.

ARP

Address Resolution Protocol (ARP) is used to convert logical IP addresses to physical MAC addresses. This is an essential part of the packet delivery process.

Network cards use a MAC address to filter irrelevant packets. When a packet is received, the network card verifies that the destination MAC address matches the MAC address of the network card or is a broadcast MAC address. For example, if the receiving computer has a MAC address of A1:B2:C3:D4:E5:F6, then the network card of the receiving computer passes the packet up to IP if the destination MAC address of the packet is A1:B2:C3:D4:E5:F6 or FF:FF:FF:FF:FF:FF (broadcast MAC address). This process offloads the responsibility for analyzing all the network packets from IP to the network card. This reduces CPU utilization on the computer.

Data packets have four addresses: source IP address, destination IP address, source MAC address, and destination MAC address. When a packet is created, the source computer must find the MAC address of the destination computer based on the destination IP address.

ARP uses a two-packet process to find the MAC address of the destination computer. The first packet is an ARP Request that is broadcast to all computers on the local network asking for the MAC address of the computer with the destination IP address. The destination computer sees this packet and sends an ARP Reply containing its MAC address. The sending computer can then create data packets using the destination MAC address. Figure 3-3 shows an example of a small computer network. Computer A needs to find the MAC address of Computer B before data packets can be delivered.

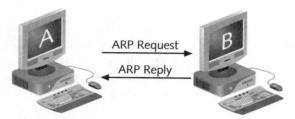

IP Address: 192.30.0.24   IP Address: 172.30.0.25
MAC: 00:10:5A:5D:BA:62   MAC: 00:50:DA:23:15:2D

Figure 3-3   Computer A communicates with Computer B

Figure 3-4 shows the structure of an ARP Request packet sent as the first step of the resolution process. The ETHERNET section of the packet contains the MAC address information used by network cards when they analyze whether the packet should be passed up to IP. In this packet, the source MAC address is the MAC address of computer A, and the destination MAC address is the broadcast MAC address of FF:FF:FF:FF:FF:FF. All computers on the local segment process this packet and pass it up to ARP because the broadcast MAC address is the destination MAC address.

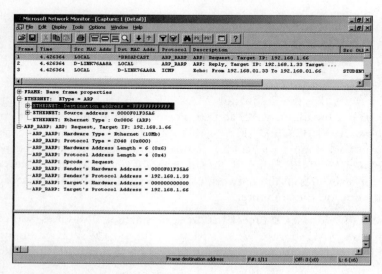

Figure 3-4   ARP Request packet

The ARP_RARP section of the packet shown in Figure 3-4 is the ARP information that is processed by ARP on the receiving computer. The most important information in this part of the packet is the Target's Protocol Address. This is the IP address of the destination computer. If the Target's Protocol Address matches the IP address of computer B, then an ARP Reply packet is created. If the Target's Protocol Address does not match the IP address of computer B, then the packet is discarded.

Figure 3-5 shows the structure of an ARP Reply packet sent as the second step of the resolution process. The ETHERNET section of the packet contains the MAC address information used by network cards when they analyze whether the packet should be passed up to IP. In this packet, the source MAC address is the MAC address of computer B and the destination MAC address is the MAC address of computer A. The ARP_RARP section of the packet has the ARP information required by computer A to create proper data packets. The Sender's Hardware Address is the MAC address that is required by computer A.

If routers are forwarding packets, then the ARP process is modified. The first ARP Request is for the default gateway, then the ARP Response includes the MAC address of the router. The data packet is then built and sent to the router. The router removes and then replaces

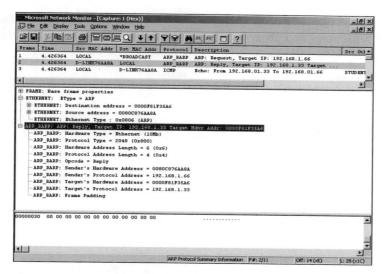

Figure 3-5   ARP Reply packet

the source MAC address with its own and uses ARP to find the MAC address of the next router, if required, or the final destination host.

In Figure 3-6, Computer A is sending a data packet to Computer B. The data packet is addressed to Computer B at the IP layer, but must be given to the router for delivery. The MAC address is used to deliver the packet to the router.

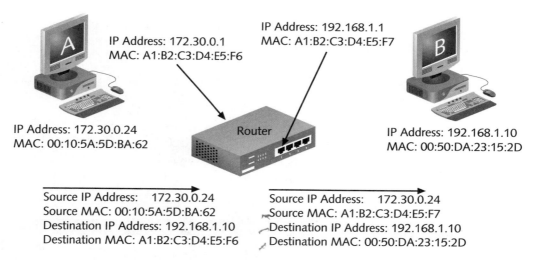

Figure 3-6   Computer A communicates with Computer B across a router

The router removes the MAC address information from the data packet and replaces it with the MAC addresses required to deliver it to computer B. The source and destination IP addresses of the packet do not change.

Activity 3-9: Viewing the ARP Cache

Time Required: 5 minutes

Objective: View the contents of the ARP cache.

Description: You are concerned that a user connectivity issue is being caused by incorrect MAC address information in the ARP. In this exercise, you view the contents of the ARP cache and clear the cache to force the rebuilding of the cache information. In this activity, your instructor will assign you a partner.

1. If necessary, start your server and log on as **Administrator**.

2. Open a command prompt (see Activity 3-2, if necessary).

3. Type **arp –d** and press **Enter**. This clears the contents of the ARP cache.

4. Type **ping** *partnercomputer* and press **Enter** (where *partnercomputer* is the IP address of your partner's computer). *Note*: Be sure that your partner's computer is on the same network as your computer.

5. Type **arp –g** and press **Enter**. This shows the contents of the ARP cache. Right now it shows the IP address and MAC address of your partner's computer.

6. Type **ping www.yahoo.com** and press **Enter**.

7. Type **arp –g** and press **Enter**. Notice that the cache does not have an entry for *www.yahoo.com*. The cache has a new entry for your default gateway.

8. Close the command prompt.

NETWORK INTERFACE LAYER PROTOCOLS

Most of the common Network Interface layer protocols are defined by the Institute of Electrical and Electronics Engineers (IEEE). The IEEE has a system of numbered committees that each defines a different Network Interface layer protocol. Table 3-3 lists some of the IEEE Network Interface layer protocols for which they are responsible.

Table 3-3   IEEE protocols

Protocol	Description
802.3	Ethernet
802.5	Token Ring
802.11	Wireless LAN
802.15	Wireless personal area network

Ethernet is the most common Network Interface layer protocol used in corporate networks today. There are many different varieties of Ethernet, all of which use Carrier Sense Multiple Access/Collision Detection (CSMA/CD) for access control. The most common version of Ethernet is implemented with twisted-pair cabling at 100 Mbps. Table 3-4 shows the different speeds of Ethernet for different cabling types.

Table 3-4   Ethernet cabling types and speeds

Cabling	Speed
Coaxial	10 Mbps
Twisted-pair (Cat 5e)	10 Mbps to 1 Gbps
Fiber-optic	10 Mbps to 10 Gbps

Token Ring is an older technology created by IBM that was implemented in the late 1980s and early 1990s. It was commonly implemented with mainframe computers. This standard uses twisted-pair cabling and operates at 4 Mbps or 16 Mbps. The access method used is token passing.

Wireless LAN is one of the fastest growing network types. The 802.11b standard defines the most common wireless standard. It uses radio signals to send data at 11 Mbps. The maximum distance of 802.11b is approximately 300 feet indoors and up to 1,000 feet outdoors.

NOTE   Microsoft has added a number of features for wireless networks to Windows Server 2003. A wireless snap-in allows you to monitor and manage wireless access points and wireless clients. Group Policy has been extended to allow the management of wireless clients, including encryption settings. Some wireless functionality for network cards is also available in the operating system to make driver development easier for hardware developers and more reliable for users.

The IEEE standard 802.15 defines the physical layer portion of the Bluetooth standard. **Bluetooth** is a short-range wireless communication system with a maximum distance of approximately 30 feet and maximum speed of 720 Kbps. This is a much shorter range and much slower data transfer rate than 802.11b. The IEEE 802.15 committee intends to increase this speed. Support for Bluetooth is built into many smaller devices that need to minimize energy consumption, such as Palm and Windows CE devices.

Infrared communication is built into many devices for wireless connectivity. It is very common on laptops, Palm devices, and Windows CE devices. The official protocol implementation for infrared communication is **Infrared Data Association (IrDA)**. This is also the name of the group responsible for defining the protocol implementation. IrDA has a maximum range of 3 feet and maximum speed of 4 Mbps. The use of IrDA is being reduced as Bluetooth becomes more popular.

CHAPTER SUMMARY

- ❑ The TCP/IP model is composed of four layers: the Application layer, the Transport layer, the Internet layer, and the Network Interface layer.

- ❑ There are many Application layer protocols, each of which is associated with a client application and service.

- ❑ HTTP is the most common protocol used on the Internet today.

- ❑ FTP is used for transferring files across the Internet.

- ❑ Telnet is used to remotely connect to UNIX and Linux systems.

- ❑ SMTP is used to send and receive e-mail messages between e-mail servers.

- ❑ POP3 is the most common protocol used for reading e-mail messages. IMAP4 is another protocol used for reading e-mail messages.

- ❑ The two Transport layer protocols are TCP and UDP.

- ❑ TCP is connection-oriented and reliable.

- ❑ UDP is connectionless and unreliable.

- ❑ Internet layer protocols are responsible for all tasks related to logical addressing and are all very specialized.

- ❑ Internet layer protocols include IP, RIP, OSPF, ICMP, IGMP, and ARP.

- ❑ Ethernet is the most common Network Interface layer protocol used in corporate networks today.

- ❑ Wireless LANs are one of the fastest growing network types.

KEY TERMS

ACK bit — A bit used in TCP communication to indicate that a packet is an acknowledgement of a previous packet.

Address Resolution Protocol (ARP) — A protocol used by hosts to find the physical MAC address of another host with a particular IP address.

Application layer — The layer of the TCP/IP architecture that provides access to network resources.

Bluetooth — A short-range wireless communication protocol.

Common Gateway Interface (CGI) — A vendor-neutral mechanism used to pass information from a Web page to an application running on a Web server.

connectionless — A term used to describe a protocol that does not establish a communication channel before sending data.

connection-oriented — A term used to describe a protocol that verifies the existence of a host and agrees on terms of communication before sending data.

File Transfer Protocol (FTP) — The most common protocol used to send files across the Internet.

graphical user interface (GUI) — A user interface for an operating system that supports graphics in addition to characters.

Hypertext Transfer Protocol (HTTP) — The protocol used to send information such as Web pages across the Internet.

Infrared Data Association (IrDA) — A standard for communication using infrared ports in mobile devices. This is also the name of the organization that created the standard.

Internet Assigned Numbers Authority (IANA) — The organization that maintains standards for Internet addressing, including well-known port numbers and ICMP packet types.

Internet Control Messaging Protocol (ICMP) — The protocol used by routers and hosts to send Internet protocol error messages.

Internet Group Management Protocol (IGMP) — The protocol used by routers to track the membership in multicast groups.

Internet layer — The layer of the TCP/IP architecture that is responsible for logical addressing and routing.

Internet Message Access Protocol version 4 (IMAP4) — A protocol used to retrieve e-mail messages from an e-mail server. It is more flexible than POP3 for managing message storage.

Internet Server Application Programmer Interface (ISAPI) — A programmer interface defined by Microsoft for passing information from Web pages to programs running on a Web server.

Netscape Server Application Programmer Interface (NSAPI) — A programmer interface defined by Netscape to pass information from Web pages to applications running on a Web server.

Network Interface layer — The layer of the TCP/IP architecture that controls placing packets on the physical network media.

Open Shortest Path First (OSPF) — A protocol that is used by routers to share information about known networks and calculate the best path through an internetwork. OSPF calculates routes based on user definable cost values.

Open Systems Interconnection (OSI) reference model — An industry standard that is used as a reference point to compare different networking technologies and protocols.

Packets — A single unit of data sent from one computer to another. It contains a source address, destination address, data, and error-checking information.

port — A TCP port or UDP port is used by Transport layer protocols to direct network information to the proper service.

Post Office Protocol version 3 (POP3) — A protocol that is used to retrieve e-mail messages from an e-mail server.

Request for Comment (RFC) — A submission to the Internet Engineering Task Force that is evaluated for use as part of the TCP/IP protocol suite.

Routing Information Protocol (RIP) — A protocol used by routers to exchange routing table information and determine the best path through an internetwork based on the number of hops.

Simple Mail Transfer Protocol (SMTP) — A protocol that is used to send e-mail across the Internet.

sliding window — A process used in the TCP protocol to track which packets have been received by the destination host.

SYN bit — A bit used in TCP communication to indicate a request to start a communication session.

Telnet — A protocol used to remotely access a command-line interface on UNIX and Linux servers.

time to live (TTL) — A parameter of IP packets used to ensure that if a packet becomes trapped in a router loop, it will expire. Each hop through a router reduces TTL by one.

Token Ring — An older Physical layer protocol developed by IBM that operated at either 4 Mbps or 16 Mbps.

Transmission Control Protocol (TCP) — A connection-oriented and reliable Transport layer protocol that is part of the TCP/IP protocol suite.

Transport layer — The layer of the TCP/IP architecture that breaks messages into smaller packets and tracks their delivery.

User Datagram Protocol (UDP) — A connectionless, unreliable Transport layer protocol used in the TCP/IP protocol suite.

Wireless LAN — A standard for wireless communication created by the IEEE. The most common variant of wireless LAN is 802.11b.

REVIEW QUESTIONS

1. Which transport protocol establishes a connection with the remote host before sending data?

   a. UDP

   b. TCP

   c. ARP

   d. FTP

2. Which protocol supports the use of multicast groups?

   a. UDP

   b. TCP

   c. ARP

   d. ICMP

   e. IGMP

3. Token Ring operates at which speed(s)? (Choose all that apply.)
   a. 1 Mbps
   b. 4 Mbps
   c. 10 Mbps
   d. 16 Mbps
   e. 1 Gbps

4. Which of the following is not an Application layer protocol?
   a. FTP
   b. HTTP
   c. IP
   d. Telnet
   e. SMTP

5. Which network layer protocol is responsible for routing packets on the network?
   a. TCP
   b. UDP
   c. IP
   d. ICMP
   e. IGMP

6. ARP is used to resolve IP addresses to what?
   a. NetBIOS names
   b. MAC addresses
   c. Fully qualified domain names
   d. Internet addresses

7. Bluetooth wireless technology is defined by which IEEE standard?
   a. 802.2
   b. 802.3
   c. 802.5
   d. 802.11
   e. 802.15

8. Which of the following statements regarding File Transfer Protocol (FTP) are true? (Choose all that apply.)
   a. FTP uses port 80.
   b. FTP uses port 23.
   c. FTP uses UDP for file transfer.
   d. FTP uses TCP for file transfer.

9. The network card operates at which layer of the IP stack?

 a. Application

 b. Transport

 c. Internet

 d. Network Interface

10. Which of the following statements regarding TCP are false?

 a. TCP is a connection-oriented protocol.

 b. TCP uses a three-way handshake to establish a connection to the remote host.

 c. Packets lost during transit are resent.

 d. HTTP and POP3 use TCP.

 e. none of the above

11. Which of the following are routing protocols? (Choose all that apply.)

 a. RIP

 b. LCR

 c. OSPF

 d. ICMP

12. Which of the following statements regarding e-mail protocols are true? (Choose all that apply.)

 a. SMTP is only used by clients to send e-mail.

 b. POP3 allows users to view multiple folders.

 c. IMAP4 can be configured to download only mail headers.

 d. POP3 stores all e-mail messages on the server.

13. Which port is used by HTTP?

 a. 21

 b. 23

 c. 25

 d. 53

 e. 80

 f. 110

14. Which of the following physical layer protocols uses Carrier Sense Multiple Access/Collision Detection?

 a. Token Ring

 b. ARCnet

 c. Ethernet

 d. FDDI

15. The time to live (TTL) of a packet is a combination of what factors? (Choose all that apply.)
    a. router hops
    b. date
    c. Internet connectivity
    d. seconds
    e. destination MAC address

16. What is the maximum distance for infrared data transfer?
    a. 2 feet
    b. 3 feet
    c. 4 feet
    d. 10 feet
    e. 30 feet

17. Which Transport layer protocol is most likely to be used for streaming media?
    a. TCP
    b. DNS
    c. UDP
    d. HTTP
    e. ARP

18. When a packet crosses a router, what happens to the packet's TTL?
    a. nothing
    b. It is decremented by one.
    c. It is incremented by one.
    d. It is reset to the default TTL.

19. What happens when a packet's TTL reaches zero?
    a. The packet is returned to the sender.
    b. The packet is discarded.
    c. The packet is forwarded to the recipient by the most direct path.
    d. The router issues a Source Quench Request to slow down the sending of packets.

20. You ping a host that is on a remote subnet. When you view your ARP cache, which MAC address do you see for the remote host?
    a. your own MAC address
    b. the MAC address of the remote host
    c. the MAC address of the router
    d. all of the above

CASE PROJECTS

Internet access has recently been installed by ZAP Internet Services and has been made available to the Arts faculty for testing. The Arts faculty is known for having demanding users and is the perfect place to find user problems.

Case Project 3-1: Slow Internet Access

Bob Jones, an Arts professor, has written an e-mail message to you complaining about the speed of his Internet connection. He regularly downloads large files from a particular Web site. Downloads from this Web site regularly pause for 10 to 15 seconds, then resume. This does not happen when he downloads information from other Web sites. Write an e-mail response to Bob explaining the likely cause of the problem and what you can do to correct it.

Case Project 3-2: Planning Physical Layer Protocols

Your supervisor has been approached by the head of the Arts faculty about redesigning the physical infrastructure for the network. Most of the Arts professors have laptop computers but are unable to use them in the classrooms because there are no LAN hookups. The offices of the Arts professors are wired with twisted-pair (CAT 5e) cabling. Write a short report with your recommendations for the Network Interface layer protocols that should be implemented to support the professors.

Case Project 3-3: Planning Application Layer Protocols

One firewall that you are evaluating has the ability to control network traffic at the Application layer. As part of your own planning process, list the Application layer protocols that you would allow through the firewall, those you would block, and your reasons for doing so.

4

DYNAMIC HOST CONFIGURATION PROTOCOL

After reading this chapter, you will be able to:

- ◆ Outline the benefits of using DHCP
- ◆ Describe the DHCP lease and renewal process
- ◆ Install and authorize the DHCP service
- ◆ Configure DHCP scopes
- ◆ Create DHCP reservations for client computers
- ◆ Configure DHCP options
- ◆ Understand and describe the purpose of a DHCP relay
- ◆ Install and configure a DHCP relay

Manually going to each workstation to configure IP addresses is a time-consuming task. You can use Dynamic Host Configuration Protocol (DHCP) to reduce the amount of time spent configuring workstations. DHCP can be used to automatically configure the TCP/IP protocol on workstations. This chapter discusses the benefits and structure of DHCP, as well as how to configure it on Windows Server 2003.

DHCP OVERVIEW

Dynamic Host Configuration Protocol (DHCP) is used to automatically deliver IP addressing information to client computers on a network. It can also deliver IP address information to servers and other devices such as printers, although most network administrators prefer to use static IP addresses for network resources such as servers and printers.

Using DHCP reduces the amount of time you spend configuring computers on your network. Imagine that a company with 500 client computers changes the IP address of its router as part of the implementation of a new firewall. If this company is not using DHCP, the network administrator has to visit each client computer and change the default gateway, which might take days. However, if this company is using DHCP, then the new default gateway can be delivered when all the users log in the next morning. In this case, the network administrator does not have to visit any client computers.

Client computers use DHCP by default unless you specify a static IP address during the installation. To confirm that a computer is using DHCP, you can view the properties of TCP/IP for a certain network interface, as shown in Figure 4-1, or view the output of the ipconfig /all command, as shown in Figure 4-2.

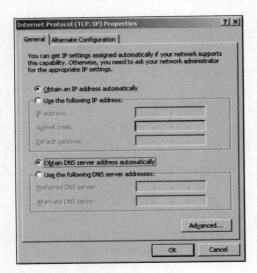

Figure 4-1   TCP/IP properties

Besides displaying the normal IP configuration for the computer, the ipconfig /all command indicates whether the configuration came from a DHCP server computer. Since DHCP Enabled is equivalent to No in Figure 4-2, the network interface did not obtain its information from DHCP.

```
C:\WINDOWS\system32\cmd.exe                                         _□×
Microsoft Windows [Version 5.2.3790]
(C) Copyright 1985-2003 Microsoft Corp.

C:\Documents and Settings\Administrator>ipconfig /all

Windows IP Configuration

        Host Name . . . . . . . . . . . . : student1
        Primary Dns Suffix  . . . . . . . :
        Node Type . . . . . . . . . . . . : Unknown
        IP Routing Enabled. . . . . . . . : No
        WINS Proxy Enabled. . . . . . . . : No

Ethernet adapter Local Area Connection:

        Connection-specific DNS Suffix  . :
        Description . . . . . . . . . . . : Intel 21140-Based PCI Fast Ethernet Adapt
er (Generic)
        Physical Address. . . . . . . . . : 00-00-F8-1F-35-A6
        DHCP Enabled. . . . . . . . . . . : No
        IP Address. . . . . . . . . . . . : 192.168.1.33
        Subnet Mask . . . . . . . . . . . : 255.255.255.0
        Default Gateway . . . . . . . . . :

C:\Documents and Settings\Administrator>
```

Figure 4-2   The ipconfig /all command

Leasing an IP Address

A client computer that is configured to use DHCP leases an IP address during the boot process when networking is initialized. The overall process to **lease** an address is composed of four packets:

- **DHCPDISCOVER**
- **DHCPOFFER**
- **DHCPREQUEST**
- **DHCPACK**

All four of these packets are broadcast packets since there are no target IP addresses involved in the communication until the client computer receives an IP address. Figure 4–3 shows the four packets transmitted as part of the DHCP process.

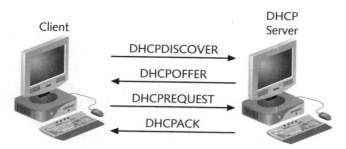

Figure 4-3   The four packets in the DHCP lease process

The DHCPDISCOVER packet is sent from the client computer to the broadcast IP address 255.255.255.255. A broadcast address must be used because the client is not configured with the address of a DHCP server. The source IP address in the packet is 0.0.0.0 because the client does not have an IP address yet. The MAC address of the client is included in the packet as an identifier.

Any DHCP server that receives the DHCPDISCOVER packet responds with a DHCPOF-FER packet. The DHCPOFFER packet contains DHCP configuration information such as an IP address, subnet mask, default gateway, and lease length. The destination IP address for the packet is the broadcast address 255.255.255.255. This destination IP address ensures that the client can receive the packet even though it does not yet have an IP address assigned. The MAC address of the client is included in the data portion of the packet as an identifier.

The DHCP client responds to the DHCPOFFER packet it receives with a DHCPRE-QUEST packet. If there are multiple DHCP servers that send DHCPOFFER packets, the client responds only to the first one. The DHCPREQUEST packet contains the lease information that has been chosen by the client. This indicates to the servers that their lease offer to the client has, or has not, been chosen.

The DHCPREQUEST packet is addressed to the broadcast IP address 255.255.255.255. This allows all of the DHCP servers to see the DHCPREQUEST. The servers that were not chosen see this packet and place their offered addresses back into their pool of available addresses.

The chosen DHCP server sends back a DHCPACK packet indicating its confirmation that the lease has been chosen and that the client is now allowed to use the lease. This packet is still being sent to the broadcast IP address 255.255.255.255 because the client has not yet initialized IP with the new address. Once DHCPACK is received by the client, the client starts using the IP address and options that were in the lease.

Renewing an IP Address

When an IP address is leased using DHCP, it can be either permanent or timed. When a permanent address is given to a client, the DHCP server never reuses that address for another client. A permanent address is a way to distribute IP address and configuration options to clients if there will never be any changes to the information.

It is very rare to find a computer network that never changes its IP addressing configuration. It is common to add additional DNS servers or change the default gateway if a new router is installed. To allow for these changes, timed leases are used.

A **timed lease** allows clients to use an IP address for a specified period of time. Windows clients attempt to renew their lease after 50% of the lease time has expired by sending a DHCPREQUEST message directly to the DHCP server from which it obtained the lease. If a DHCP client cannot renew its lease with the original DHCP server, the client broadcasts a DHCPREQUEST to contact any available DHCP server when 87.5% of the lease period has expired, and again at 100% of the lease time.

Figure 4-4 shows the two packets that are used as part of the DHCP lease renewal process.

The first packet in the renewal process is a DHCPREQUEST packet from the client to the DHCP server. This packet uses the IP address of the client as the source address and the IP address of the DHCP server as the destination address. Broadcast addresses are not required for renewing a DHCP lease because the client already has an IP address, and the client is already aware of the DHCP server's IP address.

The response from the DHCP server is either a DHCPACK packet or a **DHCPNAK** packet. A DHCPACK packet is used to confirm the renewal of the client lease, while a DHCPNAK packet is used to deny the renewal of the client lease. If the renewal is denied, the client can continue to use the current address information until the lease expires.

A client can initiate the release of an IP address before the lease time has expired. Windows NT/2000/XP/2003 uses the command **ipconfig /release** to force the release of a DHCP address. In this process, the client sends a **DHCPRELEASE** packet to the DHCP server. The DHCP server then makes the released address available to other clients if required.

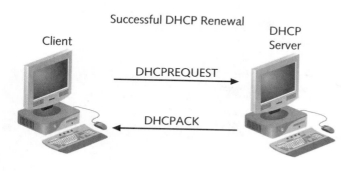

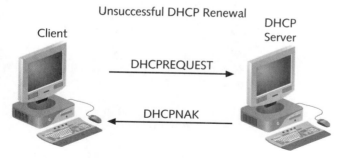

Figure 4-4   The DHCP lease renewal process

For more information on the packets sent as part of the DHCP process in various situations, view RFC 2131. It can be found at *www.ietf.org/rfc/rfc2131.txt*.

Recall from Chapter 2 that if a DHCP server cannot be contacted, the client will assign itself an Automatic Private IP Address.

INSTALLING AND AUTHORIZING THE DHCP SERVICE

Installing the DHCP Service

DHCP is a standard service that is included with Windows Server 2003. It is not installed as part of a default installation. Instead, you must add it later through Add or Remove Programs. Figure 4-5 shows the Add or Remove Programs option in Control Panel being used to install DHCP.

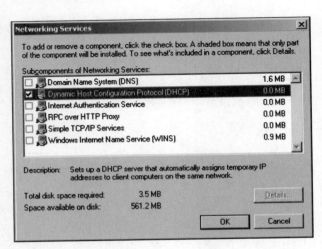

Figure 4-5   Installing DHCP

Activity 4-1: Installing DHCP

Time Required: 5 minutes

Objective: Install DHCP on Windows Server 2003.

Description: Most locations in the Great Arctic North University network are using static IP addresses for workstations. To make maintenance of the workstations easier, you are going to configure them to use DHCP. Note that the DHCP server will always have a static IP address. In this activity, you will confirm that your server has a static IP address and install DHCP.

1. If necessary, start your server and log on as **Administrator**.

2. Click **Start**, point to **Control Panel**, point to **Network Connections**, right-click **Local Area Connection**, and click **Properties**.

3. Click **Internet Protocol (TCP/IP)** and click **Properties**.

4. Verify that your network connection is statically configured, and close all open windows.

5. Click **Start**, point to **Control Panel**, and then click **Add or Remove Programs**.

6. Click **Add/Remove Windows Components**.

7. Scroll down in the components section, click **Networking Services** to highlight it, and then click **Details**.

8. Click the check box beside Dynamic Host Configuration Protocol (DHCP) to select it, and then click **OK**.

9. Click **Next**.

10. Click **Finish**.

11. Close the **Add or Remove Programs** window.

Authorizing the DHCP Service

Within a corporation's IT department, control over network resources is always important. Control over DHCP is very important, as an unauthorized DHCP server can hand out incorrect IP addressing information to hundreds of client computers very quickly. These computers are then unable to access network resources, which can be as serious as a server crashing.

To exercise control over DHCP, Windows Server 2003 must be authorized to start the DHCP Service. When the DHCP Service is starting, it checks to see that the server is authorized. If the server is authorized, then DHCP starts. If the server is not authorized, then the DHCP Service shuts itself down. Figure 4-6 shows the error message that appears in Event Viewer when an unauthorized DHCP server attempts to start.

If Active Directory is used on your network, the authorization of a DHCP server takes place in Active Directory using the DHCP management snap-in. To authorize a DHCP server, you must be a member of the **Enterprise Admins** group in Active Directory, or a member of the Enterprise Admins group must delegate permissions to you using the Active Directory Sites and Services snap-in. Figure 4-7 shows the DHCP management snap-in.

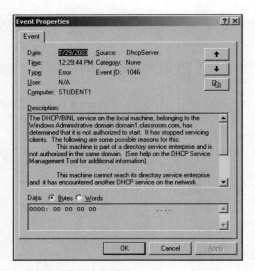

Figure 4-6   Unauthorized DHCP server error in Event Viewer

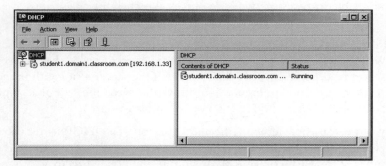

Figure 4-7   The DHCP management snap-in

Conversely, if your Windows Server 2003 is not part of an Active Directory domain and there are no other Windows Server 2003 servers on your network that run the DHCP service and participate in an Active Directory domain, then your DHCP server will automatically be authorized.

Figure 4-8 shows the information message in Event Viewer after the DHCP server is authorized and has started.

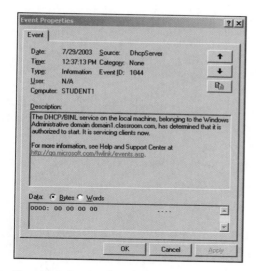

Figure 4-8   Authorized DHCP server information in Event Viewer

Activity 4-2: Starting an Authorized DHCP Server

Time Required: 10 minutes

Objective: View the results of starting a DHCP server that does not participate in an Active Directory domain.

Description: You have just installed a new DHCP server on one of your networks that does not contain an Active Directory or DHCP servers. In this exercise, you verify that the DHCP Service is started and authorized.

1. If necessary, start your server and log on as **Administrator**.

2. Click **Start**, point to **Administrative Tools**, and then click **Services**.

3. Scroll to the **DHCP Server** service, and view the status. Notice that the status is started.

4. Close the Services window.

5. Click **Start**, point to **Administrative Tools**, and then click **Event Viewer**.

6. In the left pane, click the **System log** if it is not already open.

7. Find the event generated by the DHCP Service. The type is information, the source is DHCPServer, and the event is 1043. Double-click the event.

8. Read the contents of the message, and click **OK**.

9. Close **Event Viewer**.

Activity 4-3: Installing the Active Directory Service

Time Required: 30 minutes

Objective: Install the Active Directory service on your computer and participate in an Active Directory domain.

Description: You wish to deploy the Active Directory service on your network. In this exercise, you install the Active Directory service on your computer, and you verify that the DHCP Service is started and authorized.

1. 1.If necessary, start your server and log on as **Administrator**.
2. Click **Start**, and then click **Run**. Type **dcpromo** and press **Enter**.
3. Press **Next**. Press **Next** again.
4. Ensure that **Domain controller for a new domain** is selected, and press **Next**.
5. Ensure that **Domain in a new forest** is selected, and press **Next**.
6. At the New Domain Name screen, type in **studentx.classroom.com** (where *x* is your student number assigned by the instructor) in the box provided, and press **Next**.
7. At the NetBIOS Domain Name screen, ensure that **studentx** (where *x* is your student number assigned by the instructor) is displayed in the box provided, and press **Next**.
8. At the Database and Log Folders screen, press **Next**.
9. At the Shared System Volume screen, press **Next**.
10. At the DNS Registration Diagnostics screen, ensure that Install and configure the DNS server on this computer, and set this computer to use this DNS server as its preferred DNS server is selected and press **Next**.
11. At the Permissions screen, press **Next**.
12. At the Directory Services Restore Mode Administrator Password screen, type in the password secret in both text boxes, and press **Next**.
13. At the Summary screen, press **Next**. Insert your Windows Server 2003 Enterprise Edition CD-ROM into your CD-ROM drive when prompted and press **OK**.
14. Click **Finish**.
15. Click **Restart Now**.

Activity 4-4: Starting an Unauthorized DHCP Server

Time Required: 10 minutes

Objective: View the results of starting an unauthorized DHCP server.

Description: You have just installed a new DHCP server on one of your networks that contains servers that participate in Active Directory. In this exercise, you attempt to start the DHCP Service before the server is authorized. You also view the results in the event log.

1. If necessary, start your server and log on as **Administrator**.

2. Click **Start**, point to **Administrative Tools**, and then click **Services**.

3. Scroll to the DHCP Server service, and view the status. Notice that the status is started even though the service is not authorized.

4. Close the Services window.

5. Click **Start**, point to **Administrative Tools**, and then click **Event Viewer**.

6. In the left pane, click the **System log** if it is not already open.

7. Find the error event generated by the DHCP Service. The type is error, the source is DHCPServer, and the event is 1046. Double-click the error event.

8. Read the contents of the error message, and click **OK**.

9. Close Event Viewer.

Activity 4-5: Authorizing a DHCP Server

Time Required: 10 minutes

Objective: Authorize a DHCP server in Active Directory.

Description: You have just installed a new DHCP server in one of your networks that contain servers that participate in Active Directory. In this activity, you use the DHCP management snap-in to authorize your server as a DHCP server.

1. If necessary, start your server and log on as **Administrator**.

2. Click **Start**, point to **Administrative Tools**, and click **DHCP**.

3. In the DHCP snap-in window, right-click **DHCP**, then click **Manage authorized servers**.

4. Click **Authorize**.

5. Type the IP address of your Local Area Connection, and click **OK**.

6. Click **OK** again to confirm the authorization.

7. Click **Close** to close the Manage Authorized Servers window.

8. Close the DHCP management snap-in.

9. Click **Start**, point to **Administrative Tools**, and click **Event Viewer**.

10. Click the **System log** if it is not already open.

11. Find the information event generated by the DHCP Service. The type is information, the source is DHCPServer, and the event is 1044. Double-click the information event.

12. Read the contents of the information event, and click **OK**.

13. Close Event Viewer.

Configuring DHCP Scopes

Once DHCP has been installed and authorized, you must configure it with the IP address information that is to be handed out to client computers. All configuration of DHCP is normally done with the DHCP management snap-in. However, in larger organizations where there is a need to make changes programmatically using batch files, you can also use the **NETSH** command to configure the DHCP Service.

A **scope** is used to define a range of IP addresses for the DHCP server to hand out to client computers. Each scope is configured with a name, description, starting IP address, ending IP address, subnet mask, **exclusions**, and lease duration, as shown in Figure 4-9.

The name and description of a scope are what appears in the DHCP management snap-in. These are for your use as an administrator to make it as easy as possible to manage the system. The DHCP Service does not vary its functionality based on scope names or descriptions.

The starting and ending IP addresses define the range of IP addresses that can be handed out by the DHCP server with this scope. These addresses correspond to the different subnets in your network. Each range of addresses must be within a single subnet.

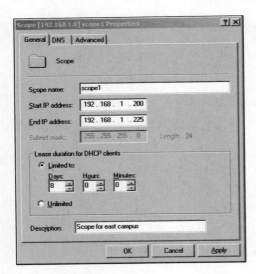

Figure 4-9   Scope settings

There are two different strategies to use when you are defining the starting and ending IP addresses. The first strategy is to configure the scope to use all available addresses on a subnet, and then exclude the static IP addresses being used by hosts such as printers. This strategy is very flexible because additional exclusions can always be added as required. An exclusion is an IP address, or range of IP addresses, within a scope that are not handed out by the DHCP server. The second strategy is to configure the scope to use only addresses that are not already in use. This strategy is used when statically configured hosts use a range of addresses at the beginning or end of a subnet. For example, many administrators place all statically configured hosts in the first few IP addresses on a subnet, and then allocate the remaining IP addresses to DHCP.

> The subnet mask for a scope is the subnet mask that is required for hosts on that subnet. If you wish to change the subnet mask after creating the scope, you must delete the scope and recreate it with the new subnet mask.

NOTE

4

Exclusions are used to prevent some IP addresses in a scope from being handed out dynamically. Choose to use exclusions when any statically configured devices such as servers and network printers have IP addresses that fall between the starting and ending IP address of a scope. If exclusions are not used for statically configured devices, then IP address conflicts can occur if the DHCP server leases out those addresses.

The lease duration for a scope defines how long client computers are allowed to use an IP address. The default lease duration used by Windows Server 2003 is eight days. Windows clients attempt to renew their lease after 50% (or 4 days, using the default setting) of the lease time has passed, then again at 87.5% (or 7 days) if the first attempt failed, and again at the end of the lease time if the second attempt fails. If a lease expires, then the client can no longer use the IP address and cannot communicate on the network. The client will then obtain an APIPA address and attempt to contact a DHCP server every 5 minutes afterward.

A DHCP server does not begin using a scope immediately after creation. A scope must be activated before the DHCP Service can begin using the scope. This is useful because it means you get a chance to confirm that the configuration of a scope is correct before addresses are handed out.

ACTIVITY

Activity 4-6: Creating a Scope

Time Required: 5 minutes

Objective: Create a scope to distribute IP addresses to client computers.

Description: You must create a scope on your newly installed DHCP server so that it can hand out IP addresses to client computers on a new network of computers at Great White Arctic University. You first configure a second NIC on your computer that is connected to this new network. Next, you create the scope for this network. You should ensure that your second NIC is connected to your partner's second NIC via a crossover cable to complete this exercise.

1. If necessary, start your server and log on as **Administrator**.

2. Click **Start**, point to **Control Panel**, point to **Network Connections**, right-click **Local Area Connection 2**, and click **Properties**.

3. Click the **Internet Protocol (TCP/IP)** option, and click the **Properties** button.

4. Enter the following IP configuration information:

- IP address: x.0.0.1 (where x is your student number)
- Subnet mask: 255.0.0.0
- Default gateway: leave blank
- Preferred DNS server: leave blank

Document your settings for later exercises.

5. Click the **OK** button to close the Internet Protocol (TCP/IP) Properties screen. Press **OK** again to accept the DNS configuration.

6. Click the **Close** button to close the Local Area Connection 2 Properties screen.

7. Click **Start**, point to **Administrative Tools**, and click **DHCP**.

8. Click your server to select it, right-click your server, and click **New Scope**.

9. Click **Next** to begin configuring the new scope.

10. Type *yourname***Scope** as the name of the scope, and click **Next**.

11. Type *x***.0.0.100** as the Start IP address.

12. Type *x***.0.0.200** as the End IP address.

13. Confirm that the length of the subnet mask is 8 bits (255.0.0.0), and click **Next**.

14. Exclusions are not required. Click **Next**.

15. Change the lease duration to 1 hour, and click **Next**.

16. Click **No, I will configure these options later**, and click **Next**.

17. Click **Finish**.

18. Close the DHCP snap-in. ·

Activity 4-7: Activating and Testing a Scope

Time Required: 20 minutes

Objective: Activate a DHCP scope, and then test it with a partner.

Description: In the previous activity, you created a scope. In this activity, you allow the DHCP Service to use the information by activating the scope. You work with a partner. When your scope is activated, your partner acts as the client computer. When your partner's scope is activated, you act as the client.

1. If necessary, start your server and log on as **Administrator**.

2. Partner A: Activate the scope on your server.

   a. Click **Start**, point to **Administrative Tools**, and click **DHCP**.

   b. Click your server to select it, click your scope to select it, right-click your scope, and click **Activate**.

   c. Close the DHCP snap-in.

3. Partner B: Change your Local Area Connection 2 to be a dynamic address.

   a. Click **Start**, point to **Control Panel**, point to **Network Connections**, right-click **Local Area Connection 2**, and click **Properties**.

   b. Click **Internet Protocol (TCP/IP)**, and click **Properties**.

   c. Click **Obtain an IP address automatically**, and click **OK**.

   d. Click **Close** to save the changes.

   e. Reboot your computer and log on as **Administrator**.

4. Partner B: View the dynamic IP address on the Local Area Connection 2.

   a. Click **Start** and click **Run**.

   b. Type **cmd** and press **Enter**.

   c. Type **ipconfig /all** and press **Enter**.

   d. If the Private connection is still using an APIPA address then type **ipconfig /renew** and press **Enter**. Then, repeat step c to view the new configuration information.

   e. Close the command prompt window.

5. Partner B: Change the Local Area Connection 2 back to a static IP address.

   a. Click **Start**, point to **Control Panel**, point to **Network Connections**, right-click **Local Area Connection 2**, and then click **Properties**.

   b. Click **Internet Protocol (TCP/IP)**, and click **Properties**.

   c. Click **Use the following IP address** and supply your previous IP configuration.

   d. Click **OK**, click **OK** again to the DNS message, and then click **Close**.

6. Partner A: Deactivate the scope.

   a. Click **Start**, point to **Administrative Tools**, and click **DHCP**.

   b. Click your server to select it, click your scope to select it, right-click your scope, and click **Deactivate**.

   c. Click **Yes** to confirm the deactivation.

   d. Close the DHCP snap-in.

7. Redo this exercise and reverse your roles. If you were partner A, this time become partner B.

Superscopes

A **superscope** is used to combine multiple scopes into a single logical scope. This is used when a single physical part of the network has two subnets on it. Often a network is organized like this because the number of hosts grew too large for a single subnet.

To conceptualize a superscope, consider the following example. A midsized company that starts out with 200 workstations has a single Class C network. There are no routers required because the entire network is switched at 100 Mbps. The DHCP server is distributing addresses to the workstations using a single scope.

Over time, the network grows to the point where a single Class C network is not large enough. To increase the number of addresses, another Class C network is added to the same segment of the network. Computers with addresses from both networks are attached to the same segment and a router is added to move packets from one logical network to the other. A second scope is added to the DHCP server.

When a client broadcasts a DHCPREQUEST packet, the DHCP server sees it. However, the DHCP server does not know which logical network the client is from and offers leases from both scopes. Combining two scopes into a superscope indicates to the DHCP Service that both scopes are on the same network segment and should be treated as a single scope. If a superscope is used, then the DHCP server offers only one lease to computers on a segment with two logical networks.

Figure 4-10 shows a superscope that contains two scopes. The DHCP server treats the superscope as a single unit. Scopes inside a superscope cannot be activated individually. The superscope must be activated and this in turn activates all scopes that are part of the superscope.

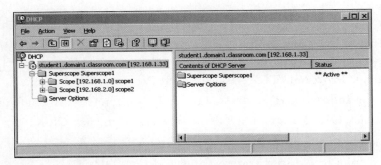

Figure 4-10   A superscope containing two scopes

Activity 4-8: Configuring a Superscope

Time Required: 5 minutes

Objective: Combine two scopes into a single logical unit using a superscope.

Description: One of the sites on your network has grown too large to use a single Class C address. It is already configured with one scope. You add a second scope, and then configure a superscope that combines the two scopes.

1. If necessary, start your server and log on as **Administrator**.
2. Click **Start**, point to **Administrative Tools**, and click **DHCP**.

3. Create a second scope.

   a. Click your server to select it, right-click your server, and click **New Scope**.

   b. Click **Next** to begin configuring the new scope.

   c. Type *yourname*Scope2 as the name of the scope, and click **Next**.

   d. Type **192.168.1.200** as the Start IP address.

   e. Type **192.168.1.225** as the End IP address.

   f. Confirm that the length of the subnet mask is 24 bits (255.255.255.0), and click **Next**.

   g. Exclusions are not required. Click **Next**.

   h. Change the lease duration to 1 hour, and click **Next**.

   i. Click **No, I will configure these options later**, and click **Next**.

   j. Click **Finish**.

4. Create a superscope.

   a. Right-click your server, and click **New Superscope**.

   b. Click **Next** to begin configuring the superscope.

   c. Type *yourname*Superscope in the Name box, and click **Next**.

   d. Press and hold **Ctrl**, click *yourname*Scope and *yourname*Scope2 to select them, and click **Next**.

   e. Click **Finish** to complete the superscope.

5. Click the **+** (plus sign) beside Superscope *yourname*Superscope to see the scopes inside the superscope.

6. Close the DHCP snap-in.

Activity 4-9: Deleting a Superscope

Time Required: 5 minutes

Objective: Delete a superscope, leaving each scope independent.

Description: A location with a superscope enabled has retired some workstations. There is no longer a need for the second scope and the superscope. You remove the superscope, and delete the second scope.

1. If necessary, start your server and log on as **Administrator**.

2. Click **Start**, point to **Administrative Tools**, and click **DHCP**.

3. Click your server to select it, right-click **Superscope** *yourname*Superscope, and click **Delete**.

4. Click **Yes** to delete the superscope without deleting any child scopes.

5. Right-click **Scope [192.168.1.0]** *yourname*Scope2, and click **Delete**.

6. Click **Yes** to delete the scope.

7. Close the DHCP snap-in.

Multicast Scopes

A **multicast scope** is used to deliver multicast addresses to applications that require it. A multicast address is used by applications to deliver packets to groups of computers rather than a single computer. Most applications that use multicast addresses are hard-coded with a single address that is used for that application rather than using DHCP to find a multicast address. Thus, using a multicast scope on a DHCP server is rare.

When you create a multicast scope, you configure start and end IP addresses, time to live (TTL), exclusions, a lease duration, and activation. The start and end IP addresses define the range of multicast addresses that the DHCP server can hand out when this multicast scope is activated. The allowable range of addresses is from 224.0.0.0 to 239.255.255.255.

The TTL of the multicast scope defines the number of routers through which a multicast packet can move. If the TTL is set to 5, then the packet is discarded by routers after five hops. This is used to control the movement of multicast packets across wide area networks. The default value for the TTL is 32.

Exclusions define addresses between the start and end IP addresses that are not handed out. Exclusions are used if there are applications using hard-coded multicast addresses within the range of the scope.

The lease duration is the length of time that an application can use a multicast address. The default lease length is 30 days.

Activity 4-10: Creating a Multicast Scope

Time Required: 5 minutes

Objective: Create a multicast scope to deliver multicast addresses to applications.

Description: You have installed a new application that requires a multicast address delivered through DHCP. You must create and activate the multicast scope on your DHCP server.

1. If necessary, start your server and log on as **Administrator**.

2. Click **Start**, point to **Administrative Tools**, and click **DHCP**.

3. Click your server to select it, right-click your server, and click **New Multicast Scope**.

4. Click **Next** to begin creating the multicast scope.

5. Type *yourname***MulticastScope** in the Name box, and click **Next**.

6. In the Start IP address box, type **224.0.0.0**.

7. In the End IP address box, type **224.0.0.255**.

8. In the TTL box, type **1**, and click **Next**. Setting the TTL to 1 ensures that your server does not start to distribute to other networks.

9. Click **Next**. There are no exclusions that need to be configured.

10. Click **Next** to confirm the default lease time of 30 days.

11. Click **Next** to activate the scope now.

12. Click **Finish** to complete the creation of the multicast scope.

13. Close the DHCP management snap-in.

Activity 4-11: Deleting a Multicast Scope

Time Required: 5 minutes

Objective: Delete a multicast scope.

Description: A location with a multicast scope enabled no longer requires that these addresses be available to workstations. You remove the multicast scope.

1. If necessary, start your server and log on as **Administrator**.

2. Click **Start**, point to **Administrative Tools**, and click **DHCP**.

3. Click your server to select it, right-click **Multicast Scope [*yourname*MulticastScope]**, and click **Delete**.

4. Click **Yes** to delete the multicast scope while it is active.

5. Close the DHCP snap-in.

CREATING DHCP RESERVATIONS

A **reservation** is used to hand out a specific IP address to a particular client computer or device on the network. This can be useful when delivering IP addresses to devices that would normally use static addresses, such as printers and servers. If the IP addresses of these devices ever need to be changed, it is easier to centrally manage the process through DHCP reservations rather than visiting each device that needs to be reconfigured.

Reservations can also be beneficial when firewalls are in place. Some companies use firewalls internally to limit which client computers can communicate with sensitive resources such as accounting and human resources information. Normally, DHCP-delivered addresses have the potential to change, which means that firewall rules based on IP addresses would not be effective. With reservations for secure clients, the firewall rules can be configured to allow packets from the IP address specified in the reservations.

Reservations are created based on the MAC address of the network card. The MAC address is used as the identifier for the client workstation that is matched to a reservation. If the MAC address of the client matches the MAC address defined in the reservation, then the IP address of the reservation is leased to the client. However, as the reserved IP address is tied to a set MAC address, if the MAC address on the device changes, such as when a NIC is replaced, then the reservation will have to be remade using the new MAC address. Figure 4–11 shows the creation of a reservation.

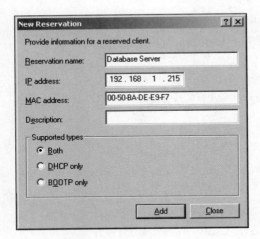

Figure 4-11   Creating a reservation

There are software utilities that override the MAC address built into the network card. This makes it possible to falsify the MAC address in a data packet and obtain an improper reservation. Consequently, using DHCP reservations with a firewall offers limited security.

Activity 4-12: Creating and Testing a Reservation

Time Required: 25 minutes

Objective: Create a DHCP reservation, and test it with a client.

Description: In an effort to control access to the Internet, you have configured a firewall to restrict the use of the Telnet protocol. However, internal technical staff needs to use Telnet on occasion to manage Linux servers. To allow this, you have created rules on the firewall that allow Telnet traffic from a few internal addresses. You now configure the DHCP server to hand out those addresses to a few specific computers using reservations. You work with a partner to complete this exercise. Partner A is the DHCP client and Partner B is the DHCP server.

1. If necessary, start your server and log on as **Administrator**.

2. Partner A: Get the MAC address of the network card on your private connection.

    a. Click **Start** and click **Run**.

    b. Type **cmd** and press **Enter**.

    c. Type **ipconfig /all** and press **Enter**.

    d. Write down the Physical Address of the network card listed under Ethernet adapter Local Area Connection 2. This address is a 12-character hexadecimal number.

    e. Close the command prompt window.

3. Partner B: Create a reservation for Partner A.

    a. Click **Start**, point to **Administrative Tools**, and click **DHCP**.

    b. Click your server to see the scopes that are configured.

    c. Click your scope to expand the contents.

    d. Click **Reservations** to view the reservations that are configured. There should be none at this time.

    e. Right-click **Reservations**, and click **New Reservation**.

    f. In the Reservation name box, type *yourname*Reservation.

    g. In the IP address box, type **x.0.0.150** (where x is your student number).

    h. In the MAC address box, type the physical address of student A.

    i. In the Description box, type **Telnet Reservation**, and click **Add**.

    j. Click **Close** to stop adding reservations.

4. Partner B: Right-click your scope, and click **Activate**.

5. Partner A: Test the client reservation.

    a. Click **Start**, point to **Control Panel**, point to **Network Connections**, right-click **Local Area Connection 2**, and click **Properties**.

    b. Click **Internet Protocol (TCP/IP)**, and click **Properties**.

    c. Take note of the IP address configuration, because this information is required again at the end of the exercise.

    d. Click **Obtain an IP address automatically**, and click **OK**.

    e. Click **Close** to save the changes.

    f. Reboot your computer and log on as **Administrator**.

    g. Click **Start** and click **Run**.

    h. Type **cmd** and press **Enter**.

    i. Type **ipconfig /all** and press **Enter**.

    j. The IP address of the Private connection should be x.0.0.150 (where x is your partner's student number). If it is not, verify that the MAC address was entered correctly in the reservation.

    k. Close the command prompt window.

6. Partner A: Change the Local Area Connection 2 back to a static IP address.

    a. Click **Start**, point to **Control Panel**, point to **Network Connections**, right-click **Local Area Connection 2**, and click **Properties**.

    b. Click **Internet Protocol (TCP/IP)**, and click **Properties**.

   c. Click **Use the following IP address**.

   d. Type in the IP address and subnet mask that were configured before you changed the address to DHCP, and click OK.

   e. Click **OK** to the message, and then click **Close**.

7. Partner B: Right-click your scope, click **Deactivate**, and click **Yes** to confirm.

8. Partner B: Close the DHCP snap-in.

9. If time permits, reverse roles and repeat the activity.

CONFIGURING DHCP OPTIONS

In addition to handing out IP addresses and subnet masks, DHCP can hand out a variety of other IP configuration options such as default gateway, DNS server, WINS server, and many more. These options can be configured for the entire server, a scope, or a single reservation. If the same option is configured twice, the option that is most specific to the computer applies. Thus, an option that is configured for a reservation will always override the same option configured for a particular scope, which will in turn override the same option configured at the server level.

It is quite common that all workstations within an entire organization use the same DNS servers. Therefore, DNS is often configured at the server level so that it applies to all scopes on that server. The same is true for WINS servers. Figure 4-12 shows the setting of server options.

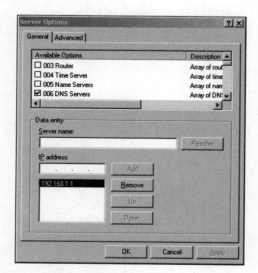

Figure 4-12   Setting server options

The default gateway is different for every subnet and is set in the options for a scope. Figure 4-13 shows the setting of scope options.

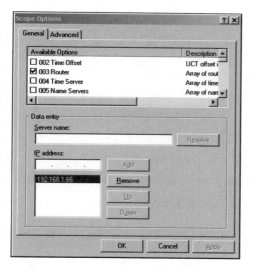

Figure 4-13 Setting scope options

It is unusual to set options in a reservation, but this may be necessary for some users with a special configuration. For example, accounting staff may use a different default gateway than other staff to allow them access to the accounting systems.

Activity 4-13: Setting Server Options

Time Required: 5 minutes

Objective: Set the DNS server option for a DHCP server.

Description: All of the computers serviced by this DHCP server are using the same DNS server. Rather than configuring each scope with a DNS server option, you have decided to configure the DHCP server with the DNS server option.

1. If necessary, start your server and log on as **Administrator**.
2. Click **Start**, point to **Administrative Tools**, and click **DHCP**.
3. Expand your server and right-click the **Server Options** folder and click **Configure Options**.
4. In the Server Options box, click the down arrow, and check **006 DNS Servers**.
5. In the IP address box, type **x.0.0.250** (where x is your student number) and click **Add**.
6. Click **OK** to save the changes to the server-level options.
7. Close the DHCP snap-in.

Activity 4-14: Setting Scope Options

Time Required: 5 minutes

Objective: Set the default gateway in the scope options.

Description: You have configured a new scope to lease IP addresses to clients. The server is already configured to include the DNS server option as part of the lease. However, for the clients to access resources outside of their own network, you must configure the default gateway option in the scope.

1. If necessary, start your server and log on as **Administrator**.
2. Click **Start**, point to **Administrative Tools**, and click **DHCP**.
3. Click your server to expand it and see the scopes inside.
4. Click your scope to see the options inside the scope.
5. Click **Scope Options** to select it, right-click **Scope Options**, and click **Configure Options**.
6. Click the check box beside 003 Router.
7. In the IP address box, type **x.0.0.251** (where *x* is your student number), and click **Add**.
8. Click **OK** to save the option.
9. Close the DHCP snap-in.

Activity 4-15: Testing Server & Scope Options

Time Required: 20 minutes

Objective: Activate a DHCP scope, and then test it with a partner to ensure that scope options are handed out.

Description: In the previous activity, you set options at the server and scope level. In this activity, you work with a partner to test whether these options are handed out to client computers alongside the normal IP configuration.

1. If necessary, start your server and log on as **Administrator**.
2. Partner A: Activate the scope on your server.
   a. Click **Start**, point to **Administrative Tools**, and click **DHCP**.
   b. Click your server to select it, click your scope to select it, right-click your scope, and click **Activate**.
   c. Close the DHCP snap-in.
3. Partner B: Change your Local Area Connection 2 to be a dynamic address.
   a. Click **Start**, point to **Control Panel**, point to **Network Connections**, right-click **Local Area Connection 2**, and click **Properties**.
   b. Click **Internet Protocol (TCP/IP)**, and click **Properties**.

4

   c. Click **Obtain an IP address automatically**, and click **OK**.

   d. Click **Close** to save the changes.

   e. Reboot your computer and log on as **Administrator**.

4. Partner B: View the dynamic IP address on the Local Area Connection 2.

   a. Click **Start** and click **Run**.

   b. Type **cmd** and press **Enter**.

   c. Type **ipconfig /all** and press **Enter**. Note the DNS and default gateway configuration.

   d. If the Private connection is still using an APIPA address, then type **ipconfig /renew** and press **Enter**. Repeat the previous step to view the new configuration information.

   e. Close the command prompt window.

5. Partner B: Change the Local Area Connection 2 back to a static IP address.

   a. Click **Start**, point to **Control Panel**, point to **Network Connections**, right-click **Local Area Connection 2**, and then click **Properties**.

   b. Click **Internet Protocol (TCP/IP)**, and click **Properties**.

   c. Click **Use the following IP address** and supply your previous IP configuration.

   d. Click **OK**, click **OK** again to the DNS message, and then click **Close**.

6. Partner A: Deactivate the scope.

   a. Click **Start**, point to **Administrative Tools**, and click **DHCP**.

   b. Click your server to select it, click your scope to select it, right-click your scope, and click **Deactivate**.

   c. Click **Yes** to confirm the deactivation.

   d. Close the DHCP snap-in.

7. Redo this exercise and reverse your roles. If you were partner A, this time become partner B.

Vendor and User Classes

Vendor and user classes can be used to differentiate between clients within a scope. Each different **vendor class** and **user class** can be configured to get its own set of options.

Vendor classes are based on the operating system being used. The vendor classes predefined within the DHCP server of Windows Server 2003 are:

- *DHCP Standard Options*—Used by all clients regardless of operating system
- *Microsoft Options*—Used by Windows 2000/XP/2003 and Windows 98 clients

- *Microsoft Windows 2000 Options*—Used only by Windows 2000/XP/2003 clients
- *Microsoft Windows 98 Options*—Used only by Windows 98 clients

Figure 4-14 shows the setting of options for vendor classes.

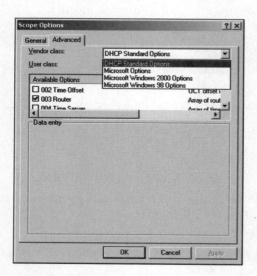

Figure 4-14   Vendor classes

User classes are defined based on how a client is connected to the network or by the network administrator. You can use the **ipconfig /setclassid** command to set the DHCP user class ID. Figure 4-15 shows the setting of a user class ID on a client.

Figure 4-15   Setting a class ID

The DHCP server included with Windows Server 2003 has three predefined user classes:

- *Default User Class*—This is used for all clients, including those that do not specify a user class or if the user class is unknown to the server.
- *Default Routing and Remote Access Class*—This class is used by clients that are assigned an IP address through DHCP when remotely accessing the network through a dial-up or VPN connection. The client computer can be running any

operating system because Routing and Remote Access obtains the IP address and options on behalf of the client computer.

■ *Default BOOTP Class*—This class is used by clients using the older BOOTP protocol rather than DHCP.

Figure 4-16 shows the setting of user class options.

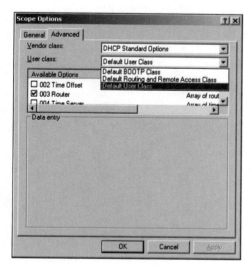

Figure 4-16   User classes

CONFIGURING A DHCP RELAY

Recall from earlier in this chapter that all DHCP packets during the leasing process are broadcast packets, which makes it impossible for these packets to travel across a router. Consequently, a DHCP server must be present on the local network in order to lease IP addresses to clients. DHCP packets cannot travel across a router.

In many larger networks, it is desirable to have a single DHCP server handle all leasing even if there are routers. To do this, you must install a **DHCP relay agent**. This can be either Windows Server 2003 with the DHCP Relay Agent protocol installed or a router that is configured as a relay (RFC 1542 compliant).

A DHCP relay agent receives broadcast DHCP packets from clients and forwards them as unicast packets to a DHCP server on behalf of the client. The DHCP relay agent must be configured with the IP address of the DHCP server to deliver the unicast packets. The DHCP server will then send the IP configuration for these clients back to the DHCP relay agent, which then distributes the configuration to the clients. Figure 4-17 shows how DHCP relay agents may be used on a routed network to distribute IP configuration to all client computers.

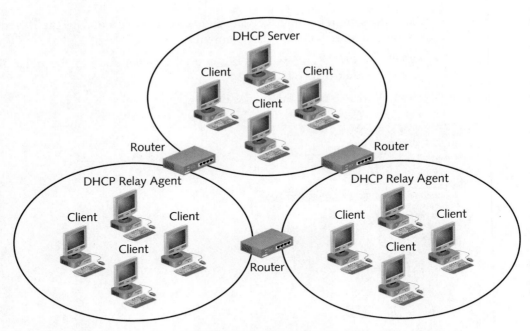

Figure 4-17 Using DHCP relay agents on a routed network

The DHCP relay agent cannot be installed on the same server as the DHCP service. Both services listen at the same port numbers. If both are installed, the performance is erratic. In Windows Server 2003, you install the DHCP relay agent through the Routing and Remote Access service, as shown in Figure 4-18.

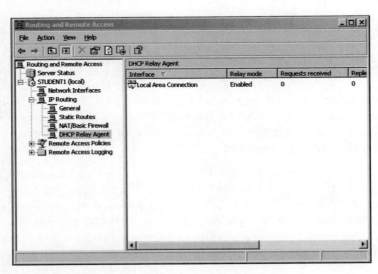

Figure 4-18 The Routing and Remote Access tool

To specify the IP address of the target DHCP server, simply view the properties of the DHCP Relay shown in Figure 4-18.

Activity 4-16: Configuring a DHCP Relay

Time Required: 20 minutes

Objective: Uninstall the DHCP service from your computer and configure it as a DHCP relay.

Description: You wish to centralize DHCP administration in the Great Arctic North University. As a result, you have configured scopes on a DHCP server that resides on a network that is available only across a router. To continue providing IP configuration for the client computers on your subnet, you uninstall the unneeded DHCP service from your computer and configure the Routing and Remote Access service to forward all DHCP requests to the remote DHCP server.

1. If necessary, start your server and log on as **Administrator**.

2. Click **Start**, point to **Control Panel**, and then click **Add or Remove Programs**.

3. Click **Add/Remove Windows Components**.

4. Scroll down in the components section, click **Networking Services** to highlight it, and then click **Details**.

5. Click the check box beside **Dynamic Host Configuration Protocol (DHCP)** to deselect it, and then click **OK**.

6. Click **Next**.

7. Click **Finish**.

8. Close the **Add or Remove Programs** window.

9. Click **Start**, point to **Administrative Tools**, and click **Routing and Remote Access**.

10. Expand your server in the left pane. Next, right-click your server and choose **Configure and Enable Routing and Remote Access**.

11. Click **Next**.

12. Select **Custom configuration** and click **Next**.

13. Select **LAN routing** and click **Next**.

14. Click **Finish**.

15. Click **Yes** to start the Routing and Remote Access service.

16. In the Routing and Remote Access screen, right-click **General** under IP Routing, and select **New Routing Protocol**.

17. Select **DHCP Relay Agent** and press **OK**.

18. Right-click **DHCP Relay Agent** under IP Routing, and select **New Interface**.

19. Select your **Local Area Connection 2** and press **OK**. This will allow the DHCP Relay Agent to respond to DHCP requests that are received on this network interface.

20. Press **OK** to accept the default settings for the DHCP Relay Agent.

21. Right-click **DHCP Relay Agent** under IP Routing, and select **Properties**. Enter the IP Address **192.168.1.99** in the box provided, and press **Add**. Press **OK**. Add DHCP requests will now be forwarded to the server with this IP address.

22. Right-click your server, and choose **Disable Routing and Remote Access**. Click **Yes** to proceed.

23. Close the Routing and Remote Access snap-in.

CHAPTER SUMMARY

- ◻ DHCP is used to dynamically assign IP address information to clients on a network. It can also be used to assign multicast IP addresses to applications that request them.

- ◻ The DHCP lease process is composed of four packets: DHCPDISCOVER, DHCPOFFER, DHCPREQUEST, and DHCPACK. DHCPNAK packets are used by DHCP servers to decline the renewal of a lease. DHCPRELEASE packets are used by clients to inform a DHCP server that their lease is no longer required.

- ◻ A DHCP client attempts to renew its lease at 50%, 87.5%, and 100% of the lease time. If it is unsuccessful in renewing the lease before it expires, then it loses the ability to access network resources and will attempt to renew its lease at 5-minute intervals afterward.

- ◻ The commands ipconfig /release and ipconfig /renew can be used to release and renew DHCP leases, respectively.

- ◻ If the Active Directory service is present on your network, each DHCP server must be authorized in Active Directory to lease addresses to clients. To authorize a DHCP in Active Directory, you must be a member of Enterprise Admins.

- ◻ A scope defines a range of IP addresses that are leased to clients. A scope must be activated before the DHCP server leases addresses in the scope.

- ◻ A superscope combines two scopes into a single logical unit to service network segments with two subnets.

- ◻ An exclusion in a scope can be used to stop a DHCP server from handing out specific addresses or a range of addresses within a scope.

- ◻ A reservation allows you to give a specific workstation a defined IP address by tying the DHCP lease to the MAC address of the client.

❑ Vendor and user classes can be used to configure some client computers with different options, depending on the class to which they belong.

❑ A DHCP relay agent is required on each network that requires IP configuration from a DHCP server across a router.

4

KEY TERMS

DHCP relay agent — A service that accepts DHCP broadcasts on one subnet and forwards them to a DHCP server on another subnet using unicast packets.

DHCPACK — The fourth and final packet in the DHCP lease process. This packet is a broadcast from the DHCP server confirming the lease.

DHCPDISCOVER — The first packet in the DHCP lease process. This packet is broadcast on the local network to find a DHCP server.

DHCPNAK — This packet is sent from a DHCP server to a client when it denies a renewal attempt.

DHCPOFFER — The second packet in the DHCP lease process. This packet is a broadcast from the DHCP server to the client with an offered lease.

DHCPRELEASE — This packet is sent from a DHCP client to a DHCP server to indicate it is no longer using a leased IP address.

DHCPREQUEST — The third packet in the DHCP lease process. This packet is a broadcast from the DHCP client indicating which DHCPOFFER has been chosen.

Enterprise Admins — A default group in Active Directory with administrative rights for the entire forest.

exclusion — An IP address or range of IP addresses within a scope that are not leased to clients.

ipconfig /release — A command used to force a client to relinquish the IP address it has obtained from a DHCP server.

ipconfig /setclassid — A command used to configure a class code on a computer.

lease — The length of time a DHCP client computer is allowed to use IP address information from the DHCP server.

multicast scope — A range of multicast IP addresses that are handed out to applications that request them.

NETSH — A command-line utility that can be used to manage many IP configuration settings and IP services.

reservation — A DHCP IP address that is leased only to a computer with a specific MAC address.

scope — A range of addresses that are leased by a DHCP server.

superscope — A logical grouping of scopes that is used to service network segments with more than one subnet in use.

timed lease — An IP address and configuration option given to a client computer from a DHCP server for a limited period of time.

user class — An identifier from the DHCP client that is sent as part of the DHCP lease process. This can be set manually by the administrator on workstations.

vendor class — An identifier from the DHCP client that is sent as part of the DHCP lease process. This is based on the operating system in use.

REVIEW QUESTIONS

1. After installing the DHCP Service, what must be done in Active Directory before it begins delivering leased IP addresses?

   a. Authorize it.

   b. Reboot the computer.

   c. Activate it.

   d. Modify the firewall rules.

2. After creating a scope, what must be done before the DHCP Service begins servicing the scope?

   a. Authorize it.

   b. Reboot the computer.

   c. Activate it.

   d. Modify the firewall rules.

3. Which of the following types of packets is used during the DHCP leasing process?

   a. unicast

   b. multicast

   c. broadcast

   d. None—it is all performed internally on the client.

4. How many packets are transmitted as part of the DHCP renewal process?

   a. 1

   b. 2

   c. 3

   d. 4

5. Which type of packet is sent if a request to renew a lease is denied?

   a. DHCPDISCOVER

   b. DHCPACK

   c. DHCPOFFER

   d. DHCPNACK

6. Which command can be used on Windows XP and Windows Server 2003 clients to force the renewal of a DHCP lease?
   a. ipconfig /release
   b. ipconfig /renew
   c. dhcpcon /renew
   d. winipcfg /release
   e. winipcfg /renew

7. Which type of packet is first in the DHCP lease process?
   a. DHCPACK
   b. DHCPOFFER
   c. DHCPDISCOVER
   d. DHCPREQUEST

8. Which utility is used to configure DHCP?
   a. DHCP management snap-in
   b. Active Directory Users and Computers
   c. Active Directory Sites and Services
   d. ipconfig

9. At what levels can you apply different options for leased IP addresses? (Choose all that apply.)
   a. server
   b. scope
   c. exclusion
   d. reservation

10. Exclusions are used to allow certain computers to use a predefined IP address. True or false?

11. Which of the following allow DHCP packets to cross over a router? (Choose all that apply.)
    a. DHCP relay agent
    b. switch
    c. RFC 1542–compliant router
    d. IPSec

12. What is used to logically combine multiple scopes into a single unit?
    a. megascope
    b. superscope
    c. metascope
    d. It is not possible.

13. What is the default lease length used by a scope created in the Windows Server 2003 DHCP Service?

   a. 3 hours

   b. 3 days

   c. 7 days

   d. 8 days

   e. 30 days

14. Which characteristic of a multicast scope controls how many routers a multicast packet travels through?

   a. lease duration

   b. time to live

   c. hop count

   d. half-life

15. Which DHCP feature allows you to distribute a chosen IP address to a particular computer?

   a. exclusion

   b. scope

   c. reservation

   d. user class

   e. vendor class

16. What characteristic of a client computer is used to match a client computer with a reservation?

   a. vendor class

   b. user class

   c. operating system

   d. computer name

   e. MAC address

17. What happens when a DHCP client cannot contact a DHCP server when the lease time is at 100%?

   a. It disables the network interface.

   b. It increases the lease to 200% of its original value.

   c. It attempts to contact another DHCP server in 5 minutes.

   d. none of the above

18. What tool is used to configure a DHCP relay agent?

   a. Routing and Remote Access

   b. DHCP snap-in

   c. DHCP Relay snap-in

   d. Add/Remove Programs

19. You configure the 003 Router option at the server level to be 192.168.1.88. For a scope called scope1, this same option is configured as 192.168.1.89. What will happen when clients obtain a DHCP lease? (Choose all that apply.)

   a. DHCP clients that obtain an IP address from scope1 will receive the 003 Router option configured as 192.168.1.89.

   b. DHCP clients that obtain an IP address from a scope other than scope1 will receive the 003 Router option configured as 192.168.1.89.

   c. DHCP clients that obtain an IP address from scope1 will receive the 003 Router option configured as 192.168.1.88.

   d. DHCP clients that obtain an IP address from a scope other than scope1 will receive the 003 Router option configured as 192.168.1.88.

20. Which of the following are client options that can be set at the scope level? (Choose all that apply.)

   a. DNS

   b. WINS

   c. ROUTER

   d. MAC address

CASE PROJECTS

The planning for new IP address allocations has been done for all of the Great Arctic North University campuses. All campuses will have at least one subnet and some will have several, depending upon the size of the campus. To make the configuration of clients easier, it has been decided that DHCP will be implemented.

CASE
PROJECTS

Case Project 4-1: Multiple Subnets

You are planning how DHCP will be used to deliver IP addresses to clients on one of your larger campuses with five different subnets. Write a short memo describing the pros and cons of using a single DHCP server versus multiple DHCP servers.

Case Project 4-2: Avoiding IP Address Conflicts

One of your newly configured sites is having a problem with IP address conflicts. Some of the addresses being leased by the DHCP server are already configured on servers, printers, and workstations. The DHCP servers are using 192.168.1.10 through 192.168.1.19. The printers are using 192.168.1.20 through 192.168.1.29. What are your options for eliminating these conflicts?

Case Project 4-3: DHCP and Firewalls

As a security measure, you have stopped all of the faculty and students from using instant messaging clients by blocking their ports. However, some of the faculty use an application based on instant messaging. How can you use DHCP to help you allow just these clients access to instant messaging ports?

CHAPTER

5

MANAGING AND
MONITORING DHCP

After reading this chapter, you will be able to:

♦ Back up and restore DHCP databases

♦ Reconcile DHCP scopes

♦ Use the jetpack utility to repair a DHCP database

♦ View DHCP statistics

♦ Enable and interpret DHCP audit logs

♦ Configure conflict detection

♦ Bind the DHCP service to certain network cards

♦ View and interpret DHCP events in Event Viewer

♦ Troubleshoot common DHCP problems

I t is important to effectively manage and monitor your DHCP server. This involves a variety of tasks that can be done and features that can be configured. In this chapter, you manage the DHCP database itself by backing it up, reconciling scopes and repairing it. In addition, you view DHCP statistics, audit logs, and event viewer messages as well as configure conflict detection and bindings. The last part of this chapter discusses common problems and their solutions.

BACKING UP AND RESTORING DHCP DATABASES

The DHCP Service provides an important function on networks; it assigns IP configuration information to client computers so that they can access other network resources. As a result, it is important to ensure that the server that hosts the DHCP Service is reliable and that the information stored on it does not become corrupted.

The DHCP Service has several files that are stored in the C:\WINDOWS\system32\dhcp directory. The file Dhcp.mdb is the database holding the addressing information that has been assigned to client computers. Another file, Dhcp.tmp, is a temporary database file only present during maintenance operations. The files J50.log and J50#####.log (where ##### is a five-digit code for uniqueness) are transaction logs of changes to the DHCP database. The file J50.chk is a checkpoint file that keeps track of which entries in the log files have been applied to the database. To ensure that DHCP server information is not lost due to corruption, you should back up the data contained within these files. Backing up the DHCP database in Windows Server 2003 backs up all of these files, as well as DHCP registry entries.

By default, the DHCP database is backed up every 60 minutes to the C:\WINDOWS\system32\dhcp\backup\new directory. You can back up the DHCP database manually by right-clicking the server in the DHCP snap-in and clicking Backup, as shown in Figure 5-1, and specifying a folder in which to create the backup.

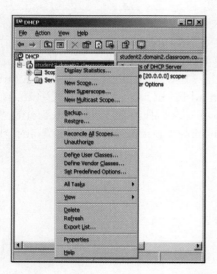

Figure 5-1   Backing up the DHCP database

You can also modify the automatic backup time by editing the registry key HKEY_LOCAL_MACHINE\SYSTEM\CurrentControlSet\Services\DHCPServer\Parameters\BackupInterval, as shown in Figure 5-2.

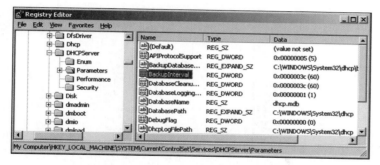

Figure 5-2   The BackupInterval registry parameter

To restore the DHCP database, right-click the server in the DHCP management snap-in, and click Restore. You will then be prompted to select the folder containing the backup, as shown in Figure 5-3.

Figure 5-3   Restoring the DHCP database

You may also modify the default paths where the DHCP database files and backups are stored. Simply access the Advanced tab of the DHCP server properties in the DHCP management snap-in, as shown in Figure 5-4, and specify alternate pathnames for the Database path and Backup path.

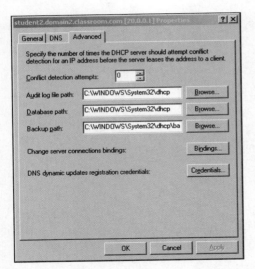

Figure 5-4   Changing the default DHCP database and backup locations

Activity 5-1: Installing and Authorizing DHCP

Time Required: 30 minutes

Objective: Install and authorize DHCP on Windows Server 2003.

Description: You wish to install a DHCP server in a test lab network at Great Arctic North University to practice common DHCP maintenance and troubleshooting procedures. Since Active Directory is used in the test lab, you must also authorize the DHCP service such that it will service clients, as well as configure a scope and activate it.

1. If necessary, start your server and log on as **Administrator**.

2. Click **Start**, point to **Control Panel**, and then click **Add or Remove Programs**.

3. Click **Add/Remove Windows Components**.

4. Scroll down in the components section, click **Networking Services** to highlight it, and then click **Details**.

5. Click the check box beside Dynamic Host Configuration Protocol (DHCP) to select it, and then click **OK**.

6. Click **Next**.

7. Click **Finish**.

8. Close the **Add or Remove Programs** window.

9. Click **Start**, point to **Administrative Tools**, and click **DHCP**.

10. In the DHCP snap-in window, right-click **DHCP**, then click **Manage authorized servers**.

11. Click **Authorize**.

12. Type the IP address of your local area connection, and click **OK**.

13. Click **OK** again to confirm the authorization.

14. Click **Close** to close the Manage Authorized Servers window.

15. Click your server to select it, right-click your server, and click **New Scope**.

16. Click **Next** to begin configuring the new scope.

17. Type *yourname*Scope as the name of the scope, and click **Next**.

18. Type *x*.**0.0.100** as the Start IP address (where *x* is your student number).

19. Type *x*.**0.0.200** as the End IP address (where *x* is your student number).

20. Confirm that the length of the subnet mask is 8 bits (255.0.0.0), and click **Next**.

21. Exclusions are not required. Click **Next**.

22. Change the lease duration to 1 hour, and click **Next**.

23. Click **No, I will configure these options later**, and click **Next**.

24. Click **Finish**.

25. Click your server to select it, click your scope to select it, right-click your scope, and click **Activate**.

26. Close the DHCP snap-in.

Activity 5-2: Backing up a DHCP Database

Time Required: 15 minutes

Objective: Back up a DHCP database.

Description: You are about to change the default file path used for the DHCP database. To prevent the loss of DHCP database information, you want to first back up the DHCP database. Next, you wish to verify that the database has been backed up to the desired location.

1. If necessary, start your server and log on as **Administrator**.

2. Click **Start**, point to **Administrative Tools**, and click **DHCP**.

3. Click your server, then right-click your server and choose **Backup**.

4. Ensure that **C:\WINDOWS\system32\dhcp\backup** is the target folder displayed, and click **OK**.

5. Close the DHCP snap-in.

6. Use My Computer to browse to the directory **C:\WINDOWS\system32\dhcp\backup\new**. View the file contents that were created as a result of the backup procedure.

7. Close My Computer.

Activity 5-3: Changing the Default Location of the DHCP Database

Time Required: 10 minutes

Objective: Change the default directory used to store the DHCP database.

Description: Great Arctic North University wishes to standardize the location of network service information across all servers. The DHCP database should be stored in the C:\DHCP directory. In this exercise, you create the C:\DHCP directory, change the default DHCP database location to C:\DHCP and ensure that the database has been moved to the new location.

1. If necessary, start your server and log on as **Administrator**.
2. Use My Computer to create the directory **C:\DHCP**.
3. Close My Computer.
4. Click **Start**, point to **Administrative Tools**, and click **DHCP**.
5. Click your server, then right-click your server and choose **Properties**.
6. Click on the **Advanced** tab and enter **C:\DHCP** in the Database path text box and click **OK**.
7. Click **Yes** when prompted to restart the DHCP service. If the service does not restart successfully, right-click your server, choose **All Tasks**, and then **Restart** to manually restart your DHCP service.
8. Close the DHCP snap-in.
9. Use My Computer to browse to the directory **C:\DHCP**. View the file contents of the DHCP database.
10. Close My Computer.

Activity 5-4: Restoring a DHCP Database

Time Required: 15 minutes

Objective: Restore DHCP database information from a backup location.

Description: You have just changed the default path for the DHCP database and noticed that your scope information is not available. As a result, you restore a backup of your DHCP database that you created prior to the change.

1. If necessary, start your server and log on as **Administrator**.
2. Click **Start**, point to **Administrative Tools**, and click **DHCP**. Click on your server. Note that your scope is not displayed.
3. Right-click your server and choose **Restore**.

4. Ensure that **C:\WINDOWS\system32\dhcp\backup** is the target folder displayed, and click **OK**. Click **Yes** to restart the service. Note that your scope is now displayed in the DHCP snap-in.

5. Close the DHCP snap-in.

Maintaining the DHCP Database

5

Over time, the DHCP database will grow in size and will be used more frequently. As a result, the DHCP database may contain inconsistencies that need to be remedied; this is typically done by reconciling a scope or repairing the DHCP database itself.

Reconciling Scopes

The DHCP database holds a summary version and a detailed version of the IP address lease information for a server. If there is a discrepancy between the two versions of information, then you must reconcile the scope to synchronize the information. If information regarding leased addresses is not appearing properly in the DHCP management snap-in, you may need to reconcile the scope. The scope may also need to be reconciled to properly show leased addresses after restoring the DHCP database. To reconcile a scope, right-click it and click Reconcile, as shown in Figure 5-5.

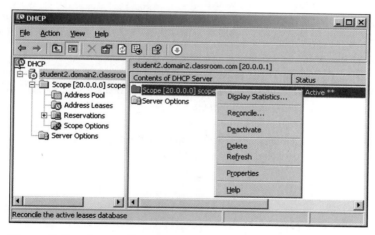

Figure 5-5   Reconciling a scope

Activity 5-5: Reconciling a Scope

Time Required: 10 minutes

Objective: Reconcile a DHCP scope.

Description: You have just restored a DHCP database from a backup location and the scope information displayed in the DHCP snap-in seems inconsistent. To solve this inconsistency, you reconcile your scope.

1. If necessary, start your server and log on as **Administrator**.
2. Click **Start**, point to **Administrative Tools**, and click **DHCP**.
3. Click your scope, and then right-click your scope and choose **Reconcile**.
4. At the Reconcile screen, click the **Verify** button.
5. Click **OK** to acknowledge that the DHCP database is consistent.
6. Close the Reconcile screen.
7. Close the DHCP snap-in.

REPAIRING THE DHCP DATABASE

As the DHCP database grows in size, the potential for it to become corrupted increases as well. When the DHCP Service starts, it checks the structure of the DHCP database files. If an inconsistency is found, it creates entries in the Event Log that indicate the DHCP database has been corrupted.

You may repair a corrupted DHCP database by using the jetpack command-line utility. Simply specify the location of the dhcp.mdb file as well as a temporary file used in the repair process using the syntax *jetpack dhcp.mdb tempfilename*.

Before running the jetpack utility, you should back up the DHCP database to ensure that data is not lost should the jetpack utility fail.

Activity 5-6: Running the Jetpack Utility

Time Required: 10 minutes

Objective: Repair a corrupted DHCP database.

Description: You have just viewed a message in Event Viewer stating that your DHCP database requires repairing. To repair your DHCP database, you run the jetpack utility.

1. If necessary, start your server and log on as **Administrator**.

2. Click **Start** and click **Run**.

3. Type **cmd** and press **Enter**.

4. Type **cd C:\DHCP** and press **Enter**.

5. Type **jetpack dhcp.mdb tmpfile** and press **Enter**.

6. Close the command prompt window.

5

Viewing DHCP Statistics

The Windows Server 2003 DHCP Service automatically tracks statistics that you can view for your server as a whole or a particular scope. To view these statistics, right-click on the server or scope, and click Display Statistics. Figure 5-6 depicts sample statistics for a DHCP server.

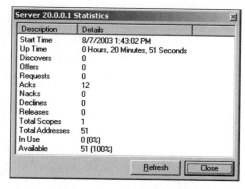

Figure 5-6   Viewing DHCP server statistics

By default, to update these statistics, you must manually click the Refresh button while the statistics window is open. You can configure these statistics to be updated automatically by selecting the Automatically update statistics every option and specifying how often they are to be updated.

The Performance snap-in may also be used to monitor DHCP statistics. When DHCP is installed on Windows Server 2003, new objects and counters are added to the Performance snap-in. You can monitor these counters to track the performance of DHCP over time. If you establish an initial benchmark of DHCP performance under average conditions, then you can tell if something is functioning abnormally later.

Figure 5-7 shows some of the DHCP performance counters that can be monitored. The number of Discovers/sec indicates how many new clients are being added to the network. If this number is higher than normal, it may indicate that the lease length is too short, and computers are not able to renew their lease before it expires. Any number of Declines/sec indicates that some computers are using dynamic IP addresses not assigned by this DHCP server. This may be an indication that someone has installed an unauthorized DHCP server on an operating system such as Linux.

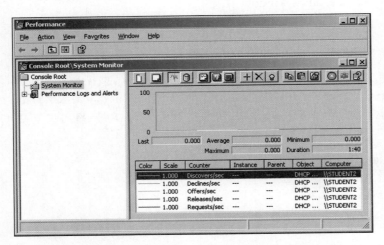

Figure 5-7   Viewing DHCP statistics in the Performance snap-in

DHCP Audit Logging

DHCP audit logs keep detailed information about DHCP server activity. This logging is enabled by default and keeps up to seven audit logs that represent the most recent seven days. The audit logs are named DhcpSrvLog-*XXX*.log, where *XXX* is the day of the week. These logs can be used to troubleshoot why a DHCP server is not functioning as you would expect.

To enable DHCP audit logging, select the option Enable DHCP audit logging in the properties of the DHCP server in the DHCP management snap-in, as shown in Figure 5-8.

Audit logs are stored in the C:\WINDOWS\system32\dhcp directory by default; however, this may be changed. To change the default location used for audit logs, simply access the Advanced tab of the DHCP server properties in the DHCP management snap-in, as shown earlier in Figure 5-4, and change the Audit log file path.

Audit logs contain detailed text information about the events that occur in the DHCP service. To view this information, open the audit log for a particular day in a text editor such as Notepad, as shown in Figure 5-9.

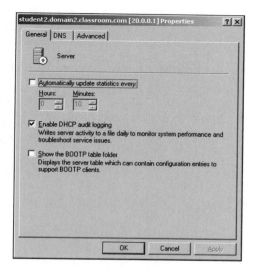

Figure 5-8   Enabling audit logging

Figure 5-9   A sample audit log

Each line in an audit log contains an event ID that states the nature of the event. Some common event IDs that you may find in a DHCP audit log are listed in Table 5-1.

Table 5-1   Common DHCP audit log events

Event ID	Event Description
00	The audit log was started.
01	The audit log was stopped.
02	The audit log was stopped due to low available disk space.
10	A new IP address was leased to a DHCP client.
11	A lease was renewed by a DHCP client.
12	A lease was released by a DHCP client.
13	A certain IP address was found to be in use on the network.
14	A DHCP client could not obtain a lease because there were no available addresses in the scope.
15	A DHCP lease was denied.
16	A DHCP lease was deleted.

Table 5-1   Common DHCP audit log events (continued)

Event ID	Event Description
17	A DHCP lease was expired.
50+	Messages relating to DHCP server authorization, including Rogue Server Detection information.

It is important to review log files on a regular basis for security reasons. Other protective measures, such as securing the physical network, site surveys and faraday cages for wireless networks, are covered in Chapter 13.

NOTE

Activity 5-7: Viewing an Audit Log

Time Required: 10 minutes

Objective: View sample events in an audit log.

Description: You have just installed a DHCP server on your network and wish to identify the tasks that it is performing. To find out what tasks are being performed, you examine the audit log for the current day.

1. If necessary, start your server and log on as **Administrator**.

2. Open My Computer and navigate to the **C:\WINDOWS\system32\dhcp** directory.

3. Double-click on the file **DhcpSrvLog-XXX.log** where *XXX* represents the current day of the week.

4. View the different events that were logged today.

5. Close the Notepad window.

CONFLICT DETECTION

Using DHCP to assign IP configuration to client computers on a network does not prevent other clients on the network from configuring IP addresses statically. Although DHCP will not hand out the same IP address from a scope to two different computers, it may hand out an IP address from a scope that another computer on the network may have configured statically. The DHCP client computer and the statically configured computer would then have identical IP addresses, and neither may be able to communicate on the network.

Conflict detection prevents a DHCP server from creating IP address conflicts. When conflict detection is enabled, a DHCP server pings an IP address before it is leased to a client computer. This ensures that even if another device is statically configured with that IP address, it is not leased.

You can configure how many ping attempts are made before an IP address is leased. The default is zero ping attempts. Each ping attempt adds approximately one second to the overall length of the leasing process. The number of pings for conflict detection is configured in the DHCP server properties in the DHCP management snap-in. Figure 5-10 shows a DHCP server that is configured to send two ping requests before leasing IP addresses from a scope.

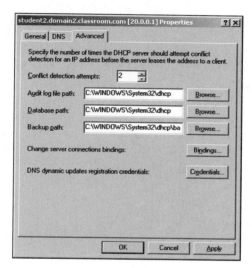

Figure 5-10   Configuring conflict detection

Activity 5-8: Configuring Conflict Detection

Time Required: 10 minutes

Objective: Conflict detection on a DHCP server.

Description: You have just installed a DHCP server on your network. Many client computers are still statically configured. You wish to prevent any IP conflicts as a result of handing out IP configuration information to client computers by forcing the DHCP service to ping any IP addresses twice before handing them out to DHCP clients.

1. If necessary, start your server and log on as **Administrator**.

2. Click **Start**, point to **Administrative Tools**, and click **DHCP**.

3. Right-click your server and choose **Properties**.

4. Click on the **Advanced** tab and enter **2** in the Conflict detection attempts box, and click **OK**.

5. Close the DHCP snap-in.

CONFIGURING DHCP BINDINGS

If a DHCP server has multiple network cards, then you can choose which network cards the DHCP Service is bound to. The DHCP server only hands out IP addresses through a network card that has the DHCP Service bound. The bindings are controlled in the Advanced tab of the server Properties in the DHCP management snap-in, as shown earlier in Figure 5-10. Clicking on the Bindings button in Figure 5-10 will allow you to select which network cards the DHCP Service will bind to, as shown in Figure 5-11.

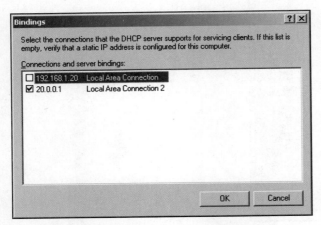

Figure 5-11   Binding the DHCP Service to one network card

Activity 5-9: Setting Bindings for DHCP

Time Required: 10 minutes

Objective: Bind the DHCP Service to one NIC only.

Description: You have just installed a DHCP server on your network. Your DHCP server has two network cards; however, only one of these network cards is connected to a network with DHCP client computers. To ensure that the other network card is not used to service DHCP clients, you bind the DHCP service only to the second network card.

1. If necessary, start your server and log on as **Administrator**.
2. Click **Start**, point to **Administrative Tools**, and click **DHCP**.
3. Click your server, then right-click your server and choose **Properties**.
4. Click the **Advanced** tab.
5. Click on **Bindings**.
6. Ensure that there is only a check mark beside your **Local Area Connection 2**, and click **OK**.
7. Close the DHCP snap-in.

VIEWING DHCP EVENTS IN EVENT VIEWER

In addition to audit logging, some summary information generated by the DHCP Service is placed in the system event log. You can view these events using Event Viewer. Some common DHCP-related events that you may see in Event Viewer are summarized in Table 5-2.

Table 5-2   Common DHCP audit log events

Event ID	Description
1040	Successfully restored the DHCP database
1044	The DHCP server is authorized
1045/1046	The DHCP server is not authorized
1052	Duplicate IP address was detected
1056	Dynamic DNS credentials are not configured
1059	Could not contact a domain controller for authorization

ACTIVITY

Activity 5-10: Viewing DHCP Events in Event Viewer

Time Required: 5 minutes

Objective: See the events placed into the system log by the DHCP Service.

Description: Some of the users on the network have been complaining that they occasionally cannot get an IP address from the DHCP server. As a starting point, you view the system event log to see if the service has been stopped and restarted recently.

1. If necessary, start your server and log on as **Administrator**.
2. Click **Start**, point to **Administrative Tools**, and click **Event Viewer**.
3. Click **System** to view the system log.
4. Click **View** and click **Filter**.
5. Click the down arrow in the Event source list box, and click **DHCPServer**.
6. Click **OK** to filter the system log.
7. View the DHCPServer events.
8. Click the **View** menu, and click **All Records** to remove the filter.
9. Close Event Viewer.

DHCP TROUBLESHOOTING

DHCP is a fairly simple broadcast-based protocol that seldom has problems. However, some problems that you may encounter include:

- *All computers are unable to lease addresses*—Confirm that the DHCP Service is running and authorized. If the DHCP Service is authorized, confirm that the proper scope has been activated and that the DHCP Service is bound to the proper adapter.

- *A single computer is unable to lease an address*—Confirm that the cabling is correct and that the proper network driver is loaded. If the TCP/IP configuration is corrupt, repairing the network connection may also fix the problem.

- *Some computers have incorrect address information*—If the computers have addresses in the range 169.254.X.X, then they were unable to contact the DHCP server. Confirm that the DHCP server is functional. Be aware that Windows XP can also be configured with alternate addresses to use when DHCP is unavailable.

- *A single computer has incorrect address information*—If this computer has a reservation, check the configuration of the reservation. Options set in a reservation override options set in a scope or at the server level.

- *A rogue DHCP server is leasing addresses*—Windows 2000 and Windows Server 2003 must be authorized to function as DHCP servers. However, other operating systems such as Linux, UNIX, and NetWare are not aware of authorization information. These servers are called **rogue DHCP servers**.

- *Two DHCP servers configured to be redundant on a network segment are leasing the same range of IP addresses and causing conflicts*—DHCP servers are not designed to be redundant. A better solution is to **cluster** your DHCP Service. However, if you cannot cluster the service, and you still require redundancy, then you should configure the servers to each handle only a portion of the entire subnet. Microsoft recommends that the available addresses be split 25/75 between the two servers.

- *IP address conflicts are created when the DHCP server hands out addresses already used by hosts with static IP addresses*—The ideal solution to this problem is to create exclusions in the scope for the IP addresses used by hosts that are statically configured. However, if this information is not documented, then turning on conflict detection ensures that a DHCP server does not hand out an IP address that is already in use.

- *A client is using an Automatic Private IP Addressing (APIPA) address*—If a DHCP server was down briefly, some clients may be using APIPA addresses. If you would like a client to reattempt leasing an IP address, then use the command ipconfig /renew.

Activity 5-11: Remove DHCP

Time Required: 5 minutes

Objective: Remove the DHCP Server service from your server.

Description: Remove the DHCP Server service to ensure that it does not interfere with activities later in this book.

1. If necessary, start your server and log on as **Administrator**.

2. Click **Start**, point to **Control Panel**, and click **Add or Remove Programs**.

3. Click **Add/Remove Windows Components**.

4. Scroll down in the Components box, double-click **Networking Services**, and click the check box beside **Dynamic Host Configuration Protocol (DHCP)** to deselect it.

5. Click **OK**, and click **Next**.

6. Click **Finish** to complete removing the DHCP Server service, and close the Add or Remove Programs window.

CHAPTER SUMMARY

- The DHCP database normally resides in the C:\WINDOWS\system32\dhcp folder; however, this location may be changed. It is backed up on a regular basis to prevent the loss of information.

- Reconciling scopes will synchronize scope information in the DHCP database.

- The jetpack command-line utility may be used to repair a corrupted DHCP database.

- You may view DHCP statistics in the DHCP snap-in or via the Performance snap-in.

- Audit logging enables you to view detailed information about the operation of the DHCP Service. It is enabled by default.

- Conflict detection sends a ping packet before leasing an IP address to ensure that it is not in use.

- You may configure the DHCP service binding such that it will respond to DHCP clients on certain network cards only.

- Troubleshooting DHCP problems is a valuable skill when implementing Windows Server 2003.

KEY TERMS

cluster — A group of computers that coordinate the provision of services. When one computer in a cluster fails, the others take over its services.

conflict detection — When in use, a DHCP server pings an IP address before attempting to lease it. This ensures that IP address conflicts do not occur.

rogue DHCP server — A non–Windows 2000/2003 class DHCP server that exists on a Windows 2003 network.

REVIEW QUESTIONS

1. Which file stores the list of IP addresses leased through DHCP?
   a. Dhcp.mdb
   b. Dhcp.tmp
   c. J50.log
   d. J50.chk
   e. J50#####.log

2. What is the default location for the DHCP database?
   a. C:\WINDOWS\dhcp
   b. C:\WINDOWS\dhcp\new
   c. C:\WINDOWS\system32\dhcp\backup
   d. C:\WINDOWS\system32\dhcp

3. Which utility can you use to create a baseline of DHCP functionality?
   a. Active Directory Sites and Services
   b. Event Viewer
   c. Performance
   d. Task Manager

4. Which of the following locations may be changed? (Choose all that apply.)
   a. DHCP database path
   b. DHCP audit log path
   c. DHCP backup path
   d. DHCP event log path

5. Which of the following commands may be used to repair a DHCP database?
   a. jetpack
   b. verify
   c. reconcile
   d. audit_log

6. Which two utilities may be used to view DHCP statistics?
   a. DHCP snap-in
   b. Event Viewer
   c. Performance snap-in
   d. audit log

7. Which feature do you enable to ensure that a DHCP server does not hand out IP addresses that are already in use on the network?
   a. audit logging
   b. conflict detection
   c. dynamic DNS
   d. bindings

8. Which DHCP event in Event Viewer would indicate that a DHCP database was restored successfully?
   a. 1040
   b. 1044
   c. 1045/1046
   d. 1052

9. Which DHCP event in Event Viewer would indicate that a DHCP service was authorized?
   a. 1040
   b. 1044
   c. 1045/1046
   d. 1052

10. To provide redundancy, what ratio does Microsoft recommend when splitting the address range for a subnet between two DHCP servers?
    a. 50/50
    b. 25/75
    c. 30/70
    d. 100/0

11. What should you do following a successful restore of the DHCP database to ensure that scope information is synchronized?

    a. back up the DHCP database

    b. repair the DHCP database using the jetpack utility

    c. change the location of the DHCP database

    d. reconcile scopes

12. By default, audit logging must be enabled before it is used on a newly installed DHCP server. True or false?

13. How can you modify the default backup interval for the DHCP database?

    a. by using the Advanced tab of the server properties in the DHCP snap-in

    b. by accessing the properties of a scope in the DHCP snap-in

    c. by editing the Dhcp.tmp file

    d. by editing the registry

14. Which code in a DHCP audit log represents a new IP address that was leased to a client computer?

    a. 01

    b. 02

    c. 10

    d. 15

15. Which of the following troubleshooting procedures would be appropriate if a single computer is unable to lease an IP address, but other computers on the subnet have no trouble leasing an IP address from your DHCP server? (Choose all that apply.)

    a. Ensure that the network cable is functional to the client.

    b. Repair the network connection.

    c. Ensure that the scope is activated.

    d. Ensure that the appropriate network card driver is loaded.

16. Which of the following troubleshooting procedures would be appropriate if all computers on a subnet are unable to lease an IP address from your DHCP server? (Choose all that apply.)

    a. Ensure that the DHCP server is authorized.

    b. Ensure that the DHCP service is bound to the appropriate network card.

    c. Ensure that the scope is activated.

    d. Ensure that the appropriate network card driver is loaded on each client computer.

17. Clients on your network have been obtaining IP addresses without problems for some time; however, there have been several IP conflicts among DHCP clients in the past two days. What are possible causes for this problem? (Choose all that apply.)

    a. A new Linux DHCP server has been handing out addresses on the network.

    b. The DHCP service has been installed twice on the DHCP server.

    c. Some client computers have been statically configured with IP information that is contained within a scope on the DHCP server.

    d. There are two overlapping scopes configured on the same DHCP server.

18. Audit logging is enabled on your DHCP server, and you wish to view the audit log for yesterday (Wednesday). What file do you need to locate?

    a. C:\WINDOWS\system32\dhcp\logs\DhcpSrvLog-003.log

    b. C:\WINDOWS\system32\dhcp\logs\DhcpSrvLog-Wed.log

    c. C:\WINDOWS\system32\dhcp\DhcpSrvLog-003.log

    d. C:\WINDOWS\system32\dhcp\DhcpSrvLog-Wed.log

19. Which Performance snap-in counter may be used to detect the presence of a rogue (non-Windows) DHCP server on your network?

    a. Discovers/sec

    b. Declines/sec

    c. Offers/sec

    d. Releases/sec

20. Which code in a DHCP audit log indicates that a DHCP lease was denied?

    a. 01

    b. 02

    c. 10

    d. 15

CASE PROJECTS

DHCP has been implemented for all of the Great Arctic North University campuses. All campuses have at least one subnet and some will have several, depending upon the size of the campus. Great Arctic North University wishes to monitor the network to ensure that any problems relating to DHCP are minimized.

Case Project 5-1: Maintaining DHCP Servers

After implementing DHCP on all subnets at Great Arctic North University, your supervisor has asked you to prepare a list of maintenance tasks that are required on each server and a schedule of how often they should be performed. Most sites on the campus have one DHCP server, however some sites have two DHCP servers, and other sites have three DHCP servers. Write a short maintenance schedule that describes the tasks that need to be performed on sites that have one, two, and three DHCP servers.

Case Project 5-2: Optimizing DHCP Servers

DHCP has been implemented for a few months now at Great Arctic North University. You wish to ensure that the performance of the DHCP Service on all DHCP servers is optimized. Write a short memo describing the different Performance snap-in counters you would use to create a performance baseline and the settings that you could change to improve the performance of your DHCP servers.

Case Project 5-3: Troubleshooting DHCP Problems

You find several messages on your answering machine from users on different subnets across Great Arctic North University. All users in the Engineering Department complain that they do not have Internet access and cannot obtain access to shared network resources. A user in the Accounting Department is experiencing the same problem, and has noted that her IP address is 169.254.1.88. Three users in the operations building keep getting messages stating that their IP address conflicts with another IP address already on the network. Nobody in the arts faculty can print to a certain shared network printer; however, they can access other network resources. Write a brief list of the possible causes for these problems and their resolutions. Next, indicate on this list what steps you would take in order to investigate these problems.

CHAPTER

6

NAME RESOLUTION

After reading this chapter, you will be able to:

♦ Describe the different name types available on Windows Server 2003

♦ View and configure NetBIOS names

♦ Describe the host name resolution process

♦ Discuss the different methods used to resolve NetBIOS names

♦ Configure NetBIOS name resolution using the LMHOSTS file and WINS

♦ Troubleshoot name resolution

In Chapter 2, you configured a network interface with the IP address of a DNS server and WINS server for name resolution. This chapter focuses on how to configure computer names that are resolved to IP addresses in order to communicate on a TCP/IP network such as the Internet. In addition, this chapter introduces the different methods used to resolve host names and NetBIOS names to IP addresses and their configuration.

NAME TYPES

Windows Sockets (WinSock) and NetBIOS are the two standard methods Windows applications can use to access network resources. Both mechanisms can be used to access IP-based resources.

When a name is used to access a resource through WinSock it is referred to as a **host name**. Host names are easier to remember than IP addresses, can be up to 255 characters in length and can contain alphanumeric characters, hyphens and periods only. When a program such as a Web browser or e-mail client uses a host name, the host name must be converted to an IP address before the resource can be contacted.

As described in Chapter 2, servers on the Internet typically have a **fully qualified domain name (FQDN)** such as www.course.com that identifies them. The FQDN is simply a host name followed by the appropriate **DNS domain name** (also called a **DNS suffix**) that represents the organization to which the server belongs. Thus, the server with the FQDN www.course.com has the host name www and the DNS suffix course.com.

Many people use the words FQDN and host name interchangeably.

Microsoft uses the term Full computer name and FQDN interchangeably.

Domain Name System (DNS) domain names consist of an organization name followed by a **top-level domain** that represents the country or organization category. The country codes are standard two-character abbreviations for country names. The Internet Corporation for Assigned Names and Numbers (ICANN) defines the category names. Table 6-1 shows some of the top-level domains that are used on the Internet.

Table 6-1   Top-level domains

Category-based	Country Code-based
.com (Commercial)	.us (United States)
.edu (Educational)	.ca (Canada)
.org (Nonprofit organization)	.uk (United Kingdom)
.net (Networking)	.de (Germany)
.biz (Business)	.au (Australia)
.name (Personal use)	.tw (Taiwan)
.pro (Professionals)	.ru (Russia)

To merge with the worldwide DNS lookup system you must register your domain name with a **registrar**. Registrars have the ability to put domain information into the top-level domain DNS servers. For instance, if you register the domain course.com, then the registrar would put records into the .com DNS server that point to the DNS servers for your course.com domain. You would then be responsible for creating and maintaining the records in the course.com domain.

You may use the **hostname** command in Windows Server 2003 to view your host name. In addition, you may use ipconfig /all command to view your host name and DNS suffix as shown in Figure 6-1.

```
C:\WINDOWS\system32\cmd.exe                                    _|□|×|
C:\Documents and Settings\Administrator>ipconfig /all

Windows IP Configuration

     Host Name . . . . . . . . . . . . : student1
     Primary Dns Suffix  . . . . . . . : domain1.classroom.com
     Node Type . . . . . . . . . . . . : Unknown
     IP Routing Enabled. . . . . . . . : No
     WINS Proxy Enabled. . . . . . . . : No
     DNS Suffix Search List. . . . . . : domain1.classroom.com
                                         classroom.com

Ethernet adapter Local Area Connection:

     Connection-specific DNS Suffix  . :
     Description . . . . . . . . . . . : Intel 21140-Based PCI Fast Ethernet Adapt
er (Generic)
     Physical Address. . . . . . . . . : 00-00-F8-1F-35-A6
     DHCP Enabled. . . . . . . . . . . : No
     IP Address. . . . . . . . . . . . : 192.168.1.33
     Subnet Mask . . . . . . . . . . . : 255.255.255.0
     Default Gateway . . . . . . . . . :
     DHCP Class ID . . . . . . . . . . : FireWallUsers
     DNS Servers . . . . . . . . . . . : 192.168.1.33

C:\Documents and Settings\Administrator>
```

Figure 6-1   The ipconfig /all command

You may use DHCP to configure client computers with a DNS domain name. Simply configure the DHCP option 015 DNS Domain Name with the desired DNS domain name.

When a name is used to access a resource through NetBIOS, it is called a **NetBIOS name**. The NetBIOS name of the remote resource must be resolved to an IP address before gaining access to the resource.

NetBIOS names can also be used to represent groups of computers, not just a single computer; Active Directory domain names are one example.

All of the networking functions in pre-Windows 2000 operating systems, such as UNC paths, use NetBIOS names. In addition, many older applications that access database application servers, such as Microsoft SQL Server, use NetBIOS names. An example of using a NetBIOS name is a Windows NT computer attempting to access a share using the UNC path \\server5\datashare. The name "server5" is a NetBIOS name, and must be resolved to an IP address before the Windows NT client can contact the server. After the name is resolved to an IP address, the share named "datashare" can be accessed.

NOTE

You may disable the use of NetBIOS over the TCP/IP protocol in Windows Server 2003 on the WINS tab of Advanced TCP/IP Properties.

NetBIOS name are limited to 15 characters in length and have a 16th character that identifies the target resource or service on the computer. For example, a computer with the NetBIOS name STUDENT1 may represent its Messenger service as STUDENT1 <03>, where <03> is the 16th character in hexadecimal format. Common networking services and their associated NetBIOS characters are shown in Table 6-2.

Table 6-2   Common services represented by NetBIOS names

Character	Networking Service
00	Workstation Service
03	Messenger Service
20	File Server service
21	RAS Client Service
87	Microsoft Exchange MTA

To view the NetBIOS names attached to services that you offer, you may use the nbtstat −n command in Windows Server 2003. A sample output from this command is shown in Figure 6-2.

```
C:\WINDOWS\system32\cmd.exe                                          _|□|x|

C:\Documents and Settings\Administrator>nbtstat -n

Local Area Connection:
Node IpAddress: [192.168.1.33] Scope Id: []

              NetBIOS Local Name Table

       Name              Type         Status
    -----------------------------------------------
    STUDENT1       <00>  UNIQUE       Registered
    DOMAIN1        <00>  GROUP        Registered
    DOMAIN1        <1C>  GROUP        Registered
    STUDENT1       <20>  UNIQUE       Registered
    DOMAIN1        <1B>  UNIQUE       Registered
    DOMAIN1        <1E>  GROUP        Registered
    DOMAIN1        <1D>  UNIQUE       Registered
    ..__MSBROWSE__.<01>  GROUP        Registered

C:\Documents and Settings\Administrator>
```

Figure 6-2   The nbtstat -n command

When you install Windows Server 2003, you are required to supply a **computer name**, which is used to identify your computer on the network. This computer name is used to generate both the host name and the NetBIOS name for your computer. The computer name, host name, and NetBIOS name are identical for most Windows Server 2003 computers. However, if your computer name is greater than 15 characters, your host name will be identical to your computer name and your NetBIOS name will be the first 15 characters of your computer name.

To change your computer name, simply click the Change button on the Computer Name tab of System properties in Control Panel and you will see the screen shown in Figure 6-3.

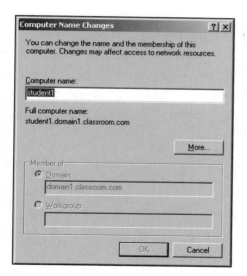

Figure 6-3   Changing a computer name

If you change your computer name, you will change both your host name and NetBIOS name.

Figure 6–3 also displays the Full computer name or FQDN for the computer. To change the DNS suffix of your FQDN, simply click the More button shown in Figure 6–3 and supply the appropriate DNS domain name as shown in Figure 6–4.

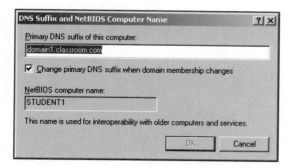

Figure 6-4   Changing the DNS suffix

The NetBIOS name is also shown in Figure 6–4, but cannot be changed. You must instead change the computer name to change the NetBIOS name. The DNS suffix shown in Figure 6–4 is called the Primary DNS suffix as it applies to all network interfaces in your computer. Instead, you may choose a different DNS suffix for each network interface that will override the Primary DNS suffix. To do this, simply access the TCP/IP Properties for a network interface, choose the Advanced button, click the DNS tab, and supply a specific DNS suffix for the connection, as shown in Figure 6-5.

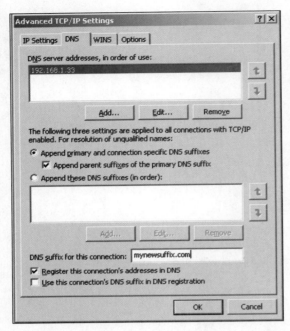

Figure 6-5   Changing a DNS suffix for a single network interface

Activity 6-1: Viewing Computer Names

Time Required: 15 minutes

Objective: View the host name, DNS suffix, and NetBIOS name of your computer.

Description: You must document the configuration of a server in a remote department of Great Arctic North University. To start, you log in to the computer and record the host name, DNS suffix, and NetBIOS name.

1. If necessary, start your server and log on as **Administrator**.

2. Click **Start**, click **Run**, type **cmd.exe**, and press **Enter**.

3. In the Command Prompt window, type **ipconfig /all** and press **Enter**. Note that your host name is studentx and your DNS suffix is domainx.classroom.com, where *x* is your student number.

4. In the Command Prompt window, type **nbtstat –n** and press **Enter**. Note that your NetBIOS name is STUDENT*x*, where *x* is your student number. Also note that there are NetBIOS name entries for the Active Directory domain on your computer.

5. Close the Command Prompt window.

6. Click **Start**, point to **Control Panel**, and then click **System**.

7. Highlight the **Computer Name** tab, and click the **Change** button.

8. Press **OK** at the warning screen. Note that your computer name is student*x* and your FQDN is student*x*.domain*x*.classroom.com, where *x* is your student number.

9. Click the **More** button. Note that your Primary DNS suffix is domain*x*.classroom.com and that your NetBIOS name is STUDENT*x*, where *x* is your student number.

10. Close all open windows.

Activity 6-2: Removing Active Directory and the DNS Service

Time Required: 45 minutes

Objective: View the host name, DNS suffix, and NetBIOS name of your computer after the Active Directory and DNS service have been removed from your computer.

Description: You wish to view the naming effects of removing Active Directory and the DNS service on a server in Great Arctic North University. After removing the Active Directory service, you remove the DNS service, change the properties of your Local Area Connection to refer to a DNS on the Internet, and view the host name, DNS suffix and NetBIOS name of your computer.

In the following steps, you remove the Active Directory service from your computer.

1. If necessary, start your server and log on as **Administrator**.

2. Click **Start**, and then click **Run**. Type **dcpromo** and press **Enter**.

3. Press **Next** and then press **OK** when the warning appears.

4. At the Remove Active Directory screen, place a check mark in the **This server is the last domain controller in the domain** box, and press **Next**.

5. At the Application Directory Partitions screen, press **Next**.

6. At the Confirm Deletion screen, place a check mark in the **Delete all application directory partitions on this domain controller** box, and press **Next**.

7. At the Administrator Password screen, type **secret;5** in the two boxes supplied, and press **Next**. You are required to enter a password that meets stricter security requirements than the Windows Server 2003 installation, since Active Directory altered the security settings of your computer when it was installed in Chapter 4. Write this password and save it for future use.

8. At the Summary screen, press **Next**.

9. Click **Finish**.

10. Click **Restart Now**.

11. When your computer has rebooted, log on as **Administrator**.

In the following steps, you remove the DNS service from your computer.

1. Click **Start**, point to **Control Panel**, and then click **Add or Remove Programs**.

2. Click **Add/Remove Windows Components**.

3. Scroll down in the components section, click **Networking Services** to highlight it, and then click **Details**.

4. Click the check box beside Domain Name System (DNS) to deselect it, and then click **OK**.

5. Click **Next**.

6. Click **Finish**.

7. Close the **Add or Remove Programs** window.

In the following steps, you configure your computer as a DNS client to gain Internet access.

1. Click **Start**, point to **Control Panel**, point to **Network Connections**, right-click **Local Area Connection**, and click **Properties**.

2. Click **Internet Protocol (TCP/IP)** and click **Properties**.

3. Ensure that the IP Address for the default gateway used for Internet access is correct, then enter the IP address for the DNS server used for Internet access in the Preferred DNS Server box and click **OK**.

4. Press **Close** to close the Local Area Connection screen and close the Network Connections screen.

In the following steps, you view your host name, DNS suffix, and NetBIOS names.

1. Click **Start**, click **Run**, type **cmd.exe**, and press **Enter**.

2. In the Command Prompt window, type **ipconfig /all** and press **Enter**. Note that your host name is student$x$ and that your DNS suffix is domain$x$.classroom.com, where x is your student number.

3. In the Command Prompt window, type **nbtstat –n** and press **Enter**. Note that your NetBIOS name is STUDENTx, where x is your student number. Also note that there are no longer any NetBIOS name entries for the Active Directory domain on your computer.

4. Close the Command Prompt window.

HOST NAME RESOLUTION

WinSock applications on Windows Server 2003 use more than one method to resolve host names or FQDNs to IP addresses. These steps are as follows:

1. *Host name*—Windows Server 2003 first checks to see if the host name being resolved is the same as its own host name. If it is, then it uses its own IP address and the resolution process stops. If the host name being resolved is not the host name of this server, then Step 2 is performed.

2. **HOSTS** *file is loaded into cache*—Upon system startup, Windows Server 2003 loads the HOSTS file into its cache so it can be evaluated in the next step. A HOSTS file is used to list host names and IP addresses for resolution. This is a static text file located on the workstation. The contents of the HOSTS file are placed in the **DNS cache**. Since this step does not actually attempt to resolve the host name, the resolution process always continues to Step 3.

3. *DNS cache*—After the HOSTS file is loaded into the DNS cache, Windows Server 2003 evaluates the contents of the DNS cache. If the host name being resolved is in the DNS cache, then the IP address in the cache is used and no further resolution is performed. The DNS cache also contains the results of previous DNS resolution attempts.

4. *DNS*—If the required host name is not the host name of this server and has not been found in DNS cache, then Windows Server 2003 submits a request to a DNS server for resolution. Using DNS as the final host name resolution method limits the amount of network traffic and speeds the resolution process.

5. If the name cannot be resolved by the preceding steps, the system attempts NetBIOS name resolution. If the host name is longer than 15 characters, the name is truncated and the first 15 characters are used to perform the NetBIOS name resolution (as discussed later in this chapter).

Configuring a HOSTS File for Name Resolution

A HOSTS file is a simple text file that stores host name information. This was the original method used to convert host names to IP addresses. For the HOSTS file to work in Windows Server 2003 it must be located in C:\WINDOWS\system32\drivers\etc.

NOTE

A HOSTS file does not have a file extension. If you create or edit this file in Notepad, it often appends the .txt file extension to the file when it is saved. To avoid this, change the Save as type option from Text Documents (*.txt) to All Files.

The contents of a HOSTS file are a list of IP addresses and host names. Each host name entry in the file has the IP address on the left, one or multiple spaces, then the host name on the right. In addition, comments can be added to the file using the # symbol. Any information after the # symbol is ignored.

Figure 6-6 shows an example of a HOSTS file. Three hosts are defined in the figure. The host name localhost resolves to the IP address 127.0.0.1. The host name oracleserver.course. com resolves to the IP address 192.168.1.33, and the host name fileserver.course.com resolves to the IP address 192.168.1.34.

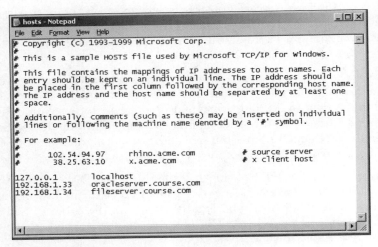

```
# Copyright (c) 1993-1999 Microsoft Corp.
#
# This is a sample HOSTS file used by Microsoft TCP/IP for Windows.
#
# This file contains the mappings of IP addresses to host names. Each
# entry should be kept on an individual line. The IP address should
# be placed in the first column followed by the corresponding host name.
# The IP address and the host name should be separated by at least one
# space.
#
# Additionally, comments (such as these) may be inserted on individual
# lines or following the machine name denoted by a '#' symbol.
#
# For example:
#
#      102.54.94.97     rhino.acme.com          # source server
#       38.25.63.10     x.acme.com              # x client host

127.0.0.1          localhost
192.168.1.33       oracleserver.course.com
192.168.1.34       fileserver.course.com
```

Figure 6-6   A sample HOSTS file

Activity 6-3: Configuring a HOSTS File

Time Required: 15 minutes

Objective: Configure and test a HOSTS file.

Description: You are testing the configuration of a new application. This application is hard coded to access the host name applicationserver.classroom.com. When the application is rolled out to all of the users, you put this entry in DNS. However, for testing, you use a HOSTS file.

1. If necessary, start your server and log on as **Administrator**.

2. Right-click **Start**, and click **Explore**.

3. In Windows Explorer go to the C:\WINDOWS\system32\drivers\etc directory, and double-click **hosts**.

4. In the Open With dialog box, click **Notepad**, and then click **OK**.

5. Place your cursor at the end of the very last line in the HOSTS file, and press **Enter**.

6. Type the IP address of your Local Area Connection on your server, press **Tab**, and then type **applicationserver.classroom.com**.

7. Exit **Notepad**, click **Yes** when asked if you want to save changes, and then close Windows Explorer.

8. Click **Start**, click **Run**, type **cmd.exe**, and press **Enter**.

9. In the Command Prompt window, type **ping applicationserver. classroom.com** and press **Enter**.

10. The ping should be successful. The HOSTS file entry you created in this activity is used to resolve the name applicationserver.classroom.com to the IP address of your server.

11. Close the Command Prompt window.

MANAGING THE DNS CACHE

Recall from earlier that the DNS cache is queried for host name resolution before DNS is contacted. The DNS cache, also called the Client resolver cache, contains the contents of the HOSTS file as well as previous DNS query results. DNS query results are only kept in the DNS cache for a certain period of time determined by the resolving DNS server. This period of time is called **time to live**; once the time to live for an entry in the DNS cache has expired, the entry is removed to ensure that stale, outdated information is not used and to prevent the DNS cache from growing too large. To view the contents of the DNS cache on your computer, simply run the command ipconfig /displaydns, as shown in Figure 6-7.

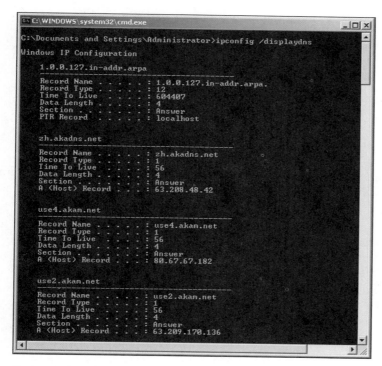

Figure 6-7   The ipconfig /displaydns command

If there are too many entries in the DNS cache, or you have changed DNS servers, you should purge the entries in the DNS cache. To do this, simply run the command ipconfig /flushdns at a command prompt.

Activity 6-4: Viewing and Purging the DNS Cache

Time Required: 10 minutes

Objective: View the contents of the DNS cache on your computer and clear its contents.

Description: You have just changed the DNS server that one of your servers is configured to use at Great Arctic North University. To prevent problems, you clear the contents of the DNS cache.

1. If necessary, start your server and log on as **Administrator**.

2. Open Internet Explorer and access the website **www.yahoo.com**.

3. Close Internet Explorer.

4. Click **Start**, click **Run**, type **cmd.exe**, and press **Enter**.

5. In the Command Prompt window, type **ipconfig /displaydns** and press **Enter**. View and note the various entries. An entry for www.yahoo.com should appear in the list.

6. In the Command Prompt window, type **ipconfig /flushdns** and press **Enter**.

7. In the Command Prompt window, type **ipconfig /displaydns** and press **Enter**. Note that the only entries contained in the DNS Cache were loaded from the HOSTS file.

8. Close the Command Prompt window.

USING DNS FOR NAME RESOLUTION

If the TCP/IP properties of your network interface is configured with the IP address of a DNS server, as shown in Figure 6-8, your computer will attempt to contact a DNS server for name resolution.

You may configure several DNS servers in Windows Server 2003. Simply click the Advanced button shown in Figure 6-8, choose the DNS tab, and add the servers to the DNS server's address list. If the first DNS server cannot be contacted, Windows Server 2003 will attempt to contact the second DNS server in the list, and so on.

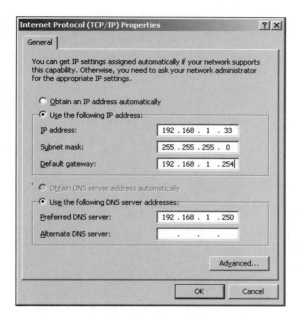

Figure 6-8   Configuring DNS settings in TCP/IP Properties.

Forward Lookup

The most common task a DNS server performs is resolving a host name to an IP address. This is called a **forward lookup.**

Resolving host names within an organization is a two-packet process. The first packet is a request from the DNS client to the DNS server containing the host name to be resolved. The second packet is the response from the server to the client, containing the IP address of the requested host name. The DNS Service on a DNS server listens for host name resolution requests on UDP port 53.

When host names are resolved on the Internet, the process is more complex. There are 13 **root servers** that control the overall DNS lookup process for the entire Internet. These servers are located around the world and are maintained by various organizations under the direction of the ICANN DNS Root Server System Advisory Committee. The root servers are responsible for directing requests to DNS servers responsible for top-level domain names such as .com and .net. If these 13 servers were to become unavailable, then much of the Internet would be inaccessible. Resources would have to be accessed via IP address, and not by host name.

On October 21, 2002, hackers attempted to perform a denial-of-service attack on the 13 DNS root servers. This attack resulted in degraded performance on 11 of 13 servers. However, because other DNS servers cache much of the root server information, Internet users did not even notice.

Figure 6-9 shows the DNS lookup process that is used when the local DNS server does not hold the requested information. This is called a **recursive lookup** and is a type of forward lookup. In this example, the client computer is attempting to resolve the host name www.microsoft.com. The request is sent from the client computer to the local DNS server. In a corporate environment, the local DNS server is installed and managed by the internal technical staff. In a home or small office environment, the local DNS server is likely to be the DNS server of the ISP.

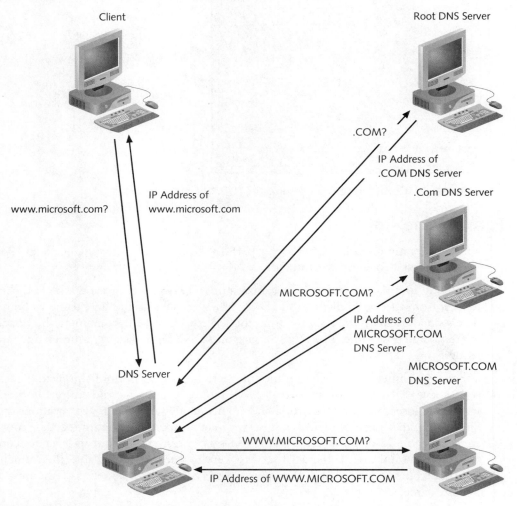

Figure 6-9   The DNS lookup process

When the local DNS server receives the request, it looks to see if it has the information that is being requested. Information could be on this server because it is authoritative for the domain or because it has previously looked up the information and has cached it. If the local

DNS server does have the information, then it responds to the client with the IP address of the host name. If the local DNS server does not have information about the host name, then it starts resolving the name by sending a request to a root server on the Internet.

The request from the local DNS server to the root server asks for the location of a DNS server that can help further resolve the host name. In this case, the name being resolved is www.microsoft.com, and the first step to resolve it is to find a server that knows about the .com domain. The local DNS server asks the root server for the IP address of a DNS server that has information about .com DNS servers. The root server responds with the IP address of a DNS server responsible for the .com domain.

The local DNS server then contacts the .com DNS server and requests the IP address of a DNS server responsible for the microsoft.com domain. The .com DNS server responds with the IP address of the DNS server responsible for the microsoft.com domain.

The local DNS server then contacts the microsoft.com DNS server and requests the IP address of www.microsoft.com. The microsoft.com DNS server responds with the IP address of the host name www.microsoft.com. Finally, the local DNS server responds back to the original DNS client with the IP address of the host name www.microsoft.com.

Reverse Lookup

In addition to resolving host names to IP addresses, DNS can also be used to resolve IP addresses to host names. This is called a reverse lookup. A **reverse lookup** allows you to specify an IP address and the DNS server returns the host name that is defined for it.

Reverse lookups are often performed for the system logs of Internet services. A Web server can be configured to perform a reverse lookup of all clients accessing a Web site. This makes it easier to read the log files because the log files list the host names instead of IP addresses.

Reverse lookup DNS information is maintained by the organization that has been assigned an entire class of addresses. Normally this is your ISP. You must contact your ISP to ensure that the addressing information is correct.

DNS Record Types

DNS records are created on a DNS server to resolve queries. Each type of record holds different information about a service, host name, IP address, or domain. Different queries request information contained in specific DNS record types. For example, to find the server responsible for e-mail in a domain, an MX record is required.

DNS has the ability to hold many different record types. However, there are only a few record types that you use on a regular basis. Table 6-3 shows some of the DNS record types and their purpose.

Table 6-3   DNS records types

Record Type	Purpose
A	*Host*—Resolves host names to IP addresses
MX	*Mail Exchange*—Points to the mail server for a domain
CNAME (or alias)	*Canonical Name*—Resolves one host name to another host name
NS	*Name Server*—Holds the IP address of a DNS server with information about the domain
SOA	*Start of Authority*—Contains configuration information for the domain on the DNS server
SRV	*Service*—Used by Active Directory to store the location of domain controllers
AAAA	*IPv6 Host*—Resolves host names to IPv6 addresses
PTR	*Pointer*—Resolves IP addresses to host names

Using NSLOOKUP

The utility **NSLOOKUP** queries DNS records. It is an indispensable tool when trouble-shooting DNS problems. With NSLOOKUP, you can query any DNS record from a DNS server. This allows you to confirm that each DNS server is configured with the correct information.

NSLOOKUP can be used from a command prompt to resolve host names, but is most powerful in interactive mode. To run NSLOOKUP in interactive mode, open a command prompt, type nslookup, and press Enter. Inside NSLOOKUP you can use the help command to get a list of available commands, as shown in Figure 6-10.

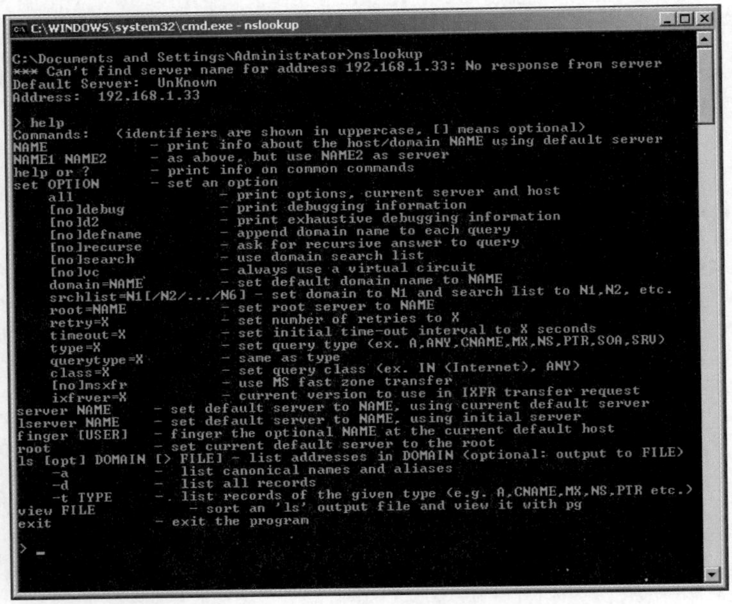

Figure 6-10   Obtaining help in NSLOOKUP

In interactive mode you can use NSLOOKUP to view any DNS records available for a zone. Figure 6-11 shows NSLOOKUP being used to find the MX records for the domain hotmail.com. MX records list the mail servers for a domain.

Figure 6-11   Using NSLOOKUP

Activity 6-5: Performing DNS Lookups with NSLOOKUP

Time Required: 10 minutes

Objective: Perform DNS lookups using the NSLOOKUP utility.

Description: You have been having trouble connecting to the www.google.com Web site and have been unable to send e-mail to the administrator of www.google.com. To confirm that the DNS is performing the host name resolution properly, you will use NSLOOKUP.

1. If necessary, start your server and log on as **Administrator**.

2. Click **Start**, click **Run**, type **nslookup**, and press **Enter**.

3. If necessary, to change the server that NSLOOKUP queries, type **server IP_address**, and press **Enter**, where *IP_address* is the IP address of the DNS server used for Internet access. Now all the queries NSLOOKUP performs are done by contacting the DNS server used for Internet access.

4. To view MX records, type **set type=mx**, and press **Enter**.

5. Type **google.com** and press **Enter** to view the MX records for the google.com DNS domain.

6. To view A records, type **set type=a** and press **Enter**.

7. Type **www.google.com** and press **Enter** to view the A record for www.google.com in DNS.

8. To close NSLOOKUP, type **exit** and press **Enter**.

NETBIOS NAME RESOLUTION

As with WinSock applications, NetBIOS applications on Windows Server 2003 use more than one name resolution method. Microsoft clients use different methods to resolve NetBIOS names to IP addresses. If the first one is not successful, the client proceeds to the next method. By default, these methods are in order:

1. *NetBIOS name cache*—When a Windows client resolves a NetBIOS name, it keeps a record of the results in the **NetBIOS name cache**. If the current NetBIOS name being resolved has a record in the cache, then the corresponding IP address in the cache is used and no further resolution is done. To view the content of the NetBIOS name cache, use the command **nbtstat –c**.

2. *Windows Internet Naming Service (WINS)*—The second method used to resolve NetBIOS names is a **Windows Internet Naming Service (WINS)** server. The client computer sends a NetBIOS name query asking for the resolution of a NetBIOS name. WINS is used early in the name resolution process because it is the resolution method most likely to be successful. By default, client computers do not know the location of a WINS server and must be configured either manually through the properties of TCP/IP or via DHCP.

3. *Broadcast*—If WINS has not been installed on the network or the client has been misconfigured, then WINS is not able to resolve the NetBIOS name. In such a case, a **broadcast** is sent on the network. The computer using the NetBIOS name being resolved receives the request and then responds with its IP address. For example, if the NetBIOS name being resolved is server5 and the computer named server5 receives a name resolution broadcast, then server5 responds with its IP address. Resolving NetBIOS names via broadcasts is not scalable to large networks because of the amount of network traffic generated and the inability to cross routers.

4. *LMHOSTS*—If no other method is successful, then an **LMHOSTS** file is parsed to find the NetBIOS name. The LMHOSTS file is a static text file located on the workstation. An LMHOSTS file is to NetBIOS name resolution what a HOSTS file is to host name resolution. LMHOSTS files are only found on Microsoft operating systems and are not commonly used. They are difficult to maintain because they must be copied to every client.

5. *Perform host name resolution*—This was discussed earlier in this chapter.

Broadcasts can slow down network communication. In the steps above, the NetBIOS name cache and WINS are used to resolve names before a broadcast is sent out onto the network, to reduce the number of broadcasts on the network.

You may choose to alter the steps used for NetBIOS name resolution in Windows Server 2003. Each grouping of steps is called a **NetBIOS node type.** The four common node types are listed in Table 6-4.

Table 6-4   NetBIOS node types

Node Type	Number	Purpose
B-node (broadcast)	1	Uses NetBIOS broadcasts only to resolve Net-BIOS names
P-node (peer-to-peer)	2	Uses WINS only to resolve NetBIOS names
M-node (mixed)	4	Uses NetBIOS broadcasts first and then WINS to resolve NetBIOS names
H-node (hybrid)	8	Uses WINS and then NetBIOS broadcasts to resolve NetBIOS names

NOTE   If a node type is not configured, the computer functions similarly to H-node. Thus, if a WINS server is configured in TCP/IP properties, it is used to resolve names before broadcasts. If a WINS server is not configured, it simply uses broadcasts to resolve names.

Each NetBIOS node type in Table 6-4 is also represented by a number. If you want to change the node type for a Windows Server 2003, simply create the registry key *HKEY_ LOCAL_MACHINE\SYSTEM\CurrentControlSet\Services\NetBT\Parameters\NodeType* and specify the correct numeric value for the desired node type.

NOTE   You may also use DHCP to configure the node type used on client computers. The DHCP option 044 WINS/NBNS Servers may be used to configure clients with the IP address of a WINS server and the DHCP option 046 WINS/NBT Node Type may be used to configure clients with a specific node type.

To view your current node type, simply run the ipconfig /all command and view the value next to Node Type. If your node type is Unknown, then your system will attempt to contact any configured WINS servers before using broadcasts to resolve NetBIOS names.

Using a LMHOSTS File for Name Resolution

Like the HOSTS file, a LMHOSTS file is a simple text file. It stores NetBIOS names and their associated IP addresses. For the LMHOSTS file to work in Windows Server 2003, it must be located in C:\WINDOWS\system32\drivers\etc.

A LMHOSTS file does not have a file extension. There is a sample LMHOSTS file in the C:\WINDOWS\system32\drivers\etc directory called LMHOSTS.SAM. If you wish to edit this file, ensure that you rename it LMHOSTS.

The format of the LMHOSTS file is similar to the format of the HOSTS file; each NetBIOS name entry in the file has the IP address on the left, one or multiple spaces, then the NetBIOS name on the right. Any lines that begin with a # symbol are comments and thus are ignored; with the exception of certain reserved words as noted in Chapter 2. For example, if you end a line with #PRE, the line will be preloaded into the NetBIOS name cache next time the system initializes. To manually reload the NetBIOS name cache with #PRE entries found in the LMHOSTS file, simply run the command **nbtstat −R** at a command prompt.

An example LMHOSTS file that contains two entries that are preloaded into the NetBIOS name cache is shown in Figure 6-12.

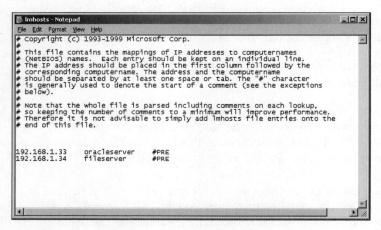

Figure 6-12   A sample LMHOSTS file

You may disable the use of an LMHOSTS file in Windows Server 2003 on the WINS tab of Advanced TCP/IP Properties.

Activity 6-6: Creating an LMHOSTS File

Time Required: 10 minutes

Objective: Create an LMHOSTS file for NetBIOS name resolution.

Description: You are installing a new accounting application for some of the finance staff. The application uses a NetBIOS name to contact the SQL database server. When you start the application, there are errors indicating that the server cannot be contacted. To ensure that NetBIOS name resolution is not a problem, you are creating an LMHOSTS file to resolve the server name, SQLSERVER, to the IP address 192.168.1.249.

1. If necessary, start your server and log on as **Administrator**.

2. Click **Start**, right-click **My Computer**, and click **Explore**.

3. In the right pane, double-click **Local Disk (C:)**, double-click **WINDOWS**, double-click **system32**, double-click **drivers**, and then double-click **etc**.

4. If LMHOSTS exists, then skip this step. If there is not already an LMHOSTS file, you must create one based on the lmhosts.sam file by following these steps:

    a. Right-click **lmhosts.sam**, and click **Copy**.

    b. Right-click the **etc** folder, and click **Paste**.

    c. Right-click **Copy of lmhosts.sam**, and click **Rename**.

    d. Type **lmhosts**, and press **Enter**.

5. Right-click **lmhosts**, click **Open**, click **Notepad**, and click **OK**.

6. On a blank line at the end of the file, type **IPaddress SQLSERVER #PRE**, where IPaddress is the IP address of your partner's Local Area Connection.

7. Click **File** and click **Save**.

8. Close Notepad and Windows Explorer.

9. Click **Start**, click **Run**, type **cmd.exe**, and press **Enter**.

10. In the Command Prompt window, type **nbtstat -R** to reload the NetBIOS name cache, and press **Enter**.

11. In the Command Prompt window, type **nbtstat -c** to view the contents of the Net-BIOS name cache, and press **Enter**. Note that SQLSERVER is listed.

12. In the Command Prompt window, type **ping SQLSERVER**. Note that your partner's IP address appears in the output of the ping command regardless of whether the ping command was successful.

13. Close the Command Prompt window.

USING WINS FOR NAME RESOLUTION

Each NetBIOS name is tied to a service such as file sharing or Windows Messenger. A WINS server is a central repository for NetBIOS name and service information. When WINS is implemented on a network, all of the client computers and servers must be configured to use the WINS server. It is important that all computers use the WINS server, or the database will be incomplete and name resolution will not be possible for some hosts. Even the server running the WINS service must be configured to use itself.

To configure a client or server to use WINS, you must edit the Advanced properties of the TCP/IP protocol. Figure 6-13 shows the configuration of a WINS server.

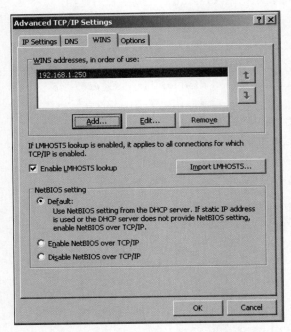

Figure 6-13   Configuring WINS name resolution

Each WINS client can have a list of multiple WINS servers as shown in Figure 6-13. If the first WINS server in the list cannot be contacted, then the WINS client queries the second WINS server in the list.

WINS offers several benefits over other NetBIOS name resolution methods because WINS:

- *Functions across routers*—WINS communication is done with unicast packets because all of the clients are configured with the IP address of the WINS server. WINS is required in routed networks because unicast packets are routable.

- *Can be dynamically updated*—The WINS database is dynamically updated as computers are added or removed from the network. Each client computer registers its name during the boot process.

- *Can be automated*—The maintenance of the WINS database contents is automatic. Once the client computers have been configured with the IP address of the WINS servers the process requires no manual updates.

- *Offers client configuration through DHCP*—WINS clients can be configured with the IP address of the WINS server using DHCP. Because this is the only client configuration required, WINS can be implemented without ever visiting the client computers on your network.

- *Offers integration with DNS*—WINS can be integrated with DNS to resolve host names. If a DNS server does not have an A record for a host name, the DNS server submits the host name (truncating it if necessary) to WINS in an attempt to resolve it. This can be useful if there are older Windows clients on your network that use WINS, but do not support dynamic DNS.

There are four common tasks performed with WINS:

- Name registration
- Name renewal
- Name release
- Name query

Name Registration

When a WINS client boots up, it performs a name registration. The name registration places NetBIOS information about the client into the WINS database. This makes the information available to other clients performing name queries. Name registration is a two-packet process.

The first packet is generated by the client and sent directly to the WINS server using a unicast packet. This packet is a **name registration request** and contains the NetBIOS name that the client computer is attempting to register.

If the NetBIOS name is not already registered by another host, then a successful **name registration response** packet is sent from the WINS server to the client computer. This packet contains the NetBIOS name that has been registered and a time to live (TTL). The computer will repeat this process for each service it has to register. Figure 6-14 shows the communication process for a successful name registration.

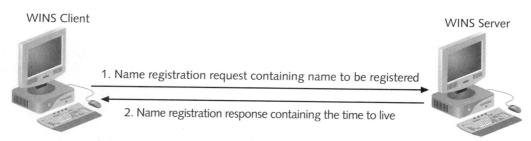

WINS Client   WINS Server

1. Name registration request containing name to be registered

2. Name registration response containing the time to live

Figure 6-14   The name registration process

If the NetBIOS name is already registered by another host, then the WINS server sends a challenge to that host. If the original owner of the name does not respond, then the NetBIOS name is registered to the new client and a successful name registration response packet is sent back to the new client. If the original owner of the name responds to the challenge, then the new client is sent a negative name registration response.

WINS clients can be configured with multiple WINS servers. If a WINS client cannot contact the first WINS server in the list after three attempts, then the second server is contacted. This process continues to the end of the list. However, the second WINS server is not contacted if a negative name registration response is received from the first WINS server.

Name Renewal

Each NetBIOS name registration is assigned a TTL. When the TTL is one-half completed, the WINS client attempts to refresh the registration. The default TTL is six days.

Name renewal is a two-packet process. The first packet is a **name refresh request** and is sent from the WINS client to the WINS server. The name refresh request contains the NetBIOS name that is being refreshed. If the WINS client is unable to contact the first WINS server for one hour, then it fails and contacts the second WINS server.

The second packet in the renewal process is a **name refresh response**. This packet is sent from the WINS server to the WINS client and contains the NetBIOS name being renewed, as well as a new TTL. Figure 6-15 shows the name renewal process. If the client is not able to renew its NetBIOS name before the end of the TTL, then the name is released.

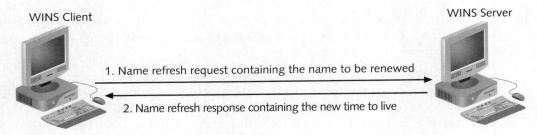

WINS Client   WINS Server

1. Name refresh request containing the name to be renewed

2. Name refresh response containing the new time to live

Figure 6-15   The name renewal process

Name Release

When a computer is properly shut down, it contacts the WINS server and releases its NetBIOS name. The first packet in this process is a **name release request** sent from the WINS client to the WINS server. This request includes the NetBIOS name being released and the IP address of the WINS client.

The WINS server sends a **name release response** to the WINS client. The name release response contains the NetBIOS name being released and a TTL of zero. Another computer can now register the released name. Figure 6-16 shows the name release process.

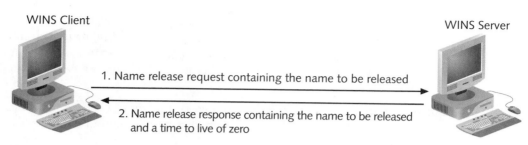

Figure 6-16   The release process

6

Name Query

A name query is used to resolve a NetBIOS name to an IP address. This is done by a client computer that is accessing resources on a server. A WINS client queries a WINS server if the NetBIOS name being resolved has not been recently resolved and stored in the NetBIOS name cache.

The first packet in the name query process is a **name query request** from the WINS client to the WINS server. This packet contains the NetBIOS name to be resolved. The second packet is a **name query response** from the WINS server to the WINS client. If the WINS server is able to resolve the query, then this packet contains the IP address registered in the WINS database for the NetBIOS name being resolved. If the WINS server is not able to resolve the query, then the packet contains a message indicating the name could not be resolved. Figure 6–17 shows the name query process.

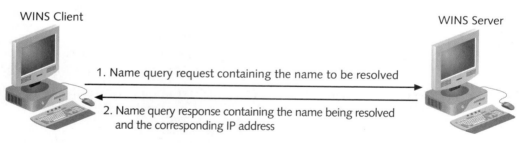

Figure 6-17   The name query process

TROUBLESHOOTING NAME RESOLUTION

Since NetBIOS and WinSock applications must resolve NetBIOS and host names to IP addresses, the failure of name resolution will prevent users from connecting to resources on the network.

If a computer is unable to connect to a remote resource, first determine whether there are any TCP/IP connectivity problems such as a bad network cable or incorrect IP configuration. The easiest method to determine whether a host has TCP/IP connectivity is to use the ping command discussed in Chapter 2.

If the ping command is successful in contacting target computers, then it is likely that the application requesting the network resource is not performing name resolution. First determine what type of name is being resolved; is it a NetBIOS name or host name? Most Internet-based applications such as Web browsers and FTP clients use WinSock, and hence, use host name resolution.

If host name resolution is failing, and the remote computer is resolved using an entry in the HOSTS file, ensure that the HOSTS file is named properly (without extension) and placed in C:\WINDOWS\system32\drivers\etc. If DNS is used, ensure that your computer is configured with the IP address of the correct DNS server in TCP/IP properties and that the computer can successfully contact the DNS server. If records for the target computer have changed on the DNS server, you may need to run the ipconfig /flushdns command to remove any old entries for the target host that are stored in the DNS cache. Finally, ensure that the DNS server has a record for the target computer.

Conversely, if NetBIOS name resolution is failing, ensure that you have a unique NetBIOS name using the netstat -n command and that NetBIOS has not been disabled on the WINS tab of Advanced TCP/IP properties. Also, determine whether your computer is configured to use WINS for name resolution in Advanced TCP/IP properties and that your computer can successfully contact the WINS server using the ping command. If the target computer is resolved using an entry in the LMHOSTS file, ensure that the LMHOSTS file does not have an extension and is in the C:\WINDOWS\system32\drivers\etc folder. Checking the NetBIOS node type using the ipconfig /all command is also useful; having a B-node type may prevent you from resolving NetBIOS names across a router.

CHAPTER SUMMARY

- Host names are used by WinSock applications to access network resources, whereas NetBIOS names are used by NetBIOS applications to access network resources.

- The Internet typically uses FQDNs to refer to computer resources. A FQDN is a combination of a host name and a DNS domain name.

- The computer name supplied during a Windows Server 2003 installation is used to determine the host name and NetBIOS name for the computer.

- Host name resolution is performed in four steps. The first step is to check if the host name being resolved matches the host name of the local computer. The second step is to load the HOSTS file into DNS cache. DNS cache is checked for the third step. Finally, DNS is used if required. If host name resolution fails and the host name is 15 characters or less, NetBIOS name resolution is used.

- A forward lookup resolves host names to IP addresses. A reverse lookup resolves an IP address to a host name.

- A recursive lookup is performed when a local DNS server queries the root servers on the Internet on behalf of a DNS client.

- Common DNS record types include: A, MX, CNAME, NS, SOA, SRV, AAAA, and PTR.

- The NSLOOKUP utility can be used to verify that a DNS server is configured with the proper records and is answering queries.

- The resolution of NetBIOS names to IP addresses is critical for pre-Windows 2000 clients. Pre-Windows 2000 clients use NetBIOS to find domain controllers and use network resources.

- There are four ways a NetBIOS name can be resolved: NetBIOS name cache, WINS, broadcast, and LMHOSTS file.

- NetBIOS node types may be used to alter the type and order of NetBIOS name resolution.

- Broadcast name resolution is not suitable for large networks because it doesn't work across routers.

- An LMHOSTS file is not suitable for large networks because the file needs to be copied to every server and workstation.

- A WINS server is a central repository for resolving NetBIOS names and offers several benefits over other NetBIOS name resolution methods. A WINS server functions across routers, can be dynamically updated, can be automated, offers client configuration through DHCP, and offers integration with DNS.

- There are four common tasks performed by a WINS server: name registration, name renewal, name releasing, and name querying.

- When a name is registered with a WINS server, the client is assigned a TTL. If the name is not renewed by the end of the TTL, then the client stops using the name.

KEY TERMS

broadcast — A packet that is addressed to all computers on a network. A broadcast for the local IP network is addressed to 255.255.255.255.

computer name — The name configured during installation for a Windows Server 2003 computer; it is used to create the host name and NetBIOS name.

DNS cache — The file in which the results of DNS name resolutions are stored for a short period of time.

DNS domain name — The name of an organization that adheres to the DNS namespace.

DNS suffix — *See* DNS domain name.

Domain Name System (DNS) — The method used to resolve Internet domain names to IP addresses.

forward lookup — The process of resolving a domain name to an IP address.

fully qualified domain name (FQDN) — A name used to locate a resource on the Internet; it consists of a host name and DNS suffix.

host name — A unique name used by WinSock that identifies the computer on the network.

hostname — A command that displays your host name in Windows Server 2003.

HOSTS — A local text file used to resolve fully qualified domain names to IP addresses.

LMHOSTS — A static text file located on the hard drive of NetBIOS clients that is used to resolve NetBIOS names to IP addresses.

name query request — A packet from a WINS client to a WINS server requesting the resolution of a NetBIOS name to an IP address.

name query response — A packet from a WINS server to a WINS client in response to a name query request. If the request is successful, this contains the IP address for the NetBIOS name in the original request.

name refresh request — A packet from a WINS client to a WINS server requesting that the registration for a NetBIOS name be renewed.

name refresh response — A packet from a WINS server to a WINS client in response to a name refresh request. If the response is successful, then the TTL of the client lease is extended.

name registration request — A packet generated by a WINS client and sent to a WINS server requesting to register the NetBIOS name and IP address.

name registration response — A packet generated by a WINS server in response to a name registration request from a WINS client. The response can be successful or negative.

name release request — A packet send from a WINS client to a WINS server when the WINS client shuts down.

name release response — A packet from a WINS server to a WINS client in response to a name release request. This packet contains the NetBIOS name being released and a TTL of zero.

nbtstat — A command in Windows Server 2003 used to troubleshoot the NetBIOS protocol.

nbtstat –c — A switch used with the nbtstat command that allows you to view the content of the NetBIOS name cache on the computer.

nbtstat –R — A switch used with the nbtstat command that allows you to manually reload the NetBIOS name cache with #PRE entries found in the LMHOSTS file on the computer.

NetBIOS name — A unique name used by the NetBIOS protocol that identifies the computer on the network.

NetBIOS name cache — The file in which the results of Windows client NetBIOS name resolutions are stored for a short period of time. The storage of these resolutions increases network performance by reducing the number of name resolutions on the network.

NetBIOS node type — A Windows setting that determines the type and order of NetBIOS name resolution.

NSLOOKUP — A command prompt- based utility for troubleshooting DNS.

recursive lookup — A DNS query that is resolved through other DNS servers until the requested information is located.

registrar — A company accredited by ICANN that has the right to distribute and register domain names.

reverse lookup — The process of resolving an IP address to a domain name.

root servers — A group of 13 DNS servers on the Internet that are authoritative for the top-level domain names such as .com, .edu, and .org.

time to live (TTL) —When referring to the DNS cache, it is the amount of time an entry may remain in the cache before being deleted. When referring to WINS, it determines the amount of time before a WINS client must renew its NetBIOS name information with the WINS server.

top-level domain — The broadest category of names in the DNS hierarchy under which all domain names fit. Some top-level domains include .com, .edu, and .gov.

Windows Internet Naming Service (WINS) — The service in Windows that resolves NetBIOS names to IP addresses and stores NetBIOS service information.

6

REVIEW QUESTIONS

1. Which port and transport protocol does the DNS Service use to listen for host name resolution requests?
   a. TCP port 53
   b. TCP port 25
   c. UDP port 53
   d. UDP port 51
   e. UDP port 389

2. The host name and the NetBIOS name are always the same on a Windows Server 2003 computer. True or false?

3. Which DNS record is used to point to a mail server for a specific domain?
   a. MX
   b. A
   c. CNAME
   d. SOA
   e. SRV

4. Resolving an IP address to a host name is what type of lookup?
   a. forward
   b. cache
   c. reverse
   d. primary

5. Which of the text files can be used to resolve domain names to IP addresses?
   a. LMHOSTS
   b. HOST
   c. HOSTS
   d. HOSTS.SAM
   e. PROTOCOL.INI

6. Which command can be used to view your DNS suffix?

   a. ipconfig

   b. hostname

   c. ipconfig /all

   d. nbtstat –n

7. The computer name configured during installation is used to set the initial host name and NetBIOS name for a Windows Server 2003 computer. True or false?

8. Which of the following situations use NetBIOS names? (Choose all that apply.)

   a. resolving a UNC path

   b. accessing the Web page www.microsoft.com

   c. opening My Network Places

   d. a Windows NT workstation logging on to the domain

9. Which command can be used to clear the DNS cache?

   a. ipconfig /flushdns

   b. nbtstat –RR

   c. ipconfig /displaydns

   d. nbtstat –R

10. Which NetBIOS name resolution method is used to resolve a name if it has recently been resolved?

   a. NetBIOS name cache

   b. WINS

   c. broadcast

   d. LMHOSTS

11. Which NetBIOS name resolution method dynamically updates a central database?

   a. NetBIOS name cache

   b. WINS

   c. broadcast

   d. LMHOSTS

12. Which NetBIOS name resolution method uses a static text configuration file on the client computers?

   a. NetBIOS name cache

   b. WINS

   c. broadcast

   d. LMHOSTS

13. What file extension is used with a LMHOSTS file?

    a. .txt

    b. .sam

    c. .dat

    d. .nbt

    e. No file extension is used.

14. What file extension is used with a HOSTS file?

    a. .txt

    b. .sam

    c. .dat

    d. .nbt

    e. No file extension is used.

15. Which of the following describe WINS? (Choose all that apply.)

    a. functions across routers

    b. uses a static text configuration file

    c. client configuration can be done with DHCP

    d. integrates with DNS

    e. uses broadcast packets

16. Which methods can be used to configure a Windows XP computer with the IP address of a WINS server? (Choose all that apply.)

    a. DNS

    b. DHCP

    c. broadcast

    d. Edit the properties of TCP/IP.

    e. multicast

17. Which WINS process is performed as the WINS client boots up?

    a. name registration

    b. name renewal

    c. name release

    d. name query

18. Which WINS process is used by WINS clients to resolve NetBIOS names to IP addresses?

    a. name registration

    b. name renewal

    c. name release

    d. name query

19. Which WINS process is initiated by WINS clients when one half of the time to live is complete?

   a. name registration

   b. name renewal

   c. name release

   d. name query

20. The default NetBIOS name resolution method used if a node type is not configured is similar to which node type?

   a. B-node

   b. P-node

   c. M-node

   d. H-node

CASE PROJECTS

A proper DNS implementation is critical to the success of your Windows Server 2003 rollout at Great Arctic North University. In addition, Great Arctic North University also has a number of different client operating systems and older applications that require NetBIOS name resolution. These case projects will present you with several situations to consider.

Case Project 6-1: Using DNS in a Windows Server 2003 Environment

FQDNs are the preferred naming convention used in Windows networks today as they integrate with Internet names and map to the structure of Active Directory. Given this, implementing DNS is vital to most Windows networks today because it is used as the primary method for resolving FQDNs to IP addresses. Use a resource such as the Internet to research the pros and cons of using FQDNs and DNS resolution. Prepare a short memo describing them.

Case Project 6-2: Accommodating Non-Windows Operating Systems

The main campus of Great Arctic North University is routed and has a variety of operating systems in use as both clients and servers. Many of the clients and servers are non-Windows operating systems such as Macintosh OS, Linux, and UNIX. Some of the non-Windows operating systems are not able to participate in WINS. How will you accommodate these operating systems?

Case Project 6-3: Choosing a NetBIOS Name Resolution Method

The Great Arctic North University network is composed of hundreds of client and server computers. All of them need to be able to resolve NetBIOS names. As part of the network design process, create a document that analyzes the benefits and drawbacks of each NetBIOS name resolution method and decide which you think is most appropriate.

6

7

DOMAIN NAME SYSTEM

After reading this chapter, you will be able to:

- Describe the functions of the Domain Name System
- Install DNS
- Explain the function and types of DNS zones
- Configure DNS zones and zone replication
- Configure a caching-only server to speed host name resolution
- Discuss the integration of Active Directory and DNS, including Dynamic DNS
- Configure and manage a DNS server
- Manage DNS zones
- Troubleshoot the DNS service

This chapter focuses on the Domain Name System (DNS), which is used to resolve host names to IP addresses. This is an essential function for the Active Directory service, large networks, and for computers accessing the Internet. In this chapter, you will learn about the functions of DNS, how to install DNS, the functions of DNS zones, and how to manage DNS servers and zones. You will also learn how to troubleshoot the Domain Name System.

FEATURES OF THE DNS SERVICE

As discussed in the previous chapter, **Domain Name System (DNS)** is the most common method used to resolve host names to IP addresses, allowing users to access resources on TCP/IP networks such as the Internet. Often, for Internet resources, your ISP handles the DNS hosting and configuration. DNS is also an essential service for a network that uses Active Directory. Windows 2000/XP client computers use DNS to find domain controllers, which the clients require to log on to Active Directory. The DNS service on Windows Server 2003 is unique because it has the ability to store DNS information in Active Directory. Once the information is stored in Active Directory, it is automatically replicated to all domain controllers, providing an easy backup mechanism.

DNS exists in various implementations; all offering the same base service and adhering to the same standards and principles, but providing different additional features and abilities. **Berkeley Internet Name Domain (BIND)** is the de facto standard for DNS implementation on UNIX and Linux systems. Many other implementations of DNS reference BIND version numbers for feature compatibility.

Microsoft offers three versions of DNS: the Windows NT4 DNS service, the Windows 2000 DNS service, and the Windows 2003 DNS service. Only the DNS service that ships with Windows 2000 and 2003 supports **service resource records** (SRV records) required for Active Directory. As a result, you may need to upgrade old Windows NT4 DNS servers on your network to take advantage of newer network technologies. Table 7-1 lists several important features of DNS alongside the Windows and BIND versions that support them. All of these features are discussed later in the chapter.

Table 7-1   Comparing DNS versions

Feature	Supported DNS Versions
Fast Zone Transfer	Windows 2003; Windows 2000; BIND 4.9.6; BIND 8.1.2; BIND 8.2.1
SRV record support (RFC 2052)	Windows 2003; Windows 2000; BIND 4.9.6; BIND 8.1.2; BIND 8.2.1
Dynamic DNS support (RFC 2136)	Windows 2003; Windows 2000; BIND 8.1.2; BIND 8.2.1
Incremental zone transfer	Windows 2003; Windows 2000; BIND 8.2.1
Secure dynamic updates	Windows 2003; Windows 2000
WINS integration	Windows 2003; Windows 2000

The Internet Software Consortium is responsible for the maintenance and development of BIND. If you would like more information about BIND, visit www.isc.org/products/BIND.

At minimum, your DNS server must have SRV record support in order to use the Active Directory service.

INSTALLING DNS

Recall from the previous section that Windows Server 2003 has the ability to act as a DNS server. In fact, most organizations using Active Directory use Windows for their DNS server.

During the installation of Active Directory, if no DNS server has been configured for the domain, then the Active Directory Installation wizard asks whether it should install DNS during the installation of Active Directory. This is a very easy way to implement DNS in a small organization with a single server.

In larger organizations, you often install DNS on multiple servers. If this is the case, then you must add DNS individually to each of these servers through Add or Remove Programs. It is not automatically added when member servers are promoted to domain controllers. Figure 7-1 shows the Add or Remove Programs option in Control Panel being used to install the DNS service.

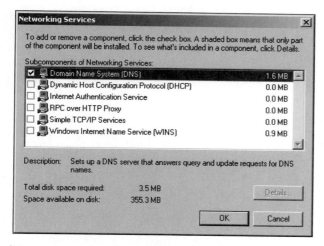

Figure 7-1   Installing the DNS service

You must have a static IP address configured on your server before installing the DNS service on Windows Server 2003.

NOTE

Activity 7-1: Installing DNS

ACTIVITY

Time Required: 10 minutes

Objective: Install DNS on your server and confirm that it is running.

Description: You wish to install a DNS server for Great Arctic North University. You have chosen a server that is highly visible by all computers in Great Arctic North University. In this activity, you will install DNS on your server and verify that it is running.

1. If necessary, start your server and log on as **Administrator**.

2. Click **Start**, point to **Control Panel**, and click **Add or Remove Programs**.

3. Click **Add/Remove Windows Components**.

4. Scroll down in the Components box, click **Networking Services** in the Components window, and click **Details**.

5. Click the check box beside **Domain Name System (DNS)** to select it, and click **OK**.

6. Click **Next** to start the installation. If prompted for the Windows Server 2003 CD-ROM, insert your Windows Server 2003 Enterprise Edition CD-ROM into your CD-ROM drive, and click **OK**.

7. Click **Finish**.

8. Close the **Add or Remove Programs** window.

9. To verify the installation, click **Start**, point to **Administrative Tools**, and click **Services**.

10. Double-click **DNS Server**.

11. Verify that the Startup type is set to **Automatic** and that the Service status is **Started**.

12. Click **OK** to close the DNS Server Properties window.

13. Close the Services window.

DNS ZONES

A **DNS zone** (commonly referred to as a zone) is the part of DNS namespace for which a DNS server is responsible. For instance, Great Arctic North University may use the domain GANU.edu to identify computers within its organization.

To store the records for this domain on a DNS server, you first create a zone on the DNS server. Once inside the zone, you can create DNS records. For example, a DNS server at Great Arctic North University may contain the zone for the GANU.edu domain. The GANU.edu zone contains the DNS resource records for computers within the GANU.edu domain. A top-level DNS server on the Internet (also called a root server) will contain the .edu zone and a DNS record that identifies the DNS server that contains the GANU.edu zone. In addition to holding the DNS records for the domain, the DNS server that contains the zone for the GANU.edu domain may also contain subdomains, which are further divisions of the DNS namespace. Thus Great Arctic North University could have the engineering.GANU.edu and business.GANU.edu **subdomains** for the faculties of engineering and business, respectively. Each subdomain may have its own DNS server and zone for its namespace, which holds the DNS records for **host names** in that subdomain.

When a zone is created, you designate whether it will hold records for forward lookups or reverse lookups. A zone that holds records for forward lookups is called a **forward lookup zone**. A zone that holds records for reverse lookups is called a **reverse lookup zone**. The DNS snap-in is used to create zones. Since you may create several zones on a single DNS server, it contains folders to organize forward and reverse lookup zones, as shown in Figure 7-2.

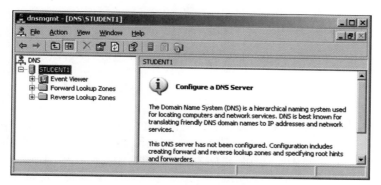

Figure 7-2   The DNS management snap-in

Primary and Secondary Zones

For fault tolerance and to reduce network traffic, it is often useful to keep copies of DNS domain information on more than one server. For instance, you might keep a copy of DNS information at each physical location in an organization to limit WAN traffic.

If you store DNS information on multiple servers, it is essential that these servers automatically synchronize information between them. This is very important if Active Directory is used on your network. If the information on multiple DNS servers gets out of synchronization, then replication of Active Directory may be affected and clients may be prevented from logging on to the network. From an administrative point of view, it is convenient to automate this process to save time and effort.

Primary and secondary zones are traditionally used to automatically synchronize DNS information between DNS servers. A **primary zone** is the first zone to be created, and all of the DNS records are created in the primary zone. A **secondary zone** has copies of primary zone information. Secondary zones contain read-only copies of DNS resource records. To create or modify resource records for a domain, you must edit the primary zone. Secondary zones will then copy the changes from the primary zone, or in some cases from other secondary zones that copy the changes from the primary zone.

The process of moving information from the primary zone to the secondary zone is called a **zone transfer**. Older DNS servers copied the entire zone database every time the secondary zone synchronized with the primary zone. Because this was time- and bandwidth-consuming, **fast zone transfer** was developed; it uses compression and sends multiple resource records per message. To further improve zone transfer speed, new implementations of DNS, including the DNS server included with Windows Server 2003, are capable of performing incremental zone transfers. An **incremental zone transfer** only copies information that has changed from the primary zone.

There can only be one primary zone in control of a domain. Secondary zones can be created as required.

NOTE

A secondary zone may receive information from another secondary zone via a zone transfer.

NOTE

To create a zone, simply right-click the Forward Lookup Zones or Reverse Lookup Zones folder shown in Figure 7-2, and click New Zone to start the New Zone Wizard shown in Figure 7-3, which will prompt you for the type of zone that you wish to create.

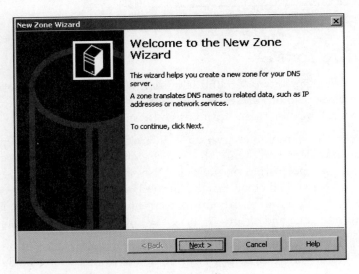

Figure 7-3   The New Zone Wizard

Recall from Table 6-3 in Chapter 6 that DNS servers contain resource records for each name that is resolved. To create a resource record in a zone, simply right-click the appropriate zone in the DNS snap-in, as shown in Figure 7-4.

Since A, CNAME, and MX records are the most common DNS resource records created, there is an option for them on the menu shown in Figure 7-4. To create other records, you must select Other New Records from the menu shown in Figure 7-4.

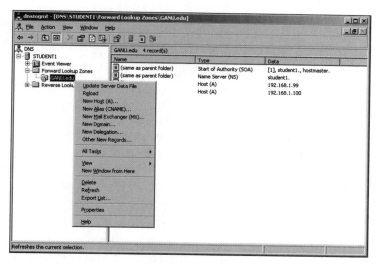

Figure 7-4   Creating DNS resource records

When primary and secondary zones are created on Windows Server 2003, the contents of the zones are held in a file on the hard drive. The name of the file is the name of the zone with a .dns extension. For example, the zone file for the domain GANU.edu is GANU. edu.dns. This file is stored in the C:\WINDOWS\system32\dns directory and adheres to BIND format so that it may be copied to another DNS server if need be. A sample zone file for the GANU.edu.dns zone is shown in Figure 7-5.

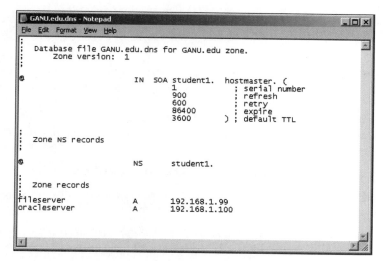

Figure 7-5   A sample GANU.edu zone file

Activity 7-2: Creating a Primary Zone

Time Required: 25 minutes

Objective: Create a primary zone to hold resource records.

Description: Great Arctic North University has just started offering online courses. This branch of the university is managed separately from the rest of the university and has been assigned the Internet domain name classroom.com. You are now creating a DNS server that will host the zone for a division of classroom.com. Because the DNS servers in your organization will be communicating with some non-Windows DNS servers, it has been decided that you will create a primary zone that can communicate with non-Windows secondary zones. You will create the required records for the mail servers in your domain and view the contents of the zone file.

1. If necessary, start your server and log on as **Administrator**

2. Click **Start**, point to **Administrative Tools**, and click **DNS**.

3. Double-click your server to expand its information.

4. Click **Forward Lookup Zones** to view the existing zones. No zones are created by default when DNS is installed.

5. Right-click **Forward Lookup Zones**, and click **New Zone**.

6. Click **Next**.

7. Confirm that **Primary zone** is selected, and click **Next**.

8. In the Zone name field, type **domainX.classroom.com**, where *X* is your student number, and click **Next**.

9. Leave the default name for the zone file of domainX.classroom.com.dns, and click **Next**.

10. Select **Allow both nonsecure and secure dynamic updates**, and click **Next**.

11. Click **Finish**.

12. Click the **Forward lookup zones** folder, then double-click **domainX.classroom.com**. Notice that only the NS and SOA records are created by default.

13. Right-click **domainX.classroom.com**, and click **New Host (A)**.

14. In the Name (uses parent domain name if blank) field, type **mail**. The fully qualified domain name is modified to mail.domainX.classroom.com.

15. In the IP address field, type **192.168.1.200**. In the classroom environment no mail server actually exists. This would be the IP address of the mail server if one existed.

16. Click **Add Host**.

17. Click **OK** to confirm the creation of the A record, and click **Done**.

18. Right-click **domainX.classroom.com**, and click **New Mail Exchanger (MX)**.

19. Leave the **Host or child domain** field blank. By leaving this blank, you are indicating that this information is for the current domain.

20. In the Fully qualified domain name (FQDN) of mail server field, type **mail.domainX.classroom.com**, where *X* is your student number, and click **OK**.

21. Right-click your server in the DNS snap-in, choose **All Tasks**, and click **Update Server Data Files**.

22. Close the DNS snap-in window.

23. Click **Start**, click **Run**, type

    notepad C:\WINDOWS\system32\dns\domainX.classroom.com.dns

    where *X* is your student number, and press **Enter**. View the records in BIND format.

24. Close the Notepad window.

Activity 7-3: Creating a Secondary Zone and Performing a Zone Transfer

Time Required: 20 minutes

Objective: Create a local copy of DNS information using a secondary zone.

Description: You will need a partner for this lab. You have found that users at some locations often need to resolve host names in other locations. To reduce the amount of WAN traffic, you have decided to create secondary zones in some of the locations. You will modify your zone to allow zone transfers and create a secondary zone of your partner's primary zone. Next, you will manually perform a zone transfer to obtain the resource records for your partner's primary zone.

1. If necessary, start your server and log on as **Administrator**.

2. Click **Start**, point to **Administrative Tools**, and click **DNS**.

3. Double-click your server, and double-click **Forward Lookup Zones** to expand their information.

4. Double-click **domainX.classroom.com**, where *X* is your student number.

5. Right-click **domainX.classroom.com** where *X* is your student number, and click **Properties**.

6. Click the **Zone Transfers** tab.

7. Confirm that **Allow zone transfers** is selected, click **To any server**, and click **OK**.

8. Right-click **Forward Lookup Zones**, and click **New Zone**.

9. Click **Next**.

10. Click **Secondary zone**, and click **Next**.

11. In the Zone name field, type **domain Y.classroom.com**, where *Y* is your partner's student number, and click **Next**.

12. In the IP address field, type the IP address of the Local Area Connection on your partner's server, click **Add**, and click **Next**.

13. Click **Finish**.

14. Click **domain Y.classroom.com**, then right-click **domain Y.classroom.com**, and click **Transfer from Master**. This will force the secondary zone to update its records from the primary zone via a zone transfer.

15. Double-click **domain Y.classroom.com**, where *Y* is your partner's student number. The records from your partner's domain are now stored on your server. You may need to press **F5** to refresh the view.

16. Close the DNS snap-in.

Activity 7-4: Testing DNS Name Resolution

Time Required: 10 minutes

Objective: Use the NSLOOKUP utility to test name resolution for a primary and secondary domain.

Description: Some users complain that they cannot use your newly created DNS to resolve host names. To rule out any server-related problems, you ensure that you can resolve names on the server itself by using the NSLOOKUP utility.

1. Click **Start**, point to **Control Panel**, point to **Network Connections**, right-click **Local Area Connection**, and click **Properties**.

2. Click **Internet Protocol (TCP/IP)** and click **Properties**.

3. Enter your Local Area Connection IP address in the Preferred DNS Server box, and click **OK**.

4. Press **Close** to close the Local Area Connection Properties screen.

5. Click **Start**, click **Run**, type **nslookup**, and press **Enter**.

6. If necessary, to change the server that NSLOOKUP queries, type **server *IP_address***, and press **Enter**, where *IP_address* is your Local Area Connection IP address. Now all the queries NSLOOKUP performs are done by contacting the local DNS server.

7. Type **mail.domain X.classroom.com**, where *X* is your student number, and press **Enter**. Note that the system resolved the record using the primary zone file on your computer for domain X.classroom.com.

8. Type **mail.domain Y.classroom.com**, where *Y* is your partner's student number, and press **Enter**. Note that the system resolved the record using the secondary zone file on your computer for domain Y.classroom.com.

9. To close NSLOOKUP, type **exit**, and press **Enter**.

Active Directory-integrated Zones

An **Active Directory–integrated zone** stores information in Active Directory rather than in a file on the local hard drive. To store DNS information in an Active Directory-integrated zone, the DNS server must also be a domain controller.

Storing DNS information in Active Directory offers the following advantages over traditional primary and secondary zones:

- *Automatic backup of zone information*—When zone information is stored in Active Directory it is automatically replicated to all domain controllers that have been configured to hold the zone information. This means that if a DNS server fails, the zone information is not lost because a copy of the zone information exists in Active Directory on other domain controllers.

- *Multimaster replication*—Active Directory-integrated zones offer the advantage of multimaster replication. In traditional DNS zones, changes are made to the primary zone and replicated to the secondary zone. With Active Directory-integrated zones, changes can be made on any DNS server servicing the zone. The changes are then replicated through Active Directory to other DNS servers. This is a benefit because when DNS servers are widely dispersed, administrators can more easily make changes to zone information via a local server. In addition, using Active Directory replication reduces complexity because only the Active Directory replication system is maintained.

- *Increased security*—Security is increased when zone information is stored in Active Directory. Traditional primary zones have no security mechanism to control which users are allowed to update DNS records. Active Directory-integrated zones use the security mechanisms built into Active Directory to control which users or computers can update DNS records.

DNS zones can be stored in two areas of Active Directory:

- The domain directory partition
- The application directory partition

The **domain directory partition** of Active Directory holds information about the objects specific to a particular Active Directory domain, such as users and computers. This partition is replicated to all domain controllers in an Active Directory domain. The information in this partition cannot be replicated to domain controllers in other Active Directory domains.

One drawback to this method of storing a DNS zone is that if a DNS zone is stored in the domain directory partition, then all domain controllers in the same domain receive copies of the zone even if they are not configured as DNS servers. This may result in unnecessary network traffic from additional AD synchronization.

If one of the servers holding the Active Directory-integrated zone is a Windows 2000 server, then the zone must be stored in the domain directory partition of Active Directory. Figure 7-6 shows a zone being created in the domain directory partition of Active Directory.

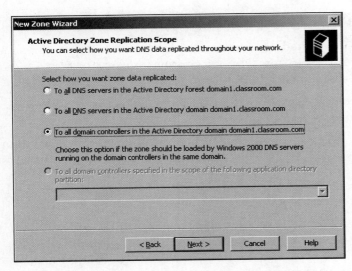

Figure 7-6 Storing a zone in the domain directory partition

Application directory partitions are a new feature of Active Directory in Windows Server 2003. They allow information to be stored in Active Directory but can only be replicated among a defined set of domain controllers. The domain controllers that hold an application directory partition must be in the same Active Directory forest but can be in different Active Directory domains.

Using an application directory partition to store a DNS zone in Active Directory offers much more flexibility than storing a DNS zone in a domain directory partition. With a zone stored in a domain directory partition, the zone cannot be replicated to domain controllers outside the Active Directory domain. A zone stored in an application directory partition can be replicated to any domain controller you choose within the same Active Directory forest.

There are three options for storing DNS zones in an application directory partition when creating an Active Directory-integrated zone:

- All DNS servers in the Active Directory forest
- All DNS servers in the Active Directory domain
- All servers specified in the scope of an application directory partition

If you choose to store a DNS zone on all DNS servers in the Active Directory forest, then an application directory partition is created to hold this information. This new application directory partition and the zone in it are automatically replicated to all domain controllers in the forest that are configured as DNS servers. In a very large organization with many DNS servers, this may not be acceptable because of the synchronization traffic that would be generated. Figure 7-7 shows a zone being created and stored on DNS servers in the Active Directory forest.

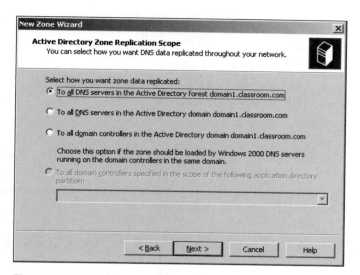

Figure 7-7   Storing a zone on all DNS servers in an Active Directory forest

Alternately, if you choose to store a DNS zone on all DNS servers in the Active Directory domain, then an application directory partition is created to hold this information. The new application directory partition and the zone in it are automatically replicated to all domain controllers in the domain that are configured as DNS servers. This is more efficient than storing the zone in the domain directory partition because synchronization can only happen between servers using the DNS information.

If you would like to be more precise with the replication of zones between domain controllers, you can create your own application directory partition. As part of creating the application directory partition, you must define the domain controllers that will hold a copy of the application directory partition you are creating. Using this option, you can replicate zone information to only a few servers throughout an Active Directory forest or domain rather than all DNS servers.

 You may convert an existing primary zone to an Active Directory-integrated zone in the General tab of the zone's properties.

Active Directory–integrated zones replicate information in a way that is fundamentally different from traditional DNS zones. Consequently, they are limited in how they interact with traditional DNS zones. Active Directory–integrated zones interact with traditional zones by acting as a primary zone to traditional secondary zones. This is useful when not all DNS servers are capable of participating in an Active Directory-integrated zone.

There are several situations where a DNS server cannot participate in an Active Directory-integrated zone:

- The DNS server is pre-Windows 2000.
- The DNS server is Windows 2000 and the Active Directory-integrated zone is stored in an application directory partition.
- The DNS server is a non-Windows server.
- The DNS server is a member server, but not a domain controller.
- The DNS server is in a different forest.

Active Directory-integrated zones can act only as primary zones when integrating with traditional DNS zones. They cannot act as secondary zones.

ACTIVITY

Activity 7-5: Promoting a Member Server to a Domain Controller

Time Required: 30 minutes

Objective: Promote a member server to a domain controller.

Description: You have decided to use the Active Directory service in the online education divisions of Great Arctic North University. You have also decided that you would like the zones to be Active Directory-integrated. To store an Active Directory-integrated zone, you must promote your server to a domain controller using the utility DCPROMO.

1. If necessary, start your server and log on as **Administrator**.
2. Click **Start**, and then click **Run**. Type **dcpromo** and press **Enter**.
3. Press **Next**. Press **Next** again.
4. Ensure that **Domain controller for a new domain** is selected, and press **Next**.
5. Ensure that **Domain in a new forest** is selected, and press **Next**.
6. At the New Domain Name screen, type in **domainX.classroom.com**, where X is your student number, and press **Next**.
7. At the NetBIOS Domain Name screen, ensure that **DOMAINX** (where X is your student number) is displayed in the box provided, and press **Next**.
8. At the Database and Log Folders screen, press **Next**.
9. At the Shared System Volume screen, press **Next**.
10. At the DNS Registration Diagnostics screen, press **Next**.
11. At the Permissions screen, press **Next**.
12. At the Directory Services Restore Mode Administrator Password screen, type the password **secret;5** in both text boxes, and press **Next**.
13. At the Summary screen, press **Next**. Insert your Windows Server 2003 Enterprise Edition CD-ROM into your CD-ROM drive when prompted, and press **OK**.

14. Click **Finish**.

15. Click **Restart Now**.

Activity 7-6: Converting a Primary Zone to an Active Directory-Integrated Zone

Time Required: 10 minutes

Objective: Convert a primary zone to an Active Directory-integrated zone.

Description: You have decided to implement Active Directory on your classroom.com networks. To enhance the fault tolerance of your DNS servers, you have promoted them to domain controllers and will change their primary zones to Active Directory integrated zones.

1. Log on to your server as **Administrator**.

2. Click **Start**, point to **Administrative Tools**, and click **DNS**.

3. Double-click **Forward Lookup Zones**.

4. Double-click your **domainX.classroom.com** domain, where *X* is your student number. Next, right-click **domainX.classroom.com** and choose **Properties**.

5. Note that the Type of this zone is set to **Primary**. Click the **Change** button.

6. Place a check mark beside **Store the zone in Active Directory** (available only if DNS server is a domain controller), and press **OK**.

7. Press **Yes** to confirm the change, and click **OK** to close the **domainX.classroom.com** Properties window.

8. Close the DNS snap-in.

Activity 7-7: Creating an Active Directory-Integrated zone

Time Required: 15 minutes

Objective: Create an Active Directory-integrated zone.

Description: Great Arctic North University has implemented a new project department in their online course division to test new technologies. The computers in the test department will use their own domain webX.classroom.com, where *X* is the test division. For added security and to reduce replication traffic, you have decided to implement an Active Directory integrated DNS zone on your DNS server for this domain and store the information in the directory partition on each domain controller.

1. Log on to your server as **Administrator**.

2. Click **Start**, point to **Administrative Tools**, and click **DNS**.

3. Right-click **Forward Lookup Zones**, and click **New Zone**.

4. Click **Next** to begin creating the zone.

5. Confirm that the options **Primary zone** and **Store the zone in Active Directory** (available only if DNS server is a domain controller) are selected, and click **Next**.

6. Click **Next** to accept the default replication option **To all domain controllers in the Active Directory domain domainX.classroom.com**.

7. In the Zone name field, type **webX.classroom.com**, where *X* is your student number, and click **Next**.

8. Click **Next** to accept the default dynamic update option of Allow only secure dynamic updates (recommended for Active Directory).

9. Click **Finish**.

10. Close the DNS snap-in.

Activity 7-8: Performing a Zone Transfer from an Active Directory-Integrated Zone

Time Required: 10 minutes

Objective: Perform a zone transfer from an Active Directory-integrated zone to a secondary zone.

Description: You have upgraded all classroom.com DNS servers to domain controllers and have converted all primary zones into Active Directory-integrated zones. The server in your department still has a secondary zone that obtained records from another primary zone before it was upgraded to Active Directory-integrated. You wish to ensure that your secondary zone can still obtain updated records via a zone transfer from the Active Directory-integrated zone.

1. If necessary, start your server and log on as **Administrator**.

2. Click **Start**, point to **Administrative Tools**, and click **DNS**.

3. Click **Forward Lookup Zones**, then click **domainY.classroom.com**. Right-click **domainY.classroom.com**, where *Y* is your partner's student number, and click **Transfer from Master**. This will force the secondary zone to update its records from the Active Directory-integrated primary zone via a zone transfer.

4. Double-click **domainY.classroom.com**, where *Y* is the student number of your partner. The records from your partner's domain are now stored on your server, including new folders that contain SRV records used by your partner's Active Directory service. You may need to press **F5** to refresh the view.

5. Close the DNS snap-in.

Stub Zones

When a DNS server does not have the information to resolve a host name, it contacts a root server on the Internet to continue the resolution process. This includes finding the DNS server that is authoritative for the domain with the requested information. However, this process works only if the domain name is registered on the Internet.

When Active Directory is implemented, many organizations choose to use a domain name that is not registered on the Internet. If a domain name is not registered on the Internet, then an alternative to using **root servers** must be implemented to ensure the lookup process is functional. In this case, DNS servers can be configured with a **stub zone** to help them resolve DNS requests.

A stub zone is a DNS zone that holds only NS records for a domain. NS records define the name servers that are responsible for a domain. When a client submits a DNS request to a server with a stub zone, the DNS server continues the lookup process by sending a request to a DNS server specified in the NS records of the stub zone.

For example, in Figure 7-8, Great Arctic North University has a subdomain for student resources called students.GANU.edu. This subdomain is created as a separate zone on the server STUDENTDNS. The STUDENTDNS server also has a stub zone for the domain GANU.edu. This stub zone has a NS record that points to the server GANUDNS, which holds the GANU.edu zone. When student computers submit DNS requests to STUDENTDNS for GANU.edu records, STUDENTDNS reads the NS record from the GANU.edu stub zone. Based on the NS record in the GANU.edu stub zone, STUDENTDNS then submits a query to GANUDNS. GANUDNS responds to STUDENTDNS, and STUDENTDNS then sends a response back to the student client computer.

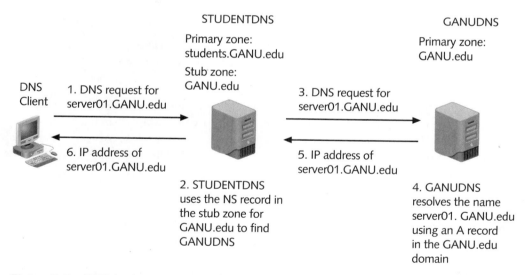

Figure 7-8   DNS lookup using a stub zone

Activity 7-9: Creating a Stub Zone

Time Required: 10 minutes

Objective: Create a stub zone to direct recursive queries.

Description: The different test divisions in the project department at Great Arctic North University requires resources to be shared between the divisions. Your DNS server is configured so that it performs a recursive query with root servers on the Internet if it does not have the appropriate information. However, the root servers on the Internet have no information about the domains used by the project department. To help your server resolve domain names in other project domains, you will create a stub zone.

1. If necessary, start your server and log on as **Administrator**.

2. Click **Start**, point to **Administrative Tools**, and click **DNS**.

3. Right-click **Forward Lookup Zones**, and click **New Zone**.

4. Click **Next** to begin creating the stub zone.

5. Click **Stub zone**, uncheck **Store the zone in Active Directory** (available only if DNS server is a domain controller), and click **Next**.

6. In the Zone name field, type **webY.classroom.com**, where *Y* is your partner's student number, and then click **Next**.

7. Accept the default file name by clicking **Next**.

8. In the IP address field, type *IP_address*, where *IP_address* is the IP address of your partner's local area connection. Click **Add**, and click **Next**.

9. Click **Finish** to finish creating the stub zone.

10. Double-click **webY.classroom.com**. The name server records for the webY. classroom.com domain have been copied to your server. When a DNS query for a record in the webY.classroom.com domain is submitted to your server, it will now submit that query directly to the proper name servers rather than the root servers on the Internet.

11. Close the DNS snap-in.

CACHING-ONLY DNS SERVERS

A **caching-only server** does not have any zones configured on it. It exists only to be a local DNS server for client computers. The first time a caching-only server performs a lookup for a client computer, it caches it. Then, if another client computer requires the same information, the caching-only server has a local copy and does not need to use the WAN or Internet to lookup the information. Over time, as the cache becomes larger, the caching-only server increases in value.

On very slow WAN links, caching-only servers may create less network traffic than storing Active Directory-integrated zones or secondary zones locally. An Active Directory-integrated zone can only be created if there is a local domain controller. If WAN links are too slow, then it may not be possible to support Active Directory synchronization. Even the zone transfers between a secondary zone and primary zone may generate more traffic than a caching-only server.

To create a caching-only server, install the DNS Service and do not create any zones. A DNS server installed on Windows Server 2003 automatically responds to client requests, forwards them to the DNS server configured in TCP/IP properties and caches all successful lookup requests before responding to the client.

7

ACTIVE DIRECTORY AND DNS

Active Directory requires DNS to function properly. The most important function that DNS performs for Active Directory is locating services, such as domain controllers. The naming structure for Active Directory domains is exactly the same as that for DNS domains so that service information about an Active Directory domain can be stored in the corresponding DNS domain. The service information that is stored in DNS helps client computers find domain controllers to log on to, and it also helps domain controllers find each other for replication of Active Directory information. For example, the DNS zone used by Active Directory will contain SRV records that describe where to find services such as **Kerberos** and **Lightweight Directory Access Protocol (LDAP)**. Client computers use these SRV records to find the domain controllers that provide these services. Figure 7-9 shows some of the DNS records created in DNS to support the Active Directory service.

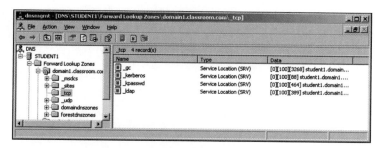

Figure 7-9 DNS records used by Active Directory

In addition to the SRV records required by Active Directory, it is preferable to have A records for the names and IP addresses of all the servers and client workstations in DNS. Many utilities such as the Microsoft Management Console (MMC) rely on host name resolution. For example, if you right-click on a client workstation in Active Directory Users and Computers and click Manage, this opens the Computer Management snap-in for that computer. To be able to do this, the MMC must be able to resolve the host name for the computer to an IP address. If DNS is not configured properly, the attempt to manage the client computer fails.

It is possible to manually add all of the required SRV and A records that an Active Directory domain requires, but this would be very difficult to manage. To simplify management of DNS records for Active Directory, you can implement **Dynamic DNS**, which is discussed in the following section.

Dynamic DNS

Dynamic DNS is a system in which records can be updated on a DNS server automatically rather than forcing an administrator to create records manually. It is defined by RFC 2136. Windows 2000/XP/2003 operating systems are compliant with RFC 2136 and have the ability to perform Dynamic DNS updates themselves. Windows 9x/NT are not compliant with RFC 2136 and rely on a DHCP server to perform Dynamic DNS updates for them.

The service records for domain controllers are placed in a DNS zone using Dynamic DNS. When the NETLOGON Service of the domain controller starts, the DNS zone is updated by Windows Server 2003. If the service records for a domain controller become corrupt or are accidentally deleted, you can recreate them by stopping and starting the NETLOGON service on the domain controller.

Windows 2000/XP clients perform their own Dynamic DNS updates. During the boot process, the clients contact their DNS server to perform a dynamic update, and then they create an A record for their host name and IP address. With this mechanism, DNS records for client computers are correct even when using DHCP because the A record is created after the IP address is leased from the DHCP server.

To manually force Windows 2000/XP clients to update their Dynamic DNS information, use the command ipconfig /registerdns.

Activity 7-10: Testing Dynamic DNS

Time Required: 10 minutes

Objective: Verify that a computer is registering a host name using Dynamic DNS.

Description: You are not sure whether your computer is properly registering its IP address and host name using Dynamic DNS. To confirm that it is working properly, you will delete the existing A record from your DNS server and force the reregistration in DNS.

1. If necessary, start your server and log on as **Administrator**.

2. Click **Start**, point to **Administrative Tools**, and click **DNS**.

3. Double-click your server to expand its information.

4. Double-click **Forward Lookup Zones** and then double-click **domainX.classroom.com**, where X is your student number. Notice that there are records for both network interfaces in your computer.

5. Right-click the A record used to map your host name to the IP address of your local area connection, and click **Delete**. Click **Yes** to confirm the deletion.

6. Click **Start**, click **Run**, type **ipconfig /registerdns**, and press **Enter**.

7. In the DNS snap-in, click **domainX.classroom.com**, where X is your student number. If you do not see a new host record for your server, press **F5** to refresh the view. If you do not see a new host record for your server, you may need to right-click your server, point to **All Tasks**, and click **Restart**. Click **Yes** if necessary.

8. Close the DNS snap-in.

Dynamic DNS and DHCP

The Dynamic DNS information updated by Windows 2000/XP is negotiated with the DHCP server during the lease process. A Windows 2000/XP client will request that the DHCP server update the PTR record for reverse lookups and that the client update its own A record. If the DHCP server does not support Dynamic DNS, then Windows 2000/XP clients can also update the PTR record. Figure 7-10 shows the options that can be configured on the scope of a Windows Server 2003 DHCP server.

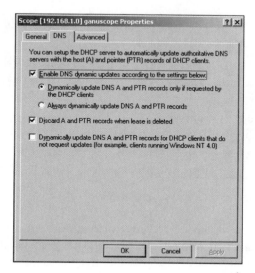

Figure 7-10   Dynamic DNS configuration of a DHCP scope

By default, a DHCP server running on Windows Server 2003 updates DNS records only for Windows 2000/XP clients and only if requested to do so. If you want the DHCP server to always update the A and PTR records for Windows 2000/XP clients, then select the Always dynamically update DNS A and PTR records option. If you want the DHCP server to update A and PTR records for clients that are not compliant with RFC 2136, then enable the Dynamically update DNS A and PTR records for DHCP clients that do not request updates (for example, clients running Windows NT 4.0) option.

To specify that the DHCP server delete DNS records it has created when a lease expires, select the Discard A and PTR records when lease is deleted option. If this option is not enabled, then A and PTR records created by the DHCP server are never deleted by the DHCP server and out-of-date information may be left in DNS.

Configuring a Zone for Dynamic DNS

A zone can be configured for Dynamic DNS during creation or by modifying the properties of the zone after configuration. Figure 7-11 shows the Dynamic DNS options that are available during the creation of an Active Directory-integrated zone.

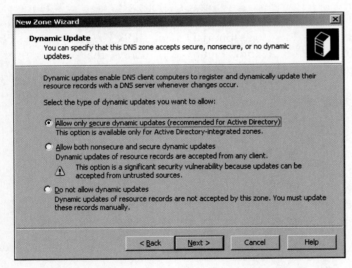

Figure 7-11   Dynamic Update options when creating an Active Directory-integrated zone

The Allow only secure dynamic updates option is available only if the zone is Active Directory-integrated. This option configures the zone to accept updates as allowed by the security permissions set in Active Directory. The DHCP service included with Windows Server 2003 allows you to configure a user and password that the DHCP server can use to securely perform Dynamic DNS updates.

If the Allow both nonsecure and secure dynamic updates option is selected, then any client can update records. This option does not have any security and can be vulnerable to hackers placing incorrect information in the zone.

The Do not allow dynamic updates option stops this zone from accepting any dynamic updates. This is not realistic for zones storing records used by Active Directory because of the high volume of record changes. However, this is the best setting to use on a DNS server that is available on the Internet and for zones that do not store records used by Active Directory.

After a zone has been created, you can change the dynamic update option by editing the properties of the zone. Figure 7-12 shows how to change the dynamic update option of a primary zone that is not Active Directory-integrated.

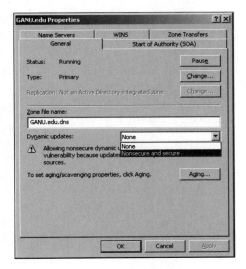

Figure 7-12   Changing the Dynamic update option

 Notice that the screen shown in Figure 7-12 does not have the option for secure dynamic updates only; this is because it is not Active Directory-integrated.

MANAGING DNS SERVERS

There are many DNS options that can be configured at the server level. Some of them are:

- Configure aging and scavenging
- Update server data files
- Clear cache

- Configure bindings
- Configure forwarding
- Edit the root hints
- Configure event and debug logging
- Set advanced options
- Configure security

Aging and Scavenging

Aging and scavenging of DNS records is a new feature of DNS in Windows Server 2003. With aging and scavenging, DNS records created by Dynamic DNS can be removed after a certain period of time if they have not been updated. This prevents out-of-date information from being stored in a zone.

For scavenging to occur, it must be enabled on the Advanced tab of the DNS server properties. Figure 7-13 shows the aging and scavenging option being enabled. Scavenging is disabled by default. The Scavenging period option specifies how often scavenging is to be performed. By default, scavenging is performed every 7 days.

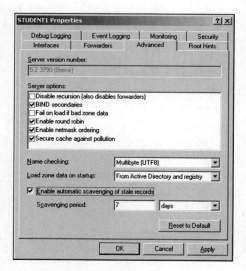

Figure 7-13 Enabling scavenging

After scavenging has been enabled at the server level, you can configure the aging of DNS records for each zone. To configure the **aging/scavenging** properties for all zones on a server, right-click the server, and select Set Aging/Scavenging for All Zones. Figure 7-14 shows the options available when you right-click on the server.

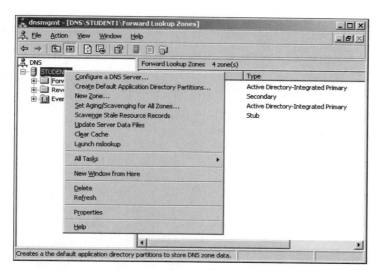

Figure 7-14 Options available when right-clicking a server in the DNS snap-in

Update Server Data Files

The Update Server Data Files option is available when you right-click on a server in the DNS snap-in, as shown earlier in Figure 7-14. If a zone is Active Directory–integrated, this has no effect. If a primary zone is not Active Directory–integrated, it forces all of the DNS changes in memory to be written to the zone file on disk.

Clear Cache

A DNS server automatically caches all lookups that it performs. Occasionally, you may have outdated information in the cache. To force a DNS server to perform a new lookup before the record in cache times out, you must clear the cache. To clear the cache, right-click the server and select Clear Cache, as shown earlier in Figure 7-14.

Configure Bindings

By default, the DNS Service listens on all IP addresses that are bound to the server it is running on. However, you can also configure DNS to only respond on certain IP addresses that are bound to the server. This may be useful if you have bound extra addresses to the server for specific purposes such as Web hosting.

The Interfaces tab of the server properties allows you to configure the IP addresses to which the DNS service listens. Figure 7-15 shows the Interfaces tab of the DNS server properties dialog box.

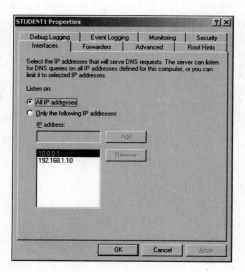

Figure 7-15   The Interfaces tab of DNS server properties

Forwarding

Ordinarily, a DNS server that cannot perform a record lookup for a domain follows a process of querying several servers to find the information. This query process begins with the root servers on the Internet.

Some internal DNS servers are restricted from accessing the Internet for security reasons, so this process is not possible. **Forwarding** allows you to configure a local DNS server to forward queries from clients to another DNS server if the local DNS server does not have the required records. DNS servers that forward requests to other DNS servers are sometimes called slave DNS servers.

For example, a company might have several physical locations, each with its own DNS server. All Internet access is routed through corporate headquarters. To ensure that each DNS server is secure from hackers on the Internet, the firewall for this company has been configured to prevent all packets from traveling from the DNS servers to the Internet or from the Internet to the DNS servers. A special Internet-accessible DNS server has been set up at corporate headquarters to perform Internet DNS lookups. The Internet-accessible DNS server does not contain any DNS information for the Active Directory domain. All of the local DNS servers at each physical location are configured to forward queries to the Internet-accessible DNS server.

In this example, when clients need to resolve a host name on the Internet, the following steps occur:

1. The client sends the query to its local DNS server.
2. The local DNS server forwards the query to the Internet-accessible DNS server.

3. The Internet-accessible DNS server performs the lookup on the Internet.

4. The Internet-accessible DNS server returns a response to the local DNS server.

5. The local DNS server returns a response to the client.

Windows Server 2003 has the ability to forward DNS queries to different DNS servers depending on the DNS domain that is being queried. This allows a very flexible forwarding system where internal DNS lookups can be forwarded to one DNS server and Internet DNS lookups can be forwarded to another DNS server.

Figure 7-16 shows the Forwarders tab for a server that has been configured to forward queries for the domain GANU.edu to the IP address 192.168.1.200. If a DNS server attempts to forward a query and it fails, it then attempts to contact the root servers on the Internet. To prevent the DNS server from attempting to further resolve the name, select the Do not use recursion for this domain option. You can also configure the number of seconds that the DNS server waits for a response before a forwarding attempt is considered a failure. The default is 5 seconds.

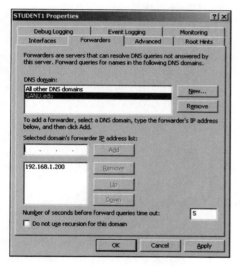

Figure 7-16   The Forwarders tab of DNS server properties

Root Hints

Root hints are servers that are used to perform recursive lookups. The Root Hints tab of the server properties is automatically populated with the names and IP addresses of the DNS root servers on the Internet. The list of root servers is loaded into the root hints from the file cache.dns stored in C:\WINDOWS\system32\dns. Figure 7-17 shows the Internet root DNS servers listed in the Root Hints tab of the server properties.

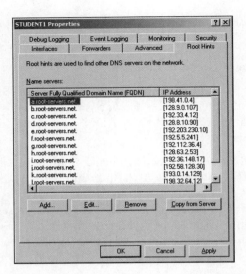

Figure 7-17   The Root Hints tab of DNS server properties

If your DNS system is completely self-contained and does not need to access the root servers on the Internet, you can configure one of your internal DNS servers to act as a root server. This is done by creating a forward lookup zone named "." (period). If a DNS server holds a zone named ".", it is considered to be a root server and will not load the list of Internet root DNS servers from cache.dns. You can then edit the list of root hints for other DNS servers to point only at the new root server you have configured.

Activity 7-11: Creating a Root Server

Time Required: 10 minutes

Objective: Configure your server as a root DNS server.

Description: Some locations on the Great Arctic North University network are not allowed access to the Internet. To keep DNS servers in these locations from performing DNS lookups, you configure your server as a DNS root server.

1. If necessary, start your server and log on as **Administrator**.

2. Click **Start**, point to **Administrative Tools**, and click **DNS**.

3. If necessary, double-click your server to expand its information.

4. Click **Forward Lookup Zones**.

5. Right-click **Forward Lookup Zones**, and click **New Zone**.

6. Click **Next**.

7. Ensure that **Primary zone** is selected, uncheck **Store the zone in Active Directory** (available only if DNS server is a domain controller), and click **Next**.

8. In the Zone name field, type "**.**" (a single period), and click **Next**. This indicates that this is to be a root zone.

9. Click **Next** to accept the default file name root.dns.

10. Click **Next** to accept the default of not allowing dynamic updates.

11. Click **Finish**. Your server will now perform DNS lookups only for zones for which it has configuration information.

12. Right-click your server, and click **Properties**.

13. Click **Root Hints**. This tab is empty because your server is configured as a root server. This tab shows the Internet root servers when not configured as a root server.

14. Click **Cancel**.

15. Close the DNS snap-in.

Logging

DNS servers are capable of **event logging** and **debug logging**. Event logging records errors, warnings, and information to the event log. Debug logging records much more detailed information.

Figure 7-18 shows the Event Logging tab of the DNS server properties. You have the option to record:

- No events
- Errors only
- Errors and warnings
- All events

Debug logging records packet-by-packet information about the queries that the DNS server is receiving. This type of logging is enabled only for troubleshooting because it records a large volume of information. To reduce the amount of information recorded, you can specify what type of information should be logged including:

- Packet direction
- Transport protocol
- Packet contents
- Packet type

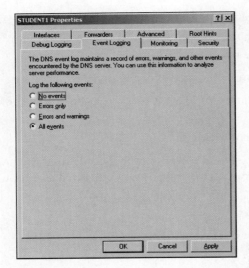

Figure 7-18   The Event Logging tab of DNS server properties

Figure 7-19 shows the configuration of debug logging in the DNS server properties dialog box.

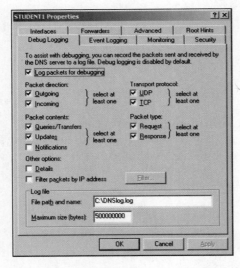

Figure 7-19   The Debug Logging tab of DNS server properties

Advanced Options

Several options can be configured on the Advanced tab of the server properties dialog box, including:

- Disable recursion (also disables forwarders)
- BIND secondaries
- Fail on load if bad zone data
- Enable round robin
- Enable netmask ordering
- Secure cache against pollution

Figure 7-20 shows the options that can be configured on the Advanced tab of the server properties dialog box.

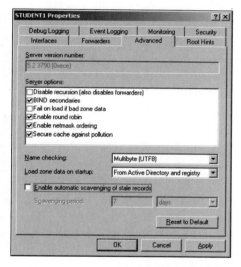

Figure 7-20   The Advanced tab of DNS server properties

The Disable recursion (also disables forwarders) option stops this DNS server from contacting any other DNS servers in an attempt to find DNS records. This DNS server recognizes DNS records configured only on this server.

The BIND secondaries option disables fast transfers between primary and secondary zones. This is necessary only if the DNS server holding the secondary zone is a non–Windows DNS server and supports a BIND version less than 4.9.4.

By default, if errors are found in a zone file, the DNS server logs the errors and ignores the affected records. You can configure the server to disable the zone when any errors are found by selecting the Fail on load if bad zone data option. You may enable this if you wish to ensure that all of the zone data is available.

Round robin DNS occurs when more than one record exists for a DNS query. For example, there may be two A records configured for a single host name, which allows a single host name to be tied to multiple IP addresses. This is sometimes done with Internet resources such as a Web server, and it is a simple way to implement "poor man's" load balancing. To enable round robin DNS, select the Enable round robin option. This option is enabled by default.

When a DNS query has multiple matches, a DNS server configured on Windows Server 2003 responds with the IP address that most closely matches the IP address of the client making the request. For instance, if a client with the IP address 192.168.5.100 makes a DNS query with valid responses 10.0.10.98 and 192.168.5.20, then the DNS server responds with IP address 192.168.5.20 because it most closely matches the IP address of the client. In most cases, this results in a response with an IP address that is physically closest to the client. This feature can be disabled by deselecting the Enable netmask ordering option.

The Secure cache against pollution option controls how the DNS server caches lookups. With this option enabled, the server does not cache lookups that result in a host name outside of the originally requested domain. For example, if a request is made for the host name www.GANU.edu, and it is redirected to www.greatarctic.edu, then the DNS server does not cache the response. This option is enabled by default.

The Name checking list box allows you to specify what characters are allowed in the zones. The default setting is Multibyte UTF8, which allows non-ASCII characters. The setting Strict RFC (ANSI) allows only characters that are defined in RFC 1123. The setting Non RFC (ANSI) allows only ASCII characters to be part of DNS names, but they do not have to conform to RFC 1123. The settings All names permits any naming convention.

The Load zone data on startup list box allows you to select from where the DNS service reads its configuration information. The default option is From Active Directory and registry. Other options include From registry and From file. If the option to start from file is chosen, then a configuration file named C:\WINDOWS\system32\dns\boot is used. This option should be chosen if configuration information has been copied from a BIND-based server.

Security

The Security tab of the server properties shown in Figure 7-21 allows you to view and modify which users and groups can modify the configuration of the DNS server. By default, the Domain Admins group, Enterprise Admins group, and DnsAdmins group are allowed to manage DNS.

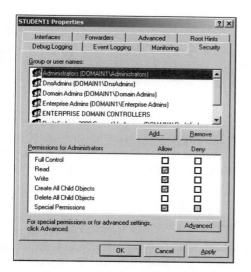

Figure 7-21   The Security tab of DNS server properties

Managing Zones

There are a variety of options that can be configured for a zone. These include:

- Reload zone information
- Create a new delegation
- Change the type of zone and replication
- Configure aging and scavenging
- Modify the Start of Authority (SOA) record
- Name servers
- Enable WINS resolution
- Enable zone transfers
- Configure security

Reload Zone Information

To perform any mass editing of DNS information stored in a non-Active Directory-integrated zone, you may find it easier to edit the zone file stored in C:\WINDOWS\system32\dns rather than using the DNS snap-in. To get the DNS server to use the newly edited zone file, you must restart the DNS service or tell it to reload the zone file. To reload the zone file, right-click on the zone, and click Reload.

Create a New Delegation

In a larger organization, you need more than one zone to hold all of the DNS information. As a zone begins to contain many subdomains, you will want to delegate responsibility for some subdomains by creating new zones for them on other servers. This allows you to choose which DNS servers hold what DNS records.

Windows Server 2003 provides a wizard to guide you through the process of delegating the authority for a subdomain to another server. To access the wizard, right-click the original zone, and click New Delegation. When the wizard is complete, DNS servers holding the original zone will redirect requests for the delegated subdomain to the DNS server specified during the delegation process.

Changing the Type of Zone and Replication

When a zone is created, you must choose whether it is a primary zone, secondary zone, or stub zone. If it is a primary zone, you must also choose whether it is stored in Active Directory. If the zone is stored in Active Directory, then you also choose how it is replicated. All of these options can be changed after the zone is created.

The zone type and replication for an existing zone can be modified on the General tab of the zone properties dialog box, as shown in Figure 7-22.

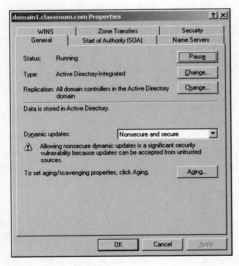

Figure 7-22   The General tab of zone properties

The button to change the replication for a zone is only available for Active Directory-integrated zones. If the button is grayed out then the zone is not stored in Active Directory.

Configure Aging and Scavenging

Once scavenging has been enabled at the server level, the aging/scavenging properties must be configured at the zone level. To configure the aging/scavenging properties of a zone, click the Aging button on the General tab of the zone properties dialog box. Figure 7-23 shows the aging/scavenging properties of a zone.

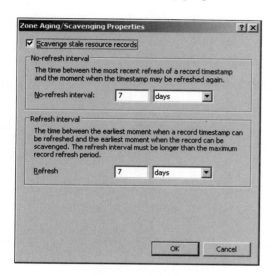

Figure 7-23 Zone Aging/Scavenging Properties

To enable the deletion of old DNS records, select the Scavenge stale resource records option. Once scavenging is enabled, the No-refresh interval option lets you specify how often a DNS record can be refreshed. By default, there is a no-refresh interval of 7 days. This means that Dynamic DNS clients cannot refresh their DNS record more than once every 7 days. A refresh is a reregistration of existing DNS information with no changes. DNS updates where there are changes to the DNS record and are always allowed regardless of the no-refresh interval. If a DNS record is updated, then the time stamp on the record is updated and the no-refresh interval begins again for that record.

The Refresh interval option is the period of time that must pass after the no-refresh interval has expired before DNS records are deleted. During the refresh interval, DNS records can be refreshed by Dynamic DNS clients. If a record is refreshed, a new time stamp is created and the no-refresh interval begins again for that record. If the record is not refreshed during the refresh interval, then the DNS server deletes the record during its next scavenging.

Manually created DNS records are never scavenged. Dynamic DNS records are scavenged only if they have not been updated or refreshed, and both the no-refresh interval and refresh interval have expired.

Activity 7-12: Configuring Aging and Scavenging

Time Required: 10 minutes

Objective: Configure a zone to automatically remove old records.

Description: Dynamic DNS is used to create host records in your zone domainX. classroom.com. To ensure that outdated information is not left in the zone, you will configure it to automatically remove Dynamic DNS records that have not been updated or refreshed for 4 weeks.

1. If necessary, start your server and log on as **Administrator**.
2. Click **Start**, point to **Administrative Tools**, click **DNS**.
3. Right-click your server, and click **Properties**.
4. Click **Advanced**, click **Enable automatic scavenging of stale records**, and click **OK**. This configures the server to look for old records to delete every 7 days.
5. Double-click your server.
6. Double-click **Forward Lookup Zones**.
7. Click **domainX.classroom.com**, where *X* is your student number.
8. Right-click **domainX.classroom.com**, where *X* is your student number, and click **Properties**.
9. Click **Aging** on the General tab.
10. Click **Scavenge stale resource records**.
11. Confirm that the No-refresh interval is set to **7 days**.
12. In the Refresh box, enter **21 days**, and press **OK**. Dynamic DNS records are now eligible to be scavenged after the total of 28 days have passed without the records' being updated or refreshed.
13. Click **OK** to close zone properties.
14. Close the DNS snap-in.

Modify the Start of Authority Record

The **Start of Authority (SOA) record** for a domain defines a number of characteristics for a zone, including serial number and caching instructions. The SOA record is configured in the Start of Authority (SOA) tab of the zone properties, as shown in Figure 7-24.

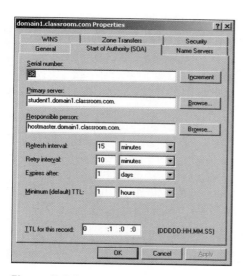

Figure 7-24   Start of Authority (SOA) tab of zone properties

The serial number of a zone is automatically updated when a change is made to the zone. This is used by secondary zones to request changes to the zone. A secondary zone requests a zone transfer if the serial number of the primary zone is higher than the serial number of the secondary zone. You can force all secondary zones to request a zone transfer by manually incrementing the serial number by one.

The Refresh interval option specifies how often secondary zones can attempt to update themselves from the primary zone. The Retry interval option specifies how long a secondary zone waits before reattempting to contact the primary zone if an initial attempt fails. The Expires after option specifies how long a secondary zone can go without contacting the primary zone before it stops functioning because its data is considered unreliable.

The Minimum (default) TTL option is used by remote DNS servers that are caching records from this zone. A record that is cached from this zone is not resolved again for the time period specified. This time is also used as the maximum time that a DNS error can be cached.

Name Servers

The name servers configured for a zone are the authoritative DNS servers for the zone. They are used in the recursive lookup process to resolve requests for the domain. In addition, they are used by Dynamic DNS clients for dynamic updates.

Dynamic DNS cannot be performed on secondary zones. A DNS server holding a secondary zone should never be added as a name server for a zone if Dynamic DNS in being used.

Figure 7-25 shows the Name Servers tab in the zone properties dialog box.

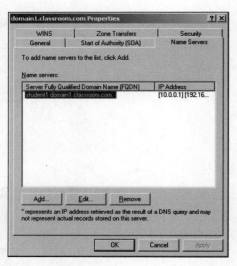

Figure 7-25   The Name Servers tab of zone properties

WINS Resolution

A DNS zone can be configured with a WINS server that is used to help resolve names. If a DNS zone receives a query for a host name for which it has no A record, it forwards the request to a WINS server. For example, if a DNS server with the zone GANU.edu receives a host name resolution request for workstation85.GANU.edu and does not have a matching A record, then the DNS server forwards a WINS lookup request for the name workstation85 to the WINS server.

Figure 7-26 shows the WINS tab in the properties of a zone. You can specify that records resolved via WINS not be replicated to other domain controllers by selecting the Do not replicate this record option.

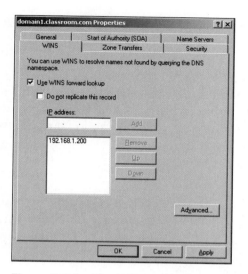

Figure 7-26   The WINS tab of zone properties

Zone Transfers

Zone transfers are used to copy zone information from a primary zone to a secondary zone. You can configure which IP addresses can request zone transfers. Figure 7-27 shows the Zone Transfers tab of the zone properties dialog box.

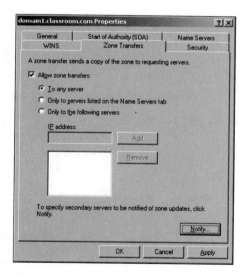

Figure 7-27   The Zone Transfers tab of zone properties

By default, zone transfers are allowed. To disable zone transfers, deselect the Allow zone transfers option. If zone transfers are enabled, you can choose whether they are enabled to any server, to only servers listed in the Name Servers tab for the zone, or to specific IP addresses. It is good security practice to ensure that zone transfers only occur to known DNS servers.

You can also specify a list of secondary zones to notify of zone changes by clicking on the Notify button. When a secondary zone is notified of a zone change, it immediately requests a zone transfer. This significantly speeds up the synchronization between primary and secondary zones. Without notification, a secondary zone checks for updates every 15 minutes.

Security

The Security tab in the zone properties dialog box allows you to control the permissions to modify the records for this zone. The security tab is only available for Active Directory-integrated zones.

TROUBLESHOOTING DNS

Most DNS problems are a result of incorrectly configured client computers, as discussed earlier in Chapter 6. If your client computers are configured correctly and can contact your DNS server, then the problem is likely due to misconfigured DNS records. To test whether a DNS server is functioning correctly, you can use the Monitoring tab of the DNS server properties dialog box, as shown in Figure 7-28.

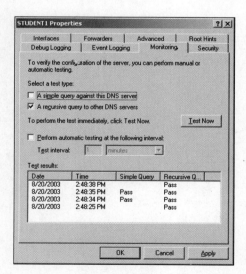

Figure 7-28   The Monitoring tab of DNS server properties

If a simple query is requested, then the server is tested for **iterative query** functionality. An iterative query is a query in which the DNS server looks only in the zones for which it is responsible.

If a **recursive query** is requested, then a NS query is submitted for the root domain ".". If this query is unsuccessful, it may be due to incorrectly configured Internet connectivity or root hints.

You can choose to perform a simple query or recursive query manually or at a scheduled interval. To manually perform a test, select the type of test you want to perform (simple, recursive, or both), then click Test Now. To perform tests at a scheduled interval, select the type of test you would like to perform, then select Perform automatic testing at the following interval. After automatic testing has been enabled, you can choose the interval at which it is repeated.

The results of automatic and manual tests appear only in the Test results box.

Activity 7-13: Removing Active Directory and the DNS Service

Time Required: 40 minutes

Objective: To remove the Active Directory and DNS services.

Description: Remove the Active Directory and DNS server services to ensure that they do not interfere with activities later in this book.

1. If necessary, start your server and log on as **Administrator**.

2. Click **Start**, and then click **Run**. Type **dcpromo** and press **Enter**.

3. Press **Next**, and then press **OK** when the warning appears.

4. At the Remove Active Directory screen, place a check mark in the **This server is the last domain controller in the domain** box, and press **Next**.

5. At the Application Directory Partitions screen, press **Next**.

6. At the Confirm Deletion screen, place a check mark in the **Delete all application directory partitions on this domain controller** box, and press **Next**.

7. At the Administrator Password screen, type **secret;5** in the two boxes supplied and press **Next**. You are required to enter a password that meets stricter security requirements than the Windows Server 2003 installation since Active Directory altered the security settings of your computer when it was installed in Chapter 4. Write this password down for future use.

8. At the Summary screen, press **Next**.

9. Click **Finish**.

10. Click **Restart Now**.

11. When your computer has rebooted, log in as **Administrator**.

12. Click **Start**, point to **Control Panel**, and then click **Add or Remove Programs**.

13. Click **Add/Remove Windows Components**.

14. Scroll down in the components section, click **Networking Services** to highlight it, and then click **Details**.

15. Click the check box beside Domain Name System (DNS) to deselect it, and then click **OK**.

16. Click **Next**.

17. Click **Finish**.

18. Close the Add or Remove Programs window.

In the following steps, you configure your computer as a DNS client to gain Internet access.

1. Click **Start**, point to **Control Panel**, point to **Network Connections**, right-click **Local Area Connection**, and click **Properties**.

2. Click **Internet Protocol (TCP/IP)**, and click **Properties**.

3. Ensure that the IP Address for the Default gateway used for Internet access is correct, enter the IP address for the DNS server used for Internet access in the Preferred DNS server box, and click **OK**.

4. Click **OK** to close the Local Area Connection Properties screen.

CHAPTER SUMMARY

- DNS is the most commonly used method for name resolution and the standard name resolution method used on the Internet.

- Once the DNS service has been added, you must create zones to hold resource records. A DNS zone holds records for a portion of DNS namespace.

- Traditional primary and secondary zones are stored in a zone file on the hard drive of the DNS server. A zone transfer is used to copy information from a primary zone to a secondary zone.

- Active Directory-integrated zones are stored in Active Directory. As a result, Active Directory-integrated zones can use the security permissions in Active Directory to control updates.

- Active Directory-integrated zones can act as primary zones to secondary zones.

- A stub zone contains name server records that are used for recursive lookups.

- A caching-only server reduces the network traffic generated by DNS queries.

❑ Dynamic DNS allows records to be automatically updated on a DNS server. Client computers create A and PTR records using Dynamic DNS. Older Windows clients are not able to use Dynamic DNS directly, and a DHCP server must perform the updates on their behalf. Domain controllers create SRV records using Dynamic DNS.

❑ Aging and scavenging remove outdated records created by Dynamic DNS.

❑ The root hints are used for recursive lookups. They are loaded from the file cache.dns.

❑ Event logging and debug logging can be used to troubleshoot DNS problems.

❑ A WINS server can be used to help resolve host names if a DNS server does not have an A record that matches a query.

❑ The Monitoring tab of DNS server properties can be used to test DNS server functionality.

7

Key Terms

Active Directory-integrated zone — A DNS zone in which DNS information is stored in Active Directory and supports multimaster updates and increased security.

aging/scavenging — The process of removing old records from DNS that have not been updated within a set time period.

application directory partition — A partition that stores information about objects that is replicated to a set of defined domain controllers within the same forest.

Berkeley Internet Name Domain (BIND) — A UNIX-based implementation of the Domain Name System created by the University of California at Berkeley.

caching-only server — A DNS server that does not store any zone information, but caches DNS queries from clients.

debug logging — The processing of logging additional DNS-related events or messages for troubleshooting purposes.

DNS zone — The part of the domain namespace for which a DNS server is authoritative. Commonly referred to as a "zone."

domain directory partition — A partition that stores information about objects in a specific domain that is replicated to all domain controllers in the domain.

Domain Name System (DNS) — The method used to resolve Internet domain names to IP addresses.

Dynamic DNS — A system in which DNS records are automatically updated by the client or a DHCP server.

event logging — The logging of status messages in an event log. This logging is less detailed than debug logging.

fast zone transfer — A zone transfer that uses compression to achieve a faster transmission time.

forward lookup zone — A zone that holds records used for forward lookups. The primary record types contained in these zones are: A records, MX records, and SRV records.

forwarding — The process of sending a DNS lookup request to another DNS server when the local DNS server does not have the requested information.

host name — The unique name that identifies the computer on the network.

incremental zone transfer — The process of updating only modified DNS records from a primary DNS server to a secondary DNS server.

iterative query — A DNS query that is resolved using local resources only.

Kerberos — An authentication protocol designed to authenticate both the client and server using secret-key cryptography.

Lightweight Directory Access Protocol (LDAP) — A protocol used to look up directory information from a server.

primary zone — A zone that is authoritative for a specific DNS zone. Updates can only be made in the primary zone. There is only one primary zone per domain name.

recursive query — A DNS query that is resolved through other DNS servers until the requested information is located.

reverse lookup zone — A zone that contains records used for reverse lookups. The primary record type in these zones is PTR records.

Root hints — The list of root servers that is used by DNS servers to perform forward lookups on the Internet.

root servers — A group of 13 DNS servers on the Internet that is authoritative for the top-level domain names such as .com, edu, and .org.

round robin DNS — The process of creating multiple IP addresses for a specific host name for fault tolerance and load balancing.

secondary zone — A DNS zone that stores a read-only copy of the DNS information from a primary zone. There can be multiple secondary zones.

service resource records — DNS resource records that contain the location of a service such as the Kerberos or LDAP services used by Active Directory.

Start of Authority (SOA) record — A DNS record that defines which DNS server is authoritative for a particular domain and defines the characteristics for the zone, including replication parameters.

stub zone — A DNS zone that stores only the NS records for a particular zone. When a client requests a DNS lookup, the request is then forwarded to the DNS server specified by the NS records.

subdomains — Divisions of a DNS domain name. The subdomain students.GANU.edu is a subdomain of GANU.edu.

zone transfer — The process of updating DNS records from a primary DNS server to a secondary DNS server.

REVIEW QUESTIONS

1. Which of the following features are supported by Windows 2003 DNS? (Choose all that apply.)
   a. fast zone transfer
   b. SRV record support
   c. Dynamic DNS support
   d. incremental zone transfer
   e. secure dynamic updates
   f. WINS integration

2. You may use the General tab of zone properties to change a primary zone to Active Directory-integrated without affecting other secondary zones for the same domain. True or false?

3. Which of the following is not a type of DNS zone in Windows Server 2003? (Choose all that apply.)
   a. Active Directory-integrated
   b. primary
   c. secondary
   d. standalone
   e. root

4. A stub DNS zone only stores which domain record?
   a. NS
   b. A
   c. CNAME
   d. SOA
   e. MX

5. Which DNS records do clients use to locate domain controllers?
   a. CNAME
   b. MX
   c. SOA
   d. NS
   e. SRV

7

6. A DHCP server running under Windows Server 2003 updates DNS records for which operating systems by default? (Choose all that apply.)

   a. Windows XP Professional

   b. Windows 2000 Professional

   c. Windows NT 4 Professional

   d. Windows 98

   e. Windows 95

7. Which of the following statements regarding Active Directory-integrated zones is false?

   a. Active Directory-integrated zones are automatically replicated to all domain controllers.

   b. Active Directory-integrated zones support multimaster replication.

   c. Only Active Directory-integrated zones support dynamic updates.

   d. Only Active Directory-integrated zones support secure dynamic updates.

8. What zone would you create if you wish to prevent recursive lookups using other DNS servers on the Internet?

   a. Active Directory-integrated

   b. primary

   c. secondary

   d. standalone

   e. root

9. Which version of BIND supports incremental zone updates?

   a. BIND 4.9.6

   b. BIND 8.1.2

   c. BIND 8.2.1

   d. all of the above

10. Which of the following zones stores a read-only copy of another zone?

    a. primary

    b. Active Directory-integrated

    c. root

    d. secondary

11. What type of zone resolves host names to IP addresses?

    a. forward lookup zone

    b. reverse lookup zone

    c. primary zone

    d. secondary zone

12. Which of the following servers can participate in Active Directory-integrated zones? (Choose all that apply.)

    a. Windows 2000 Advanced Server domain controller

    b. Windows NT 4 Server

    c. BIND version 8.2.1 DNS server

    d. Windows Server 2003 member server

    e. all the above

13. A backup network administrator accidentally deleted all the service records in DNS. What is the quickest method to recover the information?

    a. Reinstall DNS server.

    b. Reboot the server.

    c. Restore them from backup tape.

    d. Stop and start the NETLOGON Service.

    e. Manually create the deleted records.

14. Which of the following DNS records defines the primary zone?

    a. A

    b. MX

    c. NS

    d. SRV

    e. SOA

15. The process of updating information from the primary zone to a secondary zone is called?

    a. replication

    b. zone transfer

    c. forwarding

    d. scavenging

16. Your company has a remote site containing five workstations connected by a very slow link. Users are complaining of slow DNS lookups. What type of DNS server can you configure in the remote site to speed up DNS resolution without creating more WAN traffic?

    a. Active Directory-integrated

    b. primary

    c. secondary

    d. caching-only

7

17. Which command can be used to manually force a supported client's Dynamic DNS information?

    a. ipconfig /refresh

    b. ipconfig /registerdns

    c. ipconfig /flushdns

    d. ipconfig /displaydns

18. You want to configure a different list of root servers for your DNS server. Which file in \WINDOWS\ SYSTEM32\DNS do you edit?

    a. CACHE.DNS

    b. ROOTS.DNS

    c. ZONE.DNS

    d. HINTS.DNS

19. Round robin DNS is the process of:

    a. creating multiple records for a single DNS host name

    b. creating multiple host names for a single IP address

    c. creating different priorities for an MX record

    d. enabling forwarding to root hint servers

20. An administrator wants to change the replication schedule for a DNS server, but the Replication button is grayed out. What type of zone is it?

    a. primary

    b. secondary

    c. Active Directory-integrated

    d. caching-only

CASE PROJECTS

A proper DNS implementation is critical to the success of your Windows Server 2003 rollout. In the following cases you consider how DNS can be implemented for Great Arctic North University.

CASE PROJECTS

Case Project 7-1: Integrating Windows Server 2003 DNS with BIND

The university currently has seven UNIX servers providing DNS Services for the whole campus. They are all running BIND version 8.1.2. Another administrator has recommended that the UNIX DNS servers be upgraded to Windows Server 2003 to support the new Windows Server 2003 domain controllers. What options does the university have for DNS? What are the advantages and disadvantages of each option? Which do you recommend?

Case Project 7-2: Creating DNS Zones

It has been decided that the university will not replace the UNIX DNS servers with Windows Server 2003. It has also been discovered that a few small departments also have Windows NT 4 servers running DNS. In order to reduce replication traffic, not all Windows Server 2000 domain controllers will run as DNS servers. In addition, some Windows Server 2003 member servers will run DNS. The head of the Computer Services Department recommends that only Active Directory-integrated zones be created to reduce administrative and management overhead. What are the implications of such a decision? How can all DNS servers be integrated without upgrading the servers to Windows Server 2003?

Case Project 7-3: Securing DNS

The head of the Computer Services Department is very concerned about hackers improperly updating DNS information or getting a list of all the internal computer names and IP addresses. What can be implemented in Active Directory-integrated zones to secure DNS from hackers?

8

WINDOWS INTERNET NAMING SERVICE

After reading this chapter, you will be able to:

- Install WINS
- Configure WINS replication
- Manage WINS server settings
- Create static WINS mappings
- Back up and restore a WINS database
- Understand when to use a WINS proxy
- Troubleshoot the WINS service

Windows Internet Naming (or Name) Service (WINS) is required to support older Windows clients and reduces the number of NetBIOS broadcasts on a network. Pre-Windows 2000 clients typically use WINS to find domain controllers, which are required for the clients to log on to the network. WINS is also used to resolve NetBIOS names to IP addresses. This is critical in an environment with pre-Windows 2000 clients, but also important for NetBIOS applications running on Windows 2000, Windows XP, and Windows Server 2003.

INSTALLING WINS

Windows Server 2003 has the ability to act as a WINS server via the WINS service. It is very unusual to use another operating system, such as a **NetBIOS name server**. In larger organizations with expansive WANs, there are several WINS servers. If this is the case, then WINS must be installed individually on each server. WINS is never installed automatically on Windows Server 2003. Instead, you must add it later through Add or Remove Programs. Figure 8-1 shows the Add or Remove Programs option in Control Panel being used to install the WINS service.

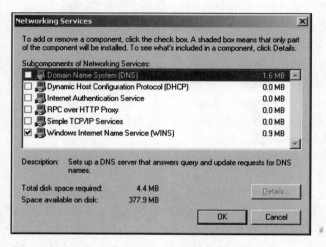

Figure 8-1   Installing the WINS service

Activity 8-1: Installing WINS

Time Required: 10 minutes

Objective: Install WINS on your server.

Description: To ensure that all of the client computers on your network can resolve the NetBIOS name servers in a routed network, you have decided to implement WINS. In this activity, you will install WINS on your server.

1. If necessary, start your server and log on as **Administrator**.

2. Click **Start**, point to **Control Panel**, and click **Add or Remove Programs**.

3. Click **Add/Remove Windows Components**.

4. Scroll down in the Components window, and double-click **Networking Services**.

5. Click the check box beside Windows Internet Name Service (WINS), and click **OK**.

6. Click **Next** to install WINS. If prompted for the Windows Server 2003 CD-ROM, insert your Windows Server 2003 Enterprise Edition CD-ROM into the CD-ROM drive and click **OK**.

7. When the installation is complete, click **Finish**, and close the Add or Remove Programs window.

Activity 8-2: Configuring a WINS Client

Time Required: 5 minutes

Objective: Configure your server to be a WINS client.

Description: It is important to remember that servers must also be configured as WINS clients. If they are not, then the NetBIOS names and IP addresses of the servers are not listed in the WINS database, and client computers cannot use NetBIOS resources on the servers. For these reasons, your server will be configured as a WINS client.

1. If necessary, start your server and log on as **Administrator**.

2. Click **Start**, point to **Control Panel**, point to **Network Connections**, right-click **Local Area Connection**, and then click **Properties**.

3. Click **Internet Protocol (TCP/IP)**, and then click **Properties**.

4. Click **Advanced**, and then click the **WINS** tab.

5. Click **Add**.

6. Type the IP address of your Local Area Connection, and click **Add**.

7. Click **OK**, click **OK** again, and click **Close**.

CONFIGURING WINS REPLICATION

A single WINS server can handle at least 5000 WINS clients. However, you may choose to implement multiple WINS servers in much smaller environments to control network traffic and provide fault tolerance.

In a large network with multiple physical locations, it may reduce network traffic across WAN links if multiple WINS servers are used. If a WINS server is located at each physical location, then WINS clients do all of their registrations and queries with the local server. This creates no WAN traffic. Smaller networks may also benefit from having multiple WINS servers. When two WINS servers are implemented, WINS clients are still able to resolve NetBIOS names if one WINS server fails.

When more than one WINS server is implemented, you must configure replication between them. This allows all the WINS servers to contain the same information; WINS servers that replicate information between themselves are called **replication partners**.

WINS is configured using the WINS snap-in shown in Figure 8-2.

8

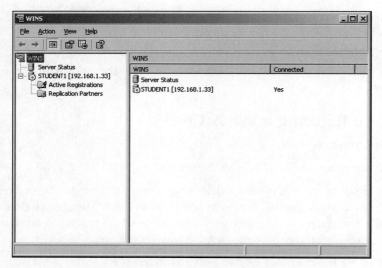

Figure 8-2   The WINS management snap-in

To configure WINS servers as replication partners, right-click on the Replication Partners folder shown in Figure 8-2, click New Replication Partner, and then enter the IP address of the replication partner.

After a replication partner has been added, you can control how replication occurs. There are three ways replication can be configured:

- Push
- Pull
- Push/pull

Default replication properties can be configured in the properties of the Replication Partners folder. You can also set the replication properties for a particular partner. To configure replication, right-click on either the Replication Partners folder or a replication partner, and click Properties.

Push replication occurs based on a certain number of changes occurring in the WINS database. When a defined number of changes occur, the replication partner is notified. The replication partner then requests a copy of the changes. Only updated information is replicated between replication partners. Figure 8-3 shows the Push Replication tab in the properties of the Replication Partners folder.

In a network with few changes, push replication may not be sufficient. If the value is set too high in the "Number of changes in version ID before replication" option, an extended period of time may pass before changes are replicated. Until the changes are replicated, WINS clients resolving queries on the out-of-date server cannot resolve the unreplicated records.

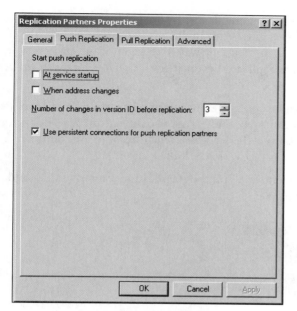

Figure 8-3   Configuring push replication

Pull replication occurs based on a set time schedule. You can set a start time for replication and the interval that replication occurs. This type of replication ensures that all changes are replicated between two WINS servers regularly. Figure 8-4 shows the Pull Replication tab in the properties of the Replication Partners folder.

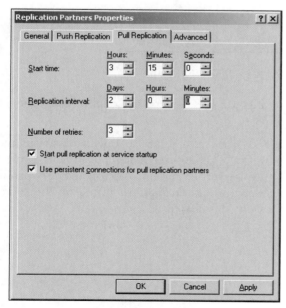

Figure 8-4   Configuring pull replication

8

By default, a combination of push and pull replication is used. This is configured by enabling both push and pull replications separately. Push replication ensures that, during periods of high change, records are replicated in a timely way. Pull replication ensures that, during periods of low change, records are replicated even if the criterion for push replication is not met.

Both push and pull replication can be configured to use **persistent connections**. Persistent connections result in faster replication because a new connection does not need to be created for each replication. However, this causes a small amount of additional network traffic that may not be appropriate for slow WAN links.

You can also force replication by right-clicking the Replication Partners folder and clicking Replicate Now, as shown in Figure 8-5.

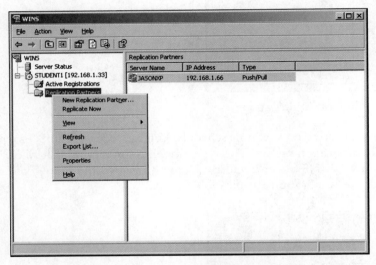

Figure 8-5   Forcing replication between replication partners

You can control two replication settings on the General tab of the Replication Partners folder properties, as shown in Figure 8-6.

The Replicate only with partners option forces a server to only replicate its records to servers configured as replication partners. This ensures that replication is two way. The Overwrite unique static mappings at this server (migrate on) option allows dynamic WINS registrations from other servers to overwrite static mappings created on this server. Static WINS mappings will be discussed later in this chapter.

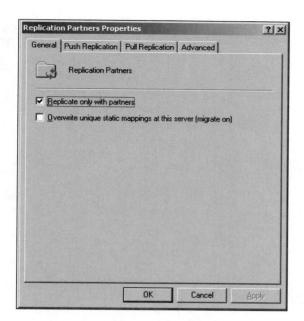

Figure 8-6   Setting general replication settings

You can enable WINS servers to automatically find replication partners. To do this, a WINS server uses multicast packets to find other replication partners. You can control how often the multicast is sent and the time to live (TTL) of the packet. A multicast TTL controls the number of routers it can pass through.

A WINS server may hold records for registrations that were not taken by itself or its direct replication partners. In the case of three WINS servers, Server1 replicates to Server2, and Server2 replicates to Server3. You can restrict the records being accepted by a server based on the owner. The owner is the server that originally accepted the registration.

Both automatically finding replication partners and restricting record replication based on the owner can be configured on the Advanced tab of the Replication Partners folder properties, as shown in Figure 8-7.

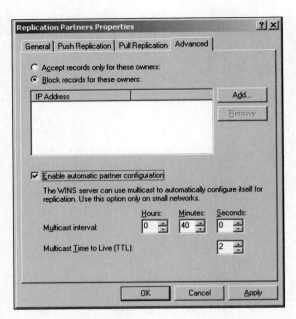

Figure 8-7   Setting advanced replication settings

Activity 8-3: Configuring Replication Partners

Time Required: 15 minutes

Objective: Configure your server to replicate WINS information with a partner.

Description: A WINS server has been installed at each physical location on your network to reduce the WAN traffic generated by NetBIOS name resolution. Replication must now be configured so each WINS server can resolve names from other locations. You will configure WINS replication with your partner. For this exercise to be completed, your partner must have successfully completed Activities 8-1 and 8-2.

1. If necessary, start your server and log on as **Administrator**.

2. Click **Start**, point to **Administrative Tools**, and click **WINS**.

3. If necessary, double-click your server to expand its information.

4. Right-click the **Replication Partners** folder, and click **New Replication Partner**.

5. Type the IP address of your partner's Local Area Connection, and click **OK**.

6. Click **Replication Partners** in the left pane to see the configured partner in the right pane of the window. Note that, by default, this replication partner uses both push and pull replication.

7. Right-click **Replication Partners**, and click **Replicate Now**. Click **Yes** to start replication, and click **OK** to close the information dialog box. The event log contains messages regarding the success or failure of replication.

8. Close the WINS snap-in.

Managing WINS

In general, the default settings for a WINS server provide adequate service. However there are some settings you can modify if required.

The General tab of the WINS server properties allows you to configure how often statistics are updated for the server, the path for backing up the WINS database, and whether the WINS database should be backed up each time the server is shut down. Figure 8-8 shows the General tab of WINS server properties.

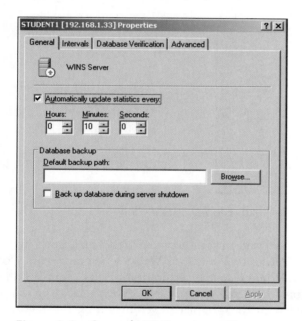

Figure 8-8   General WINS server settings

The Intervals tab of the WINS server properties allows you to configure how names expire and are deleted from the WINS database. The **renewal interval** refers to the TTL that is given to WINS clients when a name is registered with the WINS server. The **extinction interval** refers to how long an unused record exists in the WINS database before being marked as extinct. The **extinction timeout** refers to how long an extinct record is kept in the database. When an extinct record has existed in the database for the length of the extinction timeout, it is removed.

You may manually remove extinct records immediately by right-clicking your server in the WINS snap-in and choosing Scavenge Database.

The **verification interval** refers to how long a WINS server waits before validating a record that is replicated from another WINS server. Figure 8-9 shows the default values on the Intervals tab of the WINS server properties.

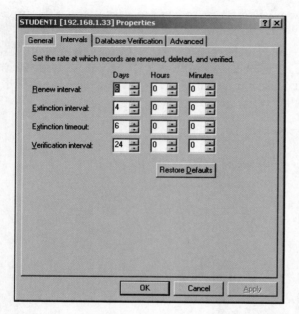

Figure 8-9   Configuring WINS record expiration and extinction

If there are a large number of WINS servers on your network, WINS replication may be slow in updating records. The Database Verification tab of the WINS server properties allows you to automate database verification. When database verification occurs, other WINS servers are contacted to confirm that they hold the same WINS information. You can choose whether the records are verified with the original server that took the registration or randomly. Figure 8-10 shows the database verification settings.

The Advanced tab of the WINS server properties allows you to set several options. Figure 8-11 shows the Advanced tab of the WINS server properties.

You can enhance the logging of events by selecting the Log detailed events to Windows event log option. This should only be used for troubleshooting because the number of events logged can adversely affect server performance.

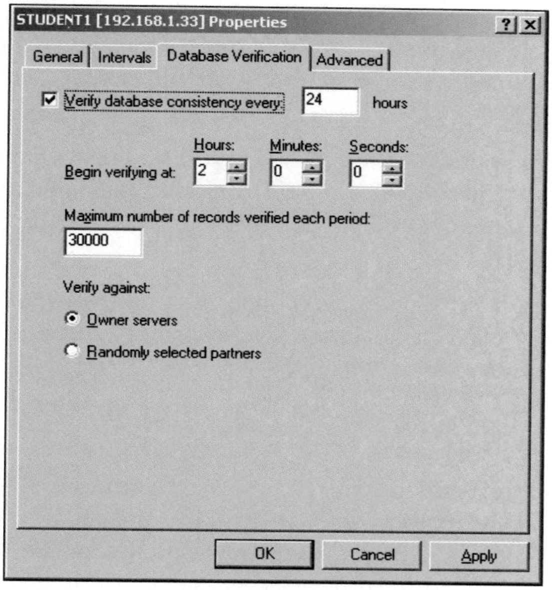

Figure 8-10   Configuring WINS database verification

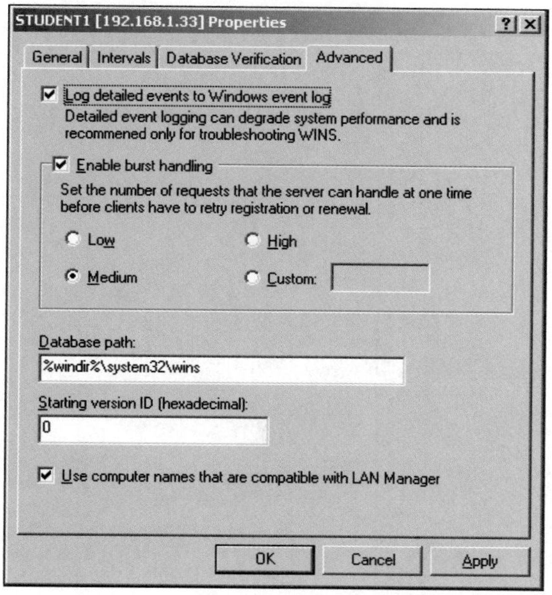

Figure 8-11   Configuring advanced WINS settings

Burst handling allows a WINS server to handle large volumes of name registration requests in a very short period of time. The WINS server does not actually perform a registration nor verify name uniqueness; it simply provides a very short TTL to the client. This will force the clients to renew themselves in a short time, but spread the requests out so the WINS server can handle the load and perform a proper registration at a later time. If the number of name registration requests becomes too large to verify in the WINS database, then the WINS server begins to send successful name registration responses without verifying whether the name is already registered. Later, the WINS server registers the name in the WINS database.

The database path indicates where the WINS database is stored. The default path is C:\WINDOWS\system32\wins. The Starting version ID (hexadecimal) field is used to force WINS replication. Incrementing this number indicates to replication partners that there is a new version of the WINS database.

The Use computer names that are compatible with LAN Manager option restricts registered names to 15 characters. Some non–Microsoft operating systems can use NetBIOS names that are 16 characters long. This option is on by default.

Viewing Database Records

To verify that a client is registered in the WINS database, you may wish to view the contents of the WINS database. To view the records that exist in the WINS database, right-click Active Registrations, and click Display Records. This opens a window that allows you to search the WINS database. You can search for records based on name, IP address, owner, or record type. Figure 8-12 shows the Display Records window used for searching the WINS database.

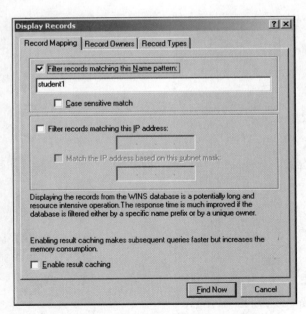

Figure 8-12   Searching the WINS database

When viewing records, you have the option to delete them as well. To delete a record, right-click the record, and select Delete. When a record is deleted, you must choose whether to delete it from just the local server or all databases. If you choose to delete it from all servers, then the record is **tombstoned**. If a record is tombstoned, it is marked for deletion. The tombstoned status replicates to all servers and is recommended when you wish to delete a record from all WINS databases. If you do not tombstone a WINS record, it may be recreated in the local WINS database via future replication from another WINS server.

Activity 8-4: Viewing WINS Records

Time Required: 5 minutes

Objective: View WINS records on your server.

Description: A client computer on your network is having problems resolving the NetBIOS name APPSERVER. You have confirmed that the client computer is correctly configured to use the WINS server. You will now verify that the record exists in the WINS database on your server.

1. If necessary, start your server and log on as **Administrator**.

2. Click **Start**, point to **Administrative Tools**, and click **WINS**.

3. Right-click **Active Registrations**, and click **Display Records**.

4. Leave the fields blank to view all records, and click **Find Now**.

5. You should see WINS records for the WORKGROUP workgroup, your server, and your partner's server. There is no record for APPSERVER.

6. Close the WINS snap-in.

Adding Static Records

If non-Microsoft servers provide NetBIOS resources on the network, they may not be able to use a WINS server to automatically register their NetBIOS name. If this is the case, then WINS clients cannot resolve their NetBIOS names. To eliminate this problem, you can create a static record in WINS for each non-Microsoft server that uses NetBIOS.

To create a static WINS record, right-click Active Registrations, and click New Static Mapping. For each **static mapping**, you enter the computer name, record type, and IP address. Figure 8-13 shows the creation of a static mapping.

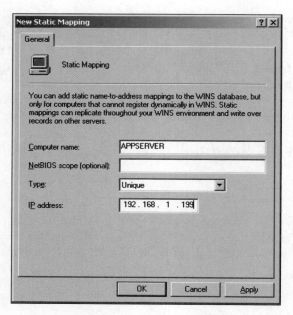

Figure 8-13   Creating a static mapping

Activity 8-5: Adding a Static Mapping

Time Required: 10 minutes

Objective: Add a static mapping to the WINS database.

Description: A UNIX server named APPSERVER runs a database required by an accounting application used by the finance staff. This application uses NetBIOS names, but APPSERVER cannot be configured to use WINS. In this activity, you will create a static mapping for APPSERVER so that client computers can use WINS to resolve the name APPSERVER to an IP address.

1. If necessary, start your server and log on as **Administrator**.

2. Click **Start**, point to **Administrative Tools**, and click **WINS**.

3. Right-click **Active Registrations**, and click **New Static Mapping**.

4. In the Computer name text box, type **APPSERVER**.

5. In the Type drop-down list, leave the default of **Unique**. "Unique" is used to identify the name of a single computer and adds records for the Workstation Service, Messenger Service, and File Server Service.

6. In the IP address text box, type **192.168.1.202**, and click **OK**.

7. To view the new records, right-click **Active Registrations**, click **Display Records**, and click **Find Now**. Notice that the expiration of the records for APPSERVER is Infinite.

8. Close the WINS snap-in.

Backing up the Database

On a network using NetBIOS-based services, WINS is essential. As a critical resource, the WINS database needs to be backed up in the same way that data needs to be backed up. If the WINS database becomes corrupted, the WINS server stops servicing clients. This results in client computers being unable to access NetBIOS-based resources because NetBIOS names cannot be resolved to IP addresses.

A corrupted WINS database can easily be fixed if you have a backup of the WINS database. Simply stop the WINS Service and restore the database. After the database has been restored, the WINS server receives changes that occurred since the backup from replication partners. The WINS servers determine the changes to replicate based on the version ID of the database records.

By default, a WINS server is not automatically backed up. To do this, you must supply a backup path on the General tab of the WINS server properties, as shown earlier in Figure 8-8. Once a backup path has been specified, the WINS server will be backed up every three hours. You may also manually back up the WINS database by right-clicking the WINS server and choosing Back Up Database, as shown in Figure 8-14.

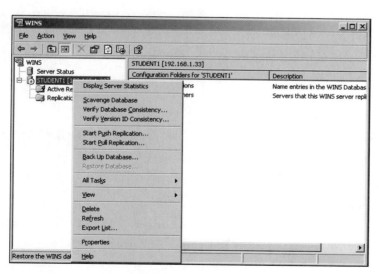

Figure 8-14   Manually backing up a WINS database

Notice that the Restore Database option displayed in Figure 8-14 is unavailable. This is because the WINS service is still running; to restore a WINS database, you must first stop the WINS service before choosing the Restore Database option.

Activity 8-6: Backing up and Restoring the WINS Database

Time Required: 25 minutes

Objective: Back up and restore the WINS database on your server.

Description: To ensure that you can quickly recover your server from a corrupt WINS database, you will configure your server to automatically back up the WINS database. Then, you will perform a manual backup and restore to test the process and ensure that it is working properly.

1. If necessary, start your server and log on as **Administrator**.

2. Create a new folder named C:\winsbak:
   a. Click **Start**, click **Run**, type **cmd**, and press **Enter**.
   b. Type **cd ** and press **Enter**.
   c. Type **md winsbak**, and press **Enter**.
   d. Type **exit**, and press **Enter**.

3. Click **Start**, point to **Administrative Tools**, and click **WINS**.

4. Right-click your server, and click **Properties**.

5. On the General tab, in the Default backup path text box, type **C:\winsbak**. After a default backup path has been specified, the database is backed up every 3 hours.

6. Click the **Back up database during server shutdown** checkbox. This ensures that your server creates a current backup every time it is rebooted.

7. Click **OK**.

8. Right-click your server, and click **Back Up Database**.

9. Click **OK** to confirm that the C:\winsbak folder is to be used for the backup.

10. Click **OK** to close the backup confirmation window.

11. Right-click your server, point to **All Tasks**, and click **Stop**.

12. Delete the WINS database:
    a. Click **Start**, click **Run**, type **cmd**, and press **Enter**.
    b. Type **cd \windows\system32\wins**, and press **Enter**.
    c. Type **del *.*** and press **Enter**.
    d. Type **Y** and press **Enter** to confirm the deletion.
    e. Type **exit** and press **Enter**.

13. Right-click your server, and click **Restore Database**.

14. Click **OK** to use the default restore path of C:\winsbak.

15. Click **OK** to close the WINS restore confirmation.

16. View the active registrations:

    a. Right-click **Active Registrations**, and click **Display Records**.

    b. Click **Find Now** to accept the default filter and view all records. You may need to click **Active Registrations** to view the records.

    c. The records should be as they were when you backed up the database.

17. Close the WINS snap-in.

Compacting the WINS database

The WINS service does not impose any limit on the number of records that can exist in a WINS database. As a result, the WINS database may grow very large over time and query time will increase. Compacting can be used to reduce the size of the WINS database and hence improve the performance of WINS queries. There are two main types of compacting that may be performed:

- Dynamic compacting
- Offline compacting

Dynamic compacting is performed automatically by the WINS service while the database is in use on a periodic basis. In this operation, any unused space used by records that have been deleted is moved to the bottom of the file to increase read efficiency. **Offline compacting** may be used to manually compact a database using the **jetpack** utility if the WINS service is stopped. In this operation, the unused space is removed altogether, resulting in a reduced file size and improved read efficiency. The path to the WINS database is C:\WINDOWS\system32\wins\Wins.mdb. To manually compact the WINS database, you could stop the WINS service, change to the \WINDOWS\system32\wins folder and run the command *jetpack Wins.mdb tmpfile.mdb* where tmpfile.mdb is a temporary file used by the jetpack utility.

ACTIVITY

Activity 8-7: Compacting the WINS database

Time Required: 10 minutes

Objective: Compact a WINS database.

Description: Users complain that WINS queries are taking a long time. You examine the size of the C:\WINDOWS\system32\wins\Wins.mdb file and note that it is very large. To improve WINS performance, you manually compact the WINS database to reduce its size.

1. If necessary, start your server, and log on as **Administrator**.

2. Click **Start** and click **Run**.

3. Type **cmd** and press **Enter**.

4. Type **cd C:\WINDOWS\system32\wins**, and press **Enter**.

5. Type **net stop wins**, and press **Enter** to stop the WINS service.

6. Type **jetpack Wins.mdb tmpfile.mdb**, and press **Enter**.

7. Type **net start wins**, and press **Enter** to start the WINS service.

8. Close the command prompt window.

Removing WINS Servers

If your Microsoft network consists of Windows 2000 or later computers, the WINS service is not necessary for normal network operations and you may uninstall the WINS service on your servers. Before removing the WINS service, however, it is important to ensure that there are no NetBIOS applications that are required on the network. Since there are several thousand mainstream NetBIOS applications that have been developed in the past decade to suit corporate needs, many Windows networks still use WINS servers and NetBIOS name resolution.

You may also choose to remove a WINS server if you have several WINS servers on your network and the number of WINS queries is low. In this case, ensure that any client computers configured with the IP address of the WINS server are reconfigured to use a different WINS server for NetBIOS name resolution.

ACTIVITY

Activity 8-8: Removing WINS

Time Required: 10 minutes

Objective: Remove WINS from your server.

Description: You have upgraded all the client computers and services on your network so that NetBIOS is no longer required. In this activity you will remove the WINS Service from your server and configure your server to no longer be a WINS client.

1. If necessary, start your server and log on as **Administrator**.

2. Click **Start**, point to **Control Panel**, and click **Add or Remove Programs**.

3. Click **Add/Remove Windows Components**.

4. Scroll down in the components window, and double-click **Networking Services**.

5. Click the check box beside Windows Internet Name Service (WINS) to remove the check mark, and click **OK**.

6. Click **Next** to remove WINS.

7. When the removal is complete, click **Finish**, and click **Close**.

8. Click **Start**, point to **Control Panel**, point to **Network Connections**, right-click **Local Area Connection**, and click **Properties**.

9. Click **Internet Protocol (TCP/IP)**, and then click **Properties**.

10. Click **Advanced**, and then click the **WINS** tab.

11. If necessary, click the IP address of your server, and click **Remove**.

12. Click **OK**, click **OK** again, click **Close** in the Local Area Connection Properties dialog box, and close the Add or Remove Programs window.

WINS PROXY

A **WINS proxy** is used for computers that need to participate in NetBIOS name resolution but that cannot be configured to use WINS. These computers are often UNIX clients that need to access NetBIOS resources. Using a WINS proxy allows these clients to resolve NetBIOS names to IP addresses using records in a WINS database.

Windows Server 2003 can be used as a WINS proxy. This is enabled by setting the registry key *KEY_LOCAL_MACHINE\SYSTEM\CurrentControlSet\Services\NetBT\Parameters\EnableProxy* to a value of 1.

All NetBIOS clients are capable of using broadcasts for name resolution. A WINS proxy receives the NetBIOS broadcasts on a local segment and forwards them to a WINS server. This allows any NetBIOS client to participate in WINS. The WINS proxy must be configured with the IP address of a WINS server in TCP/IP properties.

To prevent NetBIOS broadcasts from propagating across your network segment, place the WINS proxy in close proximity to the non-Windows NetBIOS clients.

Take the example of a UNIX client, which is unable to use WINS, accessing NetBIOS-based services on a Windows Server 2003 system. To use these services, it must resolve the name of the Windows Server 2003 system. The UNIX client sends a broadcast-based name resolution request. A WINS proxy on the local subnet sees the broadcast and forwards it to the WINS server as a properly formed WINS name query. The WINS server resolves the request and sends the response back to the WINS proxy. The WINS proxy broadcasts the response back to the UNIX client. Figure 8–15 shows the name query process when using a WINS proxy.

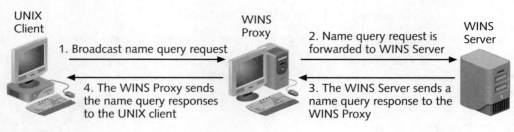

UNIX
Client

1. Broadcast name query request

WINS
Proxy

2. Name query request is
forwarded to WINS Server

WINS
Server

4. The WINS Proxy sends
the name query responses
to the UNIX client

3. The WINS Server sends a
name query response to the
WINS Proxy

Figure 8-15   Using a WINS proxy

TROUBLESHOOTING WINS

Most problems with WINS are the result of improperly configured TCP/IP settings on client computers. To simplify this configuration, you can use DHCP to hand out WINS server information using the 044 (WINS/NBNS Servers) and 046 (WINS/NBT Node Type) DHCP options as discussed earlier in Chapter 6. If clients are configured with the correct WINS information, ensure that the WINS clients can contact the WINS server using the ping utility. If the WINS clients cannot access the WINS server, the problem is network related.

Sometimes, NetBIOS name resolution problems are the result of a faulty NetBIOS name cache on the client. To flush the NetBIOS name cache and force fresh resolution, enter the command *nbtstat −R* to purge and reload the cache.

If the clients are configured properly for WINS name resolution and can contact the WINS server, first ensure that the WINS service is running on the WINS server. If it is not, start the service manually and check the event log for any errors.

If computers on the network can resolve NetBIOS names, yet cannot resolve a specific NetBIOS name, the problem may lie with records in the WINS database itself. You may search the WINS database for the record. If the record is incorrect or nonexistent, you may run the command *nbtstat −RR* on the computer you wish to have registered in the WINS database.

Failed replication may also cause name resolution problems since new records will not be propagated to other WINS servers. You may see WINS replication errors in Event Viewer. Ensure that all replication partners are configured with the correct push/pull settings and can contact each other with the ping utility. If the WINS replication partners cannot ping each other, then the problem is network-related.

Backup of the WINS database on a server may also fail. Remember that even though the database will automatically be backed up every 3 hours, this will not occur until a backup path is specified. This path must exist and be local to the server running the WINS service.

CHAPTER SUMMARY

❏ When two or more WINS servers exist on a network, replication must be configured between them to synchronize their contents. Only changes to the WINS database are replicated between servers.

❏ There are two types of WINS replication: push and pull. Push replication is based on a certain number of changes triggering replication. Pull replication is based on a certain period of time passing.

❏ A static mapping can be configured for resources that are unable to register themselves with WINS.

❏ You can view the records in a WINS database, as well as delete them.

❏ The WINS database should be backed up like any other critical resource on a network.

❏ A WINS Proxy lets non-WINS clients use the WINS Service and verify the validity of NetBIOS names over the network. The WINS Proxy forwards broadcasts from the local segment to the WINS server.

8

KEY TERMS

burst handling — A process used by a WINS server that cannot write name registrations to the WINS database fast enough to keep pace with the number of registrations. The WINS server ceases verifying that the names are not in use before sending out successful name registration requests with a short time to live.

dynamic compacting — The process whereby the WINS service deletes unused space in the WINS database automatically.

extinction interval — The period of time unused records exist in the WINS database before being marked as extinct.

extinction timeout — The period of time extinct records exist in the WINS database before being removed.

jetpack — A command-line utility that may be used to compact a WINS database.

NetBIOS name server — A server that holds a centralized repository of NetBIOS name information. The Microsoft implementation of a NetBIOS name server is WINS.

offline compacting — The process whereby the jetpack utility is used to remove unused space in the WINS database while the WINS service is stopped.

persistent connections — A connection that is created once and maintained over time for data transfer. This reduces communication overhead by reducing the number of packets used to establish connections over time.

pull replication — Replication between two WINS servers triggered by a defined amount of time passing.

push replication — Replication between two WINS servers triggered by a defined number of changes in the WINS database.

renewal interval — The time to live handed out to WINS clients when they register NetBIOS names.

replication partners — Two WINS servers that synchronize information in their databases.

static mapping — An entry manually placed in the WINS database. These are normally created for servers providing NetBIOS services that are unable to use WINS.

tombstoned — The term used to describe a WINS record that has been marked for deletion from all WINS servers. The tombstoned status is replicated among all WINS servers.

verification interval — The period of time a WINS server waits before validating a record that has been replicated from another WINS server.

WINS proxy — A service that forwards local broadcast NetBIOS requests to a WINS server. This is implemented for NetBIOS clients that are unable to use WINS.

REVIEW QUESTIONS

1. Which of the following client operating systems require WINS to function properly in a routed network? (Choose all that apply.)

   a. Windows 95

   b. Windows 98

   c. Windows NT

   d. Windows 2000

   e. Windows XP

2. Which NetBIOS name resolution method can be used by all NetBIOS clients including UNIX clients?

   a. NetBIOS name cache

   b. WINS

   c. broadcast

   d. LMHOSTS

3. What process is implemented between two WINS servers to synchronize the contents of their databases?

   a. synchronization

   b. zone transfer

   c. database transfer

   d. replication

4. Which type of replication is triggered by a defined period of time passing?

    a. push replication

    b. pull replication

5. Records are deleted from the WINS database when the _____ is complete.

    a. renewal interval

    b. extinction interval

    c. extinction timeout

    d. verification interval

6. What utility may be used to perform offline compacting of a WINS database?

    a. jetpack

    b. tombstone

    c. netstat

    d. wsdiag

7. A WINS Proxy is used to allow Windows computers the ability to access NetBIOS resources on non–Microsoft computers. True or false?

8. What status is assigned to a WINS record that is being deleted from all WINS databases, not just a singe server?

    a. extinct

    b. expired

    c. dead

    d. tombstoned

    e. irrelevant

9. What can be done to accommodate NetBIOS servers that are unable to participate in a WINS environment? (Choose all that apply.)

    a. Create a HOSTS file on each client.

    b. Configure a WINS proxy.

    c. Create static mappings in the WINS database for each server.

    d. Configure replication between WINS servers.

10. What is the default replication schedule configured when you add a new replication partner in the WINS management snap-in?

    a. push replication

    b. pull replication

    c. push/pull replication

    d. mutual replication

    e. None, you must configure this before replication will begin.

8

11. How do you configure a Windows Server 2003 server as a WINS Proxy?

  a. by using the WINS management snap-in

  b. by editing a registry key

  c. by using the Routing and Remote Access tool

  d. none of the above

12. You are considering the removal of the WINS service on all WINS servers on your network since the number of WINS queries is very low. What must you keep in mind before removing the WINS service? (Choose all that apply.)

  a. existing NetBIOS applications used by computers on the network

  b. existing TCP/IP configuration of client computers

  c. the WINS replication strategies used between WINS servers on the network

  d. none of the above

13. Your network has limited bandwidth available. As a result, you wish to replicate changes on your WINS server to all other WINS servers only when 10 changes have been made to the WINS database. What type of replication would you configure?

  a. push replication

  b. pull replication

14. You have several WINS servers configured on your network using push/pull replication. Unfortunately, you find that replication is slow between the WINS servers. What can you do to speed up replication time?

  a. Configure push replication only.

  b. Configure pull replication only.

  c. Enable persistent connections.

  d. Reduce the number of WINS servers on your network.

15. You have noticed that WINS queries on your WINS server are taking a long time to complete. What can you do to improve the performance of your WINS server?

  a. Ensure that your WINS server runs the Active Directory service.

  b. Restore the WINS database from a backup location.

  c. Enable persistent connections.

  d. Run the jetpack utility to compact the WINS database.

16. Where are WINS records stored by default?

  a. C:\WINDOWS\system32\wins

  b. C:\WINDOWS\system32\wins\Wins.mdb

  c. C:\WINDOWS\system32\wins\jetpack.mdb

  d. C:\WINDOWS\system32\wins\jetpack

17. Some users are complaining about access time when connecting to resources first thing in the morning. Most users turn their computers on each morning. What can you do to remedy the problem?

   a. Enable burst handling.

   b. Configure WINS replication.

   c. Enable persistent connections.

   d. Use a WINS proxy.

18. A UNIX server called UNIXSERVER on your network hosts a NetBIOS application that is used by other network users. Unfortunately, users are having difficulty contacting the UNIX server using the convention \\UNIXSERVER. All clients are configured to use WINS to perform name resolution. What can you do to remedy the problem?

   a. Enable burst handling.

   b. Configure a static mapping for UNIXSERVER in WINS.

   c. Configure a WINS proxy.

   d. Enable persistent connections on all WINS servers.

19. By default, a WINS database is backed up every 8 hours. True or false?

20. The WINS service stops at random times during the day on your WINS server. The Event Log does not contain information to successfully diagnose the problem. How can you force the WINS service to log detailed events to the Event Log?

   a. by editing a registry key

   b. by accessing the Advanced tab of WINS server properties

   c. by running the jetpack –d utility

   d. none of the above

CASE PROJECTS

Great Arctic North University has a number of different client operating systems and older applications that require NetBIOS name resolution. These case projects will present you with several situations to consider.

CASE
PROJECTS

Case Project 8-1: Configuring Replication

Great Arctic North University has eight physical locations connected by WAN links. Each of these WAN links is slow, so you have decided to install a WINS server at each location. Occasionally, clients at each location need to access NetBIOS resources in other locations. To accommodate this, you must configure replication. What things need to be taken into consideration when designing the replication topology? What will the replication topology look like?

Case Project 8-2: Identifying NetBIOS Applications

Before removing WINS in a Windows network environment, you must ensure that no computer run applications that require NetBIOS. Great Arctic North University would like to identify the NetBIOS applications in use on the network so that they can find suitable replacements and remove WINS from the network. Use a resource such as the Internet to compile a list of common NetBIOS applications that are used today and summarize their features and usage in a short document.

Case Project 8-3: Using WINS in a Mixed Environment

Several campuses of Great Arctic North University are routed and have a variety of non–Microsoft operating systems. Many of the Macintosh OS clients need to resolve NetBIOS names, yet cannot be configured as WINS clients. In addition, there are several UNIX servers on these networks that cannot use WINS, yet offer NetBIOS resources that Windows and Macintosh OS clients must access. In a short memo, describe how you will accommodate these operating systems. Draw a sample diagram illustrating how these operating systems will access NetBIOS resources.

9

SECURING NETWORK TRAFFIC USING IPSEC

After reading this chapter, you will be able to:

♦ Describe IP security issues and how the IPSec protocol addresses them

♦ Identify and discuss the features of different types of encryption

♦ Choose the appropriate IPSec mode for a given situation

♦ Implement authentication for IPSec

♦ Enable IPSec

♦ Create IPSec policies

♦ Create and manage IP Filter Lists and Filter Actions

♦ Monitor and troubleshoot IPSec

Although TCP/IP is very popular and used worldwide on the Internet, it is not very secure. Each IP packet that is sent on a local area network or the Internet can be read by people other than the intended recipients. Even worse, the potential exists for IP packets to contain false information that permits you or anyone else to be impersonated by someone else. IPv6 has new features that allow IP packets to be both digitally signed to prevent impersonation and encrypted to prevent unauthorized people from reading the contents of the packets. IPv4 has no such features built in. IPSec is an enhancement for IPv4 that allows packets to be digitally signed and encrypted. In this chapter, you will learn the features and functions of IPSec and how to implement them.

IPSec Overview

IPv4 has no built-in security mechanisms to protect the communication between two hosts. There are a variety of ways that hackers can corrupt or eavesdrop on IP-based communications. For example:

- *Packet sniffing*—Using special software called a **packet sniffer**, a hacker can view all of the packets traversing your network. Using these sniffed packets, a hacker can view the contents of files that are being stored on network servers, read e-mail, and possibly even view passwords. It may seem unlikely that a hacker can gain access to your premises to run a packet sniffer, but hacked Internet routers can also be used for packet sniffing.

- *Data replay*—Advanced packet sniffers can capture packets and allow the user to replay them at a later time. For example, a hacker could capture the packets involved in transferring money from one bank account to another and, even without understanding the contents of the packets, could replay the packets from one side of the communication to initiate the transaction again and again.

- *Data modification*—Some packet sniffers allow the user to modify packets before replaying them. For example, an e-mail message with a contract attached could be modified while in transit and the recipient would never know.

- *Address spoofing*—The only way IPv4 can control which users can access resources is via a firewall. Most firewall rules control access to resources based on the source IP address. Clever hackers can falsify the source IP address in a packet and gain unauthorized access to resources.

IP Security (IPSec) is a standards track protocol. It is supported by the Internet Engineering Task Force (IETF), which is designed to secure IP-based communication.

IPSec exists at the Network layer of the TCP/IP architecture. Because applications communicate with the Transport layer of the TCP/IP architecture, and because IPSec operates at the Network layer, applications are unaware of the existence of IPSec. Any TCP/IP-based application can use IPSec without being specially written to do so. This is a significant advantage over other methods used to secure data such as **Secure Socket Layer (SSL)**, which needs to be embedded in the client software.

To secure IP-based communication, IPSec uses authentication, cryptography, and digital signatures.

Authentication

Authentication describes the process whereby the identity of the sender or creator is verified. IPSec authenticates the endpoints of any IP-based conversation. This means that each participant must be known and trusted. When the two partners in a conversation using IPSec are authenticated, IP addresses are no longer used to verify the identity of the partners. Authentication stops unauthorized communication that is missed by firewalls, which are vulnerable to spoofed IP addresses. IPSec authentication identifies computers or devices involved in any IP-based communication using IPSec, not individual users.

Cryptography

Cryptography is the process of encrypting and decrypting messages and files to ensure that they are read only by the intended recipient or recipients. When a message is encrypted, it is converted to a format that is unreadable. **Decryption** is the reverse of encryption, and this process makes the data readable again. The term **ciphertext** is used to refer to encrypted information. **Encryption** can be used by IPSec to hide the contents of data packets. This prevents hackers with a simple packet sniffer from eavesdropping on network communication.

To encrypt information, an **algorithm** is used. In computerized cryptography, an algorithm is a mathematical formula that is used to modify the data. Also required for encryption and decryption are keys. A **key** is a large number that is difficult to guess, and is used in combination with an algorithm to encrypt and decrypt data. Depending on goals that need to be accomplished, one or several types of encryption may be used. The three generic types of encryption are symmetrical, asymmetrical, and hash encryption.

Symmetrical encryption uses a single key to encrypt and decrypt data. For example, if User A sends a file to User B using symmetrical encryption to encrypt the file, then User B decrypts the file using the same key that is used to encrypt the file.

This type of encryption is relatively simple from a mathematical perspective. A computer can symmetrically encrypt large amounts of data quickly. Consequently, this is this type of encryption used when encrypting files and large amounts of data across network transmissions.

Asymmetrical encryption uses two separate keys, called the **public key** and the **private key**, to encrypt and decrypt data. Anything encrypted by the public key can be decrypted with the private key, and anything encrypted by the private key can be decrypted with the public key.

When asymmetrical encryption is used, the public key is made available to anyone who wants it; hence its name. The private key is held only by the individual, or computer, to which it is assigned. If you wish to send an encrypted message to another computer using asymmetrical encryption, you would first obtain the public key of the target computer and use it to encrypt the data being sent. Since the target computer is the only computer which has the private key that can decrypt the data, the data is secure.

This type of encryption is more mathematically complex than symmetrical encryption. As a result, asymmetrical encryption requires more processing power than symmetrical encryption. Thus, it is not practical or efficient to use asymmetrical encryption for large amounts of data.

Hash encryption is unique because it is one-way encryption. A hash algorithm uses a single key to convert data to a **hash value**. The hash value is a summary of the data. For example, a 129-bit hash value might be generated for a 100-KB file. Even if the algorithm is publicly known, the hash value cannot be decrypted because the hash value does not contain enough information. The main purpose of a hash value is to be a unique identifier; it is not commonly used to secure data.

This type of encryption is often used to store passwords. This ensures that the database storing the hash values for the passwords can be publicly available, but the actual passwords are unknown. To verify a password, the system applies the hash algorithm to a submitted password and compares the newly generated hash value with the hash value in the password database. If the two hash values match, then the password is correct. If the two hash values do not match, then the password is incorrect.

Digital Signatures

A **digital signature** is used to ensure that a message has not been modified while in transit and that it truly came from the named sender. This is important for electronically delivering information such as contracts and agreements.

 A digital signature does not encrypt the contents of a message.

The public and private keys of the sender are used for a digital signature. First the sender creates the document that will be signed. Then a hash algorithm is used to create a hash value of the document, and the hash value is encrypted with the private key of the sender. Then the sender transmits the original document and the encrypted hash value. This process is shown in Figure 9-1.

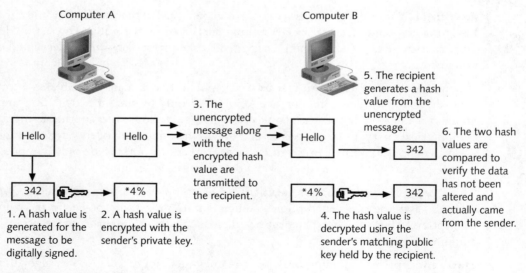

Figure 9-1   Digital signature

The recipient takes the original document and creates a hash value using the same hash algorithm as the sender. The recipient then decrypts the encrypted hash value from the sender using the public key of the sender. If the two hash values match, then the document was not modified in transit. This also verifies that the message came from the named sender, as only that sender has access to the private key that matches the public key used.

IPSec uses digital signatures on each packet of information to ensure that the packet has not been modified while in transit. Time stamps placed in the signatures ensure that the data is not being replayed.

USING IPSEC

As a standards track protocol sponsored by the IETF, IPSec is widely used by many vendors. Although it is possible that parts of IPSec may be modified in the future, the current specifications ensure at least a minimal level of compatibility between implementations from different vendors. As a result, you should be able to use a Windows Server 2003 router with IPSec to communicate with a Cisco router using IPSec.

Given the advantages of IPSec, you would think that all IP-based communications would use it. However, it is not practical or desired in all situations. Pre-Windows 2000 operating systems from Microsoft do not support the IPSec protocol. This prevents any network with Windows 9x/NT clients from implementing IPSec for all communication. You can use a mix of IPSec protected packets and unprotected packets to increase security for those operating systems that do support IPSec.

IPSec can also significantly slow communication on a network. Authentication, digitally signing each packet, and encrypting the contents of each packet consumes processing resources and time. A busy server may not have enough processing power to support using IPSec for all communication. Fortunately, you can buy network cards with dedicated processors to speed IPSec calculations.

Another drawback to using IPSec is that the majority of businesses connected to the Internet use some type of network address translation (NAT) to allow an entire office to share one IP address when accessing the Internet. IPSec is not able to be routed through NAT, and this is a very serious limitation for remote users. However, if NAT and IPSec are implemented on the same router, it functions properly. Figure 9-2 shows implementations of NAT and IPSec.

IPSec adds complexity to a network. While the Windows Server 2003 implementation of IPSec is reliable, any service added to a network has the potential to break. In real terms, a broken service translates into lost money via user downtime and additional administrative expense. Without a demonstrated need, IPSec is a waste of time and money.

IPSec can, however, be a valuable addition to a network when data integrity or confidentiality are required. On a LAN, IPSec can be implemented between client computers and specific servers holding confidential data such as financial records or human resources information. On a WAN, IPSec can be used to create a cost-effective virtual private network that allows a company to securely send private data across the Internet without fear of eavesdropping.

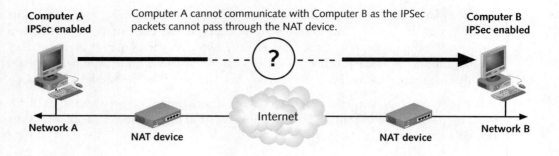

Computer A
IPSec enabled

Computer A cannot communicate with Computer B as the IPSec packets cannot pass through the NAT device.

Computer B
IPSec enabled

Network A

NAT device

Internet

NAT device

Network B

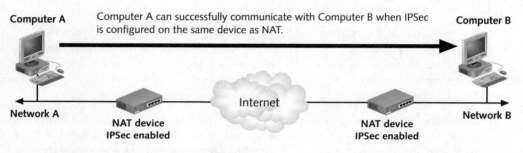

Computer A

Computer A can successfully communicate with Computer B when IPSec is configured on the same device as NAT.

Computer B

Network A

NAT device
IPSec enabled

Internet

NAT device
IPSec enabled

Network B

Figure 9-2   Implementing NAT and IPSec

IPSec Modes

When configuring IPSec, you must choose between different modes of operation. The modes of operation define whether communication is secured between two hosts or two networks, and which IPSec services are used. Attempting to use all modes of operation is not appropriate because the large amount of processing power used on routers and hosts slows down network communications.

IPSec communication between two routers is called **tunnel mode**. IPSec communication between two hosts is called **transport mode**. **Authentication headers (AH) mode** enforces authentication of the two IPSec clients and includes a digital signature on each packet. **Encapsulating security payload (ESP) mode** has all the features of AH mode plus encryption of data in the packet.

When implementing IPSec, you must choose tunnel mode or transport mode. In addition, you must choose AH mode or ESP mode. For example, you could choose to implement IPSec in tunnel mode and ESP mode if encryption is required. Or, you could choose to implement IPSec in tunnel mode and AH mode if encryption is not required.

AH Mode

The AH mode of IPSec provides authentication of the two endpoints and adds a checksum to the packet. Authentication guarantees that the two endpoints are known, and the checksum on the packet guarantees that the packet is not modified in transit, including the IP headers. AH mode does not provide data confidentiality, as the payload of the packet is unencrypted.

It would be appropriate to use AH mode in a situation where you are concerned about packets being captured with a packet sniffer and replayed later. The checksum feature ensures that packets cannot be modified to create a new connection. AH mode is less processor intensive than ESP mode because there is no need for encryption calculations.

ESP Mode

The ESP mode of IPSec provides authentication of the two endpoints, which guarantees that the two endpoints are known. It also adds a checksum to each packet, which guarantees that the packet was not modified in transit, excluding the IP headers. Finally, ESP mode encrypts the data in the packet. Encryption ensures that unintended recipients cannot read the data in the packet.

Most implementations of IPSec use ESP mode because data encryption is desired. When implementing IPSec in ESP mode, you must ensure that the devices have enough processing power to encrypt and decrypt all of the packets addressed to, or passing through, them. For example, if two routers are using IPSec in ESP mode to encrypt all of the packets transmitted across the Internet between two locations, then the processors in those routers must be able to encrypt and decrypt all the packets moving between the two networks.

Transport Mode

IPSec in transport mode is used between two hosts. Both endpoints in the communication must support IPSec. This limits the implementation of IPSec, because many devices, such as printers, rarely offer IPSec support. Figure 9-3 shows IPSec in transport mode. In this example, packets are encrypted on both internal networks as well as the Internet.

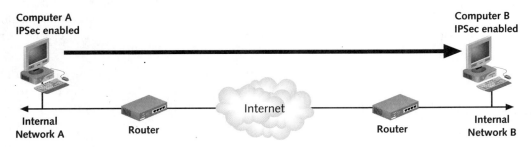

Figure 9-3   IPSec in transport mode

The two endpoints authenticated in this example are the hosts communicating when transport mode is used. Therefore, you are guaranteed to be communicating with a known host. This may be required for some secure communication.

The structure of a packet built using ESP in transport mode is shown in Figure 9-4. This packet is built locally on the host, and therefore includes all of the IPSec information inside the original IP header. There is no need to encapsulate an entire packet.

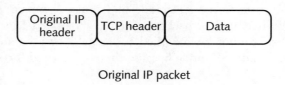

Original IP packet

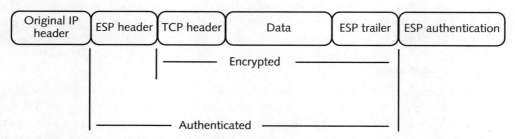

Figure 9-4   Packet structure for ESP in transport mode

Tunnel Mode

IPSec in tunnel mode is used between two routers. The two hosts communicating through the routers do not need to support IPSec; rather, the routers take the original IP packets and encapsulate them. This means that any IP devices can take advantage of routers running IPSec in tunnel mode.

Figure 9-5 shows IPSec in tunnel mode between two routers. All of the communication between computers on both internal networks is encrypted as it crosses the Internet because the routers encapsulate the original IP packets. However, communication within each internal network is not encrypted. Figure 9-6 shows the structure of a packet built using ESP in tunnel mode.

Authentication takes place between the two routers when using IPSec in tunnel mode. The computers taking part in the conversation are not authenticated. In some situations, this may be considered insecure.

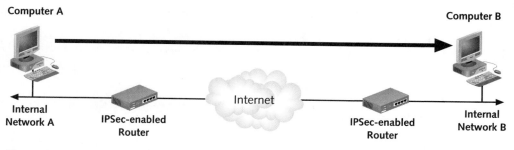

Figure 9-5   IPSec in tunnel mode

Original IP packet

9

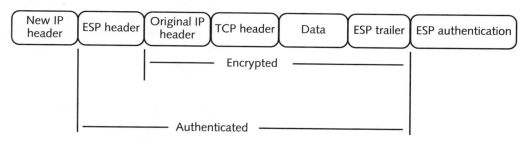

Figure 9-6   Packet structure for ESP in tunnel mode

IPSec Authentication

Both endpoints of an IPSec communication are authenticated. The authentication is for the actual devices, not the users logged into the devices. When two routers are engaged using IPSec in tunnel mode, both of the routers are authenticated to each other. When two computers are engaged using IPSec in transport mode, both of the computers are authenticated to each other.

Internet Key Exchange (IKE) is the process used by two IPSec hosts to negotiate their security parameters. The security parameters negotiated include the method of authentication, AH or ESP mode, transport or tunnel mode, encryption and hashing algorithms, and parameters for key exchange. When security parameters have been agreed upon, this is referred to as a **security association (SA)**.

There are three methods Windows Server 2003 can use to authenticate IPSec connections:

- Preshared key
- Certificates
- Kerberos

Preshared Key

A **preshared key** is simply a combination of characters entered at each endpoint of the IPSec connection. Authentication is based on the fact that both endpoints know the same secret, and no one else has been told the secret. Effectively, this is the same as configuring both ends of the IPSec connection with a password. If both ends are using the same password, then the connection is established. The major advantage of this authentication method is its simplicity. Authentication occurs as long as the preshared key is typed in correctly on each device.

The major disadvantage of this authentication method is movement of the preshared key when configuring the two devices. For example, if Bob is configuring a device in New York to use IPSec and authenticate using a key he has generated, then Bob needs to give that key to Susan in Toronto so she can configure her device before they can communicate using IPSec. When Bob gives the key to Susan using e-mail, postal mail, or the telephone, there is a risk someone might intercept the message.

Certificates

Certificates may be presented for authentication. A certificate is a file that follows the **X.509** standard created by the International Telecommunication Union – Telecommunication (ITU-T) and contains information about a user or computer, as well as a public key.

The terms "certificate," "digital certificate," and "public key certificate" are often used interchangeably when reading documentation from different vendors.

Certificates are issued by trusted organizations on the Internet called **certification authorities**.

You can buy certificates from several third-party certification authorities on the Internet, such as VeriSign.

Windows Server 2003 can become a certificate authority if **Certificate Services** is installed.

When a certificate is presented as proof of identity, it must be validated. This is accomplished using the digital signature of the certification authority. For a client application to trust that this information in the certificate is correct, it must trust the certification authority that issued the certificate.

This type of authentication is very useful when clients are from outside of your organization. The clients can obtain a certificate from a third-party certificate authority so you, as network administrator, are not responsible for maintaining the infrastructure that creates and approves certificates.

The main disadvantage of using third-party certificates is cost. Each client needs to buy a certificate. If there are hundreds or thousands of clients, then this can be expensive. In addition, many clients may not be technically savvy enough to obtain a certificate.

 Certificates can be used by many different services in addition to IPSec to provide security. These include e-mail, Encrypting File System (EFS), and smart cards.

NOTE

9

Kerberos

Kerberos is the authentication system used by Windows 2000/XP/2003 for access to network resources. Kerberos uses a security boundary called a realm. Two devices that wish to communicate must be in Kerberos realms that trust each other. In Active Directory, a domain is equivalent to a Kerberos realm.

The main benefit of Kerberos as an authentication method for IPSec is its seamless integration with domain security. The client computers do not need to be configured with any extra information if they have a computer account in the Active Directory forest.

Kerberos is not a commonly supported authentication system for IPSec on non-Microsoft products such as routers, and is not appropriate for Windows computers that are not part of the Active Directory forest.

ENABLING IPSEC

IPSec is enabled on Windows Server 2003 using **IPSec policies**. These policies can be configured manually on each server or distributed through Group Policy. IPSec policies configured on each server can be accessed through the Local Security Policy snap-in found in Administrative Tools. IPSec policies distributed through Group Policy can be configured using the Active Directory Users and Computers snap-in, or the Group Policy Object Editor snap-in.

IPSec policies define the circumstances under which IP traffic is tunneled using IPSec, permitted without using IPSec, or blocked. In addition, the policies define the type of authentication, which network connections are affected, and whether IPSec is to be used in tunnel mode or transport mode. The three policies installed by default are:

- Server (Request Security)
- Client (Respond Only)
- Secure Server (Require Security)

The default policies are configured to use Kerberos for authentication. This allows them to be used internally within an Active Directory forest with no configuration.

All ICMP traffic is permitted by the default policies. This means that network traffic generated by utilities such as ping and tracert is not encapsulated using IPSec. It is assumed that this traffic is public and does not need to be kept secure.

All of the default policies respond to requests to use IPSec. However, they differ in whether they request security. The Client (Respond Only) policy never requests IPSec for IP communication, but uses it if requested. The Server (Request Security) policy always requests IPSec for IP communication, but it can communicate without it if a security association cannot be established using IPSec. The Secure Server (Require Security) policy does not respond to any non–IPSec traffic for IP communication.

An IPSec policy must be in place to use IPSec. If there is no IPSec policy established, IPSec cannot be used.

Assigning IPSec Policies

A single server can be configured with many IPSec policies. However, no policy is used until it is assigned. Only one policy can be assigned at a time per machine. The Local Security Policy snap-in can be used to assign an IPSec policy on a single computer, as shown in Figure 9-7. The Group Policy feature of Active Directory can also be used to assign an IPSec policy to a group of computers.

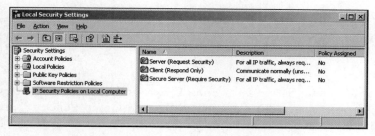

Figure 9-7   The Local Security Policy snap-in

Once a policy has been assigned, it does not take effect immediately. The IPSec Policy Agent must be restarted for the change to take effect. You can restart the IPSec Policy Agent by rebooting the server, however, the preferred method is by using the Services snap-in. In the Services snap-in, the IPSec Policy Agent is named IPSEC Services.

Activity 9-1: Assigning an IPSec Policy

Time Required: 15 minutes

Objective: Assign an IPSec policy to enable encryption of data packets.

Description: Several of your servers hold confidential student information. You want to enable IPSec on these servers to protect the information from packet sniffers. The client computers accessing your confidential servers are a mix of Windows XP/2000 and Windows 9x/NT. You will enable the Server (Request Security) policy to accommodate the older clients that do not support IPSec. As well, you will use the IPSec Monitor snap-in to verify that the policy has been assigned to your computer.

1. If necessary, start your server and log on as **Administrator**.
2. Click **Start**, point to **Administrative Tools**, and click **Local Security Policy**.
3. Under Security Settings, click **IP Security Policies on Local Computer**.
4. In the right pane, right-click **Server (Request Security)**, and click **Assign**. Notice that under the column Policy Assigned, "Yes" now appears next to the description for this policy.
5. Close the Local Security Settings window.
6. Click **Start**, point to **Administrative Tools**, and click **Services**.
7. Scroll down through the list of services, right-click **IPSEC Services**, and click **Restart**.
8. Close the Services window.
9. Click **Start**, click **Run**, type **mmc**, and press **Enter**.
10. Click **File**, click **Add/Remove Snap-in**, click **Add**, scroll through the list and double-click **IP Security Monitor**, click **Close**, and click **OK**.
11. Double-click **IP Security Monitor**.
12. Double-click your server.
13. Click **Active Policy**. Notice the information displayed in the details pane regarding your assigned policy.
14. Close all open windows. If asked if you want to save the console settings, click **No**.

Activity 9-2: Unassigning an IPSec Policy

Time Required: 15 minutes

Objective: Unassign an IPSec policy to disable encryption of data packets.

Description: You have moved a computer that has an IPSec policy enabled to the research lab. The research lab network is a private network and does not require IPSec to secure network traffic. As a result, you will disable the Server (Request Security) policy that was assigned to this computer and use the IPSec Monitor snap-in to verify that the policy has been properly unassigned to your computer.

1. If necessary, start your server and log on as **Administrator**.

2. Click **Start**, point to **Administrative Tools**, and click **Local Security Policy**.

3. Under **Security Settings**, click **IP Security Policies** on Local Computer.

4. In the right pane, right-click **Server (Request Security)**, and click **Un-assign**. Notice that under the column Policy Assigned, "No" now appears next to the description for this policy.

5. Close the **Local Security Settings** window.

6. Click **Start**, point to **Administrative Tools**, and click **Services**.

7. Scroll down through the list of services, right-click **IPSEC Services**, and click **Restart**.

8. Close the Services window.

9. Click **Start**, click **Run**, type **mmc**, and press **Enter**.

10. Click **File**, click **Add/Remove Snap-in**, click **Add**, scroll through the list and double-click **IP Security Monitor**, click **Close**, and click **OK**.

11. Double-click **IP Security Monitor**.

12. Double-click your server.

13. Click **Active Policy**. Notice that no information is displayed in the details pane.

14. Close all open windows. If asked if you want to save the console settings, click **No**.

CREATING AN IPSEC POLICY

In many circumstances, the three default policies are sufficient for your needs. However, you can create your own IPSec policies that are tailored to your environment. For example, the default policies encrypt all IP communication between two hosts. You may only wish to encrypt the traffic for one application that handles confidential information.

Each IPSec policy is composed of **IPSec rules**, as shown in Figure 9-8. Each rule is composed of an **IP filter list**, an **IPSec filter action**, authentication methods, a **tunnel endpoint**, and a connection type.

IP filter lists and IPSec filter actions are maintained in a central list by Windows Server 2003. This means that any IP filter list or IPSec filter action created can be reused by other rules within a policy or other policies. IP filter lists and IPSec filter actions can be added to this central list when using the Local Security Policy snap-in to create and edit policies, or by right-clicking IP Security Policies on Local Computer and clicking Manage IP filter lists and filter actions, as shown in Figure 9-9.

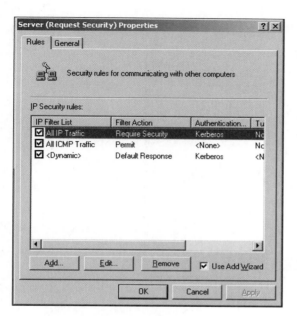

Figure 9-8   IPSec policy rules

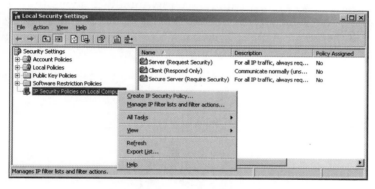

Figure 9-9   Results of right-clicking IP Security Policies on Local Computer

To create a new IPSec policy, simply choose Create IP Security Policy, as shown in Figure 9-9, and you will start the IP Security Policy Wizard. This wizard helps you create an IPSec policy, but cannot completely define it for you. It asks you for a name, a description, whether to activate the default response rule, and an authentication type.

The name and description for the policy are shown in IP Security Policies on the Local Computer when you are assigning IPSec policies. These should be descriptive so they can be easily picked from the list.

Once a name and description have been chosen, you are given the choice of activating the default response rule, as shown in Figure 9-10.

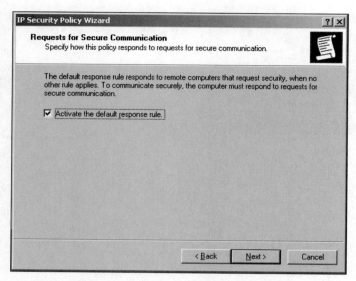

Figure 9-10   Activating the default response rule

The default response rule is used when the filters from other rules do not apply. For example, an IPSec policy may have one rule that requires security for a Web application on port 80 and the default response rule. The default response rule is used for all incoming packets not addressed to port 80. If the default response rule is not activated and a rule is not defined for a particular port, then traffic addressed to that port cannot use IPSec.

If the default response rule is activated, there are three choices for authentication, as shown in Figure 9–11.

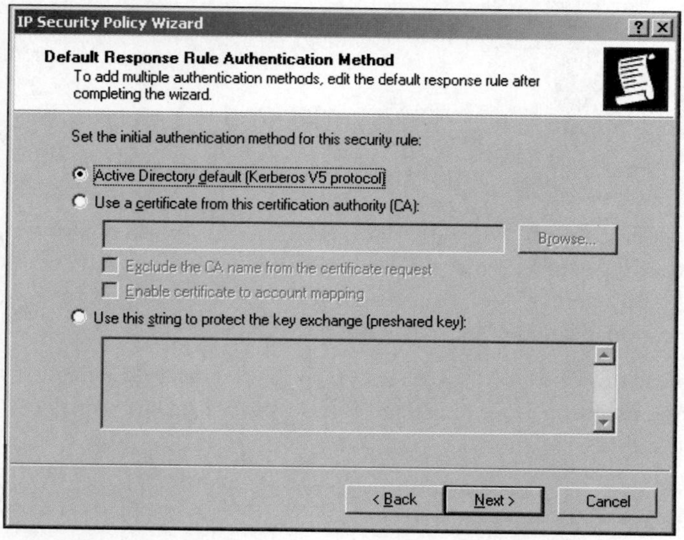

Figure 9-11   Authentication options for the default response rule

The Active Directory default (Kerberos V5 protocol) option is generally used for internal client computers and servers. The Use a certificate from this certification authority (CA) option is generally used to support external clients or in an environment where certificate services are already configured. The Use this string to protect the key exchange (preshared key) option requires both devices in an IPSec communication to be configured with the same key.

Activity 9-3: Creating an IPSec Policy

Time Required: 10 minutes

Objective: Create a new IPSec policy that is different than the default policies.

Description: All of the default IPSec policies do not restrict ICMP. The engineering department at Great Arctic North University is concerned that hackers may be using ICMP to scan available hosts in the department and hence wish to secure all ICMP traffic. To secure this traffic, you will be implementing IPSec because ICMP has no built-in security. Since the computers in the Engineering Department are not accessed by Internet users, a preshared key will be used provide authentication for IPSec.

1. If necessary, start your server and log on as **Administrator**.

2. Click **Start**, point to **Administrative Tools**, and click **Local Security Policy**.

3. Right-click **IP Security Policies** on Local Computer, and click **Create IP Security Policy**.

4. Click **Next** to start the IP Security Policy Wizard.

5. In the Name box, type **ICMP Traffic Policy**. In the description box, type **Secure ICMP Traffic**, and click **Next**.

6. Confirm that **Activate the default response rule** is selected, and click **Next**.

7. Select **Use this string to protect the key exchange (preshared key)**, type **mypresharedkey** in the text box provided, and press **Next**.

8. Click **Edit properties** to deselect it, and click **Finish**.

9. Note that the ICMP Traffic Policy now appears in the right pane as an IP Security Policy.

10. Close the Local Security Settings window.

9

Creating Rules

After an IPSec policy is created, you must edit it to add the rules that define how different types of IP traffic are handled. The only rule that may exist by default is the Default Response rule, as shown in Figure 9-12. This is present if you chose to add it during the creation process.

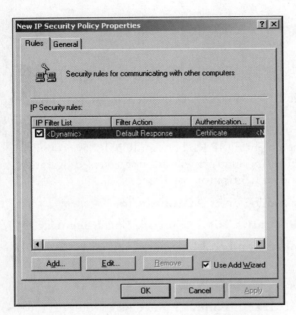

Figure 9-12   Properties of a new IPSec policy

When you add a rule to the properties of an IPSec policy, the Create IP Security Rule Wizard is used by default. This wizard allows you to configure the most commonly used options. If you prefer not to use the wizard, deselect the Use Add Wizard option shown in Figure 9-12 before clicking on the Add button.

The first screen in the Create IP Security Rule Wizard, shown in Figure 9-13, prompts you to choose tunnel mode or transport mode.

If you choose the This rule does not specify a tunnel option, then transport mode will be used. If the The tunnel endpoint is specified by the following IP address option is chosen, then tunnel mode is used between this computer and the IP address specified.

The second screen presented by the Create IP Security Rule Wizard concerns the network type, as shown in Figure 9-14. Here, you can choose whether this rule applies to all network connections, LAN connections, or remote access connections. If remote access is chosen, this applies to both dial-up and VPN connections.

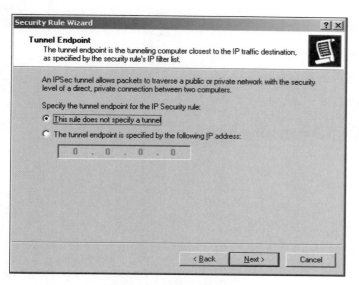

Figure 9-13   Specifying a tunnel endpoint for a new rule

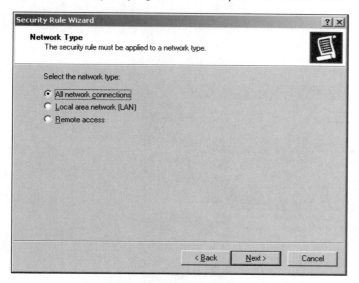

Figure 9-14   Specifying network types for a new rule

Next, you are presented with the IP Filter List window, as shown in Figure 9-15. IP filters define packet types to which actions are applied. The two IP filter lists that exist by default are All IP Traffic and All ICMP Traffic. However, you can create new IP filter lists here that suit your needs. The All IP Traffic IP filter list is normally used to specify that all IP packets be encrypted. The All ICMP Traffic IP filter list is normally used to specify that all ICMP packets not be encrypted.

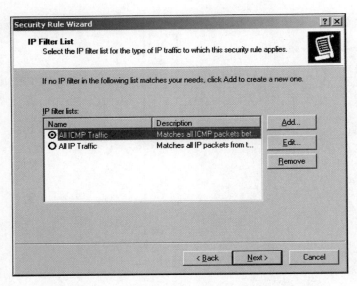

Figure 9-15   Specifying IP filter lists for a new rule

After you have selected an IP filter list, you must select an action to be performed on the packets that match the IP filter list. The Filter Action window, shown in Figure 9-16, allows you to select an existing filter action or create new actions.

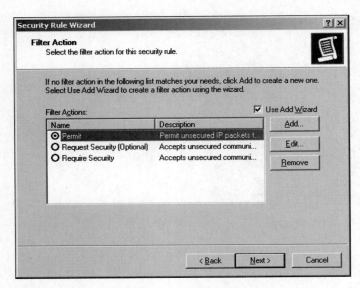

Figure 9-16   Specifying filter actions for a new rule

The three actions that exist by default are:

- *Permit*—Allows packets to pass through the IP filter unmodified
- *Request Security (Optional)*—Attempts to create IPSec connections with all other computers, but uses non–IPSec communication if a security association between the computers cannot be established using IPSec
- *Require Security*—Accepts non-IPSec packets, but responds only using IPSec packets; if Require Security is chosen, then this computer is only able to communicate with other computers using IPSec when packets match the IP filter

If you choose Request Security (Optional) or Require Security, you will also be prompted to choose the method of authentication.

Activity 9-4: Creating a New IPSec Filter Rule

Time Required: 10 minutes

Objective: Add a new IPSec filter rule that forces ICMP traffic to use IPSec.

Description: The default response rule created in the previous exercise does not force ICMP traffic to use IPSec. You will create a new IPSec filter rule that ensures that ICMP packets are always secured by IPSec.

1. If necessary, start your server and log on as **Administrator**.
2. Click **Start**, point to **Administrative Tools**, and click **Local Security Policy**.
3. Right-click **ICMP Traffic Policy**, and click **Properties**.
4. Click **Add** to create a new rule.
5. Click **Next** to start the Create IP Security Rule Wizard.
6. Confirm that **This rule does not specify a tunnel** is selected, and click **Next**.
7. Confirm that **All network connections** is selected, and click **Next**.
8. On the IP Filter List page, click the **All ICMP Traffic** option button, and click **Next**.
9. On the Filter Action page, click the **Require Security** option button, and click **Next**.
10. Select **Use this string to protect the key exchange (preshared key)**, type **mypresharedkey** in the text box provided, and press **Next**.
11. Click **Finish**.
12. Click **OK** to close the ICMP Traffic Policy Properties dialog box.
13. Close the Local Security Settings window.

IPSec Filter Lists

The two default IPSec filter lists for all IP traffic and all ICMP traffic do not allow you very much control over which traffic uses IPSec and which does not. If multiple applications are running on a server, it may be unnecessary for all IP traffic to be encrypted. For instance, if a server is running file and print services as well as SQL Server, then it may be necessary to protect the SQL Server traffic, but not the file and print services traffic. If this is the case, only traffic on TCP port 1433 used by SQL Server needs to be encrypted, and not all IP traffic.

 Encrypting only the necessary packets reduces the load on the CPU. Performing encryption and decryption can create a significant load on a busy server.

If you wish to create a new IP filter list, you must give it a name, and you have the option of giving it a description as shown in Figure 9-17. In addition, you must add IP filters that make up the list and specify the traffic to which this list will apply.

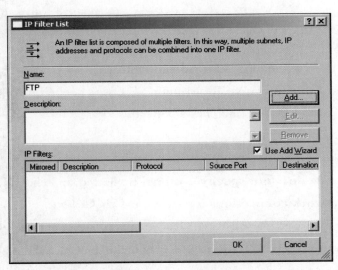

Figure 9-17   Creating a new IP filter list

By default, when an IP filter is added to a IP filter list, the IP Filter Wizard is used. If you prefer not to use the IP Filter Wizard, deselect the Use Add Wizard checkbox shown in Figure 9-17.

The IP Filter Wizard first requests a description for the new IP filter you are creating, as shown in Figure 9-18. This same screen has a Mirrored option, which automatically applies your new IP filter to the opposite source and selected destination ports specified in the IP filter. For example, if an IP filter is created for a source of any IP address, any port, and a destination of the local server and port 80, then the mirrored option automatically applies this IP filter to the return traffic with a source IP address of the local server and port 80 to a destination of any IP address and any port.

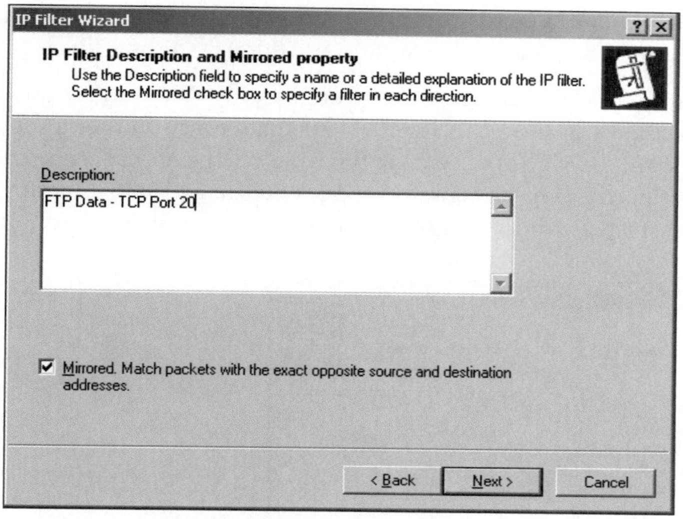

Figure 9-18   The Mirrored option for a new IP filter

The second window of the IP Filter Wizard asks for the source IP address in the filter. As shown in Figure 9–19, this can be statically configured as: My IP Address, Any IP Address, A specific DNS Name, A specific IP Address, or A specific IP Subnet. In addition, there are dynamic source IP addresses that can be configured. These are based on the IP configuration of the computer using the filter and are: DNS Servers, WINS Servers, DHCP Server, and Default Gateway.

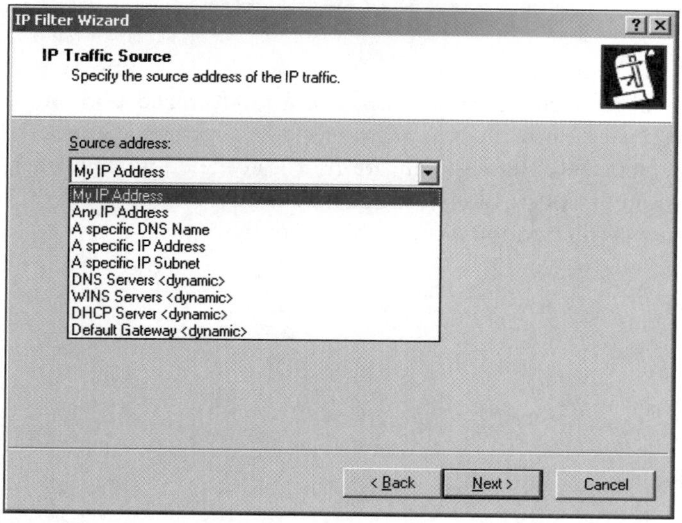

Figure 9-19   Configuring a source IP address for a new IP filter

The next window in the IP Filter Wizard asks for the destination IP address in the filter. This window provides the same choices as for the source IP address as in the filter.

Within IP packets, there is a field to describe the protocol type. You can set this as part of an IP filter in the next window, as shown in Figure 9-20. The most common protocol types used here are TCP, UDP, and ICMP. Other packet types are relatively rare. If the packet type you wish to define is not in the drop-down list, you can enter in a protocol number directly by choosing Other. An Internet standard list of protocol numbers is maintained by the IETF.

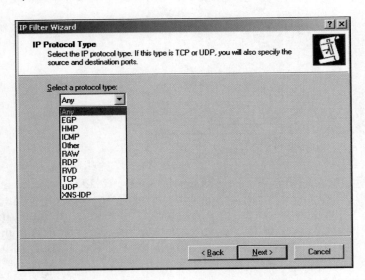

Figure 9-20   Configuring the protocol type for a new IP filter

If TCP or UDP is chosen for the packet type, then you must define the source and destination port numbers. Most client applications use a randomized port number above 1023. To affect incoming traffic from client applications, filters configured on servers should use the option From any port. Most server applications use a defined port number. To affect incoming traffic to server applications, filters configured on servers should use the option To this port. Figure 9-21 shows the window where this is configured.

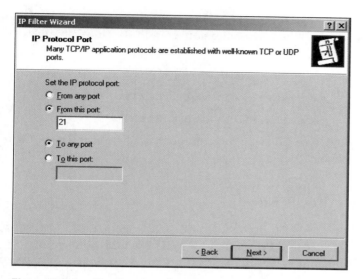

Figure 9-21   Configuring the TCP or UDP port for a new IP filter

Activity 9-5: Creating an IPSec Filter List

Time Required: 20 minutes

Objective: Create a new IPSec filter list for all FTP traffic.

Description: All of the members of the arts faculty at Great Arctic North University have agreed that they will upload final marks for the students using FTP. FTP was chosen because all of the client operating systems throughout Great Arctic North University support it. However, you are concerned that this confidential information may be viewed by unauthorized people using packet sniffers on the network. To secure this traffic, you will be implementing IPSec because FTP has no built-in security.

Before creating an IPSec Policy that is used to secure FTP, you must create a new rule that encrypts all FTP traffic. The TCP port used for control messages is 21, and the TCP port used for data transfer is 20.

1. If necessary, start your server and log on as **Administrator**.
2. Click **Start**, point to **Administrative Tools**, and click **Local Security Policy**.
3. Right-click **IP Security Policies on Local Computer**, and click **Manage IP filter lists and filter actions**.
4. Click **Add** to create a new IP filter list.
5. In the Name box, type **FTP**.
6. Click **Add** to create a new IP filter.
7. Click **Next** to start the IP Filter Wizard.

8. In the Description box, type **FTP Data – TCP Port 20**, confirm that **Mirrored. Match packets with the exact opposite source and destination addresses** is selected, and click **Next**.

9. Confirm that **My IP Address** is selected, and click **Next**.

10. Confirm that **Any IP Address** is selected, and click **Next**.

11. Click the drop-down arrow, click **TCP**, and click **Next**.

12. Click **From this port**, type **20** as the port number, confirm that **To any port** is selected, and click **Next**.

13. Click **Finish**.

14. Click **Add** to create a new IP filter.

15. Click **Next** to start the IP Filter Wizard.

16. In the Description box, type **FTP Control – TCP Port 21**, confirm that **Mirrored. Match packets with the exact opposite source and destination addresses** is selected, and click **Next**.

17. Confirm that **My IP Address** is selected, and click **Next**.

18. Confirm that **Any IP Address** is selected, and click **Next**.

19. Click the drop-down arrow, click **TCP**, and click **Next**.

20. Click **From this port**, type **21** as the port number, confirm that **To any port** is selected, and click **Next**.

21. Click **Finish**.

22. Click **OK** to close the IP Filter List dialog box.

23. Click **Close**.

24. Close the Local Security Settings window.

Filter Actions

Filter actions define what is done to traffic that matches an IP filter list. There are only three default filter actions available: Permit, Request Security (Optional), and Require Security. All the default filter actions define a number of security parameters, including the type of encryption that can be negotiated. In highly secure situations, you may wish to modify these or create your own.

To create a new filter action, you can use the IP Security Filter Action Wizard. This is invoked by default when you choose to add a new filter action. To avoid using the wizard, uncheck the Use Add Wizard option box, as shown in Figure 9-22.

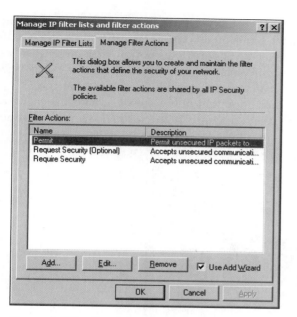

Figure 9-22   Creating an IPSec filter action

The first window of the IP Security Filter Action Wizard requests a name and description for the new filter action. The second window, shown in Figure 9-23, asks for an action behavior. Selecting the Permit option allows the traffic to move without being affected by IPSec. The Block option discards traffic that matches the IP filter list. The Negotiate security option lets you define which encryption options are used.

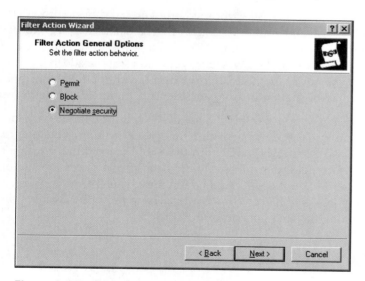

Figure 9-23   Specifying action behavior for a new filter action

In the next window, shown in Figure 9-24, you are asked whether to allow unencrypted communication with computers that do not support IPSec. If you choose the Do not communicate with computers that do not support IPSec option, then computers using this filter action cannot communicate with Windows clients that do not have an IPSec policy assigned. This is appropriate in high-security situations. If you choose the Fall back to unsecured communication option, then communication is possible with any client, whether an IPSec policy is assigned or not. This is not appropriate for high-security environments.

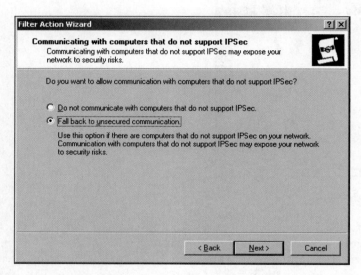

Figure 9-24   Allowing unencrypted communication in a new filter action

Each filter action requires at least one security method. The security method defines the algorithms used for encryption and authentication, as well as whether IPSec modes AH or ESP will be used. The IP Security Filter Action Wizard allows you to add only one security method, as shown in Figure 9-25. Additional security methods can be added by editing the filter action after creation. Security methods are prioritized, with the first security method listed in a filter action being the highest priority and the first attempted during negotiation.

The Integrity and encryption option specifies the use of IPSec in ESP mode with the SHA1 algorithm for data integrity and the 3DES algorithm for data encryption. The Integrity only option specifies the use of IPSec in AH mode with the SHA1 algorithm for data integrity, but no encryption is performed. Performing only the data integrity check is useful when you want to be sure the data has not been modified in transit, you are not concerned about data confidentiality, and you would like to conserve processing power by avoiding the CPU time required by encrypting the data portion of the packet.

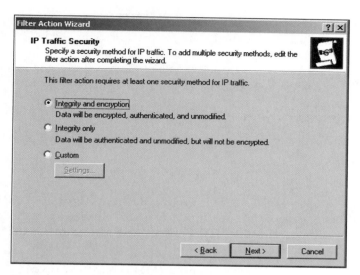

Figure 9-25 Specifying a security method for a new filter action

You can also specify custom settings for the security method, as shown in Figure 9-26. In this window, you can specify that IPSec modes AH and ESP be used. ESP mode ensures integrity and performs encryption on the data portion of the packet. AH mode ensures integrity of the data portion of the packets as well as the IP headers in the packet.

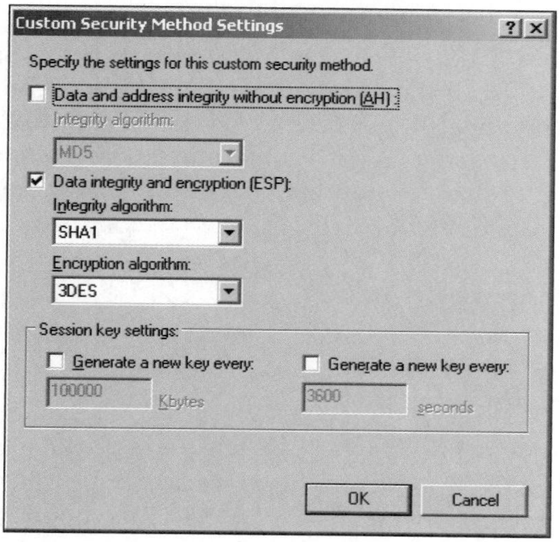

Figure 9-26 Specifying a custom security method for a new filter action

The custom settings for a security method also allow you to define how often the key used for encryption and integrity is changed. You can specify that the key be changed based on

9

the amount of data transmitted, time passed, or both. If you do not define this setting, the default values of 100 MB and 1 hour are used. The first parameter reached triggers a key change. For example, if an IPSec communication sends 100 MB of data in 20 minutes, then a key change is triggered. Likewise, if less than 100 MB of data is transmitted in an IPSec communication, then a key change is triggered after 1 hour.

Cryptography Algorithms

IPSec offers both data integrity and encryption. Each type of cryptography uses different algorithms.

The two algorithms that can be used for AH and ESP data integrity are:

- *Secure Hashing Algorithm (SHA1)*—The **Secure Hashing Algorithm (SHA1)** is a widely used hashing algorithm that produces a 160-bit message digest. Federal Information Processing Standards (FIPS) specify this algorithm for use in U.S. federal government contracts.

- *Message Digest 5* (MD5)—**Message Digest 5 (MD5)** is the most commonly used hashing algorithm for commercial applications. It produces a 129-bit message digest. It is less secure than SHA1, but it is faster.

The two algorithms that can be used for ESP data encryption are:

- *Data Encryption Standard (DES)*—The **Data Encryption Standard (DES)** is a common encryption algorithm that uses a 56-bit key. It was first designated for U.S. federal government use in 1977. Because of enhancements in computational power, it is now recommended that 3DES be used instead.

- *Triple Data Encryption Standard (3DES)*—The **Triple Data Encryption Standard (3DES)** is an encryption algorithm that performs three rounds of encryption using three different 56-bit keys, resulting in an effective key length of 169-bits. It is significantly stronger than DES and requires significantly more computational power to use. Windows 2000 computers must have installed the High Encryption Pack or have Service Pack 2 to use 3DES.

Activity 9-6: Creating a Filter Action

Time Required: 15 minutes

Objective: Create a new filter action that enforces encryption.

Description: A filter action needs to be defined to describe what will be done when the security level matches the filter list for FTP packets. The university policy dictates that secure transmissions use SHA1 for data integrity and 3DES for data encryption.

1. If necessary, start your server and log on as **Administrator**.

2. Click **Start**, point to **Administrative Tools**, and click **Local Security Policy**.

3. Right-click **IP Security Policies on Local Computer**, and click **Manage IP filter lists and filter actions**.

4. Click the **Manage Filter Actions** tab, and click **Add**.

5. Click **Next** to start the IP Security Filter Action Wizard.

6. In the Name box, type **FTP Packet Filter Action**, and click **Next**.

7. Confirm that **Negotiate security** is selected, and click **Next**.

8. Confirm that **Do not communicate with computers that do not support IPSec** is selected, and click **Next**.

9. Click **Custom**, and click **Settings**.

10. Verify that **Data integrity and encryption (ESP)** is selected. Also verify that the Integrity algorithm is set to **SHA1**, and that the Encryption algorithm is set to **3DES**. Click **OK** to close the Custom Security Method Settings dialog box.

11. When the IP Security Policy Management message box appears, indicating that the settings you have selected correspond to an encryption and integrity security level and that your security method's type will be changed to reflect this state, click **OK**.

12. Click **Next**, and click **Finish**.

13. Click **Close**.

14. Close the Local Security Settings window.

Activity 9-7: Creating an IPSec Policy Using a Customized Filter List and Filter Action

Time Required: 25 minutes

Objective: Create an IPSec policy and add a rule using the customized filter list and filter action you have created.

Description: The filter list and action you have created earlier to secure FTP traffic at Great Arctic North University are not yet part of a policy. You must create an FTP policy and add a new rule using the FTP filter list and filter action you created. Finally, to use the policy, you must assign it.

1. If necessary, start your server and log on as **Administrator**.

2. Click **Start**, point to **Administrative Tools**, and click **Local Security Policy**.

3. Right-click **IP Security Policies on Local Computer**, and click **Create IP Security Policy**.

4. Click **Next** to start the IP Security Policy Wizard.

5. In the Name box, type **FTP Traffic Policy**. In the Description box, type **Secure FTP Traffic**, and click **Next**.

6. Confirm that **Activate the default response rule** is selected, and click **Next**.

7. Select **Use a certificate from this certification authority (CA)**, and click **Browse**. Ensure that **Microsoft Root Certificate Authority** is selected and click **OK**. Click **Next**.

8. Click **Edit properties** to deselect it, and click **Finish**.

9. Note that the FTP Traffic Policy now appears in the right pane as an IP Security Policy.

10. Close the Local Security Settings window.

11. Click **Start**, point to **Administrative Tools**, and click **Local Security Policy**.

12. Right-click **FTP Traffic Policy**, and click **Properties**.

13. Click **Add**.

14. Click **Next** to start the Create IP Security Rule Wizard.

15. Confirm that **This rule does not specify a tunnel** is selected, and click **Next**.

16. Confirm that **All network connections** is selected, and click **Next**.

17. Click the **FTP** option button to select it, and click **Next**.

18. Click the **FTP Packet Filter Action** option button to select it, and click **Next**.

19. Select **Use a certificate from this certification authority (CA)**, and click **Browse**. Ensure that **Microsoft Root Certificate Authority** is selected, and click **OK**. Click **Next**.

20. Click **Finish**.

21. Click **OK**.

22. Right-click the **FTP Traffic Policy**, and click **Assign**.

23. Close the Local Security Settings window.

24. Click **Start**, point to **Administrative Tools**, and click **Services**.

25. Scroll down through the list of services, right-click **IPSEC Services**, and click **Restart**.

26. Close the Services window.

TROUBLESHOOTING IPSEC

IPSec troubleshooting can cover a wide range of possibilities dealing with general network issues, IPSec-specific configuration settings, and Group Policy settings.

NOTE

Remember that both participants in an SA must be configured to use the same modes, encryption algorithms, and authentication method.

The most common IPSec troubleshooting tools are:

- Ping
- IPSec Security Monitor
- Event Viewer
- Resultant Set of Policy
- Netsh
- Oakley logs
- Network Monitor

Ping

The ping utility is used to test network connectivity between two hosts. The default IPSec policies permit ICMP packets and do not interfere with the operation of ping. This utility does not test IPSec specifically, but it can be used to confirm that the two hosts can communicate. If they cannot communicate, they are not able to create an IPSec SA.

IPSec Security Monitor

IPSec Security Monitor is an MMC snap-in that allows you to view the status of IPSec SAs. IPSec Security Monitor can be used to confirm that an SA was negotiated between two hosts. In addition, IPSec Security Monitor can be used to view the configuration of the IPSec policy that is applied.

Activity 9-8: Verifying an IPSec Security Association

Time Required: 25 minutes

Objective: Verify that an IPSec policy that you have created is working.

Description: To verify that the ICMP Traffic Policy you created in a previous exercise is working, you will apply it to your computer and use the IPSec Monitor snap-in to show the status of IPSec security associations. The test you perform will involve using the ping utility to connect to your partner's computer using ICMP.

1. If necessary, start your server and log on as **Administrator**.
2. Click **Start**, point to **Administrative Tools**, and click **Local Security Policy**.
3. Under Security Settings, click **IP Security Policies on Local Computer**.
4. In the right pane, right-click **ICMP Traffic Policy**, and click **Assign**. Notice that under the column Policy Assigned, "Yes" now appears next to the description for this policy.
5. Close the Local Security Settings window.

6. Click **Start**, point to **Administrative Tools**, and click **Services**.

7. Scroll down through the list of services, right-click **IPSEC Services**, and click **Restart**.

8. Close the Services window.

9. Click **Start**, click **Run**, type **mmc**, and press **Enter**.

10. Click **File**, click **Add/Remove Snap-in**, click **Add**, scroll through the list and double-click **IP Security Monitor**, click **Close**, and click **OK**.

11. Double-click **IP Security Monitor**.

12. Double-click your server.

13. Click **Active Policy**. Notice the information displayed in the details pane.

14. Double-click **Main Mode**, and click **Security Associations**. At the moment, it shows that there are no items to display in this view.

15. Next, you and your partner establish a secure connection between your computers. You can view the status of security associations on your computer during the connection.

    a. Click **Start**, click **Run**, type **cmd** and press **Enter**.

    b. Next, type **ping** *IP_address* where *IP_address* is the IP address of your partner's Local Area Connection. Note that you see Negotiating IP Security in the output of the ping command on one or both of your computers. Repeat the ping command until you see replies from your partner's computer. If the policies have been applied properly on each server, a secure connection should be established.

16. In the IPSecurity Monitor window, click **Action**, and click **Refresh**. Note the details of the security association that has now been established between the two servers.

17. Close all open windows. If asked to save console settings, click **No**.

Event Viewer

The IPSec Policy Agent automatically writes events to the security event log. These show the configuration settings that IPSec is using as well as events generated during the creation of SAs. These events are only written to the log if the Audit logon events option has been enabled in the local security policy or Group Policy.

Additional information from the IPSec Policy Agent can be written to the system log. To enable this logging, you must modify the registry. Create and set the key HKEY_LOCAL_ MACHINE\SYSTEM\CurrentControlSet\Services\IPSec\EnableDiagnostics to a value of 7.

Resultant Set of Policy

Applying Group policies can be quite complex. If you are attempting to distribute and apply IPSec policies through Group Policy, and they are not functioning as you expect, then you can use the **Resultant Set of Policy (RSoP) snap-in**. The RSoP snap-in allows you to view which policies apply, and to simulate the application of new policies to test their results.

Netsh

The Netsh command allows you to configure a number of network-related settings. This is useful when batch scripts are used to remotely make changes on clients and servers. Configuration categories include: bridging, DHCP, diagnostics, IP configuration, remote access, routing, WINS, and remote procedure calls.

IPSec configuration can also be modified using Netsh, including:

- Viewing policies
- Adding policies
- Deleting policies

Oakley Logs

Oakley logs track the establishment of SAs. This type of logging is not enabled by default and must be enabled with the command "netsh ipsec dynamic set config ikelogging 1". The log file created is C:\WINDOWS\Debug\Oakley.LOG. By default, this registry key does not exist.

Network Monitor

Network Monitor can be used to view packets that are traveling on the network, and to identify IPSec traffic. However, it cannot view encrypted information inside of an IPSec packet.

Network Monitor is useful for determining whether packets are being properly transmitted between computers, but Network Monitor is not useful for troubleshooting application-level problems if the traffic is encrypted. For application troubleshooting purposes, you may need to disable IPSec, or encryption within IPSec.

Activity 9-9: Disabling IPSec

Time Required: 5 minutes

Objective: Disable IPSec policies that have been applied.

Description: In this activity, you will unassign all IPSec policies so that they do not interfere with activities later in the course.

1. If necessary, start your server and log on as **Administrator**.

2. Click **Start**, point to **Administrative Tools**, and click **Local Security Policy**.

3. Right-click **ICMP Traffic Policy**, and click **Un-assign**.

4. Close the Local Security Settings window.

5. Click **Start**, point to **Administrative Tools**, and click **Services**.

6. Scroll through the list of services until you see IPSEC Services.

7. Right-click **IPSEC Services**, and click **Restart**.

8. Close the Services window.

CHAPTER SUMMARY

- IPV4 has no built in security mechanisms and uses IPSec as an add-on protocol to make communication secure from packet sniffing, data replay, data modification, and address spoofing.

- IPSec operates at the Network layer and can be used by any IP application without the application being modified.

- Pre-Windows 2000 operating systems do not support IPSec.

- IPSec cannot be used with NAT.

- IPSec uses authentication, cryptography and digital signatures to provide secure IP communication.

- Authentication is used to verify the identity of a user or computer on the network.

- Cryptography uses algorithms and keys to encrypt and decrypt information. Symmetrical encryption uses the same key to encrypt and decrypt information. Asymmetrical encryption uses a pair of keys. Information that is encrypted by one key is decrypted by the other key. These keys are often referred to as the private key and the public key. Hash encryption is a form of one-way encryption. Anything encrypted with hash encryption cannot be decrypted.

- A digital signature does not ensure the confidentiality of the information, only its integrity and authentication.

- IPSec AH mode does not perform data encryption, but can authenticate and guarantee data integrity for an entire IP packet, including the IP headers.

- IPSec ESP mode has the ability to perform data encryption and authentication, and guarantees data integrity for the data portion of the packet, but not the IP headers.

- Transport mode is used between two hosts. Tunnel mode is used between two routers.

- The Windows Server 2003 implementation can perform authentication using a preshared key, certificates, or Kerberos. IKE is used to negotiate the security association.

- IPSec policies contain rules that control authentication, which traffic is affected, what is done to the affected traffic, the type of connections affected, and whether the computer is a tunnel endpoint.

- Filter lists are used in IPSec rules to define the packets affected by a rule. Filter actions are used to define what is done to the traffic that matches the filter list.

- The two algorithms used for data integrity are SHA1 and MD5.

- The two algorithms used for data encryption are DES and 3DES.

- Tools that can be used to troubleshoot IPSec include: ping, IPSec Security Monitor snap-in, Event Viewer, Resultant Set of Policy snap-in, Netsh, Oakley logs, and Network Monitor.

KEY TERMS

9

address spoofing — The act of falsifying the source IP address in an IP packet, usually for malicious purposes.

algorithm — A formula used to process data for encryption or decryption.

asymmetrical encryption — An encryption method that uses two different keys. When one key is used to encrypt a message, the other key must be used to decrypt it.

authentication — The process through which a computer's identity is verified.

authentication headers (AH) mode — The IPSec mode that performs authentication and ensures data integrity on the entire IP packet, including the headers.

certificate — A part of public key infrastructure that contains a public key and an expiry date. Certificates are presented for authentication and to share public keys.

Certificate Services — A service installed on Windows Server 2003 that allows it to act as a certification authority.

certification authority (CA) — A server that issues certificates.

ciphertext — Data that has been encrypted.

cryptography — The process of encrypting and decrypting messages and files using an algorithm.

Data Encryption Standard (DES) — An algorithm for data encryption defined by the U.S. government in 1977 that uses a 56-bit key.

data modification — Modifying the contents of packets that have been captured with a packet sniffer before resending them on the network.

data replay — Resending packets that have been previously captured with a packet sniffer.

decryption — The process of making encrypted data readable.

digital signature — A process that uses both hash encryption and asymmetrical encryption to ensure data integrity and nonrepudiation.

encapsulating security payload (ESP) mode — The IPSec mode that performs authentication, data integrity, and encryption on the data portion of an IP packet. Integrity checking of IP headers is not performed.

encryption — The process of rendering data unreadable by applying an algorithm.

hash encryption — A type of one-way encryption that cannot be decrypted. It is used to store information such as passwords and to create checksums.

hash value — A summary of the data being encrypted using hash encryption.

Internet Key Exchange (IKE) — A protocol used by IPSec to negotiate security parameters, perform authentication, and ensure the secure exchange of encryption keys.

IP filter list — A list of IP protocols that are affected by a rule in an IPSec policy.

IP Security (IPSec) — A protocol that adds security functions to IPv4.

IPSec filter action — Defines what is done to traffic that matches an IP filter list in an IPSec rule.

IPSec policy — A set of rules that defines how packets are treated by IPSec. An IPSec policy must be applied to be in use.

IPSec rules — The combination of an IP filter list and an IPSec filter action.

IPSec Security Monitor — An MMC snap-in that allows the monitoring of IPSec security associations and configuration.

Kerberos — The preferred authentication method used by Active Directory. It is the simplest authentication method to implement for IPSec if all devices are part of the same Active Directory forest.

key — A number, usually large to prevent it from being guessed, used in combination with an algorithm to encrypt data.

Message Digest 5 — A hashing algorithm that produces a 129-bit message digest.

Oakley logs — A type of logging that tracks the establishment of security associations.

packet sniffer — Software used to view (capture) all packets that are traveling on a network.

preshared key — An IPSec authentication method whereby each device is preconfigured with a string of text.

private key — The key in asymmetrical encryption that is seen only by the user to which it is issued.

public key — The key in asymmetrical encryption that is freely distributed to other users.

Resultant Set of Policy (RSoP) snap-in — An MMC snap-in that is used to troubleshoot the implementation of Group Policies.

Secure Hashing Algorithm (SHA1) — A hashing algorithm that produces a 160-bit message digest.

Secure Socket Layer (SSL) — A Transport layer protocol that encrypts data communication between a client and service. Both the client and service must be written to support SSL.

security association (SA) — The security terms negotiated between two hosts using IPSec.

symmetrical encryption — Encryption that uses the same key to encrypt and decrypt data.

transport mode — The IPSec mode used when two hosts create a security association directly between them.

Triple Data Encryption Standard (3DES) — A data encryption algorithm that uses three 56-bit keys in three rounds to give an effective key length of 168 bits.

tunnel endpoint — In tunnel mode, this is the other end of the tunnel with the local host.
tunnel mode — The IPSec mode used when two routers encapsulate all traffic transferred between two or more networks.
X.509 — A standard for certificates that was created by the International Telecommunication Union – Telecommunication (ITU-T).

REVIEW QUESTIONS

1. IPSec operates at what layer of the OSI model?
    a. Application
    b. Presentation
    c. Session
    d. Network
    e. Data Link
    f. Physical

2. Which operating systems do not support IPSec? (Choose all that apply.)
    a. Windows 95
    b. Windows 98
    c. Windows NT
    d. Windows 2000 Professional
    e. Windows XP Professional

3. Which of the following statements about IPSec is false?
    a. IPSec adds complexity to the network.
    b. IPSec is a standards track protocol.
    c. IPSec can be routed through NAT.
    d. IPSec requires additional processing power.

4. IPSec used between two hosts is called _____ .
    a. tunnel mode
    b. transport mode
    c. encrypted mode
    d. VPN mode

5. You want to implement IPSec to authenticate two computers and encrypt data. Which mode do you select?
    a. AH mode
    b. ESP mode
    c. tunnel mode
    d. transport mode

6. Which of the following is not encrypted with the default IPSec policy? (Choose all that apply.)

   a. FTP

   b. HTTP

   c. ping

   d. tracert

   e. SMTP

7. Once an IPSec policy has been defined, it takes effect immediately. True or false?

8. Which of the following is not an authentication option when creating an IPSec policy?

   a. password

   b. Kerberos

   c. certificate

   d. preshared key

9. Which of the following cryptography algorithms is used for U.S. government contracts?

   a. MD5

   b. SHA1

   c. DES

   d. 3DES

10. Which of the following cryptography algorithms uses three different 56-bit keys for encryption?

    a. MD5

    b. SHA1

    c. DES

    d. 3DES

11. In tunnel mode, what traffic is encrypted?

    a. all workstation-to-router traffic

    b. all workstation-to-workstation traffic

    c. only router-to-router traffic

    d. all traffic

    e. none of the above

12. The default IPSec policy is configured to use what authentication method?

    a. Kerberos

    b. preshared key

    c. certificates

    d. access token

13. You want to enable IPSec encryption on a Windows Server 2003 server and still allow communication with Windows 98 workstations. Which filter action(s) would you implement?

    a. Permit

    b. Request Security (Optional)

    c. Require Security

    d. all of the above

14. Which of the following cryptography algorithms are used for ESP data encryption? (Choose all that apply.)

    a. SHA1

    b. MD5

    c. DES

    d. 3DES

15. Which troubleshooting utility allows you to simulate the application of new IPSec policies?

    a. IPSec Monitor

    b. Resultant Set of Policy

    c. Network Monitor

    d. Oakley logs

    e. Netsh

16. AH mode performs which of the following functions? (Choose all that apply.)

    a. authenticates two endpoints

    b. generates a checksum to verify that a packet was not modified in transit

    c. encrypts data

    d. authenticates applications

17. In which of the following situations can Kerberos be used for authentication in IPSec? (Choose all that apply.)

    a. two routers on the Internet

    b. two workstations in the same Active Directory domain

    c. two workstations in the same Active Directory forest

    d. two workstations on the same subnet

18. How many IPSec policies can be assigned to a workstation?

   a. one

   b. two

   c. five

   d. ten

   e. an unlimited number

19. A combination of characters entered at both endpoints of an IPSec connection is called a _____ .

   a. password

   b. certificate

   c. preshared key

   d. shared secret

20. By default, Oakley logs are stored in which folder?

   a. \WINDOWS\OAKLEY

   b. \WINDOWS\LOGS

   c. \WINDOWS\SYSTEM32\OAKLEY

   d. \WINDOWS\DEBUG

CASE PROJECTS

Case Project 9-1: Selecting an IPSec Policy

Because of security concerns, an IPSec security policy is being evaluated for the university. The board of directors wants all communication between staff workstations and all servers encrypted. They would also like to encrypt all communication between students' computers and the servers. Student computers run various operating systems including Windows 95, UNIX, Linux, Windows 2000, and Windows XP.

How would you implement IPSec to encrypt as much TCP/IP traffic as possible with minimum overhead?

Case Project 9-2: Encrypting Remote Traffic

The university has three satellite campuses set up in various remote locations. Students can take courses and connect to the university's servers from the remote locations. Each remote campus connects to the main campus using a Cisco router. Your manager would like to encrypt all traffic from the remote sites through the Internet to the main campus. He has recommended implementing IPSec in transport mode using third-party certificates. What are your concerns?

Case Project 9-3: Evaluating IPSec

A junior administrator has commented that implementing IPSec is a waste of time. He used Network Monitor to capture ICMP packets between two systems and was able to view the packet details. He also doesn't believe that IPSec can protect the university computers from hackers. What do you tell him?

9

10

REMOTE ACCESS

After reading this chapter, you will be able to:

- Describe the purpose and features of Windows Server 2003 remote access capabilities
- Enable and configure Routing and Remote Access Service as a dial-up server
- Enable and configure Routing and Remote Access Service as a VPN server
- Configure a remote access server
- Allow remote clients access to network resources
- Create and configure remote access policies
- Troubleshoot remote access

Remote access, used to provide users outside an office access to resources on the internal network, is a vital component to many networks today. Without remote access, frequent business travelers, such as salespeople, would not have the use of the basic resources necessary to complete their jobs. In this chapter, you will learn about the remote access capabilities of Windows Server 2003. You will learn how to create and configure dial-up and VPN connections, how to grant users access to network resources, as well as how to create remote access policies. Finally, you will learn how to troubleshoot remote access problems.

Remote Access Overview

Remote access allows remote and **mobile users** access to network resources on the internal network, including files, printers, databases, and e-mail, among others. Traveling salespeople, for instance, often need network access from hotel rooms and client sites to place orders and retrieve updated price lists, and executives often need to access their e-mail from hotels and conferences when they are on the road. Network administrators also need remote access to network resources, because they can save hours of valuable time if they can repair after-hours network problems remotely from home. Windows Server 2003 has the ability to be a remote access server.

Dial-up Remote Access

Remote access using **dial-up** connections is the oldest type of remote access. In the past, this type of connection was very slow, and transferring even the smallest files was a tedious process. However, with advances in **modem** technology, current speeds are more reasonable when transferring documents less than 1 MB in size.

A dial-up connection allows two computers to connect and transfer information using modems and a phone line. The modems convert the digital signals of the computer to analog signals that can be transmitted across the phone line. Both the dial-up server and dial-up client must have a modem. When the analog signals reach the computers on each end of the phone line, the modems then convert the signals back to digital format, which can then be interpreted by the computers.

When a connection is created between a dial-up server and a dial-up client, the client can access resources on the network on which the dial-up server is located. From the perspective of the user, the modem acts like a network card to provide access to network resources. Files can be downloaded, and e-mail can be read.

Current modems can download information at 56 Kbps when using modems that are based on the **v.90** or **v.92** standards from the ITU-T. These standards are asymmetrical standards that allow faster download speeds than upload speeds. The v.90 standard allows uploads at 33.6 Kbps, and the v.92 standard allows uploads at 48 Kbps.

Line noise in the phone system can limit connection speeds. Line noise can be introduced by low-quality phones connected to the circuit, poor-quality lines from the phone system provider, or electrical interference. The existence of line noise can likely cause modem connections to be limited to 50 Kbps or less.

The main benefit of dial-up connections is availability. Roaming users almost always have access to a phone line. Most hotels include a data port for dial-up connectivity as a standard feature in rooms.

The main drawback of dial-up connections is their speed. When compared with connectivity options, such as cable modems and DSL modems, a dial-up connection is very slow.

In addition, maintenance of a **modem pool** at the office for dial-up users can be expensive and time-consuming as new standards are introduced and modems need to be replaced.

VPN Remote Access

A **virtual private network (VPN)** uses a public network to transmit private information. Encryption is used to keep the private information from being read by unauthorized persons as it traverses the public network. This allows a relatively inexpensive public network to be used in the place of a relatively expensive private network.

The public network most commonly used for VPN connections is the Internet. The client computers can be connected to the Internet via a dial-up connection, a company LAN, or broadband such as cable modem, or DSL modem. VPN remote access started to become popular in the mid 1990s. As the Internet became popular and more available, the popularity of VPN remote access increased.

Once connected to the Internet, client computers initiate a VPN connection with a VPN server. The VPN client is then able to access the network on which the VPN server is located, in the same way that a dial-up client is able to access the network on which the dial-up server is located.

Maintaining a VPN server is much easier than maintaining a dial-up server. A VPN server generally uses a standard network card to communicate with the Internet; thus, no special hardware, such as a modem pool, is required.

The speed of VPN connections is potentially much higher than that of dial-up connections. When high-speed access to the Internet is available through broadband or a company LAN, a VPN connection may be as fast as 10 Mbps. However, if Internet access is provided through a dial-up connection, then the VPN connection is limited to the speed of the dial-up connection.

The main advantages of VPN connections are their potentially high speed and the reduced maintenance achieved by eliminating a modem pool. The main drawback to VPN connections is the security risk presented by allowing access to network resources from the Internet.

ENABLING AND CONFIGURING A DIAL-UP SERVER

Windows Server 2003 uses the **Routing and Remote Access Service (RRAS)** to act as a dial-up server. This service is always installed, but is not configured by default. Using the Routing and Remote Access Setup Wizard, you can configure RRAS as a dial-up server, a VPN server, or a router.

For your server to act as a dial-up server, it must have a modem installed. Modems are installed using Phone and Modem Options in Control Panel. The first time you open Phone and Modem Options you are forced to configure a **location**, as shown in Figure 10-1.

Figure 10-1   Configuring a location

Locations are used to control how Windows Server 2003 creates dial-up connections. For instance, locations allow you to specify whether any special codes need to be dialed from this location. This is useful if the internal phone system in a company requires you to dial 9 to get an outside line.

To add a modem to your server, click the Modems tab of Phone and Modem Options, and click Add. This starts the Add Hardware Wizard, as shown in Figure 10-2.

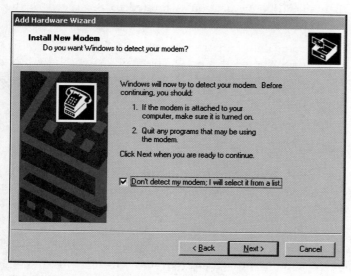

Figure 10-2   Add Hardware Wizard

By default, Windows Server 2003 attempts to find the modem through Plug and Play. However, if the modem is not a Plug-and-Play device, or has known Plug-and-Play detection problems, you can instead choose to select your modem from a list of known vendors. This can also be used in a test environment when a physical modem is not present, but a modem driver must be configured for other software to be installed or configured.

If Plug and Play is unable to find a modem, or if you have chosen to manually add your modem, then you are prompted to choose a driver from a list, as shown in Figure 10-3. Windows Server 2003 ships with several standard modem drivers, but you can also use drivers from a vendor by clicking the Have Disk option, and browsing to the location of the driver.

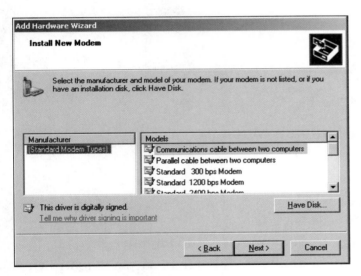

Figure 10-3   Modem drivers

After choosing a driver, you must choose the **COM port** to which the driver is connected, as shown in Figure 10-4. A COM port is a serial port. External modems normally use either COM1 or COM2, because these represent internal serial ports that are built into the computers. Internal modems normally use a COM port numbered from COM3 to COM8 that is chosen by Plug and Play.

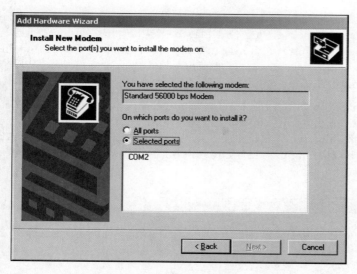

Figure 10-4   Selecting a COM port

Activity 10-1: Installing a Modem

Time Required: 10 minutes

Objective: Install a modem on your server.

Description: You want to configure Windows Server 2003 as a dial-up server. Before configuring RRAS, you must install a modem.

1. If necessary, start your server and log on as **Administrator**.

2. Click **Start**, point to **Control Panel**, and click **Phone and Modem Options**.

3. In the What area code (or city code) are you in now box, type **555**, and click **OK**.

4. Click the **Modems** tab.

5. Click **Add**.

6. Click the **Don't detect my modem; I will select it from a list** checkbox to select this option.

You are selecting this option because your server does not have a modem physically installed. You are installing the software manually to simulate a modem being installed. If a modem were physically installed in this server, then you would allow the wizard to detect the modem.

7. Click **Next**.

8. In the Models box, click **Standard 56000 bps Modem**, and click **Next**.

9. Click **COM1** to select this as the serial port on which the modem is installed, and click **Next**.

10. Click **Finish** to close the Add Hardware Wizard.

11. Click **OK** to close the Phone and Modem Options window.

Enabling RRAS for Dial-up Connections

Management of RRAS is done with the Routing and Remote Access snap-in available in the Administrative Tools menu. When the Routing and Remote Access snap-in is started for the first time, you will notice a red arrow pointing down beside the name of your server, as shown in Figure 10-5. This indicates that RRAS is not started. In this case, it is because RRAS has not yet been configured.

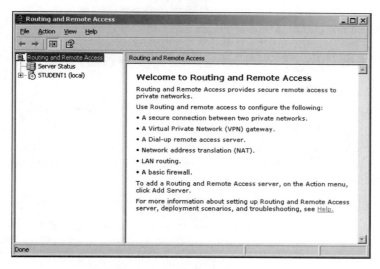

Figure 10-5   RRAS not configured

The Routing and Remote Access Wizard is used to enable and configure RRAS for the first time. After you have completed the wizard and RRAS is started, the arrow beside your server in the Routing and Remote Access snap-in will point up and be green, as shown in Figure 10-6.

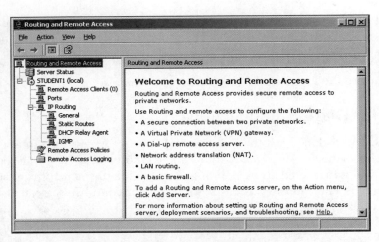

Figure 10-6   RRAS configured and functional

Activity 10-2: Enabling RRAS as a Dial-up Server

Time Required: 15 minutes

Objective: Configure RRAS on your server to act as a remote access server.

Description: Great Arctic North University needs to provide professors with access to the network file system when they are away on conferences. Most professors will be accessing the remote access server using a laptop computer and hotel phone line. To support this, you will configure your server as a dial-up server.

1. If necessary, start your server and log on as **Administrator**.

2. Click **Start**, point to **Administrative Tools**, and click **Routing and Remote Access**. Notice that your server has a red down arrow beside it to indicate that RRAS is not functional.

3. Right-click your server, and click **Configure and Enable Routing and Remote Access**.

4. Click **Next** to begin the Routing and Remote Access Server Setup Wizard.

5. Confirm that the Remote access (dial-up or VPN) option is selected, as shown in Figure 10-7, and click **Next**.

6. Click the **Dial-up** checkbox to allow this server to be a dial-up server, as shown in Figure 10-8, and click **Next**.

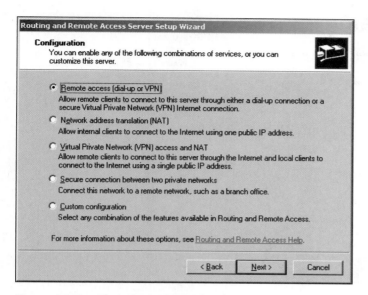

Figure 10-7   Choosing a RRAS configuration

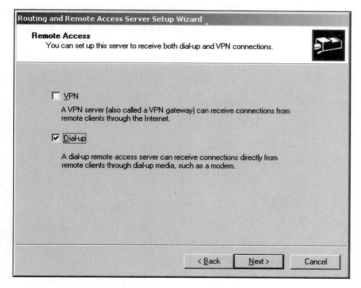

Figure 10-8   Choosing a RRAS server type

7. If necessary, click **Local Area Connection** in the Network Interfaces box to select it, as shown in Figure 10-9, and click **Next**. This indicates that dial–up clients receive IP addresses on the Local Area Connection network.

8. Confirm that **Automatically** is selected as the method of IP address assignment, as shown in Figure 10-10, and click **Next**.

10

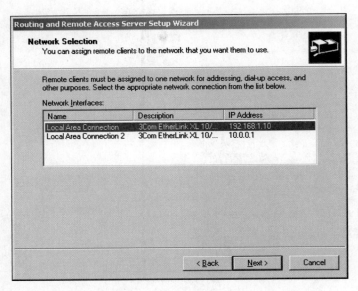

Figure 10-9   Choosing an interface for dial-up clients

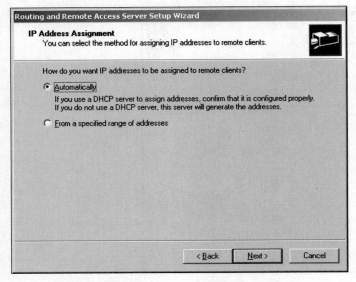

Figure 10-10   Choosing how IP addresses are assigned to dial-up clients

9. Confirm that **No, use Routing and Remote Access to authenticate connection requests** is selected, as shown in Figure 10-11, and click **Next**. RADIUS authentication will be discussed later in Chapter 11.

10. Click **Finish** to complete the Routing and Remote Access Server Setup Wizard.

11. Click **OK** to close the warning dialog box about DHCP relay.

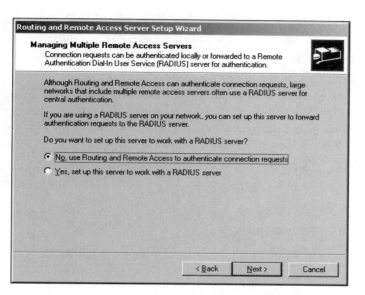

Figure 10-11 Configuring authentication for dial-up clients

12. Notice that the arrow next to your server is now green and pointing up to indicate that RRAS is configured and started.

13. Close the Routing and Remote Access snap-in.

Dial-up Protocols

LAN protocols and **remote access protocols** need to be considered when configuring Windows Server 2003 for dial-up networking. The LAN protocols supported by RRAS for dial-up networking are TCP/IP, IPX/SPX, and AppleTalk. Remote access protocols supported by RRAS for dial-up networking are **Point-to-Point Protocol (PPP)** and **Serial Line Internet Protocol (SLIP)**.

When a dial-up client is connected to the dial-up server, it has access to the resources on the LAN. The same protocols required by client computers to access resources on the LAN are required by dial-up clients to access resources on the LAN through the dial-up server. Most dial-up clients use TCP/IP, but support for IPX/SPX is included to support older applications, and support for AppleTalk is included to support Macintosh clients. These LAN protocols can also be used for VPN connections.

Remote access protocols are used only for dial-up connections, not VPN connections. SLIP is an older, and rarely used, remote access protocol supported only when Windows Server 2003 is acting as a dial-up client. SLIP cannot be used when Windows Server 2003 is a dial-up server. The only time SLIP is used is when dialing up to older UNIX remote access servers, and TCP/IP is the only LAN protocol required.

PPP is a newer remote access protocol that is in common use. Windows Server 2003 can use PPP when acting as a dial-up client or server. PPP has a number of advantages over SLIP, including the ability to automatically configure clients with IP configuration information, wide availability, and the ability to use multiple LAN protocols.

Two remote access protocols supported in Windows 2000 Server have been removed in Windows Server 2003. The Microsoft RAS protocol used to support older Microsoft clients using the NetBEUI protocol has been removed. As well, the AppleTalk Remote Access Protocol used to support older Macintosh clients has been removed.

The selection of a remote access protocol when using Windows Server 2003 as a dial-up client is made in the properties of the dial-up connection on the Networking tab, as shown in Figure 10-12.

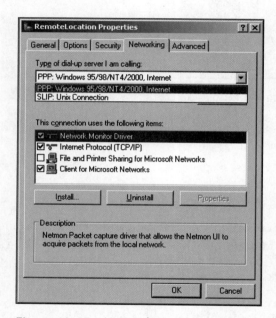

Figure 10-12   Networking tab in the properties of a dial-up connection

Activity 10-3: Creating a Dial-up Connection

Time required: 10 minutes

Objective: Configure your server with a dial-up connection.

Description: One of the more remote locations for Great Arctic North University is unable to use Internet connectivity to communicate with the other locations. As a short-term solution, you would like to dial up the server in the remote location to download data on a daily basis. You have configured an old UNIX server in the remote location to act as a dial-up server. You now need to configure your server to be a dial-up client using the SLIP remote access protocol.

1. If necessary, start your server and log on as **Administrator**.

2. Click **Start**, point to **Control Panel**, and double-click **Network Connections**.

3. Double-click **New Connection Wizard** to start the New Connection Wizard.

4. Click **Next** to begin the New Connection Wizard.

5. Click **Connect to the network at my workplace**, and click **Next**.

6. Confirm that **Dial-up connection** is selected, and click **Next**.

7. In the Company Name box, type **RemoteLocation**, and click **Next**. This is the name you see for the connection after it is created. It is best to use a descriptive name here.

8. In the Phone number box, type **555-1212**, and click **Next**.

9. In the next window, confirm that **Anyone's use** is selected, and click **Next**. If the My use only option were selected, only the user account that is creating the dial-up connection could initiate the dial-up connection at a later time.

10. Click **Finish**.

11. In the Connect RemoteLocation window, click **Properties**, and click the **Networking** tab.

12. Click the **Type of dial-up server I am calling** box, and click **SLIP: Unix Connection**.

13. Click **OK** to save the new settings.

14. Click **Cancel** because you don't want to connect to the remote server right now.

15. Close the Network Connections window.

PPP has several options that can be enabled to enhance performance. These options are enabled using the Routing and Remote Access snap-in on the PPP tab of the server properties, as shown in Figure 10-13.

Enabling the **Multilink** connections option allows Windows Server 2003 to combine multiple dial-up connections into a single logical connection to speed up data transfer. For example, a client computer with two modems can dial up the remote access server and connect to two modems on the remote access server. When data is transferred between the client and the server, the speed of the connection is twice as fast as a single dial-up connection. To use two modems, there must be two phone lines.

If the Dynamic bandwidth control using BAP or BACP option is enabled, it allows the multilink connection to dynamically add and drop modems from a dial-up connection as the amount of data transferred varies. This is very useful for long-term connections between physical locations, particularly if long-distance charges are incurred, because phone line use is minimized. The criteria used for controlling the addition or removal of modems from the multilink connection are set in remote access policies. **Remote access policies** are covered later in this chapter.

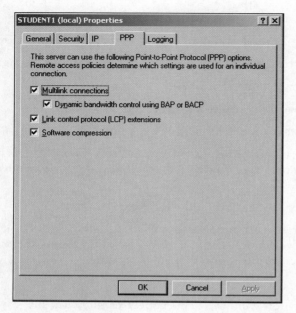

Figure 10-13   PPP tab of RRAS server properties

Enabling the Link control protocol (LCP) extensions option allows the dial-in server to use enhancements to **Link Control Protocol (LCP)** that control **callbacks** and other options. LCP is a protocol that controls the establishment of PPP sessions. If this option is disabled, then using callback is not possible.

If the Software compression option is enabled, then data transferred on this connection is compressed using Microsoft Point-to-Point Compression Protocol.

ENABLING AND CONFIGURING A VPN SERVER

Windows Server 2003 also uses RRAS to act as a VPN server. In many ways, VPN connections behave like dial-up connections. However, when a remote access server is configured to provide VPN connections, no special equipment is required. All connectivity is accomplished through a regular network card.

Enabling a VPN server is accomplished using the Routing and Remote Access Server Setup Wizard. If RRAS has already been configured, then you must disable routing and remote access before you can reconfigure it with the Routing and Remote Access Server Setup Wizard. You can reconfigure the server manually without the wizard, but this often takes longer and is more prone to error.

The first few windows of the Routing and Remote Access Server Setup Wizard are the same when configuring a VPN server and a dial-up server, including choosing to configure the server as a remote access server. However, when asked the type of remote access server, choose VPN instead of Dial-up, as shown in Figure 10-14.

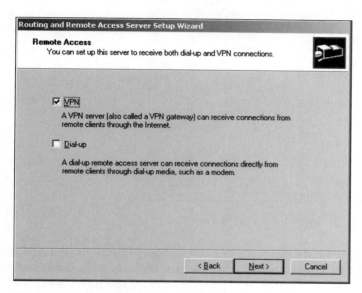

Figure 10-14   Choosing a VPN RRAS server type

The next window, shown in Figure 10-15, asks you to select the network interface that is connected to the Internet. This is the network interface to which VPN clients will be connecting. Checking the Enable security on the selected interface by setting up static packet filters option stops all packets going in and out of the selected interface unless they are part of a VPN connection.

The option to enable **packet filters** should only be chosen if the server has multiple network cards with the filtered card connected to the Internet and the unfiltered cards connected to the LAN. In this configuration, the interface connected to the Internet only responds to VPN traffic, and the VPN clients can connect to the interface on the Internet. After the VPN connection is created, the VPN clients can access any services on the LAN because the internal interface does not restrict traffic. All requests are tunneled inside VPN packets to the VPN server, then unpacked and delivered to the LAN. Responses are tunneled inside VPN packets by the VPN server and sent to the VPN client.

If a VPN server has multiple network interfaces, then VPN clients receive an IP address from an interface not connected to the Internet.

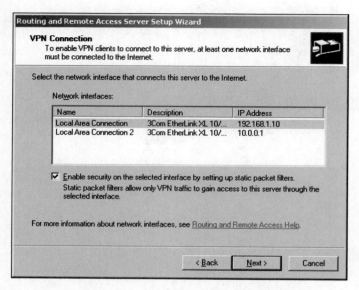

Figure 10-15   Choosing an interface for VPN clients

Just as with a dial–up server, the next window asks you to choose how IP addresses are handed out to VPN clients. If you choose the Automatically option, then the remote access server leases IP addresses from a DHCP server on the network and passes the IP addresses to the VPN clients. If you choose the From a specified range of IP addresses option, then you must configure the remote access server with a static range of IP addresses for it to hand out to VPN clients.

If you use a DHCP server on the network to lease IP addresses to remote access clients, ensure that the DHCP server has enough addresses to accommodate the remote access clients as well as local DHCP clients.

Finally, you must choose how authentication is performed, just as with the dial–up server. Your first choice is the No, use Routing and Remote Access to authenticate connection requests option, and this means that each remote access server performs its own authentication by querying Active Directory and using policies that exist on that server. Your second choice is the Yes, set up this server to work with a RADIUS server option, and this means that all authentication requests are forwarded to a RADIUS server, and the remote access server allows connections based on results from the RADIUS server. The details of how RADIUS functions are covered later in this chapter.

Activity 10-4: Enabling RRAS as a VPN Server

Time Required: 15 minutes

Objective: Enable RRAS as a VPN server.

Description: Several professors have high-speed Internet access at home and would like to use it for remotely accessing files on campus. You will reconfigure your server as a VPN server. The classroom connection will simulate the Internet-connected interface, and the private connection will simulate the LAN interface. The private interface will be configured with a static IP address. For this exercise, your instructor will provide you with your student number and group number.

1. If necessary, start your server and log on as **Administrator**.

2. Click **Start**, point to **Control Panel**, point to **Network Connections**, right-click **Local Area Connection 2**, and click **Properties**.

3. Click **Internet Protocol (TCP/IP)**, and click **Properties**.

4. Ensure that your IP address is $x.0.0.1$ where x is your student number, and the subnet mask is **255.0.0.0**. Click **OK**.

5. Click **Close**.

6. Click **Start**, point to **Administrative Tools**, click **Routing and Remote Access**.

7. Right-click your server, and click **Disable Routing and Remote Access**.

8. Click **Yes** to confirm you want to continue. When RRAS is disabled, a red arrow appears beside your server.

9. Right-click your server, and click **Configure and Enable Routing and Remote Access**.

10. Click **Next** to begin the Routing and Remote Access Server Setup Wizard.

11. Confirm that **Remote access (dial-up or VPN)** is selected, and click **Next**.

12. Click the **VPN** checkbox to configure the server as a VPN server, and click **Next**.

13. Click **Local Area Connection** to select it as the interface that is connected to the Internet.

14. Click the **Enable security on the selected interface by setting up static packet filters** checkbox to disable this option, and click **Next**. In a real-life situation where this server is connected to the Internet, you would normally leave this option on unless the server were providing services in addition to VPN remote access.

15. Click **From a specified range of addresses**, and click **Next**. In the classroom, you are not using DHCP, so you are choosing to hand out IP addresses from a static range. Most networks use DHCP to assign the addresses automatically.

16. Click **New** to create a new address range.

17. In the Start IP address box, type $x.0.0.50$, where x is your student number.

10

18. In the Number of addresses box, type **10**, and click **OK**. For the purposes of this exercise, you only need one IP address to hand out. When a VPN server is put into production, it is configured to hand out one IP address for each simultaneous client connection. This may be many more than the 10 you have just configured.

19. Click **Next**.

20. Confirm that **No, use Routing and Remote Access to authenticate connection requests** is selected, and click **Next**.

21. Click **Finish**.

22. Click **OK** to close the warning dialog box about DHCP relay.

23. Notice that the arrow next to your server is now green and pointing up to indicate that RRAS is configured and started.

24. Close the Routing and Remote Access snap-in.

VPN Protocols

Point-to-Point Tunneling Protocol (PPTP) and **Layer Two Tunneling Protocol (L2TP)** are supported for VPN connections by Windows Server 2003 when configured as a VPN server. By default, 128 PPTP ports and 128 L2TP ports are provided, as shown in Figure 10-16.

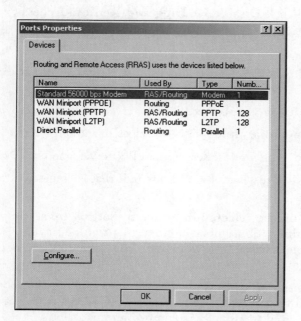

Figure 10-16   PPTP and L2TP port configuration

If your VPN server needs to support more than 128 VPN clients using either protocol, then the number of ports must be increased. If you choose not to allow PPTP because it is less secure than L2TP, then the number of PPTP ports can be reduced to zero. Conversely, if you only want to support PPTP because of its ease of configuration, then the number of L2TP ports can be reduced to zero.

Activity 10-5: Modifying the Default Number of VPN Ports

Time Required: 10 minutes

Objective: Reduce the number of PPTP and L2TP VPN ports to 10 each.

Description: You have a server with RRAS configured to be a VPN server. By default, 128 PPTP ports and 128 L2TP ports have been created. You are concerned that if this number of connections were ever created on the server, your Internet connection would become congested. You have decided to limit the number of PPTP and L2TP connections to 10 each.

1. If necessary, start your server and log on as **Administrator**.

2. Click **Start**, point to **Administrative Tools**, and click **Routing and Remote Access**.

3. If necessary, double-click your server to expand its information.

4. Right-click **Ports**, and click **Properties** to view the port drivers that are installed.

5. Double-click **WAN Miniport (PPTP)**.

6. In the **Maximum ports** box, type **10**, and click **OK**.

7. Click **Yes** to close the warning and continue.

8. Double-click **WAN miniport (L2TP)**.

9. In the **Maximum ports** box, type **10**, and click **OK**.

10. Click **Yes** to close the warning and continue.

11. Click **OK** to close the Ports Properties window.

12. Close the Routing and Remote Access snap-in.

PPTP

PPTP was developed in 1996 by Microsoft, 3Com, U.S. Robotics, and several other companies. As one of the oldest VPN protocols, it is also the most popular and widely supported. It is supported by all versions of Windows starting with Windows 95.

One of the main advantages offered by PPTP is the ability to function properly through NAT. This is very important because many times roaming users are not assigned an Internet-addressable IP address, but are behind NAT implemented at a hotel or client site.

10

Authentication for PPTP is based on a user name and password, and does not authenticate the computers involved in the connection. This means that there is no assurance that the VPN server or VPN client is authorized. For example, a hacker could obtain control of a router and redirect packets destined for a company VPN server to a VPN server controlled by the hacker where passwords are collected. Because the server and client computers are not authenticated, there is no way that the client can prevent this or be warned about it.

The encryption used by PPTP is Microsoft Point-to-Point Encryption (MPPE) protocol. This is a part of PPTP, and no extra configuration is required.

L2TP

L2TP alone is not sufficient to provide a VPN connection. It is designed only for tunneling data, not encrypting it. The L2TP implementation used by Microsoft for VPN connections uses IPSec for encryption of data packets. This protocol is only supported by Windows 2000 and newer Microsoft operating systems.

A data packet is first encapsulated in an L2TP packet. This allows non-IP protocols to travel across an IP-based network. Then, the L2TP packet is encapsulated in an IPSec packet using ESP for data encryption. The encrypted IPSec packet travels from VPN client to VPN server where the L2TP packet is decrypted and removed from the IPSec packet, and the data packet is removed from the L2TP packet. The structure of an L2TP/IPSec packet is shown in Figure 10-17.

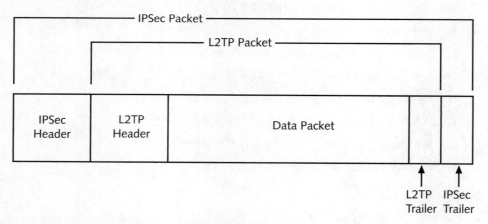

Figure 10-17   Structure of an L2TP/IPSec packet

Until recently, L2TP/IPSec connections could not function properly through NAT. However, if the devices implementing IPSec conform to the specifications laid out in the IPSec Protocol Working Group drafts "Negotiation of NAT-Traversal in the IKE" (draft–ietf–ipsec–nat–t–ike–01.txt) and "UDP Encapsulation of IPSec Packets" (draft–ietf–ipsec–udp–encaps–01.txt), then operation over NAT is possible. Windows Server 2003 supports these drafts. The only Microsoft client operating system that supports these drafts is Windows XP with Service Pack 1.

NOTE

You can find more information about the latest IPSec drafts at *www.ietf.org/html.charters/ipsec-charter.html.*

The authentication used by L2TP is based on a user name and password, just like that used by PPTP. However, the addition of IPSec adds computer–level authentication as well. This means that IPSec authentication needs to be configured on the VPN clients and VPN server. The options for IPSec authentication include certificates, and preshared keys. Kerberos authentication is not supported for L2TP/IPSec connections.

The main disadvantage of L2TP/IPSec VPN connections is the relative complexity involved in configuring them as compared to PPTP. The second main disadvantage of L2TP/IPSec VPN connections is the limited support for traversing NAT. However, L2TP/IPSec VPN connections are more secure than PPTP connections because in addition to the user authentication performed by L2TP, IPSec performs tunnel authentication which confirms the identity of both the VPN server and the VPN client.

10

CONFIGURING REMOTE ACCESS SERVERS

The default configuration options for a remote access server are generally sufficient for day-to-day operations, but there may be some situations where you need to modify these settings to allow particular types of clients to connect, or to modify the performance of the system.

The General tab in the Properties of the server, as shown in Figure 10-18, allows you to specify whether the server is a remote access server. This is normally configured using the Routing and Remote Access Server Setup Wizard, but you can enable it manually if this server is already functioning and you do not wish to lose the current configuration.

The Security tab in the Properties of the server, as shown in Figure 10-19, allows you to control authentication and logging. The Authentication Methods button allows you to specify which authentication methods this server supports for dial-up, PPTP, and L2TP connections. The Authentication provider box controls whether authentication is performed by Windows or a RADIUS server. The Accounting provider box defines whether logging of connections is disabled, stored on the local server, or passed to a RADIUS server.

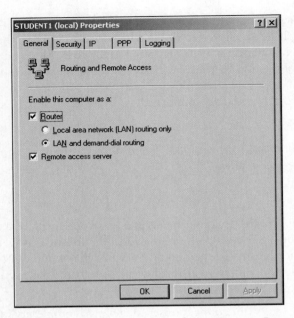

Figure 10-18   General tab of RRAS server Properties

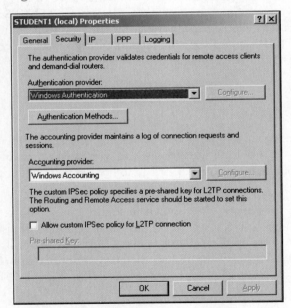

Figure 10-19   Security tab of RRAS server Properties

The Allow custom IPSec policy for L2TP connection option is used when an IPSec policy is already in place for use on the LAN. Using this option you can specify a preshared key used by L2TP/IPSec clients when connecting to the VPN server. This reduces the complexity of configuring IPSec policies for a VPN server.

The IP tab in the properties of the server, as shown in Figure 10-20, allows you to configure whether or not this server is a router for IP, and if it allows IP-based remote access connections. The IP address assignment for the client can be configured here to allow automatic assignment via DHCP or manual assignment via a static pool of addresses. You can also choose the adapter used to obtain DHCP, DNS, and WINS configuration for clients. All of these are normally configured using the Routing and Remote Access Server Setup Wizard.

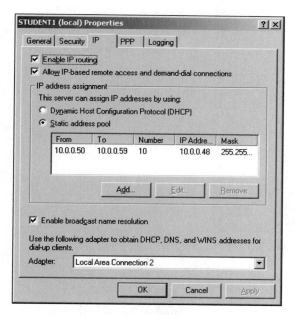

Figure 10-20   IP tab of RRAS server Properties

The Enable broadcast name resolution option is new in Windows Server 2003. In the past, because the VPN server acts as a router for VPN clients, NetBIOS name resolution by broadcast was not possible; a WINS server was required. Even with a WINS server, browsing in My Network places was sometimes unreliable. With this option enabled, the VPN server acts as a proxy for NetBIOS broadcasts, and the VPN client does not need to be configured with a WINS server if the network being connected is a single subnet (not routed).

The Logging tab in the Properties dialog box of the server, shown in Figure 10-21, allows you to control the events that are written to the event log. In addition, you can enable the Log additional Routing and Remote Access information (used for debugging) option to create C:\WINDOWS\tracing\ppp.log to track detailed information on the establishment of PPP connections.

The logging configured on the Logging tab is not the same as the accounting information configured on the Security tab.

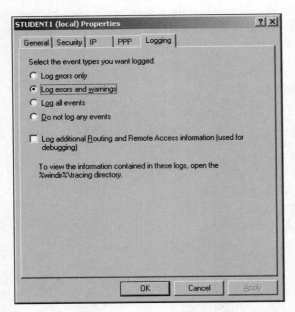

Figure 10-21   Logging tab of RRAS server Properties

Authentication Methods

Windows Server 2003 has the ability to use a number of different authentication methods. These authentication methods can be used for authenticating dial-up, PPTP, and L2TP connections:

- *No Authentication*—If you choose to have no authentication, then all users are permitted access regardless of their user name and password.

- *Password Authentication Protocol (PAP)*—**Password Authentication Protocol (PAP)** transmits passwords across the network in plain text. This makes it unsuitable for use except as a last resort for clients that support no other authentication methods. MPPE cannot be used in conjunction with PAP, which means that a PPTP VPN cannot encrypt the data packets when PAP is used. PAP also cannot change the password during the authentication process. This authentication method is disabled by default.

- *Shiva Password Authentication Protocol (SPAP)*—**Shiva Password Authentication Protocol (SPAP)** uses reversible encryption to transmit passwords. This means that the password can be decrypted if captured with a packet sniffer. It is also vulnerable to replay attacks because the password is encrypted exactly the same each time it is transmitted on the network. MPPE cannot be used in conjunction with SPAP, which means that a PPTP VPN connection cannot encrypt the data packets when SPAP is used. SPAP also cannot change the password during the authentication process. This authentication method is disabled by default.

- *Challenge Handshake Authentication Protocol (CHAP)*—**Challenge Handshake Authentication Protocol (CHAP)** is a significant enhancement over SPAP because it uses the one-way hashing algorithm MD5 to secure passwords in transit. However, it does require passwords stored in Active Directory to be encrypted in a reversible format, which is a security risk. This authentication method is widely supported by many vendors. MPPE cannot be used in conjunction with CHAP, which means that a PPTP VPN connection cannot encrypt the data packets when CHAP is used. CHAP also cannot change the password during the authentication process. This authentication method is disabled by default.

- *Microsoft Challenge Handshake Authentication Protocol (MS-CHAP)*—**Microsoft Challenge Handshake Authentication Protocol (MS-CHAP)**—is an enhancement to CHAP that allows Active Directory passwords to be stored using nonreversible encryption. MPPE can be used in conjunction with MS-CHAP, which means that a PPTP VPN can encrypt the data packets. In addition MS-CHAP can be used to change the password during the authentication process if the password has expired. Passwords are limited to 14 characters. This authentication method is enabled by default. MS-CHAP reuses the same encryption key for each connection.

- *Microsoft Challenge Handshake Authentication Protocol version 2 (MS-CHAPv2)*—**Microsoft Challenge Handshake Authentication Protocol version 2 (MS-CHAPv2)** is an enhanced version of MS-CHAP that corrects several problems. LAN Manager support for older Windows clients is no longer supported because of their weak encryption algorithms. Authentication is performed for both computers in the communication and not just the client, similarly to the mutual authentication provided by IPSec. Encryption keys vary with each connection, unlike MS-CHAP, which reused the same encryption key for each connection.

- *Extensible Authentication Protocol (EAP)*— **Extensible Authentication Protocol (EAP)** is not an authentication method as much as it is an authentication system. EAP allows multiple authentication mechanisms to be configured. The client and server can negotiate which authentication mechanism to use. The authentication mechanism options included with Windows Server 2003 are MD5-Challenge, Protected EAP (PEAP), and Smart Card or other certificate. In Windows 2000, the Smart Card or other certificate option was known as Transport Layer Security (EAP-TLS). Authentication mechanisms are also known as EAP types.

10

IP Address Management

When dial-up and VPN clients connect to Windows Server 2003 configured as a remote access server, they are assigned an IP address. The IP address can be from a static pool configured on the remote access server or leased from a DHCP server.

Regardless of which IP allocation method is used, the options for the DNS server and the WINS server assigned to the client are taken from the configuration of a specified interface on the remote access server. As you can see below in Figure 10-22, the remote access server is configured to use DHCP for assigning IP addresses to clients. The internal network interface is chosen to provide the DNS option to clients; WINS is not configured. The remote access server leases an IP address from the DHCP server for the client. This is the IP address that is assigned to the remote access client. The DNS option sent to the remote access client is obtained from the internal network interface of the remote access server. The options in the DHCP lease are not used.

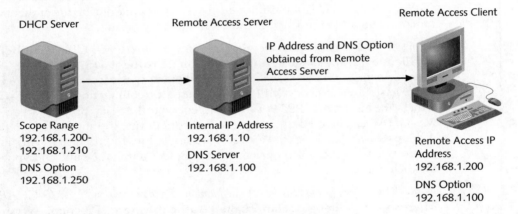

Figure 10-22   IP options configured from a RRAS server

Windows 2000 and newer clients have the ability to send a **DHCPINFORM** packet after a remote access connection has been established. This allows clients to query a DHCP server for configuration options. If the query is successful, then the options from the DHCP server override the options from the network interface of the remote access server. For this system to work, the **DHCP relay agent** on the remote access server must be configured to pass the DHCPINFORM messages on to a DHCP server. DHCP relay agents are also called DHCP proxies and were discussed earlier in Chapter 4.

In Figure 10-23, a remote access connection has been established between the remote access client and the remote access server. The remote access client sends a DHCPINFORM message to the remote access server. The DHCP relay agent on the remote access server forwards the DHCPINFORM message to the DHCP server. The DHCP Server sends the DNS configuration option back to the DHCP relay agent on the remote access server. Finally, the remote access server passes the DNS configuration option to the remote access client where the remote access client overwrites the existing DNS server option with the new configuration.

 If a remote access client attempts to use a DHCPINFORM packet and does not receive a response, then the IP options configured by RRAS continue to be used.

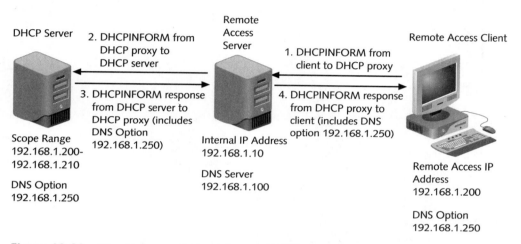

Figure 10-23   IP options configured from a DHCP server via a DHCP relay agent on a RRAS server

ALLOWING CLIENT ACCESS

In most organizations, not all users are allowed to access network resources remotely. When remote access is first configured on Windows Server 2003, none of the users are granted remote access permission. Remote access permission allows users to act as dial-up or VPN clients.

Remote access permission for users is controlled by their user object. If the RRAS server does not participate in an Active Directory domain, this user object is stored in the local user account database. However, if the RRAS server belongs to an Active Directory domain, the user object is stored in the Active Directory database located on domain controllers in the network. In a mixed mode Active Directory domain with pre-Windows 2000 domain controllers, the dial-in permission is either allowed or denied. When all domain controllers are Windows 2000 or later, and the domain has been switched to at least Windows 2000 **native mode**, then remote access policies can be used to control remote access permission as well.

To configure remote access user settings, simply access the Dial–in tab of the user object Properties dialog box, as shown in Figure 10-24. Some of the options on this tab are not available to user objects that are a member of a mixed mode Active Directory domain.

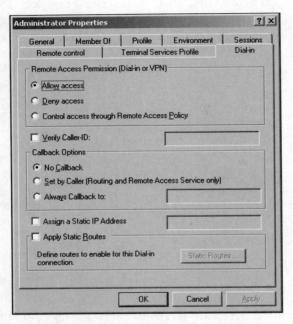

Figure 10-24   Dial-in tab of user object Properties

The Remote Access Permission box on the Dial–in tab allows you to control whether a user has access or not. The Allow access option means that a user is allowed to connect remotely. The Deny access option means that a user is not allowed to connect remotely. The Control access through Remote Access Policy option means that a remote access policy allows or denies the user access. By default, all users are denied access.

The Verify Caller–ID option allows the user to connect only if they are calling from a particular phone number. For this option to work, the modems used must be capable of reading caller-ID information, the phone company must provide caller-ID information, and the domain must be in native mode if Active Directory is used. This option is useful to prevent stolen user accounts and passwords from being used anywhere except from a designated location. Requiring the use of a particular phone line makes remotely hacking into a system much more difficult.

The Callback Options box has settings that allow you to enable or disable callback. If the No Callback option is selected, then the user is allowed to connect immediately and stay connected. If the Set by Caller (Routing and Remote Access Service only) option is selected, first the client computer gives the remote access server a phone number as part of the connection establishment process, then both client and server hang up, and then the server calls the client. This is useful for ensuring that long-distance charges are borne by the main office, and for logging where all calls come from. If the Always Callback to option is selected, then a phone number must be entered, and when the user dials in, the server always calls the user back at the configured number. This provides the same type of protection against stolen user accounts and passwords as the caller-ID option.

The Assign a Static IP Address option ensures that a user gets the same IP address each time he or she dials in. This overrides the settings configured at the server level for DHCP-based addresses or a static pool. This is useful if firewalls are configured to allow this particular IP address access to network resources not accessible to most users. This option is not available if your Active Directory domain is in mixed mode.

The Apply Static Routes option is designed for use with demand dial connections configured between routers. The demand dial connection logs in with the user account, then static routes are added to the routing table of the remote access server. These static routes allow the remote access server to route packets back to the network of the demand dial router. This option is not available if your Active Directory domain is in mixed mode. Routing and demand dial connections are discussed later in Chapter 12.

10

Activity 10-6: Allowing a User Remote Access Permission

Time Required: 15 minutes

Objective: Create a new user, and allow it remote access permission.

Description: A new professor that requires VPN access has started working for Great Arctic North University. You must create a new account for him in on your RRAS server and allow him remote access permission.

1. If necessary, start your server and log on as **Administrator**.

2. Click **Start**, point to **Administrative Tools**, and click **Computer Management**.

3. Double-click **Local Users and Groups** in the left pane, right-click the **Users** folder, and click **New User**.

4. In the User name box, type **SKlumpX**, where X is your student number and in the Full name box, type **Sherman KlumpX**, where X is your student number.

5. In the Password box, type **Password!**, and in the Confirm password box, type **Password!**.

6. Click the **User must change password at next logon** option to deselect it, and click **Create**.

7. Click **Close**.

8. In the left pane, click **Users**.

9. In the right pane, right-click **Sherman KlumpX**, where X is your student number, and click **Properties**.

10. Click the **Dial-in** tab.

11. Click **Allow access**, and click **OK**.

12. Close the Computer Management window.

Creating a VPN Client Connection

Most of the time, VPN clients are configured on client operating systems such as Windows XP. However, Windows Server 2003 can also be configured as a VPN client. This can be useful when Windows Server 2003 is configured to act as a router between two locations. VPN connections can be used to encrypt traffic sent between the two routers.

VPN client connections are created using the same New Connection Wizard that is used when configuring dial-up connections. If you have a dial-up connection created, you are asked if an initial connection should be dialed before attempting to create the VPN connection. You can select the Do not dial the initial connection option if it is not required. This is the appropriate setting if you are connecting via a LAN. You can also choose the Automatically dial this initial connection option, and then choose an existing dial-up connection, as shown in Figure 10-25.

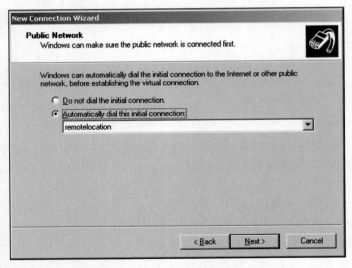

Figure 10-25   Dial initial connection option for a VPN connection

Activity 10-7: Creating a Client VPN Connection

Time Required: 20 minutes

Objective: Create a client VPN connection and then test it.

Description: After installing and configuring a VPN server, you would like to test it using one of the servers in your test lab. In this activity, you will create a VPN client connection on your server and connect to the VPN server configured on your partner's server.

1. If necessary, start your server and log on as **Administrator**.

2. Click **Start**, point to **Control Panel**, right-click **Network Connections**, and click **Open**.

3. Double-click **New Connection wizard**.

4. Click **Next** to begin the New Connection Wizard.

5. Click **Connect to the network at my workplace**, and click **Next**.

6. Click **Virtual Private Network connection**, and click **Next**.

7. In the Company Name box, type **Great Arctic North VPN**, and click **Next**.

8. Click **Do not dial the initial connection**. This feature is not required because you are connecting across the LAN using a network card. Click **Next**.

9. In the Host name or IP address box, type **IP_address**, where IP_address is the IP address of your partner's local area connection.

10. Click **Next**.

11. Click **Anyone's use**, so that all users can use this connection, and click **Next**.

12. Click **Finish**.

13. In the User name box, type **SKlumpX**, where X is your student number. This is the user you created and allowed remote access permission in Activity 10-6.

14. In the Password box, type **Password!**.

15. Click **Connect** to enable the connection. Once the connection is established, you should see an icon of two computers in the system tray.

16. Click **Start** and click **Run**. Type **cmd**, and press **Enter** to open a command prompt.

17. At the command prompt, type **ipconfig**. Note that you now have a VPN network adapter in addition to your local area connection and Local Area Connection 2. This adapter will have an IP address on the $x.0.0.0$ network where x is your partner's student number and will be between $x.0.0.50$ and $x.0.0.59$.

18. At the command prompt type **ping x.0.0.1** where x is your partner's student number. Note that your ping attempt was successful.

10

19. In the Network Connections window, double-click **Great Arctic North VPN**. On the **General** tab you can view how long the VPN connection has been active and the amount of data that has traveled through it.

20. Click the **Details** tab. Here, you can view the authentication protocol, encryption protocol, server IP address on the VPN, and the client IP address on the VPN.

21. Click the **General** tab, and click **Disconnect**.

22. Close the **Network Connections** window.

23. At the command prompt type **ping _x_.0.0.1** where _x_ is your partner's student number. Note that your ping attempt was unsuccessful since the VPN is no longer connected.

24. Close the command prompt window.

Configuring a VPN Client Connection

Most configuration of a VPN client connection is done with the New Connection Wizard. However, you can configure all of the same options in the properties of the VPN connection.

The General tab of the VPN connection properties, as shown in Figure 10-26, allows you to configure the IP address of the VPN server to which you are connecting. In addition, you can configure whether an initial connection is created, and control whether or not an icon is placed in the system tray when this connection is active.

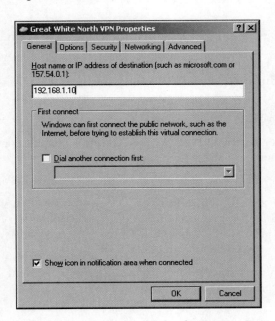

Figure 10-26   General tab of VPN Properties

The Options tab of the VPN Properties dialog box, shown in Figure 10-27, allows you to configure dialing options and redialing options. The redialing options are useful primarily for busy dial-up connections. VPN connections are less likely to be successful with redial attempts.

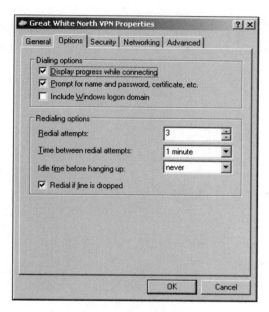

Figure 10-27   Options tab of VPN Properties

The Security tab of the VPN Properties dialog box, shown in Figure 10-28, allows you to set whether or not password encryption and data encryption are required. Based on those settings, only certain authentication methods are allowed. You can also manually choose the authentication methods by clicking Advanced. The IPSec Settings option allows you to configure a preshared key that is used for L2TP/IPSec connections.

The Networking tab of the VPN Properties dialog box, shown in Figure 10-29, allows you to configure the network configuration for the VPN connection. This includes setting a static IP address if required. You can also set the type of VPN connection to PPTP or L2TP. By default, the type of VPN connection is negotiated between the client and the server.

The Advanced tab of the VPN Properties dialog box allows you to configure an Internet connection firewall and Internet connection sharing for this connection. Both of these topics are covered later in Chapter 12.

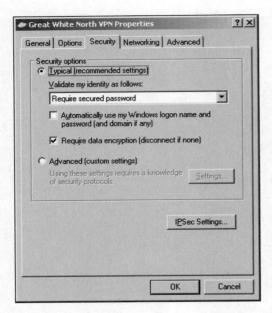

Figure 10-28   Security tab of VPN Properties

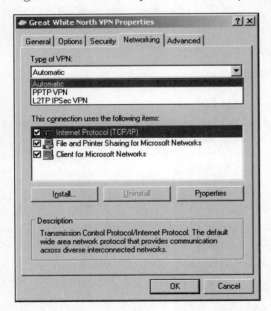

Figure 10-29   Networking tab of VPN Properties

REMOTE ACCESS POLICIES

Remote access policies are a critical part of controlling and allowing remote access. How remote access policies are applied varies depending on whether the domain is in mixed mode or native mode. Figure 10-30 shows the properties of a default remote access policy.

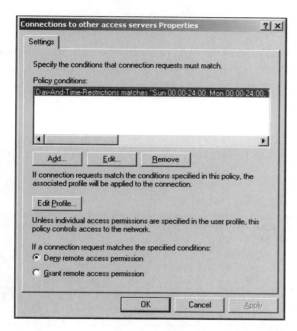

Figure 10-30   Default remote access policy Properties

These policies are stored on each individual remote access server, not in Active Directory. This means that the policies applied to a user creating a remote access connection will vary depending on the remote access server to which the user connects. As an administrator, this offers you the extra flexibility to provide remote access servers that service only certain types of users. For example, you may configure one remote access server that services all remote users, and another that services only executives. In this way, you can be sure that the executives are never blocked out of a busy remote access server. Or you may configure one remote access server that allows connections for an unlimited period, and another that only allows connections for up to 10 minutes. This ensures that all users that need to quickly check e-mail are able to do so, and are not blocked out of a busy remote access server.

Configuring remote access servers with different policies can be confusing for users. If you do this, be sure to provide documentation for your users describing exactly what is different between the remote access servers, so they understand which one to use for a given situation.

To effectively use remote access policies, you must understand:

- Remote access policy components
- Remote access policy evaluation
- Default remote access policies

Remote Access Policy Components

Remote access policies are composed of **conditions**, **remote access permissions**, and a **profile**. When a domain is in native mode, all three of these components are used. When a domain is in mixed mode, only the conditions and profile are used.

Conditions

Conditions are criteria that must be met in order for a remote access policy to apply to a connection. A variety of conditions can be set. Some of the more common conditions are listed in Table 10-1.

Table 10-1   Common remote access policy conditions

Condition	Description
Authentication type	The authentication method being used by the client; these include CHAP, MS-CHAP, and MS-CHAPv2
Called station ID	This is the phone number phoned by the user; this information is only available if arranged with the phone company
Calling station ID	This is the phone number that the user is calling from; this information is only available if arranged with the phone company
Day and time restrictions	Sets specific days of the week and times of the day; the time is based on the time set on the server providing authorization, which is either the remote access server or RADIUS server.
NAS port type	Identifies the media used to make the connection, including phone lines (async), ISDN, VPN (virtual), IEEE 802.11 wireless, and Ethernet switches
Tunnel type	The VPN protocol being used (either PPTP or L2TP)
Windows group	Group membership for the user attempting the connection. To create a policy with multiple groups you can add this condition several times with different groups, or use nested groups.

Several conditions can be combined in a single remote access policy. All of the conditions in a remote access policy must be matched for a remote access policy to apply.

Remote Access Permission

If the conditions of a remote access policy are met, then the remote access permission is checked. The remote access permission set in a remote access policy has only two options:

- Deny remote access permission
- Grant remote access permission

The permission setting in a remote access policy can only be used for native mode domains. If the domain is in mixed mode, then the permission is always taken from the user object in Active Directory.

Profile

The profile of a remote policy contains settings that are applied to a remote access connection if the conditions have been matched and permission has been allowed. If the settings in a profile, such as the authentication method, cannot be applied, then the connection is denied.

The Dial-in Constraints tab of the profile, as shown in Figure 10-31, allows you to set the number of minutes a connection can be idle before it is disconnected, the maximum number of minutes for a connection, and day and time restrictions. As well, you can configure caller ID settings and port type settings, such as Wireless – IEEE 802.11, ISDN, or Async (modem).

10

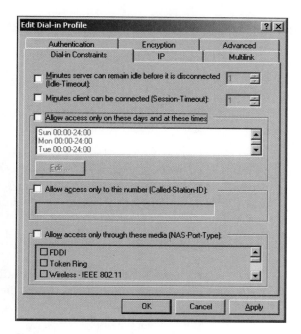

Figure 10-31   Dial-in Constraints tab of a profile

The IP tab of the profile, as shown in Figure 10-32, allows you to not only configure how IP addresses are assigned for a connection, but also to set filters to control traffic across the VPN connection. The IP address assignment setting configured in the policy overrides the settings configured on the server and the client. The IP filters can be used to control traffic based on source and destination IP addresses, source and destination port numbers, and packet type. You can use these to control what services are allowed on a connection. For example, to restrict Web-browsing traffic, you can configure a profile that denies outgoing packets where the destination TCP port is 80.

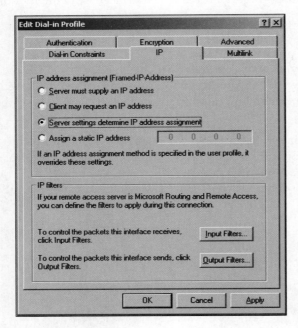

Figure 10-32   IP tab of a profile

The Multilink tab of the profile, as shown in Figure 10-33, allows you to control the maximum number of lines used for a multilink connection, and if multilink is allowed at all. In addition, you can set the capacity percentage at which the multilink connection is reduced by a line, and how long it must be at that capacity. If you select the Require BAP for dynamic Multilink requests option, then multilink connections are not allowed unless **Bandwidth Allocation Protocol (BAP)** can be used to control the number of phone lines used.

The Authentication tab of the profile allows you to control the types of authentication that are allowed. These authentication methods must be enabled on the client and on the server in order for them to be used.

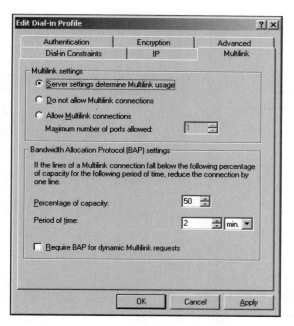

Figure 10-33   Multilink tab of a profile

The Encryption tab of the profile, as shown in Figure 10-34, allows you to control the types of encryption that are allowed. Table 10-2 lists the types of encryption allowed for each option when PPTP and L2TP/IPSec VPN connections are used.

Table 10-2   Allowed encryption types

Encryption Level	PPTP Encryption	L2TP/IPSec Encryption
Basic encryption	40-bit MPPE	56-bit DES
Strong encryption	56-bit MPPE	56-bit DES
Strongest encryption	128-bit MPPE	Triple DES (3DES)
No encryption	None	None

The Advanced tab of the profile contains settings that are generally intended to be configured when Windows Server 2003 is used as a RADIUS server. The **Ignore-User-Dialin-Properties** attribute can be configured here. If this attribute is false, then remote access policies are processed normally. If this attribute is true, then the dial-in settings in the properties of a user account are ignored.

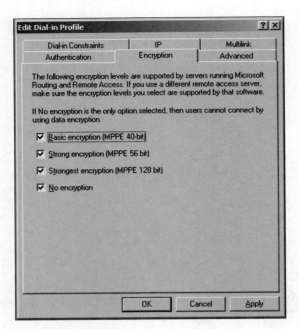

Figure 10-34   Encryption tab of a profile

Activity 10-8: Creating a Remote Access Policy

Time Required: 15 minutes

Objective: Create a new remote access policy on your server.

Description: Great Arctic North University has a wide variety of users accessing resources through remote access. You would like to force all of the department heads to use high levels of data encryption and MS-CHAPv2 for authentication when they connect via VPN. The easiest way to implement this is by creating a new policy with a condition for a Windows Group, and a profile with the encryption settings.

1. If necessary, start your server and log on as **Administrator**.

2. Click **Start**, point to **Administrative Tools**, and click **Computer Management**.

3. Double-click **Local Users and Groups** in the left pane, right-click the **Groups** folder, and click **New Group**.

4. In the Group name box, type **HighSecX**, where X is your student number.

5. Click **Add**. In the text box provided, type **SKlumpX**, where X is your student number, and click **OK**.

6. Click **Create**. Click **Close**.

7. Close the **Computer Management** window.

8. Click **Start**, point to **Administrative Tools**, and click **Routing and Remote Access**.

9. In the left pane, click **Remote Access Policies**. Notice that there are two policies already created by default.

10. Right-click **Remote Access Policies**, and click **New Remote Access Policy**.

11. Click **Next** to start the New Remote Access Policy Wizard.

12. Confirm that the setting **Use the wizard to set up a typical policy for a common scenario** is selected.

13. In the Policy name box, type **HighSecurity**, and click **Next**.

14. Confirm that the **VPN** option is selected, and click **Next**.

15. Confirm that the **Group** option is selected, click **Add**, type **HighSecX**, where *X* is your student number, click **OK**, and click **Next**.

16. Verify that the only option selected is **Microsoft Encrypted Authentication version 2 (MS-CHAPv2)**, and click **Next**.

17. Click the **Basic encryption (IPSec 56-bit DES or MPPE 40-bit)** checkbox to deselect it.

18. Click the **Strong encryption (IPSec 56-bit DES or MPPE 56-bit)** checkbox to deselect it.

19. Verify that the **Strongest encryption (IPSec Triple DES or MPPE 128-bit)** checkbox is selected, and click **Next**.

20. Click **Finish**.

21. Notice that your new policy has been placed first in the priority order.

22. If time permits, view the properties of your policy to verify the settings.

23. Close the Routing and Remote Access snap-in.

Remote Access Policy Evaluation

To create remote access policies and understand what their results will be, you need to understand not only the contents of remote access policies, but also how they are evaluated by RRAS. If you do not understand this process, you may find users who should be able to create remote access connections unable to do so. The evaluation process varies depending on whether the domain is in mixed mode or native mode.

Evaluate Conditions

Evaluating conditions follows the same process for mixed mode domain and native mode domains, and is shown in Figure 10-35. The first step in the process checks to see if there are any policies at all. If no remote access policies exist, then the connection attempt is rejected. If remote access policies exist, then their conditions are evaluated.

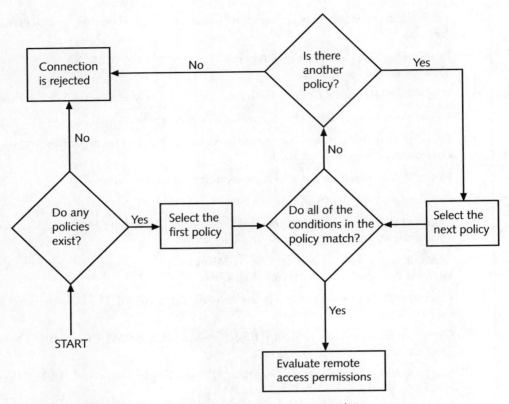

Figure 10-35 Evaluating conditions for remote access policies

The second step is to compare the conditions set in the remote access policies with the actual conditions of the connection being attempted. Remote access policies are assigned an order. The attempt to match conditions of the remote access policies starts with the remote access policy that comes first in order and continues until a match is found or no remote access policies remain. If no match is found, the connection attempt is rejected.

If multiple remote access policies match the conditions, then only the first one evaluated is used. For example, if a user is attempting to create a VPN connection and the remote access policy that comes second in order and the remote access policy fourth in order both match, then only the remote access policy second in order is used.

Evaluate Permissions

After a condition match has been found, the permissions of the user attempting the connection must be evaluated, as shown in Figure 10-36. The first step is to check for the Ignore-User-Dialin-Properties attribute in the profile of the remote access policy. This is true for mixed mode and native mode domains.

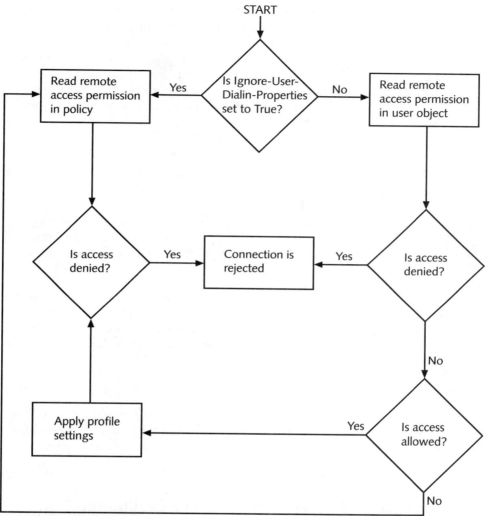

Note: If your remote access server participates in an Active Directory domain in mixed mode, then the remote access permission in the user object will always be used to allow or deny access.

Figure 10-36   Evaluating permissions for remote access policies

In a mixed mode Active Directory domain, if the Ignore-User-Dialin-Properties attribute is set to False, then the remote access permission from the user object is used to determine whether a user is allowed or denied remote access permission. If the Ignore-User-Dialin-Properties attribute is set to True, then the permission setting of the remote access policy is used to determine whether a user is granted or denied remote access permission.

In a native mode Active Directory domain, or if Active Directory is not used, and the Ignore-User-Dialin-Properties attribute is set to False, then the remote access permission from the user object is used to determine whether a user is allowed or denied access, unless the user object is configured with the remote access permission Control Access Through Remote Access policy. If this option is configured, then the remote access policy defines whether the user is granted or denied remote access permission. If the Ignore-User-Dialin-Properties attribute is set to True, then the remote access policy always defines whether the user is granted or denied remote access permission.

The Ignore-User-Dialin-Properties attribute is new in Windows Server 2003.

If a Windows NT 4.0 remote access server attempts to read the remote access permissions from a native mode Active Directory domain and the setting is Control Access Through Remote Access policy, then it is read as "Deny access."

If permission is denied based on this remote access policy, no other policies are evaluated. For example, if a user is attempting to create a VPN connection and the remote access policy second in order, which denies remote access permission, and the remote access policy fourth in order, which grants remote access permission, both match, then only the remote access policy second in order is used.

Profile Settings

Even if remote access permission is granted, it does not guarantee that a remote access connection will be successful. Some of the profile settings, such as allowed authentication methods and encryption levels, force a connection attempt to be disconnected.

Profile settings are applied in the same way for mixed mode and native mode domains.

Activity 10-9: Testing Remote Policy Evaluation

Time Required: 30 minutes

Objective: Verify the process by which remote access permission is granted.

Description: In this activity, you will perform a series of steps to illustrate the process used to evaluate remote access policies and grant remote access permission. These steps are not meant to simulate any real-world situation. You will work with a partner on this activity. One partner will perform configuration tasks on their server; the other will test the changes by initiating a VPN connection from their server.

1. If necessary, start your server and log on as **Administrator**.

2. Partner A: Verify that the existing VPN is functional.

   a. Click **Start**, point to **Control Panel**, point to **Network Connections**, click **Great Arctic North VPN**.

   b. If necessary, type **SKlumpX** in the User name box, where *X* is your partner's student number.

   c. In the Password box, type **Password!**, and click **Connect**.

   d. The VPN connection should now be active and using the settings configured in the HighSecurity policy on the remote access server.

   e. Right-click the **VPN** icon in the system tray, and click **Status**.

   f. Click the **Details** tab, and verify that Authentication is MS CHAP V2 and Encryption is MPPE 128.

   g. Right-click the **VPN** icon in the system tray, and click **Disconnect**.

3. Partner B: Create a new low-security policy, and place it first in order.

   a. Click **Start**, point to **Administrative Tools**, and click **Routing and Remote Access**.

   b. Right-click **Remote Access Policies**, and click **New Remote Access Policy**.

   c. Click **Next** to start the New Remote Access Policy Wizard.

   d. In the Policy name box, type **LowSecurity**, and click **Next**.

   e. Confirm that **VPN** is selected, and click **Next**.

   f. Click **User**, and click **Next**. This policy applies to all users, because "user" was selected.

   g. Verify that the only option selected is **Microsoft Encrypted Authentication version 2 (MS-CHAPv2)**, and click **Next**.

   h. Verify that the **Basic encryption (IPSec 56-bit DES or MPPE 40-bit)** checkbox is selected.

   i. Click the **Strong encryption (IPSec 56-bit DES or MPPE 56-bit)** checkbox to deselect it.

   j. Click the **Strongest encryption (IPSec Triple DES or MPPE 128-bit)** checkbox to deselect it, and click **Next**.

   k. Click **Finish**.

   l. The LowSecurity remote access policy is now listed as the first and will be applied before any other policy.

4. Partner A: Verify the policy application.

   a. Click **Start**, point to **Control Panel**, point to **Network Connections**, and click **Great Arctic North VPN**.

   b. In the Password box, type **Password!**, and click **Connect**.

10

    c. The VPN connection should now be active and using the settings configured in the LowSecurity policy on the remote access server.

    d. Right-click the **VPN** icon in the system tray, and click **Status**.

    e. Click the **Details** tab, and verify that Authentication is **MS CHAP V2** and Encryption is **MPPE 40**. These settings are from the new LowSecurity remote access policy created on your partner's server. The settings are taken from this remote access policy because it has higher priority than the HighSecurity remote access policy.

    f. Right-click the **VPN** icon in the system tray, and click **Disconnect**.

5. Partner B: Verify remote access permission.

    a. Right-click **LowSecurity**, and click **Properties**.

    b. By default, the remote access permission setting in this policy is set to Deny remote access permission. However, this setting is not used because the remote access permission for the user SKlumpX is set to Allow access. That is why Partner A was able to connect in Step 4.

    c. Click **Cancel**.

6. Partner B: Set the Ignore-User-Dialin-Properties attribute to True.

    a. Right-click **LowSecurity**, and click **Properties**.

    b. Click **Edit Profile**.

    c. Click the **Advanced** tab.

    d. Click **Add**.

    e. Scroll down the list of attributes, and double-click **Ignore-User-Dialin-Properties**. Microsoft is listed as the vendor.

    f. Click **True**, and click **OK**.

    g. Click **Close** to close the Add Attribute window.

    h. Click **OK** to save the profile changes.

    i. Verify that the **Deny remote access permission** option is still selected, and click **OK** to save the remote access policy changes.

7. Partner A: Verify the policy application.

    a. Click **Start**, point to **Control Panel**, point to **Network Connections**, and click **Great Arctic North VPN**.

    b. In the Password box, type **Password!**, and click **Connect**.

    c. You receive this error message: Error 649: The account does not have permission to dial in. When the attribute Ignore-User-Dialin-Properties is set to True, then the remote access permission setting on the user object is ignored, and the remote access permission from the remote access policy is used instead—even in mixed mode domains.

    d. Click **Close**.

8. Partner B: Delete the LowSecurity remote access policy.
   a. Right-click **LowSecurity**, and click **Delete**.
   b. Click **Yes** to confirm that you want to delete LowSecurity.
   c. Close the Routing and Remote Access snap-in.
9. If sufficient time exists, trade roles and repeat the exercise.

Default Remote Access Policies

The default remote access policies are created to make managing remote access easier. These default settings reduce the amount of configuration required to have a functional remote access server.

The first default remote access policy listed is named Connections to Microsoft Routing and Remote Access server. This policy has a condition where the attribute MS-RAS-Vendor must contain the characters "311". This applies to all Microsoft remote access servers. This profile for this policy does not allow unencrypted communication.

The second default remote access policy listed is named Connections to other access servers. This policy has a condition where the Day-And-Time-Restrictions attribute matches Sunday to Monday, 24 hours per day. This policy does allow unencrypted communication.

Remote access permission is denied in both of the default policies. For user objects with remote access permission set to Control access through Remote Access policy, this ensures that a new remote access policy must be created that explicitly grants the user remote access permission. This means that users cannot be accidentally granted remote access permission.

For user objects with remote access permission set to Allow access, the Control Access Through Remote Access policy remote access policy ensures that they do obtain access. If no policy exists, the users with remote access permission set to Allow access are rejected. For example, assume that all of the default remote access policies have been deleted from a remote access server. When a user attempts to connect, the first part of the remote access policy evaluation process is to find a remote access policy with matching conditions. Because no remote access policy with matching conditions is found, the connection attempt is rejected.

TROUBLESHOOTING REMOTE ACCESS

Providing remote access for users is a very complex process. The more complex a process, the more difficult it is to troubleshoot. Most of the problems with remote access are due to software configuration errors introduced by users and administrators. Occasionally, however, hardware errors may occur.

Your best troubleshooting tools for remote access are log files and error messages. Other troubleshooting tools include network monitor and ipconfig.

Software Configuration Errors

Users cannot connect remotely if the software on their computers is not configured correctly. The following are some configuration errors to look for:

- *Incorrect phone numbers and IP addresses*—Users cannot connect if they are attempting to connect to a phone number or IP address that does not exist. To reduce client configuration problems, you can use the **Connection Manager Administration Kit (CMAK)**. CMAK allows you to create remote access connections for dial-up and VPN and distribute them to client computers. For more information on CMAK, search for CMAK in Help and Support.

- *Incorrect authentication settings*—Ensure that clients, servers, and remote access policies are configured properly to allow authentication to occur. Authentication errors often result in client errors indicating that the user is not authorized. The error messages do not indicate that an authentication method could not be negotiated.

- *Incorrectly configured remote access policies*—Review your remote access policies to ensure that they really do perform the tasks you think they do. Ensure that the remote access policies are in the proper order. The only remote access policy used is the first one that the conditions match.

- *Name resolution is not configured*—When a remote access client connects to the remote access server, name resolution must be configured to access resources on the LAN. Ensure that DNS and WINS are configured properly if resources are not accessible when the connection is made.

- *Clients receive incorrect IP options*—A remote access server gives remote access clients the WINS and DNS configuration from a designated interface on the remote access server. If you want these settings to come from a DHCP server, then you must configure the DHCP proxy on the remote access server.

- *The remote access server leases 10 IP addresses from DHCP at startup*—This is not an error. RRAS is designed to do this if it is configured to hand out IP addresses from a DHCP server. Leasing 10 addresses at a time is faster and more efficient than leasing IP addresses as required.

Hardware Errors

Hardware errors are less common than software configuration errors. They are most common when new hardware is being installed. The following are some considerations for hardware troubleshooting:

- Ideally, new remote access hardware should be on the hardware compatibility list (HCL). Many times, hardware that is not on this list works, but hardware on the list has been tested and approved by Microsoft.

- If a VPN connection cannot find the server, use the ping utility to see if the IP address is reachable. You can ping other servers on the Internet to confirm that your Internet connectivity is functional.

- If you cannot dial in using a new modem, see if you can dial in to a different remote access server. This confirms that the hardware is working properly.

- If you have installed a new network card, ensure that you have reconnected the patch cable and there is a link light on the network card. "Is it plugged in?" and "Is it turned on?" are the two most valuable troubleshooting questions there are. Remember the basics.

- Is the type of hardware you are trying to use supported? When configured as a remote access server, RRAS supports analog modems, ISDN, X.25, frame relay, ATM, cable modems, and DSL modems.

Logging

Logging for remote access can be configured in many places. If RRAS is unable to start or is not performing as expected, one of the first places to check is the event log. You can control the events that are placed in the System log from the Logging tab in the properties of the remote access server using the Routing and Remote Access snap-in.

From this same logging tab, you can configure detailed connection logs. To enable this, select the Log additional Routing and Remote Access information (used for debugging) option. This creates a log file named C:\WINDOWS\tracing \ppp.log to track PPP connections. You can also record a log of modem communications. The log file is named C:\WINDOWS\Modemlog_modemname.txt.

Activity 10-10: Modem Logging

Time Required: 5 minutes

Objective: Enable modem logging.

Description: One particular professor has been complaining that he is often unable to connect to the dial-up server. You have checked all of the configuration settings on his laptop and everything seems correct. As a last attempt to troubleshoot the problem, you are enabling modem logging on the server. Then the next time the professor has problems, you can look in the log to see if there are any clues for further troubleshooting.

1. If necessary, start your server, and log on as **Administrator**.

2. Click **Start**, point to **Control Panel**, and click **Phone and Modem Options**.

3. Click the **Modems** tab.

4. Click **Properties**.

5. Click the **Diagnostics** tab.

6. Click **Record a Log**, and click **OK**.

7. Click **OK** to close the Phone and Modem Options window.

Troubleshooting Tools

The ping utility can be used to confirm that a host is reachable. If a host responds to ping attempts, then the host is reachable through the network. However, this does not confirm that RRAS is functioning.

The ipconfig utility can be used to confirm that the correct IP settings are being delivered to the remote access client. If incorrect settings are being delivered to the client, the most likely cause is incorrect configuration of the DHCP relay agent on the remote access server.

Many of the error messages viewed on the client side of a remote access VPN connection do not give many clues as to what the cause of the actual error is. Network Monitor can be used to perform packet captures, which may give you some further clues as to the cause of the error.

CHAPTER SUMMARY

- ❑ RRAS in Windows Server 2003 can be configured as a remote access server for dial-up and VPN connections. Dial-up connections are slow, but available from almost anywhere. VPN connections are usually faster, but Internet access is required.

- ❑ The LAN protocols supported by RRAS for dial-up networking are TCP/IP, IPX/SPX, and AppleTalk. The remote access protocols supported are PPP and SLIP. SLIP is only supported when acting as a dial-up client.

- ❑ A VPN server is easier to maintain than a dial-up server because no specialized hardware such as a modem pool is required.

- ❑ VPN connections can use PPTP or L2TP/IPSec. PPTP is more common and works properly through NAT. L2TP/IPSec is more difficult to configure and only works through NAT if the latest options are implemented.

- ❑ L2TP does not perform encryption; IPSec is used to perform encryption.

- ❑ Many authentication methods are supported by RRAS and include: PAP, SPAP, CHAP, MS-CHAP, MS-CHAPv2, and EAP. PPTP VPNs cannot encrypt data if PAP, SPAP, or CHAP is used. Smart cards can only be used with EAP.

- ❑ Windows 2000 and newer remote access clients can receive IP configuration options from a DHCP server rather than the interface of a remote access server. To do this they send a DHCPINFORM packet after the remote access connection is created. The DHCP relay agent must be configured on the remote access server for this to work.

❑ In a mixed mode Active Directory domain, remote access permission is controlled using the properties of the user object in Active Directory. If you do not use Active Directory or participate in a native mode Active Directory domain, remote access policies can also be used.

❑ Remote access policies are composed of conditions, remote access permissions, and a profile. All conditions in a remote access policy must be met for the policy to apply. Remote access permissions grant or deny access. The profile contains settings that apply to the connection.

❑ The most common problem with remote access connections is improper software configuration. Hardware configuration problems occur less often, and occur mostly when new hardware is installed.

❑ A variety of logs can be configured to help you troubleshoot remote access problems. RRAS logs events to the system log. You can configure PPP logging to obtain detailed information about PPP connections. Logging can be configured for a modem if dial-up remote access is configured.

❑ The most common troubleshooting tools for remote access are ipconfig, ping, and Network Monitor.

10

Key Terms

Bandwidth Allocation Protocol (BAP) — A protocol used to dynamically control the number of phone lines multilink uses based on bandwidth utilization.

callback — A security enhancement wherein a dial-up user initiates a connection, the connection is dropped, and the server then calls the dial-up client back.

Challenge Handshake Authentication Protocol (CHAP) — An authentication method that encrypts passwords using a one-way hash, but requires that passwords in Active Directory be stored using reversible encryption.

COM port — The Windows term for a serial port in a computer.

conditions — Criteria in a remote access policy, or a connection request policy, that must be met for the policy to be applied.

Connection Manager Administration Kit (CMAK) — A utility that can be used to configure dial-up and VPN connections on client computers.

DHCP relay agent — A service that forwards DHCP broadcasts from a network to a DHCP server on another network. It is required when DHCP broadcasts need to cross a router.

DHCPINFORM — A DHCP packet sent by Windows 2000 and newer remote access clients to retrieve IP configuration options from a DHCP server.

dial-up — Connectivity between two computers using modems and a phone line.

Extensible Authentication Protocol (EAP) — An authentication system that uses EAP types as plug-in authentication modules. This is used for smart cards.

Ignore-User-Dialin-Properties — An attribute that can be configured in the profile of a remote access policy that prevents the processing of the dial-in properties of a user object.

LAN protocol — A networking protocol required to communicate over a LAN or over a remote access connection. The same LAN protocol that is used by clients on the LAN must be used by dial-up and VPN clients to access LAN resources remotely.

Layer Two Tunneling Protocol (L2TP) — A VPN protocol that works with IPSec to provide secure communication. Only the latest versions traverse NAT properly.

Link Control Protocol (LCP) — An extension to PPP that allows the use of enhancements such as callback.

location — A dial-up attribute configured in Phone and Modem Options to allow Windows to vary procedures for dialing a connection based on your location.

Microsoft Challenge Handshake Authentication Protocol (MS-CHAP) — An enhancement to CHAP that allows Active Directory passwords to be stored using nonreversible encryption.

Microsoft Challenge Handshake Authentication Protocol version 2 (MS-CHAPv2) — An authentication method that adds computer authentication and several other enhancements to MS-CHAP. This is the preferred authentication protocol for most remote access connections.

mobile users — Users that move from one location to another outside of the local network. They require remote access to use network resources.

modem — A hardware device that enables computers to communicate over a phone line. It converts digital signals from the computer to analog signals that can travel on a phone line, and then back to digital format.

modem pool — A group of modems connected to a remote access dial-up server. In high-volume situations, it is implemented as specialized hardware.

Multilink — A system for dial-up connections that allows multiple phone lines to be treated as a single logical unit to increase connection speeds.

native mode — An Active Directory domain that can only have Windows 2000 and Windows Server 2003 domain controllers.

packet filters — Rules that control the forwarding of packets through a firewall based on IP address, port number, and packet type.

Password Authentication Protocol (PAP) — An authentication method that transmits passwords in clear text.

Point-to-Point Protocol (PPP) — The most common remote access protocol used for dial-up connections. It supports the use of TCP/IP, IPX/SPX, and AppleTalk for remote access.

Point-to-Point Tunneling Protocol (PPTP) — A VPN protocol that can be used with multiple LAN protocols and functions properly through NAT.

profile — The part of a remote access policy, or connection request policy, that contains settings that are applied to the connection.

Remote access — Accessing network resources from a location away from the physical network. Connections can be made using a dial-up connection or a VPN.

remote access permissions — The part of a remote access policy that defines whether the policy denies remote access or grants remote access.

remote access policies — Policies configured on remote access servers to control how remote access connections are created. They are composed of conditions, remote access permissions, and a profile.

remote access protocol — A protocol that is required for dial-up remote access. PPP is the most common remote access protocol

Routing and Remote Access Service (RRAS) — A service that allows Windows Server 2003 to act as a router or remote access server.

Serial Line Internet Protocol (SLIP) — An older remote access protocol that only supports using TCP/IP as a LAN protocol. It is used by Windows Server 2003 only when acting as a client.

Shiva Password Authentication Protocol (SPAP) — An authentication method that uses reversible encryption when transmitting passwords.

v.90 — A standard for modems that allows downloads at 56 Kbps and uploads at 33.6 Kbps.

v.92 — A standard for modems that allows downloads at 56 Kbps and uploads at 48 Kbps.

Virtual Private Network (VPN) — A means of encrypted communication across a public network such as the Internet. This is cheaper than implementing private lines for connectivity.

10

REVIEW QUESTIONS

1. Which of the following network resources can be used by remote access clients? (Choose all that apply.)

   a. files

   b. e-mail

   c. applications

   d. databases

2. A VPN connection is often slower than a dial-up connection because of the time required to perform encryption. True or false?

3. How many locations must be configured in Phone and Modem Options?

   a. none

   b. one

   c. two

   d. three

4. What hardware is required for dial-up remote access? (Choose all that apply.)

   a. network card

   b. modem

   c. phone line

   d. cable modem

5. Immediately after enabling remote access in RRAS, without further configuration, from where do remote access clients obtain IP configuration options?

   a. the properties of the remote access server

   b. a DHCP server

   c. a DHCP relay agent

   d. a defined interface on the remote access server

6. How many IP addresses does a remote access server lease from a DHCP server at one time?

   a. 1

   b. 3

   c. 5

   d. 10

   e. 20

7. Which remote access protocol can be used by Windows Server 2003 only when it is acting as a dial-up client?

   a. PPP

   b. TCP/IP

   c. AppleTalk

   d. SLIP

   e. IPX/SPX

8. Which option allows multiple phone lines to be configured into a single logical unit to increase the speed of dial-up connections?

   a. multilink

   b. LCP

   c. TurboDial

   d. PPTP

9. Which VPN protocol uses IPSec to provide data encryption?

   a. PPTP

   b. PPP

   c. SLIP

   d. L2TP

   e. TCP/IP

10. Which VPN protocol functions easily through NAT?

   a. PPTP

   b. PPP

    c. SLIP

    d. L2TP

    e. TCP/IP

11. Which of the following authentication methods can be used when PPTP is required to encrypt data? (Choose all that apply.)

    a. PAP

    b. SPAP

    c. CHAP

    d. MS-CHAP

    e. MS-CHAPv2

12. Which configuration options can be used to ensure that users call from a predefined location? (Choose all that apply.)

    a. Packet filters

    b. Verify–Caller–ID

    c. Callback

    d. Assign a static IP address

13. Which of the following is a component of a remote access policy? (Choose all that apply.)

    a. conditions

    b. profile

    c. encryption protocols

    d. authentication methods

    e. remote access permissions

14. If you require strongest encryption in a remote access policy, what level of encryption must be performed for L2TP/IPSec connections?

    a. 56–bit MPPE

    b. 128–bit MPPE

    c. 56–bit DES

    d. Triple DES (3DES)

15. If the Ignore-User-Dialin-Properties attribute is set to true when a domain is in mixed mode, there is no effect. True or false?

16. Which Windows service functions as a VPN server?

    a. RRAS

    b. Dial-up Networking

    c. IAS

10

    d. Active Directory

    e. IIS

17. Which utility can be used to configure connections for client computers?

    a. Connection Manager Administration Kit

    b. Active Directory Users and Computers

    c. ipconfig

    d. Network Monitor

18. You have set the option to Log additional Routing and Remote Access information (used for debugging) on the Logging tab of your RRAS server. Which log file is used to store this information?

    a. C:\WINDOWS\SYSTEM32\TRACING\PPP.LOG

    b. C:\WINDOWS\TRACING\PPP.LOG

    c. C:\WINDOWS\SYSTEM32\MODEMLOG_MODEMNAME.TXT

    d. C:\WINDOWS\MODEMLOG_MODEMNAME.TXT

19. You must install a DHCP relay agent on your RRAS server such that your RRAS server may obtain IP addresses from a DHCP server on the network and assign them to remote access clients. True or false?

20. How many PPTP and L2TP VPN ports are normally created by default on a RRAS server?

    a. 128 PPTP, 128 L2TP

    b. 10 PPTP, 128 L2TP

    c. 128 PPTP, 10 L2TP

    d. 10 PPTP, 10 L2TP

CASE PROJECTS

The staff at Great Arctic North University are under increasing pressure to get more work done in less time, and often take work home in an attempt to meet this pressure. You think that configuring remote access can help solve many problems that are being experienced.

CASE PROJECTS

Case Project 10-1: Traveling Professors

Many of the professors at Great Arctic North University have laptops and are taking them home to finish work on evenings and weekends. However, often when they arrive at home, they find that they are missing a file that they need. Write a short proposal indicating how remote access could help solve this problem.

Case Project 10-2: Protocol Problems

You are about to implement remote access for the arts faculty. As part of the planning process, you need to decide which protocols you will implement. Which LAN protocols, remote access protocols, and VPN protocols do you think should be used and why?

Case Project 10-3: Securing Remote Access

The Engineering Department is concerned about security issues surrounding the use of remote access in their department. What remote access guidelines should you follow to improve security for those professors who use remote access to access university resources? What configuration options on the remote access servers and remote access clients would minimize security threats? Prepare a short memo that summarizes your points for the Engineering Department.

10

11

INTERNET AUTHENTICATION SERVICE

After reading this chapter, you will be able to:

♦ Understand and describe the purpose of the RADIUS protocol

♦ Describe the function of RADIUS servers, clients, and proxies

♦ Configure a RADIUS server using the Internet Authentication Service

♦ Configure a RADIUS proxy using the Internet Authentication Service

♦ Configure RRAS as a RADIUS client

♦ Troubleshoot RADIUS

A s discussed in Chapter 10, remote access is a vital component in many networks today because it is used to provide users outside of an office with access to resources on the internal network. To centralize remote access authentication and logging for organizations that deploy many remote access servers, you may use RADIUS. In this chapter, you will learn the various components that comprise RADIUS as well as how to configure them in Windows Server 2003. In addition, you will learn how to load balance RADIUS servers and make them fault tolerant. Finally, you will learn how to troubleshoot RADIUS.

RADIUS OVERVIEW

Remote Authentication Dial-In User Service (RADIUS) is a protocol designed to centralize the authentication process for large distributed networks. Originally intended for dial-up networks, RADIUS can now be used for many other types of devices, including VPN servers, switches, and wireless access points.

When using Windows Server 2003 for remote access, each server performs its own authentication using local remote access policies or user objects. It also keeps a local access log. A benefit of using RADIUS is that both of these tasks can be centralized on a single server. As well, remote access policies do not have to be synchronized between multiple remote access servers. Log analysis is also much easier if the logs are centralized on a single server.

The RADIUS process has two mandatory server roles:

- RADIUS client
- RADIUS server

A **RADIUS client** accepts authentication information from users or devices and forwards the authentication information to a RADIUS server. The RADIUS client is an access point to the network. Traditionally, a RADIUS client is a dial-up remote access server or VPN remote access server. However, in high-security situations, wireless access points and switches can be configured as RADIUS clients to force authentication before allowing network access.

A **RADIUS server** accepts authentication information from a RADIUS client. The RADIUS server then authorizes or denies the request based on the authentication information. RADIUS servers may use the local user database or an Active Directory database to authorize requests from RADIUS clients. The authorization or denial is returned to the RADIUS client, which then allows or denies a connection attempt. This process is shown in Figure 11-1.

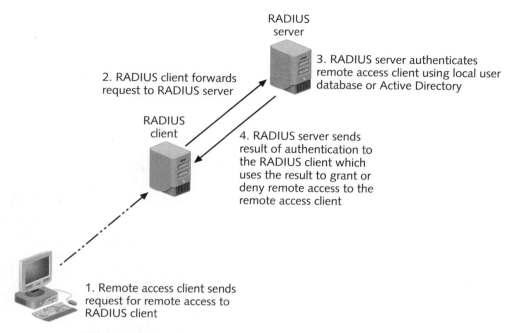

Figure 11-1   RADIUS authentication

Windows Server 2003 can act as a RADIUS client or a RADIUS server. RRAS can be configured as a RADIUS client when used for remote access. For Windows Server 2003 to act as a RADIUS server, **Internet Authentication Service (IAS)** must be installed.

A **RADIUS proxy** is an optional component that is used by organizations employing multiple RADIUS servers. The job of a RADIUS proxy is to act as an intermediary between RADIUS clients and RADIUS servers.

If a RADIUS proxy is used, it accepts authentication information from RADIUS clients, and passes the authentication information on to the appropriate RADIUS server. The RADIUS server passes the authorization or denial back to the RADIUS proxy, which then passes the authorization or denial back to the appropriate RADIUS client. This process is shown in Figure 11-2.

IAS can be configured as a RADIUS proxy. This feature is new in Windows Server 2003.

NOTE

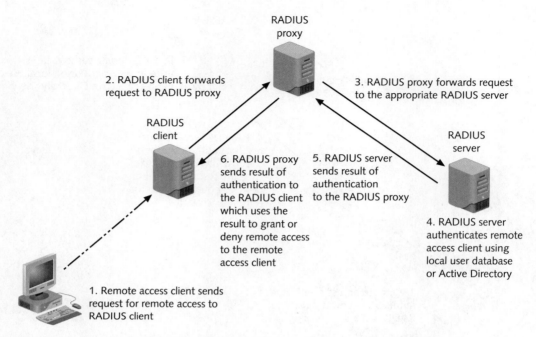

RADIUS
proxy

2. RADIUS client forwards
request to RADIUS proxy

3. RADIUS proxy forwards request
to the appropriate RADIUS server

RADIUS
client

RADIUS
server

6. RADIUS proxy
sends result of
authentication to
the RADIUS client
which uses the
result to grant or
deny remote access
to the remote
access client

5. RADIUS server
sends result of
authentication
to the RADIUS proxy

4. RADIUS server
authenticates remote
access client using
local user database
or Active Directory

1. Remote access client sends
request for remote access to
RADIUS client

Figure 11-2   Using a RADIUS proxy

Outsourcing Dial-up Requirements

You can use IAS to outsource your dial-up requirements and allow your roaming users to continue logging on using their Active Directory user name and password. To do this, you must coordinate configuration with a remote access provider, usually an ISP. Long-distance charges can be avoided if you choose an ISP with wide geographical coverage.

The ISP supplies a remote access server that is the RADIUS client. The ISP also supplies a server that acts as the RADIUS proxy. One of your servers with IAS installed is the RADIUS server.

Your users dial in to the ISP, and the dial-up software on the laptop passes the authentication information to the remote access server of the ISP. The remote access server of the ISP does not hold any user or password information for authenticating users. As a RADIUS client, it forwards all authentication requests to the RADIUS proxy.

The RADIUS proxy is configured with information that allows it to determine to which RADIUS server an authentication request should be forwarded. The authentication requests from your users are forwarded to your RADIUS server.

When your server running IAS receives authentication requests, it passes them on to an Active Directory domain controller. If IAS successfully authenticates users to Active Directory and remote access policies permit the connections, then IAS authorizes the connections.

If the connections are authorized, then IAS sends the authorizations to the RADIUS proxy. The RADIUS proxy sends the authorizations to the appropriate remote access servers. The remote access servers then connect the dial-up users and allow them access to the network. This process is shown in Figure 11-3

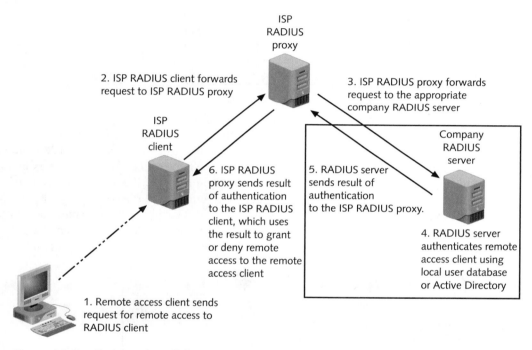

Figure 11-3   Outsourcing dial-up connections

CONFIGURING IAS AS A RADIUS SERVER

IAS is a standard component in Windows Server 2003 and is installed through Add or Remove Programs, Networking Services, as shown in Figure 11-4.

After IAS is installed, it must be configured using the Internet Authentication Service snap-in before it can be used.

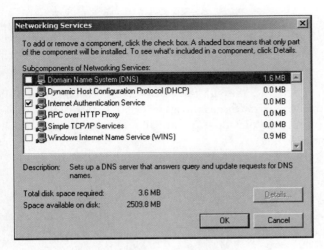

Figure 11-4 Installing the IAS service

If your IAS server does not use Active Directory to authenticate RADIUS clients, your IAS service is ready to be configured for RADIUS clients. However, if your IAS server authenticates users against an Active Directory database, it must be registered in Active Directory before it can read the remote access properties of users. To register an IAS server in the Internet Authentication Service snap-in, right-click Internet Authentication Service (Local), as shown in Figure 11-5, and click Register Server in Active Directory. This places the computer account for the server in a domain local group named RAS and IAS Servers. Membership in this group grants the proper rights to read the remote access properties of users.

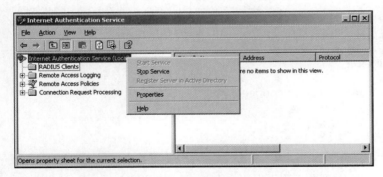

Figure 11-5 Registering an IAS server

IAS servers do not respond to requests from RADIUS clients unless the RADIUS clients are listed in the configuration of IAS. If a RADIUS proxy is used, it is listed as a RADIUS client.

To add a RADIUS client, simply right-click the RADIUS Clients folder in the Internet Authentication Service snap-in and choose New RADIUS Client. When a new RADIUS client is added, you are asked for a friendly name, and an IP address or DNS name, as shown in Figure 11-6.

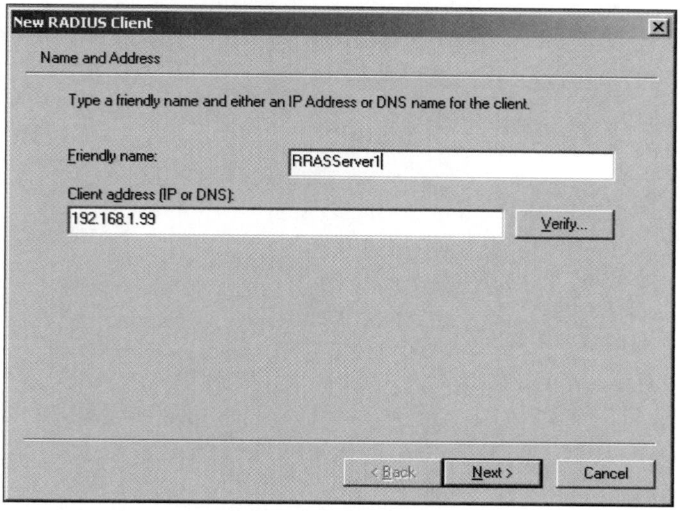

Figure 11-6   Specifying a RADIUS client in IAS

Next, you are also asked for the vendor of the RADIUS client, as shown in Figure 11-7. If you are not sure of the vendor type, choose RADIUS Standard to select a generic RADIUS vendor type.

This screen also allows you to set a shared secret that is used to authenticate connections between the RADIUS client and RADIUS server. In addition, the Request must contain the Message Authenticator attribute option requires that RADIUS clients include an MD5 hash of their request based on the shared secret. The MD5 hash prevents spoofed requests for authentication.

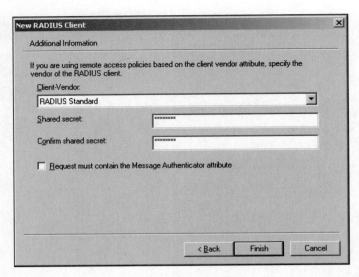

Figure 11-7   Specifying the configuration of a RADIUS client in IAS

Activity 11-1: Configuring IAS as a Radius Server

Time Required: 25 minutes

Objective: Install IAS so your server can act as a RADIUS server.

Description: Many of the professors at Great Arctic North University do not have access to high-speed Internet for VPN remote access at home. Until now, you have been providing a modem pool for them to dial into. However, this is awkward to maintain, and the cost of phone lines is very expensive. To solve this problem, you have struck a deal with a worldwide ISP with 1-800 access. The ISP will configure its RADIUS proxy to forward authentication attempts for your professors back to your RADIUS server. You must now install IAS on your server to act as a RADIUS server.

1. If necessary, start your server and log on as **Administrator**.

2. Click **Start**, point to **Control Panel**, and click **Add or Remove Programs**.

3. Click **Add/Remove Windows Components**.

4. Scroll down in the **Components** box, and double-click **Networking Services**.

5. Click the check box beside **Internet Authentication Service** to select it, and click **OK**.

6. Click **Next** to install IAS.

7. Click **Finish**, and close the Add or Remove Programs window.

8. Click **Start**, point to **Administrative Tools**, and click **Internet Authentication Service**.

9. Right-click **Internet Authentication Service**. Note that the option to Register Server in Active Directory is not selectable because your server is not a member of an Active Directory domain.

10. Click **RADIUS Clients** to view the list of remote access servers and RADIUS proxy servers that can use this RADIUS server for authentication. None are listed by default.

11. Right-click **RADIUS Clients**, and click **New RADIUS Client**.

12. In the Friendly name box, type **ISP RADIUS Proxy**.

13. In the Client address (IP or DNS) box, type **IP_Address**, where IP_Address is the IP Address of your partner's Local Area Connection, and click **Next**.

14. Click the **Client-Vendor** box, and click **Microsoft**.

15. In the Shared secret box, type **mysecret**. For a real implementation, you would pick a more secure password than this. Microsoft recommends that a RADIUS shared secret be at least 22 characters long and changed frequently.

16. In the Confirm shared secret box, type **mysecret**, and click **Finish**.

17. Close the Internet Authentication Service snap-in.

11

CONFIGURING RRAS AS A RADIUS CLIENT

Recall from earlier that a RRAS server acts as a RADIUS client if it passes authentication requests to it. You may specify that a RADIUS server be used for authentication when configuring RRAS for the first time by using the Routing and Remote Access Server Setup Wizard, as shown in Figure 11-8, or via the Security tab of RRAS server properties after RRAS has been configured, as shown in Figure 11-9.

Regardless of the method used to configure RRAS as a RADIUS client, you must specify the name or IP address of the RADIUS server as well as the shared secret used to validate RADIUS requests between the RADIUS client and server.

HANDS-ON
PROJECTS

Activity 11-2: Configuring a RRAS Client

Time Required: 15 minutes

Objective: Configure a RRAS server to use IAS for authentication.

Description: You have several VPN servers at different locations. You would like all of those VPN servers to authenticate users via a central IAS server. To do this, you will configure your remote access server to use RADIUS for authentication.

1. If necessary, start your server and log on as **Administrator**.

2. Click **Start**, point to **Administrative Tools**, and click **Routing and Remote Access**.

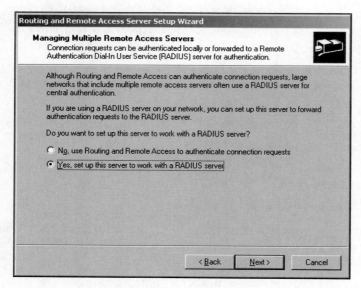

Figure 11-8   Configuring a RADIUS client using the Routing and Remote Access Server Setup Wizard

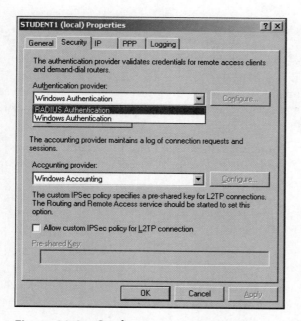

Figure 11-9   Configuring a RADIUS client using the Security tab of RRAS server Properties

3. Right-click your server, and click **Properties**.

4. Click the **Security** tab.

5. Click the **Authentication provider** box, and click **RADIUS Authentication**.

6. Click **Configure**.

7. Click **Add** to add a new RADIUS server to the list.

8. In the Server name box, type *IP_Address*, where *IP_Address* is the IP Address of your partner's Local Area Connection.

9. Click **Change** to configure a shared secret for authentication between the remote access server and the RADIUS server.

10. In the New secret box, type **mysecret**. This shared secret is also configured in IAS on your partner's computer.

11. In the Confirm new secret box, type **mysecret**, and click **OK**.

12. Click **OK** to close the Add RADIUS Server window.

13. Click **OK**, and click **OK**.

14. Read the warning message about restarting RRAS, and click **OK**.

15. Right-click your server, point to **All Tasks**, and click **Restart**.

16. Close the Routing and Remote Access snap-in.

Activity 11-3: Testing Radius

Time Required: 15 minutes

Objective: Create a VPN connection to your RRAS server to test RADIUS authentication.

Description: In the previous exercise, you configured your VPN server to use your partner's IAS service for authentication requests. To test whether the configuration was successful, you will create a VPN connection to your VPN server and log on with a user name that is defined in your partner's local user database.

1. If necessary, start your server and log on as **Administrator**.

2. Click **Start**, point to **Control Panel**, right-click **Network Connections**, and click **Open**.

3. Double-click **New Connection Wizard**.

4. Click **Next** to begin the New Connection Wizard.

5. Click **Connect to the network at my workplace**, and click **Next**.

6. Click **Virtual Private Network connection**, and click **Next**.

7. In the Company Name box, type **RADIUS Test**, and click **Next**.

8. Click **Do not dial the initial connection**, and click **Next**.

9. In the Host name or IP address box, type **IP_address**, where IP_address is the IP address of your Local Area Connection.

10. Click **Next**.

11. Click **Anyone's use**, so that all users can use this connection, and click **Next**.

12. Click **Finish**.

13. In the User name box, type **SKlump*X***, where *X* is your partner's student number. This is the user that your partner created and allowed remote access permission in Activity 10-6.

14. In the Password box, type **Password!**.

15. Click **Connect** to enable the connection. If RADIUS was configured successfully, your RRAS server contacted the IAS service on your partner's computer to authenticate the SKlump*X* user, where *X* is your partner's student number.

16. In the Network Connections window, double-click **RADIUS Test**.

17. Click the **General** tab, and click **Disconnect**.

18. Close the Network Connections window.

CONFIGURING IAS AS A RADIUS PROXY

A new feature of IAS in Windows Server 2003 is the ability to act as a RADIUS proxy. The previous version of IAS could only function as a RADIUS server.

IAS has the ability to act as both a RADIUS proxy and a RADIUS server at the same time. As a result, a mechanism is required to determine which RADIUS requests received are authenticated locally and which are forwarded to another RADIUS server. Connection request policies are used to determine how a RADIUS request is handled.

Remote RADIUS Server Groups

Remote RADIUS server groups are required for IAS to act as a RADIUS proxy. RADIUS requests and logging information are forwarded to remote RADIUS server groups, not individual RADIUS servers. However, you can create a **remote RADIUS server group** with a single RADIUS server in it.

Remote RADIUS server groups allow you to perform **load balancing** and **fault tolerance** between RADIUS servers. Each server in a remote RADIUS server group is assigned a priority number and weight, as shown in Figure 11-10. All RADIUS requests are sent to the RADIUS server with the highest priority (1 is the highest possible). If the RADIUS server with the highest priority is unavailable, then the request is forwarded to the RADIUS server with the next highest priority. This system allows fault tolerance between RADIUS servers.

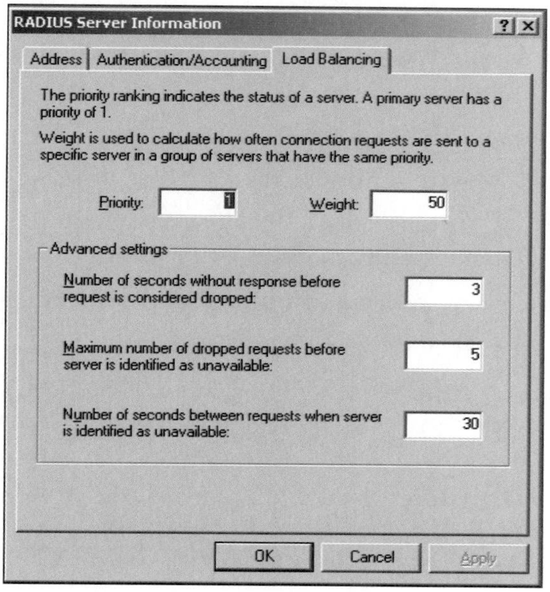

Figure 11-10   Load Balancing tab of RADIUS server Properties

To provide load balancing between RADIUS servers, the weight setting is used. If two RADIUS servers are configured with the same priority, then load balancing is performed between them. The weight is used to determine the proportion of requests sent to each RADIUS server. For example, if two RADIUS servers in a remote RADIUS server group are configured with the same priority, but one has a weight of 75 and the other a weight of 25, then the RADIUS server configured with a weight of 75 is sent 75% of RADIUS requests by the RADIUS proxy.

Activity 11-4: Creating a Remote RADIUS Server Group

Time Required: 15 minutes

Objective: Create a remote RADIUS server group that can be used when IAS is configured as a RADIUS proxy.

Description: The engineering college in Great Arctic North University uses a number of UNIX systems for their day-to-day work. All of their user accounts are held on these machines. You would like to configure your remote access system so that engineering users can use your VPN servers to access university resources remotely. To implement this, you will configure IAS to act as a RADIUS proxy and forward RADIUS requests for engineering users to the engineering RADIUS servers. The Engineering Department has configured two RADIUS servers to be used for fault tolerance. Load balancing will not be performed.

1. If necessary, start your server and log on as **Administrator**.

2. Click **Start**, point to **Administrative Tools**, and click **Internet Authentication Service**.

3. Double-click **Connection Request Processing**.

4. Right-click **Remote RADIUS Server Groups**, and click **New Remote RADIUS Server Group**.

5. Click **Next** to start the New Remote RADIUS Server Group Wizard.

6. Confirm that **Typical (one primary server and one backup server)** is selected.

7. In the Group name box, type **Engineering**, and click **Next**.

8. In the Primary server box, type **IP_Address**, where IP_address is the IP Address of your partner's Local Area Connection. All RADIUS requests will first be sent to IAS on your partner's RADIUS server.

9. In the Backup server box, type **IP_Address**, where IP_address is the IP Address of your Local Area Connection. Any RADIUS requests that could not be sent to IAS on your partner's RADIUS server will now be sent to IAS on your RADIUS server.

10. In the Shared secret box, type **mysecret**.

11. In the Confirm shared secret box, type **mysecret**, and click **Next**.

12. Click the **Start the New Connection Request Policy Wizard**. When this wizard closes, check the box to deselect it, and click **Finish**.

13. If necessary, click **Remote RADIUS Server Groups** to view the remote RADIUS server groups that are created. One named Engineering should be here.

14. Double-click **Engineering** to view its properties. Two RADIUS servers are listed as part of the group. The first is listed with a priority of 1, the second with a priority of 2. If the first RADIUS server fails, then the second is used.

15. Click **OK** to close the Engineering Properties window.

16. Close the Internet Authentication Service snap-in.

Connection Request Policies

A **connection request policy** is constructed similarly to a remote access policy. Each connection request policy has conditions. If the conditions match the request, then a profile is applied. It should be noted that there are no permissions in a connection request policy.

The conditions of a connection request policy are a subset of the conditions found in remote access policies. These include Day-And-Time-Restrictions, Client-IP-Address, and Client-Vendor.

The profile in a connection request policy has very different options than the profile in a remote access policy. It defines the location for authentication, log settings, rules to modify attributes in requests, and attributes that can be added to requests.

When the location for authentication is defined, as shown in Figure 11-11, you have three choices. The Authenticate requests on this server option means that this server acts as the RADIUS server. The Forward requests to the following remote RADIUS server group for authentication option means that this server acts as a RADIUS proxy and forwards the request to one of a defined group of RADIUS servers. The Accept users without validating credentials option means the users matching the conditions of this policy are authorized regardless of their user name and password.

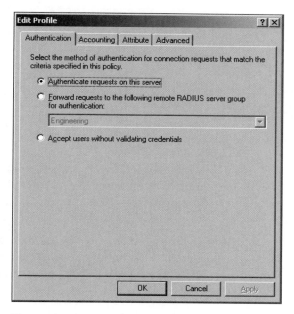

Figure 11-11   Authentication tab in a remote connection policy profile

The Accounting tab of the profile allows you to pick a RADIUS server group to handle logging for this policy.

The Attribute tab of the profile, as shown in Figure 11-12, allows you to create search and replace rules for values of certain attributes. For example, you could configure this connection request policy so that all forwarded RADIUS requests have a single Calling-Station-ID. This could then be used by the RADIUS server to identify requests from this RADIUS proxy and apply special rules.

The Advanced tab of the profile allows you to specify the value of attributes that are added to the RADIUS request. This is similar to the Advanced tab of the profile in a remote access policy.

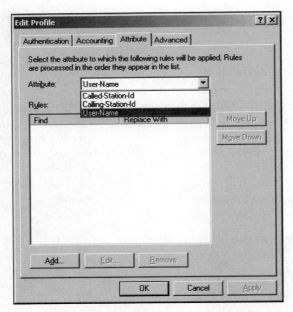

Figure 11-12 Attribute tab in a remote connection policy profile

Only one connection request policy exists by default. It is named Use Windows authentication for all users. This connection request policy is configured so that all RADIUS requests received by this server are authenticated by this server. This means that this server act as a RADIUS server for all requests it receives.

Connection request policies have an order, just as remote access policies have an order. If you would like your server to act as a RADIUS proxy for some requests, then the policy that defines those conditions must be a higher priority than Use Windows authentication for all users.

Activity 11-5: Creating a Connection Request Policy

Time Required: 15 minutes

Objective: Create a new connection request policy to configure your server as a RADIUS proxy.

Description: In Activity 11-4, you started the configuration process for your server to act as a RADIUS proxy for the Engineering Department. You must now create a new connection request policy that forwards RADIUS requests from engineering users to the Engineering remote RADIUS server group.

1. If necessary, start your server and log on as **Administrator**.

2. Click **Start**, point to **Administrative Tools**, and click **Internet Authentication Service**.

3. Double-click **Connection Request Processing** to expand it.

4. Right-click **Connection Request Policies**, and click **New Connection Request Policy**.

5. Click **Next** to start the New Connection Request Policy Wizard.

6. Click **A custom policy**.

7. In the Policy name box, type **EngineeringProxy**, and click **Next**.

8. Click **Add** to add a condition to the connection request policy.

9. Click **User–Name**, click **Add**, type *-E, and click **OK**. This connection request policy now applies to all users with "-E" at the end of their user name. All Engineering users add this to their regular user name when they remotely log on.

10. Click **Next**.

11. Click **Edit Profile**.

12. Click **Forward requests to the following remote RADIUS server group for authentication**, and confirm that Engineering is selected.

13. Click the **Attribute** tab.

14. Confirm that **User–Name** is selected in the Attribute box.

15. Click **Add** to configure a new rule for the User-Name attribute.

16. In the Find box, type **–E**, leave the **Replace with** box empty, and click **OK**. This removes the "-E" from the user name of Engineering users before it is forwarded to the engineering RADIUS server.

17. Click **OK** to finish editing the profile, and click **Next**.

18. Click **Finish** to complete the wizard.

19. Notice that the EngineeringProxy connection request policy has been added as the first in the processing order. This ensures that RADIUS requests for engineering users with "-E" in their user name are forwarded to the Engineering remote RADIUS server group. All other RADIUS requests for users without "-E" in their user name are handled by the default connection request policy.

20. Close the Internet Authentication Service snap-in.

TROUBLESHOOTING RADIUS

Using RADIUS to authenticate remote access users adds little complexity to the process of allowing remote access for users. As a result, most remote access problems are not related to RADIUS.

To determine whether RADIUS is preventing remote access, first ensure that users can obtain remote access without RADIUS. This can be done by creating a test user account on a remote access server and configuring the remote access server properties in RRAS to use Windows Authentication instead of RADIUS Authentication. If users cannot gain access, then the problem is not related to RADIUS and may be caused by a variety of hardware and software factors discussed previously in Chapter 10.

Alternately, if users can obtain remote access without RADIUS, then the problem is likely the result of an incorrect configuration of the RADIUS server, proxy or client. First, ensure that the RADIUS client, proxy and server can communicate via TCP/IP; this can be done using the ping utility. If they cannot communicate, then the problem is network related.

If the RADIUS client, proxy and server can communicate, ensure that the Internet Authentication Service is started on the RADIUS proxy and server and that all components use the same shared secret. If your RADIUS server is configured to use Active Directory for authentication, ensure that it is authorized in Active Directory and that the required user objects exist in the Active Directory database and are not disabled or locked out. If Remote RADIUS Server Groups on a RADIUS proxy are used, ensure that settings in any connection request policies are correct and allow requests to be forwarded to the appropriate RADIUS server.

Log files are a valuable troubleshooting tool. You should check the Event Log regularly for any messages related to IAS. IAS can also log authentication requests to a local file or a SQL server, as shown in Figure 11-13.

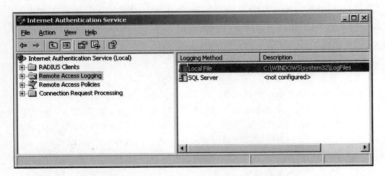

Figure 11-13   The Remote Access Logging folder

To control logging, simply view the properties of the SQL Server or Local File object, as shown in Figure 11-14. Regardless of the destination used for logging, you can control which events are logged, including accounting requests, authentication requests, and periodic status. No events are logged by default.

When logging to a local file, you can also choose the format of the log and how often a new log file is created, as shown in Figure 11-15. By default, the file location of this log is C:\WINDOWS\system32\LogFiles\IN*yymm*.log, where *yy* is the year, and *mm* is the month.

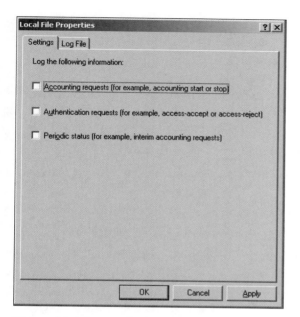

Figure 11-14   Local File Properties

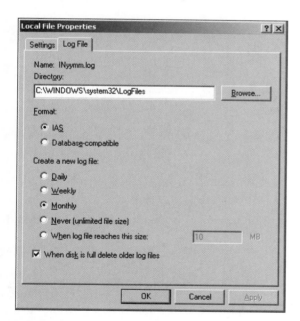

Figure 11-15   Log File tab of Local File Properties

Activity 11-6: Logging IAS Information to a File

Time Required: 5 minutes

Objective: Enable IAS event logging.

Description: A user in the Arts Department is having difficulty gaining remote access. You suspect that RADIUS may be the problem. To troubleshoot it, you enable IAS logging to a file and view the contents of the log file after a failed remote access attempt.

1. If necessary, start your server and log on as **Administrator**.

2. Click **Start**, point to **Administrative Tools**, and click **Internet Authentication Service**.

3. Double-click **Remote Access Logging** to expand its information.

4. Right-click **Local File** in the right pane, and click **Properties**.

5. Place a check mark beside Accounting requests to ensure that all accounting requests are logged.

6. Place a check mark beside Authentication requests to ensure that all valid and non-valid authentication requests are logged.

7. Place a check mark beside Periodic status to ensure that all interim accounting requests are logged.

8. Press **OK** to close the Local File Properties.

9. Close the Internet Authentication Service snap-in.

CHAPTER SUMMARY

- RADIUS may be used to centralize remote access authentication and logging.

- RADIUS is composed of the RADIUS clients, RADIUS servers, and RADIUS proxies.

- RADIUS clients forward authentication requests to RADIUS servers. RADIUS servers then authenticate the requests and authorize the connections.

- A RADIUS proxy can be used as an intermediary between RADIUS clients and servers in large environments.

- IAS allows Windows Server 2003 to act as a RADIUS server.

- RRAS can act as a RADIUS client when configured as a remote access server.

- IAS can also be configured as a RADIUS proxy.

- Connection request policies are used for each request to determine whether IAS acts as a RADIUS server or a RADIUS proxy. Connection request policies are composed of conditions and a profile.

- IAS can log information to a file or SQL server.

KEY TERMS

connection request policy — A policy used by IAS to determine whether a request is authenticated locally or passed on to a RADIUS server. Such policies are composed of conditions and a profile.

fault tolerance — Configuring a system in such a way that if a single component fails an alternate can be used.

Internet Authentication Service (IAS) — A service that allows Windows Server 2003 to act as a RADIUS server and a RADIUS proxy.

load balancing — Splitting network requests between two or more servers to reduce the load on each server.

RADIUS client — A server or device that passes authentication requests to a RADIUS proxy or RADIUS server. Most commonly, these are remote access servers.

RADIUS proxy — An intelligent server that acts as an intermediary between RADIUS clients and RADIUS servers. This server decides which RADIUS server should be used to authenticate a request.

RADIUS server — A server in the RADIUS process that accepts and authorizes authentication requests from RADIUS clients and RADIUS proxies.

Remote Authentication Dial–In User Service (RADIUS) — A service that allows remote access servers (RADIUS clients) to delegate responsibility for authentication to a central server (RADIUS server).

remote RADIUS server group — A grouping of RADIUS servers to which IAS forwards connection requests when acting as a RADIUS proxy. Load balancing and fault tolerance can be configured.

11

REVIEW QUESTIONS

1. Which RADIUS component authorizes connections?
   a. RADIUS client
   b. RADIUS server
   c. RADIUS proxy
   d. RADIUS service

2. Which RADIUS component is optional?
   a. RADIUS client
   b. RADIUS server
   c. RADIUS proxy
   d. none of the above

3. Which Windows service functions as a RADIUS server and RADIUS proxy?
   a. RRAS
   b. dial-up networking

   c. IAS

   d. Active Directory

4. In a remote RADIUS server group with two servers, which of the servers handles the incoming requests?

   a. the server with the highest priority

   b. the server with the highest weight

   c. the server with the lowest weight

   d. neither server, they use load balancing

5. If a connection request policy specifies that authentication happens on the local server, then IAS acts as what type of RADIUS component?

   a. RADIUS client

   b. RADIUS server

   c. RADIUS proxy

   d. RADIUS service

6. Which Windows service functions as a RADIUS client?

   a. RRAS

   b. dial-up networking

   c. IAS

   d. Active Directory

7. When specifying a RADIUS client in the Internet Authentication Service snap-in, which vendor type should you choose if you are unsure of the vendor type?

   a. RADIUS-MD5

   b. RADIUS Standard

   c. Microsoft

   d. Generic RADIUS

8. Your remote RADIUS server group has three servers with equal priority. Which of the servers will handle incoming requests?

   a. the first server added to the RADIUS server group

   b. the server with the highest weight

   c. the server with the lowest weight

   d. all servers

9. What must be done before a RADIUS server can authenticate remote access users in an Active Directory database?

   a. The RADIUS server must be registered in Active Directory.

   b. The computer account for the RADIUS server must be placed in the IAS group in Active Directory.

c. The computer account for the RADIUS client must be placed in the RAS and IAS Servers group in Active Directory.

d. none of the above

10. IAS can function as a RADIUS proxy and a RADIUS server at the same time. True or false?

11. What is used to authenticate connections between a RADIUS client and a RADIUS server?

a. Kerberos

b. a shared secret

c. a certificate

d. Active Directory

12. What is the highest priority that can be assigned to a RADIUS server in a remote RADIUS server group?

a. 1

b. 5

c. 10

d. 99

13. What are the two components of a connection request policy? (Choose two answers.)

a. conditions

b. permissions

c. profile

d. rights

14. RADIUS server groups perform two important functions between RADIUS servers. What are they? (Choose all that apply.)

a. load balancing

b. authentication

c. security

d. fault tolerance

15. The conditions of a connection request policy are a subset of the conditions found in remote access policies. True or false?

16. You can enable logging in IAS; however, this logging can only occur to a SQL server. True or false?

17. What is the default location for a RADIUS authentication log file?

a. C:\WINDOWS\system32\LogFiles\

b. C:\VAR\ADM\logfiles

    c. C:\WINNT\system32\LogFiles\

    d. C:\WINDOWS\system32\RADIUS\LogFiles

18. You need to access a RADIUS authentication log that was originally generated in March of 2001. Assuming that the default settings are used, how would you go about this?

    a. Look for a file named IN0103.log.

    b. Look for a file named IN0301.log.

    c. You will have to open and examine each file; this is why you should have named them so their names are intuitive.

    d. Open and examine the Properties of each file, looking for a creation date in March 2001.

19. Which Active Directory group contains registered RADIUS servers?

    a. Enterprise Admins

    b. RRAS Servers

    c. RAS and IAS Servers

    d. RADIUS Servers

20. Which RADIUS events may be logged? (Choose all that apply.)

    a. Accounting requests

    b. Authentications requests

    c. RRAS failure attempts

    d. Periodic status

CASE PROJECTS

The number of staff who use remote access at Great Arctic North University is growing larger each month. As a result, the university has decided to centralize the authentication of remote access users using RADIUS and Active Directory.

CASE
PROJECTS

Case Project 11-1: Comparing Remote Access and RADIUS

Most departments at Great Arctic North University maintain their own remote access servers and password databases. As a result, many people at Great Arctic North University are skeptical about using RADIUS to authenticate users. They feel that RADIUS would add complexity to their remote access servers. Write a short memo to alleviate their concerns.

Case Project 11-2: Configuring RADIUS Proxies

You are about to implement RADIUS for the Arts faculty. Different staff in the Arts faculty are authenticated to different Active Directory databases. As part of the planning process, describe how you can use RADIUS proxies and connection request policies to ensure that staff members in the Arts faculty are authenticated using the correct Active Directory database.

Case Project 11-3: Outsourcing RADIUS

Since remote access has become more popular at Great Arctic North University, you are considering outsourcing the remote access requirements to a local ISP. You wish to ensure that all users are authenticated using the RADIUS servers within the university. What do you need to configure for this to work properly? What are the benefits and disadvantages of outsourcing remote access?

11

12

ROUTING

After reading this chapter, you will be able to:

- Configure Windows Server 2003 as a router
- Interpret and manage routing tables
- Describe the function of dynamic routing
- Implement a dynamic routing protocol on Windows Server 2003
- Control traffic sent through a router using packet filters
- Create and configure demand-dial connections for routing
- Troubleshoot routing

Many technical professionals do not realize that Windows Server 2003 can be used as a very flexible router when required. For instance, in order to decrease network bandwidth requirements and connectivity charges, it can be configured to connect to other offices in your organization only when there is network traffic. It can also allow connectivity to the Internet for small and medium-sized organizations. In this chapter, you will learn about the routing capabilities of Windows Server 2003 as well as how to configure and manage routing using the Routing and Remote Access snap-in.

CONFIGURING ROUTERS

Recall from Chapter 2 that a router is a network device that moves packets from one network to another. More specifically, a router may be a computer or network device with more than one network interface. Each network interface will be connected to a different TCP/IP network, and the router will forward packets back and forth between the networks. Separating TCP/IP networks in this fashion reduces the number of packet collisions that may occur on physical network media since computers typically communicate more frequently with computers on the same TCP/IP network. TCP/IP, IPX/SPX, and Apple-Talk are protocols that can be routed.

 Computer devices that have more than one network interface are called **multihomed devices**.

 The routing of packets from one network to another is often called **IP forwarding**.

Most large organizations have specialized hardware from Cisco or other vendors that act as routers on their networks. However, Windows Server 2003 can be used as a router for many small and medium-sized organizations. It is able to perform routing for the TCP/IP and AppleTalk protocols. IPX/SPX routing is not supported.

The main benefit of implementing Windows Server 2003 as a router is cost. If you already have a server, you only need to add a network card and configure Windows to make it a router. This is useful if the routing requirements for your organization are simple, and a server has unused capacity. Large organizations are more likely to require the advanced features that a hardware-based router provides.

When connecting to the Internet, other advanced features, such as a proxy for network requests, are also often required. In fact, if advanced Internet connectivity features are required, Microsoft has a product called **Internet Security and Acceleration Server (ISA)** that provides proxy services.

To be a router, the server must be connected to at least two networks. A network interface in the server is connected to each network and has an IP address on that network.

Routing is part of RRAS and can be configured using the same wizard that is used to configure dial-up and VPN servers. If RRAS is already configured on a server, such as a VPN server, then routing can be configured as an additional service without losing the existing configuration.

To add routing as an additional service using the Routing and Remote Access snap-in, open the properties of the server, as shown in Figure 12-1. To enable general routing, click Router. When this option is checked, the server becomes a router. However, for it to act as an IP router, you must also select the Enable IP routing option on the IP tab, as shown in Figure 12-2.

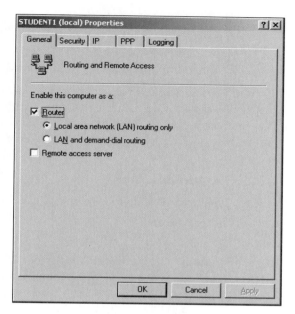

Figure 12-1   Enabling routing

12

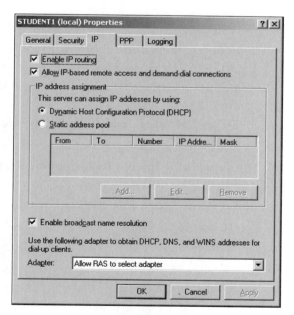

Figure 12-2   Enabling IP routing

Activity 12-1: Configuring RRAS as a Router

Time Required: 15 minutes

Objective: Configure Windows Server 2003 as a router.

Description: You have decided to use Windows Server 2003 as a router in several smaller campus locations where the cost of a specialized hardware router cannot be justified. You will confirm that both network cards in your computer are configured with an appropriate IP address, and then enable routing using the Routing and Remote Access Server Setup Wizard.

1. If necessary, start your server and log on as **Administrator**.

2. Confirm that your server has correctly configured IP addresses on both network cards.

   a. Click **Start**, click **Run**, type **cmd**, and press **Enter**.

   b. Type **ipconfig** and press **Enter**.

   c. The adapter Local Area Connection should be configured with the IP address **192.168.1.X**, where X is your student number, and a subnet mask of **255.255.255.0**. If it is not configured properly, configure it now.

   d. The adapter Local Area Connection 2 should be configured with the IP address **X.0.0.1**, where X is your student number, and a subnet mask of **255.0.0.0**. If it is not configured properly, configure it now.

   e. Close the command prompt.

3. Click **Start**, point to **Administrative Tools**, click **Routing and Remote Access**.

4. Before configuring this server as a router, you must remove the existing configuration. The existing configuration was created in Chapters 10 and 11. If RRAS is not configured, this step can be skipped.

   a. Right-click your server, and click **Disable Routing and Remote Access**.

   b. Click **Yes** to confirm.

5. Right-click your server, and click **Configure and Enable Routing and Remote Access**.

6. Click **Next** to begin the Routing and Remote Access Server Setup Wizard.

7. Click **Custom configuration** and click **Next**. You want to configure a LAN router, and that is not a standard wizard option.

8. Click the **LAN routing** check box, and click **Next**.

9. Click **Finish**.

10. Click **Yes** to start the Routing and Remote Access Service.

11. View the configuration that has been enabled by the Routing and Remote Access Server Setup Wizard.

   a. Right-click your server, and click **Properties**.

   b. On the **General** tab, the options Router and Local area network (LAN) routing only are selected.

   c. Click the **IP** tab.

   d. The **Enable IP routing** option is selected.

   e. Click **Cancel**.

12. Close the Routing and Remote Access snap-in.

ROUTING TABLES

Routers are responsible for making intelligent decisions about how to move packets from one network to another in the fastest way possible. To keep track of the different networks that are available, a **routing table** is used.

The routing table is a list of the networks that are known to the router. Each network entry is called a route. If a router wishes to communicate with computers on a particular TCP/IP network, it must locate a **route** to that network from the routing table. On Windows Server 2003, these routes are stored in the Windows registry and loaded into memory at system startup so that routes may be retrieved quickly.

Each entry in an IP routing table contains the IP address of the network, the subnet mask of the network, the gateway that is used to reach the network, the router interface that is used to reach the gateway, and the metric that measures how far away the network is.

 The meaning of the metric value in a routing table varies depending on which routing protocol is being used.

 All computers have a routing table, whether they function as a router or not. This routing table lists the networks that the computer is attached to so that it can send packets onto the correct network interface.

To view the routing table on a server, you can right-click the Static Routes folder under the IP Routing folder in the Routing and Remote Access snap-in and choose Show IP Routing Table. You can also use the **netstat –r command**, or the **route print** command to view the routing table. Sample output of the route print command is shown in Figure 12-3. This figure shows the routing table for a router with two network cards, configured with the IP addresses 192.168.1.33/24 and 1.0.0.1/8, where /24 and /8 represent the number of bits in the network ID for the 192.168.1.33 and 1.0.0.1 network cards, respectively. The entry with the network destination 0.0.0.0 listed in the routing table represents the default gateway for the router. The subnet mask 255.255.255.255 is used to refer to an individual IP address.

Figure 12-3   Output of the route print command

Windows Server 2003 automatically configures the default gateway route and routes to local networks from the contents of TCP/IP properties for each network interface. If there is no route that lists a specific destination network for a TCP/IP packet, it is forwarded to the IP address of the default gateway. The default gateway is a router that may contain a route to the destination network; if it does not, it will forward the TCP/IP packet to its configured default gateway, and so on until the packet reaches its destination.

You may manually add routes to the routing table to specify networks that are not local to the computer by using the **route command**. The route command normally affects the routing table stored in memory; you must use the −p option to force the route command to write the information to the Windows registry so that it may be used on each system at startup. Some common route commands and their descriptions are listed in Table 12-1.

Table 12-1   Common route commands

Command	Description
route print	Displays the routing table
route print 8*	Displays all routes to networks that start with 8
route −f	Removes all entries from the routing table
route add 8.0.0.0 mask 255.0.0.0 192.168.1.88	Adds a route to the 8.0.0.0/8 network via the gateway 192.168.1.88
route add 8.0.0.0 mask 255.0.0.0 192.168.1.88 IF 1 METRIC 4	Adds a route to the 8.0.0.0/8 network via the gateway 192.168.1.88. This route has a metric of 4 and must use the first interface in the computer to reach the gateway

Table 12-1   Common route commands (continued)

Command	Description
route add 8.0.0.1 mask 255.0.0.0 192.168.1.88	Adds a route to the host 8.0.0.1 via the gateway 192.168.1.88
route delete 8.0.0.0	Deletes the route to the 8.0.0.0 network in the routing table
route change 8.0.0.0 mask 255.255.0.0	Changes the route to the 8.0.0.0 network so that is uses a 16-bit subnet mask

You may also add routes to the routing table in the Routing and Remote Access snap-in. To do so, simply right-click the Static Routes folder underneath the IP Routing folder, choose New Static Route, and supply the appropriate information, as shown in Figure 12-4.

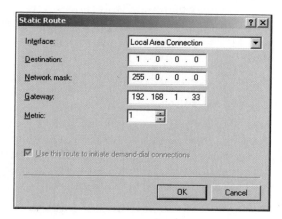

Figure 12-4   Creating a new Static Route

By default, the only networks of which a router is aware are the ones it is attached to with a network card. Any other entries in the routing table must be added. If entries are added manually, the router uses static routing. If entries are added automatically, based on a routing protocol, then the router uses dynamic routing.

Static routing is generally used when security is required. With static routing tables, you know exactly what is in each routing table and can control how packets move between networks. For example, in a campus environment, to reduce the chances of a packet sniffer being able to capture traffic, you may configure only one backbone path on which all network traffic travels.

The maintenance of a static routing table on each router can become cumbersome. Each time a new network is added, the routing table of each server must be changed. Each time a change is made, there is also a chance of an error being made in the entry and functionality being lost, even if only for a short period of time.

12

Dynamic routing is used in most environments. In this system, the routers talk to each other to build their routing tables. By setting the metric on network interfaces, you can still control how packets move through the network without the hassle of configuring each router separately.

Activity 12-2: Configuring a Static Route

Time Required: 20 minutes

Objective: Configure a static route to a remote network.

Description: Users in the Science faculty at Great Arctic North University have installed a research network that is attached to the second NIC on a server. Members of the Engineering faculty require access to the computers on this network; however, the router in the Engineering Department does not have a route to the remote research network. You will configure a route on your router that specifies how to reach the network connected to the second NIC on your partner's computer.

1. If necessary, start your server and log on as **Administrator**.

2. Click **Start**, click **Run**, type **cmd**, and press **Enter**.

3. Type **route print** and press **Enter**. There are only two networks in the routing table. These are the two networks you are connected to on the Local Area Connection and Local Area Connection 2 interfaces. Also notice that for each of these two entries, the metrics are different. If your computer is configured with a default gateway for Internet access, you will also see a route for the default gateway.

4. Type **ping** *IP_address*, where *IP_address* is the IP address of your partner's Local Area Connection 2. Note that the ping attempt is unsuccessful because your computer does not contain a route to the network configured on your partner's Local Area Connection 2.

5. Type **route add** *x*.0.0.0 **mask 255.0.0.0** *IP_address* **-p** where *x* is your partner's student number and *IP_address* is the IP address of your partner's Local Area Connection on the 192.168.1.0 network. This configures a route on your local computer to the network on your partner's Local Area Connection 2 via your partner's Local Area Connection. This route will be saved to the Windows registry for future use.

6. Type **route print** and press **Enter**. Note that the new route is available.

7. Type **ping** *IP_address*, where *IP_address* is the IP address of your partner's Local Area Connection 2. Note that the ping attempt is successful because your computer contains a route to the network configured on your partner's Local Area Connection 2.

8. Close the command prompt.

ROUTING PROTOCOLS

Routing protocols are responsible for calculating the best path from one network to another, and advertising routes for dynamic routing. When calculating the path, each routing protocol uses a different routing algorithm. When advertising routing, each routing protocol advertises different amounts of information and with a different frequency.

The two routing protocols used in Windows Server 2003 for IP routing are:

- **Routing Information Protocol (RIP)**
- **Open Shortest Path First (OSPF)**

RIP

Of the protocols supported by Windows Server 2003, RIP is the simpler of the two routing protocols and consequently the most popular. No configuration is necessary under most circumstances.

RIP is a **distance-vector routing** protocol. The distance between networks is measured by the number of routers through which the data must pass, or hops. For example, if one router must be passed through to reach a network, it is one **hop** away. The best path from one network to another is the path with the least number of hops. Routing using this method is known as distance-vector routing.

The maximum number of hops used by RIP is 15. A network is considered unreachable at 16 hops.

RIP does not differentiate between different link speeds. One hop across an ISDN line is treated the same as one hop across a T-1 line. In larger environments, this is unacceptable and leads to inefficient routing.

Each RIP router sends a broadcast packet every 30 seconds. A complete copy of the routing table is contained in this packet. RIP version 2 is capable of using multicasts instead of broadcast packets for these announcements.

Activity 12-3: Installing and Using RIP

Time Required: 20 minutes

Objective: Configure your server as an RIP router.

Description: The default configuration of the routers you have configured is static routing. You are tired of making manual changes to these routers every time there is a routing change. To implement automatic updating of the routing tables in your routers, you will configure RIP on your server.

12

1. If necessary, start your server and log on as **Administrator**.

2. Click **Start**, point to **Administrative Tools**, and click **Routing and Remote Access**.

3. If necessary, double-click your server to expand it.

4. If necessary, double-click **IP Routing** to expand it.

5. Right-click **General**, and click **New Routing Protocol**.

6. In the New Routing Protocol window, click **RIP version 2 for Internet Protocol**, and click **OK**. Notice that RIP is added as an option underneath IP Routing.

7. Click **RIP**. Interfaces using RIP are listed here. By default, there are none.

8. Right-click **RIP**, and click **New Interface**.

9. If necessary, click **Local Area Connection**, and click **OK**.

10. Click **OK** to accept the default configuration

11. Right-click **RIP**, click **New Interface**, click **Local Area Connection 2** if necessary, and click **OK**.

12. Click **OK** to accept the default configuration.

13. As your router communicates with other routers in the classroom that have enabled RIP, the routing table grows.

14. View the new routing table.

    a. Right-click **Static Routes**, and click **Show IP Routing Table**.

    b. Expand the window so that you can view all of the columns.

    c. The routing table entries with RIP listed in the protocol column are learned through RIP.

    d. Close the IP Routing Table window.

15. Close the Routing and Remote Access snap-in.

Although RIP is a relatively simple protocol to manage, there are still many options that can be configured, if required. A few RIP options can be configured globally for the entire server in the properties of the RIP protocol, but most are configured separately for each interface.

In the properties of the RIP protocol in the Routing and Remote Access snap-in, you can configure the type of events to be logged. In addition, you can configure from which IP addresses this router accepts updates, as shown in Figure 12-5. The default setting is the Accept announcements from all routers option. This is a security risk, and should be changed to the Accept announcements from listed routers only option.

In the properties of the interfaces listed in the RIP protocol, you can configure settings for each interface. The General tab is shown in Figure 12-6. The Operation mode is set to Periodic update mode, which removes entries from the routing table if the router that originally advertised them is disabled or unreachable. You can also choose Auto static update mode, which adds RIP learned routes to the routing table as static entries, which are never removed. This is useful for routing with dial-up connections to maintain a consistent routing table.

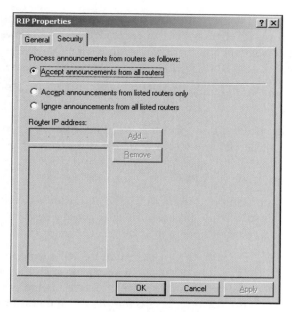

Figure 12-5   Security tab of RIP Properties

12

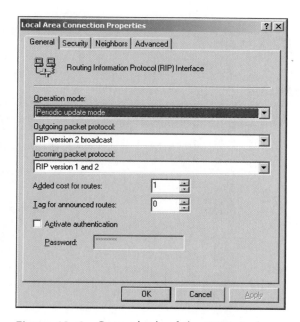

Figure 12-6   General tab of the RIP interface properties dialog box

RIP can use broadcasts or multicasts when sending information to other RIP routers. As shown in Figure 12-6, the Outgoing packet protocol can be configured as RIP version 1 broadcast, RIP version 2 broadcast, RIP version 2 multicast, and Silent RIP. The default setting is RIP version 2 broadcast. Silent RIP disables outgoing RIP announcements.

The Incoming packet protocol can be configured as Ignore incoming packets, RIP version 1 and 2, RIP version 1 only, and RIP version 2 only. The default is RIP version 1 and 2.

RIP routers advertise the routes they learn from other routers. This allows each router to build a large routing table that lists all possible networks. When a router advertises a route learned from another router, the number of hops is incremented by 1. However, you can change this default by modifying the value in Added **cost** for routes.

You can also select the Activate authentication option to force authentication between routers when announcements are sent. For this to function properly, the feature must be enabled on all routers. The password is sent in plain text and is not an effective form of security.

The Security tab, as shown in Figure 12-7, allows you to configure which incoming and outgoing routes are accepted on this interface. In addition to accepting all routes, you can choose to accept or ignore a range of addresses. If you use only a defined range of network numbers, then it is a good idea to configure the interface to use the Accept all routes in the ranges listed option. The options are the same for announcing outgoing routes as for accepting incoming routes.

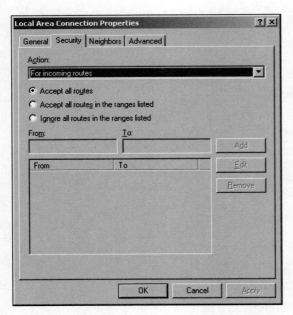

Figure 12-7   Security tab of the RIP interface properties dialog box

The Neighbors tab, as shown in Figure 12-8, is used only if broadcasts and multicasts are limited on the network. You can configure unicast IP addresses that are neighbors. This interface then communicates with the neighbors instead of, or in addition to, making broadcast and multicast announcements.

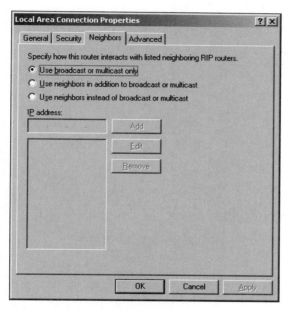

Figure 12-8 Neighbors tab of the RIP interface properties dialog box

The Advanced tab, as shown in Figure 12-9, allows you to configure a wide variety of settings. You can adjust how often routing table announcements are sent, how long entries in the routing table last before they expire, and how long after they expire they are removed from the routing table.

Split-horizon processing, which stops information from going back in the direction it was received from, and **poison-reverse processing**, which marks a network as unreachable if it goes down, are used to prevent routing loops in the case of a router failure. Triggered updates are sent when a change is made to the routing table, if this feature is enabled. If the Send clean-up updates when stopping feature is enabled, then a router announcement that expires all of the routes it has been advertising is sent when the router is shut down.

Other options disable the processing or sending of host routes and default routes in router announcements. The Disable subnet summarization option stops the router from aggregating multiple subnets as a single router entry.

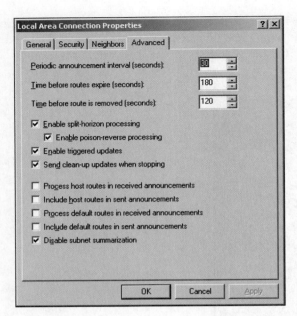

Figure 12-9   Advanced tab of the RIP interface properties dialog box

OSPF

OSPF is a **link–state routing** algorithm that determines the best path from one network to another based on a configurable value called cost. This makes OSPF more flexible than RIP and better suited to complex routing environments. Since complex routing environments normally use hardware routers, OSPF is not normally implemented on Windows routers.

Each interface on a router using OSPF is assigned a cost. The total cost of a route is calculated by adding the cost value of each router interface that is traveled through. The best path from one network to another is the one with the lowest cost.

Administrators can use the variable cost of router interfaces to differentiate between slower and faster WAN links. For example, a T-1 line may be configured with a cost of 10, while a backup ISDN line may be configured with a cost of 30. Only if the T-1 goes down is the ISDN line used.

When the routing table is built, each router builds a picture of the entire network. This is referred to as link-state routing.

When communicating with other routers, an OSPF router sends only changes in its routing table, not the entire routing table. In addition, the changes are sent only when they occur, not every 30 seconds.

OSPF is not available in the 64-bit versions of Windows Server 2003.

FILTERING ROUTER TRAFFIC

You may control the packets that are allowed to pass between routed networks by using packet filters. More specifically, **packet filters** can be placed on the router's network interfaces to control what type of information is allowed to flow in and out of a router. As well, packet filters are directional; you may specify a packet filter to filter TCP/IP traffic that leaves the router on one network interface and a different packet filter to filter TCP/IP traffic that enters the router on another network interface.

Packet filters can be used to filter network traffic based on several criteria such as protocol, source address, destination address, or port number. Once configured, these filters will either:

- Allow all traffic except that specified by the filter to pass through the interface
- Block all traffic except that specified by the filter from passing through the interface

An example of a packet filtering is shown in Figure 12-10.

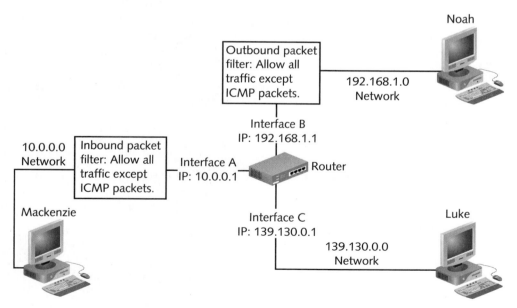

Figure 12-10   Using packet filters on a routed network

In this example, the router has three interfaces with packet filters configured on two of the three interfaces. Interface A is connected to the 10.0.0.0 network and has an inbound filter allowing all traffic except for ICMP traffic to pass. Interface B is connected to the 192.168.1.0 network and has an outbound filter allowing all traffic except for ICMP traffic to pass out of the interface. Interface C is connected to the 139.130.0.0 network and has no packet filters configured.

The computer Mackenzie exists on the 10.0.0.0 network, the computer Luke exists on the 139.130.0.0 network, and the computer Noah exists on the 192.168.1.0 network. Mackenzie can successfully use FTP to exchange files with Luke on the 139.130.0.0 network, but when Mackenzie tries to use the ping utility to reach the same computer, the ping is unsuccessful. This is so because the inbound ICMP packet filter on Interface A blocks the ping packet from entering the router; thus it cannot be forwarded. However, if Luke uses the ping utility to reach Mackenzie, the ping attempt will be successful since there are no filters on Interface C, and the filter on Interface A filters only inbound ICMP traffic.

Similarly, Noah can ping both Mackenzie and Luke because the filter on Interface B only filters outbound ICMP traffic. However, if Luke attempted to ping Noah, the ping packet could enter the router on Interface C, but the outbound ICMP packet filter on Interface B would prevent the ping from leaving the router on Interface B.

Configuring Packet Filters

Packet filters are configured using the properties of a network interface in the Routing and Remote Access snap-in, as shown in Figure 12-11. Simply expand the IP Routing folder under the General folder in the Routing and Remote Access snap-in, right-click the interface object in the right pane that you wish to configure packet filtering on, and choose Properties.

 To configure packet filtering, you must be logged on as an Administrator on the local computer.

Regardless of whether you choose to configure inbound or outbound filters by selecting the appropriate button in Figure 12-11, you are prompted to configure individual filters for the interface as well as a filter action that will allow or block packets that match the filters, as shown in Figure 12-12.

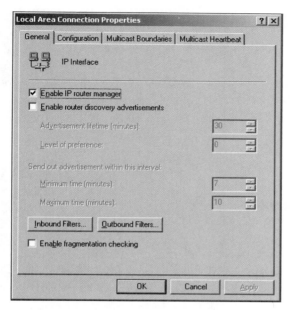

Figure 12-11   Network interface properties in RRAS

12

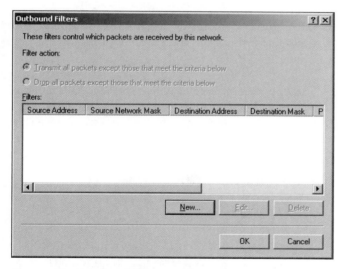

Figure 12-12   Configuring outbound packet filters

If you select the New button shown in Figure 12-12 when adding a new filter, you will be prompted to specify a source network, a destination network, and the protocol of traffic that you wish to filter, as shown in Figure 12-13.

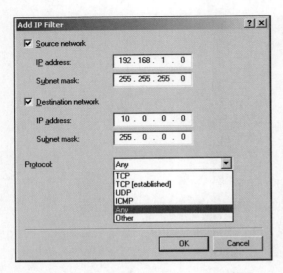

Figure 12-13   Adding a new packet filter

If you select the TCP or UDP protocol, you will also be prompted to provide the specific source or destination ports that will be matched by the packet filter. This would permit you, for instance, to allow only FTP traffic to enter a subnet containing an FTP server.

Conversely, if you select the ICMP protocol, you will be prompted to supply the particular ICMP type and code, and if you select Other from the protocol drop-down list, you will be prompted for the protocol number.

The protocol number is an industry standard number used to identify a specific protocol. A short listing of these numbers can be found in the %systemroot%/system32/drivers/etc/protocol file on your computer. For a more comprehensive list, visit *http://www.iana.org/assignments/protocol-numbers*.

Activity 12-4: Creating a Packet Filter

Time Required: 30 minutes

Objective: Create and test an outbound packet filter to block ICMP request packets.

Description: You are a network administrator at Great Arctic North University. You need to secure the network your FTP servers are on to protect them from ping flood attacks. Ping is a useful troubleshooting utility, and you do not want to impede its use on another network. You must create and test a packet filter that allows ICMP request packets to leave a network, but not enter it. You need to work with a partner to complete this exercise.

1. If necessary, start your server and log on as **Administrator**.

2. Click **Start**, click **Run**, type **cmd**, and press **Enter**.

3. At the command prompt, type **ping 192.168.1.*x***, where *x* is your partner's student number, and press **Enter**. Note that the ping attempt is successful. Wait until your partner has completed this step before proceeding to the next step.

4. At the command prompt, type **ping *x*.0.0.1**, where *x* is your partner's student number, and press **Enter**. Note that the ping attempt is successful because of the route that you configured in Activity 12-2.

5. Close the command prompt.

6. Click **Start**, point to **Administrative Tools**, and click **Routing and Remote Access**.

7. In the left-hand tree, double-click on your server to expand its information, then double-click **IP Routing** to expand its information. Click **General** to select it.

8. In the right pane, right-click **Local Area Connection**, and click **Properties**.

9. Click the **Inbound Filters** button.

10. In the Inbound Filters window, click the **New** button.

11. Click the drop-down button next to the Protocol window, and select **ICMP** from the resulting list. In the ICMP type box, type **8**. In the ICMP code box, type **0**. Click **OK**. This ICMP type and code match ping requests.

12. In the Inbound Filters window, ensure that **Receive all packets except those that meet the criteria below** is selected, and click **OK**. Click **OK** again to close Local Area Connection Properties.

13. Close the Routing and Remote Access window.

14. Wait until both partners have completed step 13, then click **Start**, click **Run**, type **cmd**, and press **Enter**.

15. At the command prompt, type **ping *x*.0.0.1**, where *x* is your partner's student number, and press **Enter**. Note that the ping attempt is unsuccessful because an inbound packet filter is configured on the Local Area Connection of your partner's router.

16. Close the command prompt.

17. Click **Start**, click **Run**, type ***x*.0.0.1**, where *x* is your partner's student number. You should see a list of shares on your partner's computer. You were successful because the inbound packet filter on your partner's Local Area Connection only restricts ICMP traffic. Close all open windows.

18. Wait until both partners have completed Step 17, then click **Start**, point to **Administrative Tools**, and click **Routing and Remote Access**.

19. In the left-hand tree, double-click your server to expand its information, then double-click **IP Routing** to expand its information. Click **General** to select it.

20. In the right pane, right-click **Local Area Connection**, and click **Properties**.

21. Click the **Inbound Filters** button.

12

22. In the Inbound Filters window, click the **Delete** button, and click **OK**. Click **OK** again to close Local Area Connection Properties dialog box.

23. Close the Routing and Remote Access window.

DEMAND-DIAL CONNECTIONS

A **demand-dial** connection is used to establish a connection between two routers only when there is data to send. When a router with a demand-dial interface receives packets destined for a remote network, a connection is created so the packets can be sent. The connection can also be configured so that if there are no packets for the remote network, it is disconnected.

Traditionally, demand-dial connections are used to minimize the amount of phone time used on dial-up connection between routers. In this case, the connection is configured to disconnect after a certain period of time if no traffic has crossed the network. Additionally, you can configure the connection to be operational only during a time period when phone rates are minimized.

Demand-dial can also be used to initiate VPN connections between Windows routers. In this situation, the purpose of demand-dial is not to minimize connection time, but to automate the establishment of a connection. This is required when the router is rebooted or when a connection is lost because of a network interruption.

Demand-dial connections can also be created for **Point-to-Point Protocol over Ethernet (PPPoE)** connections. PPPOE is used by many high-speed Internet providers to control access to their network. Just like a dial-up or VPN connection, PPPOE requires a user name and password to authenticate the connection. Only after the connection is authenticated does the ISP configure the server with an IP address and allow it on the Internet. Configuring PPPoE for a demand-dial connection ensures the automatic establishment of Internet connectivity when the router is rebooted or connectivity is interrupted.

Creating Demand-dial Connections

For a demand-dial connection to function properly, you must enable the server to perform demand-dial routing, configure a port to allow demand-dial routing, and then create a demand-dial interface. All of these tasks are completed using the Routing and Remote Access snap-in.

Enabling the server to allow demand dial connections is done in the Properties of the server, as shown in Figure 12-14. Choose the LAN and demand-dial routing option to allow demand-dial connections.

After demand-dial routing has been enabled, a Ports option will appear under the server in the Routing and Remote Access snap-in. In the properties of Ports, you can configure

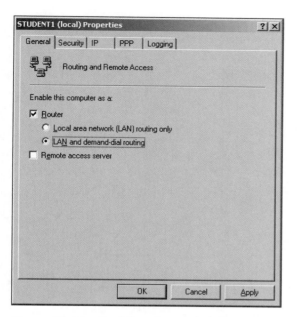

Figure 12-14   Enabling demand-dial routing

whether particular port types can be used for demand-dial connections. Port types include modems, PPPoE, PPTP, and L2TP.

Configuring the PPTP port type is shown in Figure 12-15. To enable demand-dial connections, you must select the Demand-dial routing connections (inbound and outbound) option or the Demand-dial routing connections (outbound only) option.

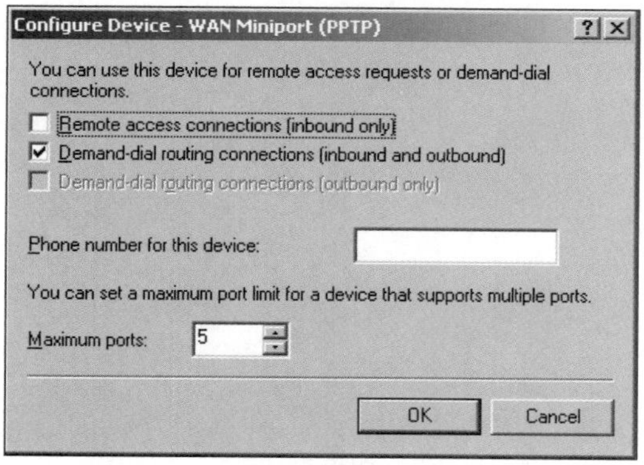

Figure 12-15   Configuring a port for demand-dial routing

New demand-dial connections are created using the Demand-Dial Interface Wizard. To start this wizard in the Routing and Remote Access snap-in, right-click Network Interfaces, and click New Demand-dial Interface. The first option you are asked to configure is the name for the demand-dial interface, as shown in Figure 12-16.

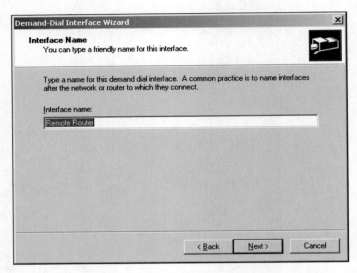

Figure 12-16   Configuring the interface name for a new demand-dial interface

The next screen in the wizard asks you what type of demand-dial connection you would like to create, as shown in Figure 12-17. The three options are dial-up, VPN, or PPPoE. Dial-up and VPN are used for connectivity between a remote office and a central office. PPPoE is used to connect to the Internet.

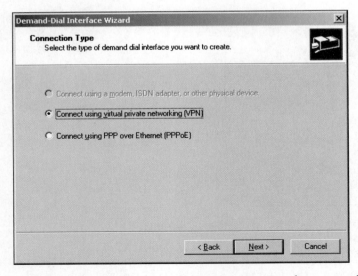

Figure 12-17   Configuring the connection type for a new demand-dial interface

If you choose to create a VPN connection, then the next step asks you what type of VPN connection to create, as shown in Figure 12-18. Choosing the Automatic selection option causes the computer to negotiate with the remote VPN server to choose PPTP or L2TP. Otherwise, you can force it to be PPTP only, or L2TP only. After the type of VPN is chosen, you must also configure the IP address of the remote server.

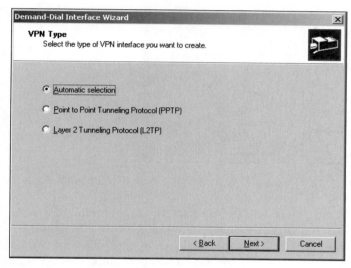

Figure 12-18   Configuring a VPN type for a new demand-dial interface

The next window asks you about protocol and security options, as shown in Figure 12-19. If the Route IP packets on this interface option is selected, then this server routes packets between the networks it is connected to and the remote network. If it is not selected, then only the server running Routing and Remote Access is able to access the remote network. This may be desired if the connection is only used for remote maintenance or data synchronization.

A user account with remote access permission is required to establish a demand–dial connection. If the Add a user account so a remote router can dial in option is chosen, then a user account is automatically created for inbound demand-dial connections. On a member server, the account created is a local user account.

Using the Send a plain-text password if that is the only way to connect option should be avoided if possible. If this option is selected, ensure that the user account is only used for connection establishment and has no rights to the remainder of the system.

Enabling the Use scripting to complete the connection with the remote router option allows you to run a script that modifies the connection settings, or adds routing table entries. This is not normally required.

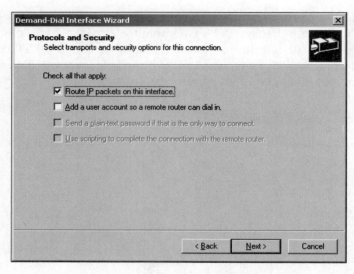

Figure 12-19   Configuring protocols and security for a new demand-dial interface

The next window, shown in Figure 12–20, asks you to configure static routes. At least one **static route** is required to trigger the demand-dial interface. Static routes must be added for each network on the other side of the demand-dial connection. The demand-dial connection is activated when a packet addressed to a host on one of the static routes needs to be forwarded.

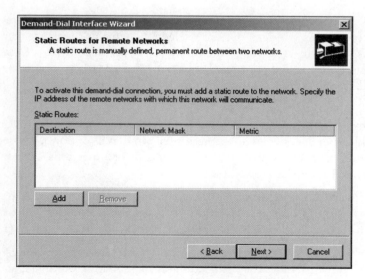

Figure 12-20   Configuring a static route for a new demand-dial interface

When a packet arrives at the demand-dial router, the router looks in its routing table to see where it should be sent. The static route for the remote network specifies the demand-dial interface to reach the remote network. If a packet is addressed to the remote network, then the demand-dial connection is activated. After the demand-dial connection is activated, the packet is forwarded across the demand-dial connection to the remote network.

If you selected the Add a user account so a remote router can dial in option shown in Figure 12-19, then the next window asks for dial-in credentials, as shown in Figure 12-21. This information is used to create the user account that is used by the remote router to connect to this router. The user name is the same as the name for the demand-dial connection.

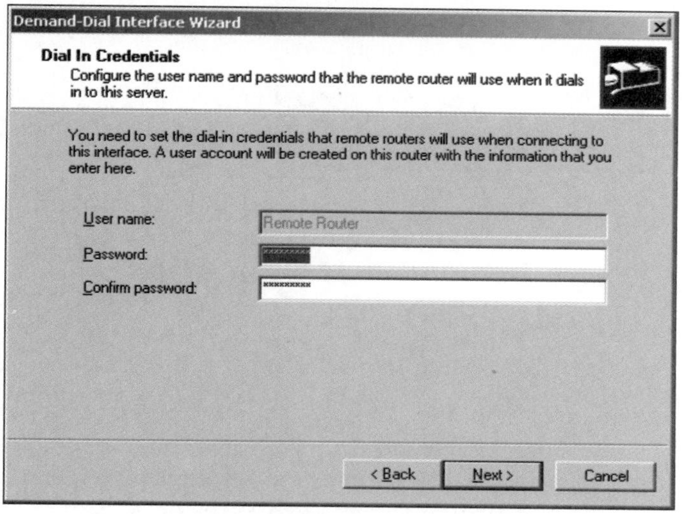

Figure 12-21   Configuring dial-in credentials for a new demand-dial interface

Next, you are prompted for dial-out credentials, as shown in Figure 12-22. These are the user name, domain, and password that are used by the demand-dial connection to log on to the remote system. If this information is not correct, the demand-dial connection is unable to connect.

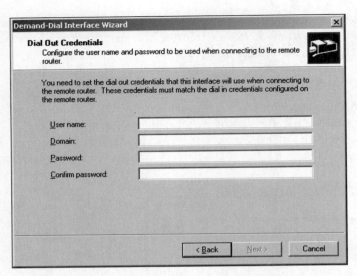

Figure 12-22   Configuring dial-out credentials for a new demand-dial interface

Activity 12-5: Creating a Demand-dial Connection

Time Required: 30 minutes

Objective: Create a demand-dial VPN connection.

Description: You have configured Windows Server 2003 as a router between sites. To enhance security, you would like to configure a dial-up VPN between the locations. In this activity, you will configure a demand-dial VPN interface on your server, and test it by connecting to a VPN server on your partner's server.

1. If necessary, start your server and log on as **Administrator**.
2. Click **Start**, point to **Administrative Tools**, and click **Routing and Remote Access**.
3. Right-click your server, and click **Properties**.
4. Click **LAN and demand-dial routing**, and click **OK**.
5. Click **Yes** to continue, and restart RRAS.
6. Right-click **Network Interfaces**, and click **New Demand-dial Interface**.
7. Click **Next** to begin the Demand-Dial Interface Wizard.
8. In the Interface name box, type **GreatArcticNorthDemand***x*, where *x* is your partner's student number, and click **Next**.
9. Click **Connect using virtual private networking (VPN)**, and click **Next**.
10. Confirm that the VPN Type selected is **Automatic selection**, and click **Next**.

11. In the Host name or IP address box, type **192.168.1.x**, where x is your partner's student number, and click **Next**. This is the IP address of your partner's server.

12. Confirm that the **Route IP packets on this interface** check box is selected.

13. Click the **Add a user account so a remote router can dial in** check box to select it, and click **Next**.

14. Click **Add** to add a static route.

15. In the Destination box, type **10.100.x.0**, where x is your partner's student number. This network does not really exist in the classroom, but is used to trigger the demand-dial interface.

16. In the Network Mask box, type **255.255.255.0**, and click **OK**.

17. Click **Next**.

18. In the Password box of the Dial In Credentials window, type **Password!**, in the Confirm password box, type **Password!**, and click **Next**. This window gathers the password for the user that is created by the wizard for remote routers to log on with.

19. In the User name box of the Dial Out Credentials window, type **GreatArcticNorthDemand$y$**, where y is your student number. This account is created by your partner during the creation of the demand-dial interface.

20. In the Password box, type **Password!**. In the Confirm password box, type **Password!**, and click **Next**.

21. Click **Finish**.

22. Configure your server as a VPN server.

    a. Right-click your server, and click **Properties**.

    b. Click the **Remote access server** check box to select it, and click **OK**. Even when configured as a router, RRAS creates five PPTP and five L2TP ports automatically. This enables them to be used.

    c. Click **Yes** to restart the router.

23. View the Connection State of your demand-dial connection in Network Interfaces. It should be Disconnected.

24. Wait until your partner has completed Step 23, then test your demand-dial interface.

    a. Click **Start**, click **Run**, type **cmd**, and press **Enter**.

    b. Type **ping 10.100.x.5**, where x is your partner's student number, and press Enter. This IP address does not exist on the network, but triggers the demand-dial connection based on the static route you configured in the Demand-Dial Interface Wizard.

12

c. You receive error messages. This is normal. If you receive the error Destination host unreachable, then the interface is not connected yet. It takes a few moments for the demand-dial connection to be completed. If you receive only this error, then repeat Step b. If after two attempts you are still receiving this error, then verify that your configuration is correct. To verify the authentication credentials, right-click your demand-dial connection, and click **Set Credentials**.

d. After the demand-dial connection is connected, the error message will change. If the error changes to Request timed out, this indicates that the demand-dial connection connected, but the host is not responding. This is normal because the host does exist on our network. If the host really existed on the remote network, then you would get a positive response. If the error changes to TTL expired in transit, then the demand-dial connection is connected and a routing loop has been created.

e. Close the command prompt.

25. View the Connection State of your demand-dial connection in Network Interfaces. It should be Connected. If the state is not Connected, then press **F5** to refresh the screen.

26. Right-click **GreatArcticNorthDemand*x***, where *x* is your partner's student number, and click **Disconnect**. This manually disconnects the demand-dial interface.

27. Close the Routing and Remote Access snap-in.

Configuring Demand-dial Settings

Most options for a demand-dial interface can be configured with the Demand-Dial Interface Wizard during creation, but some can only be configured after the interface has been created.

The properties of the demand-dial interface can be used to configure security settings and the idle timeout. The idle timeout is on the Options tab, as shown in Figure 12-23. If the Connection type chosen is the Persistent connection option, then the servers are connected whenever RRAS is functional. This is the normal configuration for a VPN demand-dial connection with a permanent Internet connection.

If the Connection type chosen is Demand dial, then you can set an idle timeout. The default setting for the Idle time before hanging up option is 5 minutes. If you are using a dial-up connection, you want to set the idle timeout to be 5 or 10 minutes. Then, when there is no traffic to be transmitted, the connection is disconnected to reduce phone charges.

A demand-dial connection can also be configured with a set of **dial-out hours** that control when it can be active. This is very useful for controlling dial-up connections that might otherwise result in large long-distance charges.

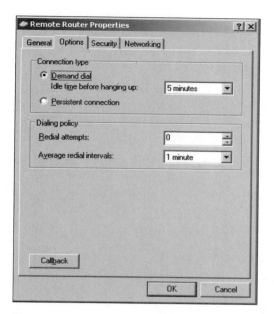

Figure 12-23   Options tab of demand-dial interface Properties

12

Typically, dial-out hours are configured to allow a connection every few hours. This results in data being moved from one network to another in batches every few hours. This is useful for Active Directory replication and data synchronization.

If users are expected to access resources using the demand-dial connection at all times, then the dial-out hours should be left at the default of 24 hours per day, 7 days per week. To set the dial-out hours, right-click on the demand-dial interface and click Dial-out hours. The window that allows you to set the dial-out hours is shown in Figure 12-24.

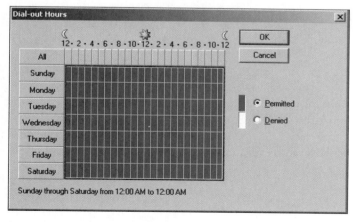

Figure 12-24   Specifying dial-out hours for a demand-dial interface

Demand-dial Filters

With the default configuration, a demand–dial connection is triggered by any IP traffic that needs to be routed. This includes relatively unimportant traffic such as ICMP packets.

To reduce the amount of time a demand–dial connection is active, you can configure demand–dial filters. **Demand–dial filters** control which types of network traffic trigger a demand–dial connection. This reduces the number of connections activated and reduces the amount of long-distance charges.

The demand–dial filters are configured the same way as a firewall rule. You can set the default option to initiate a demand–dial connection for only specific traffic or for all traffic except that specified by a rule, as shown in Figure 12-25. For each rule, you can specify a source and destination network as well as a protocol type, which includes TCP and UDP port numbers, as shown in Figure 12-26.

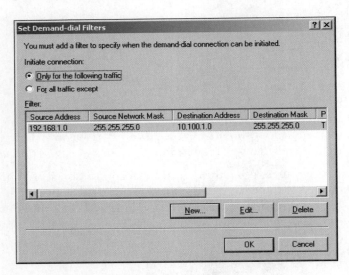

Figure 12-25   Demand-dial filters

Demand-dial filters can be used with a dial-up Internet connection to ensure that the connection is not dialed except for allowed traffic. For example, you could configure rules that limit connection establishment to packets that have a source IP address on your internal network and have a destination TCP port of either 80 or 25. Then only communication with Web servers and e-mail servers can cause the Internet connection to be activated. An attempt to ping an Internet server would not activate the Internet connection.

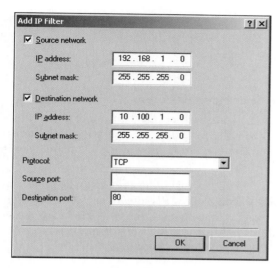

Figure 12-26   Adding a demand-dial filter

Activity 12-6: Configuring Demand-dial Filters

Time required: 20 minutes

Objective: Configure demand-dial filters to control the activation of demand-dial connections.

Description: Great Arctic North University is charged a fee for bandwidth usage on their Internet connection. You would like to reduce the amount of the fee by stopping ICMP packets from triggering the demand-dial connection.

1. If necessary, start your server and log on as **Administrator**.
2. Click **Start**, point to **Administrative Tools**, and click **Routing and Remote Access**.
3. Right-click **GreatArcticNorthDemand*x***, where *x* is your partner's student number, and click **Set IP Demand-dial Filters**.
4. Click **New** to create a new demand-dial filter.
5. Confirm that **Source network** is not selected. This acts as a wildcard to match any source address.
6. Confirm that **Destination network** is not selected. This acts as a wildcard to match any destination address.
7. Click the drop-down arrow for the Protocol list box, and click **ICMP**.
8. Leave the ICMP type box and ICMP code box empty. This setting acts as a wildcard to match any ICMP type and code.
9. Click **OK**.

12

10. Confirm that **For all traffic except** is selected. This means that any traffic can initiate the demand-dial connection except the listed filters, in this case ICMP traffic.

11. Click **OK**.

12. Test the new filter.

   a. Click **Start**, click **Run**, type **cmd**, and press **Enter**.

   b. Type **ping 10.100.*x*.5**, where *x* is your partner's student number, and press **Enter**. This IP address does not exist on the network, but can trigger the demand-dial connection based on the static route you configured in the Demand-Dial Interface Wizard.

   c. You receive an error message. This is normal. The only error is Destination host unreachable. This means that the path to the IP address that you are pinging is not available because the demand-dial interface is disconnected. This error message does not change because the filter does not allow ICMP packets to trigger the connection.

   d. Close the command prompt.

   e. Click **Start**, point to **All Programs**, and click **Internet Explorer**.

   f. In the Address box, type **http://10.100.*x*.5**, where *x* is your partner's student number, and press **Enter**. Internet Explorer cannot connect to a Web site because there is no Web server at this address, but it triggers the demand-dial interface.

   g. After 5 to 10 seconds, close Internet Explorer.

13. View the Connection State of your demand-dial connection in Network Interfaces. It should be Connected. If the state is not Connected, then press **F5** to refresh the screen.

14. Right-click **GreatArcticNorthDemand*x***, where *x* is your partner's student number, and click **Disconnect**. This manually disconnects the demand-dial interface.

15. Close the Routing and Remote Access snap-in.

TROUBLESHOOTING ROUTING

Most problems related to routing are a result of misconfiguration. Regardless of whether you are using static or dynamic routing, the first place to check for configuration problems is the routing table. If no default gateway route exists, then the routing table must contain routes to all networks that the router needs to send packets to. As well, routers on distant networks must have routes in their routing tables for the networks local to your router if those routers wish to send packets to your local networks. If these routes are placed in the routing table by a dynamic routing protocol such as RIP or OSPF, ensure that the protocol is configured properly.

If a default gateway entry exists in the routing table, then packets that do not match a destination network listed in the routing table will be forwarded to the default gateway router and hopefully reach the destination network. Sometimes, a remote router may prevent the packet from reaching its destination network. To see the path a packet takes from one router to another on its route to a destination host, you may use the tracert command. Simply specify the host name or IP address of a remote host and the **tracert command** will list up to 30 routers it has contacted in sequence between your computer and the destination. An example of using the tracert command is shown in Figure 12-27.

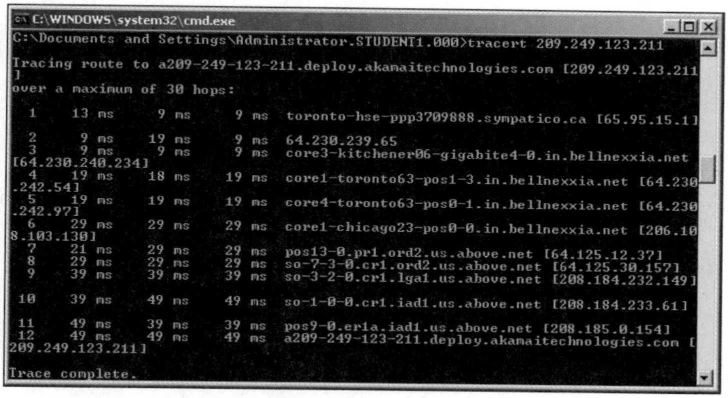

Figure 12-27   The tracert command

If the routes listed in the routing table allow traffic to pass to other destination networks correctly and the tracert command indicates no remote router problems, ensure that no packet filters are configured on the router's network interfaces to filter certain packet types. In addition, if your computer uses a demand-dial connection to another router, ensure that the static route used to trigger the connection is specified properly and that all authentication information is correct. Also ensure that no demand-dial filters or dial out hours are configured for the demand-dial connection that prevent the connection from being triggered.

CHAPTER SUMMARY

- Windows Server 2003 can be configured as a low-cost router for TCP/IP and AppleTalk. IPX/SPX is not supported.
- Each router maintains a routing table that stores routes to local and remote networks.
- Entries in the routing table may be configured automatically, using the route command, using the Routing and Remote Access snap-in, or by using a dynamic routing protocol.

❑ RIP is a distance-vector routing algorithm that calculates paths based on hops. If a route is 16 hops away, it is considered unreachable. RIP advertises its entire routing table every 30 seconds.

❑ OSPF is a link-state routing algorithm that calculates paths based on a configurable metric called cost. Each interface in a router can be assigned a cost. OSPF only advertises changes to a routing table when they happen. The 64-bit versions of Windows Server 2003 do not support OSPF.

❑ Packet filters may be applied to network interfaces on a router to control the flow of incoming or outgoing IP packets.

❑ Demand-dial connections are activated only when network traffic requires them. They can also be configured to disconnect after a specified period if there is no more traffic to cross the link.

❑ Static routes are required for demand-dial connections.

❑ Demand-dial connections can be configured with dial-out hours to limit the times they are active. They can also be configured with demand-dial filters to limit the types of traffic that can trigger the connection.

❑ The tracert command may be used to list the routers a packet crosses to reach a destination computer.

KEY TERMS

cost — In routing, a configurable value assigned to a packet being forwarded through a router interface.

demand-dial — A dial-up/VPN/PPPoE connection that is only activated when required to move network traffic.

demand-dial filters — Rules that limit the types of traffic that can trigger the activation of a demand-dial connection.

dial-out hours — A limit for demand-dial connections that allows connections only during certain time periods.

distance-vector routing — Any routing algorithm based on simple hop calculation. RIP is the most common example.

dynamic routing — When routing tables are automatically generated by routers based on communication with other routers.

hop — In routing, a packet being forwarded by a single router.

Internet Security and Acceleration Server (ISA) — A firewall and proxy server product from Microsoft.

IP forwarding — The process of forwarding TCP/IP packets from one network to another.

link-state routing — A routing algorithm where routers use a configurable cost metric to build a picture of the entire network. OSPF is the most common example.

multihomed devices — Computers or network devices that have more than one network interface.

netstat –r command — A command that lists the routing table on the local computer.

Open Shortest Path First (OSPF) — A link-state routing protocol that calculates paths based on a configurable metric called cost. Changes to the routing table are advertised only when they occur.

packet filters — A set of rules that may be applied to a network interface on a router to allow and deny different types of network traffic entering or leaving the network interface.

Point-to-Point Protocol over Ethernet (PPPoE) — A protocol used for authentication and traffic control on high-speed Internet connections such as DSL.

poison-reverse processing — An option for RIP routing where a router advertises a route as unreachable on the interface from which it was learned.

route — An entry in a routing table that lists a network and how to reach it.

route command — A command that may be used to list and configure routes in the routing table on the local computer.

route print — A command-line utility used to view the contents of a routing table.

Routing Information Protocol (RIP) — A distance-vector routing protocol that calculates paths based on hops. Complete routing tables are advertised every 30 seconds.

routing table — The list of networks and how to reach them that is maintained by a router.

split-horizon processing — An option for RIP routing where a router is not advertised back on the same interface from which it was learned to prevent routing loops

static route — An entry in a routing table that is permanently added by an administrator.

static routing — When routing tables are maintained manually by an administrator.

tracert command — A command used to trace the hops a packet takes from the local computer to the destination computer.

12

REVIEW QUESTIONS

1. The most likely place you will find Windows Server 2003 used as a router is in large corporations with very complex network routing requirements. True or false?

2. Which type of routing allows routers to automatically build their routing tables?

   a. static routing

   b. manual routing

   c. automatic routing

   d. dynamic routing

3. Which of the following commands may be used to view the routing table on a Windows Server 2003 computer? (Choose all that apply.)

    a. route

    b. route print

    c. netstat –r

    d. netstat print

4. Which of the following route commands may be used to configure a route to the 5.0.0.0/8 remote network via the gateway 192.168.1.99?

    a. route add 5.0.0.0 mask 255.0.0.0 192.168.1.99

    b. route add 5.0.0.0 mask 255.0.0.0 gw 192.168.1.99

    c. route add 5.0.0.0/8 dest 192.168.1.99

    d. route add 5.0.0.0/8 gw 192.168.1.99

5. Which option to the route command will ensure that a route is loaded into the routing table at each system startup?

    a. –e

    b. –r

    c. –p

    d. –w

6. Which routing protocol announces its entire routing table every 30 seconds?

    a. RIP

    b. SAP

    c. OSPF

    d. AppleTalk

7. A router must have a minimum of three network interfaces. True or false?

8. How often does OSPF send copies of its entire routing table to other routers?

    a. every 30 seconds

    b. every 60 seconds

    c. every 120 seconds

    d. never

9. What number of hops is considered unreachable for RIP routing?

    a. 8

    b. 16

    c. 32

    d. 64

    e. 128

10. Why would you enable Auto static update mode for RIP?

    a. to permanently keep routes learned from a demand-dial connection

    b. for higher security

    c. to limit the packets that can trigger a demand-dial connection

    d. to limit a demand-dial connection to only certain users

11. When authentication is activated for the RIP protocol, which authentication method is used to send the password?

    a. plain text

    b. CHAP

    c. MS-CHAP

    d. MS-CHAPv2

    e. PKI certificates on smart cards

12. What type of traffic may a packet filter be applied to?

    a. incoming traffic on a network interface only

    b. outgoing traffic on a network interface only

    c. both incoming and outgoing traffic on a network interface

    d. none of the above

13. Where are packet filters set on a Windows Server 2003 computer that functions as a router?

    a. the properties of individual interfaces listed in Network Connections of Control Panel

    b. the properties of the routing interface in the Routing and Remote Access snap-in

    c. the properties of the RRAS server in the Routing and Remote Access snap-in

    d. the properties of the Packet Filters folder in the Routing and Remote Access snap-in

14. Which types of connections can demand-dial be used to activate? (Choose all that apply.)

    a. VPN

    b. dial-up

    c. IPX/SPX

    d. PPPoE

    e. FTP

12

15. If a user account is created when the Demand-Dial Interface Wizard is run on a member server, where does the account exist?

    a. in Active Directory

    b. on all remote access servers

    c. in the local SAM database

    d. on all DNS servers

16. Which criteria can be used to limit how demand-dial connections are activated? (Choose all that apply.)

    a. time of day

    b. month

    c. type of traffic

    d. user

17. When creating a demand-dial interface, what setting that you specify is used to trigger the demand dial connection?

    a. a protocol number

    b. a static route

    c. a demand-dial filter

    d. a time of day

18. After a demand-dial interface has been created, what can you configure to specify a type of network traffic that is used to trigger a demand-dial connection?

    a. a protocol number

    b. a static route

    c. a demand-dial filter

    d. a time of day

19. Which entry in a routing table refers to the default gateway for the computer?

    a. the entry with a network destination of 0.0.0.0

    b. the entry with a gateway of 0.0.0.0

    c. the entry with a network destination of 255.255.255.255

    d. the entry with a gateway of 255.255.255.255

20. If you specify a packet filter that filters TCP or UDP packets, what else can you specify regarding the TCP or UDP packets?

    a. a protocol number and code

    b. a custom protocol number

    c. the number of TCP or UDP packets that may be sent on the interface

    d. specific source and destination ports

CASE PROJECTS

Case Project 12-1: Hardware Routers vs. Software Routers

As a cost-cutting measure for smaller locations, you have decided to use Windows Server 2003 as a router rather than buying hardware routers. This decision has just been announced to the rest of the IT Department. Some of your colleagues with certifications from hardware router vendors are quite upset and have complained to your supervisor.

Write a report justifying your decision. As part of the report, include a list of routing services provided with Windows Server 2003 and where they can be used in Great Arctic North University.

Case Project 12-2: Packet Filtering

One of your colleagues is concerned about implementing packet filters on routers in the campus network. He is worried that once packet filters have been implemented, some of the services on the network may not be available to remote users, and that network trouble-shooting will be more difficult. Explain how packet filters can be configured on selected network interfaces to provide extra security on the network and how to minimize troubleshooting problems related to packet filters.

12

Case Project 12-3: Demand-dial Routing

You have been approached by one of the professors at Great Arctic North University to help his small business connect to the Internet. He already has Windows Server 2003, and the network in his business connects to an ISP using a PPPoE connection. The ISP charges a fee based on the amount of time the business is connected to the Internet. Explain how demand-dial routing may be set up to allow users on his business network the ability to connect to the Internet as needed and reduce costs.

13

SECURITY TEMPLATES

After reading this chapter, you will be able to:

- Identify the components of the Security Configuration Manager tools
- Describe the different predefined security templates available on Windows Server 2003
- Apply security templates to a local computer and GPO
- Create security templates and modify their settings
- Analyze security settings on a computer using Secedit.exe and the Security Configuration and Analysis snap-in

An important component of Windows Server 2003 administration is the implementation and management of security on computers within the network. This chapter focuses on using security templates to apply security settings to computers that require various levels of security as well as the monitoring and maintenance of these security settings. More specifically, this chapter introduces you to the Security Configuration Manager tools, predefined security templates, and the tools that allow you to create, modify, and apply security templates. Finally, this chapter discusses tools that can be used to maintain and troubleshoot the design and application of security templates.

USING THE SECURITY CONFIGURATION MANAGER TOOLS

In the past, as network systems increased in size and complexity, administering security across the enterprise also became increasingly complex. Older Windows NT 4 systems did not provide adequate tools or utilities to implement and manage an effective network security policy. For example, if administrators wanted to implement security auditing on a particular group of workstations, they would either have to visit each machine individually or try to find adequate third-party tools to assist in the configuration.

Another common problem with managing security policies in Windows NT 4 involved maintaining the configuration. If a company or department has more than one administrator in charge of applying and maintaining the security settings, it can be difficult to keep track of configuration changes to the policy. Without proper documentation and good communication between the administrators, a great deal of time may be spent figuring out which auditing and security settings each administrator has changed.

There are many components in Windows Server 2003 that allow you to create and maintain security configurations across the network. Tools included for this purpose are collectively referred to as the **Security Configuration Manager tools**.

The Security Configuration Manager tools consist of the following core components:

- Security templates
- Security settings in GPO objects
- Security Configuration and Analysis snap-in
- Secedit command-line tool

An administrator uses a **security template** to define, edit, and save baseline security settings that are applied to computers with common security requirements to meet organizational security standards. These templates help ensure that a consistent setting can be applied to multiple machines and be easily maintained.

 When designing the baseline security settings for a security template, it is good practice to follow the **method of least privilege**. That is, you should restrict all components other than those that are required for a certain computer to function.

Security templates are text-based files that can be read but should not be changed or edited using any text editor. Be sure to use the Security Templates snap-in to create and edit the templates. The Security Templates snap-in is shown in Figure 13-1.

Using the Security Templates snap-in, you can configure settings such as audit or security policies and then save them as a security template to be applied to any number of computers locally using the Local Security Settings snap-in, as shown in Figure 13-2.

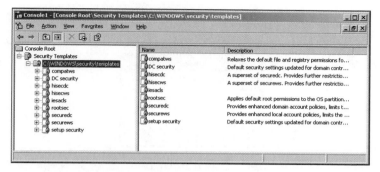

Figure 13-1   The Security Templates snap-in

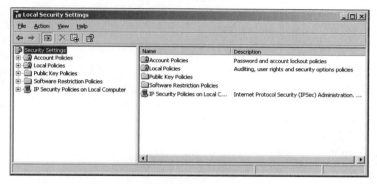

Figure 13-2   The Local Security Settings snap-in

You may also import the settings found in a security template to a **Group Policy Object (GPO)** in Active Directory. This GPO, commonly called a Security Policy template, can then be automatically applied to a large number of computers in an Active Directory domain and administered centrally. To apply a **Security Policy template** to a domain or organizational unit (OU) object in Active Directory, you can use the Active Directory Users and Computers snap-in, as shown in Figure 13-3. Conversely, to apply a Security Policy template to a site object in Active Directory, you can use the Active Directory Sites and Services snap-in, as shown in Figure 13-4.

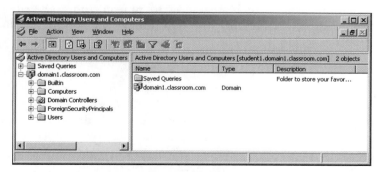

Figure 13-3   The Active Directory Users and Computers snap-in

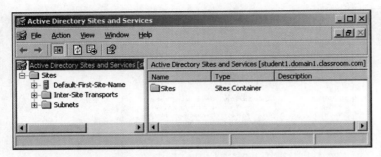

Figure 13-4   The Active Directory Sites and Services snap-in

You may also use the **Group Policy Management Console (GPMC)** to apply Security Policy Templates to domains, OUs and sites. The GPMC is available for downloading at *http://www.microsoft.com*.

To assist with security policy changes, the Security Configuration Manager tools can also be used to analyze and implement security settings on a computer system. In the analysis, a comparison can be made between a computer system's security settings and a previously defined security template file which contains the baseline security settings for the computer. Differences between the computer system and the policy template can then be viewed and reported, and action can then be taken to change the settings on the computer to the desired settings.

For example, your security plan may provide detailed information on the security settings for the company's computers. Creating the design is only the first step, however. You also need to implement the design, which could mean making changes to every computer on the network. The Security Configuration Manager tools are designed to make the implementation of the security policy much easier. When the security policy has been designed and approved, the settings can then be defined in a security template. This template can then be compared to the current settings on the network by using the **Security Configuration and Analysis snap-in** or the **Secedit.exe** command-line tool. This will show which current settings match the security policy and which do not. You can then apply and implement the new settings.

The Security Configuration Manager tools are also useful in maintaining security settings; they can check security settings on a regular basis and reapply any settings that may have been changed.

PREDEFINED SECURITY TEMPLATES

Although an administrator can design a custom security template that may be applied to computers within the network, there are several predefined security templates that come with Windows Server 2003. Since workstations, servers, and domain controllers typically have different security settings in a network environment, Microsoft provides different templates for each category of computer. Also keep in mind that only computers running Windows Server 2003, Windows XP, and Windows 2000 can take advantage of security template configurations and deployments.

The Default Template

When Windows Server 2003 is installed, the default security settings applied to the computer are stored in a template called Setup Security.inf. The contents of this template will be different depending upon the original configuration of the computer, for example, whether the operating system was freshly installed or upgraded from a previous version of Windows. The purpose of this template is to provide a single file in which all of the original computer security settings are stored. If the security settings of a computer are ever changed and an administrator wishes to easily return the system to its original settings, the Setup Security.inf template can simply be reapplied.

The Setup Security.inf template should never be applied using GPOs because it contains a large number of settings that can seriously degrade Group Policy processing performance.

Incremental Templates

If the basic security settings do not meet your security needs, you can apply various additional security configurations using incremental templates. These templates modify security settings incrementally. However, these templates should only be applied to machines already running the default security settings because they do not include any of the initial configurations that the template created during the initial installation. Following is a list of the standard **incremental templates** available in Windows Server 2003. Additional services that are installed on Windows Server 2003 may add other incremental templates that define security settings required by those services.

- *Compatws.inf*—This template can be applied to workstations or servers. Windows Server 2003 has increased the default security considerably over previous versions such as Windows NT. In some cases, this increased security results in application compatibility problems, especially for noncertified applications that require user access to the registry. One way to run these applications is to make the user a member of the **Power Users group**, which has a higher level of rights and permissions than a normal user. Another option is for the administrator to increase the security permissions for the Users group. The Compatws.inf template provides a third alternative by weakening the default security to allow legacy applications to run under Windows Server 2003.

- *Securews.inf and Securedc.inf*—These templates provide increased security for areas such as account policy, auditing, and registry permissions. The securews template is for any workstation or server, whereas the securedc template should only be applied to domain controllers.

13

- *Hisecws.inf and Hisecdc.inf*—These templates can be incrementally applied after the secure templates have been applied. Security is increased in the areas that affect network communication protocols through the use of such features as packet signing. These templates should only be applied to client computers running Windows 2000 or higher, and all domain controllers must be running Windows 2000 or Windows Server 2003. These templates should not be applied to all machines to ensure proper connectivity. The hisecws template is for workstations or servers, whereas the hisecdc template should only be applied to domain controllers.

- *DC Security.inf*—This template is applied automatically whenever a Windows 2000 or Windows Server 2003 member server is promoted to a domain controller. This is available to give the administrator the option to reapply the initial domain controller security settings if the need arises.

- *Rootsec.inf*—This template specifies the original permissions assigned to the root of the system drive. The main purpose of this template is for use in reapplying security permissions to resources on the system drive that have been changed, whether on purpose or by accident.

The security templates included in Windows Server 2003 are stored in the C:\WINDOWS\security\templates directory and provide the administrator with acceptable security configurations for a variety of situations. If there is a unique situation where a preconfigured template is not suitable, you can also create custom templates to meet your needs, as discussed in the next section.

Activity 13-1: Browsing Predefined Security Templates

Time Required: 25 minutes

Objective: Explore settings associated with built-in security templates.

Description: Windows Server 2003 includes a number of predefined templates that can be used to configure security settings on domain workstations and servers. The IT manager at Great Arctic North University is interested in evaluating the potential impact of using these settings but wants to be sure that increasing the overall level of security will not render certain systems unable to communicate. In this activity, you will browse through some of the default security templates included with Windows Server 2003 to evaluate their configuration settings.

1. Click **Start**, **Run** and type **mmc**. Press **Enter**.

2. Click **File** on the menu bar, click **Add/Remove Snap-in**, and then click **Add**.

3. In the Available Standalone Snap-ins window, click **Security Templates** and click **Add**.

4. Click **Close** to close the window, and then click **OK**.

5. Click the **plus sign (+)** next to Security Templates to expand it, and then click the **plus sign (+)** next to C:\WINDOWS\security\templates to view the available templates.

6. Click the **plus sign (+)** next to hisecdc to view its contents.

7. Click the **plus sign (+)** next to Account Policies, and then click **Password Policy**. Browse through the password settings associated with the hisecdc security template.

8. Click **Account Lockout Policy** to view the template's associated settings.

9. Click the **plus sign (+)** next to the securedc template to expand its information, and then click the **plus sign (+)** next to Account Policies.

10. Click **Account Lockout Policy** to view its settings. Compare the account lockout settings configured in the hisecdc template to those found in the securedc template.

11. As time permits, browse through some additional security templates to compare differences between settings configured in the various security templates.

12. Close the Security Templates snap-in. Click **No** in the Microsoft Management Console dialog box.

APPLYING SECURITY TEMPLATES

Security templates can be applied to either the local machine or the domain via GPOs. To apply a security template to a local machine, simply open the Local Security Settings snap-in by running secpol.msc. Right-click Security Settings in the console pane, and choose Import Policy. You can then select the template file to be imported, as shown in Figure 13-5.

Figure 13-5   Selecting a security template to apply to the local computer

To apply a security template to several computers using a GPO, simply navigate to the properties of the domain or OU object in the Active Directory Users and Computers snap-in or the properties of the site object in the Active Directory Sites and Services snap-in and navigate to the Group Policy tab, as shown in Figure 13-6.

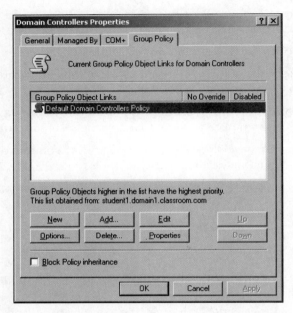

Figure 13-6   The Group Policy tab of an Active Directory object

You may then create a new GPO or edit an existing GPO and import the security settings. If you click on the Edit button shown in Figure 13-6, simply expand the Windows Settings folder under Computer Configuration, right-click the Security Settings folder and choose Import Policy, as shown in Figure 13-7. The program will prompt you for the location of the security template file.

Security settings that are applied using Group Policy will always override local settings. Group Policy security settings are refreshed any time the machine is rebooted, at 90-minute intervals for servers and workstations, and every 5 minutes on domain controllers. Even if there have been no changes, the security settings are refreshed every 16 hours. You may also use the **Gpupdate.exe** command-line tool to manually update GPO settings on your computer.

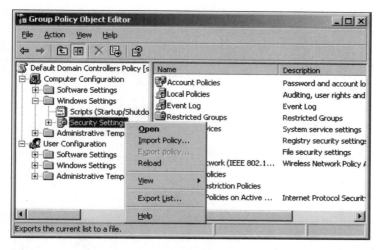

Figure 13-7   Importing a security template into a GPO

Activity 13-2: Applying a Security Template

Time Required: 5 minutes

Objective: Apply a security template to a single computer.

Description: You have recently applied a higher security baseline to all workstations at Great Arctic North University by using security templates. One user now complains that she cannot access an application that worked before. She needs this application to perform her job, so you apply the Compatws.inf security policy to her computer to weaken the higher security baseline so that she can run her application.

1. Click **Start**, **Run** and type **secpol.msc**. Press **Enter**.

2. Right-click **Security Settings** and choose **Import Policy**.

3. Highlight **compatws.inf** and click **Open**.

4. Close the Local Security Settings snap-in.

CREATING SECURITY TEMPLATES

In some cases, the predefined security templates that come with Windows Server 2003 are not sufficient to meet the security baseline settings required by your organization. As a result, you may wish to modify a predefined security template or create a new one using the Security Templates snap-in. To make a new template, simply right-click the C:\WINDOWS\security\templates folder shown in Figure 13-8 and choose New Template. Alternately, you may also right-click a preconfigured template and choose Save As to make a copy of a template that can be modified.

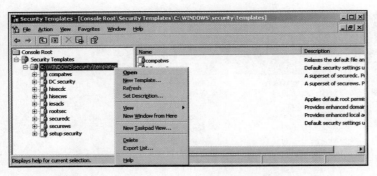

Figure 13-8   Creating a new security template

New security templates are not preconfigured with any security-related settings. Instead, you must expand the template and the categories within it and define the security settings that you require for your baseline. Afterward, you may edit any settings in a security template in the same manner.

One category within a security template that deserves special attention is the Account Policies node. This node includes configuration settings that are typically the initial step to securing the computer network. The Account Policies node, as shown in Figure 13-9, includes three subcategories: Password Policy, Account Lockout Policy, and Kerberos Policy.

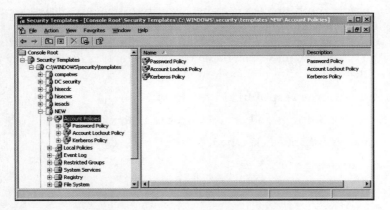

Figure 13-9   The Account Policies node of a security template

The Password Policy node contains configuration settings that refer to the password's history, length, and complexity. Table 13-1 describes each setting.

Table 13-1   Password policy settings

Configuration Setting	Description
Enforce password history	Defines the number of passwords (between 0 and 24) that have to be unique before a user can reuse an old password
Maximum password age	Defines the number of days that a password can be used before the user is required to change it; if you never want the passwords to expire, set the number of days to 0
Minimum password age	Defines the number of days that a password must be used before a user is allowed to change it
Minimum password length	Defines the least number of characters required in a password (values can be from 1 to 14 characters); if no password is required, set the value to 0
Password must meet complexity requirements	Increases password complexity by enforcing rules that passwords must follow
Store password using reversible encryption	This setting is the same as storing passwords in clear text; this policy provides support for applications using protocols that need the passwords in clear text for authentication

The Account Lockout Policy node contains configuration settings that refer to the password lockout threshold and duration, as well as reset options. Table 13-2 describes each setting.

Table 13-2   Account lockout policy settings

Configuration Setting	Description
Account lockout threshold	Determines the number of failed logon attempts that results in the user account being locked
Account lockout duration	Determines the number of minutes that a locked account remains locked; after the specified number of minutes, the account automatically becomes unlocked; you can specify that an administrator must unlock the account by setting the value to 0
Reset account lockout counter after	Determines the number of minutes that must elapse after a single failed logon attempt before the bad logon counter is reset to 0

The Kerberos Policy node contains configuration settings that refer to the Kerberos settings used primarily by Active Directory when authenticating domain logons. Table 13-3 describes each setting.

Table 13-3   Kerberos policy settings

Configuration Setting	Description
Enforce user logon restrictions	Requires the Key Distribution Center (KDC) service of Kerberos V5 to validate every request for a session ticket against the user rights policy of the target computer; if enforced, there may be performance degradation on network access
Maximum lifetime for service ticket	Determines the maximum amount of time, in minutes, that a service ticket is valid to access a resource; the default is 600 minutes (10 hours)

Table 13-3 Kerberos policy settings (continued)

Configuration Setting	Description
Maximum lifetime for user ticket	Determines the maximum amount of time, in hours, that a ticket granting ticket (TGT) may be used; the default is 10 hours
Maximum lifetime for user ticket renewal	Determines the amount of time, in days, that a user's TGT may be renewed; the default is 7 days
Maximum tolerance for computer clock synchronization	Determines the amount of time difference, in minutes, that Kerberos V5 tolerates between the client machine's clock and the time on the server's clock; the default is 5 minutes

When configuring the account policy for use by computers in an Active Directory domain, the GPO that contains the security template settings must be linked to a domain object. Account policy configurations applied at an OU or site level only affect the local SAM database of the computers within the OU and do not affect domain logons.

The other nodes available for a security template can be applied to site, domain, and OU levels if the security template is applied using a GPO. Here is a summary of the functions of each node:

- *Local Policies*—This category applies security settings to the local account database of the workstation or server. These may be overwritten at the site, domain, or OU level but remain in effect if there are no other policies at those levels. There are three subcategories that can be configured:

  - *Audit Policy*—Defines various successful or unsuccessful events that can be audited and recorded in the event logs

  - *User Rights Assignment*—Controls local computer rights that may be assigned to users or groups (for example, the right to log on locally or to shut down the computer)

  - *Security Options*—Defines a wide variety of configuration settings that adjust the registry (for example, logon banner configurations, restricting floppy or CD-ROM access, and removing the last logged-on user name from the logon screen)

- *Event Log*—This category defines configuration settings in relation to event log size, retention period, and access restrictions.

- *Restricted Groups*—This category gives the administrator the ability to control who is a member of any security group. Each time that the policy is refreshed, any users that have been added to the group by any means other than the security template are removed automatically. This category can also control the other groups to which a particular security group belongs.

- *System Services*—This category allows an administrator control over service startup mode, disabling of a service, permissions to edit the service mode, and auditing of the service.

- *Registry*—This category defines security and auditing access control list (ACL) settings for Registry keys and subkeys. This allows an administrator to control who has the ability to change or overwrite various registry settings.

- *File System*—This category defines and maintains NTFS security permissions and auditing permissions for any folder or file listed in the policy. Files or folders must reside on an NTFS partition.

Activity 13-3: Creating a Security Template

Time Required: 25 minutes

Objective: Define a new security template to meet custom requirements.

Description: Although the default security templates include a variety of different settings that can be used to increase the security level of Great Arctic North University's servers and workstations, the IT manager has decided to explore the possibility of defining a custom template containing settings specific to the University's requirements. Ultimately, a custom template will be defined that will be distributed to faculties to standardize the security process. In this activity, you will create a custom security template.

1. Click **Start**, **Run** and type **mmc**. Press **Enter**.
2. Click **File** on the menu bar, click **Add/Remove Snap-in**, and then click **Add**.
3. In the Available Standalone Snap-ins window, click **Security Templates** and click **Add**.
4. Click **Close** to close the window, and then click **OK**.
5. Click the **plus sign (+)** next to Security Templates to expand it.
6. Right-click **C:\WINDOWS\security\templates** and click **New Template**.
7. In the Template name text box, type **GANUtest**. In the Description text box, type **Test security template for Great Arctic North University**. Click **OK**.
8. Expand the **C:\WINDOWS\security\templates** folder and then expand your **GANUtest** security template. Browse through the configuration settings of the new GANUtest security template. Notice that because the template is new, no settings have yet been configured.
9. Click Account Policies and in the Password Policy section of the GANUtest security template, configure the following settings:

   Enforce password history -- 5 passwords remembered

   Maximum password age --20 days

   Minimum password age --19 days

   Minimum password length -- 6 characters

   Password must meet complexity requirements -- Enabled

13

10. Click on **Account Lockout Policy**, and then configure the following settings:

    Account lockout duration -- 5 minutes

    Account lockout threshold -- 3 invalid logon attempts

    Reset account lockout counter after -- 5 minutes

11. Right-click the **GANUtest** security template, and click **Save**. Close the Security Templates snap-in. Click **No** in the Microsoft Management Console dialog box.

12. Open My Computer and browse to **C:\WINDOWS\security\templates**. Double-click the **GANUtest.inf** file to open it in the Notepad text editor. Notice that the settings originally configured in the Security Templates tool now appear in the text file.

13. Close all open windows.

MANAGING AND TROUBLESHOOTING SECURITY TEMPLATES

After planning and implementing security settings using security templates, you should periodically check to ensure that these security settings are being applied. A **security baseline template** is simply a security template that contains a set of security settings that define the minimum security settings that must be applied to a particular computer. To ensure that security is maintained in your organization, simply compare your security baseline template to the actual configuration of the computers in your organization.

Analyzing System Security Using the Security Configuration and Analysis Snap-in

The Security Configuration and Analysis snap-in illustrated in Figure 13-10 allows administrators to compare current system settings to a previously configured security template. The comparison identifies any changes to the original security configurations and any possible security weaknesses that may be evident when compared to a stronger security baseline template.

The Security Configuration and Analysis snap-in uses a container, also referred to as a security database, to store the imported templates that will be compared to the current system. To create a database, simply right-click Security Configuration and Analysis, as shown in Figure 13-10, choose Open Database, and choose a filename for the security database, as shown in Figure 13-11. Security database files have the .sdb extension.

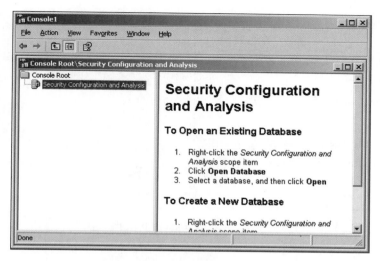

Figure 13-10   The Security Configuration and Analysis snap-in

Figure 13-11   Specifying the pathname to a security database

Next, you are prompted to import a template into the database. You may also import other templates into a database by right-clicking Security Configuration and Analysis, choosing Import Template, and selecting a security template file, as shown in Figure 13–12. This allows you to view the effects of combining security templates on the local computer.

Next, you may compare the settings of security templates in the security database to the actual computer settings; simply right-click Security Configuration and Analysis and choose Analyze Computer Now. You are then prompted to specify a log file location; by default, the

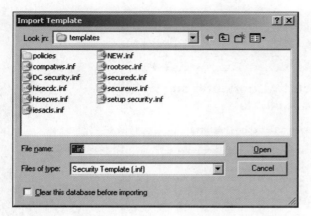

Figure 13-12 Inserting additional templates into a security database

Security Configuration and Analysis snap-in logs all information to My Documents\Security\Logs*database*.log, where *database* is the name of the security database.

After the analysis process is complete, security categories will appear. As each node is expanded, you will see the comparison between the database (imported templates) and the computer's current configuration, as shown in Figure 13-13. A green check mark indicates that your computer meets or exceeds the security settings defined in the database; a red X indicates that your computer does not meet the security settings defined in the database.

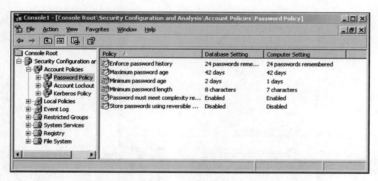

Figure 13-13 Results of an analysis

After you examine the differences between the database and the local computer, you can apply the settings in the database to the local computer, or make changes to the database settings and export the database settings to a new security template file.

To apply the settings in the database to the local computer, simply right-click Security Configuration and Analysis and choose Configure Computer Now, as shown in Figure 13-14.

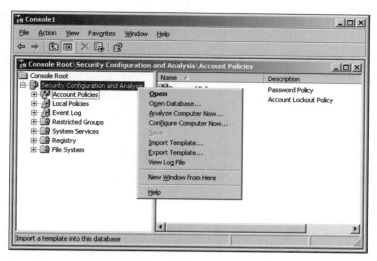

Figure 13-14   Right-clicking Security Configuration and Analysis

To make changes to the settings in the database, simply double-click any configuration entry in the results of an analysis and select the desired configuration. Next, you can export the settings in the database to a new security template file by right-clicking Security Configuration and Analysis and choosing Export Template, as shown earlier in Figure 13-14. This security template file can then be applied to other computers or applied to a GPO.

Activity 13-4: Analyzing Security Settings Using Security Configuration and Analysis

Time Required: 25 minutes

Objective: Use the Security Configuration and Analysis snap-in to compare security template settings to settings on the local computer.

Description: As part of a new security initiative, the IT manager at Great Arctic North University has decided that a mechanism must exist to allow systems to be periodically evaluated to ensure that they meet the University's security baseline. You have been asked to evaluate the Security Configuration and Analysis snap-in to determine whether or not this application will meet the stated requirements. In this activity, you will compare the current configuration of your computer with the settings found in the built-in hisecws.inf security template.

1. Click **Start**, **Run** and type **mmc**. Press **Enter**.
2. Click **File** on the menu bar, click **Add/Remove Snap-in**, and then click **Add**.
3. On the Available Standalone Snap-ins window, click **Security Configuration and Analysis** and click **Add**.
4. Click **Close** to close the window, and then click **OK**.

13

5. Right-click the **Security Configuration and Analysis** icon, and click **Open Database**.

6. In the Open database window, type **SecurityTest** in the File name text box, and then click **Open**.

7. In the Import Template window, click **hisecws.inf** and click Open.

8. Right-click the **Security Configuration and Analysis** icon, and click **Analyze Computer Now**.

9. In the Perform Analysis dialog box, click **OK** to accept the default log file location.

10. Click the **plus sign (+)** next to Security Configuration and Analysis and Account Policies to expand them, and then click **Password Policy**.

11. Review both the Database Setting column and the Computer Setting column. The first column outlines the settings found in the database that relate to the template, whereas the second column outlines the settings currently configured on your server. Note that the icons displayed as part of each setting outline whether or not your server's current configuration meets or exceeds the settings outlined in the security database.

12. As time permits, browse through additional settings such as those found in the Account Lockout Policy, User Rights Assignment, and Security Options sections.

13. Close the Security Configuration and Analysis snap-in. Click **No** in the Microsoft Management Console dialog box.

Using the Secedit Command-line Tool

Secedit.exe is a command-line tool used to create and apply security templates, as well as analyze security settings. This tool can be used in situations where Group Policy cannot be applied, such as in workgroup configurations. Secedit.exe, along with the Task Scheduler, can ensure that every computer in the workgroup maintains consistent security policy settings. The secedit.exe command uses 11 main switches:

- */analyze*—Analyzes database settings and compares them to a computer configuration

- */CFG filename*—Specifies the path to a security template file that is imported into a database specified using the /DB switch.

- */configure*—Configures a system with database (security template) settings

- */DB filename*—Specifies the path to a database file (*.sdb) that is to be used when analyzing a system

- */export*—Exports database information to a security template file

- */GenerateRollback*—Generates a security template that saves the current security settings of a system; this template can be used to return to previous security settings in the event that settings are changed

- *import*—Imports security template information into a database file for analysis purposes
- *log filename*—Specifies the path to a log file written to during an analysis; if this switch is not specified, the default log file is used
- *quiet*—Prevents all screen and log output
- *validate*—Verifies the syntax of a security template
- *verbose*—Specifies that detailed information should be logged during an analysis

For example, if you wish to regularly analyze a computer's security settings against a database called C:\baseline.sdb that contains the security template C:\baseline.inf and log verbose information to the log file C:\baseline.log, you could schedule the command secedit /analyze /DB C:\baseline.sdb /CFG C:\baseline.inf /log C:\baseline.log /verbose in Task Scheduler.

NOTE The Windows Server 2003 version of secedit.exe no longer includes the /refreshpolicy switch that was used to manually refresh computer and user Group Policy settings in Windows 2000. Refreshing Group Policy settings is now accomplished using the command-line tool gpupdate.exe.

Activity 13-5: Analyzing Security Settings Using Secedit.exe   **13**

Time Required: 15 minutes

Objective: Use the Secedit.exe utility to compare security template settings to settings on the local computer.

Description: You wish to automate the evaluation of security settings on computers at Great Arctic North University. As a result, you run the secedit command on a test computer to compare the current security settings to the hisecws.inf predefined security template.

1. Click **Start**, **Run** and type **cmd**. Press **Enter**.
2. Type **secedit /analyze /DB C:\baseline.sdb /CFG C:\WINDOWS\ security\templates\hisecws.inf /log C:\baseline.log /verbose** and press **Enter**.
3. Type **notepad C:\baseline.log** and press **Enter**. Browse through the file and note any mismatched settings and compare them to the results of Activity 13-4.
4. Close all open windows.

Chapter Summary

- Windows Server 2003 simplifies the management of security-related settings on computers using Security Configuration Manager tools.
- Security templates define baseline security settings for use on computers.

- Each security template organizes security-related settings into seven categories: Account Policies, Local Policies, Event Log, Restricted Groups, System Services, Registry, and File System.

- Windows Server 2003 comes with several predefined security templates; the default security template and a series of incremental templates that may be used to modify the default security template.

- You may create security templates using the Security Templates snap-in.

- You may apply the settings in a security template to the local computer or to a GPO in an Active Directory database. If applying a security template to a GPO, the GPO must be attached to a domain object if Account Policies settings are configured.

- The Security Configuration and Analysis snap-in can be used to analyze a computer's security settings, modify security template settings, and apply security templates to computers.

- Like the Security Configuration and Analysis snap-in, the Secedit.exe command-line utility can analyze and set security-related settings on a computer, but can also be automated using the Task Scheduler.

Key Terms

Gpupdate.exe — A command-line utility that can manually update the local computer with settings from GPOs in Active Directory.

Group Policy Management Console (GPMC) — A Windows Server 2003 tool that allows you to centrally manage GPOs in Active Directory.

Group Policy Object (GPO) — An Active Directory object that is configured to apply settings to users and computers in Active Directory. It may be linked to a site, domain, or OU object in Active Directory.

incremental templates — A set of text-based security template files that you can use to apply uniform security settings on computers within an enterprise. The templates modify security settings incrementally and do not include the default security settings.

method of least privilege — A common security practice whereby you restrict all but the necessary security settings on a computer.

Power Users group — Power users have less system access than administrators, but more than users. By default, members of this group have Read/Write permissions to other parts of the system in addition to their own profile. Power users can perform many system-wide operations, such as changing system time and display settings, and creating user accounts and shares.

Secedit.exe — A command-line tool that allows you to apply security templates to computers and analyze local computer security settings.

security baseline template — A security template that contains the minimum security settings for a computer required by an organization.

Security Configuration and Analysis snap-in — A security tool that allows you to analyze local computer security settings against a baseline. It may also be used to modify or apply security settings to the local computer.

Security Configuration Manager tools — A security toolset consisting of security templates and utilities that can be used to analyze and apply security configurations.

Security Policy template — A security template used to apply various security settings to an Active Directory container or object using a GPO.

security template — A file that contains security-related settings that may be applied to a computer.

REVIEW QUESTIONS

1. The method of least privilege states that you should restrict security settings on a computer to only those that are required to meet baseline security for the organization. True or false?

2. Which security template is automatically defined during the Windows Server 2003 installation process?
   a. Setup Security.inf
   b. Compatws.inf
   c. Securews.inf
   d. Rootsec.inf

3. Which security template can you use to relax the security settings on a computer in order for certain applications to run properly?
   a. Setup Security.inf
   b. Compatws.inf
   c. Securews.inf
   d. Rootsec.inf

4. What is the default location of security templates in Windows Server 2003?
   a. C:\WINDOWS\templates
   b. C:\WINDOWS\security\templates
   c. C:\WINDOWS
   d. C:\WINDOWS\security\logs

5. In most cases, the predefined templates that come with Windows Server 2003 satisfy the security requirements for an organization. True or false?

13

6. Which security template can you use to specify the original permissions assigned to the system drive in your computer?

   a. Setup Security.inf

   b. Compatws.inf

   c. Securews.inf

   d. Rootsec.inf

7. You wish to use the most restrictive security settings on your Windows Server 2000 domain controller. What predefined security template should you assign?

   a. Securedc.inf

   b. Compatws.inf

   c. Hisecdc.inf

   d. Rootsec.inf

8. Which of the following tools may be used to apply a security template to a computer or group of computers? (Choose all that apply.)

   a. Active Directory Users and Computers

   b. Active Directory Sites and Services

   c. Local Security Settings

   d. Group Policy Management Console (GPMC)

9. In order to return to a computer's original security settings, you should apply an incremental security template. True or false?

10. Which node in a security template allows an administrator the ability to control group membership on a computer?

    a. Registry

    b. Account Policies

    c. Restricted Groups

    d. Local Policies

11. Which node in a security template may be used to enforce password history for a computer?

    a. Registry

    b. Account Policies

    c. Restricted Groups

    d. Local Policies

12. Which node in a security template allows an administrator the ability to audit events on a computer?

   a. Registry

   b. Account Policies

   c. Restricted Groups

   d. Local Policies

13. Which node in a security template must be applied to a domain object if imported into a GPO?

   a. Registry

   b. Account Policies

   c. Restricted Groups

   d. Local Policies

14. Before analyzing security settings on computers within your organization, it is good form to define a(an) _____ .

   a. security baseline template

   b. account policy

   c. default template

   d. none of the above

15. What must you do in the Security Configuration and Analysis snap-in before analyzing the security settings on your computer? (Choose all that apply.)

   a. create a database

   b. export a security template from the database

   c. import a security template into the database

   d. configure your system with the settings from the database

16. You may analyze the settings on a computer against the security settings in multiple security templates. True or false?

17. After comparing the settings on your computer to a security baseline template using the Security Configuration and Analysis snap-in, you wish to modify the settings in the security baseline template and save it as baseline2.inf. What should you do? (Choose all that apply.)

   a. Create a new security template using the Security Templates snap-in and import it into the database in the Security Configuration and Analysis snap-in.

   b. Double-click the settings in the Security Configuration and Analysis snap-in and change their values.

13

   c. Export the database to a file called baseline2.inf using the Security Configuration and Analysis snap-in.

   d. Create a new security template using the Security Templates snap-in and enter the desired settings from the log file used by the Security Configuration and Analysis snap-in.

18. Which Secedit switch specifies the path to a security template file?

   a. /DB

   b. /CFG

   c. /export

   d. /verbose

19. Which Secedit switch suppresses all screen and log output?

   a. /log

   b. /validate

   c. /quiet

   d. /verbose

20. Which Secedit switch may be used to generate a security template based on the existing computer configuration?

   a. /log

   b. /export

   c. /GenerateRollback

   d. /validate

CASE PROJECTS

CASE
PROJECTS

Case Project 13-1: Method of Least Privilege

Several computers have been added to the Great Arctic North University network in the past few years. Several people from various faculties have expressed concerns that there are no standardized security settings on these computers. You are designing a general security policy that will be implemented on all computers at Great Arctic North University. Write a short memo that describes how security templates that follow the method of least privilege can be used to standardize security across the Great Arctic North University network.

Case Project 13-2: Applying Security Templates

Great Arctic North University has decided to implement GPOs to configure different security settings for all computers within the Arts and Engineering faculties. Other faculties do not use Active Directory, yet require a standardized security policy for servers and workstations in their departments. The IT manager for Great Arctic North University notes that the predefined templates are sufficient for use within the University and that no new templates need to be created. Given these requirements, how would you implement security templates in the Great Arctic North University network?

Case Project 13-3: Auditing Security Templates

You have successfully administered security templates to all servers and workstations in the Great Arctic North University network. You have used different templates for workstations, servers, and domain controllers. Every 2 weeks, you wish to audit the settings on each computer to ensure that no changes have been made. How will you accomplish this? What tools will you use?

13

TROUBLESHOOTING WINDOWS SERVER 2003 NETWORKS

After reading this chapter, you will be able to:

♦ Outline the maintenance cycle

♦ Understand common troubleshooting methodology

♦ Use common Windows Server 2003 tools to troubleshoot server and network problems

♦ Describe common network connectivity problems and their solutions

Many businesses today rely heavily on their servers for day-to-day operations. Expectations are set for network server availability and performance. If a network service on a server fails or performs poorly, many routine functions are affected and the complaints soon filter in. This means that as a network administrator, you need to ensure that a server is capable of meeting performance expectations and that all services are available to network users.

This chapter begins by looking at the maintenance cycle and troubleshooting methodology. Next, you are introduced to tools that can be used to monitor server and network performance. Finally, this chapter discusses various network connectivity problems and troubleshooting steps that may be used to solve the problem.

TROUBLESHOOTING METHODOLOGY

Once you have successfully installed Windows Server 2003, configured services on the system, and documented settings, you must maintain the system's integrity over time. This includes **monitoring**, proactive maintenance, and reactive maintenance, as illustrated in Figure 14-1.

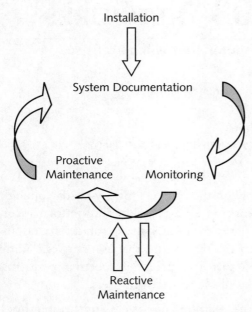

Installation

System Documentation

Proactive Maintenance   Monitoring

Reactive Maintenance

Figure 14-1   The maintenance cycle

Monitoring is one of the largest activities that network administrators do; it involves examining network connectivity, viewing log files and running performance utilities periodically to identify any problems and their causes. **Proactive maintenance** involves taking the necessary steps required to minimize the chance of future problems as well as their impact. Performing regular system backups and identifying potential problem areas are examples of proactive maintenance. All proactive maintenance tasks should be documented for future reference; this information, along with any data backups, is vital to the reconstruction of your system, should it suffer catastrophic failure.

Reactive maintenance is used to correct problems when they arise during monitoring. When a problem is solved, it should be documented and the system adjusted proactively to reduce the likelihood that the same problem will occur in the future. Furthermore, documenting the solution to problems will create a template for action, allowing subsequent or similar problems to be remedied faster. Any system documentation should be printed and kept in a logbook, because this information may be lost during a system failure if kept on the system itself.

Reactive maintenance is further composed of many procedures known as **troubleshooting procedures**, which can be used to efficiently solve a problem in a systematic manner.

When a problem occurs, you should gather as much information about the problem as possible; this may include examining **system log** files and viewing configuration settings as well as running monitoring programs. In addition to this, you could research the symptoms of the problem on the Internet; Web sites and newsgroups often list troubleshooting steps that may help solve certain problems.

Following this, you should try to isolate the problem by examining the information gathered. Determine whether the problem is persistent or intermittent, and whether it affects all users or just one.

Given this information, you may then generate a list of possible causes and solutions organized by placing the most probable solution at the top of the list and the least probable solution at the bottom of the list. Using the Internet at this stage is beneficial since solutions for many network-related problems are posted on newsgroups or Web sites such as *http://www.microsoft.com*.

Next, you should implement and test each possible solution for results until the problem is resolved. When implementing possible solutions, it is very important that you only apply one change at a time. If you make multiple modifications, it will be unclear as to what worked and why.

Once the problem has been solved, document the solution for future reference and proceed to take proactive maintenance measures to reduce the chance of the same problem reoccurring in the future. These troubleshooting procedures are outlined in Figure 14-2.

14

The troubleshooting procedures listed in Figure 14-2 serve as a guideline only; they may need to be adjusted for certain problems since troubleshooting is an art that network administrators will improve on over time. There are, however, two golden rules that should guide you during any troubleshooting process:

1. *Prioritize problems*—If there are multiple problems to be solved, prioritize the problems according to severity and spend a reasonable amount of time on each problem given its priority. Becoming fixated on a small problem and ignoring larger issues results in much lower productivity. If a problem is too difficult to solve in a given period of time, it is good practice to ask for help.

2. *Try to solve the root of the problem*—Some solutions may appear successful in the short term, yet reoccur since there may be an underlying cause to the problem. Effective troubleshooting also relies a great deal on instinct, which comes from a solid knowledge of the system hardware and configuration. To avoid missing the underlying cause of any problem, try to justify why a certain solution was successful. If it is unclear why a certain solution was successful, then there is likely an underlying cause to the problem that may need to be remedied in the future to prevent the same problem from reoccurring.

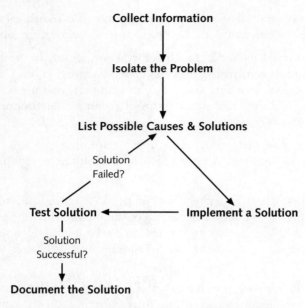

Figure 14-2   Troubleshooting procedures

TROUBLESHOOTING TOOLS

Windows Server 2003 comes with several built-in tools that can be used to obtain information as well as monitor network and server performance. The most common of these include:

- Network Monitor
- System Monitor
- Performance Logs and Alerts
- Event Viewer
- Task Manager
- Services snap-in

The following sections introduce you to these tools, providing you with a description of how they can be used to monitor your server and network.

Network Monitor

Windows Server 2003 **Network Monitor** may be used to view and log network activity by capturing the different frames and packets that are received on a network interface.

Network Monitor consists of two main components that work together to capture network information:

- Network Monitor
- The **Network Monitor driver**

Network Monitor is a Windows component that you install using the Add or Remove Programs option in Control Panel. It is a Microsoft tool that captures and organizes network information.

The Network Monitor driver can be installed on a server or workstation and enables a computer's network interface to collect statistics about network performance, such as the number of packets sent and received at that computer. Because the Network Monitor driver is a protocol that works along with the Network Monitor, you install the Network Monitor driver using the Network Connections option in Control Panel. When you install Network Monitor, the Network Monitor Driver is automatically installed as a protocol on all network interfaces.

When you run Network Monitor to monitor traffic across a network, the Network Monitor driver detects many forms of network traffic and captures packets and frames for analysis and reporting by Network Monitor. All packets and frames that pass through the server's network interface are monitored (although not all contents are viewed) so that it is possible to determine basic information about the network, such as the amount of traffic, the types of packets, and the source and destination addresses of computers transmitting data.

The version of Network Monitor that is included with Windows Server 2003 is only designed to capture data at the computer's local network interface. Microsoft's System Management Server comes with a version of Network Monitor that can connect to and monitor activity from a network interface on any computer in the network that has the Network Monitor driver installed.

14

To capture traffic in Network Monitor, simply press the F10 key. Information will then be presented in four panes:

- Graph pane (upper–left pane)
- Total pane (upper–right pane)
- Session pane (lower–left pane)
- Station pane (bottom pane)

These panes are shown in Figure 14–3 and described in Table 14–1.

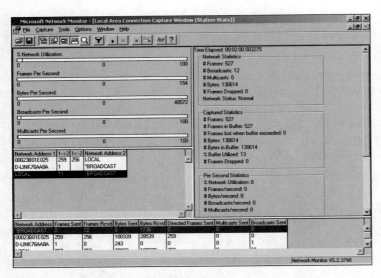

Figure 14-3   Network Monitor

Table 14-1   Network Monitor panes

Pane	Information Provided in the Pane
Graph	Shows bar graphs of the following: % Network Utilization, Frames Per Second, Bytes Per Second, Broadcasts Per Second, and Multicasts Per Second
Total	Provides total statistics about network activity that originates from, or is sent to, the computer (station) that is using Network Monitor, and includes many statistics in each of the following categories: Network Statistics, Captured Statistics, Per Second Statistics, Network Card (MAC) Statistics, Network Card (MAC) Error Statistics
Session	Shows statistics about traffic from other computers on the network which include the MAC (device) address of each computer's NIC and data about the number of frames sent from, and received by, each computer
Station	Provides total statistics on all communicating network stations, which include: Network (device) address of each communicating computer, Frames Sent, Frames Received, Bytes Sent, Bytes Received, Directed Frames Sent, Multicasts Sent, and Broadcasts Sent

The data bars in the Graph pane provide useful information that you can collect about network performance in order to establish a **baseline** for network activity at different times of the day. Four of the most helpful statistics are the following:

- *% Network Utilization*—Shows how much of the network bandwidth is in use
- *Frames Per Second*—Shows total traffic in frames for broadcasts, unicasts, and multicasts
- *Broadcasts Per Second*—Shows how much network traffic is the result of broadcasts from servers, workstations, and print servers
- *Multicasts Per Second*—Shows how much network traffic is due to multimedia servers

If % Network Utilization is frequently over 40% that means the network is experiencing collisions, and there may be bottlenecks due to the network design, possibly indicating the need to create subnets and implement routers. Network utilization that is regularly over 60% to 70% indicates a serious need to modify the network to address bottlenecks or increase network speed. Network utilization that is over 90% for a sustained period requires immediate attention in terms of locating the network problem or redesigning the network.

To view the details within each packet captured, you must first stop Network Monitor (simply press F11 to stop the capture) and press F12 to view the captured data, as shown in Figure 14-4.

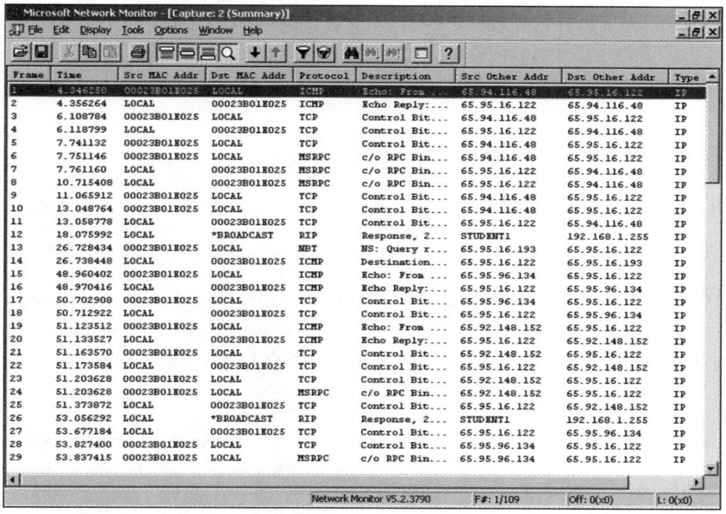

14

Figure 14-4 Viewing captured data in Network Monitor

Each line in Figure 14-4 represents a packet or frame of information that has been captured on the network. Only summary information is displayed for each packet such as source and destination IP addresses and protocol type. To view the headers and data of a particular packet, simply double-click the appropriate line shown in Figure 14-4 and you will be able to browse the structure of the packet, as shown in Figure 14-5.

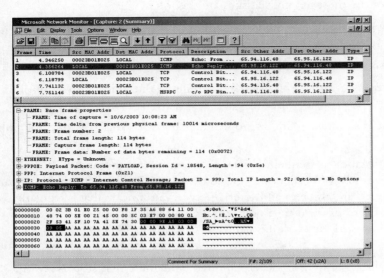

Figure 14-5   Viewing packet details in Network Monitor

Once you have captured and analyzed network traffic using Network Monitor, you may save the captured information to a file that may be opened later using Network Monitor; simply choose Save As from the File menu in Network Monitor. Network Monitor files end with a .cap extension.

Activity 14-1: Installing Network Monitor

Time Required: 15 minutes

Objective: Install Network Monitor.

Description: To facilitate troubleshooting, the IT manager at Great Arctic North University has requested that all servers in the university have Network Monitor installed on them. In this activity, you install Network Monitor and verify the installation of the Network Monitor driver.

1. Click **Start**, point to **Control Panel**, and click **Add or Remove Programs**.

2. Click **Add/Remove Windows Components**.

3. Double-click **Management and Monitoring Tools**.

4. Click **Network Monitor Tools**, and click **OK**.

5. Click **Next** and wait a few moments for the installation to be completed. Insert the Windows Server 2003 CD-ROM if prompted, and click **OK**.

6. Click **Finish**.

7. Close the **Add or Remove Programs** window.

8. Click **Start**, point to **Control Panel**, point to **Network Connections**, right-click **Local Area Connection**, and click **Properties**.

9. On the Networking tab in the box labeled This connection uses the following items, verify that the Network Monitor driver is installed. If it is installed, click **OK** to close the Local Area Connection dialog box. If it is not installed, you can install it manually at this point. Click **Install**, double-click **Protocol**, click **Network Monitor Driver**, and click **OK**, then click **Close** to close the Local Area Connection dialog box.

Activity 14-2 Using Network Monitor

Time Required: Approximately 15 minutes

Objective: Use Network Monitor to monitor traffic on a network.

Description: To prepare yourself for future network troubleshooting, you wish to familiarize yourself with Network Monitor. In this activity, you start Network Monitor and capture live network data for analysis.

1. Click **Start**, point to **Administrative Tools**, and click **Network Monitor**.

2. Click **OK** if an information box is displayed to remind you to select the network to monitor or to use the local area network as the default. Then, in the **Select a network** dialog box, click the network you want to monitor. For this activity, click **Local Computer**, click **Local Area Connection**, and click **OK**.

3. Maximize one or both Network Monitor screens if the display is not maximized.

4. Press **F10** to start capturing network performance data. View the data displayed on the screen, such as % Network Utilization or Network Statistics. Use the scroll bars in each of the four panes to view the information.

5. Click **Start**, **Run** and type **cmd**. Press **Enter**. Next, type **ping** *IP_address* where *IP_address* is the IP address of your partner's local area connection.

6. Close the command prompt and return to Network Monitor.

7. Press **F11** to stop the capture.

8. Press **F12** to display the captured data. Using protocol (ICMP), source and destination addresses, locate the lines that were generated when you contacted your partner's local area connection using the Ping utility. Double-click on these packets to view their contents.

9. If time permits, view the details of other packets shown in Network Monitor.

10. Close Network Monitor. When prompted to save the capture, choose **No**.

11. When asked if you wish to save the unsaved database entries click **No**, if necessary.

14

Network Monitor supports event management, in which you set up **filters** to capture a certain event or type of network activity. For example, you may only wish to observe traffic that is sent between your computer and a specific workstation. Another possibility is to track only IP activity related to Internet traffic into the server.

To create a filter in Network Monitor, simply press F8 and you will receive the screen shown in Figure 14-6.

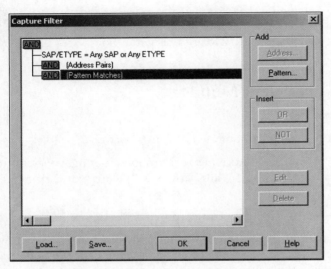

Figure 14-6   Specifying a filter in Network Monitor

Network Monitor can filter frames and packets on the basis of two property types, Service Access Point (SAP) or Ethertype (ETYPE). SAP refers to the service access point which specifies the network process that should accept a frame at the destination, such as TCP/IP, BPDU (a frame type used by network bridges), and special manufacturers, including Novell (for IPX/SPX). ETYPE refers to a property of an Ethernet frame that includes a 2-byte code for the protocol type and is used in Ethernet communications by some vendors, but is not a part of the Ethernet standard. For some protocols, such as IP, you can choose from either property or you can monitor for both. If you are in doubt, monitor both types or select SAP, which conforms to the Ethernet standard.

Activity 14-3: Creating a Filter in Network Monitor

Time Required: Approximately 15 minutes

Objective: Create a filter in Network Monitor.

Description: Great Arctic North University has an older NetWare server that runs a database application, which uses NetWare's Service Advertising Protocol (SAP). You want to create a filter to monitor only NetWare SAP frames that are received and sent by the NetWare server to determine if they are creating excessive network traffic.

1. Click **Start**, point to **Administrative Tools**, and click **Network Monitor**.

2. Press **F8**. If you are using the Network Monitor version installed from the Windows Server 2003 CD-ROM, you will see a warning that this version only captures data coming across the local computer. Click **OK**.

3. Double-click **SAP/ETYPE = Any SAP or Any ETYPE**. Note some of the protocols that you can monitor.

4. Click the **Disable All** button.

5. Click **Netware SAP** in the Disabled Protocols box, and click the **Enable** button. Click **OK**.

6. Double-click **(Address Pairs)**. Although the default settings monitor all traffic, you will manually specify that the filter monitors traffic to or from all computers. Ensure that the **Include** option button is selected and that ***ANY GROUP** is selected in the Station 1 box. Ensure that the two-way arrows are selected in the Direction box, and that ***ANY** is selected in the Station 2 box. Click **OK**.

7. Click **OK**.

8. Press **F10** to start a new capture. After 30 seconds, press **F11** to stop the capture. Note that no packets were captured because the filter specified only NetWare traffic and no NetWare servers exist on the network.

9. Close Network Monitor. When prompted to save the capture, click **No**.

System Monitor

System Monitor is one of the most useful tools for collecting data on real-time server performance. As part of the Windows Server 2003 Performance snap-in, this tool allows you to track how system resources are being used and how they are behaving under the current workload. System Monitor collects data that you can use for the following tasks:

- *Server performance*—If you use System Monitor on a regular basis, it can help you understand how the server performs under the current workload.

- *Problem diagnosis*—You can use the data that is collected to diagnose server components that may not be performing optimally, causing a bottleneck within the server.

- *Capacity planning*—You can use the information to see how server usage is changing over time and plan ahead for future upgrades.

- *Testing*—If configuration changes are made, you can use the data to observe the impact that the changes have on the server.

System Monitor is similar to the Performance Monitor tool included in Windows
NT Server 4.0.

Using System Monitor, you can define the components you want to monitor and the type
of data you want to collect. You choose the **performance objects** you want to monitor,
such as memory, and the specific type of performance counters or data associated with the
object for which you want to gather data. You can further customize the data you want to
capture by specifying the source or computer you want to monitor. You can use System
Monitor to gather data from the local computer or from a network computer for which you
have appropriate permissions. Although the System Monitor tool includes a number of
performance objects and associated counters to monitor by default, additional objects and
counters are added when various services and applications are added to a server. For
example, when the DNS service is installed, counters specifically designed to troubleshoot
the DNS service on the local computer are also added.

When you first open the Performance snap-in, System Monitor automatically begins
displaying performance data. By default, it displays data related to the memory, processor, and
physical disk objects for the local computer, as displayed in Figure 14-7.

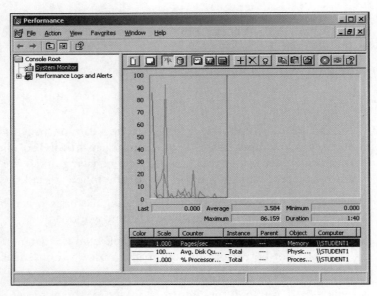

Figure 14-7   System Monitor

The information that System Monitor captures can be displayed in one of three views:

- *Graph*—Displays **performance counter**, or counter for short, information as a
  continuous graph updated on-screen in real time

- *Histogram*—Displays counter information as a bar graph, with information updated on-screen in real time

- *Report*—Displays a text-based report view of counters, with information updated on-screen in real time

The System Monitor interface provides a number of options for viewing performance data, including the ability to add additional performance counters as required, switch between display views, highlight a selected counter, copy and paste selected information, and freeze the display for analysis purposes. The System Monitor toolbar, found at the top of the details pane in System Monitor, allows you to easily control these functions. In Activity 14-4, you will explore the various settings of the System Monitor tool.

Activity 14-4: Exploring System Monitor Settings

Time Required: 10 minutes

Objective: Explore Windows Server 2003 System Monitor settings.

Description: The IT manager at Great Arctic North University has informed you that all servers will eventually be monitored for performance purposes using the Windows Server 2003 System Monitor utility. He has asked you to become familiar with the tool and explore its various features because all networking-related staff will eventually need to be trained on this tool. In this activity, you will explore the various features of System Monitor.

1. Click **Start**, select **Administrative Tools**, and click **Performance**. The Performance console opens, and System Monitor begins running automatically using the three default counters.

2. Click the **View Histogram** button on the toolbar at the top of the System Monitor details pane. This illustrates the same counter information as a histogram.

3. Click the **View Report** button on the System Monitor toolbar. This shows the same counter information using the report view.

4. Click the **View Graph** button to return to the original graph view.

5. Click the **% Processor Time** counter at the bottom in the details screen, and then click the **Highlight** button. Notice that the % Processor Time counter in the graph now appears as a thick white line to make it easier to distinguish from the other counters. Click the **Highlight** button again to remove highlighting from the counter.

6. Right-click on any area within the counter listing at the bottom of the details pane, and click **Properties**.

7. In the System Monitor Properties dialog box, click **\Processor(_Total)\% Processor Time** if necessary, and then click on the largest line thickness in the Width list box. Click **OK**. The % Processor Time counter now appears as a thick red line on the graph.

8. Click the **Freeze Display** button on the System Monitor toolbar. This pauses the System Monitor view until the button is pressed again.

14

9. Click the **Update Data** button four or five times to allow the graph to move forward. This button allows you to update the on-screen data manually.

10. Click the **Freeze Display** button again to allow data to be gathered.

11. Click the **Clear Display** button on the System Monitor toolbar to clear and restart all on-screen counters.

12. Leave the Performance console window open.

Monitoring performance on your server should be a regular maintenance task. The information you gather can help to establish a baseline of server performance and identify what is considered normal server performance under typical operating conditions. As you continue to monitor your server over time, you can compare the data against the baseline to identify how performance is changing as the network changes and workloads increase. Doing so allows you to pinpoint bottlenecks, such as components that may be hindering server performance, before they become a serious problem.

Any time you upgrade or add a component to a system, whether it is a hardware or software component, you should run System Monitor to determine the effect the change has on server performance.

When monitoring server performance, there are a few performance objects that should be included, as well as specific performance counters associated with each one.

■ *% Processor Time*—This processor counter measures the percentage of time that the processor is executing a nonidle thread. If the value is continually at or over 80%, a CPU upgrade may be required.

■ *% Interrupt Time*—This processor counter measures hardware interrupts. If you experience a combination of Processor Time exceeding 90% and % Interrupt Time exceeding 15%, check for malfunctioning hardware or device drivers.

■ *Pages/Second*—This memory counter measures the number of pages read in or out to disk to resolve hard page faults. If this number exceeds 20 or more page faults per second, add more RAM to the computer.

■ *Page Faults/Second*—This memory counter measures the number of hard and soft page faults per second. A hard page fault refers to a request that required hard disk access, whereas a soft page fault refers to a request found in another part of memory.

■ *% Disk Time*—This physical and logical disk counter measures the percentage of elapsed time that the selected disk drive is busy. If it is above 90%, try moving the page file to another physical drive or upgrade the hard drive.

■ *Average Disk Queue Length*—This physical and logical disk counter measures the average number of requests currently outstanding for a volume or partition. If it averages over two, then drive access may be a bottleneck. You may want to upgrade the drive or hard drive controller. Implementing a stripe set with multiple drives may also fix this problem.

In Windows NT, all disk counters were turned off by default. In Windows 2000, the physical disk object is turned on by default and the logical disk object is turned off by default. In Windows Server 2003, all disk counters are enabled by default.

In Activity 14-5, you will add various counters to the System Monitor interface.

Activity 14-5: Adding Counters to System Monitor

Time Required: 10 minutes

Objective: Add object counters to the System Monitor tool.

Description: After exploring the various features of the System Monitor interface, you decide to add various counters to the tool to get a better sense of server performance and the purpose of the various counters. In this activity, you will add counters to the System Monitor interface, explore the Explain feature for counter objects, and view the counter results using the graph, histogram, and report views.

1. In the Performance console, click the **New Counter Set** button on the System Monitor toolbar. Notice that all counters are removed from the System Monitor details pane.

2. Click the **Add** button on the System Monitor toolbar. The Add Counters dialog box opens.

3. In the Performance object list box, click **PhysicalDisk**.

4. In the Select counters from list list box, click **% Disk Read Time**. In the Select instances from list box, click the first entry under **_Total**, and then click **Add**.

5. In the Performance object list box, click **Memory**.

6. In the Select counters from list list box, click **Available MBytes**. In the Select instances from list box, click **_Total** if possible.

7. Click the **Explain** button. This opens a window that explains the purpose of the selected counter.

8. Close the **Explain Text** window.

9. Click the **Add** button to add the counter to System Monitor.

10. In the Performance object list box, click **Network Interface**.

11. Click the **All counters** option button, and then click **Add**. This will add all of the performance counters for the Network Interface object to the graph.

12. Click **Close**.

13. Notice that the number of counters now available on the graph has increased dramatically. Click the **View Histogram** button to view the counter data using that method, and then click the **View Report** button.

14

14. Click the **New Counter Set** button to clear all counters from System Monitor.

15. Close the Performance console window.

There are many performance counters available in System Monitor, and it is very difficult to know what each one does. Use the Explain button in the Add Counters window to view the description of each counter associated with an object.

Gathering the data is the easy part. The difficult part is interpreting the information to determine what component is affecting performance. The difficulty lies in the fact that the performance of some components can affect other components. It may appear from the data that one component is performing poorly when this can be the result of another component performing poorly, or even too well. For example, if you determine that your processor is running over 80%, your first instinct may tell you to upgrade the processor or install multiple processors if the motherboard supports it. Through further analysis, however, you may find a lack of memory is the bottleneck that is causing excess paging. You would have discovered this by monitoring the Pages/Second Memory counter. Thus, monitoring multiple components on a regular basis should give you an idea of how they perform together and make troubleshooting server performance that much easier.

The System Monitor tool provides a number of alternatives in terms of saving or viewing historical performance data. One particularly interesting feature is the ability to save System Monitor data to an HTML file. This allows an administrator to post performance data on a Web server, such that it could subsequently be easily viewed and retrieved. When System Monitor data is saved in this format, many of the control functions of the tool are still available through the Web interface. In other words, the data presented in not a simple graphics file, but rather an interactive interface.

The System Monitor tool is also capable of displaying older data that may have been saved to a log file or database using the **Performance Logs and Alerts** tool. This tool will be looked at in more detail in the next section.

In Activity 14-6, you will use the System Monitor tool to save and view a System Monitor graph.

Activity 14-6: Saving and Viewing System Monitor Data

Time Required: 10 minutes

Objective: Explore options for saving System Monitor data.

Description: Although the IT manager at Great Arctic North University is aware of the fact that multiple servers can be monitored on a single System Monitor graph, he has asked you to explore the possibility of making counter data available via a Web browser for those users who will not have access to the MMC. In this activity, you will save the output of various System Monitor counters to an HTML file and then access that HTML file using Internet Explorer to monitor your server.

1. Click **Start**, select **Administrative Tools**, and then click **Performance**.

2. Allow the System Monitor graph to gather information until the end right side of the window is almost reached, and then click the **Freeze Display** button.

3. Right-click on an area within the graph and click **Save As**.

4. In the **Save As** dialog box, click the **C:** drive in the Save in list box.

5. In the File name text box, type **sysmon**, and then click the **Save** button.

6. Open My Computer. Browse to the C: drive, and then double-click the file **sysmon.htm**.

7. The sysmon.htm file will open in Internet Explorer and will display the System Monitor details pane.

8. In the Internet Explorer window, click the **Avg. Disk Queue Length** counter at the bottom of the window, and then click the **Highlight** button. Notice that even though the System Monitor information is displayed in a Web browser, some of its ordinary functions are still available.

9. Click the **View Histogram** button, and then click the **View Report** button. Notice that both of these functions are also supported from the Web browser interface.

10. Click the **Freeze Display** button in the Internet Explorer window to deselect it. When the System Monitor Control dialog box opens, click **Yes**. Notice that the Web page automatically begins updating counter data again.

11. Close Internet Explorer.

12. Click the **New Counter Set** button to clear all counters from System Monitor.

13. Close the Performance console window, and close all open windows.

Performance Logs and Alerts

Another tool available within the Performance snap-in is Performance Logs and Alerts. This tool allows you to automatically collect data on the local computer or from another computer on the network, and then view it using System Monitor or another program such as Microsoft Excel or a relational database such as Microsoft SQL Server.

Performance Logs and Alerts allows you to perform the following tasks:

- Collect data in a binary, comma-separated, or tab-separated format. The binary versions of the log files can be read with System Monitor, but comma- and tab-separated data can easily be imported into another program for analysis.

- View data both while it is being collected and after it has been collected.

- Configure parameters such as start and stop times for log generation, file names, and file size.

14

- Configure and manage multiple logging sessions from a single console window.
- Set up alerts so that a message is sent, a program is run, or a log file is started when a specific counter exceeds or drops below a configured value.

You can access Performance Logs and Alerts through the Performance console. There are three options available under Performance Logs and Alerts, as shown in Figure 14-8: Counter Logs, Trace Logs, and Alerts.

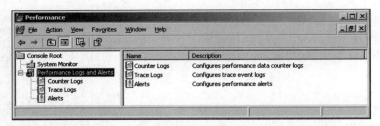

Figure 14-8   Performance Logs and Alerts

Counter logs take the information that you view using System Monitor and save it to a log file. One of the main advantages of using counter logs is that you can configure logging to start and stop at different intervals. **Trace logs** are similar to counter logs but are triggered to start when an event occurs. You can use **alerts** to configure an event to occur when a counter meets a predefined value. For example, you might choose to run a specific program or utility automatically when a certain threshold is reached, or send a message to a network administrator.

Logging does increase overhead on a server, so it is not something you want to have running all the time. It is essential that you set up a regular schedule for collecting data and ensure that the data is reviewed to make sure no problems are developing or occurring. Because logging should not be running all the time, it is good form to set up alerts that can notify you of a potential problem. For example, you can configure an alert to monitor the processor usage and notify you if it exceeds 80%. Once an alert is created, you simply double-click on it in Performance Logs and Alerts and view the Action tab to configure the event that is performed when an alert is triggered. The different actions available are listed in Table 14-2.

Table 14-2   Actions that can be taken when an alert is triggered

Option	Description
Log an entry in the application event log	An entry is added to the application log when the event is triggered.
Send a network message to	Messenger service sends a message to the specified computer when the alert is triggered.
Start performance data log	Counter log is run when the alert is triggered.
Run this program	Specified program is run when the alert is triggered.

Table 14-2   Actions that can be taken when an alert is triggered (continued)

Option	Description
Command Line Arguments	Specified command-line arguments are copied when the Run this program option is used.

In Activity 14-7, you will configure Performance Logs and Alerts settings on your Windows Server 2003 computer.

Activity 14-7: Configuring Performance Logs and Alerts

Time Required: 15 minutes

Objective: Configure performance logging and alerts.

Description: Although the servers at Great Arctic North University are monitored regularly during business hours, the company still does not have staff on hand outside of business hours to monitor system performance. Because of this, the IT manager has asked you to look into features of the Performance console that will allow data to be gathered after hours. Similarly, he would also like to have alerts configured such that an administrator would receive an on-screen message in the event that a critical server threshold is reached. In this activity, you will explore and configure various logging options as well as configure alerts using Performance Logs and Alerts.

1. Click **Start**, select **Administrative Tools**, and then click **Performance**.

2. Click the **plus sign (+)** next to Performance Logs and Alerts to expand its contents.

3. Click the **Counter Logs** icon to view its contents. Notice that a single sample log exists by default with the name System Overview.

4. Double-click the **System Overview** icon to view its properties. The System Overview Properties dialog box opens.

5. Notice the log file name associated with the log, the counters that the log includes, and the interval at which data is being gathered.

6. Click the **Log Files** tab.

7. Click the **Log file type** list arrow to view all of the different log type options available.

8. Click the **Schedule** tab. This tab allows you to schedule stop and start times for the log if necessary.

9. Click **Cancel**.

10. Right-click the **System Overview** icon and click **Start**. Notice that the icon turns from red to green.

11. Wait approximately 2 minutes, and then right-click the **System Overview** icon and click **Stop**.

14

12. Click the **System Monitor** icon. On the System Monitor tool bar, click the **View Log Data** button.

13. When the System Monitor Properties dialog box opens, click the **Log files** radio button, and then click **Add**.

14. In the Select Log File dialog box, browse to **C:\PerfLogs**, click the **System_Overview.blg** file to select it, click **Open**, and then click **OK**. This loads the data stored in the System_Overview.blg log file into the System Monitor window.

15. Under Performance Logs and Alerts, click the **Alerts** icon to view its contents. There are no alerts configured by default.

16. Click **Start**, select **Administrative Tools**, and then click **Services**.

17. Right-click the **Alerter** service icon, and click **Properties**.

18. In the Startup type list box, click **Automatic**. Click **OK**.

19. Right-click the **Alerter** service, and click **Start**.

20. Right-click the **Messenger** service icon, and click **Properties**.

21. In the Startup type list box, click **Automatic**. Click **OK**.

22. Right-click the **Messenger** service, and click **Start**.

23. In the Performance window, right-click **Alerts** and click **New Alert Settings**.

24. In the New Alert Settings dialog box, type **CPU Utilization** in the Name text box and click **OK**.

25. On the **General** tab of the CPU Utilization dialog box, click the **Add** button.

26. In the Add Counters dialog box, click the **Add** button to add the % Processor Time counter, and then click **Close**.

27. Type **30** in the Limit text box to have the alert triggered when CPU utilization reaches a value over 30%.

28. In the Interval spin box, type **1**.

29. Click the **Action** tab. Click the check box next to **Send a network message to**, and then type **localhost** in the associated text box. Click **OK**.

30. Click **Start**, click **Run**, and type **wmplayer.exe** in the Open text box. Click **OK**. The Windows Media Player opens, which will usually increase the CPU utilization for brief periods.

31. When the Messenger Service dialog box opens on-screen, read its contents and click **OK**.

32. Close all open windows.

Event Viewer

Perhaps the most common and effective monitoring and troubleshooting tool in Windows Server 2003 is **Event Viewer**, shown in Figure 14-9. You can use Event Viewer to gather information and troubleshoot services, hardware, and system problems.

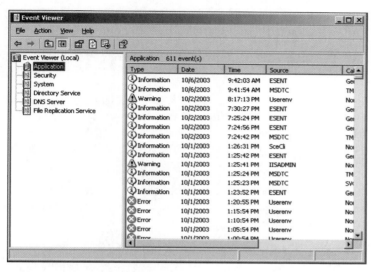

Figure 14-9   Event Viewer

 14

Events that occur on a system are tracked and recorded in different log files. You can use Event Viewer to view the contents of the log files. For example, you can use Event Viewer to view the contents of the system log to determine when, and possibly why, a specific service failed to start.

Whenever you are troubleshooting a problem with a server, one of the first places to look to gather information about the cause is Event Viewer. Entries in the log files can alert you to warnings and errors that are occurring, the component or application that is generating the message, and possibly why the problem is happening. Most entries also include an event ID that you can research on Microsoft's Web site (or the vendor's Web site in the case of third-party counters) to gather more detailed information on the problem and find a possible solution.

NOTE You can use both the *support.microsoft.com* Web site and the Windows Server 2003 Help and Support tool to research event ID messages.

Events are typically written to one of three log files:

- *Application log*—Information, warnings, and errors generated by programs installed on the system are written to the **application log**.

- *Security log*—Events pertaining to the audit policy are written to the **security log**. For example, if the audit policy is tracking failed logon attempts, an event is written to the security log each time a user is unsuccessful in logging on. By default, security logging is disabled until an audit policy is configured.

- *System log*—Information, warnings, and errors generated by Windows Server 2003 system components, such as drivers and services, are written to the system log.

A domain controller has two additional logs: the directory service log, which records events logged by Active Directory, and the file replication service log, which logs file replication events. A server installed with the DNS service also includes the DNS server log, which records events related to the DNS server service.

By default, any user can view the contents of the application and system log. The security log can only be viewed by administrators and those users who have been assigned the Manage Auditing and Security Log right.

The system and application logs display the following types of events:

- *Information*—When a component or application successfully performs an operation; information events are identified by an "I" icon.

- *Warning*—When an event occurs that may not be a problem at the current time, but may become a problem in the future; an exclamation point icon indicates warnings.

- *Error*—When a significant event has occurred, such as a service failing to start or a device driver failing to load; an "x" icon indicates errors.

There are two other types of events that are logged. These are successes and failures of actions that are performed on the network based on the configuration of an audit policy. Refer to Chapter 5 for the configuration of security audit policies.

When you click a log file within Event Viewer, the details pane lists all the events that have occurred and provides general information about each one, such as:

- Type of event (information, warning, or error)
- The date and time that the event occurred
- The source of the event (the component or application that logged the event)
- The category and event ID
- The computer on which the event occurred

An example of an event message is shown in Figure 14-10.

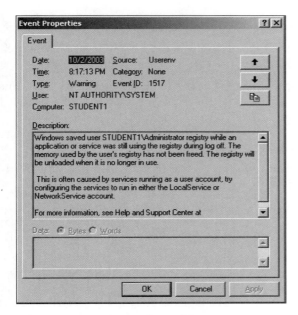

Figure 14-10 A sample event message

14

The header for an event provides information just listed. The event description provides an administrator with a description of what occurred and why the event is significant, which is usually the most useful information.

The data field of an event displays information that is generated by the program or component. It contains binary data that can be used to support technicians to troubleshoot the problem.

In Activity 14-8, you will explore events in your server's system and application logs.

Activity 14-8: Viewing Event Viewer System and Application Log Events

Time Required: 10 minutes

Objective: View events in the Event Viewer system and application logs.

Description: The IT manager at Great Arctic North University has decided that all IT staff will need to be familiar with using the Windows Server 2003 Event Viewer tool to monitor system and application events on servers within each faculty. In this activity, you will explore events in both the Event Viewer system and application logs.

1. Click **Start**, select **Administrative Tools**, and then click **Event Viewer**. Event Viewer opens.

2. Click the **Application** icon to view the contents of the application log.

3. Double-click the first information event found in the list to view its properties. The Event Properties dialog box will open.

4. Read the information contained in the event header and Description fields, and then click the down arrow button. The next event in the application log is displayed.

5. Click the **Cancel** button.

6. Click the **System** icon to view the contents of the system log.

7. Double-click the first error event found in the list to view its properties. Read through the details of the event header and Description fields.

8. Scroll to the bottom of the description field if necessary, and then click the hyperlink at the bottom of the section to visit the Microsoft events Web site. Click **Yes** in the Event Viewer dialog box. The site will open in Internet Explorer automatically.

9. Close all open windows.

Task Manager

Another tool that you can use to monitor server health and performance is Task Manager. This tool provides one of the fastest ways to check server and network performance and determine what processes are running on the system.

The **Task Manager** tool consists of five different tabs: Applications, Processes, Performance, Networking, and Users, as shown in Figure 14-11.

The Applications tab displays the interactive programs that are currently running and what their status is (running or not responding). This tab is most useful for ending a program that is frozen or that has stopped responding.

The Processes tab displays information about the processes currently running on a Windows Server 2003 system. By default, it displays information such as the name of the process, the percentage of CPU time being used by the process, and the amount of memory each process is consuming.

The Performance tab provides a quick view of a system's current performance. It is not meant to provide detailed performance information but is a quick way of checking performance to determine if there is a problem. You can then use another tool such as System Monitor for further investigation. Table 14-3 summarizes the information that is provided on the Performance tab.

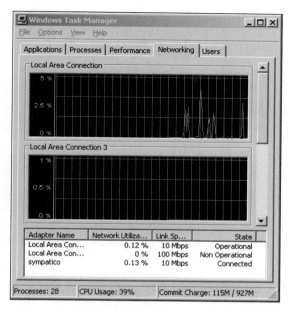

Figure 14-11   Task Manager

Table 14-3   Performance tab information

Component	Description
CPU Usage/CPU Usage History	Shows the percentage of CPU being used and graphs both current and historical CPU usage
PF Usage/Page File Usage History	Shows the amount of memory currently in use
Totals	Displays the total number of handles, threads, and processes
Physical Memory	Displays the total amount of memory, how much is available, and the amount of memory used for the system cache
Commit Charge	Displays the amount of memory that has been committed to all applications currently running
Kernel Memory	Displays the amount of memory that has been allocated to kernel functions, the amount of memory that could be paged to disk, and the amount of non-paged memory

The Networking tab provides a graphical representation of the current network utilization for a given network connection. This includes information about the status of a network connection, the speed at which it is connected, and the level of network utilization in both a percentage and graphical format.

Windows Server 2003 also includes a fifth tab named Users in the Task Manager interface. This tab allows you to disconnect, log off, or send messages to other users who may be connected to the server via technologies such as Remote Desktop or Terminal Services.

In Activity 14-9, you will explore the Windows Server 2003 Task Manager tool.

Activity 14-9: Using Task Manager

Time Required: 15 minutes

Objective: Use Task Manager to control applications and processes and gather basic system performance data.

Description: Although System Monitor provides detailed system performance information, it can be time-consuming to configure and interpret in cases where only a basic snapshot of system information is required. In this activity, you will review how you can use Task Manager to control applications and processes, as well as gather basic information about the performance and network utilization of your server.

1. Click **Start**, and then click **My Computer**.

2. Press **Ctrl+Alt+Delete** to access the Windows Security program.

3. Click the **Task Manager** button. The Applications tab will list the My Computer program as running, along with any other applications that you may have open.

4. Ensure that the entry for **My Computer** is selected, and then click the **Switch To** button. The My Computer window moves to the foreground. Click on the **Task Manager** button in the taskbar to return Task Manager to the foreground.

5. On the Task Manager **Applications** tab, click the **End Task** button. The My Computer window will close.

6. Click the **Processes** tab. This tab lists all currently running processes including their current CPU and memory usage.

7. Click the **dns.exe** entry and click the **End Process** button. This stops the DNS process on your server. Click **Yes** in the Task Manager Warning dialog box.

8. Right-click the **taskmgr.exe** entry, select **Set Priority**, and then click **AboveNormal**. This will give the taskmgr.exe process higher priority to the system processor. When the warning message appears on-screen, read it and then click **Yes**.

9. Click the **Performance** tab. Review the performance data for your server, noting that this tab displays information about the memory and CPU usage of your PC.

10. Click **View** on the menu bar, and then click **Show Kernel Times**. Notice that a new red line is added to both the CPU Usage and CPU Usage History graphs. This red line indicates the percentages of processor usage attributed to kernel rather than user processes.

11. Click the **Networking** tab. This tab displays a graph of network activity.

12. Click **Start**, click **Run**, and type **cmd** in the Open text box. Click **OK**.

13. On the command line, type **ping –t –l 1000 IP_address,** where *IP_address* is the IP address of your partner's Local Area Connection, and press **Enter**. Switch back to Task Manager to view the graph on the Networking tab.

14. Close all open windows.

Services Snap-in

When it comes to optimizing and securing your server, one of the first things you can do is disable any unnecessary components, such as services. When a service is unnecessarily installed during setup or is no longer used, it should be disabled. Running unnecessary services consumes additional system resources such as memory and CPU, thus adding overhead to a system. For example, if you have installed the DHCP service on a server for test purposes and then no longer require it, the service should be uninstalled, or disabled via the Services snap-in. If not, it will continue to run in the background and will consume resources, even though it may not be performing any valuable system function. The services that you disable depend on the role the server plays on the network. For example, a DHCP server requires different services than a DNS server. Some standard services on a Windows Server 2003 computer are listed in Table 14-4. Each network service added will also add the corresponding service to the list in Table 14-4.

Table 14-4   Standard Windows Server 2003 services

Service	Description
Alerter	Sends notification of alerts or problems on the server to users designated by the network administrator
Computer Browser	Keeps a listing of computers and domain resources to be accessed
Event Log	Enables server events to be logged for later review or diagnosis in case problems occur
File Replication Service	Replicates the Active Directory elements on multiple DCs when Active Directory is installed
Intersite Messaging	Transfers messages between different Windows Server 2003 sites
IPSec Services	Enables IPSec security
Kerberos Key Distribution Center	Enables Kerberos authentication and the server as a center from which to issue Kerberos security keys and tickets
License Logging	Enables the monitoring of server and other licensing
Logical Disk Manager	Monitors for disk problems, such as a disk that is nearly full
Messenger	Handles messages sent for administrative purposes

14

Table 14-4   Standard Windows Server 2003 services (continued)

Service	Description
Net Logon	Maintains logon services such as verifying users who are logging onto the server or a domain
Plug and Play	Enables automatic detection and installation of new hardware devices or devices that have changed
Print Spooler	Enables print spooling
Protected Storage	Enables data and services to be stored and protected by using private key authentication
Remote Procedure Call (RPC)	Provides Remote Procedure Call services
Remote Procedure Call (RPC) Locator	Used in communications with clients using remote procedure calls to locate available programs to run
Remote Registry	Enables the registry to be managed remotely
Removable Storage	Enables management of removable storage media, such as tapes, CD-RWs, and Zip and Jaz drives
Security Accounts Manager	Keeps information about user accounts and their related security setup
Server	A critical service that supports shared objects, log on services, print services, and remote procedure calls
System Event Notification	Enables the detection and reporting of important system events, such as a hardware or network problem
Task Scheduler	Used to start a program at a specified time and works with the software Task Scheduler
TCP/IP NetBIOS Helper	Activated when TCP/IP is installed and used to enable NetBIOS name resolution and NetBIOS network transport
Uninterruptible Power Supply	Used with a UPS to supply power to the server during power failures
Windows Time	Enables updating the clock
Workstation	Enables network communications and access by clients over the network

The Services snap-in allows you to configure a variety of settings related to how services function and respond to potential problems on a Windows Server 2003 system. The properties of a service include four different configuration tabs, as follows:

- *General*—Displays a service's name, description, the path to the executable file, service startup parameters, and buttons allowing you to start, stop, pause, and resume a service.

- *Log On*—Allows you to specify the user name that a service will run as, along with the hardware profiles for which the service will be enabled.

- *Recovery*—Allows you to configure the computer's response when a service fails, including different actions depending on the number of failures; also allows you to specify a program that should be run when a service failure occurs, as shown in Figure 14-12.

- *Dependencies*—Specifies the services that a service depends upon to function correctly, as well as the services that depend on this service to function, as shown in Figure 14-13. Before you stop or disable a service, check to see if there are any other services running that depend on the service.

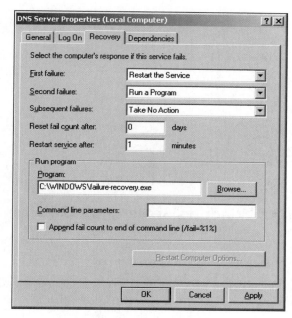

Figure 14-12   Recovery tab of a service

Many services are linked to the Server and Workstation services, including services such as Net Logon that enable users to log on to and remain logged on to a network or server. If it is necessary to stop one of these services—for example, to diagnose a problem—give the users advance warning or stop the service after work hours.

In Activity 14-10, you will configure the properties of various services on your server.

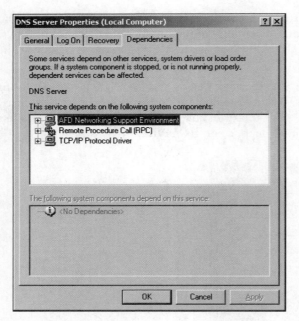

Figure 14-13   Dependencies tab of a service

Activity 14-10: Configuring Windows Server 2003 Services

Time Required: 15 minutes

Objective: Configure the startup properties and settings of Windows Server 2003 services.

Description: The IT manager at Great Arctic North University is very concerned about the levels of resource utilization of campus servers, including the impact that this ultimately has on performance for users. He is also concerned about the security risks associated with having unnecessary services running on various servers throughout the organization. In this activity, you will configure service startup settings, as well as other configuration options, such as how a service reacts to a failure.

1. Click **Start**, select **Administrative Tools**, and then click **Services**. The Services snap-in opens.

2. Right-click the **Remote Desktop Help Session Manager** service icon, and then click **Properties**. The Remote Desktop Help Session Manager Properties dialog box opens.

3. In the Startup type list box, click **Automatic**. This sets the Remote Desktop Help Session Manager service to start automatically the next time the computer restarts.

4. Click the **Apply** button, and then click the **Start** button. This manually starts the Remote Desktop Help Session Manager service.

5. Click the **Log On** tab. This displays the properties of the account under which the Remote Desktop Help Session Manager service will run.

6. Click the **Recovery** tab.

7. In the First failure list box, click **Restart the Service**.

8. In the Second failure list box, click **Run a Program**.

9. In the Program text box, type **cmd.exe**. This will cause the Command Prompt program to start in the event that the Remote Desktop Help Session Manager service fails for a second time.

10. Click the **Dependencies** tab. Review the list of services that the Remote Desktop Help Session Manager service depends upon. Click **OK**.

11. Right-click the **Remote Registry** service icon, and click **Properties**.

12. In the Startup type list box, click **Disabled**. This will prevent the Remote Registry service from starting the next time the computer reboots. Remote users will no longer be able to modify the registry; changes can only be made by users on the local computer. Click **OK**.

13. Close all open windows.

TROUBLESHOOTING NETWORK CONNECTIVITY

14

In previous chapters, you have learned troubleshooting skills for specific services such as DNS and IPSec. However, troubleshooting a network connectivity problem requires a broad knowledge of several network concepts in order to solve. The most difficult task when troubleshooting a network connectivity problem is knowing where to start. In this section, we will examine some common network connectivity problems as well as some troubleshooting procedures that will likely lead to a solution.

If a computer cannot access resources on the local network, you should perform the following troubleshooting steps:

- *Verify the IP configuration*—Ensure that the computer is configured with an IP address and subnet mask proper for the local network in TCP/IP properties. If the computer is configured to use WINS and DNS, ensure that the IP address for the WINS and DNS servers listed in TCP/IP properties is correct.

- *Ensure that DHCP is functional*—If the computer is configured to contact a DHCP server for IP configuration and it configures itself using APIPA, ensure that the computer is physically connected to a network segment that has a DHCP server or DHCP Relay Agent. On the DHCP server, ensure that a valid scope has been configured and activated and that the DHCP server is authorized in Active Directory if Active Directory is used on the network.

- *Verify the configuration of IPSec*—If IPSec is used, ensure that the IPSec service has been started and an IPSec policy has been applied to your computer using the IPSec Monitor snap-in. Also check the configuration of the IPSec policy and any filters to ensure that computers on the network use the same method of IPSec authentication (Preshared Key, Certificate, or Kerberos) and encryption.

- *Check network media*—If all software configuration is correct, ensure that there are no problems with the physical media connecting the computer to the network.

If a computer cannot access the Internet or a remote network, but can communicate on the local network, you should perform the following troubleshooting steps:

- *Verify the IP configuration*—Ensure that the computer is configured with the correct default gateway for the local network in TCP/IP properties. If the computer is configured to use WINS and DNS, ensure that the WINS and DNS servers used for name resolution contain entries for computers on the remote networks.

- *Check router configuration*—Ensure that the router contains routes in its routing table for the remote network. If a dynamic routing protocol is used, ensure that it is configured properly. Also ensure that the Routing and Remote Access service is started and that no packet filters exist that block desired network traffic across networks.

- *Check the network media*—If all software configurations are correct, ensure that there are no problems with the physical media connecting the computers on each network to the router.

If a computer cannot access resources on the local network using name resolution, you should perform the following troubleshooting steps:

- *Verify IP configuration*—Ensure that the computer is configured with an IP address of a WINS and DNS server. If the WINS or DNS server is on a remote network, ensure that routes exist between the computer and the remote WINS or DNS server.

- *Ensure that DHCP is functional*—If the computer is configured to contact a DHCP server for IP configuration, ensure that the DHCP server assigns correct scope options for WINS or DNS servers to the clients. Also ensure that static WINS or DNS options configured on the client do not overwrite correct WINS or DNS options configured on the DHCP server.

- *Ensure that DNS is functional*—Ensure that the client computer can contact the DNS server by IP address and that the DNS server service has been started on the DNS server. Also ensure that the DNS server is configured with the appropriate zone information for the client queries or uses recursion or forwarding to pass client queries off to other DNS servers. Also ensure that the client computers do not contain old information in their DNS cache that does not match the entries in DNS. If this is the case, clear the DNS cache on each client using the ipconfig /flushdns command. Recall that the local Hosts file is not only the first entity checked when performing host name resolution; it is also used to prepopulate the DNS name cache, thus all entries in it should be verified as being correct.

- *Ensure that WINS is functional*—Ensure that the client computer can contact the WINS server by IP address and that the WINS server service has been started on the WINS server. If clients cannot access resources on computers on distant subnets, ensure that the WINS server contains records for those computers or performs replication with a WINS server that contains those records. If clients cannot access resources on the WINS server itself, ensure that the WINS server is configured as a client of itself such that it can register its own NetBIOS name in its WINS database.

If a computer cannot access remote resources, you should perform the following trouble-shooting steps:

- *Verify network interface settings*—For dial-up remote access, ensure that the correct modem driver has been added to the system. For VPN clients, ensure that the network interface is configured to allow network access and that the client can contact the RRAS server on the network without a VPN.

- *Ensure that the user has dial-in permission*—Check the properties of the user account on the RRAS server or Active Directory to ensure that dial-in permission is set to Allow. If remote access policies are used to set dial-in permission, ensure that the first remote access policy with conditions that match the remote access connection allows access. If RADIUS is used to perform authentication, also ensure that the RADIUS server, RADIUS proxy, and RADIUS client are configured correctly and can contact each other on the network.

- *Confirm the configuration of remote access policies*—Examine the remote access policies configured on the RRAS server and ensure that they are configured properly. Also ensure that the profile for each policy is configured to allow the same levels of encryption and types of authentication that the remote access clients use.

- *Ensure that remote access clients are given correct IP configuration*—Ensure that the remote access client is configured with an IP address and subnet mask for the remote network. If the remote access client requires options from a DHCP server on the remote network, ensure that a DHCP relay agent is configured on the RRAS server. Also ensure that the remote access client is receiving the correct WINS and DNS server configuration for accessing remote resources.

CHAPTER SUMMARY

- Network administrators monitor the network and servers on a regular basis, perform proactive and reactive maintenance, as well as document important system and network information.

- Common troubleshooting procedures involve collecting data to isolate and determine the cause of system problems, as well as implementing and testing solutions that can be documented for future use.

❑ Network Monitor is used to gather information about network performance and is installed with the Network Monitor driver.

❑ The Performance console has two tools that you can use to monitor server health and performance: System Monitor and Performance Logs and Alerts.

❑ You can configure alerts for specific objects and counters. Once a counter exceeds or drops below the configured value, an alert is triggered. The alert can send a message, start a counter log, write an event to the application log, or run a program.

❑ You can use Event Viewer to view the contents of the system logs, application logs, and security logs. Processes and applications write events to the log files. Administrators can use this information to identify and troubleshoot server problems.

❑ Task Manager provides information on processes and applications running on a system. It also provides general information on a system's current performance.

❑ When optimizing the performance of your computer, use the Services icon to disable any unnecessary services to eliminate overhead.

❑ Troubleshooting network connectivity requires a broad knowledge of network concepts and may be broken down into different troubleshooting steps.

Key Terms

alerts — An alert performs a specified action once a counter meets the specified setting. Once an alert is triggered, a message can be sent, a program can be run, a counter log started, or an event can be written to the application log.

application log — The location where applications that are written to Microsoft standards record event information. The application developer determines the type of information an application writes to the log file.

baseline — A performance benchmark that is used to determine what is normal server performance under a specific workload.

counter log — A location where performance data that is collected into a comma-separated or tab-separated format.

Event Viewer — A utility used to view the contents of the system, security, and application logs.

filters — A function in Network Monitor that enables a network administrator to view only designated protocols, network events, network nodes, or other specialized views of the network.

monitoring — The process by which the system and network are observed for problems or irregularities.

Network Monitor — A Windows Server 2003 network monitoring tool that can capture and display network performance data.

Network Monitor driver — This enables a Microsoft-based server or workstation NIC to gather network performance data for assessment by Network Monitor.

performance counter — A data item associated with a particular performance object used to measure a certain aspect of performance.

Performance Logs and Alerts — A tool included with Windows Server 2003 that enables you to create counter logs, trace logs, and configure alerts.

performance objects — A system component that you can monitor using System Monitor.

proactive maintenance — The measures taken to reduce future system and network problems.

reactive maintenance — The measures taken when system or network problems arise.

security log — Events pertaining to the audit policy are written to the security log.

system log — A location where system components, such as services and device drivers, record information, warnings, and errors.

System Monitor — A tool that allows you to gather and view the real-time performance statistics of a local or network computer.

Task Manager — A tool used to view the processes and applications currently running on a system; also provides basic resource usage statistics.

trace logs — A location where a data provider collects performance data when an event occurs.

troubleshooting procedures — The tasks performed when solving system and network problems.

REVIEW QUESTIONS

1. On which part of the maintenance cycle do network administrators spend the most time?
   a. monitoring
   b. proactive maintenance
   c. reactive maintenance
   d. documentation

2. Network administrators should always keep a copy of all documentation in a reserved directory on the file system. True or false?

3. What feature of Windows Server 2003 can you use to have a message sent to your computer when a performance counter exceeds a certain value?
   a. counter logs
   b. alerts
   c. Event Viewer
   d. Task Manager

4. What tool can you use to view the contents of the system log?
   a. System Monitor
   b. Performance console
   c. Event Viewer
   d. Task Manager

14

5. You are running several services on your network server. One of them appears to have stopped responding. What tool can you use to check the status of the application?

   a. Performance Monitor

   b. System Monitor

   c. Application Manager

   d. Task Manager

6. What type of log would you create to have performance data collected and saved into a comma-separated file?

   a. trace log

   b. database log

   c. counter log

   d. system log

7. Only administrators can view the contents of the system and application logs. True or false?

8. You have started to receive complaints from users on the network that the server has been performing poorly. What tool can you use to monitor and view real-time performance of the server?

   a. Event Viewer

   b. Performance Monitor

   c. Performance Logs and Alerts

   d. System Monitor

9. A service fails to start on your server. In which log file is the event recorded?

   a. application

   b. system

   c. services

   d. counter

10. Which of the following actions can be taken when an alert is triggered? (Choose all that apply.)

    a. A message can be sent to a computer.

    b. An event can be written to the application log.

    c. A program can be run.

    d. A counter log can be started.

11. Which of the following are Windows Server 2003 services? (Choose all that apply.)

    a. Net Logon

    b. Protected Storage

    c. Remove Procedure Call (RPC) Locator

    d. Alerter

12. One of your server administrator colleagues in another company is struggling to understand the data produced by System Monitor. The servers and network at that company have been in place for about 5 months, but he has been too busy setting up clients to gather information about server performance. Now he does not know how to interpret the information so as to determine in what areas performance is normal and in what areas it is not. What should he have done in advance?

    a. Gathered server and network benchmarks

    b. Started the System Monitor from day one and left it running continuously to gather data on the 10 most critical monitor objects

    c. Run a trace log at least two full days a week, every week, monitoring system provider events

    d. Run Task Manager constantly to gather performance information, and then periodically taken screen captures

13. You want to stop the Network DDE Service, but are not sure what other services depend on it. How can you most easily find out?

    a. Use the Task Manager Applications tab.

    b. View the properties for the Network DDE Service in the Services portion of the Computer Management tool, and access the Dependencies tab.

    c. Stop the services that you think it might depend on, and look for the error messages.

    d. Look in the System Information option under the console tree in the Computer Management tool.

14. Which of the following can you view in the Graph pane in Network Monitor? (Choose all that apply.)

    a. % Network Utilization

    b. Bytes Per Hour

    c. Broadcasts Per Second

    d. Number of Connected Stations

15. You want to create a filter in Network Monitor, but the Edit Capture Filter button is deactivated. What is the problem?

    a. You must set the Network Monitor properties to enable filtering.

    b. You must set the Network Monitor driver properties to enable filtering.

    c. Network Monitor is already capturing data, and you must pause or stop capturing.

    d. You can only create a filter in the Session pane, but you have deactivated that pane.

16. You have been monitoring a network that normally has network utilization at 20% to 30%, but during the past month the typical network utilization has risen to 75%. What should you do?

    a. This percentage represents an acceptable figure, and there is no need to do anything.

    b. This percentage is not a serious problem, but you should plan to examine how to tune network performance during the next couple of months.

    c. This percentage represents a serious problem, and you should begin more intense monitoring to locate problems and possibly upgrade portions of the network.

    d. This percentage means that a majority of your servers are overloaded and should be upgraded immediately.

17. You have opened Network Monitor, but it does not seem to be able to capture data from your server's NIC. Which of the following is the most likely cause?

    a. Network Monitor Driver is not installed.

    b. SNMP Service is not set up to enable traps.

    c. You have not previously run netperf in the Command Prompt window.

    d. all of the above

18. Your server is running slowly, and you suspect there is a program or program process that is causing the problem, because you just installed eight new programs on a Windows 2003 server, which are run by you on the server and by clients using Terminal Services. Which of the following tools enable you to monitor for the problem? (Choose all that apply.)

    a. Computer Management tool using the Services option

    b. System Monitor using the Process object

    c. Task Manager using the Processes tab

    d. Dcpromo using the Application Management option

19. Your boss is trying to find some statistics about the network traffic across the Windows 2003 server that processes student degree checks at a college. What tool might you use to determine the number of broadcasts and multicasts seen by that server?

    a. Task Manager

    b. Network Monitor

    c. Broadcast Monitor

    d. DHCP Monitor

20. You want to use Network Monitor to monitor only NWLink traffic on a network. How can you do this?

    a. Create a trigger.

    b. Use the NWLink object.

    c. Create a trap.

    d. Create a filter.

CASE PROJECTS

Case Project 14-1: Managing Services

You are responsible for the administration of three Great Arctic North University servers. You have recently installed a new service on your server. The service is set to start automatically and runs continuously to service user requests. Your manager is concerned about server performance after the service is installed, and you assure him that performance should not suffer. Answer the following questions based on the scenario.

1. After you install the service, what is one of the first things you should do?

2. During peak hours, your manager stops in to see how the server is performing under the added workload. What tool can you use to quickly show your manager the current processor usage on the server?

3. You have a slight concern that the service may indeed have an impact on the amount of time the processor is utilized. The % utilization was running at times near 50% before the service was installed. You would like to be notified if the processor utilization goes above 60%. Explain how this can be done. What other actions can you configure if this occurs?

4. Because the server is working under an increased workload, you want to disable any unnecessary services to eliminate the overhead associated with running them. What should you consider before disabling any services on the server?

14

Case Project 14-2: Solving a Network Problem

The Arts faculty at Great Arctic North University complains that the network seems to be saturated with heavy traffic, but none of the server administrators can determine the source of the problem or if the excessive traffic is TCP/IP-based or IPX-based. How would you explain to them in a fast e-mail how they might use Network Monitor, System Monitor, or both to locate the problem? Can either of these network monitoring tools be used to monitor the IPX-based NetWare servers in case they are a source of the problem, and if so, how?

Case Project 14-3: Troubleshooting Network Connectivity

After a serious server failure in the Engineering faculty at Great Arctic North University, users complain that they can no longer access resources in other faculties. Some users complain that they cannot access resources in their own faculty as well. Upon closer investigation, you realize that the server that failed was overloaded with several services including RRAS, DHCP, DNS, and WINS. In a brief memo, describe how the clients could be affected by this server failure and the steps you will take to restore resource access to the clients in the Engineering faculty.

A

EXAM OBJECTIVES FOR MCSE/MCSA CERTIFICATION

Exam #70-291: Implementing, Managing, and Maintaining a Microsoft Windows Server 2003 Network Infrastructure

Implementing, Managing, and Maintaining IP Addressing

Objective	Chapter	Activity
Configure TCP/IP addressing on a server computer	Chapter 2	Activity 2-2
Manage DHCP • Manage DHCP clients and leases. • Manage DHCP Relay Agent. • Manage DHCP databases. • Manage DHCP scope options. • Manage reservations and reserved clients.	Chapter 4 Chapter 5	Activity 4-16 Activity 5-2 Activity 5-3 Activity 5-4 Activity 4-6 Activity 4-7 Activity 4-8 Activity 4-9 Activity 4-10 Activity 4-11 Activity 4-13 Activity 4-14 Activity 4-12
Troubleshoot TCP/IP addressing • Diagnose and resolve issues related to Automatic Private IP Addressing (APIPA). • Diagnose and resolve issues related to incorrect TCP/IP configuration.	Chapter 2	Activity 2-4 Activity 2-6 Activity 2-5 Activity 2-1 Activity 2-3
Troubleshoot DHCP • Diagnose and resolve issues related to DHCP authorization. • Verify DHCP reservation configuration • Examine the system event log and DHCP server audit log files to find related events. • Diagnose and resolve issues related to configuration of DHCP server and scope options. • Verify that the DHCP relay agent is working correctly. • Verify database integrity.	Chapter 4 Chapter 5 Chapter 14	Activity 4-2 Activity 4-4 Activity 4-5 Activity 4-12 Activity 5-7 Activity 5-6 Activity 5-9 Activity 5-4 Activity 5-5 Activity 4-15

Implementing, Managing, and Maintaining Name Resolution

Objective	Chapter: Section	Hands-on Activity
Install and configure the DNS server service • Configure DNS server options. • Configure DNS zone options. • Configure DNS forwarding.	Chapter 7	Activity 7-1 Activity 7-2 Activity 7-3 Activity 7-4 Activity 7-6 Activity 7-7 Activity 7-8 Activity 7-9 Activity 7-10
Manage DNS • Manage DNS zone settings. • Manage DNS record settings. • Manage DNS server options.	Chapter 7	Activity 7-12 Activity 7-2
Monitor DNS • System Monitor. • Event Viewer. • Replication Monitor. • DNS debug logs.	Chapter 7 Chapter 14	Activity 14-8

Implementing, Managing, and Maintaining Network Security

Objective	Chapter: Section	Hands-on Activity
Implement secure network administration procedures • Implement security baseline settings and audit security settings by using security templates. • Implement the principle of least privilege.	Chapter 13	Activity 13-1 Activity 13-2 Activity 13-3 Activity 13-4 Activity 13-5
Monitor network protocol security • IP Security Monitor Microsoft Management Console (MMC) snap-in. • Kerberos support tools.	Chapter 9	Activity 9-8
Troubleshoot network protocol security • IP Security Monitor MMC snap-in. • Event Viewer. • Network Monitor.	Chapter 9 Chapter 14	Activity 9-8 Activity 14-3

Implementing, Managing, and Maintaining Routing and Remote Access

Objective	Chapter: Section	Hands-on Activity
Configure Routing and Remote Access user authentication • Configure remote access authentication protocols. • Configure Internet Authentication Service (IAS) to provide authentication for Routing and Remote Access clients. • Configure Routing and Remote Access policies to permit or deny access.	Chapter 10 Chapter 11	Activity 10-6 Activity 10-7 Activity 11-1 Activity 11-2 Activity 11-3 Activity 11-4 Activity 10-8 Activity 10-9 Activity 11-5
Manage remote access • Manage packet filters. • Manage Routing and Remote Access routing interfaces. • Manage devices and ports. • Manage routing protocols. • Manage Routing and Remote Access clients.	Chapter 10	Activity 10-1 Activity 10-2 Activity 10-3 Activity 10-6 Activity 10-7 Activity 10-8 Activity 11-3
Manage TCP/IP routing • Manage routing protocols. • Manage routing tables. • Manage routing ports.	Chapter 12	Activity 12-3 Activity 12-2 Activity 12-4 Activity 12-5 Activity 12-6
Implement secure access between private networks	Chapter 10	Activity 10-4 Activity 10-5
Troubleshoot user access to remote access services • Diagnose and resolve issues related to remote access VPNs. • Diagnose and resolve issues related to establishing a remote access connection. • Diagnose and resolve user access to resources beyond the remote access server.	Chapter 10	Activity 10-9 Activity 11-6 Activity 10-10
Troubleshoot Routing and Remote Access routing • Troubleshoot demand-dial routing. • Troubleshoot router-to-router VPNs.	Chapter 10 Chapter 12 Chapter 14	

Maintaining a Network Infrastructure

Objective	Chapter: Section	Hands-on Activity
Monitor network traffic • Network Monitor. • System Monitor.	Chapter 14	Activity 14-1 Activity 14-2 Activity 14-3 Activity 14-4 Activity 14-5 Activity 14-6 Activity 14-7
Troubleshoot connectivity to the Internet	Chapter 14	
Troubleshoot server services • Diagnose and resolve issues related to service dependency. • Use service recovery options to diagnose and resolve service-related issues.	Chapter 14	

A

B

DETAILED LAB SETUP GUIDE

HARDWARE

Classroom PCs should be configured as follows:

- Pentium 233 MHz processor or faster
- At least 128 megabytes of RAM
- At least 1.5 gigabytes of available hard disk space
- CD-RW or DVD-RW drive
- Keyboard and mouse or some other compatible pointing device
- Super VGA video adapter that supports 800 × 600 or higher resolution
- Monitor
- Sound card for the Instructor PC
- Self-powered amplified speakers for the Instructor PC
- Internal or external fax/modem (for Activities 10-1 through 10-3)
- Two Ethernet network interface controllers per PC
- 3.5" floppy disk drive
- An Ethernet hub or switch with at least as many ports as there are PCs in the classroom
- 1 twisted-pair, category 5 straight-through cable per PC

Other equipment that may be needed:

- An additional Instructor PC, which will be used as an additional domain controller
- A generic printer
- A crossover cable for each PC

Consumable items that students should bring to class:

- 5 blank CD-R disks
- 5 blank 3.5" floppy disks

SOFTWARE

The following software is needed:

- Microsoft Windows Server 2003 Enterprise Edition operating system (1 CD media per student)
- Adobe Acrobat Reader (version 4 or higher)

- Microsoft Virtual PC (*www.microsoft.com/windows/virtualpc*) (optional)
- The latest Windows Server 2003 service pack, if available (optional)

Setup Instructions

To work on the Activities and Case Projects in this book, students need to have administrative privileges over their PCs. In a classroom setting, students should have the freedom to make administrative-level configuration errors. Normally such errors can render a PC unbootable or otherwise unusable for participation in the classroom. However, a student's mistakes should never impede completion of lab assignments. In this light, the lab should have a data recovery system and working backups that are both easy to use and reliable.

Ensure that all hardware used in the classroom is compatible with Windows Server 2003. To do this, you may need to perform a test installation. Once the installation process is complete, use Device Manager to ensure that all devices are functioning correctly and that the appropriate drivers are installed. If a device has a driver that is not functioning, you may need to go to the manufacturer's Web site to locate a device for Windows Server 2003.

Because students will have administrative control of their computers, you may need to perform data recovery if a student cannot recover from a configuration change. The most straightforward method of data recovery is the reinstallation of the operating system from the Microsoft factory CDs. However, having to reinstall the operating system from the factory CD every time a student corrupts his or her system can be time consuming and frustrating. There are no activities in the book that cover a Windows Server 2003 installation. This leaves some flexibility for the instructor to decide on how the students should install Windows Server 2003. Therefore, to ensure rapid and reliable data recovery, consider the following guidelines when setting up the lab:

- Microsoft's Virtual PC provides quick access to an operating system from a previous state. The ability to use undoable disks will give students the opportunity to restore their computers to the state before the lab. Students will have to Save State in Virtual PC after each successful lab. Virtual PC requires a high level of computer resources, so the student computers should exceed the minimum hardware requirements if the program is used.

- Consider using an imaging product such as Norton Ghost. With it a single image file that contains all of the data stored on the reference installation is created. This image file even contains the partition table of the hard disk along with the master boot record. Restoring data from such an image brings the machine back into its original state at the time the backup was created.

- When creating a reference image file, remember that the image file will be an exact copy of the reference PC's hard disk drive. This means that data such as NetBIOS computer names and SIDs (Security Identifiers) will be preserved as they were on the reference PC. This also means that unless further steps are taken, all PCs that are imaged from this reference image will have the *same* NetBIOS computer name, SID, and perhaps even IP address (if the IP addresses are set up statically). However, you do *not* want a classroom where all the PCs have the same NetBIOS name or IP address, as such duplication can cause conflicts throughout the class. You may be able to get away with all the SIDs being the same for a while, but this should not be a permanent state. You especially do not want identical SIDs in an environment that uses Active Directory domains.

- In order to make a classroom of uniquely identifiable PCs, you can execute utilities such as Microsoft's SysPrep, Norton Ghost Walker, or REMBO Toolkit (the NTChangeName command) on each PC. The easiest to use is Ghost Walker, an MS-DOS program that not only changes the NetBIOS computer name, but also creates a randomly generated SID in one easy step. If you don't feel the need to change the SID, you can manually change the NetBIOS name by right-clicking the My Computer icon, clicking Properties, clicking the Computer Name tab, clicking the Change button, and typing in the desired NetBIOS computer name in the Computer name field. Click OK when finished.

Keep the following in mind if imaging or Virtual PC is not available:

- The instructor needs to decide on the following key points and make them available to all students during their installs:
  - Computer naming convention
  - IP addressing (default gateways, DNS, and WINS, if necessary)
  - Workgroup and domain names
- Students should install Windows Server 2003 Enterprise Edition from the CD.

Expanded Chapter Summaries

CHAPTER 1 SUMMARY

Before installing Windows Server 2003, you must first determine which version meets the needs of your organization. Each version's unique features are appropriate for different functions.

Windows Server 2003, Web Edition is optimized for Web services. It is designed to compete directly with Linux Web servers. The Web Edition supports up to 2 GB of RAM and two processors.

Windows Server 2003, Standard Edition is designed for departmental servers. These can be used as a domain controller, a Remote Installation Server (RIS) server, and/or a terminal server. The Standard Edition supports up to 4 GB of RAM and four processors.

Windows Server 2003, Enterprise Edition offers high availability through its clustering support. It supports 64-bit processing and NUMA. Windows Server 2003, Enterprise Edition can still perform all the other services that Standard Edition can. The Enterprise Edition supports up to 32 GB of RAM and eight processors.

Windows Server 2003, Datacenter Edition works with applications that require high availability and scalability. This edition cannot be purchased from a retail store but must be purchased through an OEM. The Datacenter Edition supports up to 64 GB of RAM and 64 processors.

Computers communicate with each other on networks. There are three different types of networks that are used today. A local area network (LAN) connects computers within a single physical office with twisted pair cabling or wireless. A metropolitan area network (MAN) can span multiple buildings in the same city. A wide area network (WAN) connects LANs using technologies like fiber optics, satellites, asynchronous transfer mode (ATM), and frame relay.

Once computers are on the same network, they need to speak the same language with the other devices on the network. For this to occur, they must use networking protocols. Network protocols are chosen based on the clients and servers that are running in the network and commonly consist of the following:

- TCP/IP 4
- TCP/IP 6
- IPX/SPX
- AppleTalk

The Open Systems Interconnection (OSI) model is used to show how computers send and receive data. It is a seven-layer model that computers use to send and receive information. The seven layers of the OSI model are as follows:

- *Application*—User interface
- *Presentation*—Translates and encrypts data

- *Session*—Synchronization and session setup
- *Transport*—Flow control and error handling
- *Network*—Addressing and routing
- *Data Link/Media Access*—Framing of packets
- *Physical*—Contains the hardware

The Windows Server 2003 networking architecture conforms to the OSI model, which allows the operating system to talk to other networking devices. Windows Server 2003 supports two components that make this process very easy:

- Network Driver Interface Specification (NDIS) allows developers to write code to NDIS and not to any specific network cards or protocols. Without NDIS, the developer has to write code for each protocol that is used by each hardware device. Bindings allow the operating system to bind multiple protocols to a network adapter or multiple network adapters to a single protocol.

- Transport Driver Interface (TDI) is a layer that clients and servers access when using networking resources. TDI can emulate NetBIOS and WinSock. Application developers write their applications to use either NetBIOS or WinSock, and the TDI layer passes information from the clients and servers to either NetBIOS or WinSock.

Windows Server 2003 can run common networking services that are critical to a network infrastructure. These services include the following:

- *DHCP*—IP addressing service
- *DNS*—Host name resolution service
- *WINS*—NetBIOS name resolution service
- *RRAS*—Routing and Remote Access Service
- *NAT*—Translates private addresses into one or more public addresses
- *ICS*—Provides DHCP, DNS proxy, and NAT services for small companies
- *IAS*—Remote authentication service
- *IPSec*—Can encrypt and/or digitally sign IP traffic
- *ICF*—Windows-based firewall
- *PKI*—Certificates services
- *Load Balancing*—Provides high availability for Web applications
- *ASR*—One-step recovery for operating system
- *Media Services*—Streaming media services

CHAPTER 2 SUMMARY

Transmission Control Protocol/Internet Protocol (TCP/IP) is the most commonly used protocol today. Many vendors besides Microsoft support it, and without it, no one would have access to the Internet. In fact, Windows Server 2003 relies on it for several key services; for example, without TCP/IP, you would not be able to install Active Directory.

The addressing scheme TCP/IP uses has four 8-bit numbers (called octets), separated by a period or dot. The four 8-bit numbers are presented in decimal in the configuration tool, but the computer sees the four 8-bit numbers as binary. This notation is called dotted decimal, and it looks to the user like 10.15.1.9 and to the computer as 000001010. 00001111.00000001.00001001. You can convert from binary to decimal using the following number sequence:

128   64   32   16   8   4   2   1

As stated, using simple addition and subtraction, you can go from binary to decimal and decimal to binary. For example, if you had the number 181 in decimal and the preceding number sequence for your reference, you could convert 181 to binary by asking the following eight questions:

1. Can you subtract 128 from 181? If yes, put a 1 under the 128 position in the chart.
2. Can you subtract 64 from 54? If no, put a 0 under the 64 position.
3. Can you subtract 32 from 54? If yes, put a 1 under the 32 position.
4. Can you subtract 16 from 22? If yes, then put a 1 under the 16 position.
5. Can you subtract 8 from 6? If no, put a 0 under the 8 position.
6. Can you subtract 4 from 6? If yes, put a 1 under the 4 position.
7. Can you subtract 2 from 2? If yes, put a 1 under the 2 position.
8. Can you subtract 1 from 0? If no, put a 0 under the 1 position.

Your number sequence will now look like this:

128   64   32   16   8   4   2   1
1   0   1   1   0   1   1   0   = 181 in binary

To convert from binary to decimal is just as easy. For example, given the binary number 00110011, you could fill in the chart from left to right with the number provided:

128   64   32   16   8   4   2   1
0   0   1   1   0   0   1   1

When you add up the positions where the 1s are, you get the decimal number 51, as follows:

32 + 16 + 2 + 1 = 51

C

There are several fields involved when configuring IP addressing information for Windows Server 2003. The first field is the IP address that is used to identify the host. Each IP address consists of two parts: a network portion and a host portion, which can be compared to a street address and to the actual house number on that street, respectively. The second field is the subnet mask. The subnet mask defines which part of the IP address is the network ID and which part is the host ID. An IP address and subnet mask are required for every host on a TCP/IP network.

If a client needs to access resources outside its network, then a default gateway must be configured. If you want a client to communicate using a Fully Qualified Domain Name (FQDN), then you would have to configure a DNS server's IP address. If your clients used NetBIOS name resolution, then you would have to configure a WINS server's IP address.

IP addresses can be configured in different ways. When you manually enter an IP address into the TCP/IP settings, you are performing a static IP configuration. Errors occur using this method more so than any other method. You can also use a DHCP server to assign the TCP/IP settings. This way, clients that are configured to obtain IP addresses automatically will get the settings out of a configured pool of addresses and options. If clients cannot access a DHCP server, they will use Automatic Private IP Addressing (APIPA).

The three classes of IP addresses used to address hosts on networks are called A, B, and C. Classes D and E are not used for clients that communicate on a LAN. The following table shows where each address belongs in the IP address classes.

Class	First Octet	Default Mask	# of Hosts Per Network
Class A	1 – 127*	255.0.0.0 or /8	16,777,214
Class B	128-191	255.255.0.0 or /16	64,534
Class C	192-223	255.255.255.0 or /24	254

*Even though 127 is considered a Class A Network, you cannot use it for addressing because it is reserved for loop-back functions only.

As networks grow in size, it becomes more difficult to manage network traffic. One way to help with this management is to subnet TCP/IP networks. Subnetting larger networks into smaller ones has three benefits:

- Reduces collisions, thus improving throughput
- Limits network broadcasts to the current subnet that the broadcast originated
- Controls where traffic goes through routes

To fully understand addressing, it is important to understand the value of the subnet mask in binary. The number 255 can be represented in binary as 1 1 1 1 1 1 1 1 or all 8 bits on. Thus, the subnet mask of 255.0.0.0 would appear as 11111111.00000000.00000000.00000000, and wherever you see a 1 in the subnet mask, that 1 is a network bit. In addition, wherever you see a 0 in the subnet mask, that 0 is a host bit. Here is an example of determining which portion of the IP address is for the host and which is for the network: Using the address 10.15.1.9 and a subnet mask of 255.0.0.0, the network portion would be 10 and the host portion would be 15.1.9. If the subnet mask were 255.255.0.0 or 11111111.11111111. 00000000.00000000, the 10.15 of the address would be the network address and the 1.9 would consist of the host address.

The value of the subnet can be different from the default address in two ways. If you take bits that by default would be 0s and make them 1s, you are taking from your hosts to make more networks. This is called subnetting. If you take bits that would be 1s and make them 0s, you are borrowing from your networks to make more hosts per network. This is called supernetting.

There are three ranges of IP addresses that are reserved for your internal network and therefore cannot be routed on the public Internet. You should use one of the three reserved ranges of IP addresses and have a firewall that handles translation from the internal network to the external network (the Internet) using a protocol called Network Address Translation (NAT). The three ranges are 10.0.0.0 in class A, 172.16.0.0–172.31.0.0 in class B, and 192.168.0.0–192.168.255.0 in class C.

Larger networks must be subnetted into smaller networks to maintain performance. In large networks that have not been broken up, collisions can occur and broadcast traffic can overwhelm the network. One of the best ways to control both of these is to take an existing network and divide it into smaller networks which are divided by routers or switches.

Internetwork Packet eXchange/Sequenced Packet eXchange was the most commonly used protocol in the 1980s and early 1990s. NetWare used this as their primary protocol for their Networking Operating System (NOS). Microsoft created NWLink, which is an IPX/SPX-compatible protocol.

While TCP/IP uses DNS for locating services on a network, IPX/SPX uses the Service Advertising Protocol (SAP) to locate services. It does so by having each device broadcast every 60 seconds the services that it is providing. One drawback to SAP is that routers do not forward these types of broadcast by default.

IPX/SPX addresses contain a network and host portion, like TCP/IP does. The network ID is an eight-character hexadecimal number that is followed by a twelve-character hexadecimal number that represents the host. The host portion is taken from the network card's MAC address.

Computers that use IPX/SPX to communicate must use the same frame type. Windows allows you to configure a type manually or automatically. If the operating system detects multiple types on the network, Windows Server 2003 will default to 802.2. The three types of frame types that are supported are as follows:

- Ethernet 802.3
- Ethernet 802.2
- Ethernet SNAP

AppleTalk is used to connect Microsoft computers to Macintosh computers. With this installed, Windows Server 2003 can emulate a Macintosh file or print server.

A binding is the order in which protocols will be used on a network adapter. If there are multiple protocols installed, then each network adapter will use all of them. You can configure the bindings on each network adapter to optimize network connectivity.

CHAPTER 3 SUMMARY

The four layers in the TCP/IP model are Application, Transport, Internet, and Network Interface.

The Application layer handles the actual data protocols, as follows:

- *Hypertext Transfer Protocol (HTTP)*—The foundation of the World Wide Web, this protocol allows a graphical view of documents that can contain text, pictures, sounds, backgrounds, and executable scripts.

- *File Transfer Protocol (FTP)*—This protocol allows files to be transferred from a server to a client using Unix-like commands and directory structures. It also gives the administrator the ability to upload and/or download files into directories.

- *Telnet*—This terminal emulation protocol is used to connect to UNIX systems for remote management through a command-line interface. The server is responsible for the user environment.

- *Simple Mail Transport Protocol (SMTP)*—This is the protocol that transfers mail from an outgoing mail server to the destination mail server for receipt by a mail user.

- *Post Office Protocol version 3 (POP3)*—A client uses this protocol to connect to a mail server and download or read e-mail over the Internet. Programs such as Outlook Express and Outlook can be configured to do this. POP3 does not allow sending of messages (that must be done through SMTP).

- *Internet Message Access Protocol version 4 (IMAP4)*—This is similar to POP3 in that it is used to read e-mail messages. IMAP4 allows clients to download just the headers of the message and then let the end user choose if he or she wants to download the entire message.

The Transport layer handles the mapping of Application layer protocols to their appropriate port or passageway across the network. The ports are separated into two types, as follows:

- *Transmission Control Protocol (TCP) ports*—These ports are called "connection oriented" because they require a negotiated connection between the sender and receiver before data can be exchanged. This connection uses a three-way hand-shake process, often abbreviated as SYN-ACK-ACK. It starts with a SYN (synchronization) packet from sender to receiver, then an ACK (acknowledgement) packet from receiver to sender, and finally an ACK from sender to receiver to complete the handshake. During this process, the receiver also sets the reception window size to accommodate the packets from the sender. This sizing is called the TCP sliding window size.

■ *User Datagram Protocol (UDP) ports*—These ports are called connectionless because they do not require a negotiated connection between the sender and receiver before data can be exchanged. The protocol relies on a "best effort" delivery to the receiver and is considered faster but less reliable than TCP.

At the Internet layer, you have the IP protocol suite. The protocols that you will encounter in this suite are as follows:

■ Internet Protocol (IP) is responsible for addressing each packet with a logical address. This address is used in routing to help determine where to send a packet.

■ Routing Information Protocol (RIP) and Open Shortest Path First (OSPF) are both dynamic routing protocols. They define the path that computers use to send information across a network.

■ Internet Control Message Protocol (ICMP) is most commonly associated with the utility PING. This program uses the ICMP protocol to test the connection between two stations on the network.

■ Internet Group Message Protocol (IGMP) is used with Multicast transmissions for routing groups.

■ Address Resolution Protocol (ARP) is used to determine the MAC address of a network card based on its logical IP address. For two devices to communicate on a network, the IP address must be resolved to the MAC address. Obtaining the other device's MAC address is done through a broadcast packet on the network. If the destination IP address is on a different network, the router that forwarded the packet will return its MAC address to the source and the source will send the packet to the router. The router will then perform the same check and send a request either to the destination or the next router in the chain toward the destination.

The Institute of Electrical and Electronics Engineers (IEEE) defines the Network Interface layer protocols. The most common protocol at this layer is 802.3, which defines Ethernet. Ethernet can use three different cabling and speeds:

■ Coaxial, 10 Mbps

■ Twister-pair (Cat 5e), 10 Mbps to 1 Gbps

■ Fiber-optic, 10 Mbps to 10 Gbps

The IEEE has also approved other network interface layer protocols such as Token Ring, which was created by IBM to operate at 4-16 Mbps. Wireless networks and Bluetooth (a short-range wireless protocol) also operate at the Network Interface layer.

CHAPTER 4 SUMMARY

The Dynamic Host Configuration Protocol (DHCP) allows you to automate the settings of workstations, servers, and printers in your network. Without DHCP, an administrator would have to manually assign IP address information.

When a client is configured to use DHCP, it broadcasts a DHCPDISCOVER packet. The packet includes the MAC address of the client. A DHCP server responds to the client with a DHCPOFFER that includes an IP address for the client. The client responds to the DHCP server with a DHCPREQUEST packet, again including its MAC address because it does not yet have an IP address. This packet officially requests the IP address from the DHCP server. The last packet in this conversation is the DHCPACK, which acknowledges that the DHCP server has successfully leased this IP address to the client.

When a DHCP server leases out an IP address, the address is leased for a specific period of time. Once 50% of that time has expired on the client, the client attempts to renew its address with the DHCP server by sending another DHCPREQUEST packet. If all goes well, the DHCP server responds with a DHCPACK packet. If the client cannot contact the DHCP server at that 50% interval, it attempts again at 87.5% of the lease. If that attempt fails, the client tries one last time when the lease reaches 100%.

To set up the DHCP service, you use the Add or Remove Programs applet in the Control Panel and then select Add/Remove Windows Components. DHCP is under the Networking Services section. If the DHCP server is going to be a member of an Active Directory domain, you need to authorize it within Active Directory. To do this, you must be a member of the Enterprise Admins group. DHCP authorization keeps servers from assigning IP addresses in a domain environment.

To configure a DHCP server to lease IP addresses, you define the scope of addresses you wish to assign. You can then set up the scope options from the DHCP Manager console in Administrative Tools.

When creating a scope, you need to come up with a unique scope name and an IP address range that will be used by clients and the subnet mask. As you go through the Add New Scope wizard, you can also configure exclusions, which prevent a block of IP addresses in a range from being assigned to clients.

One very key setting during the Add New Scope process is the lease expiration time. If a client computer's IP address expires, then it will use Automatic Private IP Addressing (APIPA) to obtain a new address. Once a scope is created, you must activate it before it will accept client requests.

Two additional scopes that can be created on a Windows Server 2003 DHCP server are superscopes and multicast scopes. If you have multiple scopes that you would like to manage in a single scope, you can create a superscope. Some multimedia programs will require clients to receive an address that is in a multicast scope. Multicast scopes use a range of addresses from 244.0.0.0 to 239.255.255.255.

A reservation is an IP address that will always be leased to a specific host. To configure a reservation, you need to know the MAC address of the workstation. You can use the reservation feature to set servers (other than the DHCP server) and printers to a specific IP address to make management of your network easier.

Scope options help configure additional TCP/IP settings on DHCP clients without you manually configuring each one. Options can be configured at the server level, scope level, and individual computer level, and they are processed in that order. If there are any conflicts, the option that is last applied will apply.

You can use the DHCP service in Windows Server 2003 to create vendor and user classes that can be used to assign IP addresses. Vendor classes are defined by the operating system the client is running, and the user classes are created by an administrator.

DHCP is a broadcast-based service. Thus, if a DHCP server and clients are on different networks, those clients cannot contact a DHCP server. Broadcast packets are not forwarded over a router. You can configure a Windows Server 2003 computer to be a DHCP relay agent. DHCP relay agents pick up DHCP requests on the network where there is no DHCP server. The relay agent then forwards the requests on to a DHCP server to service the clients.

CHAPTER 5 SUMMARY

Clients rely on the DHCP Service to receive IP configuration information. Closely managing and monitoring DHCP can result in fewer problems for the administrator.

By default, the DHCP server backs itself up into the C:\WINDOWS\system32\dhcp\ backup\new directory every 60 minutes. You can use the DHCP management tool, named dhcp.mdb, to manually back up the database. Windows Server 2003 also backs up the DHCP registry entries. Use the DHCP management tool to restore the DHCP database and to change the default backup location.

The DHCP database grows with time and as new clients lease addresses. By reconciling a DHCP scope, you can clean up inconsistencies. This is done using the DHCP management tool and is done per scope.

As the DHCP database grows, there is a greater chance that the database can be corrupted. One way to identify if the database is corrupted is by looking in the Event Log. To repair a corrupted database, run "jetpack dhcp.mdb tempfilename" at the command prompt.

The DHCP Service tracks statistics that can be viewed at the server or scope level. The Performance snap-in also can be used to monitor DHCP servers. Installing DHCP on a server will cause additional objects and counters to appear in the Performance snap-in.

You can generate detailed events about a DHCP server by using DHCP audit logging. DHCP audit logging is turned on by default and stores seven audit logs in the C:\WINDOWS\system32\dhcp directory. These logs can be read by any text editor such as Notepad. The following is a list of common DHCP audit log events (the event ID is listed first; the description is listed second):

- *00*—The audit log was started.
- *01*—The audit log was stopped.
- *02*—The audit log was stopped due to low available disk space.
- *10*—A new IP address was leased to a DHCP client.
- *11*—A lease was renewed by a DHCP client.
- *12*—A lease was released by a DHCP client.
- *13*—A certain IP address was found to be in use on the network.
- *14*—A DHCP client could not obtain a lease because there were no available addresses in the scope.
- *15*—A DHCP lease was denied.
- *16*—A DHCP lease was deleted.
- *17*—A DHCP lease was expired.
- *50+*— These messages relate to DHCP server authorization, including Rogue Server Detection information.

DHCP assigns IP addresses from a range that an administrator sets up. These addresses never conflict with the addresses in that range; however, they may conflict with addresses that were assigned statically. Conflict detection prevents DHCP servers from issuing IP addresses that would otherwise conflict with a statically assigned address. With conflict detection, a DHCP server will ping the IP address it is about to lease before it leases that address.

When a DHCP server has multiple network cards, you can configure which ones are going to be bound to the DHCP service. Bindings lets the configured network card listen to DHCP-related traffic, and bindings can be configured in the DHCP servers advanced settings.

Chapter 6 Summary

The first name-resolution type is Winsock. With Winsock, IP host name resolution is supported by the Domain Name Service (DNS) or the HOSTS files located on the workstation. DNS is also used to resolve fully qualified domain names (FQDN) on the Internet.

DNS names have an organization name followed by a top-level domain name that represents a category or country. The Internet Corporation for Assigned Names and Numbers (ICANN) defines these category names. Companies register their name with a registrar who in turn puts records in a top-level domain referring to your company's name.

The second name-resolution type is NetBIOS. This type utilizes the Windows Internet Name Service (WINS) or the LMHOSTS file on your workstation. NetBIOS names are limited to 15 characters and use a sixteenth character to identify resources or services on the computer. When a Windows Server 2003 computer is installed and given a name, the computer-friendly name is used as the host name and NetBIOS name. If the name is over 15 characters, then the first 15 are used as the NetBIOS name.

Windows Server 2003 resolves host names in the following order:

1. Host name
2. HOSTS file
3. DNS cache
4. DNS
5. NetBIOS name resolution

The HOSTS file can be modified by any text editor and is located in the C:\WINDOWS\system32\drivers\etc directory. If an entry has a # in front of it, the respective line is ignored when the system reads the HOSTS file. The only entry in a HOSTS file will be that of the local loopback address (127.0.0.1).

When Windows Server 2003 starts up, it looks in the HOSTS file and loads the entries into the local DNS cache. Included with the local DNS cache will be any other hosts with which the computer communicates. Every entry will have a time to live that defines how long it stays in the local DNS cache. To view the DNS cache, type ipconfig /displaydns from the command prompt. To clear the DNS cache, type ipconfig /flushdns from the command prompt.

If computers are configured to use a DNS server to resolve their names, then an IP address of that DNS server will need to be entered into the clients' TCP/IP configuration. DNS servers perform two types of lookups: forward and reverse.

A forward lookup is the most common type performed by a DNS server, and it resolves FQDNs to IP addresses. In addition, DNS uses the User Datagram Protocol (UDP) and works over port 53. The way your system handles DNS requests for a resource on the public Internet is through a recursive lookup. Using the example URL *http://www.microsoft.com*, consider that your workstation can make a request to the DNS server listed in the workstation's TCP/IP configuration. It requests the IP address for the *www.microsoft.com* domain. Your DNS server then makes a request to a root server, asking for the IP address of a server that handles the .com top-level domain. The root server returns the IP address of the .com name server to your DNS server. Your DNS server then makes a request to the .com name server via its IP address and asks for the IP address of a first-level domain server that handles the domain microsoft.com. This IP address is returned to your DNS server from the .com server. Your DNS server then gives that IP address to your workstation. Once your workstation receives this IP address, you see the Web site in your browser.

NSLOOKUP is a command-line utility that is used to query DNS. NSLOOKUP can be used to confirm that each DNS server is configured with the correct information. It is also a very helpful utility when troubleshooting DNS problems.

Windows Server 2003 resolves NetBIOS names in this order:

1. NetBIOS name cache
2. WINS
3. Broadcast
4. LMHOSTS
5. Host name resolution

Using a WINS server can cut down on the number of broadcasts in a network. Clients need to be configured to contact a WINS server as quickly as possible; this is done through configuring their NetBIOS node type. The following are options are available:

- B-node
- P-node
- M-node
- H-node

WINS servers allow workstations to use the NetBIOS name to locate IP addresses for devices on the LAN. This process is automatic if the client has to be given the WINS server address either by DHCP or by static assignment. Upon boot-up, the workstation gives its NetBIOS name to the WINS server with a name registration packet. If the name has not already been registered (if there are no duplicate computer names on your network) the server accepts the registration and sends an ACK (Acknowledgement) back to the station.

Troubleshooting name resolution problems can be cumbersome if you forget when each type of resolution is used. If it is the host name (Winsock), you would first look at the DNS/HOSTS file resolution. If it is a NetBIOS name issue, then you would look at WINS/LMHOSTS.

If your DNS Server appears to be handling the resolution correctly, it could be that your local DNS Cache has become unusable or corrupted. To clear the local cache, you would use the IPCONFIG command with the /flushdns switch. This deletes the local cached entries and forces your workstation to query the DNS server for new resolutions.

In the NetBIOS name resolution, you can check the node type, WINS server addresses, and the NetBIOS name table to check local resolution on your LAN. If the database gets corrupted, you can then run the utility in the WINS management tool to scavenge the database or to purge expired (tombstone) records.

CHAPTER 7 SUMMARY

The Domain Name System's (DNS) primary function is to resolve host names to IP addresses. DNS is required for a networking environment that has the Active Directory service implemented.

There are various implementations of DNS. They include Microsoft's DNS and the Berkeley Internet Name Domain (BIND) standard, which can be used on UNIX and Linux systems. Microsoft has had a DNS server ever since Windows NT, and has made advancements with each new operating system. For example, Windows 2000 and 2003 support service resource records (SRV records), which are required for an Active Directory environment.

There are several ways to install DNS on a server running Windows Server 2003. If you promote a server to a domain controller and the Active Directory Installation wizard cannot locate a DNS server that supports SRV records, it will install DNS on the new domain controller. You can also access the Add or Remove Programs applet from the Control Panel to install the DNS service. With both methods, make sure that the server has a static IP address.

A DNS zone is the part of the DNS namespace for which a DNS server is responsible. An example of a zone name that could be created is course.com. The DNS server is responsible for all the records that are stored in that zone. When a zone is initially created, you must designate it as either a forward lookup zone or reverse lookup zone. A forward lookup zone resolves host names to IP addresses. A reverse lookup zone resolves IP addresses to host names.

Primary and secondary zones are used in traditional DNS, and their purpose is to synchronize information between DNS servers. A primary zone is the first zone created for a particular namespace. The server that hosts the primary zone is the only one that can write new records to that zone. You can create a secondary zone to help offload requests from the server that hosts the primary zone. Note, however, that it can be used only to query the zone; it is not allowed to write to the zone.

A primary zone needs to synchronize its database with secondary zones. This process is called a zone transfer. Older DNS servers would copy the entire database every time a zone transfer took place, but that action was time- and bandwidth-consuming. Windows Server 2003 can perform fast zone transfers that copy over only the incremental changes since the last time a zone transfer occurred.

Windows Server 2003 also supports Active Directory-integrated zones, which store the DNS database within Active Directory. Such a zone has the following advantages:

- Automatic backup of zone information
- Multimaster replication
- Increased security

C

When configuring DNS to work within Active Directory, you must decide the partition in which it will be stored:

- If you choose the domain directory partition, then all the domain controllers in that domain will have the DNS information replicated to them through Active Directory domain replication. However, if there is more then one domain in your forest, those domains will not have a copy of the DNS information.

- You can create an application directory partition and store DNS information in it. When you create an application partition, you manually decide which domain controllers are going to have this new application directory partition. With application partitions, the DNS information replicates only to those manually chosen DNS servers.

Stub zones are special zones that only hold a portion of the records for the zone to which they are pointing. For example, stub zones contain only a few records, including NS records. When a client sends a request to the stub zone, the stub zone checks for the NS record and forwards that request to that name server.

Caching-only servers are DNS servers that are not configured with any zone information, but clients are configured to use them to resolve names. These servers usually cache requests longer than traditional DNS servers. When they can't find what the client requests, they will forward that request to another DNS server and cache the answer.

Active Directory relies on DNS to locate services. Locating services can help clients log on and help other domain controllers find each other for replication. DNS and Active Directory can also share a common namespace.

You can turn the DNS server in Windows Server 2003 into a DNS server that supports dynamic updates. With this enabled, any client running Windows 2000/XP/2003 will update its host name within DNS automatically. If the network consists of older clients, then you need to configure DHCP and DNS to work together so that they can also update their host names in DNS.

There are three options when configuring dynamic DNS:

- *Allow only secure dynamic updates*—This option configures a DNS server to let only clients that have certain Active Directory permission update DNS.

- *Allow both nonsecure and secure dynamic updates*—This option allows any client to update information in DNS.

- *Do not allow dynamic updates (default setting)*—With this option, no dynamic updates will be allowed and all the host names must be added manually.

There are many options that can be configured at the DNS server level to help with managing DNS. A new feature in Windows Server 2003 DNS is aging and scavenging. These features help clean up the DNS database when dynamic updating is enabled. The default time of scavenging is seven days and when that threshold is met, DNS scavenges the records that haven't been updated within that time frame.

The Update Server Data Files option is used with primary zones, and it forces all DNS changes in memory to be written to disk. You can also clear the DNS cache, which cleans any outdated records that were stored in cache. DNS is configured to work on all network adapters, but can be changed by altering the bindings.

When DNS does not have the answer for a client request, it will forward the request to another DNS server. Windows Server 2003 can forward requests based on conditions. This forwarding can speed up the time to resolve names in specific domains. For example, you could add course.com as a DNS domain name and then put in the IP address for the DNS server that hosts course.com. When a client sends a request to course.com, the DNS server checks its forwarders and sees that it has a conditional forwarder for that domain name. It then forwards the request to that IP address.

If there are no forwarders set up on a DNS server, then DNS will use root hints. Root hints are servers that are automatically populated in the DNS server's properties and also are used to resolve host names on the Internet.

There are two types of logging available on a Windows Server 2003 DNS server. Event logging records events into the event log. Debug logging is more intensive; it logs DNS information to the C:\DNSlog.log file by default. You should use debug logging only when you are troubleshooting a specific problem. Once you are done with this resource-intensive logging, turn it off.

A Windows Server 2003 DNS server also has these advanced options:

- Disable recursion
- BIND secondaries
- Fail on load if bad zone data
- Enable round robin
- Enable netmask ordering
- Secure cache against pollution

DNS can be set up to use round robin DNS. Round robin DNS is known as a "poor man's load balancing" because there is no weight associated with the DNS server. When a request comes into a DNS server with round robin enabled, the request goes to the server that is designated next in line to receive the request. When another request comes into the DNS server, the next DNS server picks it up and it goes through all the DNS servers configured for round robin. This process cycles continuously through the DNS servers.

Once DNS is configured, your responsibility now switches to more management-related tasks. You may find it easier to manage DNS through the database file instead of using the console. If you make changes to the file, you have to reload zone information for the changes to take effect.

Larger companies may have too many hosts to maintain in a single zone, so they delegate subdomains to other administrators. Delegating zone information eases the burden of administration.

You may also find that you need to change zone types or replication options after you installed and configured DNS. This can all be done through the General tab of the Zone Properties dialog box. From this location, you can change a primary zone to an Active Directory-integrated zone. You can also change which servers are going to receive DNS replication data.

The Start of Authority (SOA) record contains all the relevant information about the DNS server. It has all the settings for zone transfer intervals, for how long the DNS server caches records, and for serial numbers and accountability information.

Use the Name Servers tab to manage which servers are configured as DNS servers. This can be used along with the Zone Transfers tab to include certain servers for zone transfers.

DNS can also use WINS to perform name resolution. If a DNS server does not have a record of a requested resource, it can forward that request to a WINS server to see if the name can be resolved.

When troubleshooting DNS servers, you can use the Monitoring tab of the DNS server properties. From the Monitoring tab, you can test iterative and recursive queries.

CHAPTER 8 SUMMARY

The dominant name resolution service as of this writing is the Domain Name Service (DNS). However, earlier Microsoft networks relied on the Windows Internet Naming (or Name) Service (WINS). Older Windows clients rely on WINS, and the implementation of a WINS server on the network can reduce the number of NetBIOS broadcasts generated by name-resolution requests. In a mixed network of newer and older Microsoft operating systems, WINS may still be required.

WINS is designed to resolve NetBIOS names to IP addresses. This process is referred to as name resolution. With older pre-Windows 2000 clients, NetBIOS names were used to identify hosts on the network, so name resolution was critical.

WINS is not part of the default install for Windows Server 2003. Instead, you must add it later through Add or Remove Programs. WINS is a robust service, and a single server is capable of handling a minimum of 5000 WINS clients. While this might suit most environments, adding another server can provide fault tolerance and better control for network traffic. Adding a server in branch office locations, for instance, can reduce name-resolution traffic that travels over the wide area network links. A local WINS server can handle all the name-resolution needs for the local office, and if a server fails, the other location is available as a backup. These multiple servers can also share WINS data with each other through replication. WINS servers configured to share data with each other are called replication partners.

Replication can be set up in three ways: Push, Pull, and Push/Pull. Push replication sends, or pushes, changes from one server to another server. Changes are sent after a certain number of changes have occurred. Pull replication, on the other hand, causes a server to request changes from another server. Pull replication happens on a scheduled basis. Push/Pull is a combination of Push and Pull replication.

Typically, the default settings are fine, but you can further configure the server if you choose. Configuration options include setting the renewal interval. This setting controls the TTL that is given to clients when they register with the server.

To view the records in the WINS management console, right-click the Active Registrations options and select Display Records. This opens up a search window that you can use to view some or all of the available records in the database.

Clients register with the WINS server on startup; however, you can also add static records. To add a static mapping, you must provide the computer name, record type, and IP address.

WINS keeps the records in a database. As with all databases, it is important to back up this database. A database backup allows quick recovery. A corrupt database can create numerous communication problems on the network. By default, the server is not automatically backed up. You must supply a backup path in the WINS server properties pages. After doing this, the WINS database will be backed up every three hours. You can also back up the database manually.

The WINS database can grow quite large: no limit is set on the number of records. Compacting the database can therefore increase performance, especially when query time has increased. There are two main types of compacting that you can perform: dynamic compacting, which is performed automatically at designated periods, and offline compacting, using the jetpack utility. Offline compacting improves performance the most, as all unused space is removed.

If your network has only Windows 2000 computers or newer, you may not need WINS and can remove it. Before doing so, ensure there are no legacy applications running that require NetBIOS name resolution.

WINS proxy is a solution in an environment that includes computers that cannot be configured for WINS. These are often UNIX clients. Using a WINS proxy allows these clients to query the WINS database for NetBIOS resolution.

CHAPTER 9 SUMMARY

Network communications often contain sensitive information. Data traveling over the network can include passwords, e-mails, instant messages, and data stored in documents. All of these can become security risks if the information is sensitive and exposed. IP Security Protocol (IPSec) can be used to secure traffic and avoid some of the concerns regarding communicating sensitive information.

Standard IP communication based on IPv4 has no built-in measures to aid in enhancing security. This can create several problems on a network where sensitive data is being transmitted. IPSec can enhance the security protections against some common attacks, such as the following:

- *Packet sniffing*—Using freely available tools, called packet sniffers, attackers can view traffic on the network. Much of this traffic is often transmitted as plain text, which simply means it is easily readable. This traffic can include e-mails and even passwords and logon information.

- *Data replay*—Attackers can retransmit data captured with a packet sniffer in hopes of having a certain action, such as a login or bank transaction, repeated.

- *Data modification*—An attacker could capture packets, modify them, and retransmit them. This could allow an attacker to view an e-mail attachment, modify it, and retransmit it.

- *Address spoofing*—Attackers can use this to modify the source IP address data on the network in hopes of hiding the true source of an attack.

IPSec is designed to alleviate these security concerns. It exists at the Network layer of the TCP/IP architecture and is invisible to applications.

IPSec provides authentication to communication. This verifies the identity of each endpoint of IP-based communications and ensures that both the sender and recipient of data are known and trusted parties.

Cryptography is a key part of IPSec communications. Cryptography is the process of encrypting and decrypting information. With IPSec communication, this refers to data transmitted over the network. Encryption puts the data in an unreadable format for unauthenticated parties. Decryption can be performed by authenticated parties so that the data is once again readable.

Encryption is carried out using an algorithm, or mathematical formula, to obfuscate the data being sent. To decrypt the data, a key is required. Symmetrical encryption uses the same key to encrypt and decrypt, while asymmetrical encryption uses two keys, a public key and a private key, where each key has a single role (to encrypt or decrypt).

Hash encryption is a method of encrypting that is not reversible: it is a one-way encryption method. Using hash encryption creates a hash value, which is a summary of the data. The main purpose of using a hash value is as an identifier; it is not meant to be a method to secure the data.

IPSec is an IETF standard and therefore is available for any vendor to implement. This has led to its wide adoption. There are impediments to its adoption, however; it can slow network traffic with its additional overhead, and it cannot be routed with NAT, which is a popular solution in many offices for sharing Internet access. In addition, IPSec adds another layer of complexity to the network and therefore creates additional administrative overhead.

IPSec has two main modes of operation: tunnel mode and transport mode. Tunnel mode is used to secure communication between two routers. Between two hosts, IPSec's transport mode is used.

IPSec authentication can take place using three main methods. The Preshared key method is a key, or group, of characters, that is entered at each endpoint. Authentication relies on each endpoint having the same preshared key. This is simple to set up; however, it can be difficult to ensure security of the key when it has to be shared at remote locations. The certificates method can be used for authentication as well. These are files that follow the X.509 standard. Finally, the Kerberos method can be used. This is the authentication system used by Windows 2000, XP, and 2003.

IPSec is enabled based on IPSec policies. These policies determine which traffic is encrypted using IPSec. Three policies installed by default are Server (Request Security), Client (Respond Only), and Secure Server (Require Security). Assigning a policy implements it; however, it does not take effect immediately. The IPSec Policy Agent must be restarted.

When creating an IPSec policy, you define rules. Rules consist of an IP filter list, a filter action, the authentication methods, a tunnel endpoint, and a connection type. Rules are created to determine if traffic is permitted, if IPSec is requested, or if it is required. Filter lists determine which traffic is affected by the policy. The Filter action determines what is done with traffic that matches the filter list.

Troubleshooting IPSec can be accomplished with different tools. The most common IPSec troubleshooting tools are as follows:

- Ping
- IPSec Security Monitor
- Event Viewer
- Resultant Set of Policy
- Netsh
- Oakley logs
- Network Monitor

Ping can be used to test connectivity between hosts to see if they can communicate when IPSec is implemented. The IPSec Security Monitor is an MMC snap-in. It shows the status of IPSec security associations. Event Viewer can be used to review log events that may be recorded by the IPSec Policy Agent. The Resultant Set of Policy shows how Group Policy settings are in effect. Netsh allows you to configure IPSec from a command line. Oakley logs also log SA-specific information, but it must be enabled using the netsh command. Network Monitor can be used to monitor traffic over the network and view (but not decrypt) IPSec traffic.

CHAPTER 10 SUMMARY

Remote access allows mobile use of your network. This important capability increases productivity and allows mobile users to communicate even while away from a traditional office. Administering the remote access features of Windows Server 2003 requires a thorough understanding of the various processes on which remote access relies.

The oldest method of remote access is through a dial-up connection. In the past, this has been a slow method of data transfer, but advances in modem technology have made this an effective method to transfer small files. Current modem capabilities allow download speeds of 56 Kbps when using the v.90 or v.92 standards.

A virtual private network (VPN) connection is a newer and faster method of remote access. VPN access relies on an existing connection to the Internet. The VPN client then creates a VPN connection to the server. This tunnel to the server can then be used to communicate as if the client is on the same LAN as the server. If the existing connection is a broadband connection, then the client's VPN connection may be as fast as 10 MBps. If the existing connection is a dial-up connection, then the speed will be slower.

The Routing and Remote Access Service (RRAS) must be configured for Windows Server 2003 to act as a dial-up server. It is installed by default, but it is not enabled. RRAS acting as a dial-up server also requires a modem.

Your RRAS server uses both LAN and remote access protocols for communication. LAN protocols supported by RRAS include TCP/IP, IPS/SPX, and AppleTalk. Remote access supports Point-to-Point Protocol (PPP) and Serial Line Internet Protocol (SLIP).

You can enable Multilink, which allows clients to utilize multiple connections to the server to aggregate bandwidth. You need multiple modems on the server and the client. In addition, you can set up Bandwidth Allocation Protocol (BAP) to add and drop modems from the dial-up connection.

Just as with a dial-up server, RRAS must be enabled, if it is not already, to configure a VPN server. While configuring a server, you can set up packet filters. This option is best used when the server has multiple network cards. The filtered card is used for the Internet connection, and the unfiltered card connects to the LAN.

VPN protocols supported by the server include Point to Point Tunneling Protocol (PPTP) and Layer Two Tunneling Protocol (L2TP). PPTP is typically chosen over L2TP when NAT is in use, as PPTP functions with NAT. PPTP also provides encryption. L2TP alone does not provide encryption, so it must be combined with an encryption method such as IPSec.

There are different authentication method choices. The weakest is no authentication at all. In this situation, a username and password are not used to verify identity. Others include the Password Authentication Protocol (PAP), which transmits passwords in plain text, making it an undesirable method as well. The Shiva Password Authentication Protocol (SPAP) uses reversible encryption for the transmission of credentials. This allows the decryption of the password, which is dangerous for security reasons. Challenge Handshake Authentication

Protocol (CHAP) is significantly better than the prior choices, because the password is not transmitted over the wire, and therefore is better protected. Microsoft Challenge Handshake Authentication Protocol (MS-CHAP) works more securely with Active Directory than CHAP does, and MS-CHAP v2 is an improvement that corrects several flaws in the original MS-CHAP. Another option is Extensible Authentication Protocol (EAP), which allows the use of smart cards and certificates for authentication.

Client access to the remote access server can be controlled. All users of an organization may not require access. Permissions are controlled by the user object. They may be granted through the user accounts or through a remote access policy on the server.

Windows Server 2003 can also act as a VPN client, if you configure a client connection using the New Connection Wizard.

Remote access policies can be configured to control access. Effectively implementing and managing such a policy requires understanding the different components, the policy evaluation principles, and the default remote access policies.

Remote access policies are composed of conditions, permissions, and a profile. The conditions are the criteria that must be met for the policy to apply to a connection. The criteria include station ID, authentication type, and day and time restrictions. Remote access permissions include either grant or deny permission to access the server remotely. The profile contains the settings applied to a connection once the conditions and permissions have been identified.

Remote access policy evaluation begins by evaluating whether policies even exist. If policies exist, their conditions are compared to the conditions of the attempted connection. If no match is found for the conditions, the attempt is rejected. If a match is found, permissions are evaluated, to determine if the conditions lead to the attempt being accepted or rejected. Finally, profile settings are used to determine the authentication methods and encryption levels. All three parts must pass for the connection to be successful.

Problems establishing connections are generally due to software configuration errors (such as the wrong phone number or IP address) and authentication-setting mistakes. Hardware errors include hardware that is not on the HCL, or other general connectivity issues. To help resolve issues, logging can be enabled. You can create detailed connection logs from the Logging tab of the remote access server's Properties dialog box, located in the Routing and Remote Access snap-in.

CHAPTER 11 SUMMARY

Many corporations allow remote access to their networks. However, it is important, if they do so, to allow access in a secure method. To achieve this, Windows Server 2003 includes a feature called Remote Authentication Dial-In User Service (RADIUS). RADIUS is a standard, and it is important to know how it works so that you can implement it effectively to secure remote access to your network.

C

RADIUS is used to enhance remote access authentication in a network. RADIUS allows for tasks to be centralized on a single server. There are two mandatory server roles involved with the RADIUS process: RADIUS client and RADIUS server.

The client accepts authentication information from remote access users or devices and forwards the information to the RADIUS server. It is the access point to the network, and the middleman in the authentication process.

The RADIUS server accepts the authentication information sent by the end user or device to the RADIUS client and determines whether access is granted or denied. Windows Server 2003 can fulfill either role as necessary. An optional component of the process is the RADIUS proxy, which acts as an intermediary between multiple RADIUS clients and servers.

To configure Windows Server 2003 as a RADIUS server, use the Add or Remove Programs option. Under Networking Services, select Internet Authentication Service, which is the required service to set up Windows as a RADIUS server. RADIUS clients that send information to the server should be listed and configured in the IAS snap-in. Clients that are not registered will not be able to authenticate with the server. RADIUS Proxy servers are considered RADIUS clients.

RRAS can be configured as a RADIUS client. This can be done by using the Routing and Remote Access wizard if RRAS has not been enabled, or by using the Security tab of the RRAS server properties.

A new feature in Windows Server 2003 is that you can configure IAS to act simultaneously as a RADIUS server and as a proxy; older versions could provide only one server at a time.

Connection request policies determine actions taken upon receiving a connection request. They are similar to remote access policies. When a connection request is made, the options in the policy are reviewed for a match. A match to a condition results in the policy taking effect.

Typical problems when setting up RADIUS are generally not RADIUS related, but relate instead to the underlying network infrastructure. Because RADIUS operates over a network, these problems will be network-connectivity issues, such as IP address problems or general network-connectivity issues.

While not all environments require IAS, if users are connecting remotely, then IAS can further secure the network and authenticate the end users. This allows a corporation to raise the level of its security for its remote access clients.

CHAPTER 12 SUMMARY

Almost all networks today use routing, which is the act of moving data from one network to another. A router is a device that connects one or more networks to other networks. It also passes data between them. Both home and business users who connect to the Internet use routers.

Routers have multiple interfaces. Each interface is connected to a different network. The router allows the flow of packets among the networks to which it is connected. A router may be a dedicated hardware device, or even a computer with multiple network interfaces. When a computer has multiple network interfaces, the computer is said to be multihomed.

Another tool used to control the information that goes back and forth between networks is called a proxy server. Microsoft's Internet Security and Acceleration Server (ISA) product provides these features and more.

Routers must know how to get traffic from one network to another. To be able to do so, routers keep track of the different networks connected to each interface, as well as all the networks known to the router. This information is stored in a routing table. All computers that are on the network have their own routing table as well. To view the routing table, you can use the netstat –r command or the route print command from the command prompt.

The two common types of routing are static routing and dynamic routing. Static routing is more secure than dynamic routing; specific routes are manually created to control the flow of traffic and the information in routing tables. In contrast, in dynamic routing, the routers talk to each other to build their routing tables. Dynamic routing is more common than static routing.

When determining how to get data from the source to the destination, routers rely on routing protocols. The protocols are responsible for calculating the best path from one network to another. The method that the routing protocol uses to determine the best path is called its routing algorithm.

There are two routing protocols used in Windows Server 2003 for IP routing: Routing Information Protocol (RIP) and Open Shortest Path First (OSPF). RIP, the simpler and more popular of the two, is a distance-vector routing protocol, which means it takes into account the number of routers between two points to determine the best path. Each router along the way is referred to as a hop.

RIP does not, however, take into account the speed of each link; in small environments, this may be acceptable, but in larger environments, this may lead to the inefficient routing of traffic. RIP exchanges information with other routers every 30 seconds. It sends a complete copy of the routing table in each packet. This can also be inefficient in larger networks.

To ensure routing accuracy, two common features, split-horizon processing and poison-reverse processing, are used in RIP. Split-horizon processing works by not sending routing information out of the same interface upon which it was received. Poison-reverse processing marks a network as unreachable when it goes down. Both methods are designed to prevent routing loops.

C

In contrast to RIP is OSPF. OSPF takes into account the links between routers, using a link-state routing algorithm. This gives OSPF more flexibility. In environments that are more complex, OSPF performs well. However, complex environments typically use hardware routers, so it is not common to find OSPF implemented on Windows Server 2003.

After ensuring that packets can find their remote destinations through correct router configuration, you may need to implement controls over the traffic. Packet filters enable you to control the flow of traffic by determining what traffic is allowed to pass through the routers and what traffic is dropped. Filter conditions can be the protocol, the source address, the destination address, and the port number.

Packet filters are configured in the Routing and Remote Access console. You need to choose an interface under the General folder and use its Properties page to configure filters. You have the option of selecting inbound and outbound filters and the conditions to be met by the filter. You can then either allow all traffic or drop all traffic, depending on the filter condition.

Demand-dial connections are also used in routing. As the name implies, these connections are created upon the demand, or need, for the connection. When a router receives data for a remote network that is accessible via the demand-dial interface, it creates the connection and sends the data. When the data transmission is complete, the connection is disconnected. Demand-dial connections can be used with dial-up connections between routers or when using VPN connections between routers. In addition, Point-to-Point Protocol over Ethernet (PPPoE) can be used for demand-dial connections. Note, however, that it requires authentication. This is a popular method for ISPs to control access to their networks.

Demand-dial connections are created in the Routing and Remote Access snap-in. The server's Properties page must be configured to allow demand-dial connections. Once it has been enabled, configure a port that allows demand-dial routing, and then create a demand-dial interface. To set up the port, go to the Ports option in the console and select the appropriate port type.

New connections are created using the Demand-Dial Interface Wizard. This walks an administrator through the process of creating the demand-dial connection by helping select the protocol and other parameters.

Some configuration parameters must be set after the initial demand-dial interface is created. The idle timeout setting is set to 5 minutes, but this can be modified. Dial-out hours can be set to control when the connection dials out and to keep it from dialing out constantly.

Demand-dial filters are used to control what traffic can initiate the connection. For instance, it may be undesirable to allow ICMP traffic, such as a ping or tracert command, to initiate the connection. Demand-dial filters, therefore, define the traffic that can create the connection to the remote location.

Troubleshooting routing issues is easier when you understand the common problems. With routing, the most common problem is misconfigurations. These can be spotted by examining the routing table to see where packets "think" they are supposed to go. Also examine the default gateway entry to see where packets will go when no other entry is found in the routing table.

CHAPTER 13 SUMMARY

Security continues to be an extremely important part of administering a network. The number of security issues faced by administrators continues to rise. Effectively managing the risks is key to being successful. To manage the security issues in a network, it is important to know the capabilities of the operating system and the tools on the network.

Windows 2003 includes tools that allow you to manage your security configuration. Tools included for this purpose are collectively referred to as the Security Configuration Manager tools. This collection of tools can be used to ease your administrative workload when you are implementing security policies. The bundle of tools includes security templates, security settings in GPO objects, the Security Configuration and Analysis snap-in, and the secedit command-line tool (which is defined later in this summary).

Security templates are a collection of settings—and a baseline for you to implement security. They allow you to easily implement the security requirements that most organizations require. When setting these up, use the principle of least privilege; that is, don't allow more privileges than the client requires.

You can use Group Policy Objects (GPO) in Active Directory to apply template settings in your network. GPO can then be automatically applied to a large number of computers in an Active Directory domain and administered centrally. This is done through Active Directory, using the Active Directory Users and Computers snap-in.

Windows Server 2003 includes several templates which you can use to design your organization's security. If you apply templates and decide you want to restore the default security settings, you can apply the Setup Security.inf template, which is created during the installation process.

You can use default templates when creating your own templates. These templates include:

- *Compatws.inf*—Windows Server 2003 increases default security levels. This can cause programs not to run. The Compatws.inf template weakens the default security to allow legacy applications to run under Windows Server 2003.

- *Securews.inf and Securedc.inf*—These increase security for account policies, the registry, and auditing.

- *Hisecws.inf and Hisecdc.inf*—These templates increase security further by implementing advanced features such as packet signing.

- *DC Security.inf*—This template is applied to increase security when a server is promoted to a domain controller.

- *Rootsec.inf*—This template is designed to reapply permissions that are assigned to the root of the system drive. It can be used if the permissions have been modified and need to be reset.

Some of the key settings in policies apply to password security. The following settings are commonly used and can enhance the password security of your environment:

- *Enforce password history*—This sets the number of passwords (between 0 and 24) that have to be unique before a user can repeat an older password.

- *Maximum password age*—This defines the maximum number of days that goes by before a password must be changed.

- *Minimum password age*—This sets the minimum number of days that must pass before a user can change a password.

- *Minimum password length*—This sets the minimum allowed length for a password.

- *Password must meet complexity requirements*—This increases password security by requiring complex passwords, such as those that include numbers, uppercase and lowercase letters, and symbols.

- *Store password using reversible encryption*—This weakens security by allowing passwords to be decrypted.

Security can be analyzed using the Security Configuration and Analysis snap-in. It allows comparison of settings between a template and the computer and displays any inconsistent settings. You can create a database to store information by choosing the Open Database option and creating a filename. Then, you import a template into the database. The database can then be used to perform an analysis.

You can also configure the settings based on the database. If the template settings are different and you would like to rectify the inconsistencies, the Configure Computer Now option will do so.

Your final tool is the secedit command-line tool. It can be used to create and apply security templates and analyze settings. Because it is a command-line tool, it can be used in scripts as well. It provides the capability to analyze and configure a computer and to export information to a template file. You can also generate a rollback template to reset your settings to their default.

Graphical tools make it simple to apply settings; however, it may be necessary to perform functions from a command line. Secedit.exe is a command-line tool used to create and apply security templates and analyze security settings. The secedit.exe command uses 11 main switches:

- */analyze*—Analyzes database settings and compares them to a computer configuration.

- */CFG filename*—Specifies the path to a security template file that is imported into a database specified using the /DB switch.

- */configure*—Configures a system with database (security template) settings.

- */DB filename*—Specifies the path to a database file (*.sdb) that is to be used when analyzing a system.

- */export*—Exports database information to a security template file.

- */GenerateRollback*—Generates a security template that saves the current security settings of a system; this template can be used to return to previous security settings in the event that settings are changed.

- */import*—Imports security template information into a database file for analysis purposes.

- */log filename*—Specifies the path to a log file written to during an analysis; if this switch is not specified, the default log file is used.

- */quiet*—Prevents all screen and log output.

- */validate*—Verifies the syntax of a security template.

- */verbose*—Specifies that detailed information should be logged during an analysis.

By understanding the tools available to you, you can most effectively manage the security issues that arise in your network. Proactive security management is not optional, but required, and the tools provided in Windows Server 2003 greatly simplify the task.

CHAPTER 14 SUMMARY

A vital skill for all administrators is the ability to monitor and troubleshoot problems. The rapid resolution of problems can save a company thousands of dollars. An effective monitoring program and proactive administration can also circumvent problems before they become outages or otherwise impact performance. Getting a system up and running initially is the first step. However, keeping it up and running optimally over time is just as important.

In particular, note these two types of maintenance:

- Proactive maintenance is designed to prevent problems and to limit the scope of damage from unpreventable problems.

- Reactive maintenance corrects a problem that has already occurred.

To enhance your capabilities in resolving issues, your organization should have a defined set of troubleshooting procedures. These procedures allow employees to efficiently notifiy you of issues. When troubleshooting, the procedures should include checking the system log in Event Viewer. This can provide valuable information to you and other support personnel that may help you resolve the issue. In addition, take steps to isolate the problem. This is done by examining the information you have gathered and eliminating possible causes that are ruled out by the evidence.

Next, determine what may be causing the problem and create a list of possible causes. Research the solutions, place the most probable fix at the top of the list, and place the least probable last. Then, implement the fixes in the order of your list until the solution is reached. You should implement only a single fix at a time to pinpoint the problem and minimize additional problems. Once the issue is resolved, document the solution to help resolve future problems.

Follow these steps during any troubleshooting process:

1. *Prioritize problems*—Severe problems, such work stoppages and impending data loss, are serious problems as compared to a client who cannot surf the Internet. Work on higher-priority problems first.

2. *Try to solve the root of the problem*—Make sure you understand your solution and that it addresses the cause, and not the symptom, of the complaint.

Windows Server 2003 includes different tools to assist you in troubleshooting and monitoring system performance. The most common of these include:

- Network Monitor
- System Monitor
- Performance Logs and Alerts
- Event Viewer
- Task Manager
- Services snap-in

Network Monitor is used to view and log network traffic. You can capture and analyze traffic on your network, sort and filter traffic, and view the source and destination of traffic. It has two components that work together:

- Network Monitor
- The Network Monitor driver

Network Monitor allows detailed viewing of the traffic that is on the network, including the amount of data, the type of traffic, and the contents of packets.

To make it simpler to manage and view the traffic, filters can be used. Such use allows you to view, for example, traffic sent to a specific PC or traffic using a specific protocol.

The System Monitor tool allows you to collect real-time information on your server's performance. It collects data that allows you to examine the server's performance under its current workload and to diagnose problems such as bottlenecks. The data collected can also be used for capacity planning by pointing out server usage issues and load. Testing can be done by examining changes and observing the effect in System Monitor as well.

Information can be represented in a graph, a histogram (which shows data as a bar graph updated in real time), and a report (which gives a text-based view of the counters).

Several performance objects are commonly monitored to ensure a smooth-running network. It is a good idea to memorize these objects and the values that generally indicate acceptable performance.

- *% Processor Time*—This indicator shows how busy the processor is and should be under 80%.

- *% Interrupt Time*—This processor counter measures hardware interrupts. If processor time is over 90% and this value is over 15%, you may have malfunctioning hardware.

- *Pages/Second*—This is a memory-related counter. Values over 20 are considered high.

- *% Disk Time*—This indicates how busy the disk drive is. Values over 90% indicate the disk drive may be working too much. Moving the page file may resolve the issue.

- *Average Disk Queue Length*—This indicates how busy the disk drive is.

Other capabilities of Performance Logs and Alerts allow you to collect data in various formats, such as comma- or tab-separated. You can view data in real time or after it has been collected. You can also configure start and stop times for log generation and automatic collection. All of these can be managed from a single window, including alerts designed to inform you that the server is performing outside predefined parameters.

Another excellent place to look for information is the Event Viewer. Events are typically written to one of three log files:

- *Application log*—Programs installed on the system generate events to this log.

- *Security log*—If an audit policy has been created, security events generated by the policy are recorded in this log.

- *System log*—This log contains information, warnings, and errors generated by Windows Server 2003 system components, including services and drivers.

There are three types of events reported in the system and application logs:

- *Information*—This typically minor event does not require administrative action.

- *Warning*—This indicates an event that may pose a problem in the future, but is not of immediate concern.

- *Error*—This indicates a failure, such as a service not loading or a driver failing.

Task Manager also provides useful information. It can be used to monitor the system's CPU usage history, as well as other performance information related to the CPU and memory. In addition, networking information, including utilization, is also shown.

The Services snap-in shows services installed on the computer. Services come with Windows 2003 and may also be installed by third-party software. Services, unlike programs, can run without a user being logged in.

C

Server capabilities such as DNS, DHCP, and WINS are all provided by services.

One common issue that surfaces on all networks is network connectivity. The following tasks can be useful in troubleshooting these types of issues:

- *Verify the IP configuration*—Confirm that the computer has appropriate TCP/IP settings for the network on which it is located.

- *Ensure that DHCP is functional*—If DHCP is in use, ensure that the computer is not using an APIPA address, which indicates it did not receive a lease from the DHCP server.

- *Verify the configuration of IPSec*—If IPSec is used, confirm it is working properly and the policy is implemented properly.

- *Check network media*—Make sure the cable and all connections to the network are working properly.

- *Check router configuration*—Confirm that the router has appropriate routes and is functioning properly in the network.

- *Check DNS*—Ensure that the DNS server is responding to clients and correctly resolving host names to IP addresses.

Other issues involve name resolution and require additional steps. However, the key points to remember are the importance of proactive monitoring and the use of a systematic method for troubleshooting. Document findings so that if errors arise again, they can be more quickly and easily resolved. Troubleshooting skills and monitoring skills enable administrators to excel at their jobs and manage their networks effectively.

Practice Exam

70-291 Implementing, Managing, and Maintaining a Microsoft Windows Server 2003 Network Infrastructure

Name:_____

Date:_____

1. You have assigned a server the IP address 192.168.12.1 with a subnet mask of 255.255.0.0. What is the network ID?
   a. 192.0.0.0
   b. 192.168.0.0
   c. 192.168.12.0
   d. 192.168.12.1

2. What class of IP addresses allows up to 65,534 workstations per subnet?
   a. class A
   b. class B
   c. class C
   d. class D
   e. all of the above

3. What is the term for the process of creating a large network from smaller networks?
   a. subnetting
   b. host routing
   c. classfull routing
   d. supernetting

4. You have subnetted your network into two smaller networks to improve performance. What is required to move the packets between the subnets?
   a. router
   b. switch
   c. bridge
   d. firewall

5. When will a DHCP client attempt to renew its IP address from the DHCP server? (Choose all that apply.)
   a. 25% of the lease
   b. 50% of the lease
   c. 75% of the lease
   d. 87.5% of the lease
   e. at the end of the lease

6. You have installed and configured a DHCP server on a Windows Server 2003 domain controller. However, the DHCP server is not leasing IP addresses. What must you do?
   a. Restart the DHCP service.
   b. Restart the computer.
   c. Reactivate the DHCP scope.
   d. Authorize the DHCP server in Active Directory.

7. Which group has the ability to authorize a Windows Server 2003 DHCP server?
   a. Enterprise Admins
   b. Domain Admins
   c. Schema Admins
   d. Server Operator

8. **What is the default lease duration for a multicast scope?**
   a. two days
   b. eight days
   c. thirty days
   d. unlimited

9. **You need to create an IP address reservation for a printer in the DHCP scope. What unique identifier is used to identify the printer?**
   a. IP address
   b. NetBIOS name
   c. printer port
   d. MAC address
   e. GUID number

10. **How often is the DHCP database backed up?**
    a. every 30 minutes
    b. every 60 minutes
    c. every 12 hours
    d. every 24 hours
    e. never

11. **The DHCP database has become corrupt on a Windows Server 2003 computer. What utility is used to repair the database?**
    a. ESEUTIL
    b. JETPACK
    c. NTDSUTIL
    d. SIGNERIF

12. **What is the purpose of enabling conflict detection on a DHCP server?**
    a. The DHCP server will check for other DHCP servers on the network.
    b. The DHCP server will not lease a reserved IP address.
    c. The DHCP server will ping an IP address before it is leased.
    d. The DHCP server will verify its authorization at startup.

13. **What is the maximum number of characters allowed in a host name?**
    a. 8
    b. 12
    c. 15
    d. 16
    e. 254
    f. 255

14. **What is the purpose of an LMHOSTS file?**
    a. to resolve host names to IP addresses
    b. to resolve IP addresses to host names
    c. to resolve NetBIOS names to IP addresses
    d. to resolve IP addresses to NetBIOS names

15. Which tool is used to query DNS servers to verify and test DNS functionality?

    a. PING
    b. NSLOOKUP
    c. TRACERT
    d. NETSTAT
    e. NETSH

16. Which of the following is <u>not</u> a valid NETBIOS node type?

    a. B node
    b. D node
    c. H node
    d. P node
    e. M node

17. Which of the following NetBIOS node types uses only WINS to resolve NetBIOS names to IP addresses?

    a. B node
    b. P node
    c. H node
    d. M node

18. What is the proper extension for a HOSTS file?

    a. .txt
    b. .dat
    c. .bat
    d. .ini
    e. none of the above

19. You have made changes to the LMHOSTS file. What command is used to manually reload the NetBIOS name cache?

    a. nbtstat –R
    b. nbtstat –r
    c. netstat –c
    d. netstat –A

20. An administrator has accidentally deleted all SRV records for a Windows Server 2003 domain controller in DNS. How can you re-create the SRV records in DNS?

    a. Restart the Server service on the domain controller.
    b. Restart the DNS Server service on the DNS server.
    c. Restart the Netlogon service on the domain controller.
    d. Run the command IPCONFDIG /REGISTERDNS on the domain controller.

21. Which of the following statements regarding compacting the DHCP database is incorrect? (Choose all that apply.)

    a. Dynamic compacting is performed automatically.
    b. Dynamic compacting compresses the DHCP database.
    c. Offline compacting moves space used by deleted records to the end of the file.
    d. Offline compacting uses the JETPACK utility.

22. You have installed three Linux desktop computers that need to connect to network shares using NetBIOS names. What must you do to allow these computers to query a NETBIOS name server? (Choose all that apply.)

    a. Install a WINS relay agent.
    b. Configure a local HOSTS file on each Linux computer.
    c. Install a WINS proxy.
    d. Nothing. Linux servers can query WINS natively.

23. What is the maximum amount of time that a negative query response is cached on a DNS server?

    a. one minute
    b. five minutes
    c. ten minutes
    d. never

24. What command is used to clear the DNS server cache?

    a. DNSCMD - C
    b. NBTSTAT - C
    c. IPCONFIG /FLUSHDNSCACHE
    d. NSLOOKUP /CLEAR

25. Which type of record is used to locate a network service, such as domain controller in DNS?

    a. CNAME
    b. SOA
    c. MX
    d. SRV
    e. NS

26. You are using BIND DNS servers for your Windows Server 2003 network. What symbol replaces characters in a DNS name that are <u>not</u> supported by non-Microsoft DNS servers?

    a. $
    b. %
    c. - (hyphen)
    d. _ (underscore)

27. Which of the following is a valid DNS zone type? (Choose all that apply.)

    a. primary
    b. secondary
    c. cache-only
    d. stub
    e. forwarding
    f. iterative

28. Which of the following is the reverse lookup zone name for the network range 192.168.12.0 with a subnet mask of 255.255.255.0?

    a. 0.12.168.192.in-addr.arpa
    b. 12.168.192. in-addr.arpa
    c. 168.192. in-addr.arpa
    d. 192. in-addr.arpa

29. **What type of zone transfer request is an AXFR query?**
   a. incremental zone transfer
   b. full zone transfer
   c. timed zone transfer
   d. stub zone transfer

30. **Which of the following operating systems can perform dynamic updates of their DNS records to a Windows Server 2003 DNS server? (Choose all that apply.)**
   a. Windows 9x
   b. Windows NT
   c. Windows 2000
   d. Windows XP

31. **You need to use NSLOOKUP to verify DNS functionality on a server. Which record type must exist for the DNS server for NSLOOKUP to function properly?**
   a. SRV
   b. CNAME
   c. Host
   d. PTR
   e. MX

32. **Which of the following DNS tools can be used to reregister resource records in DNS?**
   a. DNSCMD
   b. DNSLINT
   c. NSLOOKUP
   d. all of the above

33. **To troubleshoot DNS, you enabled DNS debug logging on the DNS server and set the maximum log file size to 50 MB. What happens when the log file reaches that maximum size?**
   a. DNS debug logging is stopped.
   b. A new log file is created.
   c. The oldest entries in the log file are overwritten.
   d. The DNS service is shut down.

34. **What does IPSec employ to prevent replay attacks of captured packets?**
   a. mutual authentication of both computers
   b. sequence numbers
   c. encryption of data
   d. digital signatures

35. **What protocol is used by IPSec to establish the security association for two computers to communicate?**
   a. IKE
   b. PPTP
   c. AH
   d. ESP

36. What is the function of certificates in IPSec? (Choose all that apply.)
    a. encrypting data
    b. authenticating hosts
    c. performing routing within NAT
    d. establishing the initial connection

37. You need to configure a Windows Server 2003 Routing and Remote Access server to support Windows 95, Windows 2000, and Windows XP dial-up clients. Which authentication protocol supports all three clients?
    a. PAP
    b. SPAP
    c. CHAP
    d. MS-CHAP
    e. MS-CHAPv2

38. Which of the following statements regarding PPTP is incorrect?
    a. PPTP uses Point-to-Point Protocol for authentication.
    b. PPTP uses IPSec for encryption.
    c. PPTP can be routed through NAT.
    d. none of the above

39. Which of the following protocols provides the highest form of authentication for Windows Server 2003?
    a. PAP
    b. MS-CHAPv2
    c. SPAP
    d. EAP-TLS
    e. MD5

40. You are interested in configuring a wireless LAN in the office. Which of the following wireless standards support 54 MBps transfer speeds or higher? (Choose all that apply.)
    a. 802.11
    b. 802.11a
    c. 802.11b
    d. 802.11g

41. Which of the following 802.1x wireless authentication protocols supports fast roaming?
    a. EAP-TLS
    b. EAP-MS-CHAPv2
    c. PEAP
    d. all of the above

42. What Windows Server 2003 component can function as a RADIUS server?
    a. RRAS
    b. IAS
    c. ICF
    d. ICS

43. **When IPSec is configured in tunnel mode, you can use it to make what type of connection?**
    a. server–to-router
    b. workstation-to-router
    c. server-to-server
    d. router-to-router

44. **Which of the following IPSec cryptography algorithms can be used for both authentication and data encryption? (Choose all that apply.)**
    a. SHA1
    b. MD5
    c. DES
    d. 3DES

45. **Which command is used to display the local routing table?**
    a. ROUTE VIEW
    b. ROUTE/VIEW
    c. ROUTE PRINT
    d. ROUTE /PRINT
    e. ROUTE –R

46. **What is the maximum number of hops used by RIP?**
    a. 8
    b. 10
    c. 15
    d. 24
    e. unlimited

47. **RIP sends out updates to its routing table by broadcasting. How often does RIP send a broadcast packet?**
    a. every 30 seconds
    b. every 60 seconds
    c. every 300 seconds
    d. every 600 seconds

48. **How does OSPF determine the best route to use to route a packet to its destination?**
    a. OSPF chooses the fastest route.
    b. OSPF chooses the lowest cost route.
    c. OSPF chooses the route based on a time schedule.
    d. OSPF chooses the route based on available bandwidth.

49. **When configuring multiple security policies to be applied on a Windows Server 2003 member server, which of the following policies is applied first?**
    a. domain security policy
    b. site security policy
    c. OU security policy
    d. local security policy

50. You have made changes to the local security policy on a stand-alone Windows Server 2003 computer. What tool is used to manually refresh the policy settings in Windows Server 2003?

   a. SECEDIT.EXE
   b. GPUPDATE.EXE
   c. GPRESULTS.EXE
   d. UPDATE.EXE

Glossary

ACK bit — A bit used in TCP communication to indicate that a packet is an acknowledgement of a previous packet.

Active Directory — A directory service for Windows 2000/2003 Servers that stores information about network resources.

Active Directory-integrated zone — A DNS zone in which DNS information is stored in Active Directory and supports multimaster updates and increased security.

adapter — The networking component that represents the network interface card and driver.

Address Resolution Protocol (ARP) — A protocol used by hosts to find the physical MAC address of another host with a particular IP address.

address spoofing — The act of falsifying the source IP address in an IP packet, usually for malicious purposes.

aging/scavenging — The process of removing old records from DNS that have not been updated within a set time period.

alerts — An alert performs a specified action once a counter meets the specified setting. Once an alert is triggered, a message can be sent, a program can be run, a counter log started, or an event can be written to the application log.

algorithm — A formula used to process data for encryption or decryption.

ANDing — The process in which a computer compares IP addresses against a given subnet mask to see if the IP addresses are on the same subnet or not.

AppleTalk — A protocol that is used when communicating with Apple Macintosh computers.

application directory partition — A partition that stores information about objects that is replicated to a set of defined domain controllers within the same forest.

Application layer — The layer of the TCP/IP architecture that provides access to network resources.

application log — The location where applications that are written to Microsoft standards record event information. The application developer determines the type of information an application writes to the log file.

asymmetrical encryption — An encryption method that uses two different keys. When one key is used to encrypt a message, the other key must be used to decrypt it.

authentication — The process through which a computer's identity is verified.

Authentication Headers (AH) mode — The IPSec mode that performs authentication and ensures data integrity on the entire IP packet, including the headers.

Automated System Recovery — A part of the Backup utility in Windows 2003 that allows for the backup and restoration of the operating system, system services and disks, though it should only be used as a final resort.

Automatic Private IP Addressing (APIPA) — A feature of newer Windows operating systems that automatically generates an IP address on the 169.254. x.x network when a DHCP server cannot be contacted.

Bandwidth Allocation Protocol (BAP) — A protocol used to dynamically control the number of phone lines multilink uses based on bandwidth utilization.

baseline — A performance benchmark that is used to determine what is normal server performance under a specific workload.

Berkeley Internet Name Domain (BIND) — A UNIX-based implementation of the Domain Name System created by the University of California at Berkeley.

binary — A base two numbering system, which has only two valid values for each digit: 0 and 1.

binding — The process of configuring a network protocol to use a network adapter.

bits — A single binary digit.

Bluetooth — A short-range wireless communication protocol.

bridge — A network component that controls the movement of packets between network segments based on MAC addresses.

broadcast — A packet that is addressed to all computers on a network. A broadcast for the local IP network is addressed to 255.255.255.255.

burst handling — A process used by a WINS server that cannot write name registrations to the WINS database fast enough to keep pace with the number of registrations. The WINS server ceases verifying that the names are not in use before sending out successful name registration requests with a short time to live.

caching-only server — A DNS server that does not store any zone information, but caches DNS queries from clients.

callback — A security enhancement wherein a dial-up user initiates a connection, the connection is dropped, and the server then calls the dial-up client back.

certificate – A combination of a public key and a private key that can be used to encrypt or digitally sign information.

Certificate Services — A service installed on Windows Server 2003 that allows it to act as a certification authority.

certification authority (CA) — A server that issues certificates.

Challenge Handshake Authentication Protocol (CHAP) — An authentication method that encrypts passwords using a one-way hash, but requires that passwords in Active Directory be stored using reversible encryption.

ciphertext — Data that has been encrypted.

classful routing — An older style of routing in which routing table entries would be based on Class A, B, and C networks with default subnet masks.

classless inter-domain routing (CIDR) — An addressing scheme that uses a defined number of bits for the subnet mask rather than relying on default lengths based on address classes. The number of bits in the network ID is defined as /XX after the IP address. XX is the number of bits.

client — A computer that requests resources across a network. Client software refers to the software on the client computer that performs the request.

cluster — A group of computers that coordinate the provision of services. When one computer in a cluster fails, the others take over its services.

collision — When two computers attempt to send a packet on the network at the same time, the signals collide and become unreadable.

COM port — The Windows term for a serial port in a computer.

Common Gateway Interface (CGI) — A vendor-neutral mechanism used to pass information from a Web page to an application running on a Web server.

Common Language Runtime (CLR) — A common component that runs code developed for the .NET framework regardless of the language in which it is written.

computer name — The name configured during installation for a Windows Server 2003 computer; it is used to create the host name and NetBIOS name.

conditions — Criteria in a remote access policy, or a connection request policy, that must be met for the policy to be applied.

conflict detection — When in use, a DHCP server pings an IP address before attempting to lease it. This ensures that IP address conflicts do not occur.

Connection Manager Administration Kit (CMAK) — A utility that can be used to configure dial-up and VPN connections on client computers.

connection request policy — A policy used by IAS to determine whether a request is authenticated locally or passed on to a RADIUS server. Such policies are composed of conditions and a profile.

connection-oriented — A term used to describe a protocol that verifies the existence of a host and agrees on terms of communication before sending data.

connectionless — A term used to describe a protocol that does not establish a communication channel before sending data.

cost — In routing, a configurable value assigned to a packet being forwarded through a router interface.

counter log — A location where performance data that is collected into a comma-separated or tab-separated format.

cryptography — The process of encrypting and decrypting messages and files using an algorithm.

Data Encryption Standard (DES) — An algorithm for data encryption defined by the U.S. government in 1977 that uses a 56-bit key.

Data Link Control (DLC) — A nonroutable protocol originally developed for mainframe computers. Windows Server 2003 does not support it.

data modification — Modifying the contents of packets that have been captured with a packet sniffer before resending them on the network.

data replay — Resending packets that have been previously captured with a packet sniffer.

debug logging — The processing of logging additional DNS-related events or messages for troubleshooting purposes.

decryption — The process of making encrypted data readable.

default gateway — A dedicated hardware device or computer on a network that is responsible for moving packets from one IP network to another. This is another term for IP router.

demand-dial — A dial-up/VPN/PPPoE connection that is only activated when required to move network traffic.

demand-dial filters — Rules that limit the types of traffic that can trigger the activation of a demand-dial connection.

DHCP relay agent — A service that forwards DHCP broadcasts from a network to a DHCP server on another network. It is required when DHCP broadcasts need to cross a router.

DHCPACK — The fourth and final packet in the DHCP lease process. This packet is a broadcast from the DHCP server confirming the lease.

DHCPDISCOVER — The first packet in the DHCP lease process. This packet is broadcast on the local network to find a DHCP server.

DHCPINFORM — A DHCP packet sent by Windows 2000 and newer remote access clients to retrieve IP configuration options from a DHCP server.

DHCPNAK — This packet is sent from a DHCP server to a client when it denies a renewal attempt.

DHCPOFFER — The second packet in the DHCP lease process. This packet is a broadcast from the DHCP server to the client with an offered lease.

DHCPRELEASE — This packet is sent from a DHCP client to a DHCP server to indicate it is no longer using a leased IP address.

DHCPREQUEST — The third packet in the DHCP lease process. This packet is a broadcast from the DHCP client indicating which DHCPOFFER has been chosen.

dial-out hours — A limit for demand-dial connections that allows connections only during certain time periods.

dial-up — Connectivity between two computers using modems and a phone line.

digital signature — A process that uses both hash encryption and asymmetrical encryption to ensure data integrity and nonrepudiation.

distance-vector routing — Any routing algorithm based on simple hop calculation. RIP is the most common example.

DNS cache — The file in which the results of DNS name resolutions are stored for a short period of time.

DNS suffix — See DNS domain name.

DNS zone — The part of the domain namespace for which a DNS server is authoritative. Commonly referred to as a "zone."

domain controller — A Windows 2000/2003 server that holds a copy of the Active Directory information for a domain.

domain directory partition — A partition that stores information about objects in a specific domain that is replicated to all domain controllers in the domain.

domain name — The portion of DNS namespace that can be registered and controlled by an organization or individual.

Domain Name Service (DNS) — A service used by clients running TCP/IP to resolve host names to IP addresses. Active Directory uses DNS to store service location information.

Domain Name System (DNS) — The method used to resolve Internet domain names to IP addresses.

dynamic compacting — The process whereby the WINS service deletes unused space in the WINS database automatically.

Dynamic DNS — A system in which DNS records are automatically updated by the client or a DHCP server.

Dynamic Host Configuration Protocol (DHCP) — A protocol used to automatically assign IP addressing information to clients.

dynamic routing — When routing tables are automatically generated by routers based on communication with other routers.

Encapsulating Security Payload (ESP) mode — The mode used to encapsulate and encrypt the data portion of a packet to provide a secure and confidential means of communication.

encryption — The process of rendering data unreadable by applying an algorithm.

Enterprise Admins — A default group in Active Directory with administrative rights for the entire forest.

Ethernet — The most popular media access method used today on networks.

event logging — The logging of status messages in an event log. This logging is less detailed than debug logging.

Event Viewer — A utility used to view the contents of the system, security, and application logs.

exclusion — An IP address or range of IP addresses within a scope that are not leased to clients.

Extensible Authentication Protocol (EAP) — An authentication system that uses EAP types as plug-in authentication modules. This is used for smart cards.

extinction interval — The period of time unused records exist in the WINS database before being marked as extinct.

extinction timeout — The period of time extinct records exist in the WINS database before being removed.

fast zone transfer — A zone transfer that uses compression to achieve a faster transmission time.

fault tolerance — Configuring a system in such a way that if a single component fails an alternate can be used.

File Transfer Protocol (FTP) — The most common protocol used to send files across the Internet.

filters — A function in Network Monitor that enables a network administrator to view only designated protocols, network events, network nodes, or other specialized views of the network.

forward lookup — The process of resolving a domain name to an IP address.

forward lookup zone — A zone that holds records used for forward lookups. The primary record types contained in these zones are: A records, MX records, and SRV records.

forwarding — The process of sending a DNS lookup request to another DNS server when the local DNS server does not have the requested information.

frame — A packet of information that is being transmitted on the network.

frame types — The format of IPX/SPX packets. Multiple frame types are available and two computers must be using the same frame type to communicate.

fully qualified domain name (FQDN) — The combination of a host name and domain name that completely describes the name of a computer within the global DNS system.

Gpupdate.exe — A command-line utility that can manually update the local computer with settings from GPOs in Active Directory.

graphical user interface (GUI) — A user interface for an operating system that supports graphics in addition to characters.

Group Policy Management Console (GPMC) — A Windows Server 2003 tool that allows you to centrally manage GPOs in Active Directory.

Group Policy Object (GPO) — An Active Directory object that is configured to apply settings to users and computers in Active Directory. It may be linked to a site, domain, or OU object in Active Directory.

hash encryption — A type of one-way encryption that cannot be decrypted. It is used to store information such as passwords and to create checksums.

hash value — A summary of the data being encrypted using hash encryption.

hop — In routing, a packet being forwarded by a single router.

host ID — The portion of an IP address that uniquely identifies a computer on an IP network.

host name — The unique name that identifies the computer on the network.

hostname — A command that displays your host name in Windows Server 2003.

HOSTS — A local text file used to resolve fully qualified domain names to IP addresses.

Hypertext Transfer Protocol (HTTP) — The protocol used to send information such as Web pages across the Internet.

Ignore-User-Dialin-Properties — An attribute that can be configured in the profile of a remote access policy that prevents the processing of the dial-in properties of a user object.

incremental templates — A set of text-based security template files that you can use to apply uniform security settings on computers within an enterprise. The templates modify security settings incrementally and do not include the default security settings.

incremental zone transfer — The process of updating only modified DNS records from a primary DNS server to a secondary DNS server.

Infrared Data Association (IrDA) — A standard for communication using infrared ports in mobile devices. This is also the name of the organization that created the standard.

Internal network address — A unique eight-character hexadecimal identifier used by Windows computers that are providing IPX/SPX-based services. Services are advertised as available on this network.

Internet — A worldwide public network.

Internet Assigned Numbers Authority (IANA) — The organization that maintains standards for Internet addressing, including well-known port numbers and ICMP packet types.

Internet Authentication Service (IAS) — The Microsoft implementation of a RADIUS server. It allows distributed authentication for remote access clients.

Internet Connection Firewall (ICF) — A simple firewall suitable for home use or small offices when connecting to the Internet.

Internet Connection Sharing (ICS) — An automated way to configure DHCP, NAT, and DNS proxy to share a single IP address and configuration information from an ISP.

Internet Control Messaging Protocol (ICMP) — The protocol used by routers and hosts to send Internet protocol error messages.

Internet Group Management Protocol (IGMP) — The protocol used by routers to track the membership in multicast groups.

Internet Information Services (IIS) — A popular suite of Internet services that includes a Web server and FTP server.

Internet Key Exchange (IKE) — A protocol used by IPSec to negotiate security parameters, perform authentication, and ensure the secure exchange of encryption keys.

Internet layer — The layer of the TCP/IP architecture that is responsible for logical addressing and routing.

Internet Message Access Protocol version 4 (IMAP4) — A protocol used to retrieve e-mail messages from an e-mail server. It is more flexible than POP3 for managing message storage.

Internet Protocol version 4 (IPv4) — This is the version of the Internet protocol (IP) that is used on the Internet. It is the IP part of TCP/IP.

Internet Protocol version 6 (IPv6) — An updated version of Internet protocol that uses 128-bit addresses and provides many new features.

Internet Security and Acceleration Server (ISA) — A firewall and proxy server product from Microsoft.

Internet Server Application Programmer Interface (ISAPI) — A programmer interface defined by Microsoft for passing information from Web pages to programs running on a Web server.

Internet service provider (ISP) — A company that sells Internet access.

Internetwork Packet eXchange/Sequenced Packet eXchange (IPX/SPX) — The protocol required to communicate with servers running Novell NetWare 4 and earlier.

IP address — A unique address assigned to each computer with the TCP/IP protocol installed. It is 32 bits long and is composed of a network ID and a host ID.

IP filter list — A list of IP protocols that are affected by a rule in an IPSec policy.

IP forwarding — The process of forwarding TCP/IP packets from one network to another.

IP Security (IPSec) — A service used with IPv4 to prevent eavesdropping on communication and to prevent data from being modified in transit.

ipconfig /release — A command used to force a client to relinquish the IP address it has obtained from a DHCP server.

ipconfig /setclassid — A command used to configure a class code on a computer.

IPSec filter action — Defines what is done to traffic that matches an IP filter list in an IPSec rule.

IPSec policy — A set of rules that defines how packets are treated by IPSec. An IPSec policy must be applied to be in use.

IPSec rules — The combination of an IP filter list and an IPSec filter action.

IPSec Security Monitor — An MMC snap-in that allows the monitoring of IPSec security associations and configuration.

Itanium — A 64-bit processor family manufactured by Intel.

iterative query — A DNS query that is resolved using local resources only.

jetpack — A command-line utility that may be used to compact a WINS database.

Kerberos — The preferred authentication method used by Active Directory. It is the simplest authentication method to implement for IPSec if all devices are part of the same Active Directory forest.

key — A number, usually large to prevent it from being guessed, used in combination with an algorithm to encrypt data.

LAN protocol — A networking protocol required to communicate over a LAN or over a remote access connection. The same LAN protocol that is used by clients on the LAN must be used by dial-up and VPN clients to access LAN resources remotely.

Layer Two Tunneling Protocol (L2TP) — A VPN protocol that works with IPSec to provide secure communication. Only the latest versions traverse NAT properly.

lease — The length of time a DHCP client computer is allowed to use IP address information from the DHCP server.

Lightweight Directory Access Protocol (LDAP) — A protocol used to look up directory information from a server.

Link Control Protocol (LCP) — An extension to PPP that allows the use of enhancements such as callback.

link-state routing — A routing algorithm where routers use a configurable cost metric to build a picture of the entire network. OSPF is the most common example.

Linux — An open source operating system that is very similar to UNIX.

LMHOSTS — A static text file located on the hard drive of NetBIOS clients that is used to resolve NetBIOS names to IP addresses.

load balancing — Splitting network requests between two or more servers to reduce the load on each server.

local area network (LAN) — A group of computers and other devices networked together over a relatively short distance.

location — A dial-up attribute configured in Phone and Modem Options to allow Windows to vary procedures for dialing a connection based on your location.

loopback — Any IP address that begins with 127.*x.x.x*. These addresses represent the local host.

MAC address — A number that uniquely identifies a network node. This address is hard-coded onto the NIC.

media — The material used to transfer information between computers.

media access method — The method used to send data that is formatted using a protocol to a network interface so that it may be transmitted to other computers.

Message Digest 5 — A hashing algorithm that produces a 129-bit message digest.

Metadirectory Services — A service in Windows that synchronizes Active Directory content with other directories and databases.

method of least privilege — A common security practice whereby you restrict all but the necessary security settings on a computer.

metropolitan area network (MAN) — A network where computers are located in the same city or geographic region.

Microsoft Challenge Handshake Authentication Protocol (MS-CHAP) — An enhancement to CHAP that allows Active Directory passwords to be stored using nonreversible encryption.

Microsoft Challenge Handshake Authentication Protocol version 2 (MS-CHAPv2) — An authentication method that adds computer authentication and several other enhancements to MS-CHAP. This is the preferred authentication protocol for most remote access connections.

Microsoft Management Console (MMC) — The generic utility used to manage most features and components of Windows Server 2003. Snap-ins are required to give MMC the functionality to manage components.

mobile users — Users that move from one location to another outside of the local network. They require remote access to use network resources.

modem — A hardware device that enables computers to communicate over a phone line. It converts digital signals from the computer to analog signals that can travel on a phone line, and then back to digital format.

modem pool — A group of modems connected to a remote access dial-up server. In high-volume situations, it is implemented as specialized hardware.

monitoring — The process by which the system and network are observed for problems or irregularities.

multicast — A packet that is addressed to a specific group of computers rather than a single computer. Multicast addresses range from 224.0.0.0 to 239.255.255.255.

multicast scope — A range of multicast IP addresses that are handed out to applications that request them.

multihomed devices — Computers or network devices that have more than one network interface.

Multilink — A system for dial-up connections that allows multiple phone lines to be treated as a single logical unit to increase connection speeds.

name query request — A packet from a WINS client to a WINS server requesting the resolution of a NetBIOS name to an IP address.

name query response — A packet from a WINS server to a WINS client in response to a name query request. If the request is successful, this contains the IP address for the NetBIOS name in the original request.

name refresh request — A packet from a WINS client to a WINS server requesting that the registration for a NetBIOS name be renewed.

name refresh response — A packet from a WINS server to a WINS client in response to a name refresh request. If the response is successful, then the TTL of the client lease is extended.

name registration request — A packet generated by a WINS client and sent to a WINS server requesting to register the NetBIOS name and IP address.

name registration response — A packet generated by a WINS server in response to a name registration request from a WINS client. The response can be successful or negative.

name release request — A packet send from a WINS client to a WINS server when the WINS client shuts down.

name release response — A packet from a WINS server to a WINS client in response to a name release request. This packet contains the NetBIOS name being released and a TTL of zero.

native mode — An Active Directory domain that can only have Windows 2000 and Windows Server 2003 domain controllers.

nbtstat — A command in Windows Server 2003 used to troubleshoot the NetBIOS protocol.

nbtstat-c — A switch used with the nbtstat command that allows you to view the content of the NetBIOS name cache on the computer.

nbtstat-R — A switch used with the nbtstat command that allows you to manually reload the NetBIOS name cache with #PRE entries found in the LMHOSTS file on the computer.

NetBIOS Enhanced User Interface (NetBEUI) — A nonroutable protocol commonly used in smaller Windows networks. Windows Server 2003 does not support it.

NetBIOS name — A unique name used by the NetBIOS protocol that identifies the computer on the network.

NetBIOS name cache — The file in which the results of Windows client NetBIOS name resolutions are stored for a short period of time. The storage of these resolutions increases network performance by reducing the number of name resolutions on the network.

NetBIOS name server — A server that holds a centralized repository of NetBIOS name information. The Microsoft implementation of a NetBIOS name server is WINS.

NetBIOS node type — A Windows setting that determines the type and order of NetBIOS name resolution.

Netscape Server Application Programmer Interface (NSAPI) — A programmer interface defined by Netscape to pass information from Web pages to applications running on a Web server.

NETSH — A command-line utility that can be used to manage many IP configuration settings and IP services.

netstat-r command — A command that lists the routing table on the local computer.

NetWare — A network operating system from Novell that traditionally uses the IPX/SPX protocol.

network — Two or more computers that share information.

network adapter — In Windows networking, this represents the network interface card and the driver that goes with it.

Network Address Translation (NAT) — A service that allows multiple computers to access the Internet by sharing a single public IP address.

network architecture — The physical layout and arrangement of the various components, hardware and software that make up a computer network.

Network Basic Input/Output System (NetBIOS) — An older interface used by programmers to access network resources.

Network Driver Interface Specification (NDIS) — An interface for developers that resides between protocols and adapters. It controls the bindings between protocols and adapters.

network ID — The portion of an IP address that designates the network on which a computer resides. This is defined by the subnet mask.

Network Interface layer — The layer of the TCP/IP architecture that controls placing packets on the physical network media.

network load balancing — When two or more computers share a single IP address to provide a service to clients. The load-balanced computers share the responsibility of providing the service.

Network Monitor — A Windows Server 2003 network monitoring tool that can capture and display network performance data.

Network Monitor driver — This enables a Microsoft-based server or workstation NIC to gather network performance data for assessment by Network Monitor.

network operating system (NOS) — An operating system that is optimized to act as a server rather than a client.

Non-Uniform Memory Access (NUMA) — A memory architecture for servers with multiple processors. It adds a third level of cache memory on motherboards.

NSLOOKUP — A command prompt-based utility for troubleshooting DNS.

NWLink — An IPX/SPX-compatible protocol created by Microsoft for Windows operating systems.

Oakley logs — A type of logging that tracks the establishment of security associations.

octets — A group of 8 bits. An IP address is composed of four octets, with each expressed as a decimal number.

offline compacting — The process whereby the jetpack utility is used to remove unused space in the WINS database while the WINS service is stopped.

Open Shortest Path First (OSPF) — A protocol that is used by routers to share information about known networks and calculate the best path through an internetwork. OSPF calculates routes based on user definable cost values.

Open Systems Interconnection (OSI) model — An industry standard that is used as a reference point to compare different networking technologies and protocols.

packet — A single unit of data sent from one computer to another. It contains a source address, destination address, data, and error-checking information.

packet filters — A set of rules that may be applied to a network interface on a router to allow and deny different types of network traffic entering or leaving the network interface.

packet sniffer — Software used to view (capture) all packets that are traveling on a network.

Password Authentication Protocol (PAP) — An authentication method that transmits passwords in clear text.

performance counter — A data item associated with a particular performance object used to measure a certain aspect of performance.

Performance Logs and Alerts — A tool included with Windows Server 2003 that enables you to create counter logs, trace logs, and configure alerts.

performance objects — A system component that you can monitor using System Monitor.

persistent connections — A connection that is created once and maintained over time for data transfer. This reduces communication overhead by reducing the number of packets used to establish connections over time.

Point-to-Point Protocol (PPP) — The most common remote access protocol used for dial-up connections. It supports the use of TCP/IP, IPX/SPX, and AppleTalk for remote access.

Point-to-Point Protocol over Ethernet (PPPoE) — A protocol used for authentication and traffic control on high-speed Internet connections such as DSL.

Point-to-Point Tunneling Protocol (PPTP) — A protocol that can be used to provide VPN connectivity between a Windows client and VPN server. PPTP is supported by Windows 95 and later.

poison-reverse processing — An option for RIP routing where a router advertises a route as unreachable on the interface from which it was learned.

port — A TCP port or UDP port is used by Transport layer protocols to direct network information to the proper service.

Post Office Protocol version 3 (POP3) — A protocol that is used to retrieve e-mail messages from an e-mail server.

Power Users group — Power users have less system access than administrators, but more than users. By default, members of this group have Read/Write permissions to other parts of the system in addition to their own profile. Power users can perform many system-wide operations, such as changing system time and display settings, and creating user accounts and shares.

preshared key — An IPSec authentication method whereby each device is preconfigured with a string of text.

primary zone — A zone that is authoritative for a specific DNS zone. Updates can only be made in the primary zone. There is only one primary zone per domain name.

private key — The key in asymmetrical encryption that is seen only by the user to which it is issued.

proactive maintenance — The measures taken to reduce future system and network problems.

profile — The part of a remote access policy, or connection request policy, that contains settings that are applied to the connection.

protocol — The language that two computers use to communicate on a network. Two computers must use the same protocol to communicate.

proxy server — A server that can be used to control and speed up access to the Internet. It also allows multiple computers to access the Internet through a single IP address.

public key — The key in asymmetrical encryption that is freely distributed to other users.

public key infrastructure (PKI) — A system to create and manage public keys, private keys, and certificates.

pull replication — Replication between two WINS servers triggered by a defined amount of time passing.

push replication — Replication between two WINS servers triggered by a defined number of changes in the WINS database.

RADIUS client — A server or device that passes authentication requests to a RADIUS proxy or RADIUS server. Most commonly, these are remote access servers.

RADIUS proxy — An intelligent server that acts as an intermediary between RADIUS clients and RADIUS servers. This server decides which RADIUS server should be used to authenticate a request.

RADIUS server — A server in the RADIUS process that accepts and authorizes authentication requests from RADIUS clients and RADIUS proxies.

reactive maintenance — The measures taken when system or network problems arise.

recursive lookup — A DNS query that is resolved through other DNS servers until the requested information is located.

recursive query — A DNS query that is resolved through other DNS servers until the requested information is located.

registrar — A company accredited by ICANN that has the right to distribute and register domain names.

remote access — Accessing network resources from a location away from the physical network. Connections can be made using a dial-up connection or a VPN.

remote access permissions — The part of a remote access policy that defines whether the policy denies remote access or grants remote access.

remote access policies — Policies configured on remote access servers to control how remote access connections are created. They are composed of conditions, remote access permissions, and a profile.

remote access protocol — A protocol that is required for dial-up remote access. PPP is the most common remote access protocol.

Remote Authentication Dial-In User Service (RADIUS) — A service that allows remote access servers (RADIUS clients) to delegate responsibility for authentication to a central server (RADIUS server).

Remote Installation Services (RIS) — A service in Windows that automates the installation of Windows 2000 Professional or Windows XP Professional on client workstations.

remote RADIUS server group — A grouping of RADIUS servers to which IAS forwards connection requests when acting as a RADIUS proxy. Load balancing and fault tolerance can be configured.

renewal interval — The time to live handed out to WINS clients when they register NetBIOS names.

replication partners — Two WINS servers that synchronize information in their databases.

Request for Comment (RFC) — A submission to the Internet Engineering Task Force that is evaluated for use as part of the TCP/IP protocol suite.

reservation — A DHCP IP address that is leased only to a computer with a specific MAC address.

Resultant Set of Policy (RSoP) snap-in — An MMC snap-in that is used to troubleshoot the implementation of Group Policies.

reverse lookup — The process of resolving an IP address to a domain name.

reverse lookup zone — A zone that contains records used for reverse lookups. The primary record type in these zones is PTR records.

rogue DHCP server — A non-Windows 2000/2003 class DHCP server that exists on a Windows 2003 network.

Root hints — The list of root servers that is used by DNS servers to perform forward lookups on the Internet.

root servers — A group of 13 DNS servers on the Internet that are authoritative for the top-level domain names such as .com, .edu, and .org.

round robin DNS — The process of creating multiple IP addresses for a specific host name for fault tolerance and load balancing.

route — An entry in a routing table that lists a network and how to reach it.

route command — A command that may be used to list and configure routes in the routing table on the local computer.

route print — A command-line utility used to view the contents of a routing table.

router — A network device that forwards packets from one network to another. TCP/IP, IPX/SPX, and AppleTalk can be routed.

Routing and Remote Access Service (RRAS) — A service in Windows that controls routing, dial-in access, and VPN access on a Windows Server 2003.

Routing Information Protocol (RIP) — A protocol used by routers to exchange routing table information and determine the best path through an internetwork based on the number of hops.

routing table — The list of networks and how to reach them that is maintained by a router.

scope — A range of addresses that are leased by a DHCP server.

Secedit.exe — A command-line tool that allows you to apply security templates to computers and analyze local computer security settings.

secondary zone — A DNS zone that stores a read-only copy of the DNS information from a primary zone. There can be multiple secondary zones.

Secure Hashing Algorithm (SHA1) — A hashing algorithm that produces a 160-bit message digest.

Secure Socket Layer (SSL) — A Transport layer protocol that encrypts data communication between a client and service. Both the client and service must be written to support SSL.

security association (SA) — The security terms negotiated between two hosts using IPSec.

security baseline template — A security template that contains the minimum security settings for a computer required by an organization.

Security Configuration and Analysis snap-in — A security tool that allows you to analyze local computer security settings against a baseline. It may also be used to modify or apply security settings to the local computer.

Security Configuration Manager tools — A security toolset consisting of security templates and utilities that can be used to analyze and apply security configurations.

security log — Events pertaining to the audit policy are written to the security log.

Security Policy template — A security template used to apply various security settings to an Active Directory container or object using a GPO.

Serial Line Internet Protocol (SLIP) — An older remote access protocol that only supports using TCP/IP as a LAN protocol. It is used by Windows Server 2003 only when acting as a client.

server — A computer that hosts resources for other computers on a network.

service — A networking component that provides resources to network clients. Each service communicates with corresponding client software.

Service Advertising Protocol (SAP) — A protocol used by IPX/SPX to advertise the availability of services by sending out a broadcast message every 60 seconds.

service resource records — DNS resource records that contain the location of a service such as the Kerberos or LDAP services used by Active Directory.

Shiva Password Authentication Protocol (SPAP) — An authentication method that uses reversible encryption when transmitting passwords.

Simple Mail Transfer Protocol (SMTP) — A protocol that is used to send e-mail across the Internet.

sliding window — A process used in the TCP protocol to track which packets have been received by the destination host.

split-horizon processing — An option for RIP routing where a router is not advertised back on the same interface from which it was learned to prevent routing loops.

Start of Authority (SOA) record — A DNS record that defines which DNS server is authoritative for a particular domain and defines the characteristics for the zone, including replication parameters.

static IP configuration — TCP/IP configuration settings and information manually entered onto a device such as a computer.

static mapping — An entry manually placed in the WINS database. These are normally created for servers providing NetBIOS services that are unable to use WINS.

static route — An entry in a routing table that is permanently added by an administrator.

static routing — When routing tables are maintained manually by an administrator.

stub zone — A DNS zone that stores only the NS records for a particular zone. When a client requests a DNS lookup, the request is then forwarded to the DNS server specified by the NS records.

subdomains — Divisions of a DNS domain name. The subdomain students.GANU.edu is a subdomain of GANU.edu.

subnet mask — A string of 32 bits that is used to define which portion of an IP address is the host ID and which part is the network ID.

subnetting — The process of dividing a single IP network into several smaller IP networks. Bits are taken from the host ID and made part of the network ID by adjusting the subnet mask.

supernetting — The process of combining several smaller networks into a single large network by taking bits from the network ID and making them part of the host ID.

superscope — A logical grouping of scopes that is used to service network segments with more than one subnet in use.

symmetrical encryption — Encryption that uses the same key to encrypt and decrypt data.

SYN bit — A bit used in TCP communication to indicate a request to start a communication session.

system log — A location where system components, such as services and device drivers, record information, warnings, and errors.

System Monitor — A tool that allows you to gather and view the real-time performance statistics of a local or network computer.

Task Manager — A tool used to view the processes and applications currently running on a system; also provides basic resource usage statistics.

TCP/IP protocol suite — A collection of related communication and information transfer protocols vital to communication on the Internet.

Telnet — A protocol used to remotely access a command-line interface on UNIX and Linux servers.

time to live (TTL) — A parameter of IP packets used to ensure that if a packet becomes trapped in a router loop, it will expire. Each hop through a router reduces TTL by one.

timed lease — An IP address and configuration option given to a client computer from a DHCP server for a limited period of time.

Token Ring — An older Physical layer protocol developed by IBM that operated at either 4 Mbps or 16 Mbps. This media access method allows each client equal access to the network.

tombstoned — The term used to describe a WINS record that has been marked for deletion from all WINS servers. The tombstoned status is replicated among all WINS servers.

top-level domain — The broadest category of names in the DNS hierarchy under which all domain names fit. Some top-level domains include .com, .edu, and .gov.

trace logs — A location where a data provider collects performance data when an event occurs.

tracert command — A command used to trace the hops a packet takes from the local computer to the destination computer.

Transmission Control Protocol (TCP) — A connection-oriented and reliable Transport layer protocol that is part of the TCP/IP protocol suite.

Transmission Control Protocol/Internet Protocol (TCP/IP) — A suite of protocols that allows interconnected networks to communicate with one another. It is the most common protocol in Windows networking and must be used to access the Internet.

Transport Device Interface (TDI) — A software layer that exists between client or service software and protocols. Clients and services use this layer to access network resources.

Transport layer — The layer of the TCP/IP architecture that breaks messages into smaller packets and tracks their delivery.

transport mode — The IPSec mode used when two hosts create a security association directly between them.

Triple Data Encryption Standard (3DES) — A data encryption algorithm that uses three 56-bit keys in three rounds to give an effective key length of 168 bits.

troubleshooting procedures — The tasks performed when solving system and network problems.

tunnel endpoint — In tunnel mode, this is the other end of the tunnel with the local host.

tunnel mode — The IPSec mode used when two routers encapsulate all traffic transferred between two or more networks.

unicast — Communication from one computer to a single destination computer on a TCP/IP network.

user class — An identifier from the DHCP client that is sent as part of the DHCP lease process. This can be set manually by the administrator on workstations.

User Datagram Protocol (UDP) — A connectionless, unreliable Transport layer protocol used in the TCP/IP protocol suite.

v.90 — A standard for modems that allows downloads at 56 Kbps and uploads at 33.6 Kbps.

v.92 — A standard for modems that allows downloads at 56 Kbps and uploads at 48 Kbps.

vendor class — An identifier from the DHCP client that is sent as part of the DHCP lease process. This is based on the operating system in use.

verification interval — The period of time a WINS server waits before validating a record that has been replicated from another WINS server.

Virtual Private Network (VPN) — A means of encrypted communication across a public network such as the Internet. This is cheaper than implementing private lines for connectivity.

Volume Shadow Copy — Allows the Backup Utility to copy files even if they are open, and also allows users and applications to access the data during the backup procedure.

wide area network (WAN) — Geographically dispersed networks with more than one physical location. The links between each location are relatively slow compared to local area networks.

Windows Internet Naming Service (WINS) — A service used to resolve NetBIOS names to IP addresses as well as store NetBIOS service information.

Windows Media Services — A service that provides streaming audio and video to clients.

Windows Sockets (WinSock) — A programming interface used by developers to access TCP/IP based services.

WINS (Windows Internet Name Service) server — A Windows service used to resolve NetBIOS names to IP addresses as well as store NetBIOS service information.

WINS proxy — A service that forwards local broadcast NetBIOS requests to a WINS server. This is implemented for NetBIOS clients that are unable to use WINS.

Wireless LAN — A standard for wireless communication created by the IEEE. The most common variant of wireless LAN is 802.11b.

X.509 — A standard for certificates that was created by the International Telecommunication Union - Telecommunication (ITU-T).

zone transfer — The process of updating DNS records from a primary DNS server to a secondary DNS server.

Index

S

W

W3C. *See* World Wide Web Consortium

WAN. *See* wide area network

wide area network (WAN), 8, 9, 54, 512

Windows 2000, 2, 37, 150, 337, 524, 525

Windows Calculator, binary to decimal conversion, 46

Windows CE, 91

Windows Internet Naming Service (WINS), 513

  discussed, 14, 35–36, 522, 527

  installing, 242–243

    removing, 258–259

    WINS client configuration, 243

  managing

    burst handling, 250

    extinction interval, 249

    extinction timeout, 249

    in general, 249–252

    renewal interval, 249

    verification interval, 250

  name resolution

    in general, 174, 177–179, 228–229, 260

    name query, 181

    name registration, 179–180

    name release, 180–181

    name renewal, 180

  troubleshooting, 260

  WINS database, 528

    adding static records, 253

    backing up, 255–257, 260

    compacting, 257–258

    restoring, 256–257

    static mapping, 253, 254–255

    tombstoned, 253

    viewing records, 252–253

WINS proxy, 259–260, 528

WINS replication

  configuring, 243–248, 260

  default replication, 244

  persistent connections, 246

  pull replication, 245

  push replication, 244

  replication partners, 243, 246, 247

  replication partners configuration, 248–249

Windows Media Player, 16

Windows Media Services, discussed, 16

Windows NT, 2, 436, 472, 475, 524

Windows Server 2003

  editions

    Datacenter edition, 4, 512

    Discover Features of Enterprise Edition, 8

    Enterprise edition, 3, 8, 512

    in general, 2

    Standard edition, 3, 512

    Web edition, 2–3, 512

  hardware requirements, 4

  installing, 5–7

    Determine Currently Installed Version, 7

Windows Sockets (WinSock), 158

  discussed, 13, 521

Windows Sockets Direct (WinSock Direct), 13

Windows XP, 28, 37, 525

WINS. *See* Windows Internet Naming Service

WinSock. *See* Windows Sockets

wireless network, 16, 90, 518. *See also* Bluetooth

World Wide Web Consortium (W3C), 73

X

X.509 standard, 530

Microsoft® Windows® Server 2003 Enterprise Edition 180-Day Evaluation

The software included in this kit is intended for evaluation and deployment planning purposes only. If you plan to install the software on your primary machine, it is recommended that you back up your existing data prior to installation.

System requirements

To use Microsoft Windows Server 2003 Enterprise Edition, you need:

- Computer with 550 MHz or higher processor clock speed recommended; 133 MHz minimum required; Intel Pentium/Celeron family, or AMD K6/Athlon/Duron family, or compatible processor (Windows Server 2003 Enterprise Edition supports up to eight CPUs on one server)
- 256 MB of RAM or higher recommended; 128 MB minimum required (maximum 32 GB of RAM)
- 1.25 to 2 GB of available hard-disk space*
- CD-ROM or DVD-ROM drive
- Super VGA (800 × 600) or higher-resolution monitor recommended; VGA or hardware that supports console redirection required
- Keyboard and Microsoft Mouse or compatible pointing device, or hardware that supports console redirection

Additional items or services required to use certain Windows Server 2003 Enterprise Edition features:

- For Internet access:
  - Some Internet functionality may require Internet access, a Microsoft Passport account, and payment of a separate fee to a service provider; local and/or long-distance telephone toll charges may apply
  - High-speed modem or broadband Internet connection
- For networking:
  - Network adapter appropriate for the type of local-area, wide-area, wireless, or home network to which you wish to connect, and access to an appropriate network infrastructure; access to third-party networks may require additional charges

Note: To ensure that your applications and hardware are Windows Server 2003–ready, be sure to visit **www.microsoft.com/windowsserver2003**.

* Actual requirements will vary based on your system configuration and the applications and features you choose to install. Additional available hard-disk space may be required if you are installing over a network. For more information, please see **www.microsoft.com/windowsserver2003**.

Uninstall instructions

This time-limited release of Microsoft Windows Server 2003 Enterprise Edition will expire 180 days after installation. If you decide to discontinue the use of this software, you will need to reinstall your original operating system. You may need to reformat your drive.